Captain Cook
IN THE PACIFIC

Captain Cook
IN THE PACIFIC

Nigel Rigby and
Pieter van der Merwe

With an introduction by
Glyn Williams

NATIONAL
MARITIME
MUSEUM

First published in 2002 by the National Maritime Museum, Greenwich, London, SE10 9NF.

ISBN 0 948065 43 5

Acknowledgements

Designed by AB3 Design
Cover design by Mousemat Design Ltd
Printed and bound in Spain by Grafilur

Cover images:
Resolution (left) and *Discovery* refitting in Ship Cove, Nootka Sound, April 1778; by John Webber (A8588)
A Chart of the Southern Hemisphere, an engraving by William Whitchurch after Georg Forster (A1084)
James Cook, by Nathaniel Dance (BHC2628)

Frontispiece:
James Cook, by Nathaniel Dance. Painted for Joseph Banks in 1776 it shows him in the uniform of a post-captain, with his own chart of the Southern Ocean spread out on the table (BHC2628)
All © National Maritime Museum, 2002.

Authors' note

Captain Cook in the Pacific appears in the wake of 'Oceans of Discovery', a new gallery at the National Maritime Museum, Greenwich, which features Cook in a perspective of scientific exploration at sea (and under it) from the sixteenth century up to date, as part of the Museum's 'Planet Ocean' initiative.

This book has more limited scope, although it does show how Cook deserves to be seen as the first modern scientific explorer of the oceans. It aims to outline his life and voyages in the context of his times, illustrated largely from the Museum collections; to indicate the historical significance of the voyages and to point the way for those interested to pursue the story further. It is, therefore, largely a work of summary for which the principal credit lies with the authors on whose more original and extensive writings it is based (see p. 139). We are also grateful to Professor Glyn Williams – one of the most distinguished Pacific historians of our own day – for his authoritative introduction and to colleagues both past and present at Greenwich who have contributed in many other ways. For assistance outside the Museum we would also like to thank: Katy Baron (Royal Collection), Clare Crick, Professors David Bindman and Hans-Jorg Rheinberger,and the various institutions who have kindly permitted use of their copyright illustrations.

While we hope that the evidence of joint authorship is not too apparent, the division is exact: Chapters 1, 2 and 5 are by Pieter van der Merwe, Chapters 3, 4 and 6 by Nigel Rigby.

N.R. / P.v.d.M.   Greenwich, September 2002

CONTENTS

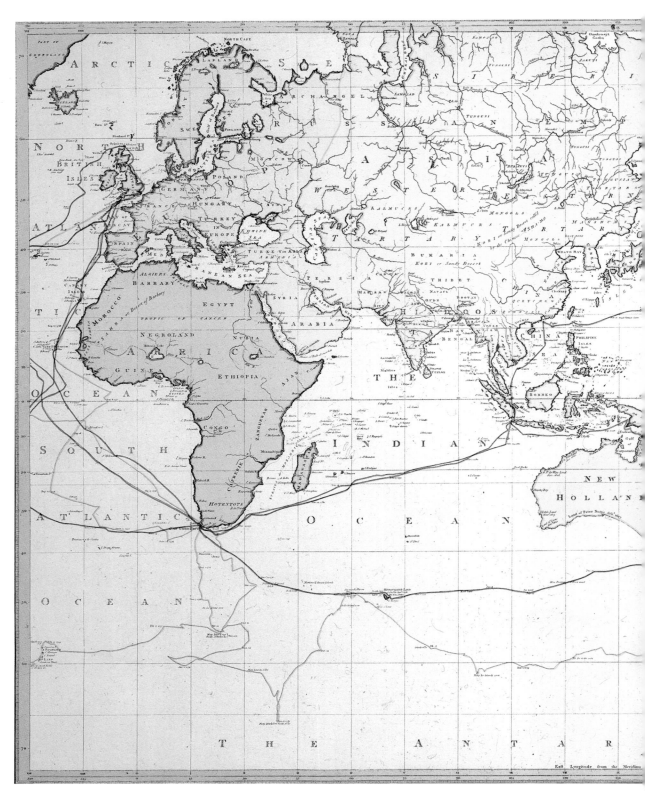

'A General Chart Exhibiting the Discoveries of Captn. James Cook ... with the Tracks of the Ships under his Command ... ', 1784. Drawn b

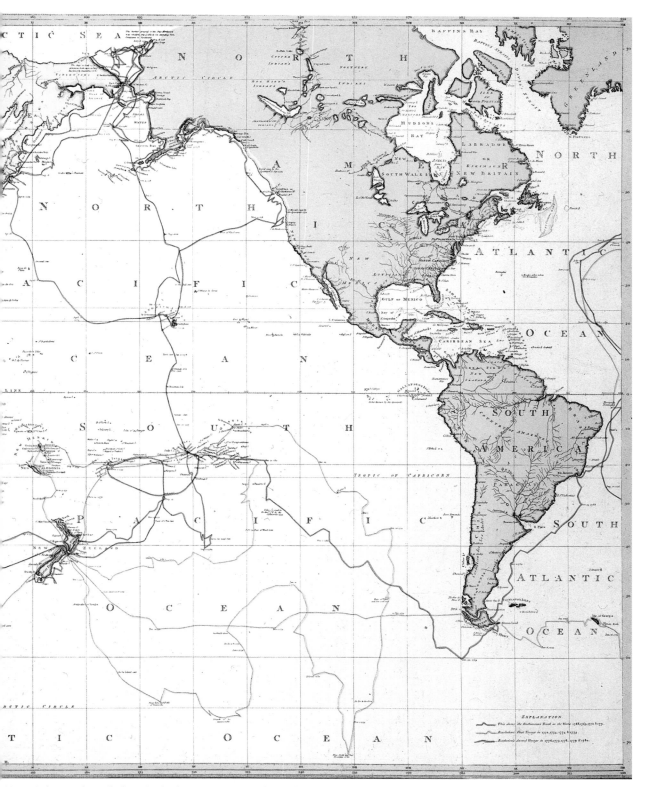

Henry Roberts, who sailed on Cook's last two voyages. The *Endeavour* track is in red, the second voyage in yellow and the third in green.

INTRODUCTION

*'... a sea so vast that the human mind
can scarcely grasp it ...'*

By the early sixteenth century the successors of Columbus were
becoming aware that beyond the newly discovered landmass of
America stretched an unknown ocean, possibly of great size. Its
waters were first sighted by Europeans in 1513 when the Spanish
conquistador, Vasco Núñez de Balboa, crossed the Isthmus of Panama
from the Caribbean to the shores of the 'Mar del Sur' or South Sea (so
called to distinguish it from the Spaniards' 'Mar del Norte' or Atlantic).
In a moment of high drama Balboa, in full armour, strode knee-deep
into the sea to claim it for Spain, but it was to take many years before
the newcomers realized the vast extent of its waters and lands.

The single most important advance in knowledge came within a
few years of Balboa's sighting. In 1519 Ferdinand Magellan left Spain
with five ships to search for a route to the new ocean from the South
Atlantic which would take him westward to the Moluccas (Spice
Islands), at this time being reached by Portuguese traders via the
Indian Ocean. Such a route would demolish the hypothesis of Ptolemy,
the Alexandrian scholar who in the second century AD had visualized
the oceans of the southern hemisphere as landlocked seas enclosed by
a huge southern continent that was joined to both Africa and Asia.
The Portuguese navigators who rounded the Cape of Good Hope had
shown that there was open water between the Atlantic and Indian
Oceans. Magellan found a route near the tip of South America in the
form of the tortuous, 350-mile (560-km) strait that was soon to bear
his name. Battling against squalls, desertions and shipwreck, Magellan
took thirty-seven days to get through the strait and reach the ocean
which he (or his chronicler, Pigafetta) named the Pacific. As later
storm-tossed mariners were to point out, it was not always the most
appropriate of names.

Picking up the south-east trades, Magellan's two remaining vessels
followed a diagonal route north-west across the ocean. For fifteen
weeks they sailed on, sighting only two small, uninhabited islands.
Men died of scurvy and starvation as the crews were reduced to eating
the leather sheathing off the rigging until in March 1521 the ships
reached the island of Guam in the North Pacific, and from there sailed

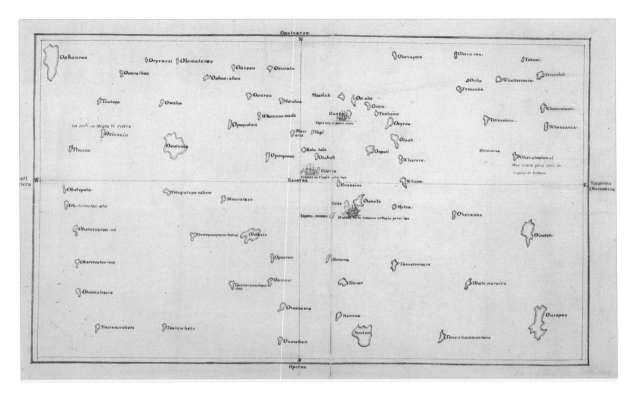

to the Philippines and the Moluccas. Magellan died in the Philippines and only one vessel, the *Victoria*, returned to Spain in 1522 to complete the first circumnavigation of the globe.

'No other single voyage has ever added so much to the dimension of the world', Oskar Spate has written, and 'dimension' is the key word, for revelation of distances rather than of new lands represented the true importance of Magellan's voyage. He had shown the daunting immensity of the Pacific, where a voyage of almost four months' continuous sailing was marked by the sighting of only two specks of land.

An ocean of unprecedented size had been revealed but to talk of its 'discovery' by Europeans hides the fact that, long before Magellan crossed the Pacific, it had already experienced a complex process of exploration, migration and settlement. The chart drawn for James Cook in 1769 by Tupaia, a priest or *arii* from the Society Islands, gives some indication of the range of geographical information held by the peoples of the Pacific before the Europeans arrived. Centred on Tahiti, the chart marked seventy-four islands, scattered over an area of ocean 3000 miles (nearly 5000 km) across and 1000 miles (over 1600 km) from north to south. The type of craft used in Pacific voyaging ranged from the small single-hulled outriggers of Micronesia to giant double-hulled outriggers in Polynesia, some of which were longer than the European discovery vessels and could make voyages of several thousand miles. Navigation was by observation of stars, currents,

Tupaia's chart, with a note by Joseph Banks stating that it was 'Drawn by Lieut Jas Cook 1769'. Tupaia joined the *Endeavour* at Tahiti in July 1769, and both in the Society Islands and in New Zealand performed valuable services as pilot, interpreter and mediator. His chart, with its seventy or more islands laid down in concentric circles to show sailing times rather than distances, has some puzzling features; but as Johann Reinhold Forster (naturalist on Cook's second voyage) wrote, it was 'a monument of the integrity and geographical knowledge of the people in the Society Islands, and of Tupaya in particular'. Tupaia never reached England, for he died at Batavia (now Jakarta) in December 1770.

Abraham Ortelius's world map, 1573. This map is typical of many of the period in that it shows an immense southern continent, though the legend, *Terra Australis*, is accompanied by the cautionary words, *Nondum Cognita* ('not yet known'). The continent occupies most of the southern temperate zone, crosses the Tropic of Capricorn near New Guinea and the East Indies, and includes Tierra del Fuego off the tip of South America.

wave and wind patterns, and the shape and loom of the land, rather than by instruments. Long-distance voyages were made which led to the peopling by Polynesians of lands as far distant from each other as the Hawaiian Islands and New Zealand. Europeans were slow to appreciate the navigational skills of the Pacific peoples and today there is still dispute about whether the great voyages of the pre-European period were planned or accidental.

Magellan's successors made slow progress in filling in the blanks on the map. Spanish attempts to follow his track and reach the Spice Islands across the Pacific from the east failed to find a commercial

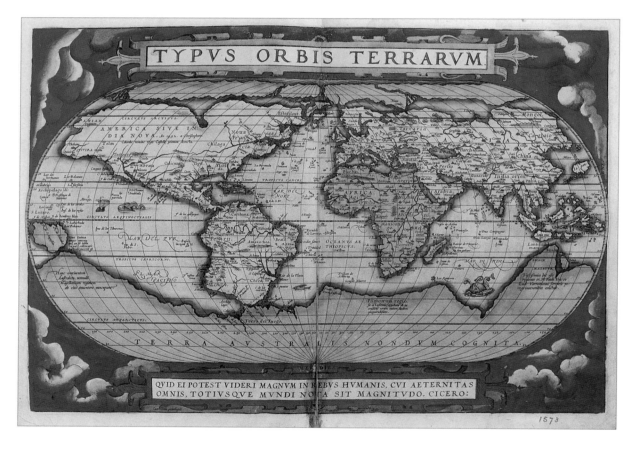

route, and in 1529 such ventures lost their point when the Treaty of Zaragoza assigned the Moluccas to Portugal, whose vessels came by way of the Cape of Good Hope. Shut out from the Spice Islands, the Spaniards turned their attention northward to the Philippines, which were conquered in the mid-1560s. On the return voyage of the Spanish invasion fleet to Mexico two vessels were pushed by wind and current far to the north. The curving track they followed soon became the regular route of the galleons sailing from the Philippines to Mexico with Chinese silks and porcelain, which were then taken overland to Vera Cruz before being shipped to Europe. At Acapulco the galleons loaded Peruvian silver for their return voyage, which followed a route well to the south of the eastbound track. West or east, it was the longest unbroken trading voyage in the world and the galleons sailing from the Philippines took five to six months to make the run.

As Spanish settlement grew in Peru so efforts began to explore the South Pacific, spurred on by the long-standing belief in the existence of an unknown southern continent *Terra Australis incognita*, a gigantic leftover from Ptolemaic concepts of the world. By the second half of the sixteenth century many world maps showed such a continent, including those constructed by the most celebrated geographers of the age, Mercator and Ortelius. In their depictions the continent covered most of the southern hemisphere, stretching towards the Equator as far as New Guinea, which was often shown as a promontory. If an unknown continent was not incentive enough, there were also fabulous islands – those rumoured to have been found by the Incas sailing west from the coast of South America, Ophir where King Solomon's ships were reported to have found gold, and Marco Polo's Locach. In 1567, ships commanded by Alvaro de Mendaña left Peru, and after two months, sailing westward, reached islands which Mendaña named 'Yslas de Salomon' (Solomon Islands). Despite the triumphant naming, no gold, silver or spices were found, and the expedition's estimate of the location of the islands was so erroneous that they were to be 'lost' for another two centuries.

Mendaña's voyage revealed the problems that faced navigators trying to establish their position in the vastnesses of the Pacific Ocean. European voyagers in the sixteenth century had no serious problems in finding latitude. Celestial observations of the Sun or stars could be made by astrolabe, simple quadrant or back-staff. Longitude was a very different matter and no straightforward solution was found until the development of the chronometer by Harrison in the eighteenth century. At this time navigators relied on keeping check of their longitude by dead reckoning. This involved a series of different estimates, a mistake in any one of which could produce significant errors. A sailing master needed to know the ship's course and how readings of the magnetic compass were affected by variation and deviation. Neither could be determined with any confidence at this time. Additional information needed before a ship's course could be plotted on a chart or traverse board included the amount of leeway caused by wind, the strength and set of currents, and the vessel's speed through the water. The effect of wind and current was almost impossible to measure precisely, and although by the end of the sixteenth century the log was used to determine a ship's speed, its operation was a chancy business as the crew timed the rate at which the line spun overboard by hour-glass or traditional chants. The long ocean crossings of the Pacific, where ships might be out of sight of land for months at a time, increased the danger of cumulative errors. For example, Mendaña's

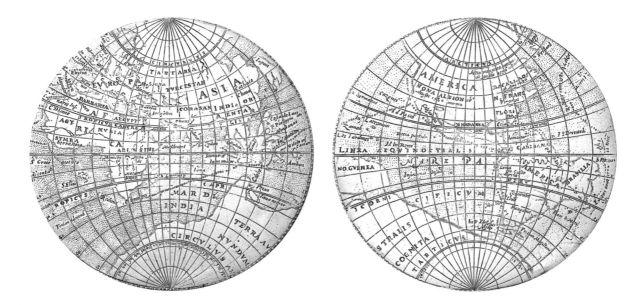

Michael Mercator's silver map of Drake's voyage, 1589. This silver medal bears the earliest dated representation of Drake's track during his celebrated voyage round the world in 1577–80. Although *Terra Australis* still looms large, Drake's sightings when he was driven south from the Pacific exit of the Strait of Magellan hinted that Tierra del Fuego was insular, not continental as shown on Ortelius's earlier map. The map is also noteworthy for the inscription 'Nova Albion' or New Albion, referring to Drake's stay on the Californian coast, and the hopes that this region might be claimed by England.

sailing master underestimated the westward drift of the Pacific Ocean Current, and placed the Solomon Islands more than 2000 nautical miles (3200 km) east of their true position.

A further handicap to comprehensive exploration of the Pacific was the system of prevailing winds. Ships entering the Pacific from the South Atlantic had to battle against gale-force westerlies, the notorious Roaring Forties of the sailors' narratives. Once in the Pacific, ships found themselves in the South-East Trades, which carried them in a diagonal line towards the Equator, skirting the main island groups, while in the North Pacific they faced the even more persistent North-East Trades. Helpful though the wind systems were once they were known, they tempted sailing ships into relatively narrow corridors across the ocean and venturing away from these could involve months of beating against head winds. It was not just a matter of time and financial loss: the longer the voyage the greater the chances of scurvy afflicting the crew. The cause of this terrible scourge of the sea – vitamin C deficiency – was not then known but its only cure was fresh food and rest on land. However, in the Pacific, ships sailed for months out of sight of land, while their crews, living on a diet of salt meat, stale biscuits and contaminated water, sickened and died.

Notwithstanding all the difficulties, by the second half of the sixteenth century the outlines of Spain's new Pacific empire were clearly visible. Its eastern rim along the American coastline had been explored from the Strait of Magellan to the Californian coast. From Peru silver was shipped to Panama on the first stage of its journey to Spain, while farther north, New Spain (Mexico) tapped the resources of China by way of the Philippines. Through diplomacy, exploration and conquest, Spain claimed an ocean whose lands and waters covered one-third of the surface of the globe. It was at this time that its position was challenged by the unexpected intrusion of another European power – the English. As relations with Spain worsened in Europe, so English mariners, supported by court and merchants, sailed for the South Sea in search of plunder. The first of these voyages was also the most famous, the circumnavigation by Francis Drake in the *Golden Hind* (1577–80), which returned to England with a cargo of treasure that captured the public imagination and the Queen's favour. None of its immediate successors enjoyed the same success but it set the pattern for a tradition of predatory raids in the Pacific. Drake's voyage and a landing somewhere along the coast of northern California or Oregon also left a tantalizing English claim to the vast region of America north of New Spain, marked as New Albion on the maps. Almost two hundred years later James Cook would be the next English navigator to sight that coast, and it was Drake's name of New Albion that he entered in his journal.

The English raids into the Pacific distracted Spanish energies from further significant exploration until 1595 when Mendaña once again sailed for the Solomon Islands, where he hoped to establish a new

'A New and Accurat Map of the World', 1626. This elaborately decorative English map, which gives prominence to Francis Drake and Thomas Cavendish, demonstrates Europe's lack of knowledge of the southern oceans in the early seventeenth century. The gigantic *Terra Australis* of the Ortelius map has been divided, rather hesitantly, into *Magallanica* and 'The Southerne Unknowne Land', but the only new feature is that of the Strait of Le Maire, passed through by the Dutch navigator of that name in 1616 on his way around Cape Horn. His track showed that there was another, more open (if often stormy) way from the Atlantic into the Pacific than the tortuous passage through the Strait of Magellan.

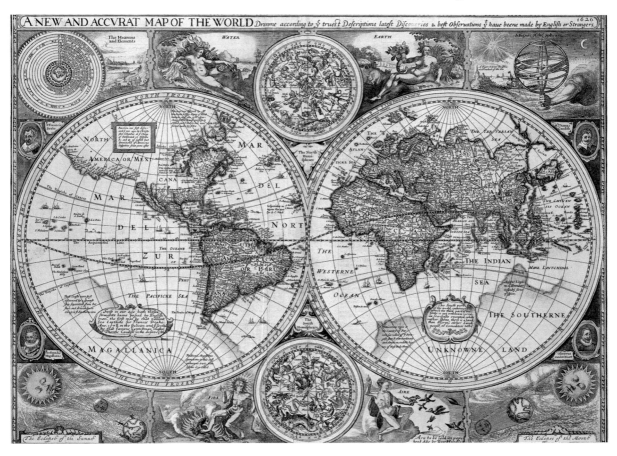

Spanish colony. He failed to find the islands of his earlier visit, although the ships touched at the Marquesas, where the slaughter of perhaps as many as 200 of the islanders made an ominous beginning to the relationship between Europeans and Polynesians.

Mendaña died on the expedition but his chief pilot, Pedro de Quiros, returned to the South Pacific ten years later in an attempt to find and settle the great southern continent. In May 1606 he sighted and named Espiritu Santo, the main island in the group later known as the New Hebrides (today's Vanuatu), and decided that it was part of the continent. Quiros's attempt to found a settlement there, New Jerusalem, ended in violence and abandonment of the venture. It was left to his second in command, Luis Vaez de Torres, to make the more significant discovery that there was a passage between New Guinea and the coast stretching away to the south. Memory of this soon faded, until in 1770 Cook proved the existence of the Torres Strait by sailing through it. The discovery of Espiritu Santo was inflated by Quiros to epic and mystical proportions. It was, he claimed, 'the fifth part of the Terrestrial Globe', an earthly paradise, rich in spices, silver and gold, with its numerous inhabitants waiting for conversion. Despite all his hopes and plans, Quiros never returned to the South Pacific and it was altogether appropriate that a different and more realistic view of the region should be taken by the Dutch, enemies to Spain both in Europe and overseas.

As the Dutch East India Company began to establish itself in the Spice Islands at the expense of the Portuguese, so it sent out expeditions to investigate the unknown seas and lands to the south. In 1605, a year before Quiros reached Espiritu Santo, the Dutch made their first landfall on the Australian coast, in the Gulf of Carpentaria. This was the first of a series of reconnaissance probes along the northern and western coasts of the continent in the first half of the century which culminated in the ambitious explorations of Abel Tasman. In 1642–43 he sailed south of New Holland (the name given by the Dutch to what is now Australia), touched on the coast of Van Diemen's Land (Tasmania) and then sailed east to a land he named New Zealand before heading north to Tonga. In 1644 he surveyed much of the northern shoreline of the Australian continent, but failed to find the Torres Strait.

By circumnavigating the Australian landmass, if at a distance, Tasman had shown that it could not be part of a greater southern continent stretching towards Cape Horn. The unknown continent was pushed back at least as far as the stretch of New Zealand coastline which he had sighted. Maps of the region made this clear but they could not convey the unenthusiastic Dutch reaction to New Holland, whose proud name flattered to deceive. Landing only briefly and for the most part along the north and west coasts of Australia, the Dutch accounts described a land which was arid and barren, devoid of exploitable resources and inhabited by a few primitive nomads who

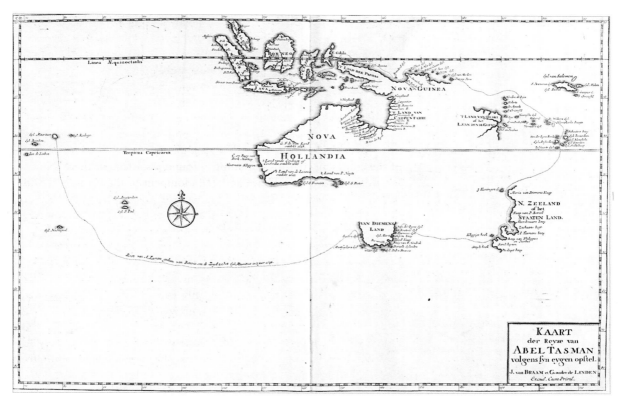

seemed as backward as any people in the world. Tasman's brief
encounter with the Maori of the South Island of New Zealand, which
left four of his men dead, strengthened the generally unfavourable
view of the region.

Amid the disappointments there were also some notable achievements, for it was in this period of Dutch exploration that the expedition
of Jacob Le Maire and Isaac Schouten (1615–16) found an alternative
route into the Pacific from the east. Their ships sailed past the Atlantic
entrance to the Strait of Magellan, round Cape Horn and into the
South Sea, and in time the passage round the Horn rather than that
through the narrow windings of the Strait became the normal route.
A postscript to the Dutch voyages of the seventeenth century came
when, in 1722, ships commanded by Jacob Roggeveen sailed far
enough south as they rounded Cape Horn to encounter icebergs,
touched at Samoa and the fringes of the Society Islands and
brought back to Europe the first reports of Easter Island and its
mysterious statues.

Juxtaposed with the discoveries, mostly disheartening in terms of
potential exploitation, was a continuing hope that somewhere in the
unexplored stretches of the southern ocean lay rich and fertile countries.
As the Americas and the Far East became known and exploited by
Europeans, so speculative attention focused on the Pacific. There the

Chart of Abel Tasman's voyage by
J. van Braam and G. de Linden,
published in François Valentyn's
and Johannes Van Keulen's, *De Zee
en Land Caarten en geigter van
steeden en Landvertooniugen van
Oost-Indien* (Amsterdam, *c.* 1726).
This summarizes the contribution of
the Dutch voyages of the first half
of the seventeenth century. The
marked track is that of Tasman's
voyage of 1642–43, which touched
on the coasts of Van Diemen's Land
(Tasmania) and New Zealand before
turning north through the Tongan
Islands. The chart also shows how
the Dutch explorations of the first
three decades of the seventeenth
century revealed the coastal outline
of the western half of New Holland
or Australia. The question of
whether New Guinea was an island
or a peninsula is left unanswered,
and Quiros's discovery of Espiritu
Santo (Vanuatu) is shown in a way
which suggests that it was part of
New Holland.

Quiros fantasy still shed its glow and utopian visionaries set extraordinary lands and societies in the region that they vaguely identified as *Terra Australis*. Accounts of voyages, real and imaginary, became bestsellers, especially in England, whose seamen were once more active in the South Sea as a multi-national wave of buccaneering raids swept along the Pacific coasts of Spanish America in the later seventeenth century. Buccaneers from Henry Morgan onwards held a place in popular esteem that reflected admiration both for their perceived role as fighters against Spain and popery and for the 'rags to riches' aspect of their depredations. An essential element in this heroising process came from their own writings, for some buccaneers went to sea with pen as well as sword in hand.

Among them was William Dampier, whose several South Sea voyages were described by him in books that became best-sellers. Dampier's visit to the western shores of Australia in 1688 produced a denigratory description of the Aborigines as 'the miserablest People in the World', which Cook turned to when in 1770 he viewed for the first time the east coast of Australia and its Aboriginal inhabitants. Although on one of his voyages Dampier discovered and named the

Title page of *A New Voyage Round the World* by William Dampier. First published in 1697, and reprinted several times, Dampier's best-known book formed the first volume of a multi-volume set of his writings published in 1729. The lengthy sub-title of the book reveals the astonishing range of his travels, while Herman Moll's accompanying map has eliminated the gigantic southern continent of earlier cartographers.

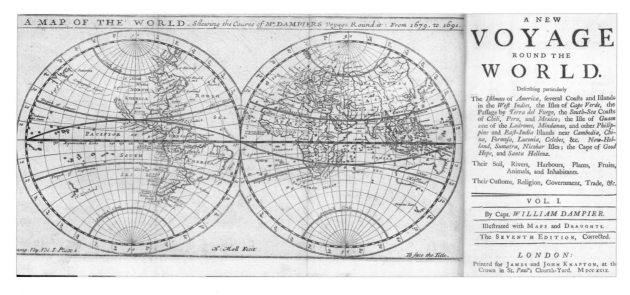

island – in fact, three islands – of New Britain just east of New Guinea, his books and those of other buccaneers and privateers such as Bartholomew Sharp, Woodes Rogers and George Shelvocke provided more in the way of literary entertainment than geographical knowledge. Certainly they influenced two of the best-known writers of early eighteenth-century England, Daniel Defoe and Jonathan Swift. The island adventures of Defoe's Robinson Crusoe were inspired by the marooning of the privateer Alexander Selkirk on Juan Fernández, while in *Gulliver's Travels* the first identifiable person named was 'My

cousin Dampier', and many of its hero's experiences were set in
Dampier's South Sea.

A map of the Pacific in the early eighteenth century makes it clear
that the uncertainties still outnumbered the certainties. Although from
Magellan onwards Europeans of several nations had ventured into and
sometimes across the great ocean, their explorations were mostly
inconclusive if not confusing. The immensity of the ocean, problems in
establishing longitude, the twin threats of scurvy and mutiny on long
voyages, and the constraints of wind and current presented formidable
obstacles to methodical exploration. In the North Pacific stretched the
one regular European trade route across the ocean, the galleon run
between the Philippines and Mexico, but little was known outside the
galleons' tracks. Japan's coasts had been charted by the Dutch but the
ocean to the north and east remained unexplored, and the Pacific
coast of America was known only as far north as California. Russian
expeditions sailing east from Kamchatka would be the first to explore
the northern waters between Asia and America but reliable information about their discoveries was slow to reach Europe. In the South
Pacific there had been sightings of some of the island groups near the
diagonal sailing course between the tip of South America and the East
Indies, but their location seemed to shift from voyage to voyage.
'There are in the South-Sea many Islands, which may be called
Wandering-Islands', the British geographer John Green complained.
The coasts of the western half of New Holland, New Guinea and
New Britain, together with short stretches of the shoreline of Van
Diemen's Land and New Zealand, had been roughly charted, but
their relationship with each other and with the hoped-for southern
continent was unknown.

If the geography of the Pacific was blurred, so was knowledge of
its inhabitants, for successive surges of migration across the ocean had
produced a complex racial and cultural pattern. European explorers
were entering a region where societies were organized in overlapping
layers, for there had been a mingling of peoples after migration and a
seeping of cultural influences from one island group to another. Once
in the Pacific the explorers found among the inhabitants a bewildering
and unpredictable variety of appearance and behaviour, the one undevi-
ating norm being that the Europeans regarded the islanders as incurably
light-fingered – a constant source of conflict which overshadowed
attempts at understanding and led to countless deaths. The observations of the discoverers were usually hasty and superficial, often the
result of a visit of only a few days, sometimes only a few hours. To the
islanders the strangers seemed apparitions, *atua* or men from the sky,
appearing and disappearing without warning. Encounters varied from
friendly to violent, but all too often ended with a blast of cannon or
musket on one side and a shower of stones and spears on the other.

The intrusion by buccaneers, privateers and illicit traders into
waters Spain regarded as its own was short-lived. The collapse in

The coat of arms of the South Sea
Company, *c*.1712. The Company was
founded in 1711 and its flamboyant
coat of arms indicates the maritime
ambitions that lay behind its
formation. Despite the oceanic
dimensions of the inset map, and
Parliament's grant to it of extensive
commercial privileges in the South
Sea, the Company never sent ships
to the Pacific. The collapse of its
stock in 1720 left Britain's credit
system badly damaged.

England and France in 1720 of a host of South Sea 'bubble' projects had a depressing effect on ventures to distant regions and the Pacific became associated with the South Sea Company, the collapse of whose stock had ruined many investors, great and small. As Defoe wrote, it was as if 'we were fully satisfied with what we have, that the enter-prising genius was buried with the old discoverers, and that there was neither room in the world nor inclination in our people to look any further'. Revival of interest came with the heightening of international tension in the middle decades of the century, and in particular after Commodore Anson's voyage across the Pacific and around the world (1740–44). This melodramatic episode of wartime achievement and disaster brought back memories of Drake and the legendary feats of English arms against the Spain of Philip II. After capturing the Acapulco treasure galleon off the Philippines, Anson brought back a

colossal treasure to wartime Britain, but at an appalling cost in lives. Out of more than 1900 men who sailed from England in 1740, almost 1400 died on the voyage – four from enemy action, a few from accidents, the rest from scurvy or other diseases. It was a grim reminder, if any were needed, of the perils of long oceanic voyages, and encouraged intensive research by James Lind and other members of the medical profession into the causes of scurvy. The official narrative of the voyage became a best-seller but it was more than a tale of adventure on the high seas. At one level it was intended to encourage 'navigation, commerce and the national interest'. At another it made an appeal to the imagination, for the life-saving months spent by Anson's scurvy-ridden crews at Juan Fernández and Tinian brought reminders of Crusoe's island, Rousseau's Nouvelle-Héloise and other tropical island fantasies.

Samuel Scott's oil painting of the engagement between Anson's *Centurion* and the *Nuestra Señora de Covadonga* off Cape Espiritu Santo in the Philippines, 20 June 1743. The action was a one-sided affair between a specialist fighting ship and a poorly armed galleon, but it redeemed a venture that until then had been marked only by its losses of men and ships. The colossal treasure taken from the galleon seemed to epitomise the wealth of the South Sea and helped to pave the way for a renewal of British interest in the great ocean.

Peircy Brett, 'A View of the Commodore's Tent at the Island of Juan Fernandes', as engraved in Richard Walter, *A Voyage Round the World by George Anson*, 1748. Juan Fernández, 120 leagues off the coast of Chile, proved a haven for Anson's surviving ships and men. There the survivors recovered from scurvy on an island which, one of Anson's officers wrote, 'seems providentially calculated for the relief of distressed adventurers'. The text described the idyllic scene of Brett's drawing, a lawn gently sloping to the beach, with bay and myrtle trees giving the whole scene the appearance of an amphitheatre. The island theme was to be given an even more vivid and appealing form in the paintings of William Hodges on Cook's second voyage.

The publicity surrounding Anson's voyage led to international speculation about the potential of the Pacific region. In France in 1756 Charles de Brosses published the first collection of voyages devoted exclusively to the Pacific, *Histoire des Navigations aux Terre Australes*, which was soon plagiarized by John Callander in an English edition. The narratives printed in these volumes confirmed that the earlier voyages had produced as much confusion as enlightenment. Islands had been sighted and resighted, identified and then lost again; low-lying clouds on the horizon had been mistaken for continental ranges; straits had become bays, and bays straits. The map of the Pacific was marked by squiggles of coastline that hinted at lands of continental dimensions, and it was dotted with island groups whose names and locations changed with the whims of cartographical fashion. But for De Brosses the exploration of the Pacific, and especially the discovery of a southern continent, was a nobler objective of French ambitions than the endless European wars. As he asked, 'What comparison can be made between the execution of a project such as this, and the conquest of some little ravaged province?' Likewise, in Britain, the geographer Alexander Dalrymple suggested that the southern continent might be 5000 miles (8000 km) across and populated by 50 million inhabitants. The 'scraps' from its economy, he

A View of the COMMODORE'S TENT at the Island of JUAN FERNANDES.

declared, 'would be sufficient to maintain the power, dominion and sovereignty of Britain, by employing all its manufactures and ships'.

After the ending of the Seven Years War in 1763 both Britain and France experienced a 'Pacific craze' in which a new kind of naval hero emerged in the shape of explorers whose ships left for the unknown, to return years later laden with specimens from the South Seas and with their crews eager to publish accounts, maps and views of the exotic places they had visited. At home enthusiasts assumed that the unexplored lands of the Pacific held resources sufficient to tilt the commercial balance of power in Europe – for Britain to confirm the overseas superiority brought by the wartime conquests, for France to redress the humiliations of an unsuccessful war and an imposed peace. The first voyage in the new era of state-sponsored Pacific exploration was Commodore John Byron's in 1764. It was an unconvincing start, for Byron – the poet's grandfather – followed the normal slanting sailing route from the tip of South America across the Pacific and made few discoveries of note. He ignored, perhaps sensibly, that part of his instructions which ordered him, after making discoveries in the South Pacific, to sail to the distant reaches of the North Pacific and there search for the entrance of the North-West Passage. That formidable task would have to wait for Cook and his final voyage. In 1766 the Admiralty sent out two more ships, commanded by Captain Samuel Wallis and Lieutenant Philip Carteret, with orders to sail into high latitudes in search of the southern continent. A few months later ships of the French navy left European waters under the command of one of the outstanding Frenchmen of the day, Louis-Antoine de Bougainville, also bound for the Pacific.

After becoming separated from Wallis's ship, the enterprising Carteret crossed the Pacific farther south than any of his predecessors and in doing so removed part of the supposed southern continent from the maps. Wallis took a more cautious route but his voyage was marked by a chance discovery whose emotional impact was out of all proportion to its geographical significance. In June 1767 he sighted Tahiti, an island of idyllic beauty which for generations was to conjure up voluptuous images of the South Seas. To the crew of a discovery vessel after months at sea, the islands of Polynesia were an earthly paradise. To the breaking surf, palm-fringed beaches and towering volcanic peaks were added sensual overtones – of women and girls, nubile, garlanded and welcoming. The opportunities, in the words of one of Wallis's officers, 'made all our men madly fond of the shore, even the sick who had been on the doctor's list for some weeks'. When Bougainville's ships reached Tahiti the following year, reactions were even more effusive and extravagant. Bougainville called the island New Cythera after Aphrodite's fabled realm. His naturalist, Commerson, preferred an even more resonant name – Utopia. From Tahiti, Bougainville sailed west through the Samoan group and on to the Espiritu Santo of Pedro de Quiros, which he found to be insular,

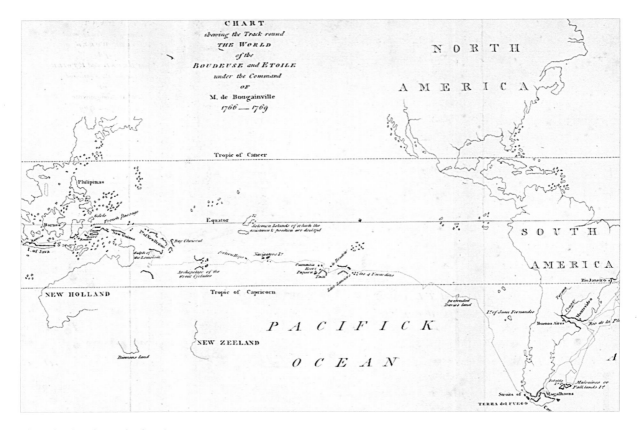

Chart showing the track of Louis Antoine de Bougainville's ships through the South Pacific in 1768. This French naval expedition immediately preceded Cook's *Endeavour* voyage and the chart shows what was known, and not known, about the Pacific just before Cook sailed. Tahiti and some of the Society Islands are marked, and farther west Bougainville identified the Spanish 'Espiritu Santo' (his 'Grandes Cyclades') as insular rather than continental. But his abrupt turn north at the Great Barrier Reef prevented Bougainville from reaching the unknown east coast of Australia or of investigating the existence of the Torres Strait.

not continental as the Spaniard navigator had imagined. The expedition continued westward in search of the unknown east coast of New Holland before the outliers of the Great Barrier Reef forced it away north.

For all the flurry of activity that these voyages represented, the central issues of Pacific geography were no nearer solution. The fabulous continent of *Terra Australis* had simply receded a little farther south; New Holland was still the western outline of a land of unknown extent; islands discovered and undiscovered remained to be properly identified and located. In the North Pacific, Russian expeditions had found a few pinpricks of land that might or might not be part of the American continent but a navigable North-West Passage remained as elusive as ever. Yet within a decade the outlines of both the North and South Pacific took shape on the maps in much the same form as they do today. The man responsible for this leap in knowledge was James Cook. His three voyages, following each other in quick succession, revealed the lands and peoples of the Pacific to Europe in a way no previous explorers had done.

1: CAPTAIN COOK AND THE VOYAGE OF *ENDEAVOUR*

'... a man, who has not the advantages of Education ... who has been constantly at sea from his youth, and who, with the Assistance of a few good friends [has] gone through all the Stations belonging to a Seaman, from a prentice boy in the Coal Trade to a Commander in the Navy ...'

Cook's description of himself, c.1775

In June 1766 the Council of the Royal Society of London resolved to send observers to various parts of the world to record the six-hour transit of the planet Venus across the face of the Sun, predicted for 3 June 1769. This rare event had first been seen in 1639, was the subject of widespread but imperfect observation on its next occurrence in 1761 and would not be repeated until 1874. The purpose of the observations, which had to be made from widely separated latitudes on the Earth's surface and precisely timed, was to calculate the distance from the Earth to the Sun. The result would provide one of the fundamental units of astronomy and enable estimation of the size of the solar system.

The difficulties of ensuring there were observers in the northern hemisphere were manageable. Finding a suitable, cloudless, daytime observation point south of the Equator – in the heart of the largely unknown Pacific – was another matter. In November 1767 the Society set up a Transit Committee which short-listed a number of locations and potential observers. As far as the Pacific was concerned, the Revd Nevil Maskelyne, Astronomer Royal and leading Transit Committee member, could only suggest a desirable general area, defined by latitude and longitude, where so-far-unknown islands might exist. Among individuals discussed, Alexander Dalrymple was proposed as 'an able Navigator and well skilled in Observation', who might be sent out in a ship which the government would be asked to provide.

Dalrymple (1737–1808) was a man of talent and ambition who was to become the Navy's first official hydrographer in 1795. Having

Alexander Dalrymple in later life, engraved from a drawing by John Brown.

gone to India in 1752 as an East India Company official, he acquired there a remarkable knowledge of early European exploration in the Indies and the Pacific. He rose to be the Company's deputy-secretary at Madras in 1758 and from 1760 to 1764 himself led several voyages through the Indonesian islands, with a professional sailing master. These opened up new trading opportunities and Dalrymple returned to England to press for Company support to develop them. In putting himself forward to observe the transit in the Pacific, Dalrymple also intended to be the expedition commander, with a greater personal mission in view. This was to prove the existence of *Terra Australis incognita*, the inhabitable but unknown 'southern continent', which geographers since classical times had suggested must exist around the South Pole in order to balance the landmasses in the northern hemisphere. His researches had made him a leader in this still widely accepted belief, which was a central tenet in his important edition of early Pacific voyage accounts, *A Historical Collection of Voyages ... in the South Pacific Ocean*, published in 1770–71.

The British authorities, less convinced, were at least alert to the potential benefits of such a continent and aware of rival French and Spanish interest. In 1764–66, they sent out Commodore John Byron to probe for it. He was instructed to examine and formally claim the Falkland Islands in the South Atlantic and to find a supposed 'Pepys Island' which, he rightly concluded, was a mis-sighting of them. Byron judged his ships, *Dolphin* and *Tamar*, were unfit to pursue his further objective of seeking an equally fabled 'north-west passage' back to the Atlantic from the Pacific coast of Canada and he only encountered Pacific islands, not continental land, as he took a circumnavigating route homeward via the East Indies. The *Dolphin* was then quickly sent out again in August 1766, under Captain Samuel Wallis and accompanied by the smaller *Swallow* under Philip Carteret, expressly to seek any landmass in the Pacific to the south of Byron's track.

Neither had returned when, in February 1768, the Royal Society petitioned George III for £4000 to mount the proposed transit expedition. It was to be a voyage of scientific prestige, not a continental search, and cited the well-proved case that advances in astronomy brought benefits to practical navigation – the basis of British sea trade and power. Maskelyne's first publication of the *Nautical Almanac* in 1766 and the 'lunar-distance' method of finding longitude which it facilitated were important recent examples. The King agreed to grant the money and the Admiralty supplied a ship, purchased for a further £2800 in the form of a stout Whitby collier. The Admirals, however, refused to have a civilian in overall command and Dalrymple was neither a naval officer nor a professional seaman. Compromise was impossible and he withdrew from the project.

The Board of Admiralty could have chosen a commander from many commissioned sea officers but accepted its Secretary's recommendation to appoint the master of the schooner *Grenville*, a well-regarded

[48] APRIL 1767.

Diftances of ☽'s Center from ☉, and from Stars weft of her

Days.	Stars Names.	12 Hours.	15 Hours.	18 Hours.	21 Hours.
		° ' ''	° ' ''	° ' ''	° ' ''
1		40. 59. 11	42. 34. 44	44. 9. 51	45. 44. 35
2		53. 32. 7	55. 4. 24	56. 36. 16	58. 7. 45
3		65. 39. 18	67. 8. 27	68. 37. 14	70. 5. 39
4	The Sun.	77. 22. 36	78. 48. 58	80. 15. 1	81. 40. 46
5		88. 45. 20	90. 9. 27	91. 33. 21	92. 57. 0
6		99. 52. 6	101. 14. 34	102. 36. 52	103. 59. 1
7		110. 47. 42	112. 9. 6	113. 30. 25	114. 51. 40
6	Aldebaran	50. 36. 10	52. 4. 5	53. 31. 57	54. 59. 44
7		62. 17. 43	63. 45. 10	65. 12. 34	66. 39. 57
8	Pollux.	31. 25. 48	32. 53. 11	34. 20. 40	35. 48. 12
9		43. 7. 5	44. 35. 4	46. 3. 8	47. 31. 15
10		17. 51. 57	19. 20. 36	20. 49. 26	22. 18. 27
11		29. 45. 36	31. 15. 26	32. 45. 26	34. 15. 35
12	Regulus.	41. 48. 49	43. 19. 55	44. 51. 10	46. 22. 36
13		54. 2. 11	55. 34. 36	57. 7. 12	58. 39. 59
14		66. 26. 28	68. 0. 18	69. 34. 20	71. 8. 33
15		25. 4. 34	26. 39. 23	28. 14. 26	29. 49. 44
16	Spica ♍	37. 49. 37	39. 26. 14	41. 3. 5	42. 40. 8
17		50. 48. 40	52. 26. 59	54. 5. 31	55. 44. 15
18		64. 1. 2	65. 41. 3	67. 21. 18	69. 1. 48
19		31. 37. 14	33. 19. 7	35. 1. 13	36. 43. 32
20	Antares.	45. 18. 29	47. 2. 10	48. 46. 5	50. 30. 12
21		59. 14. 6	60. 59. 31	62. 45. 11	64. 31. 2
22		73. 23. 37	75. 10. 43	76. 58. 2	78. 45. 31
23	Capricorni.	33. 17. 26	35. 4. 38	36. 52. 4	38. 39. 45
24		47. 41. 9	49. 29. 53	51. 18. 44	53. 7. 40
25	Aquilæ	65. 57. 35	67. 29. 54	69. 2. 36	70. 35. 39
26		78. 24. 51	79. 59. 9	81. 33. 29	83. 7. 45

MAY 1767. [49]

Days of the Month	Days of the Week	Sundays, Holidays, &c.	Phafes of the Moon.
			D. H. '
			Firft Quarter —— 5. 8. 30
			Full Moon —— 13. 8. 26
			Laft Quarter —20. 10. 14
			New Moon——27. 6. 37
1	F.	St. Philip and St. James.	
2	Sa.		
3	Su.	2d Sun. Eaft. Inv. +	Other Phenomena.
4	M.	From Eafter in 15 Days,	D.
5	Tu.	[1 ret.	1. ☾ 3 poft ♅ 2ʰ 13'.
6	W.	Johnante P.L. Termbeg.	2. ☾ ε II 5ʰ 12'.
7	Th.		3. ♂ infra Cornu bor. ♉ diff. Lat. 3'.
8	F.		4. ☾ ♃ ♋ 13ʰ 18'.
9	Sa.		8. ☾ υ ♌ 10ʰ 59'.
10	Su.	3d. Sunday after Eafter.	9. ♃ Stationary.
11	M.	From Eaft. in 3 Weeks,	13. ☾ π ♏ 21ʰ 10'.
12	Tu.	[2 ret.	14. ☾ σ ♏ 6ʰ 0'.
13	W.		☾ α ♏ 9ʰ 32'.
14	Th.		♀ infra Cornu bor. ♉ diff. Lat. 20'.
15	F.		16. ☾ λ ♐ 8ʰ 49'.
16	Sa.		☾ σ ♐ 19ʰ 26'.
17	Su.	4th Sun. after Eaft. [3 ret.	20. ☾ ⸮ ♒ 11ʰ 1'.
18	M.	From Eafter in 1 Month,	☉ enters II at 21ʰ 46'.
19	Tu.	Q.Charlotte born, 1744,	23. ☾ ε II diff. Lat. 50'.
20	W.	[Dunitan.	24. ☾ η ♓ 5ʰ 23'.
21	Th.		♀ II diff. Lat. 16'.
22	F.		27. ☾ ♂ ♀ diff. Lat. 37'.
23	Sa.		28. ☾ 3 poft ♀ ♉ 11ʰ 24'.
24	Su.	5 Su. after Eaft. Reg. Sun.	29. ☾ ε II 14ʰ 11'.
25	M.	From Eafter in 5 W. 4 ret.	☾ ♂ 22ʰ 29' : ☾ will e-clipfe ♂
26	Tu.	Auguftin, 1ft Abp.Cant. Venerable Bede.	30. ☾ ♀ 1ʰ 49' : ♀ more North.
27	W.		31. ☾ ⸮ ♋ 21ʰ 38'.
28	Th.	Afcenfion-day, H.Thurf.	
29	F.	K. Charles II. Reft. Mor-[row of Afcenf. 5 ret.	
30	Sa.		
31	Su.	Sunday after Afcenfion day.	

Maskelyne's *Nautical Almanac*, published annually from 1766 (for the subsequent year), supplied the necessary tables for seamen to calculate their longitude using 'lunar distances'. It was the most significant navigational result of work at the Royal Observatory at Greenwich since its foundation in 1675.

warrant officer and notable marine surveyor. He was a steady, married man of thirty-nine, who had proven navigational and astronomical skills and had shown much expertise in charting difficult waters, most recently in his thorough surveys of the coast of Newfoundland. His name was James Cook.

Cook's early years

Cook was born on 27 October 1728 at Marton-in-Cleveland, a small country parish in the North Riding of Yorkshire, his father – also James – being an agricultural day labourer of lowland Scots origin. His mother, Grace, was a Yorkshire girl. Young James was the second child and second son in a family of eight, but only he and two sisters lived beyond 1750.

Cook's father was a poor man and James was fortunate in gaining a modest education in reading, writing and arithmetic, principally at the charitable Postgate School at Great Ayton where James senior became a farm foreman in 1736. In 1745, at the small Yorkshire fishing port of Staithes, seventeen-year-old James junior began a trial employment as shop boy to William Sanderson, a grocer and haber-dasher, but after eighteen months both realized that this was not his *métier*. Supported by Sanderson, Cook instead went over to nearby Whitby and entered a three-year apprenticeship to become a seaman in the coastal colliers of John Walker, a respected Quaker sea captain and ship-owner. Walker was to become Cook's lifelong friend and

Harrison's first marine timekeeper (H1), 1735. The first of the Yorkshire clockmaker's three table-top experimental models proved remarkably successful at sea but was only perfected in the fourth, much smaller, 'watch' version of 1759.

their association was also the indirect start of another: that of Cook and the greatest British voyages of scientific exploration with the local 'cat-bark' colliers, the workhorses of the east coast and North Sea trade.

Cook, like most boys, entered as a 'servant' and his first voyage (with nine fellow apprentices in a crew of nineteen) was in the *Freelove*, a 341-ton Yarmouth-built ship, under John Jefferson. Two years later Cook helped him to fit out a new ship of Walker's, the *Three Brothers*, and sailed in her from June 1748 to December 1749, initially carrying coal and then taking troops home from Flanders to Dublin and London under government contract. In April 1750 Cook completed his apprenticeship and continued as an able seaman in this and other ships until December 1752. He then rose to be mate of the *Friendship*, a new Walker vessel, in which he remained for another two-and-a-half years, under three successive masters, ranging from Whitby to Norway and the Netherlands. In the *Friendship*, no doubt, his skills expanded into mature competency in North Sea coastal navigation and pilotage, since Walker invited him to become the ship's next master.

Astonishingly, it was an offer Cook declined. He instead decided to enter the Royal Navy, volunteering as an able seaman at Wapping,

London, on 17 June 1755. In terms of pay and status it was a backward step for, as Nelson later said of his own 1770s experience, merchant seamen then had 'a horror of the Royal Navy'. Cook himself gave no reason for it except a later hint, after his second Pacific voyage, that his 'ambition' led him to range further than other men. Although in 1755 he could not know how far and in what remarkable capacity this would be, the Navy was then already embroiled in the undeclared phase of the Seven Years War with France (1756–63). Fought substantially in North America and India, this was to take Cook farther than he had yet been and – not without risk – give him opportunities beyond those open to a provincial short-trade shipmaster.

Cook was assigned to the 60-gun *Eagle* at Portsmouth, and within a month was promoted to master's mate. On 1 October, after she was driven back to repair weather damage from a cruise in the western approaches, a fellow Yorkshireman who would play an important part in Cook's career took over command – the competent, energetic and experienced Hugh Palliser (1723–96). A week later, the *Eagle* sailed out again on a stormy and active cruise, taking part in the capture of one French warship before the end of October and the sinking, on fire, of another in November. In January 1756 Cook became her boatswain in addition to his mate's duties and that spring, while patrolling the southern Brittany coast, Palliser gave him temporary command of the *Cruizer*, a cutter. He subsequently brought home a merchant prize, taken in the Bay of Biscay, and in January 1757 took part in a severe fight when the *Eagle* and *Medway* captured a well-armed French Indiaman south-west of Ushant. That June, after Cook's friend Walker solicited his local MP to approach Palliser, the Captain recommended Cook's promotion to Master – the senior warrant officer of a ship of war, charged with her routine navigation and maintenance of her sailing capacity. By then he had also learnt the necessary techniques of celestial navigation for ocean voyaging. On 29 June 1757 he was successfully examined by Trinity House, Deptford, and the next day was appointed Master of the *Solebay*, a 24-gun frigate patrolling Scottish waters.

In October 1757, at Portsmouth, Cook became Master of the 64-gun *Pembroke*, under Captain John Simcoe, which in February 1758 sailed as part of Admiral Boscawen's fleet for Halifax, Nova Scotia. This appointment was to make his name in a major theatre of war, for the fleet and the troops it conveyed were being sent to help to loosen the French hold on Canada: first, by destruction of the fortress of Louisbourg, on Cape Breton Island, guarding the Gulf of St Lawrence; second by ascending the lower St Lawrence River and taking Quebec. The day after Louisbourg fell in July, Cook had a fortuitous meeting ashore with a military surveyor called Samuel Holland, whom he had watched busily taking angles with a surveyor's plane table. Holland was delighted to instruct him in its use. Cook's interest was actively

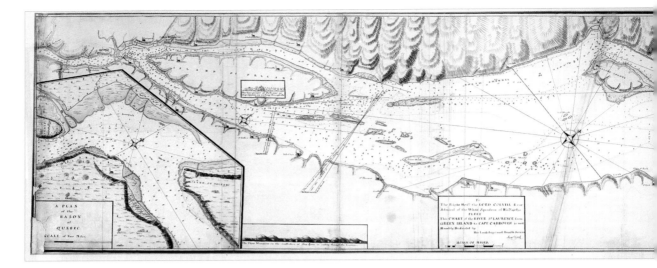

supported and shared by his scientifically minded captain, Simcoe, and
Cook himself conducted a small survey of the Bay of Gaspé in 1758.
This became his first chart to be published, in London later that year,
although Cook spent the long winter with the small squadron left at
Halifax. There, under the joint guidance of Simcoe and Holland, he
developed his skills as a cartographer and studied the higher reaches
of navigational astronomy.

Simcoe unfortunately died in the spring of 1759, which saw the
return of the main fleet from England under Admiral Sir Charles
Saunders, bringing back Major-General Wolfe for his second season's
campaign. Then followed the difficult advance up the St Lawrence
River to Quebec, in which Cook and the rest of the masters in the

'The Death of General Wolfe.'
Cook played a significant role in
the naval operations which carried
Wolfe's army up the St Lawrence
to take Quebec in 1759. This is
the enormously successful
engraving made from Benjamin
West's influential painting
of 1771.

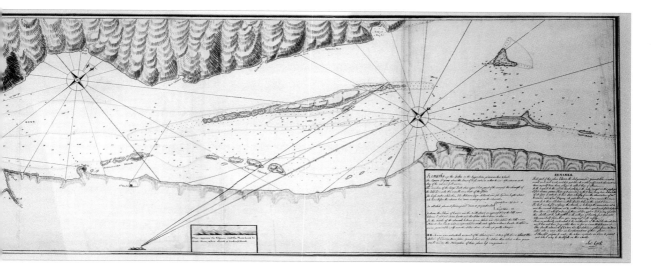

Cook's chart of the St Lawrence. One of several manuscript versions, signed by Cook, this was the result of the work that allowed the Royal Navy to land Wolfe's forces at Quebec. It was also engraved and published.

fleet were heavily involved, both as ship-handlers and in surveying and recording the passage. Quebec fell to Wolfe's assault on 13 September, with himself and his opponent, Montcalm, heading the list of dead. Cook was shortly afterwards transferred to the *Northumberland*, under Captain Lord Colville, and again spent the winter at Halifax, although the great 'New Chart of the River St Lawrence' which Saunders published in England in 1760 included a large element of his work. A French counter-siege of Quebec was lifted that May and when Montreal fell in September to British army assault from upper New York, Canada was secured. In January 1761, still at Halifax, Colville awarded Cook a bonus of £50 – over eight months' salary – for 'his indefatigable industry in making himself Master of the Pilotage of the River Saint Lawrence' and two years later in England was even more warmly to recommend his 'Genius and Capacity' as a surveyor to the Admiralty. In the interim Cook gave further proof of this. He made detailed observations of the coast of Nova Scotia and took significant part as a surveyor and pilot in operations that repelled a French assault on St John's, Newfoundland, in the summer of 1762. He then returned to England with Colville.

The charting of Newfoundland, especially its southern and western coasts, was to occupy Cook from 1763 to 1767 – the first years of peace – and on a regular pattern: systematic surveying ashore and afloat in the late spring and summer, then returning to London to work up and submit the results over the winter. He was to begin publishing them as charts in 1766. That year he also observed an eclipse of the Sun in Newfoundland, the subject of his first brief scientific communication to the Royal Society.

Set across the mouth of the St Lawrence, Newfoundland was sparsely populated but strategically placed and was the seasonal base for working the Grand Banks fishery, itself economically important to

Britain. Many nations fished the Banks but on and around Newfoundland the Royal Navy maintained jurisdiction through a naval governor, sent out each spring. Charts of the island and adjacent lesser ones were poor, and Cook was keenly sought to remedy this by the new governor, Captain Samuel Graves, who had recognized his expertise in the anti-French operations there of 1762. Palliser had also been involved and added his recommendations to those of Graves (whom he succeeded as Governor, 1764–66). The Admiralty agreed and on 15 May 1763 Cook sailed from Plymouth, in Graves's *Antelope*, to begin his work, for which the schooner *Grenville* was locally purchased. He had been back in London just over six months but only six weeks of that before he was married, on 21 December 1762, to twenty-one-year-old Elizabeth Batts of Barking, Essex. How and when they met is a mystery but, like many seamen's wives, she was to see little of him. Their six children were largely born and raised (and three died) in his absence; all were dead long before she herself died aged ninety-three, in 1835, after a widowhood of fifty-six years.

Endeavour: the voyage of 1768–71

On 29 March 1768, the Navy Board reported that they had bought, in the Thames, the Whitby-built collier *Earl of Pembroke* – fourteen months old, of 368 tons burthen and 106 ft long overall (32.3 m). The ship was seaworthy and strong, roomy for its small size and capable of being beached upright on a flat bottom. The Admiralty directed that the name be changed to '*Endeavour*, bark' (there was already an *Endeavour* in the Navy List) and the vessel armed and fitted at Deptford Dockyard to sail for the South Seas. Cook was only appointed to command in April and as the proposed complement rose to seventy (deaths being expected), the Admiralty decided to commission him Lieutenant, and gave him a second lieutenant in Zachary Hicks and later a third, John Gore – formerly a master's mate under Byron in the *Dolphin*. Others of note who had also sailed with Byron were seaman (later Lieutenant) Charles Clerke and Richard Pickersgill, master's mate. The Naval and Marine complement was eventually 98, plus the Royal Society's civilian astronomer, Samuel Green, who with Cook would observe the transit of Venus. With Green and his servant, in July, arrived an unexpected addition of nine more for the already crowded ship. Joseph Banks Esq., FRS, aged twenty-five, 'a Gentleman of large fortune … well versed in natural history', had persuaded both the Society and the Admiralty that the botanical and natural sciences would be well served by his inclusion – at his own expense – and came aboard with a 'suite' of eight: the Swedish botanist, Dr Daniel Carl Solander, a pupil of Linnaeus; the artists Alexander Buchan and Sydney Parkinson, to perform the recording roles today achieved by photography; also Banks's secretary, Dr Herman Diedrich Spöring (another Swede), four servants and two greyhounds. A famous addition – among the usual livestock which all ships carried – was a

The Australian-built replica of *Endeavour* leaving the Thames in 1996, on her first visit to Britain.

milch goat, just home from its first round-the-world voyage in the hard-worked *Dolphin*, with Captain Wallis.

Wallis had returned to England in May 1768 as first European discoverer of an earthly paradise that he called 'King George's Island', right in the centre of Maskelyne's prescribed area for the transit observation. He also had accurate latitude and longitude for it (17° 30' south, 150° west), the latter calculated by his mathematically inclined purser using 'Dr Masculine's method, which we did not understand'; that is, by lunar-distance observation. This island now became Cook's intended goal. Its local name was Tahiti.

Although only the Admiralty took note of it from the official voyage journals (all handed in as restricted documents, as were Cook's), some of Wallis's men also reported seeing extensive high land well south of the new island. Investigating this latest rumour of *Terra Australis* headed the supplementary 'Secret Instructions' Cook was to fulfil after completing the transit work. He was also to claim possession of useful places discovered, in European legal terms, although friendship with all native peoples encountered was to be cultivated. They were to be treated with respect, civility and caution, their ways observed and, where possible, fair trade conducted for fresh food and other items. Lord Morton, President of the Royal Society, also supplied an enlightened and perceptive memorandum on observations to be made and cultural and moral issues likely to arise in encounters with 'primitive' peoples. All this Cook absorbed, not as a romantic self-motivated adventurer but as a professional seaman determined to achieve objectives laid down by others. Humanity in his general dealings and a conscientious pursuit of the aims set for him were to be the hallmarks of all his Pacific voyages. His genius lay in the exceptional judgement with which he interpreted his instructions and the professional skill with which he met and surpassed their expectations.

The crowded *Endeavour* left Plymouth on 25 August 1768 and reached Rio de Janeiro on 13 November. At Madeira, Cook obtained and distributed onions among the crew and flogged two men for refusing to eat fresh meat – the start of an insistence on fresh food and greens of any palatable sort to prevent scurvy, as was his strict demand for cleanliness both of ship and crew. As a voyage on which there were few cases of scurvy and no deaths from shipboard-generated illness, the *Endeavour*'s was unprecedented and the model for both which followed. Leaving Rio on 7 December, after problems with the authorities, they landed briefly on Tierra del Fuego, where an unwise foray resulted in Banks's two black servants being frozen to death in a snowstorm and Solander narrowly escaping the same fate. Cook then passed through the Strait of Le Maire and rounded Cape Horn on 27 January 1769. He reached his farthest point south in *Endeavour* three days later, in latitude 60° 4' south, before altering course north and then west for Tahiti. This was sighted on 11 April after *Endeavour* passed through – and Cook recorded – much of the Tuamotu archipelago.

On 13 April they found the *Dolphin*'s anchorage in idyllic
Matavai Bay, on the north-west coast near modern Papeete.
Welcoming Tahitian canoes came out as soon as the ship was sighted
and, despite the language barrier, trade and cordial relations rapidly
began. The endemic South Seas problem, based on different values
and common to nearly all the islands Cook visited, was the inhabitants' persistence and expertise as thieves. Iron of any portable sort
vanished, especially nails (the common currency of trade), clothes, a
gun, a valuable quadrant and many other items. Most of any significance were recovered as the expectations and fire-power of the visitors
became clear, one Tahitian being shot dead in a rare lapse of control
which Cook greatly regretted. He also began to develop his technique
of 'detaining' local property, and sometimes people, against restitution
and flogged his own men when they could be identified for theft, or
abetting it. The usual reason was to trade for the sexual liberality of
the Tahitian women. Cook was well aware of the dangers of this and
his duty to his hosts: the Tahitians (though not all Pacific islanders)
suffered from yaws, which gave immunity to syphilis but not to
gonorrhoea. Anyone suspected of infection was confined to the ship
until pronounced clear although, as soon appeared, it had already
reached the island through Hitaa on the east coast. Cook suspected a
Spanish source but it was, in fact, the French, when Bougainville's
Boudeuse and *Etoile* had touched there shortly after Wallis, whose
own crew was another possible source of the disease.

Cook's chart of Tahiti.

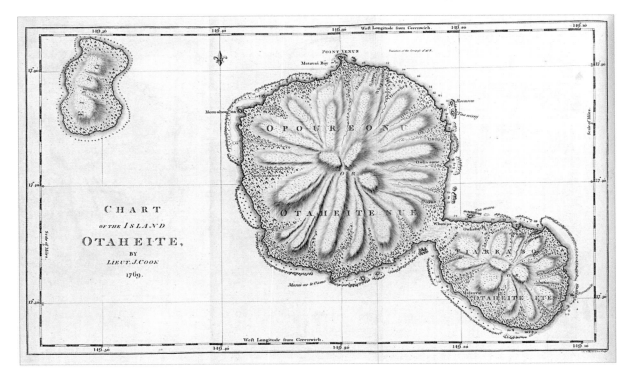

Banks and Solander were in heaven, plant collecting and recording – although their ethnographic and landscape artist, Alexander Buchan, died of an epileptic fit – and in the fort and observatory that Cook built on 'Point Venus', Green set up equipment to observe the transit. This was successfully done on 3 June in a daytime temperature of 119°F (48.3°C), two parties under Hicks and Gore also recording it from other positions as back-up.

Endeavour sailed from Tahiti on 13 July to explore islands to the north-west, which Cook named the 'Society Islands' from their close grouping. He surveyed Huahine and he made a particular friend there of the chief, Ori. Pressed by Banks, he had agreed to take a young Tahitian chief and 'priest' Tupaia, who wished to see England, and his servant boy, Taiata. Neither survived the voyage but Tupaia quickly proved an asset as an interpreter and pilot, naming well over one hundred central Pacific islands, of which Cook managed to sketch a chart of seventy-four (see p.9).

On 9 August, complying with his 'Secret Instructions', Cook sailed south. He had already scotched earlier reports of continental land farther east in his southern sweep from Cape Horn. By 2 September he had crossed well beyond latitude 40° south but there was no sign of the land reported by the *Dolphin*, neither did the long ocean swell from that direction suggest the presence of any. As also instructed, he then cast westward to seek the eastern side of New Zealand, whose western coast had first been discovered by the Dutch navigator, Abel Tasman, in 1642.

On 6 October they sighted land but on reaching it two days later found the Maori inhabitants unfriendly and unwilling to trade, although Tupaia was understood by them. Three approaches were violently repulsed by the natives and, to Cook's grief, several were killed as he and his men defended themselves. Empty-handed, the *Endeavour* left Poverty Bay, as Cook named it, heading south and finding only further hostility ashore. Having reached beyond latitude 40° south once more, with the coast still running south and west, Cook named 'Cape Turnagain' and reversed his course there. The ship then made a sweep northward to replenish water among more friendly people below East Cape, before heading north-west across the Bay of Plenty. They stayed eleven days at Mercury Bay, so named because Cook and Green observed the transit of Mercury there, which gave them an accurate longitude. Despite one more fatal incident, they established friendly relations with the people, visited an impressive Maori fortified village or *pa* and found strong evidence suggesting that they were cannibals, though this was later questioned in England. Over eighty years later a local chief, Te Horeta, who visited *Endeavour* as a child and met Cook, could recount vivid memories of it. Heading north after a further edgy landing in the Bay of Islands, Cook's running survey of the heavily fragmented coast was interrupted by a sustained gale on 13 December. This blew him out of sight of

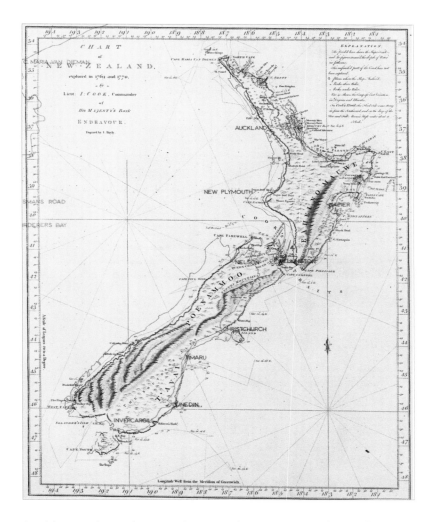

Cook's chart of New Zealand, published in 1772, with a modern overlay by the Hydrographic Office (1968) showing the remarkable accuracy he achieved in his initial survey.

land but on the 15th its resighting, and an increase in the south-western swell, showed they had passed Cape Maria van Diemen, the northern point of New Zealand.

Cook managed to plot this from a distance and with great accuracy before continuing his running survey down the dangerous west coast. On 14 January 1770 a huge bay opened to the eastward, on the south side of which Cook found what was to become a favourite harbour, Ship Cove, in the narrow Queen Charlotte Sound. Surrounded by plentiful wood, water, greenstuffs, exotic birds and a friendly, if possibly cannibalistic people, the *Endeavour* was thoroughly overhauled. Climbing a hill, Cook also confirmed what Tasman had suspected: the bay he had entered was, in fact, the wide strait which now bears his own name, dividing the two islands of New Zealand. On 6 February he sailed into it, narrowly avoiding being carried ashore by its treacherous tidal current. He then completed his survey of North Island by stretching north to resight Cape Turnagain, before reversing course once more and heading down the east coast of South Island in tempestuous weather. By 13 March he had rounded the southern end and was again sailing up the western side, completing (in Banks's phrase) 'the total demolition of our aëriel fabrick' that it might be part of a southern continent. His survey was to result in the first chart of New Zealand, compiled on a single pass to an extraordinary level of thoroughness and accuracy.

By the end of March 1770, *Endeavour* had again resupplied at Admiralty Bay in the Cook Strait, as her captain used the discretion granted by his orders to consider his route home. Although he was tempted, the state of the ship argued against further hunting for a 'southern continent' on a high-latitude Pacific passage to Cape Horn. The same applied to a route directly to the Cape of Good Hope by passing south of Van Diemen's Land (Tasmania), then suspected to be part of 'New Holland' – Australia. Cook took the views of his officers and Banks and decided to sail via the East Indies, where *Endeavour* could refit properly, but with a variation. This was to head west and fall in with the totally unknown east coast of New Holland. He hoped to confirm whether Van Diemen's Land was joined to it and then to follow it north, with luck directly to the Indies.

They sailed at daylight on 31 March and on 19 April, driven too far north to see Van Diemen's Land, sighted the main south-east Australian coast. Cook turned north along it but was prevented from landing by the weather for another ten days. On the 29th, *Endeavour* finally entered a sheltered bay inhabited by a few primitive, shy, unfriendly people, with whom Tupaia could not communicate – the first Aborigines encountered. 'Isaac, you shall land first', said Cook to his wife's young cousin, Isaac Smith, as their boat rowed ashore in

'A view of the Endeavour River on the coast of New Holland, where the ship was laid on shore, in order to repair the damage which she received on the rock.' *Endeavour* was beached in June 1770 for seven weeks of repairs. William Byrne's engraving, probably after a lost drawing by Parkinson.

what was first called 'Sting ray's Harbour'. Later, after Banks and Solander had begun studying the harvest of new plants brought aboard, it became Botany Bay. Cook left on 6 May, naming but not entering the great inlet of Port Jackson, just to the north, where modern Sydney stands. On the 23rd he entered another good haven north of modern Brisbane, which he called Bustard Bay from the birds shot there, and then began his closest and worst brushes with disaster.

Cook's method of taking a running survey of land bearings required an inshore course but doing this up the Australian coast funnelled him, almost unaware, into the open southern jaws of the completely unknown Great Barrier Reef. *Endeavour* avoided the clearly growing dangers until about 11 o'clock on the night of 10 June, when she suddenly struck on a coral outcrop, nearly 20 miles (32 km) off the land. About 50 tons of weight – ballast, stores and the carriage guns – were thrown overboard but it was high tide and the ship was stuck fast, holed and flooding badly. With great difficulty she was hauled off a day later, a broken spur of coral fortunately jamming in the hole it had made, since the pumps could not otherwise have saved her. A sail was quickly fothered over the bottom and Cook laid the ship ashore a little to the north, in what has since been called the Endeavour River. Here, far from perfect repairs were made, sick and exhausted men recuperated on fresh turtle, shellfish and wild vegetables, and more plant collecting was done. Banks's surviving dog fruitlessly chased kangaroos – first seen, shot and eaten here but the local natives proved as hard to engage as at Botany Bay and caused panic by starting a bush fire, which destroyed the remains of the shore camp. On 4 August, Cook sailed again, picking his way through the reef for a week until he found a passage to the open sea. He had sailed over 1000 miles (1600km) since mid-May, taking soundings continuously.

Two days later, having shortened sail in the night, and with an onshore wind falling to calm, their boats had to tow the *Endeavour* against an inexorable swell carrying her back into the breakers. At one point they were within eighty yards of destruction but were saved by a catspaw of breeze, before more towing and a turn of wind and tide took them safely back through a gap – the 'Providential Channel' – in the unending reef. From then on, with a boat sounding ahead, they

'This animal is called by the natives *kanguroo*'. William Byrne's engraving after a lost drawing by Parkinson, from the official account of the *Endeavour* voyage. This is the animal shot by Lt. Gore on 14 July 1770 at Endeavour River. Next day Cook reported that it made excellent eating.

pursued an intricately slow course northward within the reef and on 21 August reached the tip of the vast hinterland, which Cook named Cape York. That evening, from a hill on offshore 'Possession Island', he saw that only sea lay westward and that the 2000-mile (3000-km) coast up which he had passed and now claimed as 'New South Wales' was not joined to New Guinea. He had confirmed the existence of the strait through which Torres had unwittingly sailed from the east in 1607 and Tasman had sighted from the west in 1644.

On 29 August, *Endeavour* raised the New Guinea coast and on 11 October anchored at Batavia (Jakarta), capital of the Dutch East Indies, on Java. There Cook was able to send home first news of *Endeavour* since she had left Rio nearly two years before, while the battered ship was taken into the Dutch dockyard and repaired. Her uncoppered hull was in a desperate condition, with major damage to the keel, shipworm, and planking cut to barely ⅛ in. (3 mm) thick in places. The Dutch did a good job but it took time and the long weeks at Batavia – a sink of malarial fever and dysentery – proved far more lethal to the crew than their past voyage. Banks and Solander succumbed but recovered; seven others died, including the Tahitians,

Batavia, now Jakarta, the capital of the Dutch East Indies, in a print of 1796. Expansion of the city since the seventeenth century and the decay of its drainage canals had made it notoriously unhealthy for Europeans by Cook's time.

Tupaia and Tataia. Twenty-three more who left with Cook on 26 December also died from illness contracted there on the way to the Cape of Good Hope, including Spöring, Banks's secretary, Parkinson, the hard-working second artist, and astronomer Green. Heading north from Cape Town, Lieutenant Hicks was the final casualty, from long-standing tuberculosis, which allowed Clerke to be promoted in his place. The goat finished its second circumnavigation but Banks's last greyhound died before *Endeavour* anchored in the Downs, off Deal, on 13 July 1771.

There Cook stepped ashore with his journals and his 'charts, plans and drawings' for the Admiralty Board, under cover of a letter to its secretary. This modestly expressed hopes that the latter would 'be found sufficient to convey a Tolerable knowledge of the places they are intended to illustrate, & that the discoveries we have made, tho' not great, will Apologize for the length of the Voyage'. Given his unprecedented if not complete success – the southern continent question remained in the air – the apology must have appeared curiously unnecessary.

2: SHIPS IN COMPANY
The second and third voyages

*'... the ablest and most renowned Navigator
this or any country hath produced ...'*

Cook's epitaph by Admiral John Forbes

Early nineteenth-century Staffordshire
earthenware figure of Cook, in civilian
dress, based on the widespread
engravings from Dance's portrait.

Resolution and *Adventure*, 1772–75

Banks was a figure in society before he left England but his
triumphant return, with an epic story to tell in the highest
circles and a scientific haul of lasting value, made him even
more fêted than Cook. The more sober Admiralty was, however, well
pleased with their man: its new First Lord, the highly intelligent John
Montagu, fourth Earl of Sandwich, was henceforth Cook's most influential naval friend and quickly saw him promoted to Commander.
Unusually, he also received his new commission personally from the
King, to whom Sandwich took him with his charts and plans for an
hour's conversation.

With Dalrymple's influential *History* now in print, belief in the
'southern continent' was still strong and Cook's return tended to raise
rather than weaken confidence that it might be discoverable. Cook
himself was sure that, if there, it had to be farther south than so far
envisaged and had already sketched a plan to resolve the question by a
new voyage. This would not head west via the Horn but east round
the Cape of Good Hope, to quarter the southern Indian Ocean in the
summer season, blown before the high-latitude prevailing westerlies.
After recouping in New Zealand, he would repeat the process in the
southern Pacific at the start of the next summer. If nothing was found,
a loop back north and west on the south-east trade wind might
enlarge knowledge of islands, known and still unknown, in its central
and western basin.

The French and Spanish were now hard on British heels to establish or reinforce Pacific claims, and this was essentially the plan the
Admiralty adopted. This time Cook recommended a two-vessel expedition. *Endeavour* had firmly convinced him that only 'North Country
built ships, such as are built for the coal trade' were suitable and he
chose the *Marquis of Rockingham* and *Marquis of Granby*, both

owned by Captain William Hammond of Hull. After purchase by the Navy Board, of which Cook's friend Palliser was Comptroller from 1770, they were respectively renamed *Resolution* and *Adventure*. Both were relatively new: the former was of 462 tons; the latter, commanded by Lieutenant Tobias Furneaux (who had sailed with Wallis) was of 340 tons.

Banks enthusiastically prepared to accompany Cook with an even larger party than before, including Solander, the astronomer-physician Dr James Lind, two reputable artists, Johan Zoffany and John Cleveley junior, and draughtsmen brothers, John and James Miller. However, the necessary extra accommodation added to *Resolution* made her so unseaworthy that the Navy Board had it removed. Banks threatened to withdraw if his needs were not met and, when the Admiralty called his bluff, felt obliged to do so, although his relations with Cook were only temporarily strained. Instead, he led most of his suite on a private foray to Iceland. It was a regrettable loss to Cook's company as much as science, for Solander was replaced by the learned but difficult German naturalist, Johann Reinhold Forster, accompanied by his gifted artist son, Georg. The latter generally proved an asset but Forster senior strained everyone's patience. Some 'Endeavours' were back again in the *Resolution*'s crew of 112 (*Adventure* had 81). Clerke was second lieutenant and Pickersgill – now third lieutenant – and Midshipman Isaac Smith were among them. George Vancouver, another midshipman, was later to win fame as an explorer himself, while the work of William Hodges, the sociable landscape painter who replaced Zoffany, was to define both this voyage and the dominant visual image we still have of the eighteenth-century Pacific.

The astronomers this time were William Wales (one of Banks's team) and William Bayly, the latter going in *Adventure*. Both were appointed by the Board of Longitude, on which Maskelyne was the key figure as Astronomer Royal. Their prime task was to use lunar-distance observation, of which Maskelyne was champion, to test the reliability of four new-fangled marine timekeepers as a simpler alternative for calculating longitude at sea. One was Larcum Kendall's faithful 'K1' copy of John Harrison's great 'H4' prototype – 'our trusty friend the Watch' as the admiring Cook was later to call it – making its maiden voyage. The others were different (and unsuccessful) models by John Arnold. Their modern name of 'chronometer' only stuck after it was proposed in 1779, by Alexander Dalrymple.

The *Resolution* and *Adventure* expedition was Cook's greatest, taken as a combination of sheer sea-keeping endurance, navigation and its accumulation of geographical and related knowledge of so far unknown, or at least uncharted, Pacific islands. Longer and no less dangerous than the *Endeavour* voyage, it nevertheless lacked its two big landmarks – the surveys of New Zealand and eastern Australia – and it is only the overall pattern rather than the detail that can be summarized here.

'A View of the Cape of Good Hope, taken on the Spot, from on board the Resolution', by William Hodges; oil on canvas. This was painted in November 1772, shipped directly home and exhibited at the Free Society of Artists in 1774.

The ships sailed from Plymouth on 13 July 1772, exactly a year since *Endeavour*'s return. As she had, they replenished at Madeira and reached Cape Town on 31 October. Here Hodges painted *Adventure* lying dwarfed below Table Mountain, on a big, breezy canvas which Cook sent home from there in an Indiaman. They sailed again on 22 November heading south in search of 'Cape Circumcision', a landfall reported by the French voyager Lozier Bouvet in 1739 in latitude 54° south, longitude 10° 20' east. Instead they found a gale, cold and then ice, first in small quantities then in vast fields of pack-ice and a new phenomenon – towering 'ice islands' (icebergs) up to 200 ft (61m) high. Early in January they made the important discovery that ice taken from round a berg melted down into fine drinking water. Rigging and sails froze, however; livestock brought from the Cape died, signs of scurvy began to appear and on the 17th they became the first men in history to cross the Antarctic Circle (66° 33' south). The following day, in latitude 67° 15' south, longitude 40° east, they turned back on a long dog-leg north and then a sweep south-east again across the southern Indian Ocean to New Zealand.

On 8 February the ships were separated in fog and on 26 March Cook arrived in idyllic Dusky Bay at the tip of South Island on his own, staying for five weeks before moving to Queen Charlotte Sound on the Cook Strait, where he found Furneaux. The latter had touched on Van Diemen's Land and, although he had not resolved the question of whether it was joined to Australia, discovered a small group of islands (now named after him) to the north-east. The southern winter was now beginning but Cook did not intend to sit this out. He halted Furneaux's preparations to do so and they both sailed again early in June 1773, in a great loop west and north to revisit Tahiti and the Society Islands, where they were warmly welcomed in August. Supplies at Tahiti proved short but were made up at Huahine, where the only major incident was the stripping to his trousers of Dr Anders Sparrman – the assistant that the Forsters had recruited at the Cape – when he made a lone botanizing foray, probably on to sacred ground. His clothes were later retrieved. When they left on 7 September, Cook

'View in Pickersgill Harbour, Dusky Bay, New Zealand, April 1773', by William Hodges; oil on canvas. Cook wrote that he moored *Resolution* 'so near the shore as to reach it with a Brow or stage that nature had in a manner prepared for us by a large tree, which growed in a horizontal direction over the water [and] reached our gunwale'. Wales's observatory tent can be seen through the trees.

took a young man known as Odiddy (O-Hedidee) from Raiatea, returning him in 1774. At Huahine, Furneaux was so importuned by another called Mae that he also agreed to him joining the *Adventure*. Thus 'Omai', the first South Sea islander seen in England, steps into history and artistic celebrity, at least, in portraits by Sir Joshua Reynolds and others.

From the Society Islands, effectively Cook's central Pacific base, the expedition next sailed west to locate islands which Tasman had called Amsterdam and Middelburg (Tongatapu and Eua) some 130 years earlier. These were sighted on 1 October. The people were as light-fingered as the Tahitians and equally welcoming, though initially unwilling to trade, and Cook called the group the 'Friendly Islands' – Tonga. Red feathers obtained there were soon found to have so high a value elsewhere that Cook had to exert on-board 'exchange control' to prevent other islanders refusing to supply provisions in return for anything else. After a week both ships headed south for New Zealand again, where they were finally separated in a storm off the east coast at the end of October 1773 and *Adventure* failed to reappear.

Cook reached the Ship Cove rendezvous in Queen Charlotte Sound on 3 November 1773 and prepared for a rapid departure on his second Antarctic sweep, taking advantage of the southern summer. While there he found explicit proof of Maori cannibalism, in a shipboard experiment that Clerke rather lightheartedly initiated, with gruesomely thought-provoking results. None the less, Cook's general opinion of the Maoris remained high, not least because he found them honest among themselves and no rivals to other islanders as thieves. On 25 November he sailed, leaving a buried and marked message of his likely movements which Furneaux found a week later.

Furneaux's outlook and shipboard regime were more conventional than Cook's and his record of sickness and adverse incident less impressive. Delayed on the coast of North Island by the weather, he made Queen Charlotte Sound at the end of November, six days after Cook sailed. Following a brief respite, he was about to depart again when he lost a boat and crew: a search soon found that the men had been killed and eaten by Maori accompanying them. The facts only came out later but there had been a sudden quarrel over food, in which a seaman had first shot two natives. Furneaux buried the remains and quickly sailed for Cape Horn, searching for land in intense cold as far south as latitude 61° and continuing directly east across the south Atlantic to make another grasp for Bouvet's 'Cape Circumcision'. This remained elusive and he concluded that Bouvet had mistaken ice for land, before putting back to Cape Town in March 1774. It was a creditable performance and *Adventure* reached England on 14 July, having lost thirteen men in all, one from among her many cases of scurvy.

Resolution once more headed south through gale conditions for the Antarctic. On 7 December her crew drank toasts to home at the exact antipodes of England, north of the great Antarctic bight which

James Clark Ross would discover in 1841, now known as the Ross Sea. However, as their latitude rose from 62° to 66° south they were increasingly ensnared by loose summer sea-ice, massive bergs, fog, snow, intense cold and high winds. From latitude 67° 31' south, again beyond the Antarctic Circle, Cook prudently hauled north for over 1200 nautical miles (about 2200 km) until 11 January 1774, before making a final plunge south in deep-freeze conditions to the farthest point yet reached by man. Here, on 30 January, in latitude 71° 10', longitude 106° 54' west, he was stopped by solid ice stretching as far as the lookouts could see. Had it been farther east he would have been ashore in the mountains of Palmer Land, at the base of the 800-mile (1300-km) Antarctic Peninsula. Despite the presence of petrels and penguins, Cook was now convinced that if land lay beyond it was completely ice-bound, adding that, 'I who had ambition not only to go farther than any one had been before, but as far as it was possible for man to go, was not sorry in meeting with this interruption ...'. '*Ne plus ultra!*' ('No one further') yelled young Vancouver – literally the farthest man south, out on *Resolution*'s bowsprit – just as they turned north, leaving Antarctica itself for a future age to discover.

Having proved that no inhabitable southern continent existed, Cook would only have been using the discretion granted in his orders if he had headed home. Instead, with adequate stores, a healthy crew, a sound ship and vast areas of the central Pacific so little known, 'I was of the opinion that my remaining in this sea some time longer

'Tahiti revisited', by William Hodges; oil on canvas. This second version of Hodges's view in Vaitepiha Bay, painted for the Admiralty in 1776.

would be productive of some improvements to navigation and geography as well other sciences'. Backed by his officers and the goodwill of his men he launched north on a huge parabola which by mid-October 1774 would take him north to just below the Equator, west towards New Guinea and then back south again to his favourite New Zealand base in Queen Charlotte Sound. The passage began with a violent storm, followed in February by serious illness for Cook himself – apparently a gall-bladder and bowel problem – which caused great alarm. Fortunately he was nursed to recovery by the surgeon, James Patten, aided by the only fresh meat still on board, the last of the edible Tahitian dogs.

In March, *Resolution* briefly visited remote and deforested Easter Island, first described in any detail in 1722, of whose massive and mysterious stone figures Hodges later painted a remarkable picture. Circling north-east, Cook then rediscovered and fixed the position of the Marquesas Islands, found and named by Alvaro de Mendaña in 1595 but unseen since. This brought him back once more, via other minor landfalls, to Matavai Bay, Tahiti. The welcome was as enthusiastic as ever and the island seemed in a much more prosperous state than the previous year. Theft was just as bad and eventually, after the usual detentions of persons or property failed to be an effective remedy, Cook ceremonially flogged a Tahitian (as he did thieving seamen) to show he was both in earnest but also even-handed. He also witnessed a spectacular review of several hundred Tahitian war canoes, which were working up to attack the nearby island of Eimeo (Moorea) in a local dispute. This, too, provided the subject of one of Hodges's most famous paintings (see p.110).

From Tahiti they went on to the usual elaborate and generous welcome on Huahine and Raitaea (where Odiddy left them) and then sailed west to relocate the islands of 'Austrialia de Espiritu Santo', first found by Pedro de Quiros in 1606, although more recently relocated by Bougainville and called the 'Great Cyclades'. Cook was to rename them the New Hebrides (now Vanuatu) and to chart them with great accuracy after he fell in with them in mid-July, at Malekula, following other small discoveries and a stop for supplies at Nomuka, Tonga. The New Hebrideans, however, were Melanesians, a different race with a different language from his usual Polynesian friends. He thought them uglier, certainly cannibals and hostile – not surprisingly, since they believed the visitors to be ghosts. All attempts at friendship were met with propitiatory offerings which, when Cook misread their significance, were followed by some form of attack. Illness from eating poisonous fish was another dangerous novelty here. On Erramanga the hostility repeated itself and the Marines had to open fire, wounding several natives and killing their chief. It was not until Cook reached the bay he called Port Resolution, on the actively volcanic southern island of Tanna, that he was able to replenish wood and water in still edgy but not openly dangerous circumstances. On

'A View of the Monuments of Easter Island', by William Hodges; oil on panel.

'View of the Province of Oparree [Pare], Island of Otaheite, with part of the Island of Eimeo [Moorea]', by William Hodges; oil on panel.

25 August he finally anchored at Quiros's Espiritu Santo proper, the largest, northern island in the New Hebrides, and completed his general survey of the chain by sailing around it.

At the end of the month *Resolution* sailed south for New Zealand but on 4 September sighted a large and unknown island, later found to be the fourth largest in the Pacific, running some 300 miles north-west to south-east. It reminded Cook of New South Wales and he eventually called it New Caledonia, spending most of the month surveying the eastern side. The people were prosperous and friendly, happy to supply water and to trade. More remarkably, they neither stole nor, in the women's case, could be persuaded to bestow sexual favours on Cook's men, matters for admiration from Cook and the puritanical J. R. Forster at least. One nasty surprise was another poisonous fish, a small amount of which made Cook and the Forsters painfully ill and which killed a pig that ate part of it. At the south end of New Caledonia, on the small Isle of Pines, they first mistook the huge trees for pillars of basalt, and had a near escape from night-time shipwreck in the surrounding reefs as Cook tried to make the western

Resolution (left) and *Discovery* refitting in Ship Cove, Nootka Sound (Naniamo) during Cook's third voyage April 1778. One of Webber's 'roll drawings', nearly 5ft long (1.5m) with carpenters and blacksmiths working ashore, the astronomers' observation tents set up on a prominent rock, and a strong presence of local people and canoes.

coast. After that he reluctantly gave up any attempt to survey that side, resuming his course on 3 October for New Zealand. On the way he discovered and briefly landed on uninhabited Norfolk Island and in mid-October raised the white volcanic cone of Mount Egmont, the north-western sentinel of the Cook Strait.

On the 18th, *Resolution* anchored off Ship Cove again. Cook's message to Furneaux was missing and there were clear signs that *Adventure* had come and gone. There were also unverifiable local reports of Furneaux's casualties, although the natives eventually assured Cook that *Adventure* had left safely. Here, although very short of proper materials, Cook recaulked the ship and prepared for the last stages of the voyage. Wales, the astronomer, double-checked the longitude against an earlier result of Bayly's, and Cook, the perfectionist, was mortified to find that on the *Endeavour* voyage he had plotted South Island about 40 sea miles (about 74 km) too far east. More happily, he found that the accumulated error of Kendall's timekeeper, after nearly a year at sea in all conditions, was a mere nineteen minutes thirty seconds.

Captain Cook's sextant by Jesse Ramsden, about 1770. The sextant was Captain John Campbell's improvement on the octant, specifically to provide a longer scale for taking lunar-distance longitude observations. This is one of Cook's instruments, by one of the most famous London makers.

On 10 November 1774, in high southern hemisphere summer, *Resolution* sailed east over the Pacific, crossing the tracks of her earlier passages in about latitude 55° south, just in case any land between had been missed. They sighted Cape Deseado, the western end of the Strait of Magellan, on 17 December. There were few provisions to be found on Tierra del Fuego but, after a cheerful Yuletide in Christmas Sound, the ship passed south towards Cape Horn, with Cook still making such coastal observations as conditions allowed. In the first week of January 1775 they were in the South Atlantic, searching to just south of latitude 60° for a coastline predicted by Dalrymple, much of whose theorizing had now been disproved by the voyage. When this also vanished into air Cook turned north, stumbling instead on what he first took for an ice island before it solidified into towering peaks of rock. Cook landed briefly on the desolate shore of Possession Bay and claimed the island as South Georgia, future way-station of Antarctic voyages by Shackleton and others.

'Mr Kendall's watch' (K1), 1769. The first official copy of Harrison's revolutionary H4 chronometer of 1759, Cook took this on both his second and third voyages. He proved its efficiency and greatly admired it.

Conscientiously reasoning that, where one island existed, Bouvet's mysterious 'Cape Circumcision' might also be near, he then briefly turned back to follow the 60th parallel eastward. This brought him one last discovery in the small, remote and desolate South Sandwich Isles but took him south of the tiny speck of Bouvet Island, the hare which both he and Furneaux had so fruitlessly pursued. With the sight of a glacier calving on South Georgia, and more bergs and broken pack-ice floating north from the undiscovered Weddell Sea, Cook ended the voyage certain 'that there is a tract of land near the Pole, which is the Source of most of the ice which is spread over this vast Southern Ocean'. He was, however, correctly convinced that it lay largely within the Antarctic Circle 'for ever ... buried under everlasting snow and ice' and, quite wrongly, that it never could or would be explored.

On 21 March, after a stormy northerly passage and exchanging news and messages with passing ships, *Resolution* again anchored in hospitable Table Bay, to spend five weeks there as her rigging was refitted. She sailed on 27 April via St Helena, Ascension Island and Fernando de Noronha off the Brazilian coast, and anchored at Spithead, Portsmouth, on 30 July 1775. The ship itself and Mr Kendall's timepiece had proved their worth through a voyage of over three years and 70,000 miles (100,000 km) – well over twice round the world. Only four men on *Resolution* had died – three by accident, one of disease, none from scurvy.

Resolution and *Discovery*, 1776–80

Resolution's return saw her ever-modest captain and his achievements at the centre of public admiration. This time his glory was undimmed by the presence of Banks, who made a late return from a yachting trip to find only friendship, respect and past differences forgotten. Banks was now on the Council of the Royal Society, which unanimously elected Cook a Fellow and awarded him its prestigious Copley Medal. Royal and naval approbation came with a further visit to the King and promotion to post-captain on the establishment of Greenwich Hospital – an honourable paid retirement – although with Cook's own proviso that, if he wished, he could again request suitable active service. In the meantime there was much to do, including sitting (in his new captain's full dress) to Nathaniel Dance for a portrait that Banks had commissioned (see frontispiece).

At Cape Town, Cook had been 'mortified' to read the published account of his *Endeavour* work. This he had left to be edited by Dr John Hawkesworth as part of a more general publication of recent Pacific voyages including those of Byron, Wallis and Carteret, who reached home in 1769. He found 'his' contribution to be an erroneous conflation of his own journals with those of Banks and others, prefaced by a misleading claim that he had checked it before sailing in *Resolution*. This time, supported by Sandwich and others, he collaborated with a more meticulous editor, Dr John Douglas, who took over and polished Cook's account of his second voyage (and later edited the third), although Cook never saw the fine, illustrated two-volume result, published in May 1777. The fateful reason soon formed about him, as he began to realize that its 'fine retreat and ... pretty income' aside, 'the limits of Greenwich Hospital ... are far too small for an active mind like mine'.

With growing knowledge of the Pacific, and old rivalries soon to re-erupt as France and Spain sided with American rebellion against British rule (1775–83), a new variant on an old theme was being considered: the quest for a north-west passage between the Atlantic and Pacific, and possibly a north-eastern one above Arctic Russia. Two north-western straits were rumoured to debouch in Drake's 'New Albion', the Pacific north-west of North America: those of Juan de Fuca in about latitude 48° and one attributed to a fictional 'Admiral de Fonte' in about latitude 53°. Finding these had been the discarded object of Byron's 1764 voyage. If they existed, it had been known since 1771 that they could only connect with the Arctic Ocean somewhere north of Hudson Bay, since this had been shown to have no westerly outlets. Much clarification was also needed about the Pacific coasts south-west and south-east of the Bering Strait. Both had been substantially investigated only by the Russians, who were conducting a fur trade there. On the way, a new expedition could also return Omai to Tahiti, after his engaging but rather vacuous career as resident 'noble savage' in London.

Resolution was judged fit for another voyage, which Clerke (now a commander) would lead, and Cook advised on the purchase of her new consort, the *Discovery*. At 298 tons and with a total complement of sixty-nine, she was the smallest of Cook's ships. For shortly after-wards, around the end of January 1776, the Admiralty was gratified to hear that Cook wished to command once more, with Clerke taking *Discovery*. John Gore would be Cook's first lieutenant; the second, James King, and Cook himself would comprise *Resolution*'s astronom-ical observers, with Bayly going again in *Discovery*. *Resolution*'s previous surgeon's mate, now her surgeon, William Anderson, was also the naturalist, with the *Discovery*'s surgeon's mate, William Ellis, doubling as a natural draughtsman. David Nelson, a gardener from Kew, also joined *Discovery* as a plant collector. Dr Solander then found John Webber, another excellent and sociable draughtsman, landscape painter and portraitist, of Anglo-Swiss parentage, who agreed to join *Resolution* at short notice.

Cook had another fine navigator, William Bligh, as master of *Resolution*. His later place in the European Romantic myth of the South Seas was destined to be as commander of the ill-fated *Bounty* and of a more successful later voyage with Captain Nathaniel Portlock. The latter at this point was also a *Discovery* 'mid' as, again, was young Vancouver and Edward Riou, later to die commanding

Nelson's frigates at Copenhagen. James Burney, their first lieutenant (and brother of Fanny, the novelist), was himself to become a notable historian of Pacific voyages. Once again, on this one, they were all accompanied by 'Mr Kendall's watch', flawlessly ticking away the longitude in Cook's cabin.

Resolution, with her complement of 112, sailed on 12 July 1776 from Plymouth, a voyage anniversary which all considered lucky. Clerke was detained by family business until 1 August but the ships met at Cape Town in mid-November, where they reprovisioned for a two-year voyage. This included so much livestock, including horses, for themselves and as gifts for the islands that they seemed a floating zoo. *Resolution* had already proved wet and leaky thanks to poor dockyard work, and the continuing voyage south-east in cold weather and gales was as unpleasant as ever. Crossing the southern Indian Ocean, Cook confirmed the position of minor recent French island discoveries, the largest being the bleak Island of Desolation, later renamed Kerguelen after its finder.

After *Resolution*'s fore-topmast and main topgallant were carried away in a gale, a brief stop in Adventure Bay on Van Diemen's Land provided a necessary staging post towards the usual anchorage at Ship Cove, in New Zealand's Queen Charlotte Sound. Cook spent nearly a fortnight here, finding the Maori fearful of his possible vengeance for the death of Furneaux's men. He had no such intention and did his best to resume friendly relations, while taking sensible care against surprises. Everyone benefited from the wild celery, scurvy grass and other produce of the place, which they left for the last time on 25 February 1777, heading slowly north and east against generally contrary winds. This delay, based on ignorance of local seasonal variations, was to affect the whole progress of the voyage. By the time they touched on Mangaia in what are now the Cook Islands, Cook was short of fresh supplies and decided that he would have to visit Tonga first, delaying his planned arrival at Tahiti. Arriving at the end of April, he was to stay eleven weeks in the 'Friendly Isles', surveying, observing and pestered as ever by native theft. Clerke eventually devised the best deterrent of shaving or half shaving culprits' heads and throwing them overboard as objects of ridicule. Thirty years later it transpired that, during this visit, Tongan chiefs plotted to kill the entire party and seize the ships, one of the leaders calling it off for personal reasons at the last moment. Cook, unaware of the danger, considered the visit a success and eventually sailed for Tahiti on 17 July.

Since their last visit, Spaniards from Peru had been and gone on Tahiti, in a feeble attempt to reassert their Pacific sovereignty and 'convert the heathen'. Their leader had died there and, despite pious warnings against the British, Cook was made as welcome as before. After landing at Vaitepiha on 13 August, the old camp at Matavai Bay was recommissioned, fireworks were let off and Cook and Clerke were pleased to land the last of their livestock. Their own appearance on

'A Human Sacrifice in a Morai, in Otaheite'. William Woollett's engraving after a drawing by Webber. The chief, Tu, points out the victim to Cook and his men. The European with his back turned may be Anderson or Webber himself. From the official voyage account.

horseback, and Omai's less expert attempts, caused general astonishment. Cook declined to become involved in the continuing local war against Moorea but he did attend a human sacrifice connected with its poor progress (the victim had, in fact, been killed earlier). He also had to refuse the Tahitian chief Tu's gift of a canoe for King George as too large to take, but had Webber paint his own portrait as a present for Tu. The likeness was much treasured by Tu and Bligh was asked to repair it in 1788 when he arrived in the *Bounty*. It was last seen four years later. At the end of September, Cook moved on to Moorea, so far unvisited, where noticeable shortening of his patience with theft burst out in full fury and he burnt houses and canoes in order to gain restitution of a goat. This was followed just before they reached Huahine by a new escalation: 'in a Passion' he not only ordered a native pilferer's head to be shaved but also that his ears be cut off. The man lost his hair and one ear lobe to the barber before Cook relented and made him swim ashore. Another 'hardened Scounderal' who stole a sextant on Huahine lost both hair and ears, and was put in irons when he threatened murderous revenge. It was none the less on Huahine that Omai was finally settled, with two Maoris who had joined him from New Zealand and could not be returned, in a house and garden Cook built for him. The final parting when they sailed on 2 November was, as Bayly wrote, 'a very Afecting Scean'.

Cook next made his final visit to Raiatea, an island of delight where several men were tempted to desert and settle, a thought even entertained by Anderson and possibly Clerke, both of whom were fatally consumptive and feared the rigours of the Arctic. A simple-

minded marine called Harrison did so but was recovered. More
serious was the case of a seaman called Shaw and Alexander Mouat,
a lovelorn midshipman and son of a naval captain, both of whom fled
to nearby Borabora. Cook and Clerke rapidly and hospitably detained
on *Discovery* the son of the chief Orio, also his son-in-law and
daughter – the leading local beauty, Poetua – against his men's return.
Orio sent a message to Borabora but also unsuccessfully planned to
counter-seize Cook and Clerke when they were ashore before exerting
himself to have the fugitives returned. The happiest outcome of this
anxious drama, which only temporarily disturbed general friendship,
was the opening it gave Webber to make studies of Poetua for the fine
portrait of her which he exhibited in London in 1785. After an
emotional farewell, the ships briefly visited Borabora, obtaining there
part of one of Bougainville's anchors to convert into hatchets, and
Cook then left the Society Islands for ever.

From Raiatea they sailed north and on 24 December discovered
uninhabited Christmas Island, where Cook remained until 2 January
1778. Here an eclipse of the Sun was observed, English seeds planted
(Cook's invariable practice, for later use) and local supplies such as
yams and turtles gathered in large quantities. On the 18th, about 1300
nautical miles (2400 km) north of the Equator, they became the first
Europeans to sight the western elements of Cook's 'Sandwich Islands'
– Hawaii. Canoes quickly came out to trade and the people who came
aboard spoke Polynesian and were as light-fingered as their southerly
cousins. When a scouting party eventually landed on Kauai there was
an incident in which one native was shot dead. However, by the time
Cook himself landed the crowds seemed not only friendly but pros-
trated themselves before him (as to one of their own half-divine kings)
before he visited a nearby village and sacred site, or *heiau*. Cook
rapidly saw that he had found a very sophisticated society, stretched
over a large island group, but he was almost immediately driven from
his anchorage by weather and found it difficult to regain a safe one in
the offshore currents.

After only three days ashore in his fortnight there, he sailed again
on 2 February and sighted 'New Albion' – the coast of modern
Oregon – on 7 March, in latitude 44° 33' north. This was his southern
point on a coastline which he was to follow both north and far to the
west for over two thousand miles (3200 km), until it tailed off in the
shoals, tidal races and islands of the Aleutian chain. Although relatively low at first meeting, it was clearly backed by high ground,
which farther north piled up into the towering, snow-topped ranges of
the Canadian Rocky Mountains. The coast below, from which the
ships mostly stood well offshore in cold weeks of fog and storm from
the west, also soon became as fragmented and complex as north-
eastern New Zealand, but on a vastly grander scale. Urgently needing
to reprovision and replace some of his spars, Cook tacked north and
west in offshore gales, looking for a suitable harbour. In doing so he

missed the opening south of Vancouver Island which is now called the Juan de Fuca Strait but may not have been the first of the mythical entrances to a 'north-west passage'; the so-called Admiral de Fonte Strait was to be equally elusive.

On the western side of the island – which he did not recognize as such – he put into what became known as King George's and later Nootka Sound (now Naniamo), where the ships moored safely and refitted until 26 April. Here they cut new upper masts from the immemorial forest, set up an observatory and accurately determined their longitude, and conducted trade for fish and furs with the friendly local people. Shortly after leaving, *Resolution* sprang a leak, which the pumps kept in check as they slowly tacked their way well to seaward across the Gulf of Alaska and put in to Prince William Sound, southwest of modern Anchorage. *Resolution* was recaulked there but there was a risky incident when armed locals, now resembling Esquimaux,

'A View of Snug Corner Cove in Prince William Sound.' Engraved by W. Ellis after Webber for the official voyage account.

stormed *Discovery* in the hope of easy pickings but were driven off with cutlasses and no serious injury. Two weeks of May were subsequently spent in inconclusive probing of the nearby Cook Inlet (which leads up to Anchorage) and which Vancouver, sixteen years later, was to confirm as no more than a huge, long bay into the continental hinterland.

They were now in regions known from the earlier eighteenth-century voyages of Bering and the Russians, and there were growing signs of Russian fur-trading contact amid local people as they sailed outside Kodiak Island and west by south down the Alaska Peninsula.

Cook passed through the Aleutian Islands east of Unalaska early in July and landed on the Russian side of the Bering Strait, 800 miles (1300 km) to the north, on 10 August. On the 3rd, he had lost his excellent naturalist and surgeon in the death from tuberculosis, aged thirty, of William Anderson, whom they buried at sea.

A week after passing through the strait and heading north-east, the ships began to encounter the familiar dangers of floating Arctic ice, although the presence of large numbers of walrus – or 'sea-horses' as they were called – provided a copious supply of fresh meat. On the 18th, they were stopped by a solid wall of pack-ice at their farthest point north, latitude 70° 44', and although Cook then altered his course westward to reach longitude 179° east, well above northern Siberia, ice also stopped them there. He thus resolved to try again at an earlier stage the following summer and sailed south to Unalaska Island where there was a hospitable welcome from the local Inuit, the Russian fur-trading community and their resident factor, Gerassim Ismailov. Despite language difficulties, he added to Cook's information of the Russian coast, undertook to pass on a letter to the Admiralty via St Petersburg and provided others of introduction to the Governor of Kamchatka where Cook could have wintered. When he sailed on 26 October, however, Cook had instead already determined to winter in the Hawaiian Islands to enlarge his knowledge of the group and benefit everyone's health from fresh supplies and the warmer climate.

The passage began with a fearful storm, in which a seaman on *Discovery* was killed when rigging gave way, but a month later they sighted Maui and, late on 30 November, Hawaii itself for the first time. Cook did not land, however, until the middle of January, preferring to avoid island entanglements and to trade with canoes offshore as he recorded the group. Another storm at the end of December separated him from *Discovery* and after they rejoined on 6 January it was more than time to find a harbour for repairs to ships with leaking decks, split sails and shattered rigging. On the 17th they came to an anchor off Hawaii, in Kealakekua Bay.

Their landing brought large numbers of people and ecstatic demonstrations of honour. The strange earlier prostrations resumed. Koa, a chief and a priest whom Cook had already met, led elaborate rituals of welcome at a nearby *heiau*, where Cook was draped in red cloth and had a hog offered to him. Cook also learnt that he had been granted the style of 'Orono'. Although the matter is still much debated, what he failed to understand – fatally, as the early stages in a tragedy of cultural cross-purposes unrolled – was that the islanders may have believed his 'second coming' to be that predicted for Lono, a Hawaiian year-god. Throughout the rest of the month he was consequently honoured like a returning deity, with visits from the Hawaiian king, Kalini'opu'u, and other chiefs, ceremonies and such a quantity of 'offerings' and supplies that a natural economic anxiety for his early departure became apparent among his hosts.

'A View of Karakakooa, in Owyhee' (Kealakekua Bay, Hawaii) after the ships anchored on 17 January 1779. Cook wrote: 'The Ships very much crouded with Indians and surrounded by a multitude of Canoes. I have no where in this Sea seen such a number of people assembled at one place ... and hundreds were swimming about the Ships like shoals of fish'. In the foreground is a man on a surfboard, the first European record of one. Engraved by William Byrne, after Webber, in the official voyage account, 1784.

On 4 February 1779 Cook therefore sailed to survey the coast and find a new anchorage, sped on his way with further gifts and a fleet of canoes in final escort. Two gale-filled nights, however, split his sails and *Resolution*'s foremast. No other harbour could be found and on 11th he regretfully re-anchored at Kealakekua Bay. It proved strangely deserted and while mast repairs ashore were permitted, and the king again paid a formal visit, there were soon signs of increasing local hostility. For the Hawaiians, a disorientating and unwelcome third return for Lono was not in the script as they understood it. A spate of thefts, at which Cook protested, raised the temperature and led him to double his guards. Then, on the night of 13 February,

Discovery's cutter was stolen (and, in fact, broken up for its iron).

The next day Cook led an armed party to 'invite' king Kalini'opu'u aboard against the boat's return, following his Tahitian practice. The chief came willingly enough as far as the beach but backed by an armed crowd, who prevented him going farther. Seeking to avoid bloodshed, Cook abandoned his intention and was about to re-embark. At that moment news broke that another important chief had been shot and killed in an incident on the far side of the bay and the infuriated crowd began hurling stones. Cook was violently threatened by one man, replying first with a harmless charge of buckshot and then shooting dead another assailant. As the mob charged, his

Marine party opened fire but four of them were killed before they could reload or reach the boats. Cook was struck down and knifed from behind, then hacked and clubbed to death in the shallows.

Clerke, a sick man but no less clear-headed or humane than Cook, now took command of both the stunned expedition and the immediate situation. When a watering party was also attacked it immediately set fire to a village but he would allow no premeditated acts of vengeance. A truce was quickly established in which the *Resolution*'s foremast was finished and then re-embarked, Clerke's firm requirement being the return of Cook's body. His bones (though not the Marines') were ceremoniously restored six days later by Kalini'opu'u. The Hawaiians had sustained considerable losses themselves and equally regretted the incident, and they had treated Cook according to their custom for great men. His body had been largely burnt and the flesh stripped from the bones, of which the longer ones, the skull and the preserved hands and feet were handed back. Many small ones were beyond retrieval, having already been distributed as honoured relics. On 21 February, Clerke consigned his captain's last remains to

'View in Macao'; oil on canvas. A landscape study, with the water-stairs of a temple in the background. Webber painted this in 1784 and exhibited it at the Royal Academy the following year.

the waters of the bay, with full naval honours. The following day, with himself in command of *Resolution* and John Gore, her first lieutenant, taking *Discovery*, they weighed anchor from the beautiful but tragic scene.

Clerke, too, never returned home. He made a gallant attempt to complete Cook's Arctic mission, sailing north once more and making port on the Kamchatka peninsula, where the Russians helped him both with supplies and repairs to his increasingly weather-worn ships. On 22 August 1779, while returning to Kamchatka from a fruitless second foray beyond the Bering Strait, he died, aged thirty-eight, of the tuberculosis he had carried from England. He was buried ashore at Petropavlovsk, where the Russians again gave notable assistance, and sent home the ships' reports: their grim news broke in London five months later. Gore succeeded to command of *Resolution*. Lieutenant James King – the most adept manager of native encounters apart from Cook – took over *Discovery* and after a stormy passage down the coast of Japan both ships reached Macao, in China, in the first week of December. From there they trod the well-worn paths of the East India trade homeward, through the Sunda Strait to Cape Town, arriving there in good health on 9 May 1780.

Three months later, an Atlantic gale blew them so far north that their British landfall was at Stromness, in the Orkneys. Sailing 'north-about' and down the English east-coast route to the Thames, on which Cook first learnt his trade, they anchored off Sheerness on 4 October, after a voyage of nearly four years, three months. The news of Cook's and Clerke's deaths was already old and, whatever the private welcomes, the ships' return was both less noticed and more sombre than those of 1771 and 1775. In an idiom of that age rather than our own, it was a homecoming under the cypress of mourning rather than one crowned with laurels of triumph.

'Captn. James Cook F.R.S.' Webber published this engraving of Cook in 1784, based on his own original oil study of him painted at Cape Town in 1776, which is now in the National Portrait Gallery.

3: 'NOT AT ALL A PARTICULAR SHIP'
adapting vessels for Pacific exploration

On Monday 11 June 1770, Lieutenant Cook's *Endeavour* was sailing north by west, gently following the line of the east coast of Australia, keeping about 9 miles (about 15 km) from the shore. It was, Cook recorded in his journal, 'a clear moonlight night' and well ahead of them they could see what appeared to be two low islands. As a precaution Cook shortened sail, altering course to seaward in order to give the islands a wide berth. It was Cook's normal practice during running surveys to heave the lead at regular intervals and the leadsman soon reported the *Endeavour* was sailing safely in waters of between 14 and 21 fathoms (she drew just 2 fathoms, around 4 m). Just before 11p.m., the ship was in 17 fathoms (31 m), but 'before the Man at the lead could heave another cast the Ship Struck [a reef] and stuck fast'. They had passed safely around the seaward side of the long reef that ran roughly north to south, but in avoiding that danger they sailed into another running east–west across the tip of the first. Cook later described the events with studied under-statement but this was a moment dreaded by everyone on board: thousands of miles from the nearest help, their slim chances of surviv-ing the shipwreck would depend completely on their own seamanship and the strength of their ship, together with a bit of good fortune.

Every man on board, including Cook, Joseph Banks, the scientific party and all the ship's officers, took their turn on the pumps during that long night, trying to control the water flooding in through the hole that had been punched in the bottom of the vessel. They managed to hold their own against the water but could not gain on it. The following morning, when they were starting to try to warp *Endeavour* off the reef at high water, a misunderstanding in measuring the depth of water in the hold led them to think that the ship was suddenly about to sink beneath them. 'This mistake', wrote Cook with grim humour, 'was no sooner clear'd up than [it] acted upon every man like a charm; they redoubled their Vigour in so much that before 8 oClock in the Morning they gain'd considerably upon the leak.'

After a twenty-four-hour struggle, during which the ship's main guns and some 50 tons of surplus weight were thrown overboard,

HM Bark *Endeavour*, a modern cutaway model showing the general internal arrangement.

Cook finally did manage to get *Endeavour* off the reef and back into deep water. Two hundred years later, divers located the cannons that Cook had abandoned on the reef, and one was presented by the Australian government to the National Maritime Museum, Greenwich in 1969. Fothering a sail over the hole in order to slow down the rush of water, Cook steered back towards the coast, looking for somewhere suitable to repair the hull. After five long and exhausting days, during which the pumps had been worked round the clock, he cautiously conned *Endeavour* into a bay, which he later named Weary Bay, and beached the ship at the mouth of a river. It was only here that they found they had been saved by the coral which had nearly destroyed them: a large piece had broken off and remained jammed in the opening, keeping the inrush of water within the capacity of the pumps. The manner in which the ship was handled during the crisis sealed Cook's reputation as a practical seaman of genius, but the accident also became an important moment in the choice of ships for exploration. The episode seems to have made Cook particularly conscious of the qualities of his sturdy little vessel and the debt of gratitude that both he and his crew owed her. Up to that point on the voyage he had named nothing after her, but Endeavour Reef, Endeavour River and Endeavour Strait were named in quick succession thereafter. *Endeavour* proved the virtues of her type on the east coast of Australia as ideal for 'voyages to remote parts'.

During the late eighteenth- and early nineteenth-century boom in maritime exploration and surveying, a ship of discovery was, to use Charles Darwin's phrase of the *Beagle*, 'not at all a particular ship' but one that was adapted for the purpose, often being altered back again once the voyage was over. George Vancouver's *Discovery* of 1789, for example, was originally built as a merchant ship, finished as a ship-rigged sloop for exploration, converted into a bomb vessel in 1798 after Vancouver's voyage and finally 'hulked' as a convict ship. HM Sloop *Investigator* began its long career as a merchantman, was then bought by the Admiralty in 1798 and converted into an armed sloop for convoy duty before being adapted in 1800 for Matthew Flinders's survey of Australia. After being condemned as a hulk in Australia halfway through Flinders's voyage, the sloop was repaired and a deck taken off by the colonial authorities, who then used it as a despatch vessel. *Investigator* returned to England and served in the Navy for another five years before being condemned a second time in 1810. The hulk was sold once more, rebuilt and returned to the merchant service. After more comebacks than Frank Sinatra, *Investigator* was finally broken up in 1872 – fittingly, back in South Australia, the scene of her greatest triumph.

A ship had to be several things for exploring the mid-eighteenth-century Pacific. With no friendly ports within easy reach it had to be self-sufficient, able to carry enough stores and spare equipment to look after itself for as much as three or four years. It therefore needed plenty of storage space, which meant that tubby, deep-sided vessels were favoured. But there was also a need for ships to be manoeuvrable and responsive, able to fight their way off a dangerous lee shore and sail efficiently when short-handed. One can see a similar tension in the two extremes of sailing boats today: short, fat boats that are safe and roomy but relatively unexciting to sail, and long, lean racing yachts that sacrifice comfort to performance. Most yachts are a compromise between the two and, in the conflicting demands for storage and manoeuvrability, so were exploration vessels. A large part of the working life of a ship of discovery would be spent in uncharted coastal waters, so it also needed to have a shallow draught, be strongly made and able to survive unexpected contact with submerged hazards. No ship could be expected to survive a collision with a sunken reef but a strong bottom gave a slight but important cushion of safety. Finally, a ship of discovery had to be able to 'take the ground'; that is to say, it had to have a bottom flat enough to allow the ship to be beached safely and to sit relatively upright for any repairs, as *Endeavour* took the ground in the Endeavour River.

Endeavour was originally a Whitby-built collier named *Earl of Pembroke*, purchased by the Admiralty for £2800 in March 1768. Another ship, *Rose*, had first been considered for the voyage and work had even been started to convert it before the Navy Board wrote to the Lords of the Admiralty doubting whether *Rose* could 'stow the quantity of provisions required on such an occasion'. The Board suggested that 'if their Lordships incline to make choice of a cat-built vessel for the said service which their kind are roomly [*sic*] and will afford the advantage of stowing and carrying a large quantity of provisions so necessary on such voyages, and in this respect preferable to a man of war, a vessel of this sort of about 350 tons, may now be purchased in the River Thames if wanted'. It is often said that Cook selected the *Earl of Pembroke* himself for the voyage because he knew the virtues of colliers from his years in the east coast coal trade; in fact, the Admiralty bought the collier before they appointed Cook her captain. While Cook may not have had a hand in the selection of the ship, his long experience of the type would, however, have been invaluable in adapting and rigging the ship for its voyage.

Three sets of plans exist for *Endeavour*, one showing the vessel as purchased, a second showing how it was adapted for exploration and a third which details the alterations needed to turn it into a transport ship at the end of Cook's voyage. This was a high-profile voyage in which royalty, Parliament and an eminent scientific society took a close interest, and this attention is reflected in the unusually large number of detailed records and plans that have survived. Many of the alterations were important to the sailing and operation of the vessel but are mainly of specialist interest; here we will only look at the broader changes.

As a collier, the *Earl of Pembroke* was lightly rigged. This enabled her to be sailed in coastal waters by the dozen or so men that would

The Royal Arms of William and Mary. This handsome carving used to hang over the entrance to Deptford Dockyard, where Cook's *Endeavour* was fitted out for Pacific exploration in 1768.

Admiralty sheer draught of *Endeavour*. The red line running from bow to stern shows the extra accommodation deck inserted beneath the cabin flat and the forecastle, in what was originally the cargo hold.

Admiralty deck plan of *Endeavour*, as fitted out for Pacific exploration at Deptford Dockyard, 1768. The plans show the extra cabins that were built to accommodate Joseph Banks's scientific party in the cabin flat and those allocated to the ship's officers on the lower deck.

have normally formed her crew, but such a light rig was clearly inadequate for the rigours of oceanic exploration and the Admiralty spent nearly as much as the original purchase price in re-rigging her as *Endeavour*, with heavier masts, yards and sails. She was shallow-draughted for her size and with a relatively flat bottom – in short, she was a typical east-coast vessel, built to negotiate the shallow channels and shifting sandbanks between Newcastle-upon-Tyne and London, deliver her cargo in drying as well as deep-water ports and, when grounded on a suitable beach, unload the coal directly into carts at low tide.

The *Earl of Pembroke* had a bottom made of one layer of wooden planks about 3 in. (76 mm) thick. In preparation for Cook's voyage she was 'sheathed and filled': her bottom below the waterline was treated with a mix of pitch, tar and sulphur in order to resist 'the worm', the marine mollusc *Teredo navalis*, which could rapidly eat through a ship's bottom, especially in tropical waters. The bottom was then sheathed with an extra layer of fir planks. The new planking was given extra protection by being covered with broad-headed nails set about 3/8 in. (10 mm) apart. The practice of covering a ship's bottom with copper sheets to protect against the worm was still at an experimental stage in the 1760s. Early attempts to fit copper sheathing established that it reacted with the iron nails in the hull, causing the ironwork to disintegrate and the ship to fall apart. The cause – electrolytic action – was not understood at the time, though the practical solution of using copper rather than iron hull fastenings below the waterline was soon devised. While Captain Wallis's *Dolphin*, which had brought back the news of the 'discovery' of Tahiti in 1768, had been coppered experimentally, none of the four ships to sail on Cook's voyages were fitted with copper sheathing. Cook's vessels carried an array of new inventions and anti-scorbutic foods, but the ships themselves were uncompromisingly unexperimental.

Endeavour was fitted out for the first voyage at Deptford Dockyard in 1768, and the red ink on the plan shows the major structural changes made by the yard. As a collier, there was accommodation aft in the cabin flat for the master and mates, and accommodation forward for the crew – the normal complement of a collier like the *Earl of Pembroke* was no more than twelve or fifteen men. Separating these two living spaces and forming the largest single area of the ship was the coal-hold: it was, of course, the storage capacity of that huge space that made colliers the ideal choice for a long voyage of exploration. But *Endeavour* also needed more living space; for instead of a dozen men she would now have to find space for a crew of seventy, plus the astronomer Charles Green and his servant.

To solve this problem a completely new deck was built 7 feet (just over 2 m) below the main deck beams, giving extra living space but still leaving ample space in the hold to store the vast amounts of

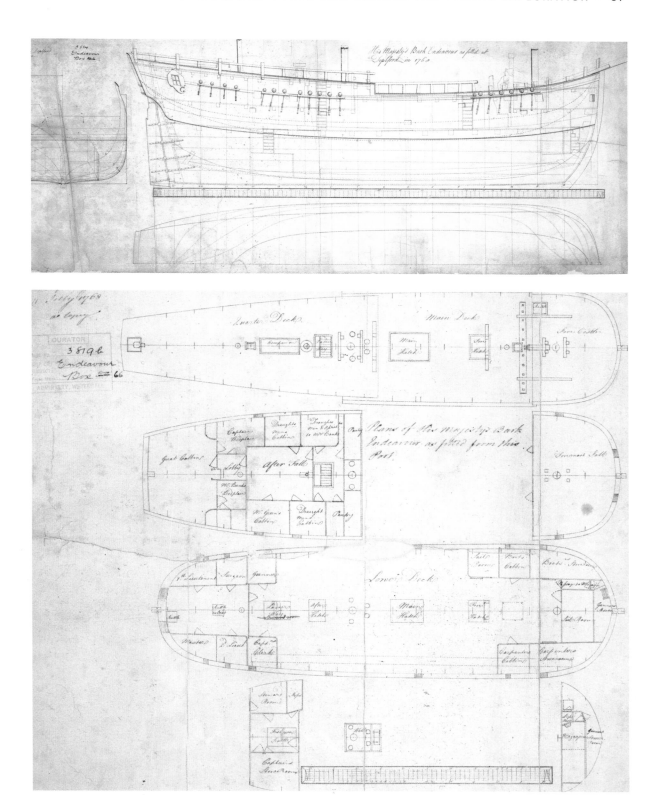

equipment and supplies for the voyage. The difficulty with this new deck was that while it gave seven feet of headroom in the waist (or middle) of the ship, at either end the existing cabin deck and the forecastle encroached on the space. This reduces the height in the new accommodation spaces beneath to around 4 ft (just over 1 m). The already cramped living conditions were made worse when it was decided shortly before *Endeavour* was due to sail that the ship's complement would be increased to eighty-five men, plus twelve marines; *Endeavour* finally left with over a hundred, the extras including the naturalist Joseph Banks and his staff of eight. The last-minute additions entailed some rapid reorganization of space and the plan shows the final alterations to the cabin flat that were actually carried out at Plymouth, just before Banks and his party joined the ship.

Under normal circumstances the great cabin would have been for the sole use of the captain, but when fitted out for exploration *Endeavour*'s was first reduced in size to make space for the extra cabins and then turned into a room that was held 'in common' among Cook, Banks and the scientists. This was an obvious and inevitable change of use, for the large windows in the stern and sides of the great cabin made it one of the few spaces in the ship with enough light for book-work. The ship's officers were originally going to be housed in the cabin flat but these cabins became the sleeping quarters of Cook and the scientific

One of the 4-pounder guns thrown overboard to lighten *Endeavour* when stuck on the Great Barrier Reef in June 1770. They were retrieved by divers in the 1960s and this one was presented to the National Maritime Museum by the Australian government in 1969.

party, while the officers were moved to the new accommodation beneath – that is, to the cabins with the 4-ft headroom.

The allocation of cabins on board *Endeavour*, as on any naval vessel, was overlaid with a lot of meaning. Cook and Banks were given equal status in spatial terms: the great cabin belonged to both of them and their sleeping quarters faced each another on either side of the ship. This was to be a voyage of Discovery and Science and their accommodation reflected the twin objectives of the expedition. Banks was a gentleman of considerable fortune and power but with no official position on board, whereas Cook was lowly born but the commander of the expedition, and the division of space was also a compromise between these two positions.

Although the scientists had the best spaces available on *Endeavour*, their sleeping cabins were little more than 6 ft (about 2 m) long and were uncomfortable quarters for a three-year voyage, especially for gentlemen used to more luxurious accommodation. In practice, Banks normally slept in the great cabin rather than in his own sleeping cabin but when preparing for the second voyage he insisted from the outset on much-improved quarters for himself and his enlarged scientific party. His ambitious plans included taking the professional botanist Daniel Solander, who had accompanied him on the first voyage, four artists (two botanical artists, one figure painter and one marine artist), the physician James Lind, some servants and a small private orchestra – a total of seventeen people. In early discussions about the proposed second voyage Banks rejected the idea of another collier, suggesting that an East Indiaman would be more suitable. These substantial merchantmen could have up to three times the capacity of *Endeavour*, with superior sailing qualities, but Banks was probably attracted to them because they were designed to carry important passengers as well as cargo and their accommodation was of a size and standard more suited to gentlemen. The Navy took Cook's recommendation, however, that its new ship would once again be a collier like *Endeavour*, and the *Marquis of Granby* was accordingly bought for the service and initially renamed *Drake*. To accompany *Drake* (for the important lesson that a second vessel could help to prevent disaster had also been learnt on Endeavour Reef) a second collier, the *Marquis of Rockingham*, was bought and named *Raleigh*. Spain, though, had always felt fiercely proprietorial about the Pacific, which it still regarded as a Spanish lake, and the Admiralty was eventually persuaded that international diplomacy would be better served by not using the names of British heroes whom Spain remembered as pirates and interlopers. *Drake* and *Raleigh* therefore became *Resolution* and *Adventure*.

At this point it was decided that, rather than Banks's party being reduced to fit the ship, the ship should be enlarged to fit the men. Banks set out in the detail the space that he thought 'absolutely necessary to be allotted to me and my people, for the carrying on of our respective Employments'. The only way these demands could be met was to build an extra deck on top of the main deck to accommodate the scientists and some of the officers, and enlarge the great cabin to 22 ft (6.7 m) long with an increased headroom of 6 ft 6 in. (1.9 m) to serve as both the scientific party's workroom and Banks's bedroom. This time, the great cabin would not be shared by Banks and Cook, but a new one would be built on the quarterdeck to house the captain, which the plans show rising above the stern carvings. Banks had argued strongly that he rather than Cook should be in overall command of the second voyage and, although he had not managed to convince the Admiralty, the proposed alterations to *Resolution* do show that the claims of science at sea were being recognized. To put the changes in perspective, the great cabin in a 74-gun ship of the line, the battleships of the day, would normally have been no more than 16 ft (4.9 m) long. The alterations were carried out at Sheerness but made *Resolution*, as one officer said after her alarming sea trials off the Downs, 'an exceeding dangerous and unsafe ship'. Another officer described her being overtaken by a small fishing vessel that kept so upright in the light airs that a marble would not have rolled from one side of her deck to the other, whereas *Resolution* heeled over so much that water was nearly lapping over her main deck. Not surprisingly,

Model of Sheerness Dockyard, where *Resolution* was adapted for Captain Cook's second voyage. The model is one of a set showing the six Royal Dockyards, presented to King George III in the 1770s. The others show Chatham, Deptford, Portsmouth, Plymouth and Woolwich.

Resolution in the Marquesas; pen and wash drawing by William Hodges.

the Navy Board decided to have the extra deck removed, the size of the great cabin reduced and the ship rebuilt like *Endeavour*.

Banks was furious. One of Cook's officers described him swearing and dancing with rage on the dockside when he saw the new deck being cut down and in an intemperate letter to Lord Sandwich, the First Lord of the Admiralty, Banks withdrew both himself and his team from the voyage. While Banks affected to be unconcerned about his own comfort in the letter, he argued that with *Resolution* restored to her original condition, 'our Great Cabbin … is too small and that is in reality the Shop w[h]ere we are all to work, which, if not sufficiently large will deprive the Workmen of a possibility of their respective Employments'. Furthermore, Banks tried to play what we might today call the health-and-safety-at-work card:

> In Expeditions of this Nature the Health and Accommodation of the People are essential to Success; when Sickness and Discontent are introduced it will be absolutely impossible to continue the Discovery; by the alterations made the Accommodations of the People are much reduced; 30 of the Crew are to be removed under the Gun Deck, before sufficiently crowded which being low and confined with a Free Air, must infallibly in so long a Voyage produce putrid Distempers and Scurvy.

Lord Sandwich would have none of Banks's crocodile tears, tartly pointing out that *Resolution* 'had been fitted with more conveniences than any ship that went to sea, not excepting the Royal Yachts; I mean conveniences for passengers; for except the Captain, Master & first Lieutenant (and there are three lieutenants belonging to her) none of the sea officers were allowed a place on the upper deck, but were all crouded between decks into that very place which you now represent as unwholesome, and as likely to endanger the lives of the common seamen who may be so unfortunate as to undertake the voyage.'

Ventilation and the belief that the foul air between decks caused shipboard disease was a big concern for the eighteenth-century navy. One of the original advantages of *Endeavour* for exploration in the tropics was that the collier had been built with five small coal-loading ports on either side, two larger ones in the bows and a further two cut into the stern below the great cabin, and these helped to keep a good flow of air through the ship. During *Endeavour*'s refit at Deptford, five more ports were added to the new cabins on the lower deck to improve ventilation further. As these ports were only just above the waterline they could not be opened at sea but Cook took every opportunity to control the spread of disease by airing the ship below decks when he could, washing out the cabins regularly and sprinkling the decks with vinegar. What may seem odd about Banks's belief that foul air could cause scurvy is that James Lind (who had already agreed to accompany Banks on the second voyage) had recently published his famous treatise on scurvy in which he quite clearly pointed to citrus fruit as the remedy for this disease, so greatly feared by seafarers. Banks himself had taken large quantities of lemon juice on the first voyage and attributed his own avoidance of scurvy to that fact. Sailors had known from the early seventeenth century at least that fruit and vegetables could prevent and cure scurvy, but it was not realized, even by Lind, that the disease was actually caused by a sustained lack of them. Cook himself believed that sauerkraut – pickled cabbage – was more effective against scurvy than preserved lemon juice but knew for a fact the importance of fresh greens and other vegetables, which he gathered at every opportunity and insisted that everyone on board consume.

Cook had initially gone along with Banks's demands to have a new deck built on *Resolution*: Lord Sandwich's reply to Banks's letter stated clearly that the original changes were made despite the 'express opinion of the principal officers of the Navy' solely because Cook had such a high opinion of the ship that he thought she could bear the extra weight. But once Banks had withdrawn from the voyage, Cook distanced himself from the alterations, saying that 'it will no doubt appear strange that Mr Banks should attempt to over rule the opinions of the two great Boards [the Navy Board and the Admiralty] who have the sole management of the whole Navy of

Admiralty sheer draught of the *Resolution*, as adapted to Joseph Banks's suggestions for the second voyage. The deck cabin intended for Captain Cook, and subsequently removed, rises above the stern carvings.

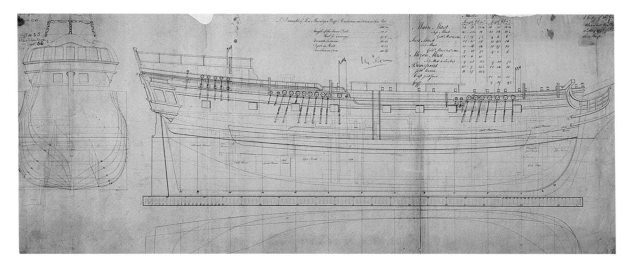

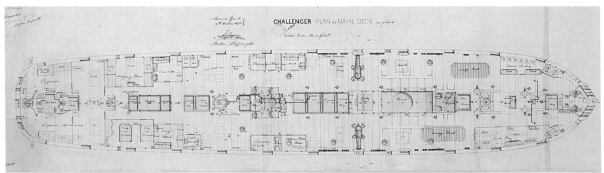

Great Britain and likewise the opinions of the principal sea officers concern'd in the expedition'. Banks had considerable power and influence and Cook had wisely decided to support rather than antagonize his young patron until it became clear that the Admiralty had complete faith in Cook.

Banks was in the wrong, of course. He neither understood nor cared about the practical problems of seamanship or the accommodation of the seamen; he tried to bully in order to get his own way and he withdrew in rash and ungenerous dudgeon when confronted with the inevitable. While Banks's motives were indeed selfish they were not

Admiralty deck plan of HMS *Challenger*, adapted in the 1860s for oceanic exploration. The rooms dedicated to specific scientific pursuits are clearly marked on the plan and the stern cabin is divided equally between the ship's captain and the senior scientist on board.

Erebus and *Terror* in New Zealand, during James Clark Ross's expedition to the Antarctic, 1839–43, by J. W. Carmichael. Ross's ships were strongly built bomb-vessels, originally firing heavy mortars, further reinforced with double-thickness planking and internal bracing to withstand polar ice pressure. They were nevertheless both later lost in the Arctic with Sir John Franklin. None of Cook's ships were reinforced for polar exploration.

completely so, however, and he deserves more credit for being one of the first people to begin thinking about ships of discovery in a totally new way. What he was arguing for, in effect, was a floating laboratory with space designed and allocated with regard to the 'respective Employments' of individuals, as he put it, rather than simply reflecting people's status within a ship's hierarchy. After the *Resolution* 'affair' scientists and artists on voyages of exploration had to fit in with the ship and the fit was not always comfortable. During the second voyage, the German naturalist Johann Reinhold Forster showed an impressive command of vernacular English when he complained bitterly about having to share his cabin with three sick sheep, 'who, raised on a stage as high as my bed, shit & pissed on one side, whilst 5 Goats did the same on the other'. An extreme example perhaps, but one that underlines the unpleasant conditions in which scientific work of the highest quality was produced on these converted colliers.

Banks's failure to get his own way on *Resolution* was a triumph for common sense but it had the effect of setting back the pursuit of science at sea for some years. Following the public argument with

Banks over accommodation, and an equally acrimonious split with
J. R. Forster three years later over the publication of the book of the
second voyage, the Navy cooled to the idea of having large numbers
of independent scientists on board who were not subject to naval
discipline. On Cook's third voyage, the responsibility for scientific
enquiry devolved more and more on the officers – the surgeon on
Resolution, William Anderson, carried out the duties of the naturalist,
and his counterpart on *Discovery*, William Ellis, took on responsibility
for drawing the botanical specimens. These men did an excellent job
and began a tradition of naval surgeon naturalists, the most famous of
whom would be Thomas Huxley, whose work on the natural history
of Australia during the *Rattlesnake* voyage of the 1860s was of an
exceptionally high standard. Science at sea would flower during the
long years of peace in the nineteenth century, the *Pax Britannica*, which
led scientifically minded officers like Robert FitzRoy, George Nares and
Robert Falcon Scott to seek promotion through science rather than
warfare. But while having some of the 'scientists' on Cook's third
voyage drawn from the service (subject to naval discipline and not

putting any extra pressure on accommodation) may have reduced tensions on board, many would say that the quality of scientific enquiry was not up to the high standards that had been set by the professional scientists on the first two voyages.

A ship adapted for exploration with what we might call a 'Banksian' vision of accommodation designed around specific scientific functions did not appear until a hundred years after the Cook voyages, when the frigate HMS *Challenger* was converted to explore the deep oceans in the 1870s. This voyage began the modern science of oceanography. It was jointly funded by Edinburgh University, the Royal Society and the Royal Navy, and gave equal importance to both scientific work and the more traditional shipboard sciences of navigation and surveying. Symbolizing these shared objectives, the great cabin in the stern was divided equally between the captain, George Nares, and Professor Charles Wyville Thomson.

The Navy's support for serious scientific work on voyages of exploration – apart from the hydrographic sciences – was variable in the wake of Cook. Darwin, the most important naturalist ever to sail on a British surveying voyage, was not appointed to the *Beagle* in the 1830s by the Navy but was invited privately by the captain, Robert FitzRoy – and Darwin had to pay for his own keep. George Vancouver's *Discovery* was probably the finest ship supplied for a voyage of exploration in the eighteenth century – it was a nearly brand-new merchantman and far more commodious than Cook's small colliers – but the Admiralty's large investment in Vancouver's *Discovery* was exceptional and was due to the strategic and commercial importance of surveying the north-west coast of America rather than to any sustained interest in the natural history of the area. The scientific party on board HM Sloop *Investigator* took delivery of some of the best and most expensive scientific equipment available for their voyage around the coasts of Australia in 1801, but this was largely supplied by Sir Joseph Banks, the main sponsor of the voyage. The ship itself was rotten. *Investigator* was chosen for Flinders's voyage, despite its structural weaknesses, because it had originally been a collier like *Endeavour* and *Resolution*.

Such was the reputation of these little ships, established by *Endeavour* on the east coast of Australia and defended so tenaciously in the Admiralty's argument with Banks, that they had become seen as the only vessels suitable for long voyages of exploration. They were also relatively cheap. While they had many advantages for this form of service, they had their disadvantages as well and the cutting comments of the botanical artist on *Investigator*, Ferdinand Bauer, about his damp, dark and confined cabin echoed those of J. R. Forster. When the conditions in which the scientists had to work are taken into account, the quantity and quality of the work they produced in their converted colliers is quite remarkable.

4: 'EXPERIMENTAL GENTLEMEN'
Science and empire in the Pacific

We dined this day upon beef, which our crew called Experimental-beef: To understand this, I only will observe, that every thing which our Sailors found not to be quite in the common way of a man of war, they call Experimental. The beer made of the Essence of beer, or Malt they called Experimental beer; the very Water distilled from Sea Water by Mr. Irwin's method was Experimental Water, Mr. Wales, the Astronomer, Mr. Hodges, the painter, Myself and my Son were comprehended under the name of Experimental Gentlemen.

Johann Reinhold Forster's Resolution *journal*

'Experimental gentlemen' sailed on all three of Captain Cook's voyages. They were scientists and artists who were taken both to help with Cook's observations and to make their own studies of the people and places in the Pacific. The practice of taking scientists on naval vessels was not in itself entirely new – Joseph Banks, for instance, had botanized on HMS *Niger*'s voyage to Newfoundland as the personal guest of the captain – but Cook's experimental gentlemen were the first to be integrated into the official aims of a voyage of discovery.

The whole character of the Cook voyages was scientific and its pursuit was generously, even lavishly funded: 'no people ever went to sea better fitted out for the purpose of Natural History, nor more elegantly', wrote a contemporary of the scientists on *Endeavour*. 'They have got a fine library of Natural History; they have all sorts of machines for catching and preserving insects; all kinds of nets, trawls, drags and hooks for coral fishing, they even have curious contrivance of a telescope, by which, put into the water, you can see the bottom at a great depth, when it is clear.' King George III gave a grant of £4000 towards scientific enquiry on the *Endeavour* voyage, and was to give a similar amount to the second. The Navy spent over £8000 in buying, refitting and victualling *Endeavour*, a sum they matched with all of Cook's ships, sending them to sea loaded with new equipment and stores, from devices for turning sea water into fresh, to sauerkraut and carrot marmalade to control scurvy, to the latest timepieces and almanacs for establishing longitude at sea. Joseph Banks, who appointed and paid for the naturalists and artists on *Endeavour*, thought that the voyage had cost him £10,000 in wages, equipment and general expenses.

The *Endeavour* voyage had at first been planned as a more modest expedition to observe the transit of Venus. The only professional scientist on board was to have been the astronomer, Charles Green, whose main task was to assist Cook's observations. The scientific side of the voyage expanded largely through the influence of Banks, a wealthy landowner with a passion for botany and a large number of well-placed friends, whose influence he was quite prepared to use in order to get a berth on the voyage to the 'new' lands of the Pacific.

> Joseph Banks Esqr Fellow of this Society [wrote the Secretary of the Royal Society], a Gentleman of large fortune, who is well versed in natural history, being Desirous of undertaking the same voyage the Council very earnestly request their Lordships [of the Admiralty], that in regard to Mr Banks's great personal merit, and for the Advancement of useful knowledge, He also, together with his Suite, being seven persons more, that is, eight persons in all, together with their baggage, be received on board of the Ship, under the Command of Captain Cook.

Although European ships had, through accident or design, touched at various parts of the Pacific for over two hundred years, these were generally brief and sometimes bloody encounters. Europe and the Pacific, particularly the islands of Polynesia, were to all intents and purposes new to each other. Scientists and philosophers were presented with a rare opportunity to observe what seemed to them to be an unspoilt natural world.

By the 1760s, science was more than the Renaissance pursuit of 'pure' knowledge and was increasingly being used to benefit commerce and industry. The Royal Society had stated a hundred years earlier that its reasons for existence were 'improv[ing] the knowledge of natural things, and all useful arts, Manufactures, Mechanic practices, Engynes and Inventions by experiment' and in 1754 the Royal Society

Sir Joseph Banks as President of the Royal Society: an engraving of Benjamin West's oil portrait, now in the Usher Art Gallery, Lincoln. It shows Banks draped in a cloak of *tapa*, the Polynesian cloth made from the mulberry tree, and surrounded by curios from the first voyage. At his feet is a sketch of the New Zealand flax plant, which was considered to have considerable commercial possibilities.

of Arts, Manufactures and Commerce was formed with the specific intention of improving all aspects of trade and industry through science, and offering cash prizes and medals as inducements. Cook was himself awarded the Royal Society's Copley Medal for his extraordinary feat of completing the second voyage without losing a man to scurvy. Scurvy had decimated the crews on Anson's expedition thirty years before and was the curse of long-distance voyaging. Cook's prevention of the disease was a great medical and humanitarian achievement in its own right but it also had important ramifications for Britain: once scurvy could be controlled, regular long-distance voyages would become far more feasible and the country's commercial and naval power would consequently increase.

The driving force behind the astronomical reason for Cook's first voyage was the Royal Society, which had persuaded King George III that Britain's prestige as a scientific nation would rise if the country were able to play a major part in observing the 1769 transit of Venus across the Sun. In many ways this was far more akin to 'pure' science, the pursuit of knowledge for the sake of knowledge, and Britain planned to establish three observation points: one in Hudson Bay, Canada; a second on the North Cape, and a third somewhere in the Pacific. The choice of Tahiti, which was to have such a tremendous impact on Europe and, indeed, on the history of the Pacific region itself, was simply chance: its existence and precise position had been reported by Captain Wallis of *Dolphin* just before *Endeavour* sailed. Other Pacific islands had originally been suggested – Tonga, for example, and the Solomon Islands – but these had not been seen by Europeans for many decades, had imperfectly known positions at best and at worst were effectively lost. To record the transit of Venus, the islands would first have to be 'rediscovered', let alone a rapport established with the local population. Wallis's reports of Tahiti, however, suggested that it satisfied all requirements at a stroke.

While recording the transit of Venus was the public reason for the voyage, Cook also carried a set of secret instructions ordering him to search for land that Wallis had reported seeing far off to the south of Tahiti. Wallis suggested that it could have been the northernmost coastline of the long-sought-after southern continent, although in reality he had probably only seen a bank of cloud on the horizon. Finding it would have been a scientific coup for Britain, a geographical achievement that would have brought far more prestige to the nation than observing the transit of Venus, but the underlying motives for Cook's secret instructions were less altruistic than imperial and commercial.

Leading the campaign in Britain for a full-scale search for the southern continent was the East India Company official, Alexander Dalrymple, who argued that the continent was vast – forming 'a greater extent than the whole civilized part of ASIA, from TURKEY to the eastern extremity of CHINA' – rich in mineral and other natural resources and with a huge population. In short, the southern continent would open up a rich empire of trade to its discoverer. Dalrymple's ideas were taken seriously and while the Admiralty refused to allow him to command their expedition it ordered Cook, if he found the continent, to 'employ [him]self diligently in exploring as great an Extent of the Coast as [he could]; carefully observing the true situation thereof both in Latitude and Longitude … and also surveying and making Charts, and taking Views of such Bays, Harbours and Parts of the Coast as may be useful to Navigation.' He was also to be mindful of the wealth of the country and 'with the Consent of the Natives to take possession of Convenient situations … in the Name of the King of England.'

No one realized it at the time, of course, but both of the voyage's main scientific goals were doomed. It was actually impossible to observe the transit of Venus with enough accuracy to calculate the distance of the Earth from the Sun, and the southern continent simply did not exist – or at least not in habitable latitudes. The outstanding success of the expedition's other objectives, however, more than compensated for the failure of the two main aims.

Cook's secret instructions also permitted him to survey the coast of New Zealand, first sighted by the Dutchman Abel Tasman in 1642 but not knowingly visited by Europeans since. Dalrymple had suggested that New Zealand might be the western extreme of the southern continent. In proving that it was not part of the continent but two large islands, Cook made a chart of New Zealand's coastline that, although being set slightly too far to the east and famously 'thin', was accurate enough in the main details to be used well into the nineteenth century.

The survey of New Zealand was completed in just six months, between October 1769 and March 1770, Cook using the 'running survey' method which he had developed himself to lay down coastlines when there was not the time or opportunity to make a full trigonometrical survey. It involved taking a series of compass bearings and horizontal sextant angles on prominent features ashore while determining the ship's track from the intersecting bearings. The method depended on being able to plot the ship's latitude and longitude with precision and on the first voyage Cook relied on Nevil Maskelyne's table of lunar distances, recently published in the *Nautical Almanac*, to find his longitude. Unfortunately, the almanac ran out on 31 December 1769 and from that point lunar distance had to be calculated by Cook and Green, which made the process rather slower and sometimes less accurate. On the second and third voyages Cook took marine chronometers which enabled him to lay down

Cook's portable observatory, from *The Original Astronomical Observations …* by William Wales.

positions with even greater accuracy and even to identify some of the errors in his first voyage. Navigation was becoming a far more precise and well-equipped science during the eighteenth century – Maskelyne's tables and Harrison's chronometer were only two of the best-known advances, all of which had a profound impact on the course of exploration.

Cook set awesome professional standards for maritime exploration: officers like William Bligh, George Vancouver, Matthew Flinders and Robert FitzRoy, who followed him to the Pacific, were always slightly apologetic and surprised when they had to correct inaccuracies in the 'great navigator's' charts. On the first voyage alone Cook charted over 5000 miles (8000 km) of previously unknown coasts, including the full extent of New Zealand, the eastern seaboard of Australia and the Torres Strait. Over his three great voyages he laid down accurately the main outlines of the Pacific, its main island groups and its approaches, opening up these seemingly remote and inaccessible parts of the world to a whole range of European activity.

An explorer who simply followed orders, Cook once told an enquirer, would never accomplish great things. Cook had an exceptional drive and determination, a stubbornness perhaps, that pushed himself and his men to the limits in the service of exploration. On his second voyage, which in terms of scientific achievements was by far the greatest of the three, Cook felt that he had sailed as far south beyond the Antarctic Circle in search of the mythical southern continent 'as I think it possible for man to go' – a claim that would not have been denied by the cold and miserable naturalist, Johann Reinhold Forster, who complained in his *Resolution* journal that 'after having circumnavigated very near half the globe, we saw nothing but water, Ice & sky'. Forster was understandably anxious not to waste time in what he saw as barren and unproductive polar seas, but to get to warmer and more fertile climes where he could start naturalizing.

The geographical and hydrographical achievements of the Cook voyages were considerable but they should not be seen in isolation, for sciences other than the navigational played equally important roles in Pacific exploration. The accounts and paintings of exotic peoples, plants, lands and animals brought back by the voyagers had, arguably, an even greater impact on eighteenth-century Europe. Orders to investigate the natural resources of the southern continent were also contained in Cook's secret instructions. He was:

> carefully to observe the Nature of the Soil, and the Products thereof; the Beasts and Fowls that inhabit or frequent it, the fishes that are to be found in the Rivers or upon the Coast and in what Plenty; and in case you find any Mines, Minerals or valuable stones you are to bring home Specimens of each, as also such Specimens of the Seeds of the Trees, Fruits and Grains as you may be able to collect, and Transmit them to our Secretary that We may cause proper Examination and Experiments to be made of them.

There is no doubt that Cook learnt a lot about how and what to 'observe' from the scientific gentlemen on his ships, and in particular from Banks and Solander on the first voyage. Banks, who came from a family of wealthy Lincolnshire landowners, was only twenty-five when the voyage began and was no scholar in the sense it would have been understood at the time, for he had little interest in the classics and had passed through school and Oxford University without leaving any great impression. Banks's passion was botany and he was rich enough to make up for any scholarly shortcomings by employing the professional botanist, Daniel Solander, who accompanied him on the voyage and spent the rest of his working life cataloguing the collections that they brought back from the South Seas. Banks and Solander were assisted on *Endeavour* by the assistant naturalist Herman Spöring and two artists: Alexander Buchan, who was employed as the topographical artist but who died from epilepsy almost as soon as *Endeavour* reached Tahiti; and Sydney Parkinson, who was contracted to Banks to draw plants and animals. Parkinson also died on the voyage, but not until the final leg from Australia to Britain and he left a large and important body of work. In addition to the drawings of plants, which formed the main part of his work, he made some 800 sketches of animals, birds and fish; he took on much of what would have been Buchan's responsibilities for people and landscapes; he recorded for his own interest the range of thermometer readings in Tahiti; he built up a Tahitian vocabulary and made many drawings of Polynesian artefacts and the various types of tattooing he came across in New Zealand.

Banks was even more ambitious in assembling a scientific team for a second voyage. Besides himself and Solander, Banks wanted to take the well-known portrait painter Johan Zoffany, John Frederick and

Sydney Parkinson; the frontispiece to his posthumously published *Journal*, 1773.

SYDNEY PARKINSON

Johann Reinhold and Georg Forster, the father-and-son team of German naturalists who replaced Banks and his party on Cook's second voyage; an oil painting by John Francis Rigaud.

James Miller, who would be responsible for the natural history drawings, and John Cleveley junior, a well-known marine draughtsman. Banks also intended to take James Lind, a physician and astronomer who had recently written an influential book on the treatment of scurvy. This team was disbanded before it had really been formed when Banks fell out with the Admiralty over the accommodation on *Resolution*. However, a similarly talented, if smaller group of scientists and artists were taken in their place. William Wales and William Bayly were the astronomers and meteorologists appointed to *Resolution* and *Adventure* respectively. Wales later taught mathematics at Christ's Hospital School, where one of his pupils would be the young Samuel Taylor Coleridge, whose long narrative poem, *The Ancient Mariner*, published in 1798, is partly based on Cook's second voyage. Another pupil would be Charles Lamb, who left an affectionate picture of Wales in his *Essays of Elia* as a man with a 'constant fund of humour' and a North Country dialect that 'absolutely took away the sting from his severities'. William Hodges was the official artist; he was a talented landscape painter and left a superb if often idealized visual record of the voyage. The responsibility for natural history fell to the German naturalist Johann Reinhold Forster, his son Georg and their Swedish assistant, Anders Sparrman, who was engaged by the Forsters when *Resolution* stopped in Cape Town on the voyage out.

Forster was educated in theological studies in Berlin and Halle and trained as pastor for a year or two after graduating before turning his energies to science. He had only arrived in England in 1766 from Russia, where he had been conducting a survey of the Russian Crown's new colonies in the Volga. Forster made the elementary mistake of being critical of his employers' methods in his report and he and his family came to Britain as penniless refugees. Once in London he set about making a living and building a reputation and soon established himself in British scientific circles. He showed a great interest in voyages of exploration and he and his son Georg translated de Bougainville's *Voyage autour du monde* into English in 1772. When Banks withdrew from the second voyage, Forster managed to have himself put forward as the replacement and succeeded in being hired on the same independent terms as Banks and with the allowance of £4000 that had been intended for James Lind – an allowance which was ten times that received by the two astronomers.

Forster described his duties as a naturalist as being 'to examine with the greatest care all of nature, lands, rocks, metals, streams and seas, unknown mountains, the composition of the atmosphere, and its changes, the plants and animals, whatever were there, and to describe more accurately new discoveries and see that they were sketched'. Forster had a formidable intellect and breadth of knowledge: he knew seventeen languages, both living and dead, was learned in philology, ancient geography, Egyptology, the study of 'man', both ancient and modern, and was well read in all branches of natural history. The sad irony with Forster was that while he probably knew as much about the scholarly study of 'man' as anyone alive in his time, he was absolutely incapable of understanding people on a practical level: his relationship with Cook was always uneasy and by the end of the voyage Forster had managed to fall out with virtually everyone on board *Resolution*.

The scientists worked closely together as teams and they used similar methods of collection, recording and classification on all three of the voyages. When *Endeavour* first landed on the east coast of Australia in 1770, Sydney Parkinson described the bay's plant life in his journal: 'There is a variety of flowering shrubs; a tree that yields gum; and a species of palm, the berries of which are of two sorts; one small and eaten by the hogs, and the other as large as a cherry, has a stone in it; it is of a pale crimson colour.' Banks and Solander picked the leaves of the gum-yielding tree, taking notes of the plant and its habitat. It was, they remarked, making the initial comparison with something already known that was the starting point of the process of classification, 'very like *Sanguis draconis*' – the dragon tree that was common in the Canary Islands and from which, according to an ancient belief, dragon's blood would flow. We know the gum tree today as the eucalyptus and the botanists had found it in a place Cook first called 'Sting ray's Harbour', from the number of large stingrays caught there. After playing around with the alternative names of Botanist Harbour and Botanist Bay, Cook eventually decided on Botany Bay in recognition of 'the great quantity of New Plants &c Mr Banks and Dr Solander collected in this place'. They saw more than just plants in Botany Bay, for the first time meeting Aborigines, who showed a complete lack of interest in the arrival of *Endeavour* and, unlike the Polynesians, no inclination to trade. The visitors also found the droppings of 'an Animal which must feed upon grass and

Eucalyptus alba, collected on the east coast of Australia in 1770 by Joseph Banks and Daniel Solander; hand-coloured engraving made from an original sketch by Sydney Parkinson.

which we judged could not be less than a deer'. The identity of this mysterious animal, the kangaroo, would not be solved until the ship was beached for repairs in the Endeavour River.

Back on board *Endeavour*, the leaves of the eucalyptus were stored temporarily in a tin chest and kept fresh by being covered by wet cloths. Parkinson then made a pencil drawing of the leaves, making some notes on their colour on the back of the sketch. Banks and Solander had been busy collecting in Botany Bay and Parkinson was kept equally busy sketching the resulting specimens. Banks noted in his journal that 'in 14 days just, [Parkinson] has made 94 sketch drawings, so quick a hand has he acquired by use'. After being sketched, the specimen was dried and pressed between sheets of heavy blotting paper in a 'drying book' – in this case, Drying Book No. 5.

By the end of this process, the naturalists would have a full record of when and where the plant had been found, the vegetation surrounding it, a description of its size and any particular features, a dried specimen and a pencil sketch. Back in London, these would help Solander and Banks in the long process of identification and classification. Even though Parkinson died before the end of the voyage, his sketches and notes were used by other artists under the supervision of Banks and Solander and a number were turned into full colour paintings and engravings for publication.

It was extraordinarily difficult to transport live plants over long distances by sea for they needed a carefully controlled climate, protection from salt spray and large amounts of fresh water, which was seldom plentiful. Yet there was a good demand in Europe for exotic and commercial species and so there were strenuous efforts during the eighteenth century to bring live plants back from foreign lands. Some plants did survive and new species were continually being established in Europe, but casualty rates of ninety or one hundred per cent were not unusual, especially on the longer voyages from Asia. No live plants were brought back from the Cook voyages but the specimens and seeds that the naturalists collected were preserved in a variety of ways, some being packed in beeswax and sugar, others dried between papers and still others sealed in glass and metal containers. Banks himself preferred to preserve seeds in paper but damp was ever-present on wooden sailing ships and the seeds needed constant attention. 'Our collection of Plants was now grown so immensely large', he wrote in his journal at Botany Bay, 'that it was necessary that some extraordinary care should be taken of them least they should spoil in the books. I therefore devoted this day to that business and carried all the drying paper, near 200 Quires of which the larger part was full, ashore and spreading them upon a sail in the sun kept them in this manner exposed the whole day, often turning them and sometimes turning the quires in which were plants inside out.'

The number of specimens brought back from the Pacific astonished European scientific circles. Banks returned with thousands of plants, 1300 of them unknown to science, including 260 from Tahiti alone. Over 500 specimens of birds were also brought back, although these were less impressive, for Banks had the habit of eating what he shot and many of the specimens were simply feet or wings. Johann Forster was tormented during the second voyage by fears that Banks and Solander had collected all the 'new' plants to be found in the Pacific, and that they were about to publish their findings and so make his own voyage seem completely pointless. Forster need not have worried. The description and classification of the flora from the first voyage was a massive task, one that remained unfinished when Solander died in 1782 and that was never completed by Banks, who had in

Ipomoea indica, collected by Sir Joseph Banks at the Endeavour River while the ship was being repaired; hand-coloured engraving from an original sketch by Sydney Parkinson.

turn been tormented by the fear that Forster would return with a collection to upstage his own. When Banks heard that *Resolution* had returned he nervously sent Solander to find out the truth, summarized by Solander in a brief note to his employer: '260 new Plants, 200 new Animals – 71°10' farthest Sth – no continent – Many Islands, some 80 Leagues long – the Bola-Bola savage an [in]corrigible Blockhead – Glorious Voyage – No man lost by sickness.' The Forsters' voyage was also a triumph for botanical science. Despite their professional rivalries, Banks gave the Forsters access to his own Pacific collections, which were housed in Banks's house in Soho Square, when they were engaged in the process of classification. These superb collections, together with those of later naturalists like Robert Brown on the *Investigator* and Archibald Menzies on the *Discovery*, who would follow Banks and Forster to the Pacific, were eventually stored at the Natural History Museum in London and are still studied by botanists to this day.

Banks may not have been a scientist of the accomplishment or range of Forster, but he could see possibilities in things that others could not. His experiences in the Pacific started him thinking more deeply about the commercial, colonial and humanitarian benefits that would come from being able to transport plants around the globe by sea: wheat, cotton, vegetables or fruit that flourished in one area of the world could be cultivated in another, helping to eliminate want and starvation; products like tea, which could only be obtained expensively through trade, could be grown at home or in the empire; new colonies could be established and grow crops of use to themselves and the home country.

The vision started to become a reality some ten years after Cook's death, once Banks had reached a position of power and influence that enabled him to put his ideas into action. His reputation had soared after the *Endeavour* – the voyage was widely known as 'Mr Banks's voyage' – and although he was sometimes ridiculed in the press as a dilettante snapper-up of unconsidered and exotic trifles, Banks was soon a valued adviser to George III on scientific matters, effectively becoming the unofficial director of the King's botanical gardens at Kew. Banks was elected President of the Royal Society in 1778, a position he kept until his death in 1820, and his advice was also sought by the Admiralty on matters concerned with exploration. With Kew as its centre, Banks built up a network of plant collectors around the world with the brief of sending as many specimens back to England as possible. Banks was a great facilitator: he encouraged the development of plant boxes that would offer plants a chance of survival at sea; he was instrumental in establishing botanical gardens in places such as St Helena where sickly plants could be 'rested' on long ocean voyages; he persuaded individual ships' captains to collect rare or commercially viable plants from foreign lands and to try to bring them back to Kew. On a higher level he badgered the East India

Company and the Royal Navy into giving the transportation of plants official sanction.

Banks promoted a whole range of official and unofficial botanical and imperial projects in the late eighteenth and early nineteenth centuries, although not all were uniformly successful. During his stay in Tahiti, he had written a long paean to the breadfruit, which, he remarked, 'is procurd with no more trouble than that of climbing a tree and pulling it down'. 'If a man should in the course of his lifetime plant 10 such trees,' he continued, '... he would as completely fulfill his duty to his own as well as future generations as we natives of less temperate climates can do by toiling in the cold of winter to sew and in the heat of summer to reap the annual produce of our soil ...'. In actual fact, breadfruit gave Banks stomach-ache, but this did not stop him from suggesting that transporting the plants from Tahiti to the Caribbean would be an ideal solution to the problem of finding cheap

A branch of the breadfruit tree. Although the breadfruit had been known for many years, as it was grown throughout Asia, it captured the European imagination on the Cook voyages as a symbol of the life without toil apparently enjoyed by the Polynesians; hand-coloured engraving by John Miller.

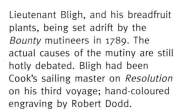
Lieutenant Bligh, and his breadfruit plants, being set adrift by the *Bounty* mutineers in 1789. The actual causes of the mutiny are still hotly debated. Bligh had been Cook's sailing master on *Resolution* on his third voyage; hand-coloured engraving by Robert Dodd.

food for Britain's slave population in the islands. Banks played a key role in the preparations for the voyage, recommending Bligh as captain of the *Bounty*, appointing the naturalist and gardener to tend the plants and helping to design the plants' accommodation and watering system. After the infamous mutiny, Banks's continued support went at least some way towards the decision to give Bligh command of the second voyage in the *Providence*, accompanied by the *Assistant* commanded by Nathaniel Portlock, who, like Bligh, had also sailed on Cook's third voyage. This expedition was successful and Bligh finally landed some 700 healthy plants at the botanical gardens in St Vincent, as well as bringing back a number of live plants and seeds to Kew Gardens. Within a few years the breadfruit tree was established throughout the Caribbean, although the enslaved Africans took a Banksian rather than a Tahitian view of its taste and the fruit never became the popular food that Banks had imagined.

When Britain was looking for somewhere to lose its growing convict population, Banks was on hand to recommend Botany Bay.

The First Fleet was duly despatched to Australia without anyone thinking that it might be worth checking that it really was the fertile haven that Cook and Banks had described in 1770. The First Fleet sailed from England in 1787, loaded down with convicts, stores, seeds and tubers, together with such a large number of live fruit trees and vines in the captains' cabins that a visitor to it described the ships as 'floating greenhouses'. Once the fleet arrived in Australia after nine long months *en route*, during which time Governor Phillip managed the not inconsiderable feat of keeping most of the convicts and plants alive, he soon found that Banks had mistaken Botany Bay's wet season for its dry and the new arrivals were faced with an arid and barren landscape that offered little hope of successful plantings. Banks's grand botanical vision would not be played out here and Phillip promptly moved the nascent colony a few miles up the coast to the larger and more promising bay of Port Jackson, which Cook had seen and named but not entered. This natural harbour would be the site of present-day Sydney.

Banks was the scientific adviser for most of the Navy's voyages of exploration between Cook's death and the early nineteenth century. He frequently lobbied for scientists to be taken on board and would recommend and even appoint particular individuals. Matthew Flinders's *Investigator* voyage of 1801–03 was planned to extend the work of Cook and Banks by charting the coastline and studying the natural history of Australia. The idea had originally been Flinders's and he sold it to Banks, who in turn persuaded the Admiralty that

An idealized view of the founding of Port Jackson in 1788.

they needed more extensive charts of and information about the continent that held Britain's youngest colony. Banks suggested that a team of seven 'men of science' would be needed for the voyage. In the end only five actually sailed but the navigational, scientific and especially the botanical achievements were at least as great as those of the Cook voyages. The naturalist Robert Brown brought 3900 plant specimens back to Britain, despite losing the larger part of his collection when the *Porpoise* (the ship that Flinders obtained to replace the rotten *Investigator*) was wrecked. It is said that Banks never really forgave Flinders for losing that collection. Brown, however, managed what Solander and Banks had not, which was to classify his collection of plants and publish the results. Flinders never managed to finish the enormous task but he completed detailed surveys of parts of the Australian coastline to a standard of which Cook would have been proud; he made the first hydrographic surveys of the future ports of Adelaide and Melbourne; and he was the first person to use the name 'Australia' instead of the more clumsy 'Terra Australis'. Flinders was captured by the French on his way home in 1803 and imprisoned for nine years on the Ile de France (Mauritius); he died in London just two days after his book of the voyage was finally published. Like Cook and Banks, Flinders and Brown are household names in Australia to this day, but unlike Cook and Banks these two men who did so much to further the causes of science and empire in the wake of the Cook voyages are virtually unknown in Britain. As Cook once put it, 'such are the Vicissitudes attending this kind of Service'.

The unlucky Matthew Flinders, who married his wife, Ann, in 1801 shortly before sailing on a three-year voyage of exploration to Australia. He intended to take Ann with him on the *Investigator* but the Admiralty prohibited it. On his way back to England in 1803 he was captured by the French and imprisoned on Mauritius until 1809.

5: ART AND ARTISTS ON COOK'S VOYAGES

At a time of competitive imperial expansion, all Cook's Pacific voyages had underlying imperial motives: the search for a southern continent and the location and claiming of so far unknown lands into Britain's sphere of influence; the noting of their resources and the nature of their populations; the compilation of geographical and navigational information on distant seas and the search for new routes both to and across them. None the less, they were also enterprises of an age of enlightenment, which believed in the perfectibility of human society and was learning to value empirically derived knowledge as both a necessary means of advance and a measure of progress made.

Against this background, the *Endeavour* voyage in particular was the first major, publicly funded 'modern' scientific expedition, both in its conception and methods of its execution. In hindsight, it also seems notably modern in its approach to funding, the state underwriting the core aims – astronomical research and geographical discovery – with Banks's private investment adding a civilian element on behalf of botany in particular. Its success set a precedent, both as the model for

'A view of the Indians of Terra del Fuego in their hut'; after Alexander Buchan. Only the hut itself and the four figures and child immediately behind the fire are fairly close to Buchan's original drawing. The seated figure on the right was completely re-posed and all the others, plus the landscape, added by Cipriani.

'A Morai or Burial Place, in the Island of Yoolea Etea' (Raiataea).
An engraving from Parkinson's *Journal*, from a drawing he probably made in July 1769, with the burial platforms on the right and an altar with offerings in the centre.

Cook's two voyages without Banks but also for later ones. In Cook's case the civilians continued to include astronomer/meteorologists, botanists and graphic artists, although now largely funded from official sources.

The voyages were the first on which artists were taken expressly to create an extensive visual record of discoveries made and the pictorial results are one of their most important features. For this Banks takes the prime credit, since he set and paid for the precedent on *Endeavour* by employing Sydney Parkinson to draw flora and fauna and Alexander Buchan to record ethnographic and landscape subjects. Parkinson took on much of Buchan's area as well after his early death, although on his own account and in his scarce leisure time, rather than for Banks. Some landscape and technical drawing was also done by Herman Spöring, whom Banks partly retasked as 'assistant draughtsman' after the loss of Buchan. Banks may also have done a few primitive but evocative drawings himself, some coloured: if they are by him it shows why he valued as well as needed the professional illustrative help his wealth enabled. If not, they are a mystery still to be conclusively solved.

Banks, no less than Cook, diligently followed the 'Hints' provided by Lord Morton for the conduct of the voyage and the gathering of scientific information. He made a record in his own journal, and through his employment of the artists, of Pacific peoples and ways of life encountered, as well as of his prime botanic interests. Although he ultimately failed to bring Parkinson's botanical work to full publication, for reasons still unclear, the latter's drawings formed the basis of most

'The Head of a Chief of New Zealand, the face curiously tattaowd, or mark'd according to their manner'; engraved by T. Chambers after Parkinson, for his *Journal*, 1773.

of the twenty engravings in the official published account of the voyage in 1773 (edited by Hawkesworth) and, more extensively, in Parkinson's own posthumous *Journal*. This was written up from his notes by a professional editor, William Kenrick, and published by Parkinson's elder brother, Stanfield, also in 1773, after an acrimonious falling-out with Banks over the rights to the drawings. A similar split occurred after the second voyage between J. R. Forster and Lord Sandwich, the guiding hand behind official publication of all the voyage proceedings, especially the second and third. Forster believed his engagement had included the honour of preparing the official account. Of this he was disabused, with the offer of a share in the process and profits, but negotiations grounded on the rock of his own intransigence. Forster's contract with the Admiralty precluded him from separate publication before the official version appeared but this did not apply to his son. The result was that Georg Forster rapidly produced a parallel but unillustrated account based on their joint knowledge. This was published in 1777 with further *Observations on a Voyage Round the World* by Forster senior in 1778. The former appeared two months before Cook's account, edited by the Revd Dr Douglas, with its twelve charts and its fifty-one engravings after Hodges. The third voyage proceedings appeared in 1784, edited by Douglas from Cook's and Surgeon Anderson's journals for the first two volumes and from Captain James King's for the third. This had sixty-one engravings after Webber and seventeen charts and coastal views, to some of which he also contributed.

Most of these illustrations were produced from worked-up drawings based on even greater quantities of sketches and studies, which remained unpublished at the time. Today, the bulk of this material is in museum collections in Britain, Australia and New

Zealand, as are most of the oil paintings of William Hodges and rather fewer by John Webber, the main artists of the two *Resolution* voyages. Some of these were painted during the expeditions but the majority later in London, especially the larger ones. Many were done expressly for the Admiralty as part of the artists' official work, which continued well after their return, others on their own account. The visual harvest of Cook's voyages therefore covers a very wide range, from natural history and navigational illustration through anthropological studies of Pacific peoples and their way of life to major exhibited works of art embodying Europe's first broad, full-colour impressions of the tropical paradise that Cook and his contemporaries found in the South Seas.

This artistic *reportage*, however, has its problems. Even a photograph is only truthful or 'real' in the limited sense of being the image that the lens records by the chemical or electronic nature of the process. Whether it is truly representative of what it purports to illustrate depends on many other factors. Not least of these are the why, where and when it is taken, the choice of what is 'in the frame', rather than left out, and the motives behind its selection for publication. The unique persuasiveness of photographic images over 'artists' impressions' – and their potential for abuse – derives from their facility, inherent credibility and capacity for undeclared manipulation.

Similar issues arise, in earlier forms, with the paintings and drawings from Cook's voyages. This has less to do with the selection of images – though the coverage is far from even – than with the European pictorial conventions within which the artists worked and which formed their conceptual framework for coming to terms with the Pacific. This particularly applied to Hodges and Webber – both of whom were trained painters with differing debts to French Classicism (indirect in Hodges's case) and also to other artists and engravers who 'worked up' material at home from sketches by minor contributors such as Buchan and Spöring.

The most important general consideration is the artists' natural tendency to use prevailing European models in the posing of figures and in aspects of landscape composition. Coincidentally, Cook's first voyage began in 1768, the year which saw the foundation of the Royal Academy in London, with Joshua Reynolds – England's greatest portrait painter – being elected as its first President. Reynolds's influential views on art, embodied in the Presidential *Discourses* which he delivered annually to 1772 and biannually thereafter, advocated a national school of 'grand manner' history painting on the heroic, Classically inspired European model. However, what then still prevailed in largely Catholic, absolutist Europe fell on less fertile ground in Protestant, mercantile and relatively libertarian England, save among an artistically educated élite. It was Reynolds's achievement to create instead a form of 'historic portraiture', in which ideal nobility of character expressed in history painting appeared instead in

modern-dress portraits of individual sitters. In parallel, the most
successful British 'history painting' of the period found its exemplar in
Benjamin West's 'Death of General Wolfe' at Quebec in 1759, painted
in 1770–71. This heroic group combined the Renaissance tradition of
'descents from the Cross' and the Antique code of martial virtue into a
popular and patriotic new British form through both the American
Revolutionary War (1775–83) and the French Wars of 1793–1815. By
comparison, Reynolds and many of his contemporaries considered
landscape painting essentially inferior to the historic mode, especially
when 'naturalistic' and modern rather than aspiring to timeless,
'typical' ideals of the seventeenth and early eighteenth-century French
and Italian schools. Reynolds's *Discourses* were published and his
judgements – which were in many ways reassertions of long-standing
views – would certainly have been known to both Hodges and
Webber. Both were still young men making their reputations when
they embarked with Cook. In this context their challenge was to
assimilate entirely new material – landscapes, climates, cultures and
peoples – and make sense of it in terms of their own artistic ambitions, and in a manner comprehensible and acceptable to their peers
and public at home.

They also faced a more immediate problem which did not affect
Parkinson, Georg Forster and the other lesser voyage 'illustrators',
whose remit was more technical. These men all worked in a well-
established tradition going back at least to the sixteenth century
which required detailed representation of scientific specimens –
be this the appearance of peoples, their dress, bodily decorations
(notably Pacific tattooing) and accoutrements, or the appearance of
plants and animals. Where figure drawing was concerned these also
tended to show the influence of a Classical repertoire of poses,
at least in finalized worked-up forms, but in Cook's day this
conventionalization was less of an issue than it would be now.
Detailed racial characteristics and distinctions were not then the
main interest, more the immediate appearances of 'primitive' life.
For Hodges and Webber, however, the very fact that part of their
work was to provide material of representational value at a technical
level created an inherent tension with the 'generalized truth' required
by the dominant aesthetic of their time.

The *Endeavour* artists

Three illustrators worked for Banks on the *Endeavour* voyage: Sydney
Parkinson, Alexander Buchan and Dr Herman Spöring. Of Buchan
nothing is known before he joined the ship and though Banks noted
that he made some views of the Cape Verde Islands at the end of
September 1768, these have vanished. He next drew studies of fish
and crabs caught off the Brazilian coast and a small number of fairly
primitive landscape and figure studies when *Endeavour* called at
Tierra del Fuego in mid-January 1769, as well as of ornaments and

equipment of the Ona people there. These show he was a very competent technical illustrator in gouache and watercolour. He was not, however, so skilled as a landscape or figure painter and when his 'View of the Indians of Terra del Fuego in their hut' was published in the official account, this was from a Classicized redrawing of the figures by G. B. Cipriani, in tune with a Utopian gloss on 'noble savagery' that Hawkesworth gratuitously added to Cook's and Banks's plain record of the encounter. Unfortunately Buchan was a sick man, both from a bowel disorder and epilepsy, which he may have concealed from Banks when recruited. He had a fit just after he arrived on Tierra del Fuego but recovered. A more severe attack proved fatal on 15 April 1769, two days after they reached Tahiti, where – at a loss to know how Tahitians might view interment ashore – Cook buried him at sea off the coast, 'with all the decency the circumstance of the place would admit of'.

Some of the work which would have been Buchan's subsequently fell to Spöring , a Swede who was born about 1733 and trained as a surgeon under his own father, the Professor of Medicine at the University of Åbo (now Turku, in Finland). He practised for only a short time before moving to London where he worked as a watchmaker for eleven years, gaining skills which proved valuable in maintaining and repairing *Endeavour*'s instruments. His family knew Linnaeus and through that connection he became Solander's clerk in London and then Banks's secretary for the voyage. As might be expected from his background, Spöring was a precise, literal but untrained technical draughtsman, a role to which Banks extended his duties on Buchan's death. He did some meticulous canoe drawings, especially of Maori prow decorations, the latter being much in the style of modern archaeological illustration; also record drawings of tattoos, some rather stiff landscape and figure studies, and a large number of coastal profiles. He copied some of his own drawings for Cook, while Parkinson was in turn allowed to copy some of Spöring's views of places he did not see himself. A number of Spöring's and Parkinson's drawings were also copied by a man called Charles Praval, who joined the crew at Batavia and was found to have sufficient talent to help by making record duplicates. Some of Spöring's work was later redrawn for engraving but his original drawings remained with Banks and were confused with Parkinson's until re-identified about 1954. He died at sea aged about thirty-eight, on 24 January 1771, two days ahead of Parkinson, both of them being among the thirty-one *Endeavour* fatalities from the malaria and dysentery contracted at Batavia. It should also be added that after both the first and second voyages a number of other artists, including Banks's recruit, John Cleveley, drew Pacific artefacts which were brought back, some for engraving. Cleveley also later painted views of the third voyage, on which his twin brother, James, was carpenter of *Resolution*. Although four related prints that he published were advertised as being from sketches by James, these are unlocated and the prints could also have been based on previously engraved views.

Sydney Parkinson was born in Edinburgh, probably in 1745, one of three children of a Quaker brewer who died leaving his family in straitened circumstances. Sydney was originally apprenticed to a woollen draper but preferred to develop a talent as a natural history draughtsman. He was apparently self-taught but was probably influenced by a number of landscape watercolourists working in Scotland and England in the 1750s and 1760s, not least by Paul Sandby, a near neighbour after the Parkinsons settled in London between 1760 and 1765. In the latter year, and in 1766, he exhibited flower paintings at the Free Society and seems to have been introduced to Banks through botanical connections early in 1767. Banks employed him from then on to draw the birds and insects he had collected on a visit to Newfoundland in 1766 (where he and Cook had just failed to meet). He then became Banks's natural history draughtsman on the *Endeavour* at the salary of £80 a year.

Parkinson was an intelligent, likeable and even-tempered young man, with an admirable Quaker revulsion for both the occasional violence and the sexual licence which coloured Cook's encounters with Pacific culture. As Cook recognized, and regretted, both aspects were unavoidable and could only be limited, by maintaining effective discipline, rather than totally prevented. The use of firearms, in particular, was both the expedition's and individuals' final guarantee of safety and, as Lord Morton's 'Hints' enjoined, Cook always tried to limit this to demonstrations or at least non-lethal levels – not always successfully. Parkinson's skills were intriguing to the islanders and clearly peaceful. This benefited the whole enterprise, since his easy manner, lively curiosity and willingness to communicate won their confidence and friendship, quite apart from being necessary to effectiveness in his work. Not least of his diplomatic achievements was his compilation of the first word-lists of Pacific languages: 400 Tahitian words and phrases, sixty-seven from the much more unpredictable Maori and 141 from the Australian Aborigines, by far the most elusive subjects to draw. He also made a collection of artefacts, intended for his cousin, and kept a much-admired fair-copy journal which, mysteriously, could not be found when he died and never has been.

All Parkinson's botanical and other natural history work was done for Banks: 955 drawings of plants, 280 of these being finished versions, and 377 of animals of one sort or another. On top of this he did studies of Pacific peoples, their activities, artefacts and landscapes for his own interest, and would probably have made much more of these at home had he lived. His work in both areas developed well over the course of the voyage but he was not trained in either and four full-length figures engraved in his *Journal* were redrawn in Classically derived poses to conform with contemporary taste. These drawings are now lost but it is unlikely that they were by Parkinson.

His lack of conventional training in this area keeps his own studies of islanders, especially those of heads, almost clear of such stereotypes. They instead show a lively individuality and were praised for their accuracy, albeit within the contemporary focus already mentioned on dress, hairstyle, ornaments and tattooed decoration, rather than exact racial definition. A similar lack of training is also apparent in his drawing of figure groups but they too gained vivacity and greater coherence as the voyage progressed. In both cases it has been suggested that Parkinson was deliberately seeking to improve his style in these areas on the lines counselled in Hogarth's *Analysis of Beauty*, which was one of the numerous books, including history and poetry, that he took with him.

He must have done some landscape work before the voyage, although none is known, and his efforts in this area also became more assured as the voyage lengthened. His views of Tahitian *marae* – the solemn, mysterious and sometimes gruesome island shrines – struck particular chords in England, both as an element in the rise of literary and artistic Romanticism and as evidence of a need for Christian missionary activity. Less immanent subjects combine specifically identified plants in picturesque landscape compositions, while others cut loose from botany and attempt to capture the mood and general appearance of the Pacific, with and without figures of the inhabitants in characteristic occupations. There is also a growing awareness, both in the text of his published *Journal* and in the drawings themselves, of the effects of weather, light and colour. Parkinson did not use watercolour except in his botanical work on the voyage – the rest is all in pencil, ink or monochrome wash. This may have been because watercolour was then seen mainly as an informational 'drawing' medium not an expressive 'painting' one like oils, because he lacked appropriate technique or because Banks wanted the limited colour stock prioritized to natural history uses. Nevertheless, the evidence of Parkinson's imaginative awareness shows how the Pacific and perhaps his association with seamen and astronomers, as well as natural historians, broadened his range from purely technical concerns.

When Parkinson died on the way home he was only twenty-six and was owed just over £150 in wages by Banks. His employer was slow in handing this and his personal effects to Stanfield Parkinson, who asked a Quaker family friend, Dr John Fothergill, to mediate in the matter. Fothergill easily persuaded Banks to pay the family a total of £500, comprising the back pay and a sum in recognition of Sydney's diligence and death in harness. Banks, however, assumed the payment would give him possession of all Parkinson's drawings, not just the botanical ones, a view with which Fothergill agreed. Stanfield disputed this and eventually got the return of his brother's working papers, which formed the basis of his published *Journal*. Its appearance was legally prevented by Hawkesworth until after that of the official account and, when published immediately afterwards, comments in Stanfield's preface created a rift with Fothergill. Banks had in the meantime ensured that Parkinson was not credited as original author of the Cook plates in Hawkesworth's edition, while the strain and cost of championing his dead brother's reputation brought Stanfield to mental collapse and an early death. Fothergill none the less attended him at the end and purchased 400 unsold copies of the *Journal* from the family. They were reissued as a second edition in 1784, prefaced with his own 'Explanatory remarks' on the affair. It was only then that Parkinson received the full credit due to him in the praise of the reviewers. The episode does not show Banks in a good light, but the fact that he retained the majority of Parkinson's work of all sorts means that the bulk survives in the British Museum and Natural History Museum.

William Hodges: 'a Landskip Painter' on *Resolution*

As on *Endeavour*, there were a number of contributors to the graphic results of Cook's subsequent voyages. On all three, Cook himself was the main cartographer but had assistants. On *Endeavour* and the first voyage of *Resolution*, one was his young cousin Isaac Smith (1752–1831), midshipman and then master's mate; he eventually retired as a rear-admiral. The talent of Henry Roberts, able seaman and master's mate on *Resolution*, was spotted on her first voyage and

Georg Forster's remarkable gouache drawing of the ships in the Antarctic in March 1773, with the loom of ice-blink reflected in the distant southern sky.

he became a skilled cartographer by the end of her second. Other help came from Midshipman John Elliott and the sailing master, Joseph Gilbert. Roberts, Smith and Elliott, according to the last, were encouraged by Cook 'either Copying Drawings for him, or Drawings for ourselves under the Eye of Mr Hodges', the principal artist of the voyage. Apart from a small watercolour of icebergs by Smith, all the known work of these men relates to charts and coastal profiles. Similarly, except for a strikingly Romantic gouache drawing of *Resolution* and *Adventure* among icebergs by Georg Forster, clearly influenced by Hodges, all his drawings were of plants and animals. The Forsters later sold 729 of these to Banks, taking others home with them to Germany, where Georg became an influential writer on Pacific subjects.

Zoffany, Cleveley and the draughtsman Miller brothers withdrew from Cook's second voyage with Banks, their employer, in May 1772. Replacing them by Admiralty order of 30 June, addressed to Cook at Plymouth, came 'Mr William Hodges, a Landskip Painter … to make Drawings and Paintings of such places in the Countries you may touch on in the Course of the said Voyage as may be proper to give a more perfect idea thereof than can be formed from written descriptions only'. Cook was to ensure that he worked diligently to produce pictures of such places '… as also of such other Objects and things as may fall within the Compass of his Abilities'.

Hodges seems to have been recommended to the Board by one of its members, Lord Palmerston, who knew his pre-voyage work, now almost completely lost. That he was a landscape artist – unlike the figure and portrait specialist, Zoffany – was significant: it matched Cook's mission to find and record any 'southern continent' and add to knowledge of the islands. Hodges, in practice, also showed himself to be at least a competent figure painter and was a far from neglible portraitist, with a penchant for working in red chalk. He produced good drawn likenesses of native sitters, which also catch the characters of named individuals as far as we know them. Among the finest is his drawing of Tu (or Otoo), the timid but politically astute Tahitian chief whose territory included Matavai Bay and who later became the first king of Tahiti as Pomare I. That said, his figures were an aspect of his work singled out for later criticism and he did not attempt to exhibit portraits from the voyage. Only two in oils are known, both probably painted in England. One of Omai, painted for the anatomist John Hunter, certainly was; the other, of Cook, was probably also painted in London as the basis for the frontispiece of the voyage proceedings. Hodges also painted two oil portraits of American Indians for Hunter but no others by him are now known.

Like Parkinson, Hodges was a man of talent from modest origins. His father was a respectable London blacksmith with a shop just south of fashionable Piccadilly, where he was born in 1744. His parents encouraged his artistic interests and placed him as an errand boy and pupil in the London drawing school run by William Shipley,

Tu (Otoo), later King Pomare I of Tahiti, by William Hodges. A red chalk drawing, probably done in August 1773.

founder in 1755 of the influential Society for the Encouragement of the Arts, Manufactures and Commerce. In 1758 his talents were noticed by the portraitist and landscape painter Richard Wilson (1714–82), who took him on as an apprentice. At around the same time he also took lessons at the Duke of Richmond's sculpture gallery under Joseph Wilton and the history painter, Cipriani. Wilton was a sculptor and Hodges showed some interest in this: in 1759 he won a modest prize for 'Modelling Bas Relief Ornaments in Clay'.

Wilton and Cipriani would have improved Hodges's figure drawing but the influence of Wilson, the earliest major English landscape painter, was crucial. Wilson himself had switched from portraiture to landscape after 1735 and spent several years in Italy. This gave him a preoccupation with light, which one also sees developed in Hodges, and he was deeply influenced by the French Classical landscape painters, Claude Lorrain and Gaspard Dughet (brother-in-law and follower of Nicholas Poussin, whose name he adopted). However, much of Wilson's work also had a simplicity, breadth and interest in specific landscape detail which Reynolds criticized as 'too near common nature' – that is, naturalistic rather than conforming to the generalized, timeless ideals required by history painting. In the event, this is why Wilson was an important forerunner to English Romantic landscape art and the work of painters like Constable and Turner. Hodges, as his pupil and follower, was in no sense a conscious pioneer of Romanticism although his work, like Wilson's, marks a stage towards it. He would none the less have known Burke's essay on the nature of the *Sublime and the Beautiful*, published in 1756 – a seminal text on the subject – and would have been familiar with general use of the term.

Cook's own attitude to landscape, like Banks's, was utilitarian and agricultural rather than poetic: one as a naval officer of limited education assessing the natural potentials of newly found lands, the other as a country landowner. On board *Resolution*, however, were the Forsters, intellectuals already sensitized to the early stirrings of Romantic thought. Hodges was inevitably influenced to some degree by his contact with them during the voyage, and in his work deriving from it. The Forsters were both well placed and well qualified to criticize Hodges's efforts, especially since relations between them cooled in the disagreements over the voyage publication, and on some points they did. However, they remained broad admirers of Hodges's work. In 1778, for example, J. R. Forster wrote of his depictions of the waterfalls in Dusky Bay, New Zealand:

> Some of these cascades with their neighbouring scenery, require the pencil and genius of a Salvator Rosa to do them justice [Rosa was noted for wild Italian mountain scenes]: however the ingenious artist, who went with us on this expedition has great merit, in having executed some of these romantic landscapes in a masterly manner.

Hodges's mature attitude to his subject came out later, in 1795:

> ... in the ancient and in many of the modern masters of landscape ...
> I confess there seemed very rarely to me any moral purpose in the
> mind of the artist ... It could not escape me that other branches of the
> art had achieved a nobler effect – History exhibited the actions of our
> heroes and patriots, and the glory of past ages – and even Portrait,
> though more confined in its influence, strengthened the ties of social
> existence. To give dignity to landscape is my object ... [and] ... to
> amend the heart while the eye is gratified...

In short, his wish was to deepen the purpose of his branch of art
within conventional bounds, not break a mould. With that in view the
interest of his *Resolution* work lies in how he managed to adjust his
own experience and ambitions to the subjects which the voyage put in
front of him and, more originally, interpret the light and atmosphere
of the Pacific. At the simplest level, in many of his sketches in all
media there is a striking naturalistic immediacy of response both to
what he sees and the often novel conditions in which he sees it. He
works with a breadth and fluency beyond Parkinson and, unlike him,
uses watercolour to tint many of his wash drawings. However, when
he launches into a formal oil composition, he then often imposes an
idealized structure to anticipate his audience's expectations, while at
the same time trying to retain the informational detail inherent in his
role as voyage *rapporteur*. The various conflicts involved explain criticism that his work met when first exhibited. Two hundred years on,
the fact that his record of the pre-European Pacific still has as much
impact as it did in the 1770s and 1780s – though for different reasons
– is a measure of his long-term success, and of how far he was ahead
of his time.

Two of the most original works are the matched pair of panels
showing the 'Monuments of Easter Island' (see p.47) and the 'View in
the Province of Oparree' – a panoramic seascape suffused in evening
light, with two figures in a canoe almost photographically half out of
frame at the bottom (see p.47). They are two of the most fluidly
painted works from the voyage, probably done together and neither
on the spot. There was no time at Easter Island and it is almost
certain that Hodges ran out of sufficient paint for such work by
September 1773, since there is only one oil done with very short
measure of colour after that date. One suggestion is that he may have
painted them during the voyage home from Cape Town, having
acquired more paints there. If he did, their liquidity and freedom, and
the fact that they were done from sketches and recall at the end of the
voyage, makes an interesting contrast with the 'View of the Cape of
Good Hope' (see p.42), painted there on the way out. This shows a
similar awareness of the unusual weather conditions that prevail
around Table Mountain, which certainly interested the astronomer

William Wales, who was one of Hodges's closest friends on the voyage. Weather conditions continued to be a notable interest of Hodges throughout the expedition and in his work in later life. However, the 'View of the Cape' is at the same time a more technical 'coastal profile' than later Pacific examples. It owes much to Wilson's influence, although sharp contrasts of shadows and light make it one of Hodges's works which also suggest that of Canaletto, well known in England.

The picture was the largest painted during the voyage and is especially remarkable for that reason. *En plein air* oil-painting was very unusual at the time and although Hodges began with a preliminary drawing, the windows of *Resolution*'s great cabin gave him a unique vantage point to finish this and do other works: if not strictly 'open-air' – which some of his small oil sketches may have been, flies and heat permitting – it was effectively so, being done in a floating studio with a panoramic and ever-changing view, as well as being the only one available. Shipped back with two small paintings of Madeira to the Admiralty, the 'View of the Cape of Good Hope' was exhibited at the Free Society in 1774 as 'painted on the Spot'. The view from *Resolution*, in Pickersgill Harbour, New Zealand (see p.43), probably also painted on the spot, is an even more unusual composition from the cabin, looking forward down the port side of the ship from the quarter-gallery window. This was probably shown at the Academy in 1776.

Several of the even larger paintings done later in London are worthy of note. The extraordinary 'View of Cape Stephens in Cook's

Waterspouts in Cook Strait, 17 May 1773; '... one of the most curious and perhaps the most extraordinary and powerful of Nature's productions', Wales wrote; 'One of them came ...within 30 or 40 yards of the ship...The annexed plate ... was engraved from a drawing of Mr Hodges, taken at the time; in which he has exhibited the appearance of one of them in three several states and also the appearance of that which approached so near to the ship.' From Wales and Bayly's *Astronomical Observations* ...(1782).

Straits with Waterspout' (*c*.1775–76) recalls an incident of 1773, in which one of several waterspouts came perilously close to the ship. Although done for the Admiralty and not publicly exhibited, it is the nearest that Hodges comes to painting 'the sublime', as defined by Burke, in which depiction of the overwhelming forces of nature aims to inspire awe or terror in the beholder. By comparison, it is a measure of Hodges's limits and that of his audience that while he made some striking drawings of the ships among Antarctic icebergs he made no attempt to paint them imaginatively in oils. This is why Forster's unique gouache 'painting', an aesthetic as much as a documentary response, is so unusually advanced.

Wales, the astronomer, saw Hodges make the sketch on which the 'Waterspout' was based as the phenomenon rapidly developed. This is no longer known, only the relatively naturalistic engraving developed from it for Wales and Bayly's *Astronomical Observations* from the voyage. The contrast between the print and the painting well illustrates the tension between Hodges's roles: on the one hand, as a recorder of observed fact; on the other, as an artist repackaging Pacific experience within established pictorial conventions. It is well known that the painting's composition reflects Wilson's 'Ceyx and Alcyone' of 1768 – which Hodges's probably helped with – and his 'Destruction of Niobe's Children' (1760). Both, and Hodges's picture, are differing

'A View of Cape Stephens in Cook's Straits with Waterspout', by William Hodges; oil on canvas. Hodges painted this version of the 1773 incident for the Admiralty, in 1776. As in the related engraving, the distant waterspout is shown in its three phases, while the general composition is based on Dughet's 'Jonah and the whale'.

'Jonah and the whale': engraved by François Vivares after Gaspar Dughet (1615–75). The painting became celebrated as a Classical example of the sublime after it was acquired by Frederick, Prince of Wales, about 1745, and this print appeared in 1748. The print is in fact a left-to-right reversal of the painting (a fairly common practice), reproduced here in the latter's orientation for comparative purposes. Lord Sandwich had known Frederick and may have had some part in Hodges's adoption of the composition.

attempts to elevate landscape by bending naturalistic elements into a Classical framework. Less familiar is the similarity of the 'Cape Stephens' to a direct French Classical source, Gaspar Dughet's 'Jonah and the Whale', certainly also known to Wilson. This was then a celebrated exemplar of the sublime, not least because it was the only sea-piece by an artist better known for pastoral landscapes. The debt is particularly noticeable in the coastline and lightning-struck buildings (Hodges's being a Maori *pa*), with Hodges's natural maritime drama presenting a modern, observed equivalent to Dughet's stormy realization of Biblical myth. Hodges also reduces the Maori figures in his foreground to a similar level of Classical, and in the woman's case European, generalization as those in the 'Jonah' and may have derived poses from two of them. Wales's description of Hodges's print shows that it firmly authenticates his own written account of how the waterspouts appeared to form. 'He has', wrote his friend, 'exhibited the appearance of one of them in three several states' as well as 'the appearance of that which approached so near to the ship'. The painting is also notably precise in this regard, despite all its other differences.

The Classical mode for showing modern subjects had some other benefits. In about 1775–76 Hodges painted two versions of a picture including naked Tahitian girls bathing at Vaitepiha Bay, the second entitled 'Tahiti revisited' (see p.45). Considering the sexual

gratifications enjoyed there by Cook's men – what he called 'the
Amours of my People at Otaheite and other places' – few hints come
through in the art of all three voyages. In this it mirrors Cook's
instruction to his editor, Douglas, after the second voyage 'not to
mention them at all' unless necessary to understanding Pacific peoples.
This was perhaps in part a reaction to Hawkesworth's sensual
popularization of the earlier voyage accounts, which prompted further
salacious retellings. If one excludes naked figure studies – which were
acceptable within both the scientific and artistic 'nude' traditions –
Hodges's two paintings are the only ones with a clear erotic element.
This, however, is neatly defused by the Arcadian setting, a prominent

Tahitian idol and a shrouded corpse on a distant burial platform (or
tupapu). The last two details firmly signal the pagan context and make
an oblique but familiar Classical reference to the transience of earthly
paradise: *et in Arcadia ego* ('I, Death, am also in Arcady'). The
particular interest of the formula in this case, however, is how it
provides a context for the unfamiliar main subject of Hodges's picture
– an idealized recollection of the improbably shaped Tahitian mountains
soaring into an iridescent blue sky, their flanks glittering in an early
morning light that streams almost upwards across the picture, through the
valley to the left, from the low and invisible sea horizon east of the bay.

Resolution and *Adventure* in Matavai
Bay, Tahiti, by William Hodges; oil on
canvas. This version of the subject
was painted for the Admiralty in
about 1776. The earlier version shows
Tahitian war canoes in the bay and
has the same seated male figures in
the canoe on the left.

'The War Boats of the island of Otaheite, and the Society islands...' by William Hodges; oil on canvas. Hodges's large Royal Academy set-piece of 1777 combines canoes which he saw at Opare, Tahiti, with a setting from Huahine. The idyllic landscape and the alarmed family group in the left foreground emphasize the warlike preparations on an agitated sea.

The first version of this picture and its pair, a view of Tahitian canoes in Matavai Bay, were probably the ones shown at the Royal Academy in 1776. The second (slightly less explicit) version was painted for the Admiralty with a variant of the same pendant, showing *Resolution* and *Adventure* in the bay. The two bay pictures are also in contrast. The former, like the Arcadian girls, evokes the pre-European purity of Tahiti. The towering island is bathed in golden, western light; the decayed earthworks of Cook's *Endeavour* 'fort' on Point Venus are barely visible, and various canoes lie suspended across the calm, intervening sea, with two Classically posed Tahitian men prominent on one in the left foreground. The latter (see p.109) almost completely transforms the scene into one of European dominance: the British camp is firmly re-established on the Point and Cook's ships, even though dwarfed by the mountains behind, command the bay at the focus of the composition, with their ensigns and pendants flying. On the foreground canoe the same men have been joined by a third and what elsewhere would pass as a 'Madonna and Child', the mother's half-naked form suggesting the innocence of the newly discovered Eden.

An even more conventional mother and child in the foreground of the large 'War Boats of the island of Otaheite', exhibited in 1777, points up the contrast between the idyllic setting with the warlike, alien preparations and equipment. This ambitious picture was one of Hodges's less successful, being criticized for 'ragged' and 'unfinished' colouring – a common complaint before Romanticism made such colour applications more acceptable as expressive in themselves. Considering that Hodges deliberately softened his painting effects in this work, its disappointing reception shows the struggle he had to fit the exotic subject and effect of Pacific light to the perceptions of an Academy audience. For similar reasons his composition also misrepresents the facts, shifting the fighting platform of the main canoe from its correct place in the prow to midships, inserting a gratuitous 'steering oar' to strengthen the prow and giving it no paddlers at all. The smaller 'Review of the War Galleys at Tahiti', which he prepared for very successful engraving in the voyage account, is more accurately informative, less contrived and a franker admission of his inventive handling of paint. It well shows the liquid, highlighting method he developed – perhaps again with aspects of Canaletto in mind – to render the sharp spot-colour and shadow contrasts of the Pacific.

While we do not know how the subjects of any of Hodges's post-voyage paintings for the Admiralty were decided, or how they were originally displayed, the relationship between the major examples, at least, was important. The 'Cape Stephens' and 'Matavai Bay' pictures are a pendant pair which contrast the awesome 'sublimity' of the

'Review of the War Galleys at Tahiti'. Hodges's small oil painting, on panel, of about 1775–76, which was engraved by William Woollett for the second voyage account.

former with the still beauty of the latter, both placing Cook's ships – interloping symbols of British power and scientific progress – in Classically influenced interpretations of alien landscapes and cultures, and the unfamiliar natural conditions which the pictures show. It is probably significant that the exhibited 'War Canoes', in further contrast, both excludes overt reference to British presence and is by far Hodges's largest single Admiralty painting (70 x 107 in./178 x 272 cm), with the Cape Stephens/Matavai Bay pictures being the largest pair (53.5 x 76 in./136 x 193 cm). Notwithstanding its classicized elements and the criticism it received, its aim was presumably to display the uncompromised native grandeur of Tahitian sea power in some central position in the old Admiralty building, possibly flanked and complemented by this smaller but still large pair.

Not all Hodges's engraved versions were either as convincing as the smaller version of the 'War Canoes', or free from criticism. While his landscapes are consistent with his general aims of elevating the form as a whole, those which show Cook's landings at various places are conventional 'history paintings' on the modern-dress pattern established by West's 'Death of General Wolfe': the contemporary hero of European discovery stepping ashore to primitive welcomes of peace, suspicion or outright hostility. All are post-voyage inventions showing Hodges's weakness in composing acceptable figure groups and considerable falsification of dress, pose and stature of native peoples (though not of all ethnographic detail) to fit the historical model. *The Landing at Tanna* (see p.129) is the most successful example, with the volcano smoking in the background, but for the 'Landing at Middleburgh' (Eua) in the Tonga group and the 'Landing at Erramanga' (see p.130) in the New Hebrides, he sought help. In the first, a peaceful scene for which only part of a drawing survives, this was probably from John Sherwin, the engraver. In the second, where the reception was so hostile that no drawings were possible anyway, Hodges's old teacher Cipriani provided him with one to use as a model for the native figure group. From this he did the preparatory painting, itself a rapid and spirited piece of work, exhibited at the Academy in 1778 as one of his two last exhibited voyage pictures. In both cases, however, the engraved versions roused the strong published criticism of Georg Forster in his *Voyage Round the World*, for their inauthentic Classicization, while an Academy reviewer objected to the Erramanga painting because 'The Europeans and the savages are not discriminated in their complexion … and neither [are] like anything in nature'.

We do not know Hodges's salary for the voyage but on his return the Admiralty retained him at £250 a year until the end of 1778 to oversee the engraving of his work for the voyage proceedings and finish the drawings and paintings which they required. He had married in May 1776 but his wife died in childbirth within the year. By early 1779 he had left to work in India, where he gained the lasting patronage of Warren Hastings, Governor-General of Bengal.

William Hodges by George Dance. This print is from a drawing of Hodges after he became a Royal Academician in 1789.

He returned to England in 1783, remarried in 1784 and again lost his wife, this time after only three months. Finally, in December 1785 he married Ann Carr, by whom he had five children, in addition to an illegitimate son whom he brought back from India. He continued to exhibit Indian and British subjects and from 1785 to 1788 published forty-four prints of *Select Views in India*, followed in 1793 by a vivid account of his travels there. He was elected Associate of the Royal Academy in 1786 and Academician in 1789 but his family and other expenses remained a burden. In 1791 he painted scenery (which he had also done in Derby when young) for the King's Theatre and after it burnt down in 1792 made an unsuccessful trip to seek patronage in St Petersburg.

Hodges's last artistic project was two large paintings called 'The Effects of Peace' and the 'Consequences of War', a pair of contrasting 'moral' landscapes exhibited in London, without great success, in November 1794. In January 1795, HRH the Duke of York – just returned from a notoriously ineffective spell commanding the army in Flanders – condemned and closed the show as subversive to the war effort against Revolutionary France. Hodges gave up, sold his remaining work at auction and retired to Brixham, Devon, becoming partner in a small bank at Dartmouth. This failed in a general banking crisis of early 1797 and he died of 'gout of the stomach' on 6 March (though suicide was rumoured) the day after he had ridden over in dreadful weather to close it down. His wife also died within a few months, leaving the six children 'in great want'.

John Webber and the last voyage

By the time of Cook's third voyage, the value of carrying artists was well proved. It also seems clear that, had Cook lived, it would still have been his last major expedition and that he had its writing-up for publication himself in mind from the beginning. To this end he would have wished to work closely with any artist he took, and did so. Who that would be was only formally resolved three weeks before he sailed when, on 24 June 1776, the Admiralty appointed twenty-four-year-old John Webber. He was recommended by Daniel Solander, now Banks's librarian, who visited the Royal Academy annual exhibition and saw two views near Paris and a fine portrait drawing by him. Solander was impressed, sought him out and canvassed him for the job.

Apart from being described as 'a Draughtsman and Landskip Painter' Webber's contract was the same as Hodges's but this time we know his voyage salary was one hundred guineas a year. There was also a second draughtsman and watercolourist, William Webb Ellis, aged about twenty. He was an educated man who began the voyage as a surgeon's mate on *Discovery* before moving to *Resolution* in February 1779, after which he was in close rather than only occasional contact with Webber. His interest was primarily in natural history, and appears to have benefited technically from Webber's

advice. They often drew the same landscape views and it is likely that some of Ellis's, whose own style tends to be rather diagrammatic, are copies made from Webber's and under his guidance. Both of them – Webber inevitably the more closely – also worked under the advice of William Anderson, *Resolution*'s surgeon but also a natural historian and botanist. His well-written journal of the voyage testifies to his intellect and imagination, although he died at sea in August 1778.

Webber was not just the youngest of the official voyage artists but the most cosmopolitan and comprehensively trained, including as an engraver. Overall he was also the most successful in accommodating the recording role to artistic convention, largely avoiding obvious stereotypes and showing frequent quiet originality. Although he was a very competent portraitist, his drawing of figure groups was comparatively weak and certainly idiosyncratic. All these tend to similarity, with small heads on elongated bodies – perhaps to add 'dignity' – although this did not apply to his single-figure studies and he improved greatly during the voyage. His work is otherwise precise, sensitive, detailed and remarkably homogeneous. A particular bonus is his frequent use of watercolour, again as an informative rather than an

'Christmas Harbour in the Island of Desolation', December 1776, by William Ellis. This example of Ellis's work repeats a view also drawn by Webber on Kerguelen Island; 'as rocky, barren, and desolate... as can be conceived,' wrote Ellis, 'which induced Captain Cook to call it the Island of Desolation.'

aesthetic medium, and a far larger number of his drawings than Hodges's have delicate colour tinting, especially the finished versions. Although the natural history results of the third voyage are less than the previous two, with Webber's limited but polished output supplementing Ellis's larger personal initiative, the expedition's visual harvest as a whole is the best of all. Webber alone brought back around two hundred drawings in a more or less finished state and many more sketches. Notably he was the only artist who appears to have summarized the work he did for the Admiralty in a catalogue list of 172 drawings of two sizes (portfolio and 'roll') and twenty portraits in oil, the whereabouts of few of the latter now being known.

Webber was the only full-time general artist with Cook who was, to all intents, foreign and foreign-trained. His father, Abraham Wäber, was a Swiss sculptor from Berne, who settled in London after 1740, anglicized his name and married a local girl in 1744. John was born in 1751, probably the second and oldest surviving child of a family which his father struggled to support. For this reason, when aged six, he was sent back to Berne to be raised by his unmarried aunt Rosina. This was in an artistic family *milieu*, since she was housekeeper for her widowed brother-in-law, Webber's uncle Matthias Funk, a notable cabinet-maker. Rosina spotted his talent and the Berne merchants corporation, to which the Wäber family had belonged since 1544, helped to fund his artistic education. It began in 1767 with his apprenticeship to a leading Swiss topographical artist and pioneer of mountain views, Johann Ludwig Aberli, who trained him in landscape watercolour and probably introduced him to oil-painting. In 1770, with Aberli's blessing, he left for Paris to study painting at the Académie Royale, with an introduction to Jean-Georges Wille, an eminent art historian and teacher of engraving and draughtsmanship. Wille became a lifetime friend and further encouraged him in these skills, with an emphasis on scenes of rustic, peasant life in the Paris area which would prove useful with Cook. In April 1775, Webber returned to London, enrolled as a student at the Royal Academy Schools and began painting portraits and mythological figure subjects. A number of the latter were as house decorations for an unnamed architect, who urged him to submit work to the Academy show of 1776. Within two months of its opening the unknown young Anglo-Swiss, barely returned from spending the last eighteen of his twenty-four years deep in inland Europe, joined *Resolution* for a four-year voyage to some of the remotest places on earth.

Parkinson had been an unassuming botanical specialist who rose creditably to other unforeseen artistic chances on the *Endeavour* voyage. Its sequel found Hodges, a creatively imaginative painter, stretched between the demands of his recording role, his own aesthetic responses and public expectations. Webber, in contrast, presents a combination of virtues which were probably as close to ideal as Cook and officialdom might have wished. While his response to light and colour was less incipiently Romantic than Hodges's and he was barely interested in atmospheric effects save in establishing a general tone, his skills as a topographical and general draughtsman certainly exceeded his predecessor's. That said, he still showed a sensitive response to quieter aspects of the 'topographical sublime', rendering the tropical luxuriance of the Pacific (perhaps rather too temperately) or the mountainous chill of Alaska with equal ease, fine washes and carefully composed detail.

The fact that Webber eventually catalogued all the work he did for the Admiralty (which as far as we know Hodges did not) also suggests organized habits. This was probably a personal trait but Cook also played a part in it, with the eventual publication of engravings to illustrate his voyage in mind. Taking his lead from Lord Morton's guidelines, his journals continued to report on dwellings, structures, arts and crafts, as indicative of levels of Pacific material civilization, and on matters suggesting local ideas of religion. All these areas were more expressly complemented by Webber than Hodges.

On approaching new land, Webber first seems to have done a coastal profile for the navigational record. He would then go ashore

only after a safe landing had been made, often with Cook, and start collecting sketches. These studies of people, activities, artefacts and landscape would then be worked up on board into full compositions. Whereas Hodges's landing scenes, conflicts included, were all done after the voyage, they were one of Webber's earliest concerns and, given both his way of working and perhaps his preference, recorded peaceful circumstances. In them he shows either Cook's arrival and first contact with the inhabitants or the ships established in the bay, often surrounded by native craft. The earliest of these 'greetings', 'An interview between Captain Cook and the natives of Van Diemen's Land' in January 1777, is perhaps the most formal and also the most tentative, as well as being the only one with completely naked Aboriginal figures. It shows Webber's awareness of witnessing history and his inexperience in doing such groups.

His view of Cook greeting the Maori the following month in Ship Cove, Queen Charlotte Sound (see p.125), is more assured and naturalistic – a scene in which his captain, an explorer rather than a conqueror, informally comes ashore in circumstances of established tranquillity, leaving most of his men and his ships well in the background. Webber's catalogue, in fact, describes it as primarily a study of the 'temporary habitations' which the Maori built when they came down to trade with the visitors. Cook (a tall man anyway), his men

'An interview between Captain Cook and the natives of Van Diemen's Land'. Webber's large drawing (670 x 972mm) probably shows Cook's second meeting with natives in Adventure Bay on 29 January 1777, since his journal mentions the presence of the hump-backed man in the right foreground.

and the New Zealanders all have Webber's elongated style but the scene is otherwise free of conventional 'elevation' of subject. A further example, of Cook's brief meeting (no more than three hours) with the Chukchi people of the Siberian coast on 10 August 1778, shows how fast Webber could gather information by then and with what results. The drawing, of a welcoming dance, is full of ethnographic detail while capturing the desolation of the area and the lively informality of the incident. Even the fact that the Europeans are seated is not a convention of implied superiority: they were asked to sit, wrote Cook, for the 'greater security' of their hosts. A study of individual Chukchi men, used in another finished drawing, also suggests Webber's initial accuracy of sketching and the few changes he made when combining elements into final compositions.

Captain Cook's meeting with the Chukchi at St Lawrence Bay, on the Chuktotski Peninsula, Siberia, 10 August 1778. David Samwell, the assistant surgeon, wrote: 'To entertain us they performed what we supposed to be their warlike exercise which consisted of dancing to the beat of the Drum.' Webber's drawing shows the drummers on the right and Cook seated (second from left) with his landing party.

Webber's Chukchi dance is an instance where first contacts overlap with another large category in his work – more formal ceremonies of honour or entertainment for Cook, or others which he attended. On occasion these are arranged as almost panoramic 'bird's-eye view' perspectives to show detail that could only be clearly seen in this way. Although there are more elaborate examples, the engraving of 'The Natche, a Ceremony in honour of the King's Son in Tongataboo' (Tonga) is of interest because we know Webber went

'The *Natche*, a Ceremony in Honour of the King's Son, in Tongataboo'. The engraving of one of Webber's slightly 'bird's-eye view' drawings, designed to include maximum detail, of the ceremonial area in front of a Tongan burial mound. It was published in the official voyage account of 1784.

with Anderson to record the landscape and burial-mound setting before the ceremony, which would have obscured them. Cook and Anderson also gave an account of some of the night dances or *heivas*, of Tonga , which Webber drew in visual parallel almost as contemporary theatre scenes illuminated by 'footlight' flares between the silhouetted spectators in the foreground and the performers behind (see p.137). This similarity was probably fortuitous, though no less dramatic for that, but the subject reflects long-standing European interest in primitive dance as a measure of culture and common humanity, often with religious connotations. Cook himself wrote of Tongan dances that

> The drawings which Mr Webber has made of these performances will give a very good idea of the order in which they range themselves but neither pen nor pencil can describe the numerous actions and motions they observe, which ... are easy and gracefull and many of them extremely so.

Of other more specifically religious ceremonies covered, the most notorious in the voyage aftermath was Cook's presence at a human sacrifice. The body was that of a slave, intemperately killed earlier by one of Tu's chiefly allies. This was being offered to the war god Oro in connection with their smouldering dispute with the island of Moorea, for which Hodges had painted the fleet preparations. Cook refused to be involved in the war but wished to see 'this extraordinary and Barbarous custom' and Webber accompanied him to make sketches at the important *marae* where it took place. His final drawing skilfully reflects Cook's and Anderson's account of the long and complex rite, by combining a number of its separate episodes into a single image. At the same time, the observing figure of Cook – with Tu, Anderson and (probably) Webber himself, all looking towards him in the foreground corner – clearly expresses the abhorrence of the visitors to the scene (see p.54).

As with Parkinson's earlier treatment of Tahitian *marae*, the published version strengthened pressure for Christian intervention in the Pacific although, also like Parkinson's, many of Webber's other drawings of burial shrines emphasized the dignified solemnity which links them to European artistic equivalents. At a period when a taste for 'gothic' melancholy was emerging in literature and art it is perhaps not surprising that Webber drew some of these on his own initiative, without reference to Cook's needs, and often in several versions. 'A Toopapaoo [burial platform] of a Chief, with a Priest Making his Offering to the Morai' is one of 1786, the original dating from 1777, and he made yet another version which he etched himself in 1789. This was as one of a series of sixteen soft-ground voyage etchings (1788–92) which were pioneering, both in the relatively new technique – which he appears to have learnt from Wille – and as a selection by their artist rather than by a commissioning publisher. They were reissued as aquatints from 1808 and continued to sell, and presumably influence attitudes to their subject, well into the 1820s. (By that time there was even Cook wallpaper, based on scenes from all three voyages, manufactured by the Paris firm of Dufour from 1806.)

Apart from his 'greeting' scenes, Webber's general views of Cook's ships at various places on the voyage are notably panoramic, both in conception and in physical format. His original watercolour of Kealakekua Bay (c.1781–83, see the print, p.58), with *Resolution* and

'A Toopapaoo of a Chief, with a Priest Making his Offering to the Morai'. This drawing by Webber, dated 1786, is one of a number of later versions of one he made of a chief's burial platform on Huahine in October 1777. It was a subject he also engraved in his series of soft-ground etchings from the voyage in 1789, later themselves reproduced as aquatints.

'A Party from his Majesties ships *Resolution* & *Discovery* Shooting Sea-Horses, Latitude 71 North'. Webber's exhibited painting of 1784, showing a walrus hunt from the ships in 1778; oil on canvas. Like many painted for the Admiralty from both the second and third voyages this remains in its original frame with its title given on a plaque fixed to it.

Discovery lying diminished beneath the towering coast and surrounded by Hawaiian craft swarming from the shore, has a sense of vertical scale comparable to Hodges's 'Cape of Good Hope'. More literally panoramic is the, 'roll-size' drawing 5 ft (1.5 m) long, of the ships refitting in Nootka Sound, Vancouver Island (see p.48). This holds a remarkable level of documentary detail – of the ships, the crews' activities ashore, the locals and their craft, the coastal geology and the enclosing forest wilderness – but is none the less a coherent, eerie achievement of the 'topographical sublime'. The activity and bustle around the ships is only brief interruption of a gloomy, anechoic, primeval silence, which will re-engulf the remote inlet as soon as they leave.

The expedition's two forays north to Alaska and beyond the Bering Strait took Webber into very different territory from Polynesia and, as the Chukchi drawing suggests, saw him do some of his best work there. Having been trained to draw snow-capped mountains by Aberli, one senses his familiar response to the peaks towering over Snug Corner Cove, Prince William Sound (see p.56). By contrast he does not rise well (as even Hodges did) to the challenge of drawing Arctic ice although, unlike Hodges, it did provide him with a subject for an impressive exhibited oil-painting of 'A Party from His Majesties ships *Resolution* & *Discovery* Shooting Sea-Horses' [walrus] amid the melting floes. While a rather grim topic now, walrus at that time were little known and this dramatic and well-received hunting scene had a documentary side. At Nootka, on the Aleutian island of Unalaska, and later in Russian Kamchatka, he also gave considerable attention to drawing the interiors of local Inuit dwellings – again very much part

'The Inside of a House, in Oonalashka'. The Unalaska Island dwellings were part sunk in the ground with a wood-frame roof covered in straw and 'a great quantity of earth & all kinds of rubbish to a considerable thickness'. All access, and light, for the four families who usually lived in them was via the roof hatch, reached by the tree-trunk ladder. Engraved by William Sharp after Webber in the official voyage account, 1784.

'Inside a Jourt' by Philippe-Jacques de Loutherbourg. The only surviving piece of 'voyage' scenery design for the 1785 Covent Garden pantomime *Omai*. It combines elements of Webber's records of the interiors of dwellings in Nootka Sound and on Unalaska, with the yurts of Kamchatka.

A woman of Oonalaska, July 1778. Cook noted: 'we met with a very beautiful young woman accompanied by her Husband... who Mr Webber was willing to have a sketch of... ; we were all charmed with the good nature & affability with which she complied... She was withal very communicative & intelligent & it was from her I learnt that the name of the Harbour... is Samgoonoodha.' This is Webber's original pencil sketch.

of Cook's brief – for which Polynesia had offered only limited opportunities. A number of these were effectively cross-sectional views, or developed on that basis. They gained a novel popularity in 1785 when Webber assisted his older friend P. J. de Loutherbourg, another eminent foreign artist in London, with his scenery for the spectacular Cook-based pantomime *Omai; or a Trip Around the World* at the Theatre Royal, Covent Garden. One of the surviving de Loutherbourg designs, 'Inside a Jourt' (a Siberian yurt), is a combination of all three dwelling types. Various related *Omai* costume designs by de Loutherbourg, based on Webber's Kamchatka figure studies, also survive and this was not the only theatre piece based on Cook's voyages.

Although Webber painted and drew portraits and individual figure studies throughout the voyage, these vary greatly. Of the twenty oil portraits he brought back only three seem to be known: one of the Tahitian chief, Tu; another which may be Omai; and his original portrait of Cook, painted at Cape Town in 1776 (see p.61). All are small 'head and shoulders' canvases. There is a famous three-quarter-length portrait – certainly his best – of the beautiful Poetua, 'princess' of Raiatea, of which three versions are recorded (see p.128). However, the size of all these suggests they were probably painted in London rather than on board *Discovery* during Poetua's brief detention there in 1777, even though there are no located sketches or oil studies. Most of Webber's other drawings are of types rather than named individuals, although a few are identifiable. Notable among these is the wash drawing of the Maori chief, Kahura – responsible for the massacre of Furneaux's men in 1773 – which Webber did at Kahura's request in Queen Charlotte Sound. As an early example of his voyage work this bears comparison with Parkinson's similar Maori heads, but exceeds them in both spirit and individuality. More generally, Webber's technique was to do initial sketches, often in pencil or chalk, and redraw later in pen and wash, only then adding colour. More of his original figure and portrait sketches, in addition to finished versions, survive from Cook's arrival on the Oregon coast onward, especially in Alaska and Kamchatka. By this time Webber's rapid fluency in pencil or chalk sketches was in many cases even more impressive than his finished versions, not least the studies of Chinese heads and figures which he did at Macao. His most impressive known landscape oil from the voyage is also of Macao (see p.60), with another botanically specific one of Krakatoa Island. Both, however, were painted in London and overall – at least to a post-Romantic view and given the relatively few Webber voyage oils still known – one has to conclude that Hodges was superior in this medium. The two canvases mentioned derive from drawings made on the way home in Feburary 1780. He did the last of his fine but relatively few natural history 'field drawings', of a deer on Prince's Island (Sunda Strait) in the same month, apparently still following the guidance of dead Anderson and Cook to make a representative record of the voyage, if not from long habit and pleasure in the task.

The Maori chief, Kahura, by Webber. Drawn at Kahura's request on board *Resolution*, on 13 February 1777 at Ship Cove, Queen Charlotte Sound.

Webber was not present at Cook's death but did draw and paint it in oils as a formal, invented historical composition in the early 1780s, and the basis of an engraving made in 1782–83. Cast very much in the spirit of West's 'Death of General Wolfe' (see p.28), it shows Cook raising his hand, as if to prevent further firing, just before being struck down by 'the murdering Dagger of a Barbarian ... the Victim of his own Humanity', as stated on the legend for the engraving. The picture is an important and rare example of Webber in full historical mode but cast a long shadow. Factually, if understandably, it distorts the degree to which Cook was responsible for his own death. More seriously, it combined

'A hog deer of Prince's Island', Sunda Strait, February 1780. This watercolour drawing is one of Webber's last and finest wildlife studies from the voyage.

with the darker pagan images that all three of the main voyage artists brought back, confirming the unredeemed nature of Pacific culture, helping to justify European intervention and hastening the end of the primitive paradise they first recorded.

When Webber returned to London he, like Hodges, was immediately re-engaged by the Admiralty at £250 a year to finish off his drawings and paintings for them, and to supervise engraving of his work in the official voyage proceedings of 1784. These were the most magnificently produced of all, as befitted the memory of both dead commanders, Cook and Clerke, and the achievements recorded. Webber's last payment from the Admiralty was in July 1785, the year he exhibited his portrait of Poetua (one of the Admiralty pictures) at the Royal Academy. The 'Seahorses' and two China sea views had preceded it in 1784, and he showed another twenty-six voyage subjects there up to 1792, most now untraced. Apart from other voyage-related work already mentioned, the rest of Webber's life was spent drawing and painting landscapes in Britain, France, the Alps and Northern Italy – following a long tour which he made in 1787, including a visit to see his Swiss relations. He also continued painting portraits and, being as industrious and sociable as he was on *Resolution*, he prospered and continued to enjoy many artistic friendships in London and elsewhere, although he never married. He was elected an Associate of the Royal Academy in 1785 and full Academician in 1791, the same year as he gave his own collection of Pacific artefacts, 101 items, to the library of Berne (where they are now in the Historical Museum). Unfortunately, Academy membership was not an honour he long enjoyed. In 1792 he became ill with kidney disease and on 29 April 1793 he died in his Oxford Street lodgings, leaving generous bequests to close friends, his Swiss relations and his loyal servants. He was still only forty-one.

John Webber by Johan Daniel Mottet, 1812, based on an earlier miniature.

6: A 'LOVE OF HUMAN KIND'
Captain Cook and Pacific Peoples

Had these possess'd, O Cook! thy gentle mind,
Thy love of arts, thy love of human kind;
Had these pursued thy mild and liberal plan
Discoverers had not been a curse to man!

Hannah More, 'The Black Slave Trade' (1788)

Captain Cook in Ship Cove, Queen Charlotte Sound: pen and wash, by Webber. Maori on the move lived in temporary hut encampments and set one up at Ship Cove while Cook was there in February 1777. He is shown greeting the group's chief and later wrote in his journal: 'Mr Webber has made a drawing of one these Villages that will convey a better idea of them than any written description.'

Early in 1777 *Resolution* and *Discovery* entered Queen Charlotte Sound at the north end of New Zealand's South Island and anchored at Cook's old mooring in Ship Cove. Queen Charlotte Sound was the first major refreshment stop on the third voyage and it had been chosen because Cook knew from previous visits that it offered good water, seemingly endless amounts of fish and large quantities of fresh greens – the last of which were now supplemented by the vegetables that the European explorers had planted there since 1770.

Resolution and *Discovery* had not long been at anchor when several canoes put out from shore and came alongside the ships. This was a familiar enough sight in the sound, for the Maori had come to value European cloth and metal goods and the arrival of British ships usually heralded brisk trading. But on this occasion Cook noted that few Maori would venture on board, 'which appeared the more extraordinary as I was well known to them all'. There was one man, indeed, that Cook 'had treated with remarkable kindness' during the whole of *Resolution*'s previous stay in 1774, but 'neither professions of friendship nor presents would induce him to come into the ship'.

There was another possible reason apart from the availability of supplies for choosing the sound as an anchorage on this particular occasion, and it was obvious from their behaviour that the Maori were as aware of this as Cook himself. Cook suspected, rightly, that they feared that the real reason for his visit was to take revenge for the killing and eating of a boat's crew from *Adventure* towards the end of the second voyage.

Resolution and *Adventure* had become separated on the voyage home in 1774 and Furneaux's ship arrived at the rendezvous in Queen Charlotte Sound to find Cook already gone. Furneaux stayed there for a little over two weeks, resting his men and stocking up on fresh provisions. The day before *Adventure* was due to sail he sent the cutter with a crew of ten to Grass Cove to collect a final load of greens, but by nightfall the boat had not returned. The next morning he sent another boat commanded by Lieutenant James Burney to find out what had happened. All morning Burney rowed along the shore-line, looking for signs of the missing boat, asking 'the Indians' if they knew of its whereabouts and firing signal guns at regular intervals. They found nothing. Then, at the entrance to Grass Cove, they saw a large canoe drawn up on the beach; as the boat approached a group of Maori sitting around the canoe leapt to their feet and ran into the woods. A suspicious Burney ordered the canoe to be searched and in it they found one of the cutter's rowlocks and some shoes; a few minutes later a seaman found a piece of flesh on the beach. At first Burney and his men took it to be salt meat, thinking that it was probably part of the cutter's supplies; on closer examination, however, it proved to be fresh. Still reluctant to accept the inevitable conclusion, Burney suggested that it could be dog meat, but he and his crew 'were soon convinced by most horrid & undeniable proofs' that the flesh was part of one of their shipmates. They found no complete bodies but 'such a shocking scene of Carnage & Barbarity as can never be mentioned or thought of, but with horror', and they finally took back to *Adventure* some twenty baskets containing pieces of roasted flesh, together with two hands – one of which they identified from a scar as belonging to a master's mate, John Rowe, and the other, from the tattooed letters

Captain James Cook by Hodges, painted in about 1775.

'TH' on the back, to a seaman called Thomas Hill – and the head of Furneaux's black servant, James Swilley.

Once the initial shock had passed, Burney wrote in his report that he was 'not inclined to think this was any premeditated plan of these Savages' but that the killings had probably been caused by 'some quarrel' or by over-confidence on the part of the boat's crew and, perhaps, opportunism on the part of the Maori. Furneaux did not stay to find out which, and in the morning *Adventure* left Queen Charlotte Sound to begin its long voyage back to Britain. Cook returned a year later, *en route* for England after the *Resolution*'s second great sweep through the westernmost islands of the Pacific, and picked up a worrying story of a ship being wrecked on the other side of the sound and its crew being killed and eaten, but the Maori assured him that *Adventure* had left safely. Concerned but not unduly worried, Cook departed for home and did not hear the truth of the incident until he reached Cape Town in 1775. But when Cook returned on his third voyage in 1777, with *Resolution* and its new consort, *Discovery*, the Maori knew that he would 'no longer [be] a stranger to that unhappy affair' and they not unsurprisingly expected reprisals.

Although there had still been relatively few meetings between Europeans and Maori by 1777, Furneaux's were not the first European sailors killed in New Zealand. The site of Abel Tasman's landing in 1642 bore the name Murderers Bay in memory of that brief and bloody encounter. In 1772 the French explorer Marion du Fresne and a number of his men had been killed by New Zealanders at the Bay of Islands. It was said that when the French philosopher Jean-Jacques Rousseau heard the news of du Fresne's death, he confessed to being shocked that the 'children of nature' could behave with such violence. Rousseau had introduced the figure of the Noble Savage to European thinking in 1755 in the essay *A Discourse on Inequality*, which argued that the natural state of primitive 'man' was one of simple happiness and freedom. The Noble Savage was always a more important figure in France than in Britain and more influential in art than in literature, but the real-life encounters between European explorers and Pacific islanders had already demonstrated that the charming ideal of primitive innocence was, like Dr Johnson's description of a second marriage, a triumph of hope over experience.

Tahiti's reputation for being a tropical paradise peopled with gentle, beautiful and welcoming natives, however, survived the realities of contact: repackaged for the Polynesian tourist trade, it still thrives today. Sex played a large part in this romantic picture, which was established immediately by the early descriptions of the beauty of the islanders, their very different sexual customs and their enthusiastic welcomes, such as Louis-Antoine de Bougainville's frankly admiring picture of his ship being covered by naked 'nymphs' the moment it dropped anchor. One particular young woman who draped herself over the main hatch seemed, to the Classically educated Frenchman, 'as

'Man of New Zealand'; an engraving from a drawing by William Hodges. Maori earned a reputation for being a fierce and warlike people when the Dutch navigator, Abel Tasman, landed on South Island in 1642 and several of his men were killed. After a series of violent encounters in Poverty Bay in 1769, Cook's dealings with Maori improved.

Samuel Wallis's *Dolphin* was the first European ship to land in Tahiti, in 1767. The sailors and the islanders were suspicious of each other and the Tahitians eventually launched an attack on the ship, which was bloodily repulsed by the *Dolphin*'s gunfire.

Venus ... herself to the Phrygian shepherd, having ... the celestial form of that goddess'. Classical allusions abounded in European descriptions of Polynesia, let alone in Hodges's paintings, and reflected the idea that Europe had discovered a new Golden Age in the Pacific. While few people really believed this, the idea of the Tahitians as 'soft primitives' persisted in Europe's popular imagination, despite an attack on Wallis's *Dolphin*, the discovery that the Tahitians practised both infanticide and human sacrifice and the lurid missionary accounts of Tahitian society that began appearing in the early nineteenth century.

Poetua, aged about nineteen, by John Webber. This was painted in England from sketches made in the great cabin of *Discovery* in 1777 while Poetua, daughter of the Raiatean chief, Orio, was being held hostage pending the return of two British deserters. It was shown at the Royal Academy in 1785 and its dreamy romanticism has come to embody the sexual fascination that the Tahitian islands held for Europe.

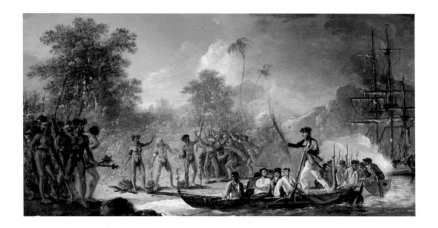

'The Landing at Tanna', by William Hodges; oil on panel, painted c.1775–76 and engraved for the third voyage account.

Before Cook met the Maori for the first time, in 1769, he and his crew had been in Tahiti for three months, during which the relationship between the islanders and Europeans had been generally peaceful. Cook's instructions from the Admiralty had ordered him 'to endeavour by all proper means to cultivate a friendship with the Natives' of Tahiti – good sense during an extended stay when the success of the ship's mission to observe the transit of Venus would be dependent on the goodwill of the islanders. But the instructions also warned him that the Tahitian attack on Captain Wallis's *Dolphin*, which had been bloodily repulsed by the British ship's cannons, showed that the inhabitants were 'rather treacherous than otherwise', so Cook was to be 'Cautious not to let [him]self be surprised by them …'. A Tahitian who attempted to steal a musket from one of Cook's men was shot by a nervous sentry a couple of days after *Endeavour* arrived and there had been several other instances of theft during the ship's stay – most notably when the astronomical quadrant was stolen from a guarded tent by an enterprising Tahitian.

Cook's response to theft was to take canoes or people, or both, hostage. While this method generally worked well for him during his three voyages and stolen goods were returned without bloodshed, the Tahitian response in this instance to both the killing and hostage-taking was to close down the trade of the fresh meat and vegetables that the crew of *Endeavour* needed. Cook worked hard to maintain cordial relations with the islanders: after the man had been shot Cook managed to persuade a group of obviously apprehensive islanders to sit down and hear Cook's attempts to 'convince them that the man was kill'd for taking away the Musquet and that we still would be friends with them'; when marking out and building the fort at Point Venus, Cook wrote that 'we endeavour'd to explain as well as we could that we wanted the ground to sleep upon such a number of nights and then we should go a way'. Whether the Tahitians understood or whether the sailors in turn understood the islanders' feelings about the fort or the dead man was uncertain, as Cook himself acknowledged. But it is clear that the Tahitian rulers worked equally hard to keep the peace – they had discovered after the attack on Wallis's *Dolphin* that they could not control the visitors by force – and so trade, which actually suited both parties, became a way of maintaining some form of stability in the relationship.

Cook's encounters with Maori, by contrast, erupted into violence immediately. He landed at Tuuranga-nui on the east coast of New Zealand's North Island on 8 October 1769, 'naming' the area Poverty Bay – a name it little deserved as both the bay and the area surrounding it were actually rich in supplies and home to four Maori tribes.

'The Landing at Erramanga' by William Hodges; oil on panel. Painted about 1776 for engraving in the voyage account and exhibited in 1778. Cook's encounters with the people of the New Hebrides in the west Pacific were often tense affairs. The Erramangans attacked and at least one islander was killed. Some fifty years later, the exploring missionary John Williams was also killed on the island. The native figure group here is based on a preparatory drawing by Cipriani.

But the bay appeared poor to Cook in contrast to the tropical luxuriance of Tahiti, and he certainly got little there. Cook left a small party of men in charge of the ship's boats while he, Banks and Solander went to explore a settlement they had spotted. While they were looking around the village they heard gunfire and hurried back to discover that a small group of Maori had approached the boats and that one had been shot and killed. The Maori had undoubtedly intimidated the crew and, while their threatening behaviour may have been ritual rather than actual, there was no way that the sailors would have known this.

The next morning Cook landed once again, this time to be faced immediately with 'a good number of the natives' who answered the British party's shouts in Tahitian 'by flourishing their weapons over their heads and dancing, as we supposed the war dance'. The Maori 'distended their Mouths, Lolling out their Tongues and Turned up the Whites of their Eyes, the whole Accompanied with a strong Hoarse Song, calculated ... to Chear Each Other and Intimidate their Enemies'. This was the *haka*, the fierce ritual challenge designed to intimidate strangers, and we are probably most familiar with it today through watching the pre-match dance of the New Zealand international rugby team, the All Blacks. Watching the challenge with *Endeavour*'s party was Tupaia, the Tahitian priest that Joseph Banks was taking back to England. Tupaia found that he was able to understand and make himself understood to the Maori as they also spoke a Polynesian language. Despite Tupaia's help in interpreting, this encounter also ended in bloodshed when another Maori was shot and killed and a further three wounded while trying to take a sword from one of the British party.

After this dreadful start, Cook thought that he would try a different tack and later that afternoon he rowed to the head of Poverty Bay, trying to find a small party of Maori that he could 'surprise', take on board his ship and 'by good treatment and presents endeavour to gain their friendship.' This plan was clearly open to misinterpretation by the Maori and such, tragically, proved to be the case when Cook approached two canoes. Although both Cook and Tupaia tried to reassure the Maori that they would be safe, they had the sudden deaths of their countrymen in their minds and understandably tried to beat a hasty retreat. Cook fired over their heads to try to make them surrender but the demonstration of fire-power had the opposite effect, 'for they immidiatly took to their arms ... and began to attack us'. A further three Maori were killed in the ensuing fight and another wounded. 'Thus ended', wrote Joseph Banks, 'the most disagreeable day My life has yet seen black be the mark for it & heaven send that such may never return to embitter future reflection.'

Cook was shocked at the killings and, in a passage of critical self-examination in his journal, tried to work out the reasons:

> I am aware that most humane men who have not experienced things of this nature will cencure my conduct in fireing upon the people in this boat nor do I my self think that the reason I had for seizing upon her will att all justify me, and had I thought that they would have made the least resistance I would not have come near them, but as they did I was not to stand still and suffer either my self or those that were with me to be knocked on the head.

There was a fundamental tension between exploration and humanitarianism that Cook sees very clearly here. Before *Endeavour* had left England, Cook had been given a set of 'Hints' by the Earl of Morton, President of the Royal Society, on how to deal with the inhabitants of the various lands the ship would visit. It was a liberal document in which the Earl stated unambiguously that the 'Natives' were the 'natural, and in the strictest sense of the word, the legal possessors' of their countries, that no 'European Nation [had] a right to occupy any part of their country' and that killing them in defence of their lands would be 'a crime of the highest nature'. The European voyages of exploration and exploitation to the Americas from the end of the fifteenth century had led to the violent colonization of the land and the murder and enslavement of the peoples but, as Cook's earliest biographer put it, the Pacific voyages were very different in intent, having 'the enlarged and benevolent design of promoting the happiness of the human species'.

These liberal ideals sat uneasily with the Admiralty's secret instructions to Cook which ordered him to explore and claim land for Britain, 'with the Consent of the Natives' where he thought it viable and valuable, and he did conduct a number of such ceremonies on the first voyage in both New Zealand and Australia. After Tahiti, a different set of rules was operating in which maintaining good relations with 'the Natives' was less important. What Cook was saying in his journal was that while he had tried to follow the principles of humanitarian exploration, landings were always going to be volatile and potentially threatening occasions. In the final analysis, his responsibility to behave humanely to the native inhabitants would always have to take second place to his responsibility to his crew and his ship, and it would depend on the sort of reception he got. This is a good point and one that shows the fears and tensions that existed on both sides of the beach on all of Cook's landings, but even Cook is not entirely convinced that the reasons 'for seizing upon' the Maori canoe could 'att all justify' his behaviour. Perhaps he could sense that violence was an inevitable part of exploration, be it never so humanitarian: the 'savage within' himself and his crew that had been artificially repressed during the stay on Tahiti.

To most historians of Pacific exploration, the deaths of both the Maori and other islanders who were killed during the three voyages were occasional lapses in difficult circumstances which were deeply regretted by Cook – who has largely remained an emblem of the humanitarian ideals of his time. To others, who are mainly writing from a Pacific point of view, Cook's killings stand for the violence inherent in European exploration and imperial expansion. The truth is probably somewhere between the two. Cook himself had few illusions about the moral superiority of European civilization and could see more clearly than most what would follow him to the Pacific: the whalers, sealers, traders, missionaries and colonists who would almost destroy Polynesian culture. The memory of the killings in Poverty Bay stayed with Cook, profoundly influencing his dealings with other native peoples and especially his handling of the situation in Queen Charlotte Sound when he arrived to find out what had happened to the boat's crew from *Adventure*.

Cook's response was restrained when he returned to New Zealand with *Resolution* and *Discovery* in 1777. He had come to respect the Maori as he got to know them better. His first response when he had heard of the incident was not outrage but a sympathetic and astute summary of the Maori that saw cannibalism as only one aspect of their character, if an unfortunate one: 'I have allways found them of a Brave, Noble, Open and benevolent disposition, but they are a people that will never put up with an insult if they have an oppertunity to resent it.' Cook took the sensible precaution of sending armed guards with every shore party and any boat that had to sail any distance from *Resolution* or *Discovery*. Although Cook felt that the deterrent was probably unnecessary, it had the effect of reassuring his men, who were understandably nervous when Maori were around. Cook then set about rebuilding a relationship with the Maori and trying to establish calmly the truth of Grass Cove. He soon discovered that the incident had happened while the cutter's crew had been eating their lunch on the beach. A group of Maori were present but as the boat's crew had no reason to suspect violence they took only a couple of muskets with them and left the cutter in the charge of James Swilley. The precise sequence of events after that point was harder to establish but it appeared that, as Burney had originally thought, there had been an argument: one version given to Cook by the Maori was that one man had attempted to steal something from the cutter and had been shot by Swilley; another version said that there had been an argument over food. Whatever the truth, the fight that followed had been as brief and brutal as it had been unpremeditated.

Local Maori identified the leader of the attack as a chief called Kahura (see p.123), telling Cook to kill him in revenge; 'they were', said Cook, 'not a little surprised that I did not'. There is no doubt that many of Cook's crew were similarly not a little surprised. Cook was also encouraged to kill the man by Omai, the Society Islander who had been taken to London on *Adventure* and who was now being returned to Tahiti. Omai told Cook that far from damaging relations with the Maori, taking Kahura's life in exchange for that of the boat's crew would be entirely compatible with the Maori custom of *utu*, or payment for the offence. Omai was almost certainly right. While in modern Europe a person could gain status through showing restraint and magnanimity, Maori saw this as weakness and several of Cook's officers thought that they noticed a growing lack of respect from the Maori in Queen Charlotte Sound once it became clear that Cook was going to stick by his humanitarian principles and not punish Kahura.

Cook took a certain amount of pleasure in not behaving as his crew, his officers, the Maoris and perhaps the public who would eventually read the account of the voyage would expect. The restraint he showed at Queen Charlotte Sound made a deservedly large contribution to his reputation for fair treatment of Pacific islanders – although a part of him was also self-consciously acting out the role of the humanitarian explorer, for Nelson was not the first sailor to see the importance of a public image. What made Cook's behaviour the more remarkable on this occasion was that the third voyage began to see a marked deterioration in his relations with Polynesians, as will be discussed later.

Cook had already had ample first-hand evidence that Maori were cannibals well before he discovered the truth about *Adventure*'s men. During the second voyage, also at Ship Cove, Lieutenant Clerke had taken the head of a young Maori killed in an inter-tribal fight back to *Resolution*, cut off a couple of slices of flesh, toasted them on the galley fire and offered them to other Maori, who obligingly ate them. When Cook himself returned to the ship he ordered the grotesque experiment to be repeated in front of himself and the two scientists, Johann Reinhold and Georg Forster, watching in astonishment as 'one of these Canibals eat [another piece of flesh] with a seeming good relish before the whole ships Company which had such an effect on some of them as to cause them to vomit'. Cook had long suspected that Maori were cannibals, but now, he wrote, the fact can 'no longer be doubted'.

The word 'cannibal' arrived in European languages as a direct result of maritime exploration, although 'anthropophagy', from the Greek for 'human beings' and 'to eat', has been an object of revulsion, horror and fascination – and humour – in Europe for thousands of years. The Ancient Greeks gave the name 'anthropophagi' to a people living beyond their borders who, they thought, ate human beings. 'Cannibal' has a much more recent origin. During his first voyage across the Atlantic in 1492, Columbus met a group of islanders who told him that on a particular island 'were people who had one eye in the forehead, and others whom they called "canibals"' who 'ate people'. The islanders were describing the Caribs, a people who also gave their name to the Caribbean, but the corrupted word 'cannibal' actually came to mean an eater of human flesh rather than the people themselves. It quickly passed into Spanish and then into English during the sixteenth century.

European explorers had been meeting cannibals, real or imagined, from that point onwards and philosophers like Montaigne and Hobbes drew on travellers' descriptions of cannibalism to illustrate their own very different theories about human behaviour. Montaigne, writing in the 1580s, did not condemn cannibalism among the American Indians, saying that it was part of an original, unformed, even innocent state of nature, which anyway was no worse than the racking, burning and shooting which went on in Europe. Hobbes was writing nearly a hundred years later and his view of an original state of nature was more hard-line: it was 'nasty, brutish and short' and cannibalism either caused or was an integral part of all three.

Montaigne and Hobbes were 'armchair philosophers' and because no reputable scientist had ever actually witnessed the eating of human flesh there was still a debate in intellectual circles about whether or

Execution and cannibalism, from Theodor de Bry, *Americae* (1599).

not cannibalism, other than that caused by starvation, really existed, and what part it might play in a primitive society. Cook and Banks had looked unsuccessfully for hard evidence of cannibalism, which they seemed to expect to find: when Banks's unfortunate artist, Alexander Buchan, died as they reached Tahiti, he was buried at sea just in case the Tahitians might be cannibalistic. What excited the naturalist Johann Reinhold Forster about the prospect of going on Cook's second voyage was that scientists were no longer dependent on 'the vague reports of unphilosophical travellers', but would have the unique opportunity to 'collect facts' about man in an original state of nature at first hand and communicate them 'with few inferences' to the 'impartial and learned world'. Forster was a man of his scientific time and he believed that it was possible to understand a society and explain how it worked through the exhaustive collection of facts. During the voyage he was rigorous in his recording of data, always taking the opportunity of adding to his comparative dictionary of Pacific languages on his often brief visits to the islands, for instance. Dickens's Thomas Gradgrind, for whom 'facts [were] all that is wanted in life', would have admired J. R. Forster.

The loss of the *Luxborough Galley*; from an oil painting by John Cleveley the Elder. The ship was destroyed by fire in the Atlantic in 1727, the incident becoming infamous when it was revealed that the survivors had eaten their fellow crewmen. The possibility of starvation cannibalism was something that all sailors might have had to face: it was seen as a necessity very different to the cannibalism for pleasure that Europeans expected native peoples to practise.

Forster recorded the demonstration of Maori cannibalism in the true spirit of Enlightenment enquiry and used the incident to develop his theory of human societies. Maori cannibalism was clearly not caused by hunger, Forster thought: while New Zealand did not have the tropical abundance of the Society Islands, there was no shortage of food. Neither was eating people evidence of an original state of savagery but, Forster speculated, of a stage towards civilization. Maori society may have been violent but it also showed considerable evidence of the arts, which he saw as evidence of progression towards a more advanced state of social living. Forster's theory was that cannibalism evolved as Maori society developed: it was a culture that bred suspicion of outsiders, that demonstrated its aggression and bravery in the *haka* and was never prepared to forget an insult. This was not an original state of nature but education, the result of succeeding generations of Maori being tutored in ways of behaviour. To Forster, eating the bodies of enemies captured in battle was simply an extension of the aggression within Maori society, something that had over the years become a habit. But it was still a step towards civilization and a habit that would eventually disappear when primitive people came to see that 'a living man is more useful than one that is dead or roasted', and that it was altogether more sensible to capture or enslave enemies. Through conquest, small, fragmented tribal societies would give way to larger, more settled ones, preparing the way for a 'more humane and benevolent scene'.

Where the first voyage had been one primarily of the botanical and navigational sciences, the character of the second was strongly anthropological as *Resolution* and *Adventure* made huge sweeps across the Pacific, landing at Easter Island, the Marquesas, the Cook Islands, the Tongan group, the New Hebrides, New Caledonia and Norfolk Island – in addition to the by now routine stops at the Society Islands and New Zealand. The voyage of *Resolution* and *Adventure* confirmed that a people with a single point of origin had settled a huge area of ocean, stretching from Easter Island in the east, to Tonga in the west and New Zealand in the south-west. The people would eventually be called Polynesians and their island groups Polynesia – from the Greek for 'many islands' – although the full extent of the 'Polynesian Triangle' did not become clear until the third voyage when Cook chanced on Hawaii, its northern point. Cook and Forster asked the questions that have preoccupied historians and scientists ever since – where did the Polynesians come from, when did they arrive and how did they get there? Scientist and sailor also came into contact with what they took to be a different race of people on islands to the west of Polynesia. Where the Polynesians, to Forster, were 'fair, well limbed, athletic, of a fine size, and a kind benevolent temper', the islands to the west were inhabited by people who were 'blacker, the hair just beginning to become woolly and crisp, the body more slender and low, and their temper, if possible more brisk'. In the nineteenth century these islands came to be called 'Melanesia', the 'black islands'.

Forster was fascinated by the differences between the people he saw in the island groups, collecting facts about their colour, physical appearance, language, density of population, degree of agricultural cultivation and variety of climate in order to develop the theories that he published in his *Observations Made During a Voyage Round the World* (1778). Tahiti, 'the queen of tropical isles' as he called it, represented the highest stage of civilization in the Pacific to him, followed by the Marquesas and the Friendly Islands. Forster observed that the largest part of the Friendly Islands – the Tongan group – was 'highly cultivated' with all private property neatly fenced in; the character of their inhabitants, 'whose complexion … partakes of a lively brown, inclining so far towards the red or copper colour, as not to deserve the appellation swarthy' were, he wrote, 'really aimiable; their friendly behaviour to us, who were utter strangers to them, would have done honour to the most civilized nation'. Cook too was impressed with the Tongans on both his second and third voyages, naming the group the Friendly Islands in recognition of their 'generous and noble' manner.

The voyagers' attempts to make sense of what they saw around them on Pacific islands were inevitably fraught with misunderstanding. In Tonga, on the third voyage, Cook was engrossed by a lavish entertainment put on by the islanders and recorded in John Webber's drawings of the night dances, blissfully unaware that the Friendly Islanders were conspiring to kill him and his crew. The plan to attack the British while they were absorbed in the dancing only fell through at the very last minute because of a disagreement between the various Tongan parties.

'A night dance by women at Hapaee.' 'The drawings that Mr Webber has made of these performances,' wrote Cook, who is sitting in the centre, 'will give a very good idea of the order in which they range themselves… '. It was during one of these events that Tongan chiefs planned to assassinate the party and seize the ships. Engraving from the official third voyage account, 1784.

This story did not emerge until 1815 with the publication of William Mariner's *An Account of the Natives of the Tonga Islands*. Mariner's ship had been captured by the Tongans in 1806, and he lived on the island for some years as the captive and confidant of Finau, the chief who had planned the attack on Cook. Mariner was not an educated man and his book was actually written by a clergyman named William Martin; it was the first book to build on the accounts of the Pacific islanders by Cook and his scientists and to attempt to describe a different culture from within. The problem with simply collecting facts about the islands, as Cook and Forster did so superbly, was neatly summed up by the hero of Herman Melville's *Typee* (1851), a semi-autobiographical novel about a young beachcomber in a village in the Marquesas: 'I saw everything, but I comprehended nothing'. Martin's study of the Tongans, by contrast, was based on Mariner's intimate knowledge of the language and a real understanding of the culture and society built up over years. It would be used to great effect by nineteenth- and twentieth-century missionary writers like William Ellis (no relation to Cook's Ellis), who were as fascinated by the Polynesian cultures as they were determined to change them, and the method would become one of the founding principles of modern ethnographical field work.

What nearly happened to Cook and his men in Tonga was typical of the deteriorating relations with Pacific islanders on the third voyage. After ten years of nearly continuous exploration Cook was exhausted. He was almost certainly a sick man as well. During the voyage he seemed to lose his judgement and sense of perspective: he became exasperated by the islanders and intolerant of theft, as well as increasingly short-tempered and dictatorial with his crew. There were several occasions when he reacted hastily and violently to instances of minor theft, which he would have normally dealt with firmly but humanely. When a goat was stolen at Moorea in the Society Islands, a furious Cook marched a party of armed Marines and sailors all over the island for two days, burning houses and war canoes in retribution. In stark contrast to their attitude to Cook's humanitarianism in the aftermath of the cannibalism at Ship Cove only a few months earlier, many of his officers were shocked by the undue savagery of Cook's revenge.

'The Death of Captain Cook.' Francesco Bartolozzi's engraving after John Webber's oil painting, now in Australia. This is generally regarded as the closest depiction of Cook's death at Kealakekua Bay, Hawaii, despite its artistic conventionalization. One scholar has even recently claimed that he can identify the man standing behind Cook and about to strike him with a dagger.

Cook's death on the beach of Kealakekua Bay in 1779 was at least partly the result of an over-reaction to the Hawaiians' theft of *Discovery*'s cutter and an inability to judge the situation as coolly as he would have done on his first two voyages. John Webber's painting has always been taken to be the most faithful account of the scene. In it, Cook stands with his gun by his side, gesturing urgently to the boats to stop firing, while behind him a Hawaiian is poised to strike him down. Even at the moment of his death, Cook is the humanitarian explorer trying to protect those who would destroy him. Four Marines and seventeen Hawaiians were killed on that beach as well as Cook. It is known that Cook did actually make a gesture, but it was unclear in all the noise and confusion whether he was trying to stop the shooting or was ordering the boats closer in to pick up the shore party. Like the mixture of scientific, imperial and humanitarian aims in the voyages, the conflicting emotions, principles and responsibilities jostling within Cook, and even the death of Cook itself, his last gesture remains ambiguous.

Sources and further reading

K. V. Austin, *The Voyage of the Investigator* (London, 1964)

J. R. Beaglehole, *The Exploration of the Pacific* (Stanford, 1934)

J. R. Beaglehole, *The Life of Captain James Cook* (London, 1974)

David Cordingly (ed.), *Capt. James Cook, Navigator: The achievements of Captain James Cook as a seaman, navigator and surveyor* (London, 1988)

James Cook, *The Journals of Captain James Cook on his Voyages of Discovery*, ed. J. R. Beaglehole (8 vols, London, 1988)

Miriam Estensen, *Discovery: The Quest for the Great South Land* (London, 1998)

Ben Finney, *Voyage of Rediscovery: A Cultural Odyssey through Polynesia* (Berkeley, Los Angeles and London, 1994)

J. R. Forster, *The* Resolution *Journal of Johann Rheinhold Forster*, ed. Michael E. Hoare (London, 1982)

Anton Gill, *The Devil's Mariner: A Life of William Dampier, Pirate and Explorer, 1651–1715* (Honolulu, 1972)

William Hauptman, *Captain Cook's Painter: John Webber 1751–1793, Pacific Voyager and Landscape Artist* [exh. cat. in German and English] (Berne, 1996)

Derek Howse (ed.), *Background to Discovery: Pacific Exploration from Dampier to Cook* (Oxford, 1990)

Rüdiger Joppien and Bernard Smith, *The Art of Captain Cook's Voyages* (3 vols [in 4], London and New Haven, 1985–88)

Margarette Lincoln (ed.), *Science and Exploration in the Pacific: European voyages to the Southern Oceans in the 18th Century* (Woodbridge, 1998)

David Mackay, *In the wake of Cook: exploration, science and empire, 1780–1801* (Beckenham, 1985)

David Phillip Miller and Peter Hans Reill (eds), *Visions of Empire: voyages, botany, and representations of nature* (Cambridge, 1996)

Neil Rennie, *Far-Fetched Facts: The Literature of Travel and the Idea of the South Seas* (Oxford, 1995)

Anne Salmond, *Two Worlds: first meetings between Maori and Europeans, 1642–1772* (London, 1991)

Bernard Smith, *European Vision and the South Pacific* (London, 1988)

Bernard Smith, *Imagining the Pacific: In the Wake of the Cook Voyages* (London, 1992)

O. H. K. Spate, *The Pacific since Magellan*, Vol. I, *The Spanish Lake* (Canberra, 1979); Vol. II, *Monopolists and Freebooters* (London and Canberra, 1983); Vol III, *Paradise Found and Lost* (Oxford, 1988)

Isabel Coombs Stuebe, *The Life and Works of William Hodges* (New York and London, 1979)

Glyn Williams, *The Great South Sea: English Voyages and Encounters 1570–1750* (London and New Haven, 1997)

Derek Wilson, *The World Encompassed: Drake's Great Voyage, 1577–1580* (London, 1977, 1998)

THE VOYAGE OF *ENDEAVOUR*

DATE	PLACE	NOTES
25 August 1768	*Endeavour* leaves Plymouth	Over a hundred people on board, including Joseph Banks's scientific party.
12 to 18 September	Funchal, Madeira	Cooks buys 3000 gallons (nearly 14,000 litres) of wine and reprovisions with fresh food over a period of six days. Master's mate, Alexander Weir, drowns in harbour.
13 November to 7 December	Portuguese colony of Rio de Janeiro	Portuguese suspect Cook of being a spy and insist that officers and crew remain on board while reprovisioning is carried out. Seaman Peter Flower is drowned in the harbour. *Endeavour* leaves on 7 December for Cape Horn.
11 to 30 January 1769	Tierra del Fuego	Banks's two servants, Thomas Richmond and George Dorlton, freeze to death during a botanzing expedition. *Endeavour* rounds Cape Horn and enters the Pacific Ocean.
13 April to 13 July	Tahiti	*Endeavour* anchors in Matavai Bay, 13 April. Alexander Buchan, artist, dies of an epileptic fit, 16 April. Transit of Venus observed, 3 June. Cook makes tour of island 26 June to 1 July.
13 July to 9 August	Society Islands	*Endeavour* cruises through Tahiti's neighbouring islands. Tahitian priest, Tupaia, and his servant, Taiata, are taken on board as Banks wants to take them back to Britain. Tupaia helps Cook to draw a map of the Pacific which shows 74 islands known to the Polynesians.
9 August to 5 October	At sea	Sailing south to search for the southern continent. Abandons search and heads for New Zealand (Aotearoa), first sighted by Abel Tasman in 1642.
October 1769 to March 1770	New Zealand	East coast of North Island sighted on 6 October by ship's boy, Nicholas Young. Cook calls landfall Young Nick's Head.
8 to 10 October 1769	Poverty Bay, NZ	Series of violent encounters with local Maori leave at least six of them dead. Cook leaves Poverty Bay and sails south along New Zealand's coastline.
16 October	Cape Turnagain, NZ	Cook turns north and retraces his course back up North Island. Begins circumnavigation of New Zealand's North and South Island.
4 November	Mercury Bay, NZ	Transit of Mercury observed on east coast of North Island.
16 January to 7 February 1770	Queen Charlotte Sound, NZ	*Endeavour* careened and watered. Leaves to continue circumnavigation of South Island.
31 March	New Zealand	*Endeavour* leaves New Zealand at Cape Farewell and heads west towards the east coast of Australia (New Holland) *en route* for Britain.
19 April	Australian coast sighted	Turns to follow the coast north.
29 April to 6 May	Botany Bay, Australia	Banks and scientific party botanize. Crewman Forby Sutherland dies on 1 May.
11 June to 4 August	Great Barrier Reef, Australia	*Endeavour* strikes reef on 10 June and is finally beached in Endeavour River on 18 June. Repairs to hull carried out. First kangaroo seen and shot by Lieutenant Gore.
10 October to 26 December	Batavia, Java	*Endeavour* arrives for badly needed repairs. Many of crew catch fever: Tupaia, Surgeon Monkhouse and five others die at Batavia; a further twenty-three men die later of illness caught here, including the astronomer Samuel Green, the artist Sydney Parkinson and the scientific assistant, Herman Spöring.
13 March to 15 April 1771	Dutch colony of Cape Town, South Africa	Sick men landed and ship reprovisioned. Cook sails for Britain via St Helena and Ascension Island.
13 July	The Downs, Britain	*Endeavour* drops anchor off east Kent and Cook leaves the ship to travel to London with his papers.

THE VOYAGE OF *RESOLUTION* AND *ADVENTURE*

DATE	PLACE	NOTES
13 July 1772	Plymouth	*Resolution* (Cook) and *Adventure* (Furneaux) set sail.
29 July to 2 August	Funchal, Madeira	Ships reprovisioned.
31 October to 22 November	Cape Town, South Africa	Hodges paints *Adventure* at anchor in Table Bay. Ships reprovision. Sail south in company towards the Antarctic in search of the southern continent.
17 January 1773	Antarctic	Ships become the first known to have crossed the Antarctic Circle.
8 February	Antarctic	*Resolution* and *Adventure* become separated in fog.
February to May	New Zealand	After losing *Adventure*, Cook sets a course for the rendezvous at Queen Charlotte Sound in New Zealand, but lands first at Dusky Bay in the south of South Island, where *Resolution* stays until 30 April. Furneaux arrives at Queen Charlotte Sound 7 April, having landed briefly in Van Diemen's Land (Tasmania) en route. Cook arrives at Queen Charlotte Sound, 17 May.
June to November	First island sweep	Rather than wintering in New Zealand, Cook orders that *Resolution* and *Adventure* should sail in company for an exploratory sweep of the central Pacific. Anchor at Vaitepiha Bay, Tahiti, 15 August, before moving to old anchorage in Matavai Bay, 26 August. 2 September, Huahine. 7 September, Omai (Mae) is taken on board *Adventure* and eventually returns to London on the ship. 2 October, land at 'Amsterdam' and 'Middelburg', two islands in the Tongan group, which Cook calls the Friendly Islands. 30 October, *Resolution* and *Adventure* become separated and do not meet again.
3 November	New Zealand	Cook arrives at rendezvous at Queen Charlotte Sound and sails 25 November to continue search south for the southern continent. *Adventure* arrives at Queen Charlotte Sound, 30 November. On 17 December, boat's crew from *Adventure* killed by Maori and Furneaux sails next day for Britain via Tierra del Fuego, arriving 14 July 1774.
November 1773 to October 1774	Second island sweep	*Resolution* sails south to look for the southern continent, crossing the Antarctic Circle on 20 December. On 30 January they reach the farthest south (71° 10' S.) before turning north to warmer climes. 13 March, land at Easter Island and on 29 March reach the Marquesas. 17 April, land at Takaroa in the Tuamotu Islands, en route for Tahiti, which they reach on 22 April. Attempt to land at Niue, but driven off by hostile reception – Cook names it Savage Island. 25 June, *Resolution* lands in the Tongan group again, before sailing farther west. Land at Malekula and Erramanga in the New Hebrides in July and August, sailing south to New Zealand via New Caledonia (4 September) and Norfolk Island (10 October). Arrive Queen Charlotte Sound, 18 October.
18 October to 10 November	Queen Charlotte Sound, NZ	Cook discovers that the message he left for Furneaux is gone; picks up a story of a ship being sunk and men killed but is also told *Adventure* sailed safely. Leaves to continue search for southern continent.
November 1774 to July 1775	*En route* to Britain	Heads south and east into the Southern Ocean towards Tierra del Fuego, landing at Desolation Island on 17 December. After a long sweep in the South Atlantic, during which they sight South Georgia, the South Sandwich Islands and Bouvet Island, *Resolution* heads north towards Table Bay, South Africa, which they reach on 21 March. They sail for Britain on 27 April via St Helena and Ascension Island, anchoring at Portsmouth on 30 July.

THE VOYAGE OF *RESOLUTION* AND *DISCOVERY*

DATE	PLACE	NOTES
12 July 1776	Plymouth	*Resolution* sails on her own; *Discovery* (Captain Clerke) sails on 1 August to rendezvous at Cape Town.
18 October	Cape Town	*Resolution* arrives on 18 October, *Discovery* on 10 November. Both ships sail for New Zealand on 1 December.
26 January 1777	Van Diemen's Land (Tasmania)	Both ships anchor in Adventure Bay in south-east Tasmania. Cook does not explore the northern coast and believes that Tasmania is joined to the Australian mainland.
12 February	Queen Charlotte Sound, NZ	Sails from Tasmania on 30 January for New Zealand. Arrives Queen Charlotte Sound, 12 February, and Cook finds out more of what had happened to the crew of *Adventure*'s cutter. Sails on 25 February for sweep of southern Pacific islands, rather than sailing north to search for the North-West Passage.
29 March	Cook Islands	Arrive at Mangaia, one of the Cook Islands (named after Cook by a Russian explorer in the early nineteenth century).
28 April	Tongan Islands	Cruise through the group escorted by Finau, a chief of Tongatapu. Tongan plot to kill Cook and his crew falls through and ships sail for Tahiti on 17 July unaware of the plan.
13 August	Tahiti	Ships anchor at Tautira, the eastern end of Tahiti, moving to Matavai Bay on 23 August. Learn that Spanish ships from Peru have called since Cook's last visit.
30 September	Moorea	Goat stolen by islanders and Cook burns canoes and houses in reprisal.
11 October	Huahine	Omai returned and ships' carpenters build him a house.
2 November	Raiatea	Two men desert. Poetua, her husband and brother are imprisoned on *Discovery* pending the return of the deserters. John Webber paints Poetua. Cook's ships leave the Society Islands on 8 December sailing north to begin search for North-West Passage.
18 January 1778	Hawaiian group	Sight Kauai, one of the Hawaiian islands. Stay in the group until 2 February.
7 March to 26 April	Oregon and Nootka Sound	Crews use local timber to replace damaged masts and spars. Sail north.
May to September	Alaska, Aleutian Islands, the Arctic and north-east coast of Russia	Follow coast of North America looking for North-West Passage, enter Bering Strait and sail as far north as 70° 44' N. until stopped by ice. Surgeon, William Anderson, dies on 3 August. Start south on 29 August, following the Asian coastline. Sail for Hawaii on 26 October.
26 November to 22 February 1779	Hawaii	Cook's ships slowly circle the Hawaiian islands, finally anchoring in Kealakekua Bay on 17 January. Ships leave on 4 February but are forced back by a broken mast on the *Resolution*. Cook killed on 14 February and ships sail on 22 February. Clerke takes command of *Resolution* and Gore of *Discovery*.
February to September	Kamchatka and the Arctic	Clerke explores the other islands in the Hawaiian group before sailing north to continue the search for North-West Passage. Arrives at Kamchatka 24 April and sails for the Arctic on 16 June. Reaches 70° 33' N. before starting south again. Clerke dies of consumption on 22 August as ships return to Kamchatka. Gore sends letters and journals back to London from here, which arrive in January 1780.
October 1779 to 21 August 1780	From Kamchatka to Britain	Leave Kamchatka on 10 October, returning to Britain via Macao and the Cape of Good Hope. Bad weather at the approach to the English Channel forces the ships north and they finally anchor at Stromness in Orkney on 21 August. Sail south to London on 20 September, reaching Deptford on 7 October.

PICTURE ACKNOWLEDGEMENTS

Page 9 by permission of the British Library, London [MS 21593.o].
Page 108 © The British Museum, London.
Pages 58 and 59 DL PXX 2 f.39; *123* DL Pe 214. Dixson Library, State Library of NSW, Australia.
Page 124 (bottom) Historisches Museum, Berne. Photograph Stefan Rebsamen.
Page 102 PXD 11 f.30. Mitchell Library, State Library of NSW, Australia.
Pages 103, 114 and 115, 124 (top) by permission of the National Library of Australia.
Page 31 by permission of Pieter van der Merwe.
Page 84 Private Collection.
Page 117 © Crown Copyright 2002. Published by permission of the Controller of Her Majesty's Stationery Office and the UK Hydrographic Office (www.ukho.gov.uk).
Page 122 V&A Picture Library, London.

The following are NMM photographic references. Pictures may be ordered from the Picture Library, National Maritime Museum, Greenwich, London, SE10 9NF (tel. 020 8312 6600). All © National Maritime Museum, London.

Cover: A8588; A1084; BHC2628.
Frontispiece: BHC2628.

INTRODUCTION
Page 6 and 7 D4761; *10* E8962; *12* E2317_1 and E2317_2; *13* B6374; *15* E8961; *16* E8947; *17* D4847_1; *18 and 19* BHC0360; *20* E8975; *22* E8974.

CHAPTER 1
Page 23 PU3117; *25* 7147; *26* D6783_1; *28 and 29 (top)* A0123, *28 (bottom)* PY7700; *33* E9025; *35* 4139_1; *36* PZ3988; *37* PT3959; *38 and 39* D3940.

CHAPTER 2
Page 40 D6072; *42* BHC1778; *43* BHC2370; *45* BHC2396; *47 (top)* BHC1795, *(bottom)* BHC1936; *48 and 49* A8588; *50 (top)* C8745, *(bottom)* A5512; *54* PW6439; *56* PZ1555; *60* BHC4214; *61* PU4633.

CHAPTER 3
Page 63 D3358_1; *66* D2284; *67 (top)* D7008, *(bottom)* D7009; *68* B4125; *70* D7824; *71* B5488; *73 (top)* E9034, *(bottom)* E9033; *74 and 75* BHC1214.

CHAPTER 4
Page 79 2961; *81* E9031; *83* E9032; *86* D9964; *87* D9965; *89* 3935; *90 and 91* B1337; *92 and 93* A1071; *93* PW3511.

CHAPTER 5
Page 94 PZ3954; *95* PW6424; *96* PU8337; *106* E9026; *107* BHC1906; *109* BHC1932; *110* BHC2374; *111* BHC2395; *112* PZ2374; *118* PT2965; *119* PAI1536; *120* PY9582; *121 (top)* BHC4212, *(bottom)* E9027; *122 (bottom)* PZ3921.

CHAPTER 6
Page 125 2338; *126* BHC4227; *127* PZ3885; *128 (top)* A4809, *(bottom)* BHC2957; *129* BHC1905; *130* BHC1903; *135 (top)* PY7637, *(bottom)* BHC2389; *137* PW6438; *138* PW6417.

INDEX

To

Amy

with love

from

Mum

x ♡

The Political Legacy of
Margaret Thatcher

The Political Legacy of

Margaret Thatcher

Edited by

Stanislao Pugliese

POLITICO'S

First published in Great Britain 2003 by
Politico's Publishing, an imprint of
Methuen Publishing Limited
215 Vauxhall Bridge Road
London SW1V 1EJ

10 9 8 7 6 5 4 3 2 1

The copyright for the individual contributions lies with the contributors

A CIP catalogue record for this book is available from the British Library

ISBN 1 84275 025 9

Printed and bound in Great Britain by Creative Print and Design

Contents

Part V: Leadership and the Monarchy

Part VI The Thatcher Legacy

Introduction

This volume brings together selected essays first presented at an international conference at Hofstra University examining the prime ministerial years of Margaret Thatcher. Lady Thatcher was the longest-serving British Prime Minister of the twentieth century (1979–1990) and the first woman to hold that office. The conference brought together scholars, journalists, and politicians in far-ranging discussions of the issues that marked her twelve years in office and the distinctive style and personality she brought to her leadership. Her address from the conference, included here, 'Reflections on Liberty' was delivered at Hofstra University as she was awarded a Doctorate of Humane Letters, honoris causa. The essays collected in this volume not only appraise Lady Thatcher but also evaluate Thatcherism, a political ideology and associated set of policies that carry her name to this day, more than a decade after her departure from 10 Downing Street. What distinguished Thatcherism from the politics of previous post-World War II Conservative British prime ministers was its author's fierce determination to attack rather than acquiesce in the fundamental premises and organisation of the social welfare state. Borrowing freely from nineteenth century conceptions of personal liberty and free enterprise, Thatcher chose to confront some of the most sacred pillars of that state, from government ownership of major economic sectors to the incorporation of unions into the governing structures of society. Some benefited from the policies associated with Thatcherism, others suffered from them. As a consequence, the period of her Prime Ministership was marked by incessant and bitter conflict – conflict that marked the conference and which still resonates today as historians struggle over the meaning of her legacy.

Abroad, Thatcher projected a muscular foreign policy, engaging in war with Argentina over the Falklands, striking a defiant stance in Northern Ireland and restraining the integration of the United Kingdom into the European Community. She aligned her government firmly with the Cold War policies of American President Ronald Reagan, enthusiastically supporting the deployment of a new generation of nuclear weapons in Europe. At the same time, Thatcher was among the first Western leaders to recognise the genuine changes occurring in the Soviet Union as a consequence of Mikhail Gorbachev's rise to power, becoming in the process a co-architect of the ordered end of the Cold War.

No other twentieth-century politician's name is synonymous with a political ideology, not even Franklin D. Roosevelt or even Lady Thatcher's hero, Winston Churchill. Yet Thatcher and Thatcherism embodied profound contradictions that surfaced at the conference. For example: although Thatcher and her proponents insist that Thatcherism was tantamount to an increase in liberty, her very public and outspoken defense of Chilean dictator General Augusto Pinochet would seem to contradict such a claim. Thatcherism as an economic policy did little to halt Britain's industrial decline and her adamant criticism of 'Europe' in the name of national sovereignty seemed to go against the historical current.

For all that, Margaret Thatcher looms as one of the major figures of twentieth-century history. Hofstra University's conference, 'The Thatcher Years: The Rebirth of Liberty?' was the first major academic event of its kind and an attempt to assess her impact on British, European and global politics and culture. As these essays demonstrate, few politicians generate the amount of admiration and indignation as does Margaret Thatcher. Fewer still have left as profound a mark on their country or the international scene.

Stanislao Pugliese
New York, July 2003

Reflections on Liberty

The Rt Hon. Baroness Thatcher, L.G., O.M., F.R.S.

Mr President, Members of Convocation, Ladies and Gentlemen. It is a great honour to be awarded this degree by your distinguished university.

It is also an honour to be the subject of one of your conferences. There is, of course, something rather unnerving about being weighed in the balance by academics. But even among the erudite, majority opinion is not always right – as 364 academic economists once learned to their cost in Britain.[1]

But looking through the names on your discussion panels, I can see that you have chosen the best minds with the sharpest insights you could possibly hope to find. Indeed, some of your participants must take their full share of the credit – or the blame – for all that happened in the 1980s. Ours was always a joint enterprise. So I warmly congratulate you and wish you well with your deliberations.

At another seminar, some years ago now, I recall listening for several hours to a number of policy advisers and technical experts – all men. They had a lot to say for themselves, and to be fair they made a lot of useful suggestions. When the time came for me to give my reaction, I began by reminding them of the proverb that it's the cock that crows but it's the hen that lays the egg. So in just the same spirit – and certainly without crowing – perhaps I can make a few observations about the testing and exhilarating years during which I had the immense privilege of serving as Britain's Prime Minister.

Isms

The subtitle of your Conference is: 'The Rebirth of Liberty'. But I note that it's

1

followed by a question mark. With the greatest of respect, that piece of punctuation is redundant. From the very beginning, liberty is what my colleagues and I believed in, and sought to secure and expand. So, at the same time, did my old friend President Reagan in the United States. And we succeeded.

Liberty – or freedom if you like – is a perfectly simple concept, understandable to all, it seems, except to the very dim or the very clever. It is the condition in which a man (or woman) is free to express their identity, exercise their God-given talents, acquire and pass on property, bring up a family, succeed or fail, and live and die in peace. And the most important requirement for that free society is a rule of law, informed by equity and upheld by impartial judges.

The single biggest intellectual error during my political lifetime has been to confuse freedom with equality. In fact, equality – being an unnatural condition which can only be enforced by the state – is usually the enemy of liberty. This was a point I made in France on the bicentennial celebration of the French Revolution, which deliberately and dangerously confused the two. My French hosts were somewhat perplexed. But the point stands.

Starting with the French Revolution, and then greatly encouraged by the Bolshevik Revolution, modern times have been plagued by '–isms', that is by ideologies, in effect secular religions. Most of them were unrelievedly bad.

Communism accounted for approaching one hundred million deaths.[2] It enslaved the East, while its first cousin, socialism, impoverished much of the West. Nazism – that other brand of socialism – and its tamer forbear, Fascism, killed about 25 million. All have left scars on our societies which perhaps will never fully heal.

The proponents of these ideologies engaged in polemics and indeed violence against each other. But they had more in common than they admitted. For their essence was that the state had the right, indeed the duty, to act like God. And the results were devilish.

Of course sometimes, in the case of socialism, they were also comical. The Russians who are lucky to have such a marvelous sense of humor, if only because they have had so little to laugh about, recount a story about Leonid Brezhnev's arrival at the pearly gates. Saint Peter tells him that he has been found wanting but that he can choose between a capitalist and a socialist hell. To Saint Peter's surprise the former Soviet leader replies that he prefers a socialist hell. Saint

Peter tells him to think carefully: this is no time for propaganda. But Brezhnev repeats that he chooses a socialist hell. St. Peter grants his wish, but asks for an explanation. To which Brezhnev replies that at least in a socialist hell they will always be short of fuel.

Of course, not all '–isms' are as bad as that. Liberalism, individualism and free enterprise capitalism are sometimes also classed as ideologies. That's arguable. But, however classified, they've certainly been far more beneficial than statism, as judged by almost any measure of human happiness and progress.

About one thing though, I would like to be clear: I don't regard Thatcherism as an '–ism' in any of these senses. And if I ever invented an ideology, that certainly wasn't my intention.

The principles in which I believe, and the policies which we tried to put into effect in the 1980s, did not constitute a system of the sort described by T. S. Eliot as being 'so perfect that no one will need to be good'[3]. Rather, they should be understood in the light of two overriding considerations.

Human Nature

The first relates to human nature. We Conservatives understood, and understand it: the socialists didn't and generally still don't.

Our experience tells us that man is neither as good nor as bad as he's painted. Given the right framework of laws, taxes and regulation, most individuals will apply their talents and energies productively. They will certainly make far more effort on behalf of themselves and their families than they ever would for an impersonal entity called 'government'. What government has to do is to set the right rules so that the game – and it's never a 'zero sum game', remember – is played to the best of every player's ability. That's on the positive side of human nature. And from it stems everything which the West has achieved and which the world calls progress.

But there is also a negative side to human nature. We Conservatives have no illusions about the perfectibility of Man. Human beings are as capable today of unspeakable brutality as they ever were. And the march of science and technology has provided new means of cruelty. If there are no assured penalties against wickedness, some people will disrupt and, if their numbers are sufficient, destroy all the good things of civilised life.

3

And it's not just the under-class but also the 'over-class' that causes the trouble. If politicians or bureaucrats are given power that is unaccountable and unrestrained they will, in the long run, be as corrupt as they can get away with. That's the best possible argument for limited government – and a pretty good one too against a centralised European superstate.

Practical Policies

The second consideration to which I would like to draw your attention isn't philosophical, or moral, or even psychological – it's really historical, a matter of the circumstances we found in Britain at the end of the 1970s. The principles and policies we held to during the decade that followed reflected the needs of Britain at the time.

The Second World War, even more than other wars, had given an enormous boost to government control. Indeed, oddly enough when you consider that it was fought against totalitarian states, the Second World War provided in many people's minds convincing proof that a planned society and a planned economy worked best. The 1960s and 1970s in Britain were decades during which this illusion was gradually, painfully dispelled. Social and economic planning led to larger, cumulative failures, and these in turn produced disillusionment and despair – even among those who once thought that socialism could achieve heaven on earth.

As the results of all this multiplied, commentators spoke wearily of the so-called 'British disease'. By this they meant an affliction of restrictive practices, low productivity, trade union militancy, penal taxes, poor profits, low investment–in short economic decline. And hardly less corrosive was the mentality which underlay, and which was itself encouraged by that decline. To put it simply, there was a resigned acceptance that Britain was finished.

This discouraged some politicians on the Right, who felt that damage limitation was the only sensible strategy, that managing decline made best sense. But a number of us felt differently. We did not believe that Britain was down, let alone out. We felt that it was socialism that had failed the country, not the country that had failed socialism. And we were determined to prove it.

Let me emphasise again: my journey along this path was never solitary. Keith Joseph gave the best political analysis of what was wrong, and what had to change. But behind him lay the wisdom of people like Friedrich Hayek, bodies like the Institute for Economic Affairs, and a host of thinkers who had swum against the tide of collectivism which at one time threatened to sweep away our national foundations.

If I were to use one phrase to sum up what had to be done – and what indeed was done – it is that we had to 'reverse the ratchet'. The notion of the ratchet, which I believe was Keith Joseph's, reflected the fact that Britain's post-World War II history had consisted of sharp swings to the left, followed by periods when the leftward lurch was arrested but never reversed. The result was that an ever greater share of a virtually stagnant economy was under the control of the state.

By the mid-1970s – the high point (if that's the word) of socialism – Britain was on a knife edge. One more jerk of the ratchet and we would create a probably irreversible shift towards state power and away from liberty. If today that statement seems alarmist, please remember that this was also the high point of Soviet expansionism, and that the same socialist politicians who were keenest to impose a left-wing blueprint on Britain were often deeply sympathetic to the advance of Soviet power abroad. What occurred in Britain in this period was not therefore just a clash between two parties, it was a struggle between two systems offering two entirely different destinies.

The policies we followed in the 1980s were therefore those required by the practical circumstances of the time. If they seemed like revolutionary propositions to many critics, this only reflected how far those critics had lost touch with common sense and abandoned the common ground of Western values. So it was that monetarism – control of the money supply – was needed to beat the ill of apparently unstoppable inflation. Public spending cuts were needed to curb runaway borrowing. Tax cuts were needed to restore incentives. Removal of controls on prices, incomes, dividends and foreign exchange was needed to allow key economic decisions to be made by the market, not by politicians. Above all, step-by-step trade union reforms were needed to curb the hugely destructive power of trade union bosses.

But the programme had to be much more than just economic. Its purpose was, in a certain sense, moral – and again it had to be, because the problem was moral. We had to give people a renewed appetite for liberty and responsibility.

5

The instinct for freedom had never been totally lost. It was too deeply rooted in the English-speaking peoples for that. But it's not enough for a free people to fight for freedom – however heroically. A free people has to live freedom, and this we now endeavoured to achieve.

Cutting taxes and curbing inflation by positive interest rates allowed people to build up savings. But we also pioneered two radical policies for wider owner-ship. First, the sale of public sector houses at large discounts to their tenants turned hundreds of thousands of families into property owners. Alongside this, the privatisation of industries with special preference for workers and for small buyers began to turn Britain into a nation of shareholders. Of course, ownership of assets brings risks as well as rewards. But the transformation it effects on a society is wholly positive, because it gives people a stake in prosperity and trains them to take control of their own lives.

So the principles and policies we developed in the 1970s, and put into effect in the 1980s, were rooted in human nature and in the requirements of the time. This assertion leads on to a question – and a pressing one for you, who presumably will be doing more than picking over the bones of my administration. That question is – what relevance does our experience have to the world today?

A Legacy Worth Preserving

I suggest that there are three reasons why the principles and policies of the 1980s should be explored, updated as necessary, and then applied in this new century too.

The first is that human nature doesn't change – and won't change unless the horrors of cloning were allowed free rein. It will therefore always be necessary to keep in good repair the institutional framework of freedom if the material benefits of freedom are also to be enjoyed. Private property, limited government, a clear and honest rule of law, light regulation and low taxes on the one hand – and rigorous prosecution of crime and discouragement of dependence on the other – will always be necessary conditions for prosperity and order. If you forget one of these elements, or concentrate on just one at the expense of the others, a free society and a free economy are in peril. Inevitably. Always. Everywhere.

Second, there is the simple fact, which pragmatic converts from the Left don't really deny, namely that today's dynamic, successful economics in Britain and, still more so in America, are the results of what Conservative administrations in our countries did in the 1980s. Neither the present British government nor the Clinton administration could be so generous with the taxpayer's money if they didn't have the economic growth to fund the taxes. And they have that growth because Conservatives created the condition for it.

Third, many of the same dangers, though in different forms, are present and pressing in the world today. And precisely because the principles applied in the eighties were neither simple pragmatism nor an inflexible dogma they are eminently applicable to our new circumstances.

I could refer here to several current and controversial areas – I might at a pinch be tempted to say something about Europe's ambitions to become a superpower and the challenge that poses both to individual sovereign nations and to American influence in the world. I could mention the extreme dangers from the proliferation of weapons of mass destruction and the missile technology to deliver them – dangers at least as great as those we faced for most of the Cold War.

But I would particularly draw your attention to a less dramatic phenomenon – the way in which the Left in the post-socialist world are driving forward their agenda by other means. For collectivism now advances far more through regulation (often international regulation) and through welfare programmes than through the old methods of state socialism. The ingenuity of the politician and the bureaucrat in devising means to keep between a third and a half of our countries' wealth in the grip of the state – even when our economies are forging ahead on a surge of enterprise and innovation – is truly astonishing. But, of course, the temptation to prefer comfortable dependency to the strenuous life of liberty is hardly less so.

Such is perhaps the most serious long-term threat to the West. And we still do not know how fully and deeply freedom will take root in countries which lack the normal, cultural, religious and historical condition that allowed it over centuries to prevail with us.

Will Russia ever develop a true rule of law and become a normal country? Will Asian capitalism ever develop the openness and honesty of America's? Will a rich China ever be a truly free and democratic China?

Even to pose these questions is to remind ourselves how little we can predict,

7

let alone control, our global future. But at least we know what works for us. And whatever else we do, we must not lose sight of it – or lose hold of it.

As Rudyard Kipling reminds us:

Dear-bought and clear, a thousand year,
Our fathers' title runs.
Make we likewise their sacrifice,
Defrauding not our sons.[4]

Visions of Glory, 1874–1932 (Boston: Little, Brown, 1983), p. 45

Mr President, Ladies and Gentlemen, may I thank this Convocation for the honour you do me – and to your distinguished Conference guests may I say 'Let battle commence!'

Notes

1   Editor's note: On 30 March, 1981, 364 British economists published an open letter in *The Times* (London) denouncing Margaret Thatcher's 1981 budget and Thatcherism. They predicted dire results for the British economy and the further decline of British industrial power.

2   Editor's note: The number has been put forth most recently in *Le livre noir du Communisme: Crimes, terreur, répression*, Stephen Courtois, et. al., eds. (Paris: Editions Robert Laffont: 1997); the book has been published in English as *The Black Book of Communism: Crimes, Terror, Repression*, translated by Jonathan Murphy and Mark Kramer (Cambridge, MA: Harvard).

3   Editor's note: T. S. Eliot, 'Choruses from 'The Rock'', in *The Complete Poems and Plays 1909-* (New York, Harcourt Brace).

4   Editor's note: Quoted in William Manchester, *The Last Lion. Winston Spencer Churchill* (Bos Little, Brown, 1983), p. 45.

Margaret Thatcher:
The Lady Who Made the Weather

Peter Riddell

———————

One of the most evocative descriptions of a leading British politician was made by Winston Churchill in his essay on Joseph Chamberlain in *Great Contemporaries*: 'Joe was the one who made the weather. He was the man the masses knew. He it was who had solutions for social problems, who was ready to advance, sword in hand if need be, upon the foes of Britain.' The same could be said of Margaret Thatcher. Although very different from Joseph Chamberlain, both in character and in accomplishments, she also 'made the weather'. She dominated the political scene for over a decade. Alone of twentieth-century British prime ministers, she became an 'ism,' a doctrine, a defining term for a whole era. She was the epitome of the transforming prime minister rather than the manager.

But nearly a decade after she was forced out of office by her own party, it is still hard to reach a clear judgement on her impact. As Zhou En Lai reportedly said when asked about the significance of the French Revolution: 'It's too soon to tell.' Just as no one was neutral about her when she was Prime Minister, so no one is neutral about her now. The battles she fought are still being re-fought by her allies and enemies. Her presence, her ability to thrill and excite a Conservative Party audience, shows her long shadow and complicates any assessment.

There is a vast literature about her impact. There are two broad views: one is the minimalist or statistical. This looks at growth rates and relative shares of world trade and concludes that the Thatcher years did not produce a steep change in Britain's position. Some political scientists at Essex University under-took research claiming that the favourable effects of the Falklands War raised the Conservatives' rating no more than three per cent above expected levels and this boost lasted for no more than three months. On this view, the real reason for the improvement in the Tory position was the start of economic recovery and a rise in living standards. This is parallel to the argument that not only did the Thatcher years fail to improve Britain's economic performance but that they also left a more divided, materialist and uncaring society.

The other main view is reverential. It is the Lady as heroine, battling against impossible odds, and often alone, against opponents in her own cabinet, in the trade unions and in the rest of Europe to change the course of history.

Neither explanation is convincing nor does it do Lady Thatcher justice. The minimalists miss the big picture. They fail to recognise the importance of mood and of attitudes. To argue that the Falklands War had a minimal impact on the Tories' standing is to lose all sense of perspective. The war changed the way that both the British public and world opinion viewed Lady Thatcher and in so doing largely created the image of 'Thatcher the warrior'. Just imagine what would have happened if the expedition to retake the islands had failed with the loss of one or more of the carriers and several thousand British servicemen dead. The Thatcher government would have fallen. The war was a decisive and defining event. The critics also fail to recognise how attempts to reform the post-war settlement by a consensus approach had failed during the 1970s creat-ing the need for more radical action.

The reverential school underestimates her skill by taking her contribution out of its historical context. No politician can be viewed on his or her own as a giant who moved mountains on their own, though the mountains sometimes took a buffeting from her handbag. To depict her as the leader who triumphed alone and was always right is paradoxically to do her a disservice. She was, and is, a politician with flaws as well as strengths, who often had to compromise, was dependent on her allies over a wide range of policy and was not always consistent. For all her clear-cut public image, she did listen to colleagues and advisers, sometimes reluc-tantly and exhausting them in the process, and she was often a pragmatist.

In practice, what mattered was timing and her own skills and will, her ability to exploit the circumstances of the time. She became Tory leader at the right time when the British public was disillusioned with the post-war settlement during that most dismal of decades, the 1970s, as a result of high inflation, strikes, rising taxes, etc. The Labour government of the late 1970s had already begun to adopt a different approach, reining back public spending and focusing on control of the money supply, though with limited success.

The successful Tory alternative – a counter-attack against trade union power, a cutting of marginal tax rates (if not of the tax burden), a check to the sharp increase in public spending, deregulation and privatisation – had various authors and implementers – ranging from Keith Joseph, via Geoffrey Howe, to Norman Tebbit and Nigel Lawson.

Her distinctive contribution was not really ideological or in new policy think-ing but more personal: her clear sense of values and her will; her single-mind-edness and determination. Her gut feelings and belief in the righteousness of her position could severely test the patience of her colleagues as much as those who worked with her. But that will and persistence enabled her to face up to challenges when other prime ministers would have backed down and compro-mised. She was a great survivor through the force of her personality.

Lady Thatcher was tested during the deep recession and inner city riots of 1981, by the Falklands conflict of spring 1982, during the miners' strike of 1984–5, in her steadfast response to the Brighton bomb of October 1984 and even when she wobbled during the Westland crisis of January 1986. The famil-iar Thatcher image emerged from these events as a prime minister who would not accept conventional warnings and who would press on, in the end to the point of imperilling her premiership.

Paradoxically, many of those features of her premiership that were most striking at the time were also the most transitory, particularly in foreign affairs: the Falklands, her crucial interventions with Ronald Reagan over arms control and the nuclear balance, in spotting the early significance of Mikhail Gorbachev, in stand-ing up against terrorism. These were all notable achievements at the time, and con-tributed to a greater sense of national self-confidence after the years of retreat, and fostered the happy illusion, for a time, that the Great was back in Great Britain.

But these impressions did not last.

To the extent that Lady Thatcher's influence with Ronald Reagan and Mikhail Gorbachev reflected their personal rapport, it did not, and could not, last. As she confesses in her own memoirs of her Downing Street years, her relations with President Bush were initially more distant, and at times, sticky, as the State Department under James Baker consciously sought to tilt US policy more towards Germany. Some of her own advisers believed that at times the personal aspects of her approach predominated too much and made her unwilling to see the limitations of President Gorbachev and the increasing weakness of his position from 1989 onwards.

These personal aspects inevitably faded over time and her distinctive international legacy dimmed. Her premiership did not produce a lasting change in Britain's place in the world. In 1990, as in 1979, Britain was still a medium-sized European power with an uncertain role.

It was on Europe – the issue that has preoccupied her and the Conservative Party in the decade since her departure from Downing Street – that her policies and attitudes were most ambiguous. Always seeing Europe from a nationalist viewpoint, she nonetheless supported, or at least acquiesced in, a key measure of European integration in the Single European Act which extended the community's role and qualified majority voting. Admittedly, the act was seen at the time mainly as a means of creating the single market but it has never been entirely convincing for the Thatcherites to claim that she did not understand the constitutional implications. Admittedly, the nature of the European debate changed when Jacques Delors became President of the Commission and launched the drive to monetary union underpinned by a network of social protection. Her own advisers also argue that, after a decade, she had become disillusioned with most other European leaders and with negotiating with them at summits.

Lady Thatcher's awakening to what she saw as the European threat was reflected in her Bruges speech of September 1988, in effect a rejection of her government's earlier approach. Her opposition to growing centralism and the creation of a European state ignited a debate about Britain's role in Europe which has dominated Conservative politics to this day. The questions she raised then, and since she left office, were and are an admission that her governments had failed to find a satisfactory position for Britain within Europe. That was reflected a year later in her mishandling of German unification. Having been a notable advocate of liberty and freedom in Eastern Europe, she appeared churlish in her response to the breaching of the Berlin Wall and in seeking to slow down German unification. The Bush administration recognised the inevitability of unification and sought to secure the best terms, keeping an enlarged Germany within NATO. It was her biggest foreign policy mistake and strained relations not only with other European leaders but also with Washington – though the breach was relatively short-lived as relations were quickly restored after the Iraqi invasion of Kuwait a few months later.

If the Thatcher legacy for foreign policy was ambivalent, her domestic impact was much greater and more long lasting. Admittedly, the path of her government was not always consistent. The agenda developed over time. There were often tactical retreats – for instance the decision to postpone a confrontation over pit closures in spring 1981 until coal stocks had been built up at power stations – and some issues were not addressed until late in her premiership, such as schools and the health service.

There were also internal contradictions. She was never a pure economic Thatcherite – always defending the interests of what she saw as her people, hard-working home-owners and savers. She was always highly sensitive over interest rates and resisted any reduction in mortgage interest tax relief.

The champion of individual liberty was also a great centraliser. She and her allies had little time for local government and other intermediary institutions such as universities, the churches (especially at times the Church of England) and voluntary bodies. This was one of the reasons why she was so disliked by many academics and people in the world of the arts and literature – as shown by the vote of her own University of Oxford against giving her an honorary degree. Many in this world disapproved of her tone and values and what they saw as the greedy materialism of the late 1980s.

She mishandled local government. The Treasury's desire for control over levels of spending usually predominated over local autonomy with the result that the proportion of local income raised by councils steadily fell. The attempt to reconcile these differing interests led to the poll tax or community charge, which, uniquely for a major tax, was introduced and repealed within a single parliament. The tax failed for a variety of reasons but mainly because it was brought in at a time when the government was anyway becoming very unpopular and interest rates and inflation were rising. The high level of evasion and non-payment symbolised a growing disaffection from the government, and

Lady Thatcher herself. The boom of the late 1980s and the conspicuous affluence of many reinforced the widespread belief that Britain had become a more
unequal and divided society (as it had in terms of income distribution). That
was particularly true in Scotland where Tory support began to fall sharply from
the mid-1980s onwards.

But many of the central problems that had preoccupied British governments
over the two decades before 1979 were successfully addressed. The power of
trade unions was tamed through a combination of recession and a skilful
step-by-step approach to reform of trade union laws to remove previous immu-
nities on industrial disputes and closed shops. Under the direction of Norman
Tebbit as Employment Secretary for two crucial years from 1981 until 1983, the
government led but never jumped far ahead of public opinion on the unions.
These changes significantly altered the climate in which British industry operated, as well as helping the Thatcher government successfully to face and defeat
the challenge from Arthur Scargill and most of the miners' union in 1984–85.
This was the symbolic turning point in the battle over union power.

The other most striking change was privatisation. In the late 1970s, the state
owned the electricity, gas, water, telephone, railways and nuclear power industries, as well as British Aerospace, the British Airports Authority, British Leyland,
British Airways and many other smaller interests. Many of these utilities had
been losing very large sums and were subject to recurrent disruption by powerful public sector unions. The idea of selling these industries to the private sector
had been debated for a long time in new right/free market circles but many senior Conservatives close to Lady Thatcher doubted whether it would ever be possible to privatise the monopoly utilities. The Conservatives' 1979 manifesto was
distinctly coy on the issue. But under pressure of mounting nationalised industry deficits, the privatisation programme developed, led by Nigel Lawson, first
as Energy Secretary, and then as Chancellor. This led to a substantial shift in the
boundaries between the public and private sectors and to an improvement in
their management. Hardly anyone under the age of forty now knows what the
term 'nationalised industry' means. The flotations were linked in some cases to
a liberalisation of what had been monopoly markets, although this was patchy
as some industries, such as gas, were sold off as monopolies.

The other main innovation was the attempt to sell shares to a large number of people rather than just to institutional investors. The number of adults holding shares increased more than threefold but most holdings were small and less financially important than home ownership or occupational pensions. The perennial Tory aim of creating a property-owning democracy was achieved more by selling council houses to their tenants, raising owner occupation from 53 to 66 per cent of households, than through privatisation. But despite later problems over the mis-selling of personal pensions and negative equity after house prices fell in the early 1990s, more people were entrenched with a greater financial stake in society. It is over-simplistic to say that privatisation and council house sales turned people into Tory voters, rather than Tory voters were more likely to buy shares and houses. The two were probably mutually reinforcing.

The Thatcher administrations' record on taxes and spending was mixed. Top marginal rates were cut: from 83 to 60 /40 per cent in the first Budget, and then down to a single rate of 40 per cent in 1988, with the basic rate down from 33 to 25 per cent. However, the tax burden – the share of taxes in national income – rose by three percentage points to 36.3 per cent because indirect taxes were increased steadily and to hold down public borrowing. This was higher than in the US and Japan but lower than in most of the rest of Europe. However, the relative size of the public sector was reduced – from 45 to less than 40 per cent – after having risen apparently inexorably over the previous two decades. The share jumped up again during the recession of the early 1990s.

The Thatcher governments – and particularly Geoffrey Howe and Nigel Lawson – can claim not only to have shifted the focus of macro-economic policy but also to have checked the previous growth of the public sector and shifted key areas to the private sector. Free market critics argue that Lady Thatcher was not bold enough, but what she did – particularly over privatisation and a series of incremental reforms to slow the growth of the welfare budget – was far more than anyone thought possible in 1979. She had to operate within tight limits. While she worked with the grain of public opinion over trade union reform, there was never any appetite for radical measures in, say, health. When some radical options about private medical insurance in a think tank (Central Policy Review Staff) paper were leaked in autumn 1982 – a few months after her triumph in the Falklands conflict when she was at the height of her powers – she immediately ordered the suppression of the document and quickly proclaimed that the 'NHS [National Health Service] is safe in our hands'. As Professor Ivor Crewe memorably remarked, Keynes was dead, but not Beveridge.

There are two central questions. Did the Thatcher government in any way halt Britain's long decline? And did she permanently change the political landscape?

The Thatcher governments cannot be said to have ended or reversed Britain's economic decline. Britain's productivity and growth performance, and the share of world trade, improved during the Thatcher years compared with the 1970s but not spectacularly and not by comparison with other leading industrial countries. Talk at the height of the economic boom about a British economic miracle was quickly shown to be premature when inflation rose sharply again and boom turned into bust. But there were lasting benefits from privatisation, from the weakening of trade unions and from a series of measures to encourage enterprise such as the ending of exchange controls, the phasing out of industrial subsidies (despite continuing support for the motor and aerospace industries) and the encouragement of inward investment. Much manufacturing capacity may have been lost in the recession of 1979–82, but industry emerged more competitive and made British industry better able to cope with the integration of world markets during the 1990s – everything that has come to be known as globalisation.

It is easy to say that such policies should have been introduced earlier – indeed the Heath government tried and failed with some of these policies – but the consensual/interventionist approach to economic management had to be seen to break down before the alternative – and the associated challenge to trade union power – became political feasible.

Lady Thatcher always said that she wanted to defeat socialism. In that she largely succeeded, both by undermining the main pillars of the old Labour order such as trade unions, local authorities and council housing and by forcing Labour leaders to shift to accept the main economic and social changes introduced by her governments. The election of Tony Blair as Labour leader in 1994 and his explicit acceptance, and praise for many of her achievements, is the clearest testament to her influence. The Blair government is interventionist and internationalist in a way that the Thatcher and post-Thatcher Conservative Party could not be, but it cannot seriously be described as socialist. The Blair government has accepted – and taken further – privatisation and the shift in the boundaries between the public and private sectors, has accepted the marginal tax rates it inherited and has modified but not rolled back the trade union laws of the Thatcher years. Of course, Mr Blair is not a Thatcherite, but his approach has been molded by the achievements of the Thatcher era and by the approach of Lady Thatcher herself.

What would have happened without her? The times were right for a shift in strategy. The weather had already begun to blow in her direction. There would probably have been a shift in fiscal and monetary policies away from the post-war Keynesian approach. This had anyway started under Labour and occurred in most other Western industrial countries, even those under left-wing governments. But the shift would probably have been slower, as in France. Similarly, it is doubtful whether, without Lady Thatcher's determination and will, privatisation or the roll back of trade union power would have been as extensive and radical as they became. Neither France nor Germany proceeded as rapidly in their privatisation programmes and they did not attempt to challenge trade union power.

Without Lady Thatcher, Britain would have changed, but less dramatically. The bruises and social divisions might have been less, but so would have been the economic changes for the better. She made a difference.

Returning in conclusion to Joseph Chamberlain – not the familiar epitaph in Enoch Powell's biography – 'all political careers end in failure . . .' – but Winston Churchill again: 'One mark of a great man is the power of making a lasting impression upon people he meets. Another is to have handled matters during his life that the course of after-events is continuously affected by what he did ... Those who met him in his vigour and heyday are always conscious of his keenly cut impression; and all our British affairs today are tangled, biased or inspired by his actions. He lighted beacon fires which are still burning; he sounded trumpet calls whose echoes still call stubborn soldiers to the field.'

Whatever caveats and reservations are made about the record of her administrations, and the unresolved conflicts she left on Europe, that epitaph could also apply to Margaret Thatcher. She defined an era in ways which all who lived through it will never forget.

I

The Intellectual and
Historical Roots of Thatcherism

The Ablation of a Mother:
Phoebe, Beatrice and Margaret

Leo Abse

I fear you will find this little essay churlish. It will hardly repay the tolerance extended to me by Hofstra University which, when engaged in a celebration that, to an outsider, seems to be an apotheosis of Margaret Thatcher, has extended this invitation to me on the basis of a hostile psycho-biography[1] and, doubtless, of the clashes I had with her on the floor of the House of Commons.

More, I do not doubt, its premises and conclusions will mobilise your resistance; and that is because not only are your political prejudices likely to be far different from mine, but because psychoanalytical interpretations of politics and politicians notoriously raise the hackles of so many political scientists, psephologists and, of course, politicians; but my legislative experience in Westminster for thirty years has long since caused me to believe that the protective armour of the practising politician, assuming the affectation of undiluted commitment to principle and community, and dismissing the ad hominem argument as a vulgar irrelevance in no way invalidating his manifesto, is paper thin. So many a politician, seeking to mask his needs and elevate his personal prejudices into principles, hates what he describes as 'personalisation' of politics even as he never ceases, narcissistically, to draw attention to his own personal attributes.

But politicians, having chosen to live upon the public stage, cannot claim the same rights of privacy to which the citizen is entitled; and in a nuclear age, when the public acting-out of private anguishes can lead to such ultimate catastrophe, we should not permit the politician to invoke the canons of taste and etiquette

21

when he seeks to protect himself against those who will not accept the old boundaries beyond which enquiry into motivation is required to halt.

On our side of the Atlantic some of us have noted, with some admiration, the courage of John McCain in placing his full psychiatric record before the nation. It is a vain hope, but I wish other politicians would follow his example; in the meantime, although denied the psychiatric or psychoanalytical material gained in the privacy of the consulting room when the therapist strives to unravel the infantile sources of current attitudes, nevertheless a psycho-biography, although necessarily more rough-hewn, can, I believe, be a needed admonitory exercise, an attempt to alert an over-acquiescent public.

That, then, is my inadequate apologia for stating dogmatically – as must be within a synoptic presentation – that there is no shortage of material in Thatcher's adult life to enable us to point unerringly at the pathogens she is carrying in her aetiolated affectional bonds with her mother which, in so many of her political stances, are so torridly displayed.

Prior to my publishing a psycho-biography of Thatcher, in her bizarre entry in *Who's Who* which she herself had composed, she brutally repudiated her mother by suppressing her very existence. In the entry she had simply described herself as the daughter of Alfred. She did not concede she was born of woman. She fantasises herself as an autochthonous Adam. 'Well of course,' she has said, 'I just owe everything to my father . . .' No acknowledgement is ever made of any indebtedness to her mother.

On one rare occasion when close questioning about her mother forced Thatcher to give some reply, her response was revealing for in the same sentence in which she protested her love she also denied she had had any relationship with her mother: 'I love my mother dearly but after I was fifteen we had nothing more to say to each other.' Realising that such an extraordinary response called for some addition, she proffered to puzzled listeners this explanation: 'It was not her fault; she was always weighed down by the home.' Since the home consisted of some rooms above a shop where two daughters and an active grandmother lived, the notion that household duties and chores weighed down the mother does not bear the slightest scrutiny. A contemporary at school and university with more accurate recall has said: 'So I used to feel just occasionally that she rather despised her mother and adored her father.'

The ablation of a parent, the denial of a biological past and an insistence upon being self-made with no umbilical link to a mother's womb is a phenomenon well-known to psychoanalysis. Such denials of one's ontology can result in an arrogant a-historicity, a blotting out of any debt to the past; the past, the parents, are erased; identity is claimed only by a depopulation of the psyche through a total exclusion of the parent figures.

In Thatcher's case, she has attempted to expel only one parent; the mother, Beatrice, has been sent into exile. But the affectation of psychological discontinuity is, of course, an illusion and achieved only by massive self-deception and inauthentic philosophy. Thatcher's selective caesura in her personal biography was part of the same condition that precipitated her 'radical' assault on the past – upon the historic Tory Party. Under Thatcher, the traditions of pragmatism and the domination of the Party by the aristocracy were swept aside; she wants no lineage. The past must be discouraged; when meeting students of history she notoriously and discouragingly informed them that their course was a luxury. She emerges from no womb, even the womb of time. And since she acknowledges no legacy she favours the self-made men. Her cabinet mirrored her own fantasised parthogenesis and the cabinet, it followed, was to consist only of men. No hint of a mother image was permitted in Downing Street, only men in her father's image.

Those whose psychic structure bears disproportionately the impact of an idealised father image, as does Thatcher's, function in such a way as to compensate for their lack of a sufficiently empathic mother. The baby needs an approving mirror for healthy exhibitionism; denied this by an unresponsive and negative mother, Thatcher turned in compensation to the father, trying first absurdly to idealise and then to integrate into her own self the father's abilities, skills and values. Thatcher's constant public recall and over-valuation of her father, a small town councillor with many frailties and of no special significance, tells us of her use of a compensatory technique enabling her to function; but the injury resulting from her denial of the mother remains. It is my belief that the deep wound the shadowy mother inflicted upon Margaret Thatcher's narcissism has never healed. All the decades I sat opposite her confirmed to me how overwhelmingly her primal narcissistic rage invaded every issue to which she addressed herself. She was happy – indeed she seemed only

23

to exist – when she was furious; only then did she regain the self-esteem she was not granted in her cradle.

It will be recalled that Margaret was Beatrice's second child, born five years after her sister Muriel. When a second daughter is born to a woman without a son it is often experienced as a disappointment and this may have contributed to the mother's lack of a positive relationship with her child, but more firmly established is the consequence of Margaret Thatcher's living-in maternal grandmother, Phoebe Stevenson, who evidently ruled the crowded household even if downstairs Alderman Roberts, the father, ruled his shop. Phoebe, Thatcher has told us, was 'very, very Victorian and very, very strict'. Margaret Thatcher's mother could not give her the warm response which she in turn had never received from her martinet mother.

The narcissistic deprivation which Thatcher endured and her constant ceaseless fury reverberated around our domestic politics and was dangerously injected into the conduct of Britain's foreign affairs. Too often the babe, denied the reassurance that her mother does belong to her, and that she has often consequently omnipotent control over her mother, becomes chronically and traumatically frustrated. Then chronic narcissistic rages with all their deleterious consequences can become established and can herald their later ideational companions – the conviction that the environment is essentially inimical. A paranoid impress is etched into the adult individual perception of the outside world. When determining patronage within her own party, Thatcher asked: 'Is he one of us?' If enemies are not in existence, they will be created; no area of consensus politics must be permitted – the split between her side and the other must be total.

While some ambivalence in all human relationships is natural and unavoidable, Thatcher will not tolerate it; persons, philosophies and institutions are all perceived as either friend or foe. Under no circumstances can she tolerate consensus. Casting herself as a prophet, she once told a rally: 'Old Testament prophets did not say 'Brothers, I want consensus'; they said 'this is my faith and vision. This is what I passionately believe.'' The lineaments of Thatcher's considerable failure to advance to a more integrated albeit slightly ambivalent phase are embossed upon her personality structure.

During all the elections I fought against Thatcher I was always aware that my real opponents were Beatrice Roberts and the grandmother who for the first ten years of Margaret Thatcher's life enveloped the household. These women of so little public importance in their lifetimes ruled us from their graves, for their denials and their imposed frustrations left Margaret Thatcher with no affection for any legislative action that could recall the qualities with which mothers less atypical than Beatrice Roberts can so bountifully endow: to nurse and nourish, to care and tolerate, improve and preserve. The welfare state, the National Health Service were, and are, for Thatcher but mother surrogates, necessary evils which only electoral considerations inhibited her from totally destroying. When she publicly considered what her aptitudes are, Thatcher declared herself as 'eminently suitable as a prime minister' but, significantly, stressed her lack of qualifications to be a nurse. The cycle of emotional deprivation inexorably and inevitably revealed itself in all her assessments of the institutional fabric of British society and continues to pervade her stamp upon every extant political issue.

The unresponsive mother is not only the precipitate prompting the content of Thatcher's political policies; the mother determined too her dangerous political style. Political journalists so often stressed how she thrived on confrontation and crisis, and languishes, in her own estimation, when calm interludes occur in public affairs. Tory political columnists, sympathising with her policies and revelling in the success of her turbulence, only mourned that her attacks were so indiscriminate. But here the style is the woman and she lacks the freedom to focus her aggression; she is driven always to attack and the force driving her is unmitigated.

Insightful paediatricians have illuminated the source of such compulsiveness. They have shown the consequences that arise in adult behaviour when the woman, as a baby, lacks the good care which allows a fusion of her aggression and eroticism. The motility which existed in the intra-uterine life as the babe kicks in the womb, and which exists when an infant of a few weeks thrashes away with its arms, is the precursor to the aggression which has to be positively and meaningfully directed at specific targets if the child is to become a well-rounded person. For some, the environmental chance which enables the baby to ensure an integration of the personality is denied and he does not become the healthy adult whose behaviour is purposive and whose aggression is meaningfully focused; these are the sick whose aggression is expressed like the babes who, without direction, kick in the womb or thrash away with their arms and upon whom we project the notion that he means to hit when, in fact, we have no right to make such an assumption. They are, in short, the men and women who have not lived their earliest times constantly discovering and redis-covering their environment by using their motility, as they snuggle and struggle within their mother's arms; they have not enjoyed that primal erotic experience within which they can fuse their aggression and love. For them, contact with the environment has been an experience of the individual; having lacked loving care, they lack a series of individual experiences helping them on their way to integration, and have suffered only an environment which was felt as an impingement.

The tragedy of men and women who have suffered such an early fate is that, as adults, they must constantly expose themselves to opposition which is vigor-ous if not dangerous. Only in aggressive reactions to impingement can they feel real; and if the opposition is not in existence it must be provoked. Thatcher illustrates the hazards to the public weal when a politician needs constant polit-ical turbulence to ward off fears of personal dissolutions.

During her leadership, Thatcher was compelled to mount new provocations – sometimes she selected the National Health Service, at other times the dock-ers, and sometimes the targets were the miners. More recently her provocations prompted the long-suffering and patient British premier John Major, in his autobiography, to describe her behaviour during his premiership as 'intolerable'. But she cannot resist, for there is no stillness in the woman; always she must be on the attack. The true base for the effective binding and modification of aggres-sive impulses is found in the essentially non-verbal communication received by the baby as he is held in love and safety in the mother's arms; and the baby can be strengthened by the mother's calm voice and by the reassuring lullaby. I believe Thatcher lacked such an early blessing and that therefore to restrain her-self from slipping into more primitive forms of aggression than is her wont, she uses words, even more than most politicians, to mollify her anxiety. For, with the end of early childhood, mitigation and control of the aggressive drive is effect-ed by verbalisation; from then on, words are expected to take the place of mus-cular action. Dirty words must take the place of dirty actions such as protesting defecation; verbal abuse must take the place of physical attack; not for nothing has the dictum stressed that the man who first hurled words of abuse against his enemy instead of a spear was the founder of civilisation. I believe that unconsciously Thatcher fears that she will yield to her aggressiveness, regress to a display of violence in a frighteningly savage form; verbalisation is the uncertain dam which resists and blocks the ebb-tide of aggression that may otherwise engulf her.

And all her intemperate prolixity, all her talk, all her evangelising, is conducted frenetically, incessantly. She unashamedly has declared herself a workaholic – as if the addiction to work had none of the pejorative overtones of an addiction to alcohol; but all the compulsive battling and interfering has in public affairs a shadowy side as well as a positive value and reflects the fragility of a basic self; work is the glue keeping her together. In an interview when she was still insisting that she was going to go on with her premiership she said: 'Why, I can never, never let up.' That was because she had not then found a worthy successor but the real explanation was that it was she, not the country, that was in danger of falling to bits if she desisted from her hyper-activity; for she had never received from her unresponsive mother the needed corroboration of a vigorous and healthy narcissism. I believe she did not see herself as the gleam in her mother's eye – for there was no gleam; the baby, deprived of the needed stimulating responses, lacking the assurance of joyful responses to her aliveness, can be depleted of self-esteem and be left with a residual disposition towards depressing emptiness in adult life; the philanderer, the promiscuous homosexual and the drug addict are all desperately seeking the over-stimulation of manic excitement to gain the stimulation initially denied them, for without their excitement they feel they will fall to pieces and the workaholic, though sometimes less obviously driven and less anti-social, is indeed no less afflicted with the syndrome.

I believe Thatcher is a woman who dare not stop; her aggressive hypo-manic activity is her defence against depression. In stillness she would collapse inwards. Her conduct in the House of Commons reflected her inner depressiveness. When an eloquent rapier thrust or some droll gaffe was made in the Commons, the whole House laughed but Thatcher rarely joined in the fun. The mothering smile was never bestowed upon her, and although she can jeer, the spontaneous laugh is not part of her equipment. The frown, not the genuine smile, is her emblem. And with that frown, affirming her independence of the mother, mocking the bonds of society – 'there is no such thing as society' – and asserting extravagantly the values of individualism, she conquers America and increasingly estranges herself from Britain.

Notes

1 Editor's note: see Leo Abse, *Margaret, Daughter of Beatrice: A Politician's Psycho-Biography of Margaret Thatcher* (London: Jonathan Cape, 1989).

Mrs Thatcher's Liberties

Alan Allport

History's lessons usually teach us what we want to learn

Margaret Thatcher, 1995[1]

Was Mrs Thatcher a freedom fighter? Ten years since her precipitous fall from office – or treacherous shove, if you will – the answer remains unsettled. To apostles of the creed, there is little question: freedom rarely received such a dogmatic protectrix as Margaret Thatcher. She reversed more than forty years of state encroachment on the property and rights of the British people. Public sector loafers, flying pickets, obfuscating Whitehall officials, loony councilors with a taste for Marxist dialectic and rate hikes – all were duly handbagged. Mrs Thatcher's great achievement was the 'rolling back of the state,' the chipping away of four decades of collectivist detritus that had stifled economic performance and personal freedom for decades. Her international achievement was perhaps even greater. By restoring pride in the core values of liberal capitalism, above all by defending British sovereignty in the Falkland Islands against fierce military opposition, she invigorated the West in its Manichean struggle with the Communist bloc and encouraged the collapse of that feeble and despotic institution.[2]

That is one version. Mrs Thatcher's critics have a rather different one. To them, all that the 'rolling back the state' amounted to in practical terms was the demolition of any intermediary institution – local government, the civil service, independent broadcasting – that stood in the way of the prime ministerial will. Far from relaxing centralised control over British life, Mrs Thatcher's administration inaugurated a decade of creeping authoritarianism in which the state was given extraordinary leeway to infringe upon traditional privileges of information, of privacy, and of public dissent. Partly, this interference was justified in the name of 'security' – though whether Zircon, Death on the Rock and the Spycatcher debacle were more about sparing ministerial blushes than national defence is a moot point. But there was more to the Nanny State than just keeping secrets. Mrs Thatcher had a taste for social engineering. Britons' faults were not in their stars but in themselves, she told them: nothing less than the reconstruction of the national character would reverse a century of decline. It was the task of her government, she felt, not merely to provide the apparatus of economic growth but also to tinker with British culture. Patriotism, temperance, thrift, piety, sexual rectitude, endless, endless self-improvement – these were the virtues to be inculcated in the people. How, it is fair to ask, did Mrs Thatcher reconcile that commitment to hands-off government with her seemingly interminable wish to stick her nose in where prime ministerial beaks had rarely ventured before?

This essay is concerned with the curious resulting phenomena, the two Margaret Thatchers. One of them, Millian Margaret, was a good nineteenth-century liberal who believed in the citizen as autonomous actor – a vessel of absolute personal sovereignty whose freedom of choice must always be maximised without regard to the pretensions of government or any nebulous concept of social justice. But then there was her High Tory alter-ego, Burkean Margaret, who insisted that society was a collection of fragile moral truths that had to be carefully husbanded, if necessary at the expense of individual preference. Millian Margaret hacked away at the paternalistic shackles of the state, selling off council houses, trimming tax burdens and deregulating industrial monopolies. Burkean Margaret harangued the BBC for its insufficient displays of patriotism, stiffened divorce laws, and fretted about the licentiousness of 'Yoof'. One sought to furnish 'a man room to breathe, to take responsibility, to make his own decisions and to chart his own course': [3] the other assailed civil servants who questioned whether government policy ought to make moral distinctions. [4] There even seemed to be a different Britain for each Prime Minister. Thatcher the libertarian yearned for a dynamic, Americanised society, cutting-edge and iconoclastic, staffed with go-getting entrepreneurs. Thatcher the traditionalist, like her successor, preferred Orwell's pastoral vision of warm beer, suet pudding and red pillar-boxes. If an old maid could not be guaranteed to cycle to Communion through the morning mists of every Conservative constituency – for old maids were a closed shop in serious decline – then a determined effort would nonetheless be made to recreate the mental atmosphere of, say, Dixon of Dock Green.

If Mrs Thatcher saw no contradiction between these world-views, it was because she felt she had a historical precedent to demonstrate their reconcilability. For all the talk of Victorian values during her premiership, it was not really the nineteenth century from which she took inspiration. As Patrick Middleton has pointed out, Mrs Thatcher's prescription for society bore little resemblance to that epoch of vast, sweeping social dislocation. Rather, she seems to have had in mind her Grantham home of the 1930s, recalled with such genuine affection and admiration in her 1995 memoir, *The Path to Power*. Depression-era Lincolnshire was the appropriate model for freedom; Alfred Roberts' specialist grocer's, the benchmark of moral and economic equity. As Middleton says,

What she has done is to recollect the moral order of her girlhood (she was born in 1925) and project it back on to the Victorian period. In other words, what she is really recommending is a return to 'Georgian' values – those which were dominant between the end of the First World War and the middle of the 1950s.[5]

Mrs Thatcher believed that her childhood world represented an effective balance between the operation of the market and a traditional, socially cohesive community – a proper equilibrium between liberty and moral order. It was this prelapsarian vision, fallen by the temptations of Mr Butskell, that she strove to recreate. But the project proved unworkable. Partly, because her model was a caricature, ignoring the traits of 1930s Britain that fitted less comfortably into the mythos. But mostly it was because she did not recognise that her economic deregulation would exacerbate, not reverse, social dissolution; that the very generation of wealth her reforms inaugurated would eat away at customary mores in a way that could not simply be blamed on fuzzy 1960s permissiveness. Baldwinian certainties – unquestioning fealty to Church, Queen, Country, and all the ancient shibboleths of Middle England – were shattered, perhaps irrevocably, by Mrs Thatcher's economic miracle.

By the time that she became Prime Minister, the 1930s were a decade in need of some rehabilitation. Damned for the miseries of the dole queue and the doomed inconstancy of the Appeasers, the political establishment agreed that the period was 'a bad thing: a class-ridden age of unnecessary poverty and inequality, led by governments who wilfully ignored the possibility of making things better'.[6] In the Academy, opinions were more divided: new histories like Stevenson and Cook's 1978 *The Slump* sought to modify the popular view by pointing out a considerable growth in ordinary living standards and opportunities during the inter-war years.[7] But the enlightened consensus remained unmoved: the 1930s were a warning, not a model. Biography played a significant part in this communal rejection. Most of the leading political figures of the late 1970s came of age somewhere between Munich and D-Day; the principal ministers in Mrs Thatcher's first cabinet had almost all served in the wartime military or won their political spurs in the Chamberlain imbroglio.[8] To politicians of their generation, the iconography of the 1930s was singularly incriminating: Love on the Dole, Jarrow, Cato's *Guilty Men*. Innocent, ignorant and ineffectual, the pre-war condition of England might be admired for its anachronistic charms in a Brideshead kind of way, but it was no sensible archetype for a modern society.

Mrs Thatcher saw things differently. Scarcely a teenager at the outbreak of war, her experience of the 1930s was juvenile, parochial and favourable. Elder Tories had personally witnessed the moral crumbling of the National Government from the vantage point of Westminster, or been seduced by the rough and ready egalitarianism of the armed forces. Margaret Roberts, cramming for her Somerville scholarship in the austere but sheltered auspices of a provincial market town, missed these defining moments. For her, the crucial turning point would be 1945, Churchill's drubbing at the polls and the triumph of the democratic Left, a tumble into the errors of economic collectivism that only served to highlight the benign characteristics of her childhood years. As Mrs Thatcher saw it, hers had been the 'normal' experience. Patrician Conservatives may have dabbled in wartime socialism as a squire's conceit, but she was the representative of the ordinary folk, unusually qualified to 'address people who spoke the same language . . . and had lived the same sort of life'.[9] The view from Grantham was the authentic experience of the common man and woman, not distorted by the aberrations of privilege guilt.

'Most of us probably recall our earliest years as a sort of blur. Mine was an idyllic blur.'[10] Indeed, the specialty grocer's shop of North Parade, Grantham, is revealed to us in Mrs Thatcher's memoirs as a seat of homespun virtue, exemplary of the mixture of Smilesian entrepreneurship and Nonconformist self-denial that characterised the essence of her 1930s. The Roberts were tireless, uncomplaining and frugal. Their lives revolved around the improving spectacle of Chapel, Sunday School, civic organisations and private charity. If Methodism had an unfortunate Peacenik bent – many Wesleyans were active pacifists – it did at least extol the requirements of thrift and practical labour. Demands were strict on the Roberts' time. But beyond the grocery lay a self-supporting town community, stitched together with fierce local patriotisms that reinforced the lessons of the hearth; and beyond that were Nation and Dominions, a vast global engine of British worthiness, owned and administered by the King-Emperor to the mutual satisfaction of all. While later generations of politicians may have dwelt in unseemly detail on the labour exchange and the means test, to Mrs Thatcher the 1930s gave a benign instruction:

The 'lessons' I drew were quite different . . . the kind of life that the people of Grantham had lived before the war was a decent and wholesome one, and its values were shaped by the community rather than by the government.[11]

Of course, even accepting that this is an accurate biographical account – which it probably is[12] – still leaves the general applicability of Mrs Thatcher's memoirs open to question. In Grantham itself, the Roberts, highly respected as they were, were considered far from ordinary in their behaviour.[13] There are even fewer grounds for supposing that many people in 1930s Britain were as energised as Mrs Thatcher's family by the appeal of PT exercises, annual stocktaking and Evening Service. Methodism was waning at an alarming rate, far faster than the long moribund Anglican Church; in the thirty years before the outbreak of war the number of Congregationalist Sunday scholars fell by almost half.[14] Malcolm Muggeridge's mischievous but invaluable record of the decade, *The Thirties* (1940), reminds us that the average newspaper reader was as concerned with the fate of the original tabloid naughty vicar, the Rector of Stiffkey, as Abyssinia. The Depression is allotted a couple of inches in Mrs Thatcher's record; she notes that the children of the unemployed were 'very neatly turned out'.[15] J.B. Priestley's obsolete Gateshead underclass, 'undisciplined and carefree, the dinghy butterflies of the back streets', has no place in this tidy backdrop.[16] By extrapolating too casually the circumstances of one relatively fortunate and conscientious household, Mrs Thatcher produces a version of history of questionable relevance to the experience of the nation.

Nonetheless, if her point is that the social milieu of the 1930s was more traditional, restrained and cohesive than that of three or four decades later – that familial and civic ties were stronger, allegiance to conventional pieties greater, and overt challenges to the standing order of God, Crown and Empire much less common – then she is clearly on the right track. Most people who lived through the period recognise that it was one of remarkable moral and social stability. The question that arises, then, is why. To Mrs Thatcher, the constancy of the inter-war order was intimately tied to the virtues of unfettered private commerce. There is a nicely drawn illustration of her introduction to this truth at the opening of *The Downing Street Years*. The scene is the shop floor of the Grantham specialist grocer's; surrounded by the mahogany spice drawers and the black lacquered tea canisters, Alfred Roberts describes the complex trade arrangements that ensure the efficient transfer of Indian rice, Kenyan coffee and Caribbean sugar from far-off plantations to the breakfast tables of North Parade. Young Margaret is instructed that:

The free market [is] like a vast sensitive nervous system, responding to events and signals all over the world to meet the ever changing needs of peoples in different countries, from different classes, of different religions, with a kind of benign indifference to their status. [17]

Mr Roberts taught that liberty of economic exchange was far more than just a useful engine of wealth creation. It underwrote a whole moral order of self-respect, attachment to the common good, and shared group identity. Reliance upon personal accomplishments instilled in communities the necessary traits of hard work, thrift, pride in oneself and one's country; it was the bedrock of genuine freedom in that it allowed the natural penalties and rewards of social behaviour to operate to their maximum extent. Industry triumphed over sloth, irreverence received its appropriate censure, wickedness was trammelled by swift public response; Smith's Invisible Hand, by the aggregation of millions of individual choices, ensured as just and favourable an outcome for society as the marketplace. In this way were Millian Margaret and Burkean Margaret reconciled.

What rotted away this happy conjunction of virtues was the ascendancy of the state in the years immediately following the end of the Second World War. The stunting of economic progress by the dead hand of nationalisation, uncontrolled public spending and punitive taxation was bad enough in itself. But what was worse was the replacement of conventional taboos by the 'callous, selfish and irresponsible'[18] influence of liberal reforms from the 1960s onwards. Just as financial liberty and the maintenance of a mutually self-supporting social order were of a pair, so statism and permissiveness were but two sides of the same tarnished coin. While sapping the entrepreneurial will, government ate away at the fragile social bonds that kept neighbourhoods together by a fallacious appeal to moral relativism and an overbearing but negligent assumption of authority in loco parentis. 'Socialism had literally demoralised communities and families, offering dependency in place of independence as well as subjecting traditional values to sustained derision'.[19] By 1979 the social indicators told the story. As the state's control of the economy grew, so did the crime and divorce figures; extended family structures crumbled, battered by repeated waves of delinquency. Respect for elders, community heritage and national symbols of authority were at their nadir. The reconstruction of Britain would involve not only a tightening of the public purse strings but also an end to faddish leftist theory and the destructive paternalism of government.

There are a couple of ways to think about this. It is worth considering, first of all, the extent to which government really did adopt a hands-off attitude to economics and society in the Thatcherite heyday of the 1930s. Certainly, one wonders if those elegant disquisitions on the free market conducted between the mahogany drawers and the tea canisters of the Roberts shop floor were ever soured by a knowledge of Imperial Preference. Expenditure by public authorities as a proportion of the national income had risen to over 30 per cent on average during the inter-war years, isolating the period far more from the laissez-faire of the pre-1914 generation than from the welfare state to come.[20] Government intervention in the form of National Insurance and Assistance, workers' compensation, pensions and health benefits inextricably combined the interests of the state with the fortunes of the masses. Whatever the properties of the Idyllic Blur may have been, a night-watchman state was not one of them; the involvement of government in the daily life of its citizenry was an established fact of the 1930s.

Why did the social cohesion that Mrs Thatcher recalled with some acuity steadily erode during the final years of the twentieth century? It is certainly reasonable to argue that a major part was played by the enlargement of just those liberties of information, social mobility and consumer choice that good Thatcherites so extol. If 1930s Britain was a cosier, more intimate, less outwardly acrimonious society than it is today, this was as much due to sheer absence of opportunity as it was some pietistic quality of the marketplace. Economic fear played its role. The inter-war years saw the cost of living fall just enough to strip some of the radical sheen off of mass politics without raising expectations sufficiently to have much social impact. Working people were materially a little better off than their Edwardian parents, but their consciousness of potential disaster made them cling just as tightly to notions of conventional respectability. Mrs Thatcher records that life for many Grantham families was a perilous balancing act between propriety and woe:

They lived on a knife edge and feared if some accident hit them, or if they relaxed their standards of thrift and diligence, they might be plunged into debt and poverty.[21]

'This precariousness,' she notes, 'often made otherwise good people hard and unforgiving.' It certainly reinforced their commitment to the status quo.

Media manipulation played its role too. The British Board of Film Censors' dictum that 'nothing will be passed which is calculated to demoralise the public' translated in practice to an avoidance of anything smacking of social dissidence, not merely in sexual or behavioural mores but in attitudes towards all of the symbols of the existing order.[22] The 1930s was a decade in which the Gentleman in Whitehall, knowing best as usual, was able to exercise extraordinary control over popular media by the powers of legal monopoly. The BBC seeded its Reithian earnestness across the stratosphere, unimpeded by the strains of competition, while the press, albeit with a more vulgar cadence, also avoided distressing the limits of conventionality. Even the fate of the Rector of Stiffkey, eaten by lions in an appropriate nod to the Early

Martyrs, was a terrible warning about the fate of the socially heterodox. With higher education still the provenance of the wealthy few, there was scant opportunity for the general public to learn about or propagate alternatives to their traditional lifestyle even if they had had the purchasing power to put change into effect.

When change did come, ten to fifteen years later, it was greatly assisted by the growth of wage-earning potential and financial independence. As the pay packets of young employees fattened, so teenagers and twenty-somethings became consumers with a viable subculture of their own. Greater flexibility in the job market allowed many women to work out of the home for the first time, and encouraged the movement of labour from old urban areas to the ribbon developments of the light industrial suburbs – both trends loosening the ties of traditional family structures. Access to exotic retail goods and services broke down parochial mindsets; working class youths went to university, travelled abroad, and saw less need for the familiar but often stultifying constraints of their parents' world. Information flowed faster and in less regulated a form. Commercial television and radio gave new outlets for opinion and ideas, encouraging scepticism about the formerly sacrosanct. Some developments were less welcome. Crime rose steadily from the mid-1950s onwards, a tribute in its perverse way to the material rewards of the post-war boom and the covetousness that it provoked in the bored, frustrated and jealous. New choices in marital behaviour and working patterns brought with them the broken home and the latchkey child. But these disagreeable novelties cannot simply be teased apart from the rest of social history or isolated in some lurid specimen jar marked 'fuzzy liberal nonsense'; they were part of the changes taking place in civic life encouraged by economic licence and an unprecedented rise in the standard of living.[23]

The point here is not that social transformation is inherently a good or a bad thing. The innocent communality of the 1930s naturally conjures up a certain amount of nostalgia, although its harsher traits – its austerity, its intolerance, its unblinking submission to authority – also remind us of the benefits we have accrued from a half-century of cultural relaxation. The point is rather that change was an inherent by-product of the free market opportunities opened up by the post-war world and accelerated by the

Conservative governments of the 1980s and 1990s. In other contexts, the liberties that created the British social revolution of the last fifty years are lauded by Mrs Thatcher and her supporters: the repeal of entrepreneurial constraints, the free flow of labour and capital, media deregulation. But the social cohesion that she admired about 1930s Grantham was backed up by the same kind of restrictive practices that her reforms as Prime Minister were intended to demolish.

Take, say, the abolition of Retail Price Maintenance in 1964. Was there ever a more indefensible curtailment of free high-street competition than RPM? Its passing allowed the creation of the supermarket giants that dominate the modern British retail economy and provide a range of choice and price sensitivity unknown forty years ago.[24] And yet it was only through the application of such arbitrary restrictions as RPM that the likes of specialist grocer Alfred Roberts could hope to stay in business. Small family-run corner shops such as the Roberts' provided limited stock and inflexible pricing; they were also an important constituent of that complex, brittle fabric of local relationships that made towns like Grantham so much more cohesive before the Second World War than today. Then we had inefficient trade and communal stability; now we have absolute consumer choice and scarcely know our neighbours. The two things are not wholly accidental.[25]

Or consider broadcasting, the legislative area that saw the Thatcher government at perhaps its most schizophrenic. The BBC and ITN duopoly offended against the administration's instinct for the expansion of market opportunities; in that sense, it was natural that reform would see the old closed shop torn down and the airwaves opened up to free competition. But, as connoisseurs of Live TV's topless darts and dwarf throwing can presumably confirm, the result has largely been to exacerbate those programming tendencies – triviality, tackiness, a disinclination 'to uphold the great institutions and liberties of the country'[26] – that brought the duopoly into such disfavour in the first place. But if she really wanted to recreate the sly, harmonising influence of the Home Service, then a small clique was exactly what she was going to need.

The political philosopher John Gray, in his 1984 work *Hayek on Liberty*, illustrates the paradox of a Burkean reverence for the past accompanied by a taste for economic liberalism: 'Curiously, that last possibility is one that Hayek never considers,'[27] says Gray. The same appears to have been true of his Finchley protégé.

———————

Notes

1   Margaret Thatcher, *The Path to Power* (New York: HarperCollins, 1995), p.118.

2   Analyses of Thatcherism can be categorised by their belief, apostasy, or agnosticism. Mrs Thatcher provides her own uncompromising defence in *The Downing Street Years* (New York: HarperCollins, 1993), while the memoirs of her former colleague, Lord Ian Gilmour, in *Dancing With Dogma* (London: Simon & Schuster, 1992) are an eloquent expression of the Tory 'wet' position. This author has found two third-party works of particular help: Lord Robert Blake's recently revised *Conservative Party from Peel to Major* (London: Heinemann, 1998) is an arresting narrative that puts Thatcherism in its broad historical context, while Hugo Young's *One of Us* (London: Pan, 1990) is the best and most detailed biographical study of Mrs Thatcher yet available.

3   Speech to the Conservative Party Conference, Blackpool, 13 October, 1989. Reprinted in Robin Harris, ed., *The Collected Speeches of Margaret Thatcher* (London: HarperCollins, 1997), p. 350.

4   Thatcher, *Downing Street Years*, p. 629.

5   Patrick Middleton, 'For 'Victorian', Read 'Georgian': Mrs Thatcher Corrected', in *Encounter*, July-August 1986, pp. 5–9.

6   John Baxendale, *Narrating the Thirties* (New York: St. Martin's Press, 1996), p. 141.

7   Ibid., pp. 161–166.

8   Carrington and Whitelaw had been in the Guards. Hailsham, as Qintin Hogg, was the establishment candidate at the notorious 1938 Oxford by-election, later renouncing his Appeasement past. Wartime service was not, of course, a sufficient condition for wetness: Sir Keith Joseph, arch iconoclast of the post-1945 consensus, had a distinguished military record.

9   Thatcher, *Downing Street Years*, p.10.

10 Thatcher, *Path to Power*, p. 3.

11 Ibid., p. 31.

12 See Young, pp. 3–13.

13 'The Roberts family were very strict Methodists and used to go to Church twice or three times on Sunday. Mr Roberts himself was a lay preacher... although he took a daily paper he wouldn't, for example, take a Sunday paper.' Grantham resident John Foster, quoted in Hugo Young and Anne Sloman, *The Thatcher Phenomenon* (London: BBC Books, 1986), p.15.

14 Angus Calder, *The People's War* (New York: Ace Books, 1969), p. 551. Calder quotes the historian of Methodism, R.F. Wearmouth, on the 'silent disappearance' of the traditional social expressions of the Wesleyan faith during the inter-war period.

15 Thatcher, *Path to Power*, p. 23.

16 J. B. Priestley, *English Journey* (Harmondsworth: Penguin, 1981), p. 288.

17 Thatcher, *Downing Street Years*, p. 11.

18 Thatcher, *Path to Power*, p. 152.

19   Thatcher, *Downing Street Years*, p. 625.

20   Figures from A.J.P. Taylor, *English History 1914–1945* (Oxford: University Press, 1965), p. xxvii.

21   Thatcher, *Path to Power*, p. 6.

22   Quoted in Middleton, p. 7.

23   See Arthur Marwick, *British Society since 1945* (Harmondsworth: Penguin, 1996), esp. pp. 141–153.

24   Mrs Thatcher personally approved of the repeal of RPM (see Thatcher, *Path to Power*, p. 131). She records that the decision, while correct, was politically ill-timed because of the dissension it created among Conservative small businessmen on the eve of a general election.

25   As John Foster notes, 'Mr Roberts had a very successful business. It's not the sort of business that would be successful these days with supermarkets.' Young and Sloman, p. 15.

26   Thatcher, *Downing Street Years*, p. 637.

27   John Gray, *Hayek on Liberty* (London: Routledge, 1998), pp. 153–154.

Two Nations:
From Disraeli to Thatcher and Beyond

Arianna Huffington

———

Two nations, between whom there is no intercourse and no sympathy; who are ignorant of each other's habits, thoughts, and feelings as if they were dwellers in different zones or inhabitants of different planets; who are formed by a different breeding, are fed by different food, are ordered by different manners, and are not governed by the same laws . . . the rich and the poor.
      Benjamin Disraeli, Sybil, or The Two Nations, *1845, book II, chapter 5*

My first exhilarating memory of Margaret Thatcher is being in my car in London in February 1975 – I was living there at the time – and hearing on the radio that she had defeated the Conservative establishment and had become the leader of the Tory Party. I remember cheering in my car, partly because up until that moment, the conventional wisdom among the pundits in England was that this could never happen; that you could never get a woman of a modest background to defeat the Tory grandees. And yet she issued her challenge and she did it, and it was a really truly exhilarating moment.

There are really two very significant lessons that Margaret Thatcher has to teach to politicians here – of both parties, incidentally, since both parties have largely become indistinguishable. The one lesson is born of her victories, her triumphs, and the other lesson is born of her defeats. And it's in the second lesson that Benjamin Disraeli will be central, but to the first lesson first.

Speaking to a group – a packed hall, actually – in Cardiff, just before the 1979 election, Margaret Thatcher said, 'I've learned something from you, in a way, because when you have a message, you preach it, wherever you are. And I too am

41

a conviction politician'. She truly was a conviction politician; and what a rare breed they are today here. When we're surrounded by politicians driven by focus groups and pollsters, who really do not utter a sentence – do not choose a tie in the morning – without consulting polling results, who can hardly remember what it is like to be a conviction politician, who are driven by ideas and a passion for ideas and not just a passion for power. We see Al Gore redefining himself as a passionate campaign finance reformer, putting forward an entire agenda for that. It is so unconvincing and so deeply shameless that it makes you long for the kind of politician that Margaret Thatcher was.

She took on the fatuity and the complacency of the Tory Party as it was before she became the leader, and it's precisely the same kind of complacency that we see in the political establishment today, as for example Trent Lott and Mitch McConnell welcomed back to the Senate, and John McCain chastened by his defeat, his tail between his legs, coming in to join the very party that he lambasted for an entire year. So there they are again, in supreme control, just as entrenched as the Tory Party looked before Margaret Thatcher became its leader.

So this is the first tremendous gift, really, that Margaret Thatcher can bring to anybody who cares to go back and study how she did it, the kind of courage she displayed, and the spine she demonstrated in the face of incredible odds. Immediately after she became the leader of the Tory Party, the same pundits who had said this would never happen vied with each other to explain why this was inevitable all along; which was my first great lesson in media group-think.

Now, to move on to her defeats. There is no question that, although in *The Path to Power*, the second volume of her memoir, she says at one point that tax cuts were not intended merely to give people more of their own money to spend, but to have more money to help the old and the sick and the handicapped, but that is really more of an aside for her. She never recognised these as a central pillar of a private enterprise revolution. And that's where she would have learned tremendous lessons herself if she had studied Benjamin Disraeli, a Tory who actually had proved that social justice and preoccupations with issues of fairness and social justice are not, and should never be, left to be the prerogatives of the Left. And when Benjamin Disraeli, in the 1840s, before he became Prime Minister, wrote of the danger of England degenerating into two nations, between whom there is no sympathy, as if they were inhabitants of different planets, that's exactly where we are today here in America. Truly, we have become two nations. One nation is benefiting from the growing prosperity, from the high Dow Jones, and is part of our political conversation. The other nation is not even part of the political conversation anymore. For the first time, both parties have abandoned it. When you have the president of the United States stand up during his State of the Union address and say, 'The state of our union has never been stronger,' it is a truly hubristic statement that ignores the realities of thirty-six million people living below the poverty line, more homeless children than we've ever had since the Great Depression. Of those people living below the poverty line, fifteen million are children. At the same time, more bankruptcies than ever before, more people living beyond their means than ever before, more college kids burdened with credit card debt. But they're all part of the other nation, because our nation – the one nation that politicians of both parties are concerned with – is the nation that votes, and the other nation has given up on voting as well. And that's another preoccupation that doesn't bother either party at all. They're very content with the diminishing universe of voters, down to 36 per cent in the last election. The more diminished, the easier it is to manipulate and control.

So as a result, what Benjamin Disraeli knew – and knew brilliantly – because even before he became Prime Minister, when he wrote his novels he said in 1867, the year before he became Prime Minister, that 'I had to prepare the mind of the country and to educate our party'. So he knew that leadership is about building a new consensus around problems before they become crises. And that's exactly what's missing today. There is no interest in building a new consensus. There is only interest in following polling results, where the public is right now. What do they want right now? We're going to tell them exactly what they tell us in the polls they want to hear. We're going to vie with each other to tell them what they want to hear. And as a result, major looming crises are not being addressed in this presidential race.

In the same way that Margaret Thatcher ignored some of the issues addressed in Alan Allport's essay – Burkean issues such as how do you build a good society? – free market may create the best conditions for wealth production, but it does not create the best conditions for a good society. And to pretend, as so many of my friends on the Right continue to pretend, that if you just deregulate everything and worship daily at the altar of supply-side economics, then a good society of which you can be proud somehow will emerge by miracle, is to really continue to preach these things in the face of overwhelming evidence to the contrary.

I remember studying economics at Cambridge and spending a lot of my time in the Marshall Library, named after Alfred Marshall, one of the founders of private enterprise economics. And he said – and said again and again – that capitalism cannot survive without economic chivalry. 'Economic chivalry' was his term for a generosity of spirit, for a kind of concern for those left out of the good times, that is lacking tremendously in our culture and in our country here today.

And that's something that Margaret Thatcher frankly was not really passionate about, and even not really greatly aware of. Just imagine how different the history of her reign, and of the Conservative Party, and of England, would have been if she had recognised this as a central pillar of a private enterprise economy. If she had used her bully pulpit and her great megaphone to preach that; to preach social responsibility, not just private responsibility, and to address the issues that we still have not addressed in this country of what happens after the Great Society programmes have been proven not to work. It's not enough to say, well, we'll just 'end welfare as we know it' and then everything will somehow take care of itself, because clearly it hasn't and it won't. And to look at new models that are being discussed everywhere around this country – but not within the political conversation – of social entrepreneurship, of identifying what works on the ground and taking it to market is exactly the debate that we need to be having. But our model here is Disraeli and not Margaret Thatcher.

Indeed, she said herself in her book, quoting a lovely phrase from Kipling that 'To have had no end of a lesson, it will do us no end of good'. And I recommend that we study her and learn a lot here, both from her great victories, her great passion for politics, for the battle of politics and for the ideas of politics, but also learn from the way that she betrayed from within her own revolution.

Mrs Thatcher and Mr Gladstone

Joseph S. Meisel

Roy Jenkins, it is well known, viewed himself as a torchbearer of Gladstonian liberalism – his claim to the succession underscored by his biographies of Asquith and recently of Gladstone himself.[1] In 1987, the former Labour Chancellor of the Exchequer and co-founder of the Liberal Democrats was elected Chancellor of the University of Oxford. This was widely interpreted as a direct and defiant affront by the University to the Prime Minister and Oxford alumna, Margaret Thatcher.[2] The new Chancellor was seen as standing for everything that was antithetical to Thatcher and Thatcherism. In this way, through the medium of Jenkins, we see Thatcher and Gladstone opposed. Nevertheless, comparisons with Gladstone – the previous late-century giant of British politics – furnish a number of suggestive and revealing ways to approach Thatcher's career as Prime Minister and political icon from a longer historical perspective.

It is significant that Thatcher seems to lend herself particularly well to comparison with eminent Victorians. David Cannadine, for example, has usefully compared Thatcher both to Benjamin Disraeli as an outsider who succeeded in climbing to the top of the greasy pole, and to Florence Nightingale as a determined woman in a male-dominated public life.[3] Since comparisons between any two people will inevitably run up against the law of diminishing returns, this discussion of Gladstone and Thatcher will be selective rather than systematic. Although there is much to compare in the areas of foreign and imperial/Commonwealth affairs,[4] this study will be confined to the domestic arena: first, by comparing Gladstone and Thatcher in relation to the political apparatus over which they presided; second, by discussing their relationship to, and effect upon the wider political culture.

Parliament and Government

Thatcher and Gladstone are two of only eight prime ministers to serve for a total of over ten years: Gladstone for a total of twelve and a half years; Thatcher for around eleven and a half (although unlike Gladstone her term in office was consecutive). Before becoming Prime Minister, Gladstone had held government office for sixteen years, Thatcher for less than half that time. The differences between their office holding are qualitative as well as quantitative. Almost from the first, Gladstone held important offices of state: the colonial office, the board of trade, the Exchequer. Thatcher held the kind of lesser offices considered appropriate for women: pensions, education. Prior to the Tory leadership contest of 1975, given the realities of being a woman in politics, Thatcher's ambition dared look no higher than the exchequer.[5] Thus, the chancellorship, which had made Gladstone a politician of national standing over a hundred years earlier, was at one time seen by Thatcher as just above the glass ceiling.

Gladstone's political career through his (orthodox) first ministry can be understood largely as the fulfilment of his school and university friends' high expectations: 'establishment as an MP, an effective period as a departmental minister, a noted premiership.'[6] At a very early stage he benefited from the patronage and mentoring of a great Prime Minister, Sir Robert Peel, and in many ways continued to be (in Richard Shannon's phrase) 'Peel's Inheritor' – nowhere more so than in the area of finance. Thatcher's career, by contrast, defied all expectations of what a woman – particularly a greengrocer's daughter and mother of two with a second-class science degree – could achieve in public life. No great statesman took her under his wing (Keith Joseph was no Peel), and she became converted to the economic philosophy that came to bear her name only later in her career.

As prime ministers, both Gladstone and Thatcher vigorously propounded their economic beliefs, and both maintained a particularly strong hold on the Treasury and fiscal policy. Gladstone even personally assumed responsibility for the exchequer during part of two ministries. Thatcher, according to one well-placed observer, was 'much more the First Lord of the Treasury than any previous holder of that office.'[7] Many have pointed to the Gladstonian heritage of fiscal Thatcherism. Samuel Beer, for example, has written that 'Margaret Thatcher proclaimed and practised a Gladstonian liberalism.'[8] In her 1996 Keith Joseph Memorial Lecture, Thatcher herself said that 'The kind of Conservatism which he [Joseph] and I . . . favoured would be best described as "liberal", in the old-fashioned sense. And I mean the liberalism of Mr Gladstone, not of the latter-day collectivists.'[9]

Very generally, however, both prime ministers believed in a minimal state, balanced budgets, the benefits of free trade, individual responsibility, and the distinction between the deserving and the undeserving poor. Though in somewhat different ways, the economic views of Thatcher and Gladstone were directly connected with their moral values and sensibilities. For both, this made their economic views *right*, and explains the tenacity – indeed vehemence – with which they adhered to them.[10] Although the centrality of economic policy and the broad principles behind those policies certainly link Gladstone and Thatcher across the century dividing them, it does not help to explain why each came to dominate the politics of their respective times and after. And here we get to one of the most interesting and important points of comparison: parliamentary style.

Thatcher, like Gladstone, rose to national prominence through demonstrating her abilities within the parliamentary context. Gladstone had been a 'coming man' almost from the time he first entered Parliament, but his demolition of Disraeli's budget in 1852, followed shortly by his own first budget in 1853 turned him into a figure of national importance. Thatcher's emergence as a political leader began in the winter of 1974–75 when, as shadow financial secretary, the former tax lawyer set out to demolish the Wilson government's Finance Bill. The credibility she gained in this episode made possible her (highly contingent) election as party leader.

Both Gladstone and Thatcher were extraordinary parliamentary performers, and in the House it proved extremely difficult to get the better of either of them. Even at the end of his long career, the rising generation might find Gladstone's long set speeches tedious, but his forensic powers remained fresh. According to Lloyd George (no mean debater himself), Gladstone in his eighties was 'far and away the best Parliamentary speaker I have ever heard. He was not so good in exposition. He was very long and often bored you, but in debate, when he was attacked, he was superb.'[11] Possessed as he was with a vast store of knowledge, long experience as a debater, and a certain vehemence of temperament, it proved virtually impossible to take Gladstone head on – hence Disraeli's and Lord Randolph Churchill's attempts to ridicule and deflate him.

In Thatcher's own words: 'I thrive on honest argument.'[12] By her time, it was no longer the practice for the First Lord of the Treasury to also serve as Leader of the House. Thus, unlike Gladstone, she was not responsible for day-to-day procedural skirmishing over the government's legislative programme. Her great vehicle in the Commons was the twice-weekly Prime Minister's Question Time (invented, in essence, by Gladstone). During 'these noisy ritual confrontations',[13] the meticulously prepared and rehearsed Thatcher proved as indomitable, and as impervious to the opposition's shafts as Gladstone had. As Hugo Young has written, she 'maintained her domination [in Parliament] partly by sheer forensic competence . . . She made her mark not by elegance but combat. She was a fighting speaker who always liked to win, preferably leaving a corpse rather than taking prisoners'.[14]

For both Thatcher and Gladstone, crucial aspects of their parliamentary style were their seriousness and perceived humourlessness. The Commons has a strong tradition of humor.[15] Gladstone's perceived lack of a sense of humour invited a great deal of ridicule, but it also provided him with strong armour to withstand even the most brilliant barbs of his opponents and retain his dominant position.[16] Thatcher too benefited from the kind of protection that humourlessness affords. Like Gladstone, Thatcher projected that most Victorian value, earnestness. Also like Gladstone, it was an earnestness that sprang from her low-church origins. She was propelled, as Young has written, 'by an inner force, to which no British Prime Minister since Gladstone had laid claim with such unembarrassed clarity'.[17]

As a woman in Parliament and as a woman in charge, it was all the more crucial for Thatcher to project an absolute seriousness of both purpose and person. With various elements of the Tory leadership cadre ranged against her (including members of her cabinet), Thatcher's reforming zeal – undiluted by parliamentary bonhomie – contributed in important ways to her ability to keep the backbenchers with her. Ultimately, much of what passes for humour in the Commons – and by this I mean not the humour of chumminess or comic relief, but the humour of political effect – are rooted in ridicule and scorn, and at these Thatcher famously excelled.

Beyond the Commons, it is also instructive to compare Gladstone's and Thatcher's dealings with their respective cabinets. Both had to balance a wide range of interests in the construction of their cabinets: Gladstone, the often stressed coalition of Whigs, Peelites, and Radicals; Thatcher, those who were 'one of us' and those who were decidedly not. Despite the Caesaristic tendencies ascribed to him by Max Weber,[18] Gladstone operated very firmly within the British tradition of cabinet government. He viewed ministers as entitled to their own opinions, and sought to handle disagreements with courtesy. In the words of Roy Jenkins, 'He never doubted their right to disagree and it would not have occurred to him to sack a minister for his views. He regarded a Secretary of State (or the equivalent), once appointed, as inviolate, as much so as a member of the College of Cardinals.'[19]

Thatcher, by contrast, exemplified the post-war trend towards a more 'presidential' style of premiership. She has even been described by one former cabinet colleague as 'absolutist'.[20] She cut back the number of cabinet meetings and used cabinet committees (a non-existent practice in Gladstone's day) as well as ad hoc groups to assert more fully her personal control over those areas of policy that concerned her most. In 1981, once her hold on power was somewhat less insecure, she took the first opportunity to sack the collectivist 'wets' who failed to see the Thatcherite light. Political differences would be the explicit or underlying cause for her many subsequent reshuffles – the one in January 1989 so sweeping (and so desperate) that it seemed to some like Macmillan's notorious night of the long knives.[21] To judge from her own memoirs, and those of some former ministers, she did not go out of her way in order to be, like Gladstone, courteous to the cabinet. She chaired from the front: 'My style of chairmanship certainly nonplused some colleagues, who knew their brief a good deal less than I did. But I adopt this technique because I believe in argument as the best way of getting to the truth.'[22]

Both prime ministers had a strong belief in the institution of the monarchy, although the nature of that institution was rather different in the 1970s than in the 1870s. Victoria was far more meddlesome in affairs of state than would be permissible for her great-great-granddaughter. Victoria disliked Gladstone's politics, his policies, his platforming, and his penchant for lecturing her. Gladstone resented the Queen's interference and lack of appropriate political neutrality. The mutual antipathy between Gladstone and Victoria is now well known. The true nature of the relationship between Thatcher and Elizabeth will not be known for some time, if ever.[23] Certainly, the press found potential divisions between the two most powerful women in Britain to be good copy. This reached crisis proportions in 1986 when *The Sunday Times* reported statements by royal advisers that the Queen 'considers the Prime Minister's approach often to be uncaring, confrontational and socially divisive.'[24] Thatcher hardly mentions the Queen in her memoirs except to dismiss these stories.[25] While it is natural for any memoir writer (even Thatcher) to smooth over the rough spots where possible, it is significant that Hugo Young – a journalist himself – also takes pains to downplay the extent of the division between monarch and minister.[26]

In the friction between Thatcher and the Queen, as in that between Gladstone and Victoria, the significance went far beyond disagreements between head of government and head of state. As the political commentator Peter Riddell wrote during the Thatcher/Palace crisis of 1986, 'at a deeper level, the episode highlights the reservations the traditional British establishment has about the social outsider Mrs Thatcher and her counter-revolution.'[27] As this suggests, comparisons between Gladstone and Thatcher cannot be limited to the formal structures of politics.

The Classes and the Masses

Of Gladstone, one great Whig lady once said, there was 'something in the tone of his voice and his way of coming into a room that is not aristocratic'.[28] And certainly he was not, nor did he ever become an aristocrat. As Colin Matthew has written: 'For all the many honours he had recommended for others, Gladstone always saw himself as a commoner.'[29] He venerated the social system built around hereditary land tenure, but also saw himself as outside the British tradition of middle-class absorption into the aristocracy. As a public figure, Gladstone's status as a commoner became iconic through such un-aristocratic activities as tree-felling, and reached its highest expression with the 'Mr' that continued invariably to precede his name well into the 1960s.[30] If Gladstone can be seen to represent the arrival of the mercantile and manufacturing classes in British political life, Thatcher has come to symbolise the arrival of the lower middle classes. Her elevation to the peerage notwithstanding, to many she will always be 'Mrs Thatcher'.

Oxford is often viewed as a forcing house of the elite. Of the total fifty-three prime ministers from Walpole to Blair, for example, twenty-six, or half went to Oxford (nearly twice the number of Cambridge-educated prime ministers). Like a number of other prime ministers, both Gladstone and Thatcher were Oxford meritocrats: Gladstone, the successful merchant's studious son at a university dominated by the aristocracy; Thatcher, the greengrocer's hard-working daughter at a university dominated by the upper middle class professional elite. Of all the university-educated prime ministers, Thatcher and Gladstone probably had the most difficult relationships with their alma mater. Gladstone represented the University in Parliament from 1847 to 1865, but his re-election was contested several times – considered a grave mark of disfavour in university constituencies.[31] There was even an unsuccessful attempt to prevent awarding Gladstone the honorary degree traditionally conferred upon the university's MPs. For his part, Gladstone came to feel that, although his constituents 'have had much reason to complain, I have not had an over-good bargain'.[32]

Thatcher's relationship with Oxford has been even more problematic. In 1985, the university bowed to faculty and student protests and declined to award her the honorary degree customarily given to Oxford prime ministers. Later, as already described, the landslide election of Roy Jenkins as Chancellor was seen as a further rebuke.[33] Despite his difficulties with the university, Gladstone retained a lifelong devotion to Oxford. Thatcher now raises money for Cambridge.[34]

Gladstone's and Thatcher's difficult relations with Oxford are but one aspect of their complex and seemingly paradoxical relationships with established institutions. Although he was a devout Anglican and believed in the hierarchical structure of society, as a modernising, reforming Prime Minister Gladstone and his ministries challenged established interests in a host of ways: competitive examinations, church disestablishment, university reform, education reform, reform of Irish land tenure, military restraint, extension of the franchise, the ballot, and Home Rule, to name the most obvious. He also came to believe that privileged groups like the army, the clergy, and the agricultural interest were encouraging the development of a more divided society through their willingness to assert their particular interests in politics – largely through the agency of the House of Lords.[35] Rhetorically, Gladstone's deeply shocking challenge to the traditional elite came in 1886, when he declared from the platform that 'in matters of truth, justice and humanity' he would 'back the masses against the classes'.[36]

Gladstone's approach was one of 'prudential conservatism radically applied'.[37] He accepted the need for change in order to maintain stability. Thatcher, on the other hand, accepted instability in order to effect change. She had, in the words of Andrew Sullivan, a 'passionate attachment to institutions which she combined with a deep desire to rattle them'.[38] Like Gladstone, she sought to uphold the traditional hierarchy by forcing it to come to terms with modern realities. As much as it was about destroying the power of the Left, Thatcherism was equally about challenging elite vested interests: the universities, the civil service, the BBC, the traditional aristocracy.[39]

The 'Victorian values' which she extolled and sought to promote by political and rhetorical means were not those which characterised the political and social elite of nineteenth-century Britain – the values, for the most part, of Gladstone – but rather the thrift, hard work, and improvement-mindedness of the Victorian shopkeeping classes. The heroine of the so-called 'peasant's revolt' against the Tory traditionalists, she seems to cherish the memory of sacking Lord Soames in the September 1981 cabinet reshuffle: 'I got the distinct impression that he felt the natural order of things was being violated and that he was, in effect, being dismissed by his housemaid.'[40]

While challenging the expectations of the elites, both Gladstone and Thatcher were also highly effective moral populists. Both were 'mobilising' prime ministers, as Dennis Kavanagh has argued,[41] and both came to adopt a 'revivalist rhetorical style'.[42] This populism arose from different sources in each case. Gladstone came out of retirement and harnessed extra-parliamentary agitation in the late 1870s largely in response to what he believed to be the fiscal irresponsibility of Disraeli's government. In his subsequent ministries, he used his distinctive style of rhetorical leadership to dominate the process of politics – at times using his popular appeal to go over the heads of his party, and even his cabinet. Thatcher in 1979 found herself to be something of an accidental prime minister – and clearly one on probation. As John Vincent has written: 'Lacking a power base in the cabinet, she turned, as Gladstone had, in other directions.'[43]

Overall, she failed to cultivate the kind of broad national popularity that Gladstone achieved, but succeeded in building a very loyal following and in discrediting the alternatives.

Their campaigns changed the way things *were* done. In 1879 and 1880, Gladstone's barnstorming Midlothian campaigns set new models for the conduct of electoral politics for the last two decades of the nineteenth century and well into the twentieth.[44] A century later, Thatcher provides an amusing description of how, under her, Conservative campaign rallies 'moved into the twentieth century with a vengeance. Dry ice shot out over the first six rows, enveloping the press in a dense fog; lasers flashed madly across the auditorium; our campaign tune, composed by Andrew Lloyd Weber for the occasion, blared out; a video of me on international visits was shown; and then on I walked to deliver my speech, feeling something of an anti-climax'.[45] At Gladstone's rallies, the music was supplied by the audience, which sang liberal songs set to the tune of hymns. In his speeches, Gladstone himself supplied both the lightning and the fog.

In comparing their relations with 'the masses', it is also important to note at least briefly the ways that both Gladstone and Thatcher harnessed the power of mass media. For the recently organised press agencies of the late-nineteenth century, a Gladstone speech was a highly profitable article of trade.[46] Gladstone's stature was such that most regional and local newspapers would carry his speeches, usually verbatim. Even Conservative papers carried the full text of his speeches. The late nineteenth century was an era of the printed word; the late twentieth, an era of image. Accordingly, Thatcher's media efforts were especially focused on television. She employed a crack team of image-makers, and during campaigns sought to ensure that she appeared in people's sitting rooms as frequently as possible.[47] Thus, whether favourable coverage or not, both Thatcher and Gladstone had their status as the dominant political figure of their times undergirded by a kind of media ubiquity.

Conclusion

Despite their powerful influence on their own times and after, both Gladstone and Thatcher left behind a mixed record and a confused political legacy. Gladstone twice failed to enact Home Rule, and its achievement a generation later hardly settled the Irish question. Other central elements of Gladstone's politics – free trade and fiscal orthodoxy – were eroded and abandoned.[48] Thatcher, despite her avowed intention to roll back socialism, succeeded only in curtailing its growth. Both also left their parties deeply divided – permanently sundered in the case of the Liberals.

But this is far from the last word on either Gladstone's or Thatcher's legacy. For example, it is a striking fact that Gladstone and Thatcher are the two predecessors in office most commonly mentioned in connection with Tony Blair. In 1996, looking ahead to a probable general election victory for Labour, one commentator wrote: 'The life, times, and government of Tony Blair may yet be seen as Margaret Thatcher's greatest victory.'[49] And indeed, the Blairite transformation of the Labour Party into New Labour has been seen by many as representing a great triumph and vindication for Thatcher.[50] Thatcher's mission was to slay post-war consensus politics. In many respects, Tony Blair symbolises that at least a modified Thatcherism has become the new consensus.

Yet, at the same time that Blair can be seen as Thatcher's legatee, he is also seen as the heir of Gladstone. This has something to do with the kind of fiscal probity that links Gladstone with Thatcher. Even more, it has to do with a policy agenda that a number of commentators have described as Gladstone's unfinished business: principally, settlement of the Irish question, UK devolution, and reform of the House of Lords.[51] For his part, Blair has hardly been shy about acknowledging Gladstone as a personal hero and political model, both at home and abroad.[52] In a number of ways, therefore, to observe Blair is to study the living connection between Gladstone and Thatcher.

Notes

1   Roy Jenkins, *Asquith,* revised edition (London: Collins, 1978); idem, *Gladstone* (London: Macmillan, 1995)
2   See, e.g. Brian Groom, 'Jenkins Wins Oxford's Traditional Tory Fiefdom,' *Financial Times,* 16 March, 1987, p. 7.
3   In essays from 1989 and 1990 reprinted in David Cannadine, *History in Our Time* (New Haven and London: Yale University Press, 1998), pp. 288, 206–7.
4   Both, for instance, believed in the rights of small nations. It is also a coincidence that Gladstone and Thatcher bracket some important long-term overseas developments. In foreign affairs, Germany

unified during Gladstone's first ministry and re-unified in the course of Thatcher's last ministry. In imperial affairs, Britain acquired Rhodesia during Gladstone's last government, and intervened to 'solve' the Rhodesian problem during Thatcher's first.

5   Hugo Young, *One of Us: A Biography of Margaret Thatcher, Final Edition* (London: Macmillan, 1991), p. 49.

6   H. C. G. Matthew, *Gladstone*, 2 vols. (Oxford: Oxford University Press, 1986–1995), vol. II, p. 79. See also p. 3.

7   The long-serving Permanent Secretary at the Treasury Douglas Wass, quoted in Young, p. 146.

8   Quoted in Samuel Beer, 'Liberalism Rediscovered,' *The Economist*, 7 February, 1998, p. 23. See also David Cannadine, *Class in Britain* (New Haven: Yale University Press, 1998), pp. 174–5.

9   The *Collected Speeches of Margaret Thatcher*, ed. Robin Harris (London: HarperCollins, 1997), p. 574. Thatcher also invoked Gladstone in order to ridicule her Liberal Democratic opposition. See Thatcher, *Speeches*, p. 143.

10 See Brian Harrison, , 'Mrs Thatcher and the Intellectuals,' *Twentieth Century British History*, vol. 5, no. 2 (1994), p. 226. A very important distinction, however, is that Thatcher's economic policies (and moral fervour) were directed at undoing the long established post-war economic orthodoxy. Gladstone's policies were the orthodoxy. His return to office in 1880 was prompted in no small measure by his desire to undo the very recent free-spending deviations of 'Beaconsfieldism', Gladstone might very well have approved of Thatcher's efforts at fiscal restraint, but their agreement in this respect cannot be carried too far in light of the very different contexts in which they led the nation. For one thing, with Britain a member of NATO in the midst of the Cold War, Thatcher did not share Gladstone's antagonism to large-scale military spending (although she was keenly interested in getting better value for money out of the military).

11 Quoted in *Lord Riddell's War Diary, 1914–1918* (London: Nicholson & Watson, 1933), p. 67.

12 Margaret Thatcher, *The Downing Street Years* (London: HarperCollins, 1993), p. 129.

13 Thatcher, *Downing Street Years*, p. 41.

14 Young, p. 242.

15 See P. J. Waller, 'Laughter in the House: A Late Nineteenth and Early Twentieth Century Parliamentary Survey,' *Twentieth Century British History*, vol. 5, no. 1 (1994), pp. 4–37.

16 See Joseph S. Meisel, 'The Importance of Being Serious: The Unexplored Connection Between Gladstone and Humour,' *History*, Vol. 84, no. 274 (1999), pp. 278–300.

17 Young, p. 352. Young also provides an example of 'that rarest of contrivances, a Thatcher joke' (p. 125) – significantly, not one delivered in Parliament, but to her image-maker, Gordon Reece. On Gladstone and Thatcher's shared low-church outlook, see Harrison, 'Mrs Thatcher and the Intellectuals,' p. 226.

18 Max Weber, 'Politics as a Vocation' (1918), in From Max Weber: *Essays in Sociology*, tr. and ed. H. H. Gerth and C. Wright Mills (New York: Oxford University Press, 1946), p. 106. See also Matthew, *Gladstone*, Vol. II, pp. 49-51.

19 Roy Jenkins, Gladstone (London: Macmillan, 1995), pp. 466–7.

20 Quoted in Peter Jenkins, *Mrs Thatcher's Revolution: The Ending of the Socialist Era* (Cambridge, MA: Harvard University Press, 1988), p. 183. On Thatcher's use of the cabinet generally, see Dennis Kavanagh, *Thatcherism and British Politics: The End of Consensus?* (Oxford: Oxford University Press, 1987), pp. 253–65.

21 Young, pp. 559–60.

22 Thatcher, *Downing Street Years*, p. 561.

23 To date, the most suggestive and thorough exploration of the relationship between Thatcher and Elizabeth II is Ben Pimlott, *The Queen: A Biography of Elizabeth II* (London: HarperCollins, 1996), pp. 459–63, 494–515.

24 Simon Freeman and Michael Jones, 'Queen Dismayed by "Uncaring" Thatcher,' *The Sunday Times*, July 20, 1986, p. 1. For a retrospective summary of the bad relations between Thatcher and the Queen, see Alan Hamilton, 'Coolness That Kept First Ladies Apart,' *The Times*, 23 November, 1990, p. 5.

25 Thatcher, *Downing Street Years*, p. 18.

26 Young, pp. 488–93.

27 Peter Riddell, 'Not so Much a Crisis, More a Midsummer Storm,' *Financial Times*, 23 July, 1986, p. 10.

28 Quoted in John Vincent, *The Formation of the Liberal Party, 1857-1868* (London: Constable, 1966), p. 228.

29 Matthew, *Gladstone*, Vol. II, p. 356.

30 Matthew, *Gladstone*, Vol. II, p. 304.

31 Oxford was the core of the Anglican establishment, and Gladstone displeased many of his constituents by taking stands that were seen as being against the interests of the Church (e.g. support for the removal of Jewish disabilities, and criticising the Church of Ireland). After Gladstone was defeated at Oxford in 1865, neither seat for the University was contested until 1918, with the exception of one by-election in 1878. Matthew, *Gladstone*, Vol. I, p. 129.

32 Quoted in John Morley, *The Life of William Ewart Gladstone*, 3 vols. (London: Macmillan, 1903), Vol. I, p. 360.

33 For Thatcher's increasingly problematic reception in intellectual and cultured circles, see Young, pp. 410–1; and Harrison, 'Thatcher and the Intellectuals,' passim. On the honorary degree scandal, see H. L. A. Hart, 'Oxford and Mrs Thatcher,' *New York Review of Books*, 28 March, 1985, pp. 7–9.

34 See Andrew Pierce, 'Thatcher Takes Revenge on Oxford,' *The Times*, 16 August, 1999, p. 1.

35 See Matthew, *Gladstone*, Vol. II, p. 95.

36 Quoted in Cannadine, *Class*, p. 109.

37 Matthew, *Gladstone*, Vol. II, p. 310.

38 Quoted in Robert S. Boynton, 'Profile [of Niall Ferguson]: Thinking the Unthinkable,' *New Yorker*, 12 April, 1999, p. 48.

39 See Cannadine, Class, pp. 176–7.

40 Thatcher, *Downing Street Years*, p. 151.

41 Kavanagh, p. 275.

42 Young, p. 119 (speaking only of Thatcher).

43 John Vincent, 'The Thatcher Governments, 1979–1987,' in *Ruling Performance: British Governments from Attlee to Thatcher*, ed. Peter Hennessy and Anthony Seldon (Oxford: Blackwell, 1987), p. 282.

44 H. C. G. Matthew, 'Rhetoric and Politics in Great Britain, 1860–1950,' in *Politics and Social Change in Britain: Essays Presented to A. F. Thompson*, ed. P. J. Waller (Hassocks: Harvester, 1987), p. 41.

45 Thatcher, *Downing Street Years*, p. 580.

46 See Alfred Kinnear, 'The Trade in Great Men's Speeches,' *The Contemporary Review*, Vol. LXXV (1889), pp. 439–44; and Matthew, 'Rhetoric and Politics,' p. 40.

47   Young, pp. 428–9; Thatcher, *Downing Street Years,* pp. 286–7.

48   See Matthew, *Gladstone,* Vol. II, p. 387ff.

49   Geoffrey Wheatcroft, 'The Paradoxical Case of Tony Blair,' *Atlantic Monthly,* June 1996, p. 40.

50   Comments along these lines were particularly in evidence in the spring of 1999, the twentieth anniversary of Thatcher's assumption of the premiership, and the conclusion of the first two years of Blair's ministry. See, e.g. 'Thatcher's Legacy: She Changed Britain and Created Blair' [leading article], *Guardian,* 3 May, 1999, p. 17.

51   See, e.g., Andrew Adonis, 'Back to the Gladstone Agenda,' *Times Literary Supplement,* January 3, 1997, pp. 4–5. More recently, numerous leader writers have pointed out the Gladstonian resonances of Blair's enthusiastic efforts in the Balkans.

52   See, e.g., Michael White, 'Blair's Praise for the Victorian Way,' *Guardian,* 6 December, 1998, p. 12; 'Gladstone's Ghost,' *The Economist, 29* May, 1999, p. 54.

Thatcher and Reagan:
Soulmates for Liberty

Larry Bumgardner

———

Former Secretary of State George Shultz, describing Margaret Thatcher in his memoirs, writes: 'Freedom in political and economic life was her trademark. In that regard, she and Ronald Reagan were soul mates.'[1] He further describes the personal relationship between Thatcher and Reagan as being 'as close as any imaginable between two major leaders'.[2] Thatcher biographer Chris Ogden, calling Thatcher and Reagan 'blood brother and sister' on matters of policy, adds that 'no president and prime minister have ever been so close philosophically'.[3] This essay will explore the development and significance of this unique partnership between two of the most important world leaders of the late twentieth century.

A review of the political careers and years in office for both Thatcher and Reagan shows remarkable parallels. With Thatcher often charting the course roughly a year ahead of Reagan, it is not surprising that another biographer, Hugo Young, calls Thatcher 'a kind of [John the] Baptist to Reagan's Messiah'.[4] Coming from the right wing of their respective conservative parties, they both rose to national political prominence by challenging their party leaders. Thatcher defeated Edward Heath for the Conservative Party leadership in 1975. A year later, Reagan almost beat President Gerald Ford for the 1976 Republican presidential nomination. Thatcher became Prime Minister in 1979, leading the Conservative Party to victory by arguing that new approaches were needed to overcome Britain's decline under the leadership of the Labour Party. A year later, Reagan was elected President after convincing Americans they were not better off after four years of Democratic President Jimmy Carter.

The parallels continued after both reached office. Both endured periods of low popularity during economic troubles in their first terms, but Thatcher and Reagan recovered to win easy re-elections in 1983 and 1984, respectively. During their second terms, each survived a major scandal involving military equipment (Thatcher and Westland; Reagan and Iran-Contra). Coincidentally, both even survived assassination attempts (Thatcher narrowly escaped injury in a bombing at Brighton, while Reagan was shot and barely survived). After leaving office, their hand-picked successors (John Major and George Bush) were able to win one national election each. Ultimately, though, Major and Bush were unable to live up to the large reputations of their predecessors and were defeated in their own re-election efforts, returning power to the opposition parties that had been greatly weakened by Thatcher and Reagan.

While both Thatcher and Reagan were in office, there were also many similarities in policy and practices. Both cut income taxes and sought to reduce the role of government (Thatcher through privatisation; Reagan through deregulation). Both restored national pride through winning a brief war on island territories (Thatcher and the Falklands; Reagan and Grenada). Both proved their power by standing firm against labour unions (Thatcher and the miners; Reagan and the air traffic controllers). Both were strong anti-Communists who ultimately were willing to deal with the Soviets. Finally, both left as their legacy a conservative revolution, forcing Tony Blair's Labour Party and Bill Clinton's Democratic Party to moderate their own views to regain power.[5]

For the most part, these parallels for Thatcher and Reagan were not mere coincidences. Rather, they vividly demonstrate the strength of their shared convictions and determination. Further, their close relationship was crucial to their success in office, as both Thatcher and Reagan assisted each other and likely even strengthened each other's already significant resolve. A brief look at some recently declassified correspondence between Thatcher and Reagan, now available at the Ronald Reagan Presidential Library and Museum in California, may provide greater insight into this relationship. (It should be noted that most of their correspondence, including all sensitive documents, remains classified and unavailable at this early date.)

Thatcher and Reagan first met in 1975, as up-and-coming leaders of their parties. Although they immediately liked each other and shared similar views, their close ties did not begin until both had taken office. Still, Thatcher was pleased enough with the result of Reagan's 1980 election that, only a few days after his inauguration, she was looking forward to being the first European head of government to visit the new President. In a speech at the Pilgrims' Dinner in London on 29 January 1981 (a copy of which was sent by British Ambassador Nicholas Henderson to Richard Allen, Reagan's national security adviser), Thatcher said:

I believe that that visit will underline the closeness of the friendship between our two countries but it will also I am certain mark the opening of a period of particularly close understanding between the two Governments and a particularly close understanding between the two Heads of Government. [. . .] So we have a common interest in liberty, in culture, in political philosophy and I might add that the economic policies of the new Administration and of Her Majesty's Government are also strikingly similar.[6]

In response, Reagan wrote Thatcher in February 1981: 'You are indeed right that we share a very special concern for democracy and for liberty. That is the essence of the special relationship between our two countries, and it is similarly an excellent basis for inaugurating an extended period of cooperation and close consultation between your government and my administration.' Reagan added in his own handwriting the salutation of 'Dear Madame Prime Minister' and signed the letter 'Ronald Reagan'.[7] This formality, although indicative of the newness of the relationship, would soon change.

After Thatcher's visit to the White House, Thatcher wrote to Reagan in March 1981 a rather typical thank-you letter, similarly using a formal salutation of 'Dear Mr President' and signing the letter 'Margaret Thatcher'. However, she added a hand-written note at the end of the typed letter, saying, 'We shall never have a happier visit.'[8] With the assassination attempt intervening, Reagan responded in April 1981: 'Despite the rush of disturbing events two weeks ago, pleasant thoughts of your visit in February are still strong in our memories. It was not only a pleasure to renew our acquaintance, but even more special to get to know each other better.'[9]

By only a few months later, the formalities were gone and they were on a first-name basis, perhaps due in part to a decision at the Ottawa G7 economic summit to have all the heads of state use each other's first names.[10] That July 1981 summit may have helped cement the relationship, as Thatcher and Reagan worked together as a team against far less conservative leaders of the other nations. In a letter a few weeks later (by this time addressed 'Dear Margaret' and signed 'Ron'), Reagan thanked Thatcher for her work in drafting the summit communiqué and added: 'I look forward to the closest possible relations between our two countries. You know, of course, the esteem in which I hold our personal friendship.'[11]

With a solid foundation for their close relationship now established, there were soon opportunities for both Thatcher and Reagan to benefit from it. Perhaps the most striking example came when the British Falkland Islands were invaded by Argentina in 1982. The United States first tried to play the role of mediator between Argentina and Britain, as Secretary of State Al Haig tried his own brand of 'shuttle diplomacy'. Once these efforts failed to provide a diplomatic resolution of the crisis, Reagan and the Pentagon then felt free to support the Thatcher effort (despite some within the Reagan administration arguing for American neutrality in hopes of not offending South American nations). The result was massive military and intelligence aid from the United States to the British forces – assistance which helped ensure British victory. 'It is difficult to exaggerate the difference that America's support made to the military outcome,' British Ambassador Henderson said.[12] Clearly, Reagan did not want to turn his back on his ally, Thatcher. Moreover, it was a strong example of Thatcher and Reagan working together as soul mates for political liberty. As Reagan told Parliament near the end of the Falklands War: 'Those young men are not fighting for mere real estate. They fight for a cause, for the belief that armed aggression must not be allowed to succeed.'[13]

A few years later, in 1986, Thatcher had an opportunity to return the favour. The United States had decided to use air strikes against Libya to retaliate for a number of terrorist activities tied to Libya and Colonel Muammar Qaddafi. Reagan sent a personal message to Thatcher, asking that she approve the use of American aircraft stationed in Britain to facilitate the strikes on Libya. Despite some initial questions posed by Thatcher, she soon approved the American request. In making what was an unpopular decision in Britain and Europe generally, Thatcher clearly had not forgotten the vital American support in the

Falklands. Thatcher later wrote in her autobiography: 'Finally, I stressed that we had to stand by the Americans as they had stood by us over the Falklands.'[14]

There were yet other instances of mutual support. Thatcher also stood by Reagan during the difficult days of the Iran-Contra scandal.[15] Reagan allowed the British to improve its nuclear capabilities with a low-cost deal on American Trident missiles, and helped expedite Thatcher's privatisation of British Airways by clearing away antitrust logjams in the United States.[16] These decisions were indications not only of the close alliance between the two nations, but also of the strong personal relationship between Thatcher and Reagan.

Perhaps an even stronger sign of this partnership was the ability of Thatcher and Reagan to overcome several serious differences. The most strident disagreement came when the United States invaded Grenada, an island nation with a pro-Soviet government but still officially part of the British Commonwealth, without first notifying Thatcher. Although Reagan justified this based on the need for secrecy in Washington, Thatcher's anger was heard directly by Reagan. According to Young, Thatcher 'was infuriated: had rarely been more so, according to people present that night. She did not hesitate to vent her rage on the President'.[17] Yet Reagan took her reaction in stride, as Ogden noted: 'He was grinning as he described her feistiness. "She was great," he told aides. She will get over it, he added, knowing that the ends – the elimination of a nasty socialist regime – would outweigh the means with a pragmatic anticommunist like Thatcher.'[18] Understanding the instincts of his friend well, Reagan had surmised correctly. Thatcher later recounted in her autobiography: 'American intervention in Grenada was, in fact, a success. Democracy was restored. [. . .] No one would weep any tears over the fate of the Marxist thugs whom the Americans had dislodged.'[19]

While Grenada was a disagreement primarily over notice and process, Reagan's insistence on the Strategic Defence Initiative and his stated goal of eliminating all nuclear weapons led to rare policy differences with Thatcher. Thatcher doubted the scientific basis for SDI (or 'Star Wars') and feared the programme would cause a major division within the NATO alliance. But rather than publicly breaking ranks with Reagan, she flew to Camp David in December 1984 to meet with Reagan in hopes of modifying, or at least clarifying, the American position. Reagan responded well to her approach, and the result was a communiqué based on a draft that Thatcher had brought with her to the meeting.[20] The communiqué, known as the Camp David accord, stressed the goal of enhanced deterrence and the need for continuing arms control talks. With this clarification in place, Thatcher then publicly supported Reagan's SDI. Continuing to show both political skills and deference to the leader of the free world, Thatcher wrote to Reagan in January 1985: 'Our discussions at Camp David had given me a valuable outline of your own thinking especially on the Strategic Defence Initiative; your message was a great help in explaining the details of your approach.'[21]

A similar pattern emerged two years later after the 1986 Reykjavik Summit, where Reagan and Mikhail Gorbachev almost reached agreement on eliminating all nuclear weapons. The only sticking point was Gorbachev's insistence that the United States give up Star Wars, which Reagan refused to do. This near agreement crystallised Thatcher's long-standing concern over Reagan's dream of eliminating all nuclear weapons, as Thatcher feared the loss of nuclear deterrence would leave Europe and the world far more susceptible to Soviet conventional forces. As she had written to Reagan first in February 1985, following another trip to Washington:

I hope that I was able to explain to you clearly my preoccupation with the need not to weaken our efforts to consolidate support in Britain for the deployment of Cruise and for the modernisation of Trident by giving the impression that a future without nuclear weapons is near at hand. We must continue to make the case for deterrence based on nuclear weapons for several years to come.[22]

By the time her worst fears were nearly realised at Reykjavik, Thatcher was truly alarmed. She later wrote in her autobiography: 'My own reaction when I heard how far the Americans had been prepared to go was as if there had been an earthquake beneath my feet.'[23] With yet another prepared statement in hand, Thatcher again met with Reagan at Camp David. Reagan once again agreed to her statement, which clarified the American position and reiterated the importance of nuclear deterrence without forcing Reagan to back off his own position – a result very similar to the SDI episode.[24] 'I had reason to be well pleased,' Thatcher concluded in her autobiography.[25]

The Reykjavik reaction was only a small part of the story of Thatcher's involvement in the Reagan-Gorbachev pairing. In fact, history may record that involvement as the most significant result of the Thatcher-Reagan partnership. Thatcher clearly shared Reagan's anti-Communist views and could even match his 'evil empire' rhetoric. As Thatcher wrote to Reagan in September 1983, after the Soviets shot down a Korean Air Lines flight, killing 269 people:

My views on the barbarity of this act are completely at one with yours. [. . .] This incident has vividly illustrated the true nature of the Soviet regime. Its rigidity and ruthlessness, its neuroses about spying and security, its mendacity, and its apparent inability to understand, let alone apply, the normal rules of civilised conduct between nations, have been an object lesson to those who believe that goodwill and reason alone will be sufficient to ensure our security and world peace.[26]

With their anti-Communist credentials never in question, Thatcher and Reagan were well positioned to negotiate with the Soviets. Moreover, their united front made it easier for both to deal, as Reagan wrote to Thatcher in June 1983 to thank her for her assistance in reaching a unified message at the Williamsburg economic summit:

That message, both in its economic and political dimensions, was crucial at this time of questioning in our own countries and of challenge from the Soviet Union and its allies. Thanks to your contribution during Saturday's dinner discussion of INF, we were able, in our statement, to send the Soviets a clear signal of allied determination and unity.[27]

The two leaders also consulted regularly on their approach to the Soviets. Reagan wrote to Thatcher in January 1984 to give her advance notice of his upcoming message on relations with the Soviets. 'Given our close relationship and the special significance that I attach to this statement of US policy, I want to share the text with you beforehand. I hope you will agree that it meets our common objectives of setting a positive tone [. . .] for George Shultz's bilateral meeting with Soviet Foreign Minister Gromyko.'[28]

Seeking an opening to the Soviet Union, Thatcher in 1984 invited to Britain a then relatively unknown Gorbachev, who had only recently been identified as a rising Soviet Politburo member. Gorbachev met with Thatcher in December

1984, only three months before he came to power. Thatcher was immediately impressed and saw him as a potentially different type of Soviet leader. Gorbachev asked Thatcher about Reagan and the United States, and Thatcher predictably defended her friend and ally.[29] After this first meeting, Thatcher delivered her now-famous and prophetic assessment of Gorbachev. 'I like Mr Gorbachev. We can do business together.'[30] Only a week later, Thatcher was at Camp David with Reagan for the meeting that yielded the Camp David accord on SDI. Even before the SDI discussion, she reported to Reagan on her good impression of Gorbachev. This endorsement by Thatcher, in particular, was meaningful in convincing Reagan to deal with Gorbachev.[31]

Throughout the Reagan-Gorbachev summits that followed, as Ogden notes, Thatcher played the role of 'honest interpreter with special skills that made her invaluable to both leaders'.[32] Although there was no doubt that she was clearly on the side of the United States, both Gorbachev and Reagan would report to Thatcher on their summit discussions. In Thatcher's own summit with Gorbachev in Moscow, Gorbachev again quizzed Thatcher about Reagan and asked her to pass his own views on to Reagan.[33] The result was that, in essence, Thatcher joined Reagan and Gorbachev to form the most important troika of world leaders since the alliance of Roosevelt, Churchill, and Stalin. As the earlier group oversaw the effort that won World War II, the Reagan-Gorbachev-Thatcher team should be credited with ending the Cold War. Reagan himself acknowledged the crucial role of Thatcher as he stopped in London on the way back from his Moscow meeting with Gorbachev in June 1988. Recalling Thatcher's early suggestion that they could 'do business' with Gorbachev, Reagan added: 'Prime Minister, the achievement of the Moscow summit, as well as the Geneva and Washington summits, say much about your valour and strength.'[34]

The question remaining about the Thatcher-Reagan relationship is what prompted such a close partnership. Certainly, the long-established 'special relationship' between the United States and Britain played a part. However, the Thatcher-Reagan friendship went far beyond the ties between virtually any other prime minister and president. Even Churchill and Roosevelt could not match the Thatcher-Reagan closeness. Political expediency or even necessity must also be mentioned as a cause, as Thatcher and Reagan had different but complementary skills.[35] Thatcher was involved in every policy detail but lacked

Reagan's personal popularity, while the delegating Reagan was the Great Communicator who could connect with the public.

Still, beyond politics, there was strong personal chemistry that solidified the Thatcher-Reagan connection. They had somewhat similar upbringings, growing up in small towns with hard-working parents. Each was especially influenced by one dominant parent (Thatcher by her father; Reagan by his mother). That gender pattern was followed throughout their careers, as Thatcher's cabinet and closest advisers were almost exclusively male.[36] Reagan obviously preferred strong women like Thatcher, as seen through his ties to his mother, his first wife (Jane Wyman), and his second wife (Nancy Reagan). Moreover, Reagan had few close male friends. Thus, gender certainly played a major role in bringing Thatcher and Reagan together.

Yet their shared beliefs and values were the primary reason for their closeness. Above all else, they agreed on freedom – free enterprise, free trade, personal freedom, and political freedom. Allied together in a world fraught with danger and far too many enemies of freedom, it is no surprise that they were indeed soul mates for liberty.

Notes

1   George P. Shultz, *Turmoil and Triumph: My Years As Secretary of State* (New York: Scribner's, 1993), p. 153.
2   Ibid., p. 154.
3   Chris Ogden, *Maggie: An Intimate Portrait of a Woman in Power* (New York: Simon & Schuster, 1990), p. 231.
4   Hugo Young, *The Iron Lady: A Biography of Margaret Thatcher* (New York: Farrar, Straus, Giroux, 1989), p. 250.
5   Geoffrey Smith, *Reagan and Thatcher* (New York: Norton, 1991), p. 259.
6   Nicholas Henderson, letter to Richard Allen, 5 February 1981, Ronald Reagan Papers, Reagan Presidential Library, Simi Valley.
7   Ronald Reagan, letter to Margaret Thatcher, 2 February 1981, Ronald Reagan Papers, Reagan Presidential Library, Simi Valley.
8   Margaret Thatcher, letter to Ronald Reagan, 5 March 1981, Ronald Reagan Papers, Reagan Presidential Library, Simi Valley.
9   Ronald Reagan, letter to Margaret Thatcher, 27 April 1981, Ronald Reagan Papers, Reagan Presidential Library, Simi Valley.

10   Smith, p. 53.

11   Ronald Reagan, letter to Margaret Thatcher, 4 August 1981, Ronald Reagan Papers, Reagan Presidential Library, Simi Valley.

12   Young, p. 289.

13   Ibid.

14   Margaret Thatcher, *The Downing Street Years* (New York: Harper, 1993), p. 446.

15   Young, p. 481.

16   Ogden, pp. 238–239.

17   Young, p. 346.

18   Ogden, p. 238.

19   Thatcher, *Downing Street Years*, pp. 334–35.

20   Ogden, p. 240.

21   Margaret Thatcher, letter to Ronald Reagan, 14 January 1985, Ronald Reagan Papers, Reagan Presidential Library, Simi Valley.

22   Margaret Thatcher, letter to Ronald Reagan, 22 February 1985, Ronald Reagan Papers, Reagan Presidential Library, Simi Valley.

23   Thatcher, Downing Street, p. 471.

24   Ogden, p. 242.

25   Thatcher, *Downing Street Years,* p. 473.

26   Margaret Thatcher, letter to Ronald Reagan, 15 September 1983, Ronald Reagan Papers, Reagan Presidential Library, Simi Valley.

27   Ronald Reagan, letter to Margaret Thatcher, 15 June 1983, Ronald Reagan Papers, Reagan Presidential Library, Simi Valley.

28   Ronald Reagan, letter to Margaret Thatcher, 15 January 1984, Ronald Reagan Papers, Reagan Presidential Library, Simi Valley.

29   Ogden, p. 282.

30   Ogden, p. 283.

31   Smith, p. 147.

32   Ogden, p. 277.

33   Ogden, p. 286.

34   Smith, p. 247.

35   Smith, p. 261.

36   Michael A. Genovese ed *Women as National Leaders* (Newbury Park: Sage, 1993), p. 205.

II

Thatcher and Domestic Policy

Margaret Thatcher's Taming of the Trade Unions

Peter Dorey

Tackling the trade unions is widely considered to be one of Margaret Thatcher's greatest successes, an achievement cited by her supporters and critics alike within the Conservative Party. Indeed, one of the latter, Lord Ian Gilmour, once declared that: 'When I am asked about the [Thatcher] governments' achievements, I always say trade union reform, then I hesitate . . .'[1]

Whereas previous Conservative leaders had either grudgingly tolerated the trade unions (such as Lord Salisbury), or actively sought to obtain their trust and co-operation (most notably Harold Macmillan), Margaret Thatcher made no secret of her profound distaste for them.[2] Her hostility towards the unions was derived from both a particular ideological perspective and from her own political experience.

Margaret Thatcher was convinced that too many previous Conservative leaders had equated Conservatism with the eschewal of ideology, and thus placed an excessive emphasis on pragmatism and the pursuit of harmony or consensus. What her predecessors had viewed commendably as governing according to circumstances and accommodating themselves to reality, thereby gently adapting Conservatism to changing conditions, Thatcher viewed as mere drift and vacillation. This hitherto emphasis on consensus and conciliation had contributed to the Conservative Party's alleged appeasement of the trade unions, thereby enabling organised Labour steadily to amass power without responsibility. By the 1970s, Thatcherite Conservatives believed, trade union power had increased to the extent of rendering Britain virtually ungovernable. Certainly, one of

71

Margaret Thatcher's closest colleagues and ideological proselytes declared that 'solving the union problem is the key to Britain's recovery'.[3]

To some extent, Thatcher's instinctive and ideological hostility towards the trade unions can also be understood in terms of her petit-bourgeois social background and outlook. Whereas many previous Conservative leaders emanated from somewhat aristocratic backgrounds, and were characterised by a philosophy of noblesse oblige (entailing a patrician concern with the welfare of the so-called lower orders, and an attempt to accommodate the organised working class, both in order to create 'one nation' and to reconcile industrial workers to liberal democratic capitalism), Thatcher was immediately noted for her more humble origins as a shopkeeper's daughter brought up in a small, provincial market town in Eastern England.[4]

This lower-middle class background tended to preclude any patrician paternalism, and instead, fostered a highly individualist perspective which viewed collectivist institutions such as trade unions with profound distaste.

Indeed, it has variously been observed how such a petit-bourgeois viewpoint often engenders a marked antagonism towards trade unionism, for organised Labour (and, to a somewhat lesser extent, big business) is seen to be crushing the middle classes and squeezing it out of existence. It is a perspective which depicts the small businessperson and the self-employed entrepreneur being destroyed by trade union militancy from below and corporate monopolies from above.

Furthermore, this petit bourgeois approach considers the middle classes – particularly the lower middle class – to provide the moral basis of a civilised society, with its emphasis on such values and principles as individualism, independence, self-reliance, hard work, and deferred gratification.[5] In this respect, Thatcher apparently viewed herself as both a representative and the saviour of Britain's petit-bourgeois, someone who would fight for their interests as vigorously as the trade unions had apparently fought for the interests of the industrial working class during the previous one hundred years.[6] Yet this would necessarily entail launching a counter-attack against the trade unions in order that the middle classes could re-establish themselves economically, morally and politically.

What also reinforced Thatcher's instinctive and ideological hostility towards the trade unions was the experience of the 1970–74 Conservative government of

Edward Heath, in which she was a cabinet minister. Heath's administration had witnessed the failure of its 1971 Industrial Relations Act (itself intended to curb trade union power), followed, in 1972 and 1974, by two major strikes by Britain's coal miners. Indeed, the latter of these disputes arguably brought down the Heath government, and starkly symbolised the apparent apotheosis of trade union power in Britain.

In the light of these experiences, New Right Conservatives like Margaret Thatcher became convinced that the Party's appeasement of the trade unions had been pursued too far, for too long. It was now deemed vital that trade union power was curbed decisively and definitively. What further underpinned this conviction was the plethora of opinion polls, during the latter half of the 1970s, which revealed that vast majority of British people (including a majority of trade unionists themselves) believed the unions had become too powerful and disruptive, and were virtually 'running the country'. Such a mood amongst the British electorate perfectly suited Margaret Thatcher's determination to portray herself as a uniquely populist leader who was 'out there' on the side of ordinary people against over-mighty vested interests, of which the trade unions were deemed a prime example.

Yet Thatcher was also a politician astute enough to recognise the need to proceed carefully in attacking the trade unions. Rather than declaring 'all-out war' on the unions, therefore, a 'guerilla warfare' approach was adopted.[7]

The Thatcherite approach was to attack the unions by stealth, aiming at different targets on different occasions, and thus constantly forcing the unions onto the defensive. Radical ends were pursued by incremental means. Or as Howell has observed, 'Conservative industrial relations policy [was] ideological in its content, direction and coherence, but pragmatic in its timing, and in the manner in which it sought to achieve its aims'.[8]

Thus it was that Margaret Thatcher presided over no less than five Acts of Parliament during the eleven and a half years of her premiership.[9] The cumulative effect of this tranche of legislation was to weaken and ultimately abolish the closed shop (i.e., compulsory trade union membership); require trade unions to conduct secret ballots of their members prior to a strike, or when electing new leaders, or in order to operate a political fund; to narrow the definition of a trade dispute, thereby significantly reducing the range of issues over which trade unions could legitimately and lawfully pursue industrial action. This last measure also ensured that secondary or 'sympathy' action was effectively prohibited, thus seriously limiting the scope for active solidarity amongst trade unions and their members.

Yet this comprehensive battery of legislation was notable for four other reasons. Firstly, of the five laws introduced during this period, four were called Employment Acts, thereby reflecting the Thatcherite premise that trade union behaviour and power was a deterrent to the investment and wealth creation upon which jobs depended. Consequently, the reduction of trade union power was presented as a prerequisite (in conjunction with anti-inflationary monetary and supply-side policies) of economic renewal, and thus of the creation of new jobs. That the first (1979–83) Thatcher government presided over a virtual trebling of unemployment to more than three million was deemed by Thatcherites merely as further evidence of the need to weaken the trade unions.

In this context, the Thatcher governments sought to deny and deflect responsibility for high unemployment by claiming that it was 'greedy' trade unions and their members who were 'pricing themselves out of work' through 'excessive' pay claims and 'militant' industrial action. Only a return to 'responsible' trade unionism, encouraged by the Thatcher governments' own reforms, would eventually facilitate lower levels of unemployment through the generation of new employment opportunities, as companies and entrepreneurs become more confident about the viability of developing or expanding their commercial ventures.

Yet until such time, Thatcherite ministers were well aware that rising unemployment was likely to provide much greater labour discipline, as employees became fearful of losing their own jobs, and consequently became much less inclined to seek 'excessive' pay increases, participate in industrial action, or challenge managerial authority in the workplace. Although they rarely expressed it explicitly, it was clear that what Thatcher and her closest ministerial colleagues (along with various backbench Conservative disciples) relished was a cowed and submissive workforce, with employees grateful to have a job at all in the context of high unemployment (and concomitant cutbacks in welfare provision).

As such, high unemployment was viewed as a major means of simultaneously weakening the trade unions, restoring managerial authority – a key phrase in the Thatcherite discourse was that of 'management's right to manage' – and fostering greater compliance amongst the workforce. Indeed, high unemployment not only made it easier for the Thatcher governments to introduce hostile trade union legislation, but also provided an intellectual and ideological rationale for doing so.

Secondly, in introducing their trade union legislation in an incremental manner, the Thatcher governments deliberately sought to maximise the perceived electoral advantages, for not only were proposals for further legislative measures included in the 1983 and 1987 election manifestos, thereby exploiting public hostility towards aspects of trade unionism in Britain, they also served to undermine the Labour Party. This was because when the Labour Party criticised the Thatcher governments' proposals for further trade union legislation, the Conservative Party depicted Labour as 'soft' on the trade unions, and warned voters that if they did elect a Labour government, then the trade unions would once again be permitted to run – and ruin – the country. On the other hand, when they were re-elected, the Thatcher governments could claim that they had been given a mandate by the electorate for further trade union legislation, especially as up to one-third of the Conservative Party's electoral support during the 1980s emanated from trade unionists.

Thirdly, the legislation was framed in such a manner that breaches of the law were deemed civil, rather than criminal, offences. This ensured that legal action against a trade union behaving in an unlawful manner would be instigated by aggrieved individuals – namely affected employers or union members themselves – rather than by ministers. Not only did this clearly accord with the renewed Conservative emphasis on individualism and individual responsibility, it also meant that any legal action against the trade unions would not emanate directly from the government, and as such, would ensure that the state did not become directly embroiled in industrial conflicts. Instead, Conservative ministers invariably claimed that any legal action was a matter for the individuals, unions and courts to resolve between themselves. Having provided the legal framework, ministers argued, it was up to aggrieved individuals or companies to use the legislation to seek redress.

Equally importantly, framing the legislation in order to ensure that breaches were classified as civil offences meant that no trade unionists would actually face imprisonment if they defied the law. Instead, recalcitrant trade unions would be subject to injunctions instructing them to desist from unlawful action, and if these were subsequently defied, damages would be awarded to those affected by the action. Indeed, trade unions who continued to flout the law were liable to face sequestration of their funds, and possible bankruptcy, the possibility of which was presumably envisaged with considerable relish by Thatcherite ministers.

These reflected the important lessons learnt from the ill-fated 1971 Industrial Relations Act, which had sought to bring Britain's trade unions within the ambit of criminal law, whereupon the state itself, via ministers and a specially created Industrial Relations Court, became directly embroiled in industrial disputes. At the same time, the occasional imprisonment of defiant trade union members served to create martyrs around whom the wider trade union movement would rally, thereby exacerbating, not eradicating, industrial conflict and union militancy in Britain. Consequently, Thatcherite ministers were determined to ensure that trade unionists would not be imprisoned as a result of their Labour relations legislation.[10]

Fourthly and finally, the Thatcher governments' trade union legislation was notable for the manner in which it claimed to be concerned to 'democratise' Britain's unions, and thereby 'hand them back to their members'. This characterisation entailed a populist distinction between ordinary, decent, hard-working and politically moderate union members on the one hand, and over-mighty, egotistical, politically motivated and often 'extremist' trade union leaders on the other.[11]

Yet following on from this dichotomy, it was clear that ballots of ordinary trade union members were intended to secure the election of more moderate leaders, and a reduced propensity to pursue strike action.

One of the – intended – consequences of weakening the trade unions and tolerating high unemployment was to restore managerial authority in the workplace. Throughout the 1980s, the Thatcher governments portrayed managers and employers as individuals courageously attempting to run their businesses in the face of trade union obstinacy and obstruction. Indeed, Thatcherite Conservatives viewed business leaders and entrepreneurs as the heroes of British society during the 1980s, depicting them as hard-working and highly motivated individuals seeking to create wealth – and thus jobs and prosperity for everyone else – in an industrial and intellectual climate which, it was alleged, had traditionally disdained wealth creation and money-making.

As such, whilst Conservative ministers routinely condemned workers and trade unions for their 'greed' in obtaining 'excessive' wage increases, no such criticism was ever levelled at the enormous salaries and bonuses which many of Britain's employers and company directors awarded themselves throughout the 1980s and 1990s. No employer was ever admonished for securing an inflationary pay rise, or warned that they were pricing themselves out of work.

Instead, the Thatcher governments sought to enhance the authority of employers and managers through a variety of means. As we have already noted, legislation was an important resource, for by weakening the trade unions, limiting the range of activities which they could lawfully undertake, and rendering it easier for employers to dismiss certain employees, managerial authority was significantly enhanced, which in turn swung the balance of power away from labour back to capital.

However, legislation was by no means the only resource deployed by the Thatcher governments in their determination to restore managerial authority in the workplace during the 1980s. Also of considerable importance was the ideological and rhetorical support given to employers, particularly when they were faced with trade union hostility and opposition. The 1980s witnessed a number of bitter industrial disputes whereby employers 'took on' the trade unions, and were given maximum support and encouragement by Conservative ministers.

For example, in 1983, Eddie Shah, the proprietor of the *Stockport Messenger* newspaper, began recruiting non-union Labour, following an unresolved dispute with the National Graphical Association. The ensuing conflict was accompanied by much bitterness, along with mass picketing, yet Conservative ministers gave full support to Eddie Shah, maintaining that he was quite entitled to employ non-union Labour if he felt unable to gain the co-operation of unions such as the NGA. At the same time, the pickets were often depicted as militants and union 'bully boys', and presented as further vindication of Eddie Shah's decision to switch to non-union Labour. Eddie Shah was thus portrayed as the brave 'little man' trying to exercise his right to manage in the face of trade union intimidation and mob-rule.

Even more notorious was the Wapping dispute which occurred in 1986 when Rupert Murdoch, proprietor of News International (publisher of the *Sun*, *The Times* and the *Sunday Times*) sacked 5,000 employees, and then replaced them with staff who were prepared to accept total managerial authority, coupled with 'no-strike contracts'. Again, the immense bitterness which emerged was plainly visible on the ensuing picket lines in Wapping, yet Murdoch too was viewed as a hero by Conservative ministers delighted at the way he had 'taken on' the trade unions.

Many previous post-war Conservative prime ministers and their Ministerial colleagues had studiously sought to convey an image of impartiality or detachment in the context of industrial disputes, anxious to avoid exacerbating tensions between management and Labour, and fearful that any political display of sympathy for employers might make the trade unions more intransigent and militant. Such Conservatives thus confined themselves to exhorting both sides in an industrial dispute to resolve their disagreements through dialogue and a greater willingness to compromise, or to seek arbitration through an ostensibly impartial institution established for just such a purpose. The Thatcher government's approach, however, was unashamedly the opposite of such conciliatory even-handedness. Thatcher and her ministers explicitly and unequivocally made clear their instinctive and wholehearted support for employers or companies embroiled in an industrial dispute with a trade union, irrespective of either the legitimacy or validity of the unions' grievances, or of any provocation deriving from the words or actions of the employers. For Thatcher and her acolytes, managerial authority in the workplace was inviolate; the sovereignty of employers over their employees indivisible. The rights which Thatcher's governments bestowed upon union members vis-a-vis their unions qua institutions were not matched by comparable rights against their employers.

The third means by which the Conservatives sought to bolster 'management's right to manage' during the 1980s was in the support they offered – material and moral – to the police when dealing with the protests and picket line incidents accompanying industrial disputes. In both of the above instances, along with the notorious miners' strike of 1984–85, Conservative ministers brooked no criticism of police tactics or behaviour on picket lines, but instead, insisted that the police were valiantly upholding law and order in the face of mob-rule, and also defending the 'right to work' of those employees 'courageously' seeking to cross the picket lines in defiance of the unions.

Needless to say, however, when workers were subsequently made redundant – as 250,000 coal miners were – little more was heard from Thatcher and her

Ministers about their 'right to work'. As strike-breakers, they had served their purpose, and so their subsequent fate was of no interest to Thatcherite Conservatives.

A fourth way in which the Conservatives sought to revive managerial authority generally was through endorsing the appointment of high-profile employers who, it was widely recognised, would 'take on' the trade unions in their respective industry. Thus, for example, having 'restructured' the steel industry, Ian MacGregor was appointed chairman of the National Coal Board in 1983, with the clear expectation that he would 'take on' the National Union of Mineworkers, and particularly its prominent left-wing leader, Arthur Scargill. Elsewhere, at British Airways, Lord King was appointed as chairman in the expectation that he too would tackle alleged trade union obstructiveness, and prepare the company for privatisation.[12]

Finally, as already noted previously, managerial authority was effectively restored as a consequence of high unemployment. With up to three million people out of work during Margaret Thatcher's premiership, many of those who were still employed were understandably fearful of losing their own jobs. This served further to shift the balance of power towards employers, enabling the more unscrupulous of them to impose new – less favourable – terms and conditions of employment on their workers or/and reduce wages. Those employees who expressed unhappiness at such treatment were invariably exhorted to be grateful that they still had a job, or asked rhetorically whether they would prefer to swap places with one of the millions on the dole.

The combined emphasis on restoring the primacy of market forces, re-establishing the authority of the state, and reviving managerial control in the workplace, all led ineluctably to a dismantling of the British variant of corporatism which had evolved incrementally during the post-war era.[13]

From the very the outset of her premiership, Margaret Thatcher gave practical effect to the intellectual attack on corporatism which a number of her colleagues had been articulating with increasing vigour during the 1970s.[14]

She clearly agreed with their claims that corporatism entailed ever greater state control over economic affairs; served to politicise decisions which ought to be made solely according to market criteria; fatally undermined individual liberty; privileged producer interests over those of the consumer; and bestowed an unacceptable and unwarranted degree of power on the trade unions. Rather that retain its relative autonomy, and govern in the interests of the whole of British society, Thatcher and her adherents believed that the state, through the drift to corporatism, was surrendering much of its power and authority to 'vested producer interests' like the trade unions, and effectively pooling, rather than protecting, its sovereignty.

Consequently, from 1979 onwards, Britain's trade unions found themselves increasing marginalised by the Thatcher governments, and the tripartite forums on which they had previously enjoyed direct representation being downgraded or displaced. The Thatcherite perspective was that:

The ability of the economy to change and adapt was hampered by the combination of corporatism and powerful unions . . . Corporatism limited competition and the birth of new firms whilst, at the same time, encouraging protectionism and restrictions designed to help existing firms.[15]

The most obvious symbol of British corporatism had been the National Economic Development Council (NEDC), which had been established by Harold Macmillan's Conservative government in 1962 in an attempt at securing a permanent economic and industrial partnership between government, trade unions and employers organisations. Such a body, however, and the consensual approach which it symbolised, were anathema to Thatcher and her ideological adherents, so it was no surprise that the during her premiership, the NEDC was steadily downgraded, with its monthly meetings reduced to just four per year, and increasingly attended by junior ministers and civil servants, rather than the relevant cabinet ministers. The contempt with which many senior Ministers viewed the NEDC was clearly expressed by the Chancellor of the Exchequer for much of the 1980s, Nigel Lawson, who declared that 'no useful purpose was being served . . . the deliberations of the Council itself were a complete waste of valuable ministerial time . . . it should therefore be abolished.'[16] However, the NEDC itself was not finally abolished until 1992, although in lieu of this, many of its thirty-eight Sector Working Parties (the so-called 'little Neddies' which corresponded to specific industries) were dismantled.

Meanwhile, the Thatcher governments also presided over changes to other tripartite institutions on which trade unions had traditionally enjoyed representation alongside employers' representatives. Some of these bodies were also abolished (such as the National Enterprise Board), whilst others had their composition altered, so that the number of employers' representatives or business interests increased considerably, whilst trade union or employee representation was correspondingly reduced.

This rejection of corporatism and tripartism also entailed a reduction in ministerial contacts and meetings with trade union leaders generally. For example, whereas there were twenty-three meetings between the TUC and Conservative ministers in 1985, along with one meeting with the Prime Minister, there were only eleven meetings between ministers and the TUC in 1987, and no meetings at all between trade union leaders and the Prime Minister. Meanwhile, when TUC leaders met the Chancellor in 1993, it was the first such meeting for five years.[17]

This reduction in the number of meetings between trade union leaders and ministers was accompanied by a corresponding diminution in the effectiveness of such meetings (from the trade unions' point of view): a qualitative and a quantitative decline. For example, whereas the TUC had adjudged 47 per cent of its meetings with (Labour) ministers to have been successful or effective back in 1978, it considered less than 19 per cent of its meetings with Conservative Ministers in 1984 to have been a success.[18] Part of the problem for the trade unions was that Conservative ministers tended to use any meetings with the TUC as an opportunity to lecture the trade unions about government policies (and the unions' obligation to accept them), rather than engaging in a genuine dialogue.

Privatisation became a defining feature of the Conservative governments during the 1980s and early 1990s, with a number of objectives being ascribed to the programme of selling nationalised industries, most notably 'rolling back the state,' widening share-ownership (a 'capital-owning democracy,' or 'popular capitalism'), and creating a dynamic, vibrant private enterprise economy freed from the 'dead hand' of government control and bureaucratic interference.

However, one other advantage accrued to the Conservative Governments as a consequence of privatisation, namely a further reduction in trade union membership and power. It was reasoned that as nationalised industries enjoyed a monopoly with regard to their particular product or service, then the trade unions and employees in those industries could cause maximum disruption by engaging in strike action; if train drivers in a nationalised railway industry withdrew their labour, for example, then immense inconvenience might be caused to millions of commuters, and to companies transporting their raw materials or finished products by rail.

Conversely, by returning nationalised industries to the private sector and opening them up to competition (in theory), their monopoly position would be eradicated, along with the power of the trade unions in these industries. Furthermore, the transfer of certain nationalised industries to the private sector has resulted in both regional and functional fragmentation. For example, having been privatised, Britain's railway industry now comprises a plethora of regional railway companies, whilst different aspects of the industry – signalling, track maintenance, train services, etc. – are also operated by different companies. This fragmentation seriously weakened the power of trade unions in the railway industry (as was fully intended) and in turn, made a national rail strike much less likely. As Howell notes, in virtually every case of privatisation, the result has been 'the end of national bargaining and instead a decentralisation to either regional centres or different business groups'.[19] Much the same can be said with regard to local government reform. Thatcherite Conservatives argued that many aspects of local government also involved the monopoly provision of public services, which in turn provided a major source of power for the trade unions; if local authority refuse collectors went on strike, for example, then maximum disruption would be caused to residents because there would be no one else to whom they could turn to collect their household waste. Local government reform remedied this situation, however, by subjecting many local services to Compulsory Competitive Tendering (CCT), which enabled private firms to provide services at local level. This served to deprive public sector workers or trade unions of their hitherto monopoly over the provision of such services. Furthermore, if they did disrupt local services through industrial action, they faced the distinct possibility that a rival firm or service provider might be awarded their contract when it came up for renewal, which, in turn, might lead to the loss of their jobs.

Meanwhile, in other parts of the public sector – most notably the NHS – the introduction of internal markets, 'cost-centres', and Trusts at local or regional level, involved the formal decentralisation of many decisions, including those pertaining to terms and conditions of employment. This, in turn, rendered it more difficult for the relevant trade unions to pursue industrial action at national level, thereby further weakening their bargaining power overall.

Through these various means, therefore, the Conservative governments which Margaret Thatcher led from May 1979 to November 1990 seriously weakened the trade unions, judiciously combining instinctive and ideological hostility towards the unions with a cautious and pragmatic approach to the actual character and timing of the measures implemented. In pursuing these reforms, Thatcher and her ministers variously claimed that they were restoring the competitiveness of the British economy after decades of relative decline, reviving the authority of democratically elected government and the state after a decade in which Britain had become virtually ungovernable, re-establishing managerial authority in the workplace (and labour market discipline generally), and 'handing back' the unions themselves to their ordinary members by wresting power away from self-serving 'bully boy' union leaders and militant activists. As Gilmour's quote at the beginning indicates, many Conservatives and political commentators thus consider Margaret Thatcher's weakening of the trade unions to have constituted her finest and most durable achievement.

Finally, it is worth noting that the Thatcherite attack on Britain's trade unions did not cease after Margaret Thatcher had been replaced by John Major as Conservative Party leader and Prime Minister in November 1990. On the contrary, those who hoped that Major would seek a rapprochement with Britain's trade unions (in accordance with his professed desire to create a nation 'at ease with itself') were subsequently to be disappointed, for the 1990–1997 Conservative governments relentlessly maintained the Thatcherite approach, as evinced by the implementation of yet more restrictive legislation, abolition of the NEDC and Wages Councils, continued promotion of individual pay bargaining and labour market flexibility, and unyielding opposition to relatively modest European Union measures intended to improve employment rights and protection.[20] Britain's trade unions soon discovered that whilst Margaret Thatcher had officially departed, Thatcherism continued unabated.

Notes

1   Quoted in the *Observer* 25 April 1999; see also Ian Gilmour, *Dancing With Dogma: Britain Under Thatcherism* (London: Simon & Schuster, 1992) p. 79.

2   For a history of the Conservative Party's policies towards the trade unions, see Peter Dorey, *The Conservative Party and the Trade Unions* (London: Routledge, 1995).

3   Keith Joseph, *Solving the Union Problem is the Key to Britain's Recovery* (London: Centre for Policy Studies, 1979).

4   See, for example: Kenneth Harris, *Thatcher* (London: Weidenfeld & Nicolson, 1988), pp.40–49; Hugo Young, *One of Us* (London: Pan, 1990), pp.3–13; Hugo Young and Anne Sloman, *The Thatcher Phenomenon* (London: BBC, 1986) pp.12-21.

5   For a discussion of the 'moral economy' of the petit-bourgeoisie, and its corresponding political perspective, see: Frank Bechhofer and Brian Elliott, 'Petty Property: the Survival of a Moral Economy' in Frank Bechhofer and Brian Elliott (eds.) *The Petit Bourgeoisie: Comparative Studies of the Uneasy Stratum* (London: Macmillan, 1981); Frank Bechhofer and Brian Elliott, 'The voice of small business and the politics of survival,' *Sociological Review*, 26,1978; Stuart Hall et al, *Policing the Crisis: Mugging, the State, and Law and Order* (London: Macmillan, 1978), pp.162–4; Roger King and Neil Nugent (eds.) *Respectable Rebels* (London: Hodder & Stoughton, 1979); Nicos Poulantzas, *Classes in Contemporary Capitalism* (London: Verso, 1978), pp.290–92; E.P. Thompson,'Writing by candlelight,' in E.P. Thompson, *Writing by Candlelight* (London: Merlin, 1980); Leon Trotsky, 'The Moralists and Sycophants against Marxism,' in *Leon Trotsky*, John Dewey and George Novack, *Their Morals and Ours* (New York: Pathfinder, 1973), pp.65–66.

6   On the apparent link between Margaret Thatcher's petit-bourgeois background and her political beliefs, see Julian Critchley's often wry observations in *The Palace of Varieties* (London: Faber, 1990), passim and *A Bag of Boiled Sweets* (London: Faber, 1994), passim. On the rise of Thatcherism within in the Conservative Party, see Peter Dorey, 'The exhaustion of a tradition: the death of "one nation" Toryism,' in *Contemporary Politics* 2:4, Winter 1996.

7   The case for which had been lucidly explained by David Mahoney, 'Union strategy wanted,' *Crossbow* (The Bow Group), Summer 1976. For a detailed account of the evolution of Conservative trade union policy during the first four years of Margaret Thatcher's leadership of the Party, see Robert Behrens, 'Blinkers for the carthorse: The Conservative Party and the trade unions 1974–1978,' *Political Quarterly*, October-December 1978; Peter Dorey, 'Between principle, pragmatism and practicability: The development of Conservative Party policy towards the trade unions 1974–1979,' in David Broughton et al (eds.) *British Elections and Parties Yearbook* 1994 (London: Frank Cass, 1995), pp.29- 44; Michael Moran, 'The Conservative Party and the trade unions since 1974,' in *Political Studies*, Vol.27, 1979.

8   Chris Howell, 'Turning to the State: Thatcherism and the Crisis of British Trade Unionism,' in *New Political Science* 1995/1996, 33:4, p.15

9   The five pieces of legislation were: The 1980 Employment Act; 1982 Employment Act; 1984 Trade Union Act;1988 Employment Act; 1990 Employment Act.

10 Norman Tebbit, *Upwardly Mobile* (London: Weidenfeld & Nicolson, 1988), p. 198.

11 See, for example, Clive Buckmaster, 'Industrial progress or political anarchy,' in *Tory Challenge* (Monday Club), September 1977; David Howell, *The Times*, 13 November 1976; Norman Tebbit, 'Don't let's be duped by Labour,' in *Industrial Outlook* (Conservative Central Office), January 1975; Margaret Thatcher, *The Times*, 10 January 1978.

12 Nigel Lawson, *The View From No. 11: Memoirs of a Tory Radical* (London: Bantam, 1992), p. 227

13   For the evolution of the British variant of corporatism up until the 1970s, see: Andrew Cox, 'The Failure of Corporatist State Forms and Policies in Post-War Britain,' in Andrew Cox and Noel O'Sullivan (eds) *The Corporate State: Corporatism and the State Tradition in Western Europe,* (Aldershot: Edward Elgar,1988); Peter Dorey, 'Corporatism in the United Kingdom',. *Politics Review,* 3:2, November 1993; Ray Pahl and Jack Winkler, 'The coming corporatism,' *New Society,* 10 October 1974.

14   See, for example: John Biffen, 'The elephant trap,' in *Conservative Monthly News* April 1977; Nicholas Budgen, House of Commons Debates, 5th series, Vol. 914, cols.1239–40; David Howell, 'Putting the boot into liberal society,' *The Times* 25 April 1972; Timothy Raison, *Power and Parliament* (Oxford: Basil Blackwell, 1979); Arthur Shenfield, 'What about the trade unions?', in Rhodes Boyson (ed.) *An Escape from Orwell's 1984* (London: Churchill Press, 1975); William Waldegrave, *The Binding of Leviathion* (London: Hamish Hamilton, 1978)

15   Department of Trade and Industry, DTI – Department for Enterprise (London: HMSO, 1988), p.1

16   Nigel Lawson, op. cit., pp.713–714. See also Norman Tebbit, op. cit, p.193; Margaret Thatcher, *The Downing Street Years* (London: HarperCollins, 1993), p.94

17   Ibid. p. 204.

18   Neil Mitchell, 'Changing pressure group politics: the case of the TUC 1976–1984,' *British Journal of Political Science,* 14:4, 1897. See also John McIlroy, 'Ten years for the locust: the TUC in the 1980s,' in Derek Cox (ed.), *Facing the Future* (Nottingham: Nottingham University, 1992).

19   Chris Howell, op cit, p.21. See also Labour Research Department, Bargaining Report, 136, February 1994.

20   Peter Dorey, 'No return to beer and sandwiches: Trade union and employment policies under John Major,' in Peter Dorey (ed.), *The Major Premiership: Politics and Policies Under John Major 1990-1997* (Basingstoke: Macmillan,1999), pp.179–198.

March, 1987:
The Foreshadowing of a General Election

E. Bruce Geelhoed

On 11 May, 1987 British Prime Minister Margaret Thatcher drove to Buckingham Palace for a meeting with Queen Elizabeth II to request a dissolution of Parliament on 18 May and a general election on June 11. In that fashion, British voters received the official answer to the question which had been on their minds for more than a year: would Thatcher announce a general election in 1987 or wait until early 1988 when the term of her government expired? Was it to be May or June, 1987, or April 1988?[1] To that point, Thatcher had wisely concealed her intentions about the timing of the election in order to give herself as much latitude as possible. The timing of the election, therefore, remained the subject of conjecture and speculation right until Thatcher spelled out her plans on 11 May.

In retrospect, it now appears that the Conservatives, and Prime Minister Thatcher, had set their sights on a June election in 1987 and a series of fortuitous events, in and around March 1987, combined to convince the government that a June date provided them with their best opportunity to win a third consecutive victory. These events included: the victories by the SDP-Liberal Alliance party at by-elections in Greenwich on 26 February and at Truro on 11 March, two victories which shook voter confidence in the Labour Party and led to a sharp decline in its standing in the public opinion polls; the presentation of the government's Budget for 1987–1988 on 16 March by Nigel Lawson, Chancellor of the Exchequer, a budget which promised typical Conservative fiscal stability on the one hand and a handful of spending programmes designed to attract voter support on the other; the visit by Neil Kinnock, leader of the Labour Party, to Washington on 23–27 March for talks with President Ronald Reagan, an event which underscored the weakness of the Labour Party on the defence issue as well as the preference of the American government for Thatcher's leadership; and, finally, Margaret Thatcher's visit to Moscow between 28–31 March for a mini-summit with Soviet President Mikhail Gorbachev, talks which enhanced Thatcher's reputation as an international leader. The combined effect of these events in March was critical for the Conservatives. At the beginning of March, the Tories held a six per cent lead over the Labour Party, 36 per cent to 30 per-cent, in *The Times* /MORI poll (the poll considered the most reliable of the numerous political polls taken in Britain). By the first week in April, the Conservatives had moved out to a twelve-point lead over Labour and were gain-ing strength while their primary opponent appeared to be trapped in a frantic attempt to stabilise itself.[2] An examination of each of these events reveals their impact, not only upon the timing of the election, but also upon its results.

An early indicator of the current state of political thinking in Britain occurred in late February and early March when British voters elected successors to Guy Barnett, Labour MP for Greenwich who died from a heart attack on Christmas Eve 1986, and David Penhaligon, Liberal MP for Truro who died in a motor vehicle accident in January 1987. Of these two by-elections, the result at Greenwich was clearly the most significant in terms of its impact upon the polit-ical environment. Since 1945, the Labour Party had controlled the Greenwich seat and, even though its margin of victory had declined in the most recent elec-tion, 1983, the seat was still considered safe for Labour.

As the successor to Guy Barnett, Labour chose Deirdre Wood, the chair of the London Inner Education Authority, as its candidate. Wood's choice turned out to be a setback for Labour, primarily because of her identification with the Party's hard-Left faction, known within Britain as 'the loony (for lunatic) Labour Left.' This noisy, cantankerous, but extremely committed and activist faction of the Party was associated with a host of left-wing causes in education, gay and lesbian rights, nuclear disarmament, and others.[3] Politically, the 'loonies' presented a threat to many of London's traditional working-class and middle-class voters who were concerned about higher taxes, rising crime, poor schools, and the threat of urban AIDS epidemic. Before long, Wood's association with the 'loonies' became a major political liability and she began losing ground rapidly in the public opinion polls.

The beneficiary of Wood's misfortune was not John Antcliffe, a 25-year-old merchant banker who was running for the Conservatives, but instead Rosie Barnes, a 40-year-old homemaker and market researcher who was the candidate of the SDP-Liberal Alliance. Married to John Barnes, a Greenwich councillor, she was an energetic mother of three children. Supremely confident and 'a natural communicator', Barnes was determined to pull out all the stops in her effort to win the seat.

To that end, Barnes enlisted the assistance of Alex McGivan, the Alliance's main strategist and organiser. A self-described workaholic, the 33-year-old McGivan was connected to Matt Reece and Associates, a Washington-based firm which had managed campaigns for several American politicians. McGivan told Barnes to concentrate on two themes: her residence in Greenwich and her 'common-sense' approach to the issues in the campaign. McGivan consistently instructed the Barnes supporters to remind the voters that 'Rosie lives here' and 'her heart's in the right place but so is her head'. Such references were direct slaps at the Conservatives, viewed as 'uncaring' toward ordinary people, as well as at Labour, whose policies were considered too costly and ineffective.

To reinforce those themes, McGivan instituted an Americanisation of Barnes's drive for the House of Commons. Using the techniques of computerised research, direct mail, and individual targeting of voters, McGivan quickly built a momentum behind the Barnes campaign which was galvanised by a small army of volunteers who worked tirelessly in the field, canvassing voters and promoting their candidate. Barnes proved to be a tireless, exceptionally attractive campaigner herself. By late January, she had passed Antcliffe in the polls and was taking aim at Deirdre Wood.

With victory in sight, McGivan and Barnes turned to an ingenious British strategem, tactical voting, a device employed by the Alliance which quickly struck fear into the hearts of both the Conservative Party and the Labour Party. As an instrument of political mischief-making, tactical voting involved convincing voters of one party, in a three-way race, to vote for the candidate who was most likely to deprive their primary opponent of victory. Once Barnes overtook Antcliffe in the polls, she began actively courting Conservative voters, urging them to vote for the Alliance and deprive Labour of a seat in the House of Commons. Her message was clear: 'The Tory can't win and you don't want a left-wing Parliament. Vote Alliance.'

Tactical voting worked for Barnes. With Antcliffe's support in decline, Conservative voters leaped at the chance to spoil the contest for Labour. In the final weeks of the campaign, the Barnes team intensified its targeting of Tory voters and, by election eve, the polls showed Barnes as the clear favourite. Professional political observers in Britain expressed astonishment at the Barnes surge.

The result of the Greenwich by-election was a smashing victory for Rosie Barnes. She tallied 19,297 votes (53 per cent) to 11,676 to Deirdre Wood (34 per cent), and 3,852 for John Antcliffe (11 per cent). Antcliffe's total was the lowest for any Conservative candidate running for the Greenwich seat since 1979. It that respect, his total revealed the degree to which tactical voting had influenced the outcome of the election. The vote total for the Alliance almost doubled from the General Election of 1983 whereas the vote for Labour declined by almost 2000 from its level in 1979. The Tory vote was down by 8,500 from 1983, proof that Tories had engaged in widespread tactical voting.[4]

Despite the tactical voting, however, Rosie Barnes's victory was clearly no fluke. In analyzing the by-election, British political commentators credited Barnes and McGivan with conducting the most 'meticulously planned' campaign which Britain had recently witnessed. Her victory margin of 6,600 votes showed that voters preferred her candidacy to that of both the Conservative and Labour candidates. On March 7, *The Economist* reported that the Alliance's 'thumping victory at the Greenwich by-election on February 26 has left [the Conservatives and Labour] rattled'.[5]

Recriminations within the Labour Party set in shortly after its defeat at Greenwich. On March 9, press reports revealed the contents of a letter sent by Patricia Hewitt, press secretary to Neil Kinnock, to a Labour supporter in Greenwich which blamed Labour's defeat on Deirdre Wood's 'loony left' reputation. Hewitt wrote: 'It's obvious that the "London effect" is now very noticeable. "The loony Labour Left" is taking its toll. [It appears] that the London party is pulling Labour down nationally.'[6]

The Alliance victory at Greenwich was repeated on 13 March when the Liberal candidate, Matthew Taylor, retained the seat held by David Penhaligon.

On this occasion, tactical voting did not factor in the outcome but a second Alliance victory in just two weeks appeared to suggest a strengthening of support for the third party throughout Britain. After Taylor's victory, David Steel, leader of the Liberal Party, captured the mood of the Alliance when he declared: 'This is a much greater triumph than we ever hoped for. I believe that this result will make Mrs Thatcher more cautious about going to a general election but her responsibility now is either to name the day or say she is going through to the end [of the term].'[7]

The strength of the Alliance caused concern within the Conservative camp, also. The fear which the Tories privately expressed was that tactical voting for Alliance candidates could deprive the Tories of victories in many 'marginal' seats in the middle of Britain, thereby leading to a hung Parliament or even a Labour victory. The Conservatives, led by Thatcher and Norman Tebbit, the party chairman, decided to take their gloves off and attack the Alliance at the next opportunity.

Between 20–22 March, the Conservatives held their Central Party Council meeting at Torquay. Tebbit was the first to launch into an attack on the Alliance. The best man on the attack in British politics at that time, Tebbit was also the most nicknamed politician in Britain. Some of the unflattering sobriquets attached to Tebbit were 'the Chingford Strangler', 'The Hound of the Baskervilles', 'Dracula', or more commonly within the party simply as 'the Assassin'. A writer for *The Economist* described Tebbit in much the same vein: 'Mr Tebbit clearly regards political opponents not as fellow practitioners of the same art who happen, sadly, to be of a different persuasion, but as a species of insect, to be crushed, if possible, underfoot.'[8]

At the conference, Tebbit lashed out at the policies of the Alliance and, personally at David Steel, with whom he had been carrying on a rhetorical feud since the Truro by-election. According to Tebbit, speaking on March 30, the 'Alliance was playing a dirty game. [Its] aim is quite simply to smile and say nothing. That is what I really dislike about the Liberal Party, the downright deceit, the selling tactics that would land a doorstop encyclopaedia salesman in jail'.[9]

On 21 March, Thatcher piled in. In her estimation, the 'SDP were retread socialists who had gone along with nationalisation and increased trade union power when in office' [as members of Labour governments]; and the Liberals were 'the least scrupulous force in British politics'.[10] Her opponents distinguished themselves by their 'full-blown socialism' (Labour); by their 'half-baked socialism' (the Alliance); and by their 'half-hearted socialism' (the Liberals). Thatcher told the party faithful that 'I gather at the next election [the Alliance] are hoping to be asked to give us an encore – the two Davids in that ever popular musical delight: "Don't Tell My Mother I'm Only Half of a Horse in a Panto". I am told that Mr Steel has been rehearsing for it this week'.[11]

In launching their attack on the Alliance, or as Tebbit put it, 'the liberal half of the Alliance', the Conservative leadership was trying to solidify Tory support and deal a blow to the prospect of tactical voting. Given some time, this strategy worked. Gains for the Alliance over the next month occurred primarily at the expense of Labour and national support for the Conservatives inched ever higher to the 40 per cent level.

Elections are decided on voters' perceptions of the state of the economy, and in the spring of 1987, the Conservatives clearly held the high ground in terms of public confidence in their economic policies. By this time, Britain had clearly rebounded from the difficult economic conditions which prevailed in the country between 1978 and 1981. In 1987, the British economy had been improving for six consecutive years and the major indices of economic activity: productivity, new business starts, the trade balance, the rate of new investment, and the rate of economic growth, were all trending in the government's favour.

To some extent, Thatcher was able to claim credit for the healthy economy. During her eight years in office, she had reduced taxes, 'privatised' several of Britain's nationalised corporations, reduced the deficit, and passed legislation restraining the power of trade unions. The expanding economy had yielded higher tax revenues and reduced the level of borrowing, known as the Public Sector Borrowing Requirement (PSBR). Most important, Thatcher's governments appeared to have whipped inflation. In 1986, inflation stood at 3.4 per cent, well below the double-digit levels of the previous decade.

Thatcher's economic record was not entirely positive, of course. In 1987, Britain's most persistent economic problem was its high level of unemployment, still hovering around per cent with three million British out of work. Britain's transition from an industrially based economy to one based on knowledge and information made life extremely painful for the large numbers of unemployed workers and miners in the North, Wales, and Scotland. By 1987, Great Britain had become two nations in economic terms: a relatively prosperous South and an economically distressed North. The prevailing high levels of unemployment, combined with Britain's changing economic demography, represented the twin issues which Thatcher's opponents planned to emphasise in their attempt to bring down her government.

Despite the claims of Thatcher's supporters and critics, several economic facts were irrefutable. Inflation was at its lowest in over fifteen years; unemployment, while high, appeared to be coming down; Britain's annual rate of economic growth, 3.4 per cent, was the highest in Europe, surpassing that of even West Germany; interest rates were down; and the average British worker's pre-tax income had increased by over 25 per cent since 1979.[12]

To the extent that the good news on the economy figured in the Conservative Party's pre-election planning, the event which highlighted the government's record was its annual budget message, delivered to the House of Commons on 16 March by Nigel Lawson, Chancellor of the Exchequer. After a successful career as a journalist, Lawson entered politics in the late 1960s. He joined Thatcher's cabinet in 1981 as Energy Secretary and became Chancellor in 1983. For the next four years, Lawson became increasingly prominent as one of Thatcher's closest advisers. Known as a radical Conservative like Thatcher, Lawson believed in tax reductions and tight restraint on the growth of public spending.

On March 16, Lawson presented the government's Budget to the House of Commons in a speech designed to bring maximum benefit to the Conservative record. He called for a 2 per cent reduction in the basic rate of personal income tax, from 29 per cent to 27 per cent; a sizeable reduction in the PSBR; and a further reduction in interest rates. He proposed no new taxes on cigarettes or alcohol and the abolition of some duties levied on the gambling industry.

That evening, Lawson gave a televised presentation of the Budget to the country. In a masterful performance, illustrated with charts and graphs, Lawson spoke glowingly about Britain's recent economic performance. After lagging well behind the rest of Europe in terms of economic growth, the British had now 'moved to the top of the league'.[13] He discussed the benefits to the average wage-earner of the government's programme of tax reductions and spending restraint. He emphasised that Conservative policies had resulted in strong economic growth, increased consumer spending, and record levels of investment. Under the Thatcher government, Lawson argued that Britain had enjoyed its most sustained period of economic growth since 1945.

The Tories greeted Lawson's Budget enthusiastically, maintaining that the Chancellor had scored a 'hat trick' by producing a programme with tax cuts, lower interest rates, and less borrowing. Likewise, the financial community responded positively and the London stock market surged the day after Lawson delivered his message.[14]

Predictably, the Labour Party's response to the government's Budget focused on its inadequate response to the problem of unemployment. Neil Kinnock scorned the Conservative Party's economic package as 'a bribes budget . . . that had little to do with the general good and everything to do with the General Election. Instead of across-the-board tax cuts, we need across-the-board cuts in unemployment'.[15] Tony Blair, a Labour MP who specialised in economic policy, echoed Kinnock's comments, warning the voters on 15 March to 'beware the bribes of March'.[16]

Kinnock's criticism of the government's Budget represented Labour's desire to appeal to its natural constituencies. Instead of reducing taxes, Kinnock proposed to use the additional revenue to finance Labour's employment programmes. Instead of reducing taxes across-the-board, Kinnock believed in more spending designed to reduce unemployment, build housing, and stimulate industrial development. Besides, Kinnock claimed, in a remark which later had serious political consequences, if people received a tax reduction, 'they'd just use the money to buy imports'.[17]

Thatcher wasted no time in pouncing on Kinnock's comments. On March 19, during question time in the House of Commons, she charged that 'the Labour Party [cannot] trust their own constituents, their own people, to spend their money, in their own way'.[18] In that fashion, the Prime Minister introduced a message which was heard repeatedly for the next several months: the Labour Party had such a patronising attitude towards British wage earners that it would not even trust them to manage their money properly.

On the same day, Lord Young, the government's Secretary of State for Employment, announced that the number of unemployed British had declined by 71,427 in February. This figure was the largest monthly decline in unemployment in Britain since 1973 and Young confidently stated that 'we have now had falls [in unemployment] for seven months. There appears little doubt that the monthly fall which has been running at 20,000 will continue, as will our stronger economic performance, particularly after the Chancellor's Budget measures'.[19]

For the Conservatives, the economic news was highly positive in March 1987, as was the improving economy's impact upon their political prospects. As Chris Ogden wrote: 'Thatcher, simultaneously broadcasting the economic news, reaped the benefits. After eight years, her programmes were kicking in.'[20] With the momentum clearly moving in the government's favour, the Labour opposition faced a daunting task as it contemplated its comeback before the announcement of a General Election.

Hardly anything went right for the Labour Party in the spring of 1987. Still stinging from their defeats in the by-elections at Greenwich and at Truro, Neil Kinnock and the Labour leadership lost further ground in the polls when the Tories trumpeted the good news about the economy in mid-March. Traditionally, British voters expressed a preference for Labour's policies on social issues, including education, but even those policies received a setback between and 11–20 March when Britain's two largest teachers unions, the National Union of Teachers (NUT) and the National Association of School Mistresses/Union of Women Teachers (NAS/UWT) conducted a nuisance strike against local school authorities throughout the country. The strike ended without incident on March 20 but the government, led by Education Secretary Kenneth Baker, took the occasion to criticise the leadership of the two unions for their 'illegal' strike, and by implication the Labour Party, for its support of the job action.

For Neil Kinnock, however, the most troublesome problem which he faced was reconciling Labour's 'non-nuclear' defence policy with the British public's support for NATO, defence co-operation with the United States, and arms control negotiations with the Soviet Union.

In 1986, Labour had adopted its non-nuclear policy, pledging that the next Labour government would dismantle Britain's independent nuclear deterrent; undertake negotiations with the United States for the removal of American nuclear forces from Britain; and cancel the agreement with the United States to purchase Trident III missiles in the 1990s. The policy represented a sharp departure not only from the policies of the Thatcher government but also with the policies of previous Labour governments led by Clement Attlee, Harold Wilson, and James Callaghan.

Within the Labour Party, the adoption of the non-nuclear policy signified a victory for the hard-Left faction and many Labour MPs expressed serious misgivings about the party's position on defence. On 8 March former Prime Minister James Callaghan broke publicly with his party in a speech before the House of Commons. 'This was no time for Britain to abandon Trident as the replacement for Polaris,' he stated. 'Multilateralism is the only route to disarmament. The decision by the last Labour government to deploy the [American] cruise missiles helped bring the Russians back to the negotiating table.'[21] Even the most ardent Thatcherite could not have given a better speech in support of the government and jubilant Tory MPs repeatedly interrupted Callaghan's speech with cheers and applause.

Faced with Callaghan's opposition, Kinnock retreated and, on March 18, he chose to modify Labour's position by saying that Labour would not insist on the removal of American cruise missiles from Britain while arms control negotiations remained in progress. Labour's anti-nuclear activists responded in fury to Kinnock's comments, leaving the British public confused as to whether the Party could make up its mind about such a vital matter. Undoubtedly, Kinnock hoped to defuse some of the tension on the defence issue before his scheduled trip to Washington in late March for meetings with President Ronald Reagan, Secretary of Defence Caspar Weinberger, and other administration officials. Kinnock placed great hope in these meetings, especially since a previous trip to the United States in December 1986 had gone poorly for him. Knowing the Reagan Administration's support for Thatcher, several of Kinnock's advisers urged him not to go to America, fearing a public relations disaster. But, as Peter Jenkins wrote: 'Kinnock was now trailing in the opinion polls with a general election imminent.'[22] Up to this point, Kinnock had failed to move the ball on the ground; now he was forced to throw the long pass.

On 27 March, Kinnock arrived at the White House for his meeting with Ronald Reagan. Controversy and confusion followed almost immediately.

According to diplomatic protocol, as the leader of an opposition party, Kinnock was entitled to a thirty-minute meeting with Reagan. Reagan arrived at the meeting ten minutes late, however. Was this an intentional snub of Kinnock? Then, during the meeting, Reagan repeatedly referred to Denis Healey, Labour's Shadow Defence Secretary, as British Ambassador Antony Acland, who was embarrassingly present during the session.

The substantive part of the discussions enabled Kinnock to inform Reagan of Labour's non-nuclear policy and its implications for future British-American relations. According to Kinnock, Reagan listened politely but neither endorsed nor expressed any 'overt criticism' of his remarks. Kinnock assured Reagan that Labour supported Britain's membership in NATO and the President assured him that the administration pledged to remain neutral in any future British election.[23] Speaking with reporters after the election, Kinnock was relaxed and optimistic. He described his talks as 'friendly and constructive', but admitted that Reagan indicated his reservations with certain aspects of Labour's defence policy. Most importantly, the meeting lasted the full thirty minutes.

White House versions of the Reagan-Kinnock meeting were considerably different. Reagan had no intention of co-operating with Kinnock and he even linked the Labour Party's position on defence with Britain's appeasement policies of the late 1930s. In a statement released by the White House after the meeting, Reagan insisted that the West must be prepared, 'as it had not been in 1939', for the risk of a world war. Casting more doubt on Labour's defence policy, Secretary Weinberger told reporters that any savings which Labour anticipated by phasing out its nuclear forces would be insufficient to fund the improvements in conventional capability which Kinnock advocated.

Instantly, Kinnock's dream of a successful visit to the United States evaporated. Not only had Reagan opposed his policy but, within days of the meeting, Kinnock found himself accused by the British press of provoking a split between Britain and the United States over the defence issue. Once the Kinnock delegation returned to Britain, the Labour leadership attempted an awkward exercise in damage control, blaming Marlin Fitzwater, Reagan's spokesman, of intentionally undermining the objectives of the visit.

The forthcoming political fallout from Kinnock's disastrous visit to America created a host of new problems for the Labour Party. A set of public opinion polls released on March 29 showed Labour in third place, 2 per cent behind the Alliance and 12 per cent behind the Conservatives. To quote Peter Jenkins, Kinnock's 'colleagues regarded his decision to go ahead as the stupidest he had ever taken. [The trip was] a total, total disaster'.[25]

Moreover, Kinnock's personal standing in the polls dropped in the post-Washington period. Prior to the Washington visit, 45 per cent of British voters surveyed had a positive opinion of Kinnock. After Washington, only 25 per cent held that view.[26] The trip reinforced the Tory caricature of Kinnock as the 'Welsh windbag', prone to astonishing rhetorical gaffes.

Incumbency has its advantages. Nigel Lawson's Budget presentation on March 16, delivered during a period when the British economy was expanding, allowed the Conservatives to seize the high ground on the economic issue. Thatcher and her advisers also used their incumbency on the issue of foreign affairs, highlighting her stature as a world leader and contrasting the Prime Minister's persona with the confusion which existed in the public's mind about Labour's positions on national security matters. Repeatedly, Thatcher had gone on to the world stage during her tenure in office, meeting with the heads of European countries as well as conferring with Soviet President Mikhail Gorbachev and American President Ronald Reagan.

Throughout her time in office, Thatcher had worked to restore Britain's status as a country with a role to play in international relations. Britain's poor economic showing during the 1970s contributed to the belief that the British had become insignificant in both world and European affairs. The British economic recovery during the 1980s, combined with Thatcher's personal diplomacy in Africa (Zimbabwe) and Asia (Hong Kong) and her re-emphasis on the 'special relationship' with the United States, illustrated the 'top table' effect by which Britain returned to the fore in world politics.

Thatcher's most skilful use of her incumbency occurred between 28 and 31 March 1987 when she visited the Soviet Union for bilateral talks with Soviet President Mikhail Gorbachev.

The stated purposes of the Moscow mini-summit were to respond to Gorbachev's visit to Britain in 1984 and also to discuss issues of European security prior to the superpower summit between Gorbachev and Reagan expected for later in 1987. In addition to the discussion of strategic issues, however,

Thatcher also intended to raise the subjects of religious freedom and human rights with Gorbachev.

Regardless of the political overtones involved with this visit, both Thatcher and Gorbachev took the occasion seriously. The Soviets scheduled Thatcher for five different series of talks with Gorbachev, with 31 March, entirely blocked out for meetings between the two leaders. On 29 March, Thatcher's first full day in Russia, the Prime Minister visited the Holy Trinity Monastery of St. Sergius in Zagorsk, forty-five miles outside of Moscow.

At Zagorsk, Thatcher lit a candle for peace and met briefly with a leader of the Russian Orthodox Church. To underscore the importance which she attached to religious freedom, Thatcher declared: 'If you are going to deny [your people] freedom of speech and freedom of worship, then you are a danger to other countries.'[27]

Direct talks between Gorbachev and Thatcher began on March 30, and such subjects as nuclear weapons policy, human rights, and the general scope of East–West relations. In a day of hard discussion, characterised by *The Times* of London as 'megaphone diplomacy', the two leaders discussed the INF negotiations, human rights, and the continued Soviet presence in Afghanistan. Thatcher clearly was hawkish on the role of nuclear weapons. Quoting from Winston Churchill, hardly a hero in the Kremlin, she recalled: 'Be careful above all things not to let go of the atomic weapon until you are sure, more than sure, that other means of preserving peace are in your hands.'[28]

For his part, Gorbachev showed in his remarks that he did not intend to take a back seat to Thatcher when it came to defending the positions of his government. Gorbachev condemned nuclear weapons as 'evil' and contended that the NATO countries were reneging on their previous proposals to reduce intermediate range nuclear weapons in Europe. He also warned Thatcher that the West should not push him too quickly on political reform in the Soviet Union and chastised her for the British government's record on human rights. 'How can you talk about human rights in the West with millions of homeless living a beggarly existence?' he asked. Gorbachev also spoke about those 'who police beat up', (a reference to alleged police brutality in London and Belfast); 'those whose human rights are subject to indignity mainly because of the colour of their skin', and 'trade unionists whose rights to defend their members has been removed'. 'Talk about human rights – talk about all rights.'[29]

In substantive terms, the Thatcher–Gorbachev summit produced no startling agreements; only a few minor accords dealing with trade and cultural exchanges. From other perspectives, however, the visit was significant. It cleared the path for a future summit between Reagan and Gorbachev and the resumption of the INF negotiations. The visit also dispelled much of the inflexible, Iron Lady image which the Soviets had cast around Thatcher's persona. Thatcher was able to talk freely with ordinary Soviet citizens during the course of her visit. One Soviet lady, interviewed by a reporter for the British Broadcasting Corporation (BBC), went so far as to say that Thatcher was 'much more good looking than I had expected from television. It is a very good thing for both our countries that she can come out and meet us like this. It will make us forget she is the Iron Lady'.[30]

Once Thatcher returned to London from Moscow, it became clear that her trip to the Soviet Union was going to yield enormous political dividends. The standing of the Conservative Party continued its upward move in national opinion polls. More important, Thatcher's reception in Moscow contrasted sharply with the rude treatment given to Neil Kinnock in Washington just a few days earlier. As a writer for *The Economist* put it: 'Gorbachev voted Tory for Thatcher; Reagan voted Tory against Kinnock. [There is] little dispute which party leader has, and has not, fallen below the level of events.'[31]

By the end of the first week in April, Thatcher and the Conservatives stood on the brink of a third electoral triumph. The economic news in March had been positive and Lawson's Budget was well received by the voters. Thatcher's mini-summit with Gorbachev reinforced her status as a world leader. The result of the *Sunday Times* poll on 5 April showed the Tories with their largest lead since 1983 and, if the poll results held up, the Conservatives were on target for at least an eighty-seat majority in the next election.[32]

Did the events of March have anything to do with the outcome of the elections? Many British political observers, as well as several individuals in both the Conservative and Labour campaigns, certainly believed so. For example, in the case of the by-election at Greenwich, sentiment existed within the Conservative Party that Labour's defeat demonstrated the vulnerability of Labour candidates nationwide. As Chris Ogden wrote: 'The catalyst for [Thatcher's decision] was the by-election only four miles down the Thames from the Tower Bridge in Greenwich.'[33] Likewise, David Butler and Dennis Kavanagh cited Labour's 'disastrous showing' in

Greenwich as a key indicator of the uphill struggle which Labour faced in the upcoming campaign. According to one Labour supporter, 'What changed everything was [the] Greenwich [defeat] and subsequent rows because they reawoke the fears which many potential Labour voters still had about Labour extremism, divisions, unfitness for government, and Kinnock's own leadership ability.'[34]

Likewise, the defence issue cut both ways by benefiting the Tories on the one hand and damaging Labour on the other. Again, to cite Butler and Kavanagh: 'The rebuff to Mr Kinnock in the White House on 27 March contrasted with Mrs Thatcher's reception in Moscow the following week. James Callaghan's public disagreement with the party's nuclear policy . . . kept the issue and the party divisions in the headlines.'[35] Moreover, during the election campaign, both the Labour Party and Neil Kinnock personally mounted a spirited effort and closed their initial gap with the Tories. One Conservative tactician, complimenting the 'evangelical fervour' of the Labour campaign, believed that 'we'd have lost the election without defence.'[36] In that respect, Thatcher's forcefulness in dealing with the Soviet leadership while in Moscow galvanised public opinion in favour of the Tory position on defence.

As Rodney Tyler wrote: 'It was the third Tory 'goal'– a solo dribble from deep in her own half – which was far and away the most spectacular. The Prime Minister's extraordinary trip to Russia at the end of March had a stunning impact both in Britain and in the host country.'[37]

However one views the effect of the March events, the fact remained: Thatcher and the Tories won their third consecutive victory on June 11. In an exciting, unpredictable, and exhausting campaign, she carved out her particular place in British history. If people no longer contemptuously referred to the 'British disease' of a poor economy and an aimless foreign policy, Thatcher must receive the lion's share of the credit.

Notes

1   Chris Ogden, *Maggie* (New York: Simon and Schuster), p. 274; Peter Jenkins, *Mrs Thatcher's Revolution* (Cambridge, MA: Harvard University Press, 1988), p. 328; Rodney Tyler, *Campaign!: The Selling of the Prime Minister* (London: Grafton Books, 1987), pp. 94–95.

2   'Thatcher To Move,' *Economist*, Vol. 303, no. 7493 (11 April 1987), pp. 14–15.

3   *The Times*, 18 March 1987.

4   *The Times*, 28 February 1987.

5   'The Fight for Second Place,' *Economist*, Vol. 302, no. 7488 (7 March 1987), p. 55.

6   *The Times*, 9 March 1987; see also David Butler and Dennis Kavanagh, T*he British General Election of 1987* (New York: St. Martin's Press, 1988), pp. 55–57.

7   E. Bruce Geelhoed, *Margaret Thatcher: In Triumph and Downfall*, 1987 and 1990 (Westport, CN: Praeger, 1992), pp. 54–56.

8   *Economist*, vol. 309, no. 7579 (3 December 1988), p.101.

9   Geelhoed, Margaret Thatcher, p. 22; Norman Tebbit, *Upwardly Mobile* (London: Weidenfeld and Nicolson, 1988), p. 259.

10   Margaret Thatcher, *Downing Street Years* (London: Harper Collins, 1993), pp. 573-574.

11   Ibid; Geelhoed, *Margaret Thatcher*, p. 23; Tyler, *Campaign*, pp. 66-67.

12   Tebbit, *Upwardly Mobile*, p. 259; Tyler, *Campaign*, pp. 83-85.

13   *Sunday Times*, 17 May 1987.

14   Geelhoed, *Margaret Thatcher*, pp. 17-18.

15   'The Pleasures of a Tory Chancellor,' *Economist*, 302, no. 7486 (21 February 1987), pp. 55-56; 'Up She Goes,' *Economist*, 302, no. 7490, (21 March 1987), pp. 13-14; Ogden, *Maggie*, pp. 275-276; Hugo Young, *The Iron Lady* (New York: Farrar, Straus, Giroux, 1989), p. 512; Butler and Kavanagh, *The British General Election of 1987*, p. 41.

16   Ogden, *Maggie*, pp. 275-276.

17   Ibid.

18   Ibid.

19   Ibid.

20   Ibid, pp. 19–20.

21   Ibid., pp. 275–276.

22   *The Times*, 9 March 1987; Butler and Kavanagh, *The British General Election of 1987*, p. 69.

23   Jenkins, *Mrs Thatcher's Revolution*, pp. 308–309.

24   Geelhoed, *Margaret Thatcher*, pp. 74–75; Ogden, *Maggie*, p. 291.

25   Geelhoed, *Margaret Thatcher*, pp. 74–75.

26   Jenkins, *Mrs Thatcher's Revolution*, pp. 308–309.

27   Ibid, p. 319.

28   Geelhoed, *Margaret Thatcher*, p. 29.

29   *The Times*, 1 April 1987.

30   Ibid, 5 April 1987.

31   Geelhoed, *Margaret Thatcher*, p. 77.

32   *Sunday Times*, 5 April 1987.

33   Ogden, *Maggie*, p. 274.

34   Butler and Kavanagh, *The British General Election of 1987*, pp. 56–57, 72.

35   Ibid., p. 69.

36   Jenkins, *Mrs Thatcher's Revolution*, p. 333.

37   Tyler, *Campaign!*, 94.

Thatcher's Half-Revolution:
Economics Was Not Enough

Candace Hetzner

———

Prime Minister Margaret Thatcher and her government set out to make Britain a robust free enterprise economy and, thus, to overcome decades of decline. The Thatcher 'revolution' had at its core the creation of an 'enterprise culture' that would encompass the values necessary to a highly productive, modern free market economy. The Thatcherite approach to securing such a flourishing culture and economy focused primarily on economic structural change such as privatising government-owned entities, ending government subsidisation of business, and deregulating in some spheres. Certainly, the economic agenda of Thatcherism contained other elements of reform such as promotion of monetarism and fiscal restraint as well as the reduction of trade union power. Nevertheless, the central strategy of the Thatcherite grand economic project was simply to take as much of the economy out of the hands of government and Whitehall as possible and to place the economy in the hands of the private sector.

As a result of this limited structural strategy, the Thatcher government could bring the enterprise culture only to partial fruition. Despite the tremendous economic successes of the Thatcher government in just over eleven years, it still gave Britain at best a half-revolution that left the economic agenda vulnerable. For the cultural transformation that Thatcherism desired required a major shift in British values. True, British culture appeared at the end of the Thatcher era to have embraced such capitalist notions as private ownership, profit, and increased consumption more than ever before. But the culture failed to have adopted other crucial ones, namely, those supportive of modernisation, in general, and the modern business enterprise and those who run it, in particular. The government needed to have overcome traditional cultural biases favouring leisure over hard work and productivity; amateur, generalist abilities over professional, specialist expertise; and theoretical over applied pursuits. Moreover, Thatcherism needed to have elevated the status of entrepreneurs, managers, or engineers from second-class professionals to cultural heroes to be admired and emulated. Though undoubtedly a fair amount of normative change did follow from reconfiguring the balance of public and private, such an approach was not sufficient for effecting many other necessary value shifts.

Because the Thatcher government focused nearly exclusively on socialist ideology and policy, the government did little to address the anti-modern, anti-business cultural values rooted in and reinforced by the evolution of the British power structure over the centuries. Thatcherism needed to have provided an ideology and policies, discourse and action, that would have shifted British values in favour of a modern business economy.

Examining what Thatcherite ideology and strategy neglected is useful in several ways. First of all, it helps to explain the failure of Thatcherism to deliver a more complete economic revolution. Secondly, it may also further understanding of the directions taken by post-Thatcher governments, most especially those of the present Blairite 'Third Wa..' Thirdly, many countries, currently adopting more capitalist economic systems, can benefit from a picture of what more is needed beyond reforming the economic structures of their societies.

No doubt Thatcherism recognised the deep cultural biases against modernisation and business. Most obvious was the working class prejudice against the bosses that had been abiding since the Industrial Revolution. It was this opposition to the immiseration of the worker that gave rise to the Labour Party and the development of its socialist ideology. The tradition of working-class antagonism to the bosses, of course, had roots that went far deeper than the Industrial Revolution, roots that lay in pre-capitalist resentment of the masters in their various incarnations from lord of the manor to master of the cottage. Interestingly, however, modern working-class antagonism to the masters has been far more focused on the business bosses than on others in positions of power, authority, and privilege in British society. Ferdinand Zweig has observed that the working classes admired hereditary wealth or that gained from gambling but despised money that had been earned.[1] The working classes have tended to be much less hostile to aristocrats or to members of the upper middle class, who have been enculturated into the manners and habits of the aristocracy, than to top business people.

Of course, the chief manifestation of the hostility had been years of labour relations strife as evidenced in slow-downs and strikes. Prior to Mrs Thatcher taking office, the Callaghan government had been paralysed by striking public workers and the famous 'Winter of Discontent'. As a result, the Thatcherites took office prepared to tackle radical trade unionism. They legislated to curb union power on several occasions during their tenure, and Mrs Thatcher famously faced down the miners. Though they did effectively quiet industrial strife, the Thatcherites did so only by weakening the power of the unions – especially in the public sector (in large measure as a result of privatisation). The government did nothing to foster better industrial relations, i.e., to improve worker-management communication, understanding, or harmony.

The closest the Thatcher government came to addressing worker-management harmony was in Thatcherite privatisation efforts involving discounted shares to workers. The policy was designed to make workers believe that they had a stake in the success of the firm and in the British economy as a whole. In fact, however, the discounted share scheme at its best enhanced only the capitalist value of quick profit-taking (as workers readily sold their shares at a profit shortly after the privatisations had taken place).[2] Thatcherism paid scant attention to the need to shift worker values in directions more supportive of bosses and companies. Thus, worker attitudes towards management did not change during the Thatcher era; if anything, they may have worsened.

In addition to their awareness of negative worker attitudes toward business, the Thatcherites knew that the gentlemanly classes, the aristocrats and meritocrats, held business in contempt. Even much of their own party – though the party of business at least since the Liberals joined the Tories at the turn of the century – adhered to the pre-capitalist, landed values of the aristocracy and gentry and, therefore, shunned business. The aristocrat had his land, the exercise of his inherited authority and associated responsibilities to his inferiors in accordance with 'noblesse oblige', and his amateur pastimes such as connoisseurship and horsemanship. Likewise, his siblings under primogeniture had their professions and a similar, if more modest, lifestyle and relationship to their inferiors. Over time the gentlemen successors in the meritocracy had their professions, their emulation of aristo-gentry pastimes, and the exercise of their earned authority and social responsibilities.[3]

All of these descendants of the aristo-gentry, gentlemanly tradition have been unutterably opposed to vulgar business and its practitioners. Moreover, they have been vocal in their contempt – a contempt expressed in their authoritative upper class accents. The accents may have changed somewhat over time or at least admitted of wider variety, now encompassing, for example, both the aristocratic cadences of Queen Elizabeth and those of the BBC. But these sounds have been readily recognisable as the voice of the governors, of those in the know, of those who establish the parameters of public discourse. In a country where accents loom so large in locating people by social class, where the sound of one's opinions often matter as much as the opinions themselves, this dimension of gentlemanly influence over cultural values is central.

Marxist analysts have claimed that the British upper classes were capitalist, just not industrialist. Hence their contempt did not prevent them from investing in business, just engaging in or expressing admiration for it. On these accounts, the aristo-gentry culture contained the forces of industrial capitalism with the result being a bourgeois culture thoroughly imbued with an aristocratic outlook that was hostile to modern economic activity. Moreover, this cultural hegemony extended beyond the upper middle class professionals and influenced even the industrialists themselves who then tended to devote themselves less than wholeheartedly to economic matters.[4] Hence, the upper classes looked down on the business middle classes for such things as striving, greed, and a narrow specialist world view, and similarly the working classes resented the bosses for striving, greed, and the abuse of authority. In the words of Charles Hampden-Turner: 'The top and bottom of the British sandwich unites against the meat.'[5]

The Thatcherites not only were aware of these anti-business prejudices among the British but also were cognisant of the British possessing a weak work ethic. For instance, shortly before Mrs Thatcher took office, a New Society poll revealed that few Britons wanted to be rich or were willing to work more to be so; they thought that people should only work as hard as they needed to lead a 'pleasant life.'[6] Mid-way through the Thatcher years, the head of Ford Europe was pointing out that West Germans produced a car in half the time of Merseyside workers.[7] And, William Rodgers, a founder of the former Social Democratic Party, could be heard saying that Mrs Thatcher 'doesn't understand the culture of which she is Prime Minister. It's her greatest flaw politically. It's no good saying that if you pay people more they'll work harder. They'll say, "What's the point?" Thank goodness! . . .We are not an enterprise culture. We like our leisure. It's the British character.'[8]

This weak work ethic had been a major topic of discussion in decades of analyses of British decline.[9] This weakness appeared to be true across social classes. The upper classes pursued an aristocratic leisurely, amateurish lifestyle, and the working classes either imitated the behaviour of those above them or refused to work in opposition to the bosses. The standard account was that the British preferred to take their leisure in work rather than to work to afford leisure as did, for example, their American and German counterparts. Moreover, critics claimed that the British were far less attentive to high standards of professional expertise, craftsmanship, and quality control. Here again, the Thatcher government made little effort to instil values of know-how, productivity, and pride in the British workforce at all levels.

For Thatcherism to have delivered a complete economic revolution, the Thatcher government needed to have routed the aristo-gentry's value hegemony or influence which had done so much to undermine the institution of business and its success. This would have required a strategy that went beyond the simple altering of economic structures and included three interrelated tactics: increasing democratisation and modernisation of the power structure in British society, reforming education, and fostering national discourse that made the business person a legitimate new cultural hero.

Thatcherism needed a liberal political and modernising ideology and policies to complement and underpin the ideology's liberal economics. So long as the majority of people in high positions continued to disdain business and the modern and so long as technically proficient, productive business people seldom rose to the apex of the society, the health of the economy continued to be at risk. This is to say that as long as the elites continued to inhabit the ranks of the aristo-gentry – the courts, the arts, academia, journalism, Parliament, and the civil service – and business could not attain top professional status, the anti-business elites would continue to dominate British thinking with respect to economic matters.

The Thatcherites were certainly conscious of the bias, for they had often been on the receiving end of the contumely of the elites. These elites had scorned Mrs Thatcher and her followers as representing the interests of business and the commercial middle classes. Prominent Thatcherites like Lord Young, Sir Keith Joseph, and Hugh Thomas (later Lord Thomas) had written articles and given speeches about the cultural prejudices against business. Hugh Thomas observed: 'In England, we have lived for a long time in an atmosphere in which private manufacturing is thought second best, to say, the Treasury or academic life for an intelligent person at a university. Napoleon had no sooner said that we were a nation of shopkeepers than we became one of proconsuls.'[10]

How could the Thatcherites have gone about rectifying the cultural prejudices against business and modernity? To start, they could have democratised and modernised Britain's political institutions. Reform of the monarchy and House of Lords, institutions steeped in hereditary privilege and legitimation, would have been a first step. The problems presented by such institutions to an economy attempting to modernise and move forward are several-fold. First of all, because the highest positions of honour in the society have been invested in an hereditary monarchy and a partially hereditary peerage with their roots deep in British history, the focus of the society will necessarily tend to be on tradition, not modernity. For example, in both the monarchy and the Lords, the importance and grandeur of tradition is ritualistically and publicly reinforced in the carrying out of state business and ceremonies. In addition, both royalty and peers provide highly visible evidence that the entitlements of some people to high prestige and authority are rooted in the past, not the present. Similarly, what one accomplishes in the present will matter less than what one's ancestors accomplished in the past. Although it is true that the House of Lords also accommodated meritocratic life peers, including some business executives, the latter usually fit the mould of the business person-cum-gentleman. This was a successful executive who tended to be more interested in grouse moors than increased revenues and more concerned about his public responsibilities than his business ones. Moreover, the rest of the meritocratic peers came straight from the professions that had always eschewed the business and technical worlds. Hence, even life peers have tended to reinforce traditional values and have looked beyond the mere economic to more noble pursuits and concerns. Finally, the top honour that one could achieve in British society was being made a member of the House of Lords which was an organisation directed to governing and public service, rather than to producing and profit.

The Thatcher government could have lessened the aristocratic influence of the monarchy in several ways. The government could have reduced some of the largely symbolic, but highly visible, public functions of the Queen and other members of the royal family. Far more importantly, the government could have taken some steps to reduce royal privileges and could have cut back public taxpayer support for the grand lifestyles of the contemporary court. Despite the exhortations of Prince Philip and Prince Charles over the years for the modernisation and productivity of British business, the monarchy has remained the most prominent institutional embodiment of the traditional landed way of life. The royals have remained emblematic of the past and ever-present reminders of the hierarchical nature of authority and the need for deference. The Thatcher government could have taken steps that would have relegated the royal family to the anachronistic status of many of their continental cousins and, thus, to a minor role in the actual life of the state. Instead, because of continuing state subsidisation of and political deference to the monarchy, the royals have attained glamorous star status, occupying centre stage in the admiration and imagination of the British public.

Similarly, because the Thatcher government did not seek to reform the House of Lords into an elected second chamber, the Lords remained a highly visible institutional reminder of the importance of heredity in the exercise of authority and possession of prestige in Britain. In addition, being a peer continued to be the primary reward for societal achievement and the most prestigious role for the execution of individual responsibility to society. Democratising the Lords would have removed an ancient and potent symbol and source of anti-modern, anti-business values.

Likewise, further democratising the civil service would also have lessened that institution's anti-modern, anti-business influence on British culture. The civil service has aristocratic roots in ancient courts, at least as far back as the Tudors, and as a sinecure for those disinherited by primogeniture until well into the late nineteenth century. However, the modern civil service has been the bastion of upper middle class, meritocratic Britain ever since the Northcote-Trevelyan Report effectively ended patronage in favour of merit appointments in the 1850s.

The public school and Oxbridge[11] architects of civil service reform in the late nineteenth century designed a new profession for the rapidly expanding gentlemanly classes of the era. Candidates demonstrated merit by passing an examination that drew on the curricula of the public schools and Oxbridge. The examination downplayed mathematics and science and anything practical or professionally specialised and emphasised the humanities, verbal and written facility, and the capacity for seeing the broad picture. Such an examination was suited to gentlemanly rule in several ways. It enabled the civil service to recruit only those from privileged backgrounds who could attend the elite institutions of learning and who could make their way in the world without acquiring practical skills. By drawing heavily on the Oxbridge curriculum and concentrating on ancient languages, especially Greek, and nothing modern, the examination encouraged students to study a corpus emphasising the need for those of superior ability and nurturing to assume power and authority over the rest of society. In addition, the bias in favour of those who could make a well-wrought written argument, and after the Leathes reforms of 1917, also a well-constructed oral argument, favoured candidates from the upper reaches of British society who possessed the right educations and accents.[12] The examination also favoured those who had studied subjects that involved learning to manipulate words rather than, for example, to deduce from hypotheses or to manipulate numbers or mathematical symbols. Finally, by tying this examination to the curriculum of the public schools and Oxbridge, the civil service obtained personnel with common concepts and habits of mind and speech. These were people who had been educated to believe that rational men, able to take in the big picture, would all ultimately arrive at the Aristotelian golden mean. The curriculum and the recruitment examination institutionalised consensual decision-making in the civil service. The disinterested, reasonable approach of the civil servant to all matters of policy combined with his skill in argument and communication meant that he has been a linchpin in fostering public policy discourse of a decidedly gentlemanly consensual variety. Over the years, the constitutional role of the civil service has become the ballast in the English ship of state, providing continuity and moderating radical change. The pivotal function of the civil service has been providing neutral policy advice to cabinet ministers of the government of the day, i.e., keeping secret the work of previous governments, and brokering policy discussion with outside constituencies, chief among them business.

The civil service has adversely affected business in Britain for a number of reasons. Unlike many nations that view business executives as top society leaders, Britain has ceded this role to civil servants. The civil servant's education, style, and prestige have always worked to keep the business person feeling inferior. Hence, business executives have often remained deferent to and imitative of civil servants.[13]

Moreover, because of the civil servant's prestige in British society, the profession has always enormously outdistanced business in recruitment of the 'best and the brightest' from Britain's universities. It almost goes without saying, therefore, that the overwhelming preponderance of those with the proper fit have been Oxford and Cambridge arts graduates although some contemporary recruitment data suggests that their numbers may have been diminishing. From 1905 to 1914, Oxford and Cambridge supplied 82 per cent of Civil Service recruits; 1925 to 1937, 78 per cent; 1948 to 1956, 78 per cent; and 1957 to 1963, 85 per cent. However, by the mid-1970s, the Oxbridge percentage had dropped to about half of the recruits, and then subsequently started climbing again in the early 1980s to about 75 per cent.[14] By the late eighties, the percentage of Oxbridge entrants began to decline yet again, only to begin to rise once more in the 1990s.[15] In 1990, shortly before Mrs Thatcher left office, the First Division Association of Civil Servants criticised the recruitment process for selecting only those who seemed to 'fit in' – the 'outgoing' but 'conformist' team leaders who were good at passing exams and who were deemed 'reasonable'. The association went on to ask: 'Will this bias continue to favour those with a preponderance of male hormones, white skin, Oxbridge arts degrees and carrying umbrellas?'[16]

In addition to these reforms, Thatcherism might have further lessened the impact of the anti-business elites through other forays into increasing democracy. For example, the government might have pursued parliamentary devolution, the reinvigoration of local government, and the promotion of freedom of information. The limited extension of self-rule in the form of legislative bodies for Northern Ireland, Scotland, and Wales along with an enlarged role and responsibilities for local government would at the very least have encouraged a greater pluralism of elites and opinions.

The government also could have pursued such constitutional or statutory issues as a written Bill of Rights and a Freedom of Information Act. Because of the unwritten nature of the British Constitution, adjudication of individual rights has arisen from past precedent and judicial decisions of the Law Lords. In other words, the successful assertion of rights-claims was heavily dependent upon the gentlemanly elite. Similarly, the governing classes, at least since the Privy Council Oath of Secrecy of 1250, has tended to be almost exclusively in the know about matters affecting the British public, and the British public has tended to be nearly totally in the dark. Whether in Number 10, Westminster, or Whitehall since the 1911 Official Secrets Act, British officials have been required to remain silent about all official business.[17] Hence, giving Britain a Freedom of Information Act would profoundly have reduced the power of the governing elite.

All of these measures would have helped to foster equal opportunity for entry to elite governing positions as well as upward mobility. The Thatcherites were not unaware of the power and influence of this governing elite and its negativity toward their economic agenda. But, Thatcherism pursued a policy of 'trickle up' economics: the notion was that by succeeding in the free market, successful Britons or their children would ultimately be able to populate the elite institutions of government. In other words, the free market would by itself deliver equal opportunity in all aspects of British life.

But, so long as the governing elites in their authoritative, upper class voices dominated normative discourse in directions demeaning the business person, along with such things as specialist expertise and professional knowledge, business would not be likely to attract top recruits. If the 'best and the brightest' in the society continued to go into government and other gentlemanly professions like academe or the arts, then the pool of talent needed to transform the economy – to work in industry, to line up venture capital for start-up hi-tech firms, and so forth – simply would not be there, or at any rate, not in sufficient numbers. Moreover, as long as the most prestigious institutions of society such as the House of Lords and the Civil Service, upheld standards of secrecy that gave them monopolistic control of great quantities of official information and propagated an anti-business discourse, it would be almost impossible for the forces of modernity and capitalism to be heard. Little value transformation supportive of a modern capitalist economy can occur until people begin to experience a new kind of individual sitting at the pinnacle of society. Until more pro-business people sit at the top, the discourse will not change. Hence, opening access to and modernizing the institutions of politics was a necessary condition of moving the economy ahead.

For despite Thatcherism's belief in 'trickle up' economics and some real evidence of social mobility throughout the Thatcher era, the gentleman and his values remained dominant. A 1990 *Sunday Times* survey of the 400 richest people in Britain showed a great deal of continuity in who comprised the British economic elite. More than one-quarter were aristocrats, and over one-third of the wealth belonged to landowners (though they had not invested all of the wealth in land) who were part of 'Old Britain.' Furthermore, much of Britain's economic elite still matched the traditional gentlemanly profile. Almost one-fifth had hereditary entitlement to a seat in the House of Lords. Seventy-eight of those surveyed had attended Eton, and eleven, Harrow. With respect to their social clubs, 36 were members of Whites; eleven, the Turf or Jockey Club; six, Boodles; and one, the Garrick. Almost all were Conservatives.[18]

One of the most telling of the survey's findings was that royals and the aristocracy continued to possess a sizable and stable portion of the wealth of the nation. The Queen was the richest with a fortune estimated at £6.7 billion (not including 267,000 acres of land including 350 London acres). The Duke of Westminster was second with £4.2 billion; whereas, the third richest Britons were commoners, the Swedish-born Rausing brothers, worth only £2.04 billion.[19]

Furthermore, a 1992 *Economist* survey of 'top people' revealed that Britain appeared to be much the same in 1992 as in 1972. The magazine composed a list of top people in politics, business and finance, academia, the learned professions, and the arts. Almost two-thirds had attended private schools, and well over 50 per cent attended Oxford or Cambridge. This represents only a 1 per cent drop in public schools' products and a 2 per cent increase in Oxbridge graduates compared to 1972. The only significant change was that fewer Etonians and people from a broader spectrum of public schools were on the 1992 list than in 1972.[20]

Of course, reforming political institutions was not the only stratagem open to the Thatcherites in their efforts to promote pro-business cultural values. They also needed to have effectively addressed problems in the educational system from bottom to top that were resulting in a workforce insufficiently skilled and expert to sustain a modern economy and inadequately possessed of the values necessary to such an economy. Reinvigorating the state schools was essential to combating the overweening influence of the public schools. In addition, reforming the schools and the higher education system was crucial to providing essential skills, expertise, and values. The Thatcher government recognised the deficiencies and attempted to address them with new educational policies. However, many of the policies failed to combat the problem, either because mis-designed or because they occurred too late in the game. Moreover, Thatcherism could have done a great deal more by way of using the curriculum to enculturate new generations of students into an interest in and belief in the importance of business.

Britain suffered from several key educational deficiencies. First of all, general literacy and numeracy were extremely low. Britain had fewer seventeen-year-olds still in school than its main industrial competitors: 53 per cent in Britain compared to 85 per cent in the United States; 87 per cent in West Germany; and 89 per cent in Japan.[21]

Secondly, the British educational system was very poor at vocational education. The proportion of school leavers age sixteen was higher than in most Western industrialised countries. Forty per cent of Britons left school with no qualifications for work compared to 10 per cent of the Germans. On standardised tests, the British scored well below their Western European counterparts in such things as computer science. A comparative study between France and Britain revealed that in the workforce per head, France produced three times as many craftsmen and two and one-half times as many technicians. *Management Today* noted in the late 1980s that the British cultural bias against training was so entrenched in the educational system that it denigrated the 'trained intelligence' requisite for making a good desk and only valued the 'don or mandarin sitting behind it.'[22]

Thirdly, the British had way too few students pursuing applied science and engineering in the universities. Government reports and business executives, from the late 1970s throughout the 1980s, expressed alarm over the lack of qualified British engineers. The Finniston Report in 1978 warned of steady economic decline if Britain did not offer higher pay and status for engineers to attract people to the profession.[23] Similarly, the Lords' Committee on Overseas Trade also warned of the shortage of engineers in British industry and noted that the Japanese produced nearly four and one-half times as many engineers per capita as Britain.[24] And the Bodmer Report of the Royal Society claimed that the British poorly understood the sciences and urged the government to provide more and better quality science education.[25]

Furthermore, Britain had failed to produce adequately educated and technically trained business executives. A National Economic Development Office study *The Making of Managers* noted that whereas in the United States 85 per cent and in West Germany 63 per cent of top management possessed degrees, in Britain only 25 per cent did. A 1987 British Institute of Management survey of 3000 managers found that two-thirds had received no formal training at a management school or other institution. In the United States, 25 per cent of undergraduates pursued some business course work; whereas in the United Kingdom, that figure was under 2 per cent. Furthermore, British companies themselves offered their employees little training. For example, in contrast to American, Japanese, and German large firms that offered at least five days 'off-the-job' training, British companies offered only one day.[26]

The Thatcher government did bring forward a substantial amount of school reform under the 1988 Education Act. The government gave parents more control of schools and enabled schools to remove themselves from Local Education Authorities (LEAs) in favour of direct grants from the Department of Education and Science. In addition, the Act provided for a national curriculum designed to broaden British secondary education away from its narrow course specialisation. These reforms also dovetailed with the implementation of the new General Certificates of Secondary Education (GCSEs) taken at 16+ which were designed to use a variety of assessment mechanisms across a wider range of fields, including technology and economics, than had previously been the case. At first the GCSE reforms appeared to be addressing the poor basic level of British education as scores began to improve dramatically. But upon further investigation over time, evidence emerged to suggest that the quality of the examinations themselves had slipped as well as the standards by which they were marked.[27] In addition, because the government left the Advanced Level General Certificates of Education or A-level examinations in place for those preparing for university, the narrow specialism proceeded apace. This had particularly negative effects on university science and mathematics places. Because in Britain students must specialise so early, at age sixteen, compared, for example, to the United States where students have several more years for this kind of academic decision-making, British universities continued to suffer from a very small pool of science and mathematics students.

At the end of the Thatcher era, the British school system still seemed unable to deliver a sufficiently educated population. In 1991, the figures from nine education authorities revealed that the number of extremely poor readers in Britain had increased over 50 per cent from 1985. In addition, only one-third of the sixteen-to-eighteen-year-old population was still in school compared to nearly four-fifths of the Americans and nearly two-thirds of the French. And only 15 per cent of Britons went on to university compared to over 50 per cent of the Americans.[28] Clearly, far greater attention to reforming the examination system would have wrought educational and productivity benefits.

With respect to vocational training, the Manpower Services Commission introduced a number of different programmes and mechanisms to deliver technical education. The most prominent programmes were what became known as Youth Training (YT) and Employment Training (ET). Begun in 1983, YT, an employer-based program enabled 16 and 17-year-old school leavers to engage in two years on-the-job training (with some off-the-job instruction). The programme was enormous, ultimately enrolling over two million people. The ET programme, begun in 1988, with places for nearly half a million trainees by 1990, aimed to help the long-term unemployed and provided for twelve-month individualised instruction. In addition, by 1988, the government created the Training and Enterprise Councils (TECs), business-government partnerships, modelled on American Private Industry Councils and German Chambers of Commerce. The TECs became the central locus for vocational training. Finally the government also introduced the National Vocational Qualifications (NVQs) in order to provide a qualification system with uniform standards into its vocational efforts.[29] All of this appears to represent a great deal of government policy effort in this area though the ETs and TECs occurred late in the Thatcher government. Furthermore, the government seems not to have promoted well-designed or well-executed programmes.

Much of the effort proved reasonably ineffective. Business people became critical and maintained that government was unwilling to spend enough and was sticking business with an inordinate amount of the cost. Moreover, business executives felt that the civil service was exercising too much control: 80 per cent of the TEC chief executives were civil servants, and 400 civil servants were TEC employees. In addition, the business community was not totally enthusiastic about the NVQs for several reasons. Businesses trained and evaluated their own trainees and received bonuses for each of the trainees who passed. Such an arrangement raised questions about the evaluative standards involved in the qualifications. Moreover, the programme was expensive with trainees being paid a higher percentage of the adult wage than in other European countries. Also, the training was so job-specific that employers claimed that they did not have sufficient manpower flexibility. At the same time, EU competitors were already designing new programs that involved combined education and training in schemes far more advanced than the British. Finally, and most importantly, British YT standards were well below those of their competitors. When Britons received their certificates for completing their two years of training, their skill levels were those of the Germans after six months. Many people who completed the programmes complained that they spent much of the time engaged in menial, unskilled work, and came away with no skills and no jobs.[30]

Thatcherism had even worse luck with its efforts to improve the professional expertise of the population in the sciences and mathematics. In large measure, because of the earlier mentioned problems presented by the continuance of the A-levels, few students opted for places even though government policy enlarged the number of university and polytechnic places. But, the failure to provide for the fundamental overhaul of undergraduate technical education proved disastrous. Of the 4,000 additional technology places created by the government in 1985, 1,100 went unfilled because students did not have the necessary A-levels. The number attempting A-levels in physics, biology, and chemistry fell, and applications in physics and mathematics declined. In 1987, of the fifty-four universities in Great Britain thirty were still seeking students in physics, chemistry, and mathematics. By the end of the Thatcher government, many universities were lowering their admissions standards in order to obtain students in these fields. And Oxford and Cambridge, though not lowering their admissions standards, were contemplating an extra year of course work in engineering and mathematics.[31]

Moreover, overall budgetary cutbacks and changes in funding mechanisms for universities, generally, and the sciences, particularly, combined to weaken the sciences. The effect of budget cuts in 1981, for example, was the reduction of University Grants Committee funding for science by 11 per cent. In addition, the government over time cut back its civil research budget from 0.72 per cent of GDP in 1981 to 0.62 per cent in 1986 placing Britain behind key Western European competitors.[32] The result was that research and patents contracted. Some of the world's leading scientists joined the brain drain and took up much higher paying positions with well-funded laboratories in the United States. Perhaps, the most depressing feature of the Thatcher years for the sciences and other technical subjects like engineering was that students were still not very interested in pursuing them.[33]

Although not entirely successful, Thatcherism had better luck with the professionalisation of business although not because of public policy intervention. Here, Thatcherism having relied on the impact of structurally freeing up the marketplace seems to have worked. As the free market began to take off, more people went to business school, and more business schools opened. In 1986, 22.85 per cent of the applicants at polytechnics were in business compared to 11.41 per cent in engineering and technology, and 1.73 per cent in social science and arts. Between 1983 and the 1990s, the number of business schools had grown four-fold. Finally, by the 1990s, even Cambridge and Oxford had begun offering MBAs.[34] But two problems remained. Attitudes toward industry and the making of things were relatively the same as always. After graduation, students did not opt to pursue manufacturing. The City was what appeared to be alluring to university graduates, but the City traditionally had had far greater status than industry. Moreover, the City itself had ultimately declined in its attractiveness in Thatcher's third term (interestingly, just as applications to the Civil Service had picked up again).[35]

Secondly, the non-interventionist stance did nothing to help with the professionalism of extant British management. One of the policy efforts that the Thatcher government made with respect to improving managerial performance was the Enterprise Initiative which was not introduced until 1988. The Department of Trade and Industry (DTI) sponsored a consultancy service for small and medium-sized firms geared to lending assistance with such things as: design, marketing, quality management, manufacturing systems, business planning, and financial and information systems. In addition, the DTI also committed itself to working with employers to give teachers, teacher-trainees, and students experience of and understanding of the workplace.[36]

Little evidence exists to suggest that market forces succeeded in improving managerial performance. In fact, many of the business success stories of the Thatcher era ended in failure – from Tony Berry of Blue Arrow to Sophie Mirman of the Sock Shop to Alan Sugar of Amstrad. Most observers attributed these failures to too little attention to management – too little professional expertise and too little delegation. Sugar says of his own failure that 'Amstrad possessed no stock control, made poor acquisitions abroad, suffered incompetent management, and failed at solving technical problems. Ultimately, he rescued his firm by hiring high quality management with technical expertise away from companies like Polaroid and Gillette'.[37]

British industry also engaged in little cultural or structural overhaul to allow technical expertise to come to the organisational forefront. A comparative study of nine production units in Britain, France, and Germany indicated that the British possessed many fewer managers or supervisors relative to workers than the French or German. The British continued to institutionalise snobbish divisions of labour and, therefore, not to place people with technical backgrounds in managerial roles.[38]

Hence, by inadequately intervening in education and training, the Thatcherites not only failed to raise knowledge and skill levels throughout the hierarchy of the workplace but also concomitantly failed to change values.

Although subscribing to productive values will tend to create workers and managers who are technically proficient and diligent, it is difficult for a society to adopt such values without the opportunity to obtain the skills necessary to productivity. Furthermore, it is difficult to come to believe in and respect such expertise unless it is embodied in the society. Thus, upping the technical and professional expertise of the entire British workforce was a necessary condition of beginning the value transformation to modernity essential to anchoring the enterprise culture.

In addition to having needed to democratise political institutions and to modernise and improve education and training, Thatcherism also needed to have consciously addressed itself to creating a new national discourse. This national discourse should have championed the modern business person as the new cultural hero. In order to have done this effectively, the Thatcherites would had to have presented a picture of a societal ideal type that people could understand, admire, and emulate. Unfortunately for Thatcherism, the Thatcher years had not been much different from the ones preceding them in terms of the picture of the greedy self-serving business person except that it had perhaps got worse.

The media certainly devoted much more attention to business than in the past with a great deal of television programming like the 'Money Show' and 'Stocks and Shares' being aired. This inclined some to believe that such increased attention indicated that the business person was rising in public esteem. And, occasionally, those in business were positively portrayed. For example, a Mills and Boon editor described the romantic figure of the late 1980s as 'a Thatcherite businessman who's pulled himself up by his bootlaces'.[39] Such figures have occurred in the novels of Jeffrey Archer such As the Crow Flies, a saga of a man's rise from barrow boy to magnate. Though this novel might be viewed as sheer propaganda considering Archer's Thatcherite credentials, the book's huge commercial success makes clear that there was a large audience for this genre. (It is noteworthy, nonetheless, that Archer created a character that after succeeding at capitalism turned to the higher pursuits of arts, philanthropic activity, public service, and ultimately a seat in the House of Lords – a very British story, indeed.) The other place in the media where the business person was allegedly portrayed positively was in advertisements. But, the advertising agencies, themselves among the most competitive of businesses, tended to portray the business person, often a City denizen, as a well-dressed, finagling operator. At the end of the Thatcher era, the business person was still nowhere to be found cast in a positive light on the stage or television, or for that matter, in high quality novels. However, he might be found in these places cast in the worst possible light, for example, Caryl Churchill's play *Serious Money* which focused on the immorality of the City or Harry Enfield's 'Loadsamoney' television character who comically portrayed Thatcherism's materialistic, newly rich. Thus, although the business person, especially in his City incarnation, loomed large in British consciousness as the Thatcher years wore on, he might possibly be someone to envy, but never someone to admire and respect.

Thatcherism needed to have made the case for a new heroic type for the Enterprise Culture. This could not be the image of a greedy, rapacious modern-day pirate or buccaneer. The Thatcherites needed to have led a national conversation about the value of the business person to the public good. The new hero would needed to have fused some of the virtues of the capitalist business person with those of the traditional gentleman. In other words, the heroic type essential to the Thatcher Revolution was a highly professional, productive capitalist who was motivated by something other than avarice and who was a contributor to the welfare of others. Thatcherism needed to have made cogent arguments about why the hard-working, highly expert business person was essential to increasing productivity and with it the comfort and well-being of the British public. The tradition of noblesse oblige had to meld with the persona of the modern capitalist.

Moreover, Thatcherism needed to have incorporated gentlemanly notions of fair play and honesty into the persona of the ideal business person who needed to embody a sense of decency. The public perception of the moral integrity of business, as well as even business' own view of itself, in these years was hardly one with moral integrity at its heart, especially given such scandals as Johnson Matthey Bankers, Guinness, and Lloyds. But Thatcherism did not choose to anchor its new cultural hero in the concepts and virtues of the traditional culture and did not choose to argue for the morality of the modern capitalist. Aside from a few Christian homilies or Victorian verities, Mrs Thatcher and her followers, by and large, ceded the moral high ground to the gentlemen and left the entire Thatcherite economic agenda vulnerable. Hence, the gentleman, whether in politics, academia, or the arts, was still free to pillory modern business as well as Thatcherism.

Interestingly, Prime Minister Tony Blair, subscribing to much of the Thatcherite free enterprise agenda, appears to be attempting to complete the Thatcher Revolution by making modernity a chief theme of his government. Mr Blair and his government have set about providing for increased democratisation of political institutions through such things as the promotion of greater governmental transparency, devolution of legislative power to Wales, Scotland, and Northern Ireland, and reform of the House of Lords. In addition, the Blair government is pursuing an ambitious education agenda involving greater investment in pre-schooling, technology in the schools, specialist schools, inner city schools, and the colleges and universities. Furthermore, the government is pressuring prestigious Oxbridge to widen the net in its recruiting to take more students from state schools.

Finally, Tony Blair might succeed at least at some elements of the creation of a new national hero – the modernising, capitalist business person. For, as Blair went about creating the 'New Labour' and the 'Third Way', he had to convince members of his own party, who have traditionally been morally opposed to business and the evils of capitalism, of the need to pursue a new economic path for the welfare of the nation. He has, thus, from the outset been involved in making legitimating arguments to the Labour Party membership on the need for a modern, capitalist system.

Notes

1   Ferdynand Zweig, *The British Worker* (Harmondsworth: Penguin 1952), p. 206.

2   United Kingdom. OECD Economic Surveys (Paris: Organisation for Economic Cooperation and Development 1985), p. 25.

3   Candace Hetzner, *The Unfinished Business of Thatcherism* (New York and London: Peter Lang, 1999), pp. 23–32.

4   Martin Weiner, *English Culture and the Decline of the Industrial Spirit 1850–1980* (Harmondsworth: Penguin, 1981), pp. 9–10.

5   Charles Hampden-Turner, *Gentlemen and Tradesmen* (London: Routledge, 1983), p. 57.

6   Hetzner, p. 192.

7   Roger Eglin, 'Why Ford Is on the Side of the Small Battalions,' *Times* (London) 3 November 1985.

8   Hetzner, p. 287.

9   See, for example, G.C. Allen, *The British Disease* (London: Institute of Economic Affairs 1979); Michael Barnes, *Britain on Borrowed Time* (Harmondsworth: Pelican 1967); Correlli Barnett, *The Pride and the Fall* (New York: Free Press 1987); Andrew Gamble, *Britain in Decline* (Houndsmills: Macmillan 1985); David Landes, *The Unbound Prometheus: Technological Change and Industrial Development* (Cambridge: Cambridge University Press 1969); Sidney Pollard, *The Wasting of the British Economy* (London: Croom Helm 1982); Alistair Mant, *The Rise and Fall of the British Manager* (London: Macmillan 1978); Michael Shanks, *The Stagnant Society* (Harmondsworth: Penguin 1968); and Weiner.

10 Candace Hetzner, 'Social Democracy and Bureaucracy: The Labour Party and Higher Civil Service Recruitment,' *Administration and Society* 17 (May 1985): 101–102.

11 Common Language,' *Public Voices 1*, no. 2 (Winter/Spring1994) 17.

12 Candace Hetzner, 'Humanities Backgrounds of British Civil Servants'

13 J.P. Nettl, 'Consensus or Elite Domination,' *Political Studies* 13 (1965) 22.

14 Hetzner, *Unfinished Business* p.17.

15 *Times* (London), 10 July 1991 and *The Economist*, 27 June 1991, p.65.

16 *Times* (London), 19 October 1990.

17 Peter Hennessy, *Whitehall* (London: Secker and Warburg 1989), pp.349 and 355-356.

18 Hetzner, *Unfinished Business*, p.320-21.

19 Ibid., p. 320.

20 Ibid., p. 321.

21 *The Economist*, 20 September 1986, p. 23.

22 Hetzner, *Unfinished Business*, p. 241-42.

23 Sir Monty Finniston, *Engineering: Our Future* (London: HMSO 1980).

24 Report From the Select Committee on Overseas Trade, 3 vols. (London: HMSO 1985), 1:51.

25 *The Economist*, 14 September 1985, p. 96.

26 Gillian Peppercorn and Gill Skoulding, *Profile of British Industry* (Corby: British Institute of Management 1987), p. 46.

27 Hetzner, *Unfinished Business*, p. 248.

28 Ibid., p. 251.

29 Ibid., p. 252.

30 Ibid., pp. 253–4.

31 Ibid., pp. 259.

32 Ibid., pp. 262.

33 Ibid., pp. 259–60.

34 Ibid., pp. 263.

35 Ibid., pp. 264.

36 Department of Trade and Industry, *Introducing the Enterprise Initiative* (London: HMSO 1989).

37 *Sunday Times* (London), 4 March 1990.

38 Christel Lane, *Management and Labour in Europe* (Aldershot: Edward Elgar 1989), pp. 41–2.

39 The Listener, 24 March 1988, p. 52.

Reprivatising Britain:
Thatcherism and Its Results

Duane Windsor

———

Thatcherism, reprivatising Britain from a socialist state, may well prove, in the long run, Margaret Thatcher's most significant accomplishment – although carried through in considerable measure by the succeeding John Major government. The acid test is what Labour does with a marketised economy. Privatisation can mean either or both: marketisation (i.e., a 'return to the market') and voluntarism (i.e., a re-emphasis of civic virtue). Narrowly, privatisation refers to the denationalisation, or at least the commercialisation (i.e., the profit reorientation), of state-owned enterprises (especially in Britain and other socialist or formerly Communist countries), the sale of public assets to private ownership (especially in the US at the federal level but illustrated as well by council housing in the UK), the contracting out of public services to private production even though still under public provision and control (especially in the US at the local level), and an abandonment of specific policy areas in favour of business or voluntary initiative. Broadly, privatisation is in practice frequently bundled up with related initiatives: deregulation of markets and private conduct, improvement of competitive conditions in markets, the introduction of business-like approaches and competitive pressures in government organisations (including state-owned enterprises), and reduction of government spending, taxing, deficits and gross debt levels. Hence, privatisation may be conceived of and implemented narrowly or broadly depending on how the term is used. The driving force behind privatisation is the conviction that democratic society should be market oriented rather than state dominated. Privatisation can be a fundamental social transformation process at the broadest application, as in Eastern Europe and in the UK. The psychological impact of the global privatisation movement has been given great force because privatisation efforts in the UK (from 1979) and US (from 1981) were followed by the dramatic destatisation of the command economies of the former communist regimes of Eastern Europe after 1990.

Margaret Thatcher, the first woman Prime Minister of any Western country has reasonable claim to be regarded as the initiator of this global privatisation movement. (Privatisation plays, however, a fundamentally different role in the formerly communist transition economies.)[1] The Thatcher government in the UK (from 1979) and the Reagan administration in the US (from 1981) undertook explicitly intended policy and political revolutions – now famous, or notorious, depending on one's viewpoint, as 'Thatcherism' and 'Reaganism'. The policy revolution aimed at reducing the role of the public sector in national life. The political revolution aimed at safeguarding the policy revolution, most desirably through continuation of the 'conservative' party (Tory or Republican) in power, but in any case through a shift in citizen attitudes and in ownership and control of national activities. Thatcherism and Reaganism were quite different phenomena, due to quite different contexts in the UK and the US. The 'Thatcher revolution' involved a 'return of the pendulum' to a capitalist market economy (conceived of in terms of the widely distributed business ownership of 'popular capitalism') and a privately oriented society in a state-dominated and substantially nationalised economy created by the post-World War II Labour government and 'accepted' in large (but not full measure) by subsequent Conservative governments until 1979. Reaganism involved much more of a 'public-private partnership' with greater emphasis on private (both business and voluntary) initiative in a regulated but essentially already popular capitalism economy. Both Thatcher and Reagan thought of privatisation in the UK and the US, respectively, in terms of a revolutionary (or at least radical) transformation of national life. The UK experiment came closer to marketising and privatising of a society, heavily socialised and government oriented.[2]

The political history of socialism and neocapitalism in Britain is, in itself, an interesting subject. Until 1979, the essentially socialist public sector created, largely but by no means exclusively, by the post war Labour government of

1945–1951, had dominated the British economy. Enjoying a large majority in the July 1945 election, the Clement Attlee government had immediately undertaken a broad program of socialisation built around three central elements explicitly stated in the Labour manifesto:

(1) Key industries were nationalised, including the Bank of England, coal mining, iron and steel, and railways. The emphasis in nationalisation was upon control of the industrial infrastructure (the 'commanding heights') of the country, particularly unionised industries with large workforces, as well as the principal instrument for monetary policy. (2) A comprehensive 'cradle-to-the-grave' social security programme was enacted, including a National Health Service (NHS), social insurance, and expanded public education. (3) Public housing provision became a major activity of local government in particular; and there was an emphasis on the rehabilitation of depressed areas. British socialism was, however, highly centralized and bureaucratic, and did not provide for workers' consultation: 'The failure of nationalisation in Britain to accomplish what had been hoped for was a major cause of the crisis of confidence which was to shake European socialism as a whole in the decade of the 1950s.'[3]

The fundamental change in the responsibilities of British government after 1945 flowed inevitably out of the wartime 'implied contract between government and people' of egalitarianism and advanced social policy in the post-victory era that must be carried out by either party.[4] The Conservatives of the wartime Churchill National Government had committed to increased public education and the NHS, as well as social insurance, public housing, and full employment.[5] The Conservatives were, however, opposed to nationalisation of industries. The parliamentary battle was waged over the nationalisation of steel,[6] which the Conservatives opposed.

Although Conservative governments (Winston Churchill, 1951–55; Anthony Eden, 1955–56; Harold Macmillan, 1956–63; Alec Douglas-Home, 1963–64) held office until 1964, when Labour (Harold Wilson) returned to power, the socialist programme of nationally owned industries, welfare state, and public housing provision was not generally dismantled. 'The Welfare State is as much our creation as it is that of the Socialists.'[7] The chief emphasis of the Conservatives was on denationalisation of steel and inland transport.[8] A key element in the 1950s was the return of middle-class voters to a newly responsible conservatism.[9] The Conservatives gradually increased NHS charges (for prescriptions, eyeglasses, dentistry) and in 1957 eliminated some housing rent controls (instituted in 1915)[10] thus encouraging private construction.[11]

In winter 1978, the trade unions refused to renew the Labour wage compact and called crippling strikes, especially in public services. The Scottish referendum insufficiently endorsed and the Welsh referendum overwhelmingly rejected Labour devolution bills. Scottish nationalists deserted James Callaghan's Labour government. At the end of March 1979, a no-confidence motion carried by a single vote (311 to 310).[12] The forced election held 3 May, 1979, gave the Conservatives a definite majority of 339 seats, and Margaret Thatcher, leading the Conservatives in succession to Edward Heath from February 1975, became Prime Minister on 4 May.[13] There was substantial voter discontent over the winter strikes. The Conservative election slogan was 'Labour isn't working'.[14]

Thatcher won three consecutive elections (the only such record in the twentieth century) and was the longest-serving British Prime Minister since 1827. The June 1983 election returned a landslide victory in the wake of the 1982 Falklands War. The 1987 election returned a large Conservative parliamentary majority, but that majority rested on only a plurality of the vote – at just over 40 per cent. Thatcher resigned in November 1990, succeeded by John Major (Chancellor of the Exchequer), in a party split over her policy towards European monetary and political integration. Major won an April 1992 election, but was decisively defeated by Tony Blair in March 1997.[15]

The initial Thatcher cabinet was a factional coalition including what the Prime Minister called 'wets' (ministers opposed to spending reductions) and 'dries' (those agreeing with her plans to cut direct taxes, government spending, and money supply growth).[16] The 'wets' were ministers who adhered to traditional Conservative policies. The 'dries' were the right or 'radical' wing of the party. The 1981 budget process facilitated Thatcher's domination of the cabinet. Inflation was very high during 1979–81, and the economy slide into recession in 1981–83. The tight money policy adopted to battle inflation bankrupted small firms and increased unemployment, which nearly tripled between 1979 and 1987 from 1,100,000 to 3,000,000.[17] Some 3,320,000 new jobs were created between March 1983 and March 1990.[18] Urban riots (which had occurred in spring–summer 1981) broke out again in the fall of 1985, and unemployment was at a post-war high of nearly four million in early 1986.[19] Coal pit closings generated a year-long miners' strike, in which Thatcher refused any concessions (unlike Heath's earlier final action). The strike collapsed in March 1985.

Thatcher's 1979 election pledge was to break the welfare state philosophy in order to reverse Britain's industrial decline.[20] The 1979 Conservative manifesto was, however, quite restricted with respect to privatisation: 'to sell back to private ownership the recently nationalised aerospace and shipbuilding concerns, giving their employees the opportunity to purchase shares' and selling 'shares in the National Freight Corporation to the general public.'[21] Privatisation implementation was hampered by the recession conditions.[22] The objective of privatisation was a radical transformation (literally the 'reprivatisation') of British politics and society.[23] Privatisation was, however, more initially a limited initiative that evolved in office with success into an expanding stream of actions.[24] Success fed privatisation strategy. What had been accomplished by the 1983 election was privatisation of British Aerospace and the National Freight Consortium (by management and worker buy-out), together with (in whole or part) Cable and Wireless, Associated British Ports, Britoil (created in 1975 for North Sea oil operations), British Rail Hotels, and Amersham International (radioactive research materials).[25] The 1983 manifesto nominated British Telephone (a bill had been introduced in the previous parliament), Rolls-Royce, British Steel, British Leyland, the National Bus Company, and airports, gas, and electricity. Some two million people purchased shares in British Telecom's 1984 privatisation.[26] Gas was privatised in 1986. The 1987 manifesto added water.[27] British Aerospace acquired British Leyland (Rover Group). 'The most technically and politically difficult privatisation . . . was that of the Electricity Supply Industry.'[28] The Major government[29] carried on with the civil list reform and accountability, British Coal, British Rail, purchaser-provider split in the NHS, a national educational curriculum and testing, and promulgation of the 1991 People's Charter.[30]

It was Thatcher's announced policy to adhere to 'strict economic principles'.[31] This policy was a return to arguably laissez-faire nineteenth-century 'liberal market economics'[32] of 'minimal government, individual initiative, and free trade.'[33] Thatcher was an ideologue as well as a practical politician.[34] The term 'ideology' has acquired a perhaps too systematic and anti-democratic connotation. To characterise someone as an ideologue is simply to emphasise an explicit connection with ideas expressed through political rhetoric, as distinct to the professional politician's operational code of pure deal-making.[35] Robert Armstrong, Cabinet Secretary during much of the Thatcher government, told Young: 'She was more skilful than anyone I've ever met in combining rhetoric which was faithful to her principles with policies that were totally pragmatic.'[36] Young comments: 'But another reading also has to be considered: that the rhetoric so far drowned out the pragmatism as fatally to complicate the most elementary task of the politician – securing popular support for the policies her government is actually pursuing. As time went on, she allowed her very personal obsessions to confuse, even corrupt, her role as a national leader.'[37]

In two articles on political philosophy for the *Daily Telegraph* (published in early 1969), Thatcher presented the following theme: 'I argued the case for the ideological clash of opposing political parties as essential to the effective functioning of democracy. The pursuit of "consensus", therefore, was fundamentally subversive of popular choice. It was wrong to talk of taking the big issues "out of politics" or to imply that different approaches to a subject involved "playing politics". I applied this specifically to the question of nationalisation versus free enterprise . . . not least education . . . where the ruthless pursuit by the socialists of comprehensivisation was threatening not just Britain's schools but long-term social progress.'[38] Thatcher refers to 'fraudulent appeal of consensus'.[39] From a visit to Russia in 1969, from which she came away impressed that 'communism was the regime for the privileged élite, capitalism the creed for the common man'.[40]

'Privatisation, no less than the tax structure, was fundamental to improving Britain's economic performance. But for me it was also far more than that: it was one of the central means of reversing the corrosive and corrupting effects of socialism.'[41] Thatcher makes specific reference to her reading of the works of F. A. Hayek[42] and to how impressed she was with A. V. Dicey's (1885) constitutional hostility to the administrative state.[43] Even so, 'Economics is too important just to be left to the economists.'[44] Much of the intellectual force for privatisation came from Keith Joseph and Nicholas Ridley, strong supporters of free markets. 'I came into 10 Downing Street with an overall conception of how to put Britain's economy right, rather than a detailed plan: progress in different areas would depend on circumstances, both economic and political.'[45] Economic strategy comprised 'four complementary elements':[46] (1) inflation control; (2) public finances control including income tax rate cuts; (3) promotion of 'private enterprise and ownership'; and (4) structural reforms for market efficiency,[47] including trade union reform through particularly the Employment Acts 1982, 1988, 1990.[48] For Thatcher, privatisation connoted individualism (in contrast to collectivism or civil society) and marketisation (in contrast to the administrative state).[49]

A key component of Thatcherism was public expenditure control, tax restructuring, and debt reduction.[50] OECD general government financial statistics are reported for the seven benchmark countries at five-year intervals 1970-2000 (the latter year estimated) as per centage of nominal GDP.[51] Sweden had the highest per centage of GDP devoted to government outlays (58.5 per cent average), while Japan and the US had the lowest per centage (about 34 per cent average). In general, Germany, France, and Italy exceeded Britain somewhat (in the range of 41 to 48 per cent average). The British deficit averaged 2.8 per cent during the period 1980–2000, compared to 1.5 per cent in the US and 1.8 per cent in Sweden, and 3.0 per cent in Japan (Germany and France falling just below Britain). The 1988 Budget (Chancellor Nigel Lawson)[52] produced a surplus for the first time since 1969. Italy had an average deficit of 8.4 per cent. Gross public debt rose in all comparison countries (most dramatically in Japan relative to 1970, and especially in Italy after 1985), except the UK, and exceeded 100 per cent of GDP in Italy at the 1995 and 2000 observation points. In the UK, the debt proportion fell to 1985 (rising somewhat in 1990), but had been projected to rise again through 2000. In 2000, Britain will still have the lowest gross public debt proportion of these countries. Government employment, expressed as per centage of total employment, has averaged 19.2 per cent in the UK, ahead of the US (15.9 per cent), Italy (15.7 per cent), and Germany (14.3 per cent), but behind France (21.2 per cent) and especially Sweden (29.1 per cent). Japan was extraordinarily low at 8.4 per cent. Roughly the same ordering (with different per centages) occurred for public employee compensation as per centage of GDP. The essential picture is that the UK is a high government employment state relative to the US, Germany, and Italy (Japan being unusually low), but more restrained than France (Sweden being unusually high relative to France).

Analysis of OECD data on composition of general government current out-lays reported in ten-year intervals (1970–90 plus 1996) by level of government reveals interesting differences among the seven benchmark countries. The data indicate proportion of such outlays in terms of central government (i.e., other than social security), social security, and state-local government. Central gov-ernment and social security can also be combined to give a sense of centralisa-tion relative to state-local activities. Although such gross analysis must be used cautiously, due to inter-country differences, the UK is over this period the most centralising and most centre-dominated state (that is, combining central gov-ernment and social security).[53] It is also the least social security-oriented state at 1996, because the social security orientation has been declining in the UK while rising elsewhere. (Overall, the central-social security combination is high and has been rising.) The nature of the British 'welfare state' is possibly concealed in these categorical data, so caution is necessary in interpretation without refer-ence to more detailed data than provided here for a general overview. Health services are typically centrally funded (recorded as final consumption), and housing may be provided locally as in the UK. Central outlays are the highest proportion in the UK, and this proportion has risen historically. The centralis-ing tendency relative to local government is seen in the reported governmental performance data.[54] France is the most centre-oriented state (combining central government and social security), with the lowest proportion of state-local out-lays, and is high (but roughly steady since 1980) in social security orientation. There has been some movement toward fiscal devolution. Italy is somewhat more centralised than the UK, with only moderate and relatively declining emphasis on directly measured social security. Germany has the lowest (and declining) central proportion, and the highest (and rising) directly measured social security orientation. Germany, a federal republic, is strongly state-local oriented. Japan is high (but declining) in state-local orientation, and is high (and rising) in social security orientation. Sweden has a high (but declining) state-local orientation and a low (but rising) social security orientation. (The data are for general government outlays only, and again what is widely perceived to be a 'welfare state' may be operated in various ways.) The US is the least cen-tralised state (in the wake of the end of the Cold War), with the highest (and ris-ing) proportion of state-local outlays and the lowest (and declining) combined central-social security proportion. Social security orientation is low relatively, but has been rising historically.

OECD data also report for the seven benchmark countries at ten-year intervals (1970–90 plus 1996) composition of general government current outlays by type of outlay data (final consumption, social security, debt interest, investments, and other). While not necessarily fully correspond with somewhat similar data presented in the previous paragraph, the general patterns and implications remain essentially the same. The UK has proportionally the highest (and rising) final consumption, together with other outlays (including transfers and subsidies) also rising, and the lowest (and here declining) social security component. Debt interest is low and declining over time. Investments are the lowest proportion among these countries and declining historically. The US exhibits moderate social security, debt interest, and investments (rising except for investments), and declining final consumption. Japan has the lowest (and declining) final consumption and the highest (but declining investments). Social security is high and rising. Germany has moderate (but rising) social security and low (but rising) debt interest. Final consumption, investments, and other outlays are declining relatively. France has high (but steady) social security and the lowest (but rising) debt interest. Italy has the highest social security and debt interest (rising in both cases), with other categories moderate to low and declining. Sweden has high (but declining) final consumption and rates moderate on the other outlay categories. Social security appears moderate. While debt interest and other outlays are rising proportionally, investments are declining.

In Thatcher's view, 'A range of . . . evidence . . . suggests that the policies of the 1980s have resulted in structural changes in the British economy which, as long as they are not reversed by wrong policies, will put us in good shape in the year 2000.'[55] UK productivity performance in the 1970s 'was by far the worst of any leading industrial nation'.[56] Thatcher attributes 'The economic record of the 1980s in both our countries [UK and US] – low inflation, more growth, more job creation, rising living standards, lower marginal tax rates' to Thatcherism and Reaganism.[57] 'The 1980s saw the rebirth in Britain of an enterprise economy.'[58] What had been a socialist economy created, without much central planning or workers' consultation, in 1945–51 by the Labour Party was managed (despite the denationalisation of steel) during the 1950s and early 1960s by the Conservative Party, which found itself compelled occasionally to carry out certain nationalisations (as with steel). During the eighteen years of Thatcher and Major's Conservative governments (1979–97), privatisation made Britain a neocapitalist economy managed from 1997 by the Labour Party. 'Mr Blair quite deliberately set out to replace Britain's class-based politics with something more like the American system, in which it is perfectly normal for businessmen to support the centre-left party, the Democrats. He junked many of the Labour policies that repelled business: in particular, his party's historic commitment to nationalisation and its traditional love of high rates of corporate and personal taxation.'[59] If so, the Thatcher revolution is likely to prove a permanent outcome in shifting Britain toward a market economy, although Labour's purpose is of course to attract the business community into its ranks without respect to recognising proper historical credit for the growing economic and political importance of that community. Blair speaks of a 'stakeholder economy',[60] language at least familiar to business.

Notes

1   As noted by Jean Pasquero, 'The Ethics of Privatisation: An Examination of Various National Experiences,' paper presented at the International Association for Business and Society (IABS), Paris, June 1999, the model appropriate to the formerly communist transition economies is quite different from either Thatcherism or Reaganism. That model is one of 'institution building' for the creation of a new, Western-like society, market, and government – where generally those institutions (except perhaps in the case of Czechoslovakia, a democratic and industrialised country prior to 1939) never existed at all before the devastation of World War II.

2   Margaret Thatcher's views are published in her two-volume autobiography: *The Downing Street Years* (New York: HarperCollins, 1993), ch. 23, 'To Cut and to Please: Tax Cuts, Tax Reform, and Privatisation,' pp. 668–687); *The Path to Power* (New York: HarperCollins, 1995), ch. 16, 'Promoting the Free-Enterprise Revolution: Economic Policy,' pp. 565–601.

3   H. Stuart Hughes and James Wilkinson, *Contemporary Europe: A History* (Englewood Cliffs, NJ: Prentice-Hall, 1987, 6th ed.), p. 404.

4   Ibid., pp. 401–402.

5   Ibid., p. 402; Thatcher, *Path to Power*, p. 44; The Industrial Charter (May 1947) of the Conservative Party endorsed economic planning, industrial partnership, and workers' consultation (Thatcher, idem, p. 49). This approach was already expressed in Harold Macmillan's prewar *The Middle Way* (London: Macmillan, 1938); Thatcher, idem, p. 50.

6   It was transparent that coal mining required government capital for modernisation (Hughes &
     Wilkinson, op. cit., p. 403). The Attlee government modified the unwritten British constitution by
     changing the Parliament Act 1911 to further reduce the power of the House of Lords, so as to
     restrict its ability to delay legislation to a single session (idem, p. 403).

7   R. A. Butler, cited by Hughes and Wilkinson, ibid., p. 478.

8   Relatively minor fees were instituted in the NHS for control of expenses (Hughes and Wilkinson,
     ibid., p. 478).

9   Ibid., p. 478.

10   Thatcher, *Path to Power*, p. 91.

11   Hughes and Wilkinson, op. cit., p. 523.

12   Thatcher, *Path to Power*, p. 635.

13   Hughes and Wilkinson, op. cit., p. 559. Scottish nationalists lost most of their seats.

14   An MP since 1959 (Finchley, North London), Thatcher had served as joint Parliamentary Secretary
     to the Ministry of Pensions and National Insurance (1960–64) and secretary of state for education
     and science (1970–74), in the Heath government, being the second woman minister ever appoint-
     ed in a Conservative government. In between, she served as shadow spokesperson on pensions,
     housing and land, and then tax (Thatcher, *Path to Power*, pp. 627–628) and in Heath's shadow cab-
     inet with responsibilities for fuel and power (from October 1967, idem, pp. 142, 628), then for
     transport (from October 1968, idem, pp. 143, 628), and then for education (from October 1969,
     idem, pp. 156, 629). This series of assignments should be regarded as important in the development
     of her views concerning privatisation and trade union reform. The Transport Bill 1968 had reor-
     ganised railways, nationalised the bus industry, and created a National Freight Authority (idem, p.
     143). In March 1974, Thatcher took over environment in the Heath shadow cabinet (idem, p. 631).
     In November 1974, she became assistant spokesperson on Treasury (idem, p. 632). In that month,
     Thatcher made the decision to challenge Heath for leadership when Keith Joseph (one of her key
     advisers on privatisation) told her he would not; Heath was being urged to call a leadership election
     from October 14 (idem, p. 632). The 4 February, 1975 first ballot was 130 for Thatcher, 119 for
     Heath (who resigned and refused to serve in the new shadow cabinet), and 16 for Hugh Fraser; the
     second ballot in her favour took place on 11 February (idem, p. 632).

15   Robert M. Worcester and Roger Mortimore, *Explaining Labour's Landslide* (London: Politico's
     Publishing, 1999) examine the election. Although an economic boom began in the mid-1990s, the
     electorate switched to Labour (*Independent on Sunday*, 8 August 1999, review of Worcester and
     Mortimore.) Subsequently, Thatcher was quoted as supporting Britain's withdrawal from the
     European Union (EU) on the grounds that it is becoming a federal superstate (*Independent on
     Sunday*, 8 August 1999). Thatcher's autobiographies suggest that Major let the Thatcher revolution
     run out of steam (*Sunday Times*, 8 August 1999), although *The Major Premiership: Politics and
     Policies Under John Major, 1990-97* recently published (by thirteen British academics, ed. Peter
     Dorey, New York: St Martin's [Macmillan], 1999) concludes differently that, "Majorism' . . . . was
     'merely Thatcherism without Thatcher – with a slightly less abrasive or strident tone' (as quoted in
     the *Sunday Times*, 8 August 1999). In a television documentary scheduled to air in October 1999
     just before the annual Conservative Party conference at Blackpool, Major was being quoted as crit-
     ical of Thatcher's conduct during the 1995 leadership crisis, when Major was challenged by a cabi-

net member (*Daily Telegraph*, 12 August 1999; *Financial Times*, 12 August 1999; The *Guardian*, 11 August 1999). The documentary was being aired with publication of Major's memoirs (*John Major: The Autobiography*, London: HarperCollins, 1999) – those of Norman Lamont, Chancellor sacked by Major and denied a peerage, being released in the same month ((*In Office*, London: Little, Brown, 1999).

16   Hughes and Wilkinson, op. cit., p. 582.

17   Riots occurred in spring-summer 1981 in major cities including London, Manchester, and Liverpool. By January 1982, poll ratings had fallen to the lowest level (25 per cent) recorded since World War II (ibid., p. 583). What aided the Conservatives was the creation out of Labour of the Social Democratic Party (SDP), which in alliance with the Liberals began taking seats in local elections from both established parties (idem, 1987, p. 583). The 1983 General Election, following the Falklands War, gave the Conservatives a strong majority, second only to the 1945 Labour victory.

18   Thatcher, *Downing Street Years*, p. 668.

19   Hughes and Wilkinson, op. cit., p. 584.

20   Ibid., p. 582.

21   Thatcher, *Downing Street Years*, p. 678.

22   Ibid., p. 678.

23   Hughes and Wilkinson, op. cit., p. 585.

24   Alan Murie, 'Privatising State Owned Housing,' in Thomas Clarke (ed.), *International Privatisation: Strategies and Practices* (Berlin: Walter de Gruyer, 1994), pp. 105-118, ch. 5, at p. 106, citing P. Bell and P. Cloke, 'The Changing Relationship between the Private and Public Sectors: Privatisation and Rural Britain,' *Journal of Rural Studies* 5 (1989): 1-15.

25   Thatcher, *Downing Street Years*, p. 678.

26   Ibid., p. 680.

27   Ibid., p. 678.

28   Ibid., p. 682.

29   Thatcher turned increasingly hostile to Britain's integration into the European Union (EU): 'once routinely favouring Europe, she became its passionate enemy. There is more than a touch of dissimulation. ... There is the preaching of illusion. ... And there is incompetence: she lost four senior ministers to the Europe question [including Nicholas Ridley, Trade and Industry Secretary, virtually her only ally in the cabinet on the issue, after he publicly insulted the Germans, Young, 1999, p. 361], a record of instability that culminated in her own eviction' in November 1990 according to Hugo Young (political columnist for the *Guardian*), *This Blessed Plot: Britain and Europe from Churchill to Blair* (Woodstock, NY: Overlook Press, 1999), p. 311. Young attributes Thatcher's fall from power to the parliamentary party's fear of losing the next election in light of her hostility to Europe and her insistence on the highly unpopular poll tax (idem, p. 369). In the European Parliament elections of summer 1989, the Conservatives received only 28 per cent. In December 1989, Sir Anthony Meyer, a backbencher, staged a failed challenge that acquired however 60 votes. Michael Heseltine, a former defence minister (who resigned in 1986 over whether to procure military helicopters from the US or, as he favoured, Europe), launched a challenge in 1990, and received 152 votes to 204 for Thatcher: she was four short of the mandatory majority for a first-round victory. The parliamentary party then elected the relatively obscure John Major (Chancellor of the

Exchequer), quite different in both leadership style and policy content from Thatcher (idem, p. 413). Major had entered parliament in 1979 with the Thatcher victory. In April 1992, Major won the General Election with only a 21-vote majority. In 1995, Major won a leadership challenge with 218 votes to 89 votes with 20 abstentions; more than a third of the parliamentary party did not vote for the Prime Minister (idem, p. 459). Labour (Blair) won the 1997 election by 179 seats ahead of all the other parties combined (idem, p. 468).

30   See Earl A. Reitan, *Margaret Thatcher, John Major, and the Transformation of Modern Britain, 1979-1998* (London: Rowman & Littlefield, 1997).

31   Hughes and Wilkinson, op. cit., p. 559.

32   Young, *Blessed Plot*, p. 310.

33   Hughes and Wilkinson, op. cit., p. 585.

34   Thatcher stated in a private interview that, 'Believing as a matter of ideology in the limits and not the power of government. ... 'My job is to let the country begin to exist within sensible and realistic economic disciplines" according to Hugo Young, *The Iron Lady: A Biography of Margaret Thatcher* (New York: Noonday Press, Farrar, Straus and Giroux. 1989), p. 207. Educated (Somerville College, Oxford, B.A. 1946, B.Sc. 1949, M.A. 1950) and employed in business as a research chemist, Thatcher subsequently married a prosperous businessman and then became a tax lawyer (the Revenue Bar) by reading for the bar examination (Thatcher, *Path to Power*, p. 83).

35   Tony Blair wrote: 'I have always believed that politics is first and foremost about ideas. Without a powerful commitment to goals and values, governments are rudderless and ineffective, however large their majorities. Furthermore, ideas need labels if they are to become popular and widely understood' ('New Politics for the New Century,' *Independent* 21 September 1998). Blair's label for a 'progressive centre-left' is the 'Third Way' of 'modernised social democracy, passionate in its commitment to social justice and the goals of the centre-left, but flexible, innovative and forward-looking in the means to achieve them'. The 'Third Way' is neither the 'old left preoccupied by state control, high taxation and producer interests' nor the 'new right treating public investment, and often the very notions of 'society' and collective endeavour, as evils to be undone' but a reconciliation of previously antagonistic themes 'to build the open, fair and prosperous society to which we aspire'. Blair articulates a fusion of democratic socialism and liberalism into a progressive politics of a civil society of 'traditional values in a changed world'.

36   Young, *Blessed Plot*, p. 307.

37   Ibid., p. 307.

38   Thatcher, *Path to Power*, pp. 149–150. In her 21 May, 1988 address on 'Christianity and Wealth' to the leaders of the Church of Scotland, Thatcher stated: 'Ideally, when Christians meet, as Christians, to take counsel together, their purpose is not (or should not be) to ascertain what is the mind of the majority but what is the mind of the Holy Spirit – something which may be quite different.' Thatcher then emphasised her enthusiasm for democracy, not because majorities will necessarily protect 'God-given human rights' because 'it most effectively safeguards the value of the individual, and, more than any other system, restrains the abuse of power by the few'."

39   Thatcher, *Path to Power*, p. 150.

40   Ibid., pp. 149–150.

41   Thatcher, *Downing Street Years*, p. 676.

42   Thatcher, *Path to Power*, pp. 50, 85.

43   Ibid., p. 84.

44   Ibid., p. 565.

45   Ibid., p. 569. Young, *Iron Lady*, p. 537, comments: 'to reduce the role of government itself in the life of the nation. ... was seen as a matter of economic efficiency: believers in market liberalism held as an axiomatic principle that state intervention in what markets did to the economy should be held to a minimum. But it was also a matter of philosophy. Big government was a socialist aberration, small government a Conservative promise reflecting what the party saw as its classic commitment – often neglected ... – to individual liberty."

46   Thatcher, *Path to Power*, p. 569.

47   Characterised by Patrick Minford, *The Supply Side Revolution in Britain* (Institute of Economic Affairs, 1991) as the 'supply side revolution' in Britain (cited by ibid., p. 575.)

48   Thatcher, *Downing Street Years*, p. 669; *Path to Power*, p. 575.

49   Thatcher's address to the leaders of the Church of Scotland on 'Christianity and Wealth' (May 21, 1988) received sharp criticism from Labour (as 'the creed of greed'). 'I believe that by taking together ... key elements from the Old and New Testaments, we gain a view of the universe, a proper attitude to work and principles to shape economic and social life. We are told we must work and use our talents to create wealth. "If a man will not work he shall not eat," wrote St. Paul to the Thessalonians. Indeed, abundance rather than poverty has a legitimacy which derives from the very nature of creation.' It is the 'love of money for its own sake' that is wrong rather than 'the creation of wealth'; the spiritual test of the latter comes with the use of wealth. 'Any set of social and economic arrangements which is not founded on the acceptance of individual responsibility will do nothing but harm.' The prominent British Conservative politician Christopher Soames told Young: 'She is an agnostic who continues to go to church. She won't become an atheist, but on the other hand she certainly won't become a true believer' (Young, *Blessed Plot*, p. 321). Thatcher makes reference to her Methodism background and her attraction to the writings of the 'High Anglican C. S. Lewis' (*Path to Power*, pp. 39, 40).

50   Some 25,000 public sector staff (teachers, firemen, policemen, civil servants) take early retirement, typically for 'ill-health', at an additional cost of £ 1 billion pounds annually (*Guardian*, 12 August 1999).

51   A complete series was not reported in the OECD source document for UK total outlays and deficit or surplus.

52   See Nigel Lawson, *The View From No. 11: Memoirs of a Tory Radical* (London: Bantam Press, 1992).

53   Compulsory Competitive Tendering (CCT) legislated by the Local Government Act 1988 is reviewed in Trevor Colling, 'Commerce Vs. Politics: Compulsory Competitive Tending and the Determination of Employment Policy in a British Local Authority,' in Thomas Clarke (ed.), *International Privatisation: Strategies and Practices* (Berlin: Walter de Gruyter, 1994), ch. 6, pp. 119–138.

54   Young, *Iron Lady*, p. 538, argues the community charge or poll tax was intended to increase central control over local spending, based on a Conservative view about the 'reckless financial irresponsibility of Labour outposts in the big cities'. Thatcher, *Downing Street Years*, discusses the community charge policy crisis in detail (ch. 22, 'A Little Local Difficulty: The Replacement of the Rating

System with the Community Charge,' pp. 642–667). She makes three general points: (1) she attributes centralisation to the failure to continue the charge; (2) she emphasises the need for central controls to lack of local government accountability; (3) she indicts the 'low' politics and ineffective administration of local government. An Audit Commission 1982 was established to monitor local government. Introduced following the 1987 election, the community charge was a flat rate on all adult residents in place of the domestic rate on property, with a partial rebate for low incomes (a flat tax on top of a partial exemption produces mild progression), joined to a national business rate. By 1985, 60 per cent of the revenues came from business rates (idem, p. 646), and rates varied greatly as a result in part of resource equalisation (so as to provide similar revenues in each area). Thatcher's expressed rationale is that local government services had shifted historically from property-serving to population-serving, and that the tax scheme should shift similarly (idem, p. 645), with income and sales tax alternatives being even worse. 'I had always disliked the rates intensely. Any property tax is essentially a tax on improving one's own home. It was manifestly unfair and un-Conservative' (idem, p. 644).

55　Thatcher, *Path to Power*, pp. 576, 578.
56　Ibid., p. 576.
57　Ibid., p. 579.
58　Thatcher, *Downing Street Years*, p. 668.
59　*The Economist*, 'A new corporatism: The new establishment' (14 August, 1999), pp. 48–50.
60　*The Economist*, 'Blair raises the stake' (13 January, 1990), pp. 53–54.

III

Thatcher and Foreign Policy

Bush and Thatcher:
Managing the End of the Cold War

Ryan J. Barilleaux and Mark J. Rozell

George H W Bush came to the presidency with a reputation for expertise in foreign affairs. This reputation had been earned through service as United States ambassador to the United Nations (1971–73), head of the American liaison office in the People's Republic of China (1974–75), and as Director of the CIA (1975–76). In these posts and as vice-president, Bush schooled himself in the intricacies of diplomacy and national security.

Bush's international experience left him with entrenched, coherent values for conducting international relations. These values placed emphasis on the need for order and stability in world affairs, good personal relations among national leaders, and sensitivity to the interests and views of other countries. By the time he became president Bush had developed an overall attitude toward world affairs that can be characterised as a 'conservative internationalism'.[1] This approach is shaped by the desire to promote values associated with the American system – including liberty, democracy, and republicanism – but to do so through means that seek to ensure international security and stability.

Two dimensions of Bush's conservative internationalism can be seen in major international developments during his presidency. In one, there was Bush's cautious reaction to the break-up of the Soviet Union's Eastern European empire and to the fall of the Soviet regime itself. As pleased as any American president would have been to hold office during such momentous events as the fall of the Berlin Wall and the 'Velvet Revolution' in Czechoslovakia, Bush hesitated to claim victory for the West. Nor did he gloat in the face of the Kremlin's problems holding together its empire, despite the obvious fact that it was exactly such developments that had been a central goal of American policy since the Truman Doctrine. Bush's caution arose from his concern that unpredictability and instability were bigger threats to international peace than Soviet imperialism or the defunct Brezhnev Doctrine. Bush wanted to promote democracy, but not at the risk of war.

The other dimension can be seen in Bush's reaction to Iraq's invasion of Kuwait in 1990. Bush saw the occupation as a violation of international law and the principle of national sovereignty, but his initial response was again cautious. He resisted making blunt statements demanding that Iraq withdraw from Kuwait, but when Arab attempts to deal with the crisis failed, Bush turned to international sanctions and ultimately a ferocious war machine to drive Iraqi forces from Baghdad's small neighbour.

Bush placed enormous emphasis in international diplomacy in his personal relationships with world leaders. He wrote: 'I believed that personal contact would be an important part of our approach to both diplomacy and leadership of the alliance and elsewhere . . . I suppose there is a danger that one can be naively lulled if one expects friendships will cause the other party to do things your way, but I thought that danger was remote. For me, personal diplomacy and leadership went hand in hand.'[2] Bush placed high emphasis on his working relationship with Margaret Thatcher, although he admitted that, 'I regret that we never were quite as close as she had been to Ronald Reagan.'[3]

Bush placed great value on personal relationships in choosing most of the top officials of his administration. Not only was his Secretary of State, James Baker, a long-time political associate and personal friend, but he had previously worked closely with his Assistant for National Security Affairs, Brent Scowcroft, and with most of his cabinet and senior Executive Office staff. Bush valued competence, but relied on personal relationships in his appointments; it is no surprise that he should value it in his interactions with his international peers. Margaret Thatcher's approach to foreign policy was closer to that of her close ally and friend Ronald Reagan. Thatcher placed great emphasis on standing for key principles, on demonstrating commitment to those principles through strong rhetoric, and on decisive action to maintain Britain's role as a great power in a rapidly-evolving international arena.

Also like Reagan, Thatcher came to power as the standard-bearer of a conservative movement that had grown dissatisfied with the direction in which her party's established leaders had taken both the party and government policy. She was proud to be the leader who called the Conservative Party and the nation to what she saw as the difficult but necessary course that would save Britain from self-destruction by socialism at home and a self-imposed weakness in world affairs. No matter how harsh the criticisms of her policies, whether from opponents or even members of her own party, she would not turn from the direction she believed to be correct. During one of the toughest periods of her premiership, in the fall of 1980, she told the Conservative Party Conference that 'To those waiting with bated breath for that favourite media catchphrase, the "U-turn," I have only one thing to say. "You turn if you want to. The lady's not for turning." I say that not only to you, but to our friends overseas – and also to those who are not our friends."[4]

For what would she take a stand? Thatcher herself summarised her principles, relating her convictions to the lessons she drew from observing the Second World War:

I drew from the failure of appeasement the lesson that aggression must always be firmly resisted . . . nations must cooperate in defence of agreed international rules if they are either to resist evils or to achieve great benefits. That is merely a platitude, however, if political leaders lack the courage and farsightedness . . . My view was – and is – that an effective internationalism can only be built by strong nations which are able to call upon the loyalty of their citizens to defend and enforce civilised rules of international conduct. An internationalism which seeks to supersede the nation-state, however, will founder quickly upon the reality that very few people are prepared to make genuine sacrifices for it. It is likely to degenerate, therefore, into a formula for endless discussion and hand-wringing.[5]

On this one point Thatcher's supporters and critics would have little trouble agreeing: that she did stand for her principles during her years in power.

Thatcher made no claims to a special eloquence, but she was probably the first British leader since Churchill who employed strong rhetoric as an instrument of policy. Again, like her counterpart Reagan and unlike the almost tongue-tied Bush, Thatcher was able to exercise international influence by focused and forceful language. For example, when George Bush asked her what she thought should be done about Iraq's invasion of Kuwait, her response was blunt. As she told an interviewer later, 'I told him that aggressors must be stopped, not only stopped, but they must be thrown out.'[6]

Thatcher used strong rhetoric to promote negotiation as well as to steel resolve against Iraq's aggression. Indeed, it was she who helped to set the stage for better relations between the Soviet Union and the West. In 1984, when Soviet premier Chernenko appeared to be dying, Thatcher invited to Britain the two men who seemed to have the best chance of becoming the next Soviet leader. After meeting with Mikhail Gorbachev, she told a television interviewer – and therefore the world – 'I like Mr Gorbachev. We can do business together.'[7]

Upon assuming the premiership, Thatcher concluded that Britain's international status did not conform to her nation's traditional role as a great power. As she put the situation in her memoirs, 'Britain was a middle-ranking power, given unusual influence by virtue of its historical distinction, skilled diplomacy and versatile military forces, but greatly weakened by economic decline.'[8] Of course, what she did not say was that Britain also remained a member of the elite club of nuclear states, held a veto in the United Nations Security Council, and enjoyed a 'special relationship' with the United States that she renewed through her close working relationship with President Reagan.

Thatcher was determined to protect Britain's international interests. To that end, she acted decisively in the international arena. She employed overwhelming force against Argentina to take back the Falkland Islands in 1982, gaining a victory that revived Britain's reputation as a military power (*Newsweek* had a cover story during the war that read 'The Empire Strikes Back') and cemented Thatcher's hold on a majority in Parliament. Later, she kept Britain (and herself) as an international player by taking an active role in the diplomacy of the end of the Cold War.

When Iraq invaded Kuwait, she was the most forceful voice pressing George Bush to be firm in dealing with Saddam Hussein. She later related to an interviewer her first reaction to the news that Kuwait had been invaded – it is expressed in the form of one of the principles she was committed to upholding: 'You've got to take some action quickly.'[9] In addition to pressing Bush, she backed up her counsel with a large British contingent in the force that drove the invaders out of Kuwait.

Thatcher's actions in office belied her initial assessment of the United Kingdom as a middle-level power. Under her direction, Whitehall behaved as if Britain were an undisputed great power.

The individual approaches of Bush and Thatcher are relevant because they help to explain the personal relationship between the two principals in the Anglo-American 'special relationship'. While each one respected the other and was committed to a good working relationship, the differences in their own ideas and styles kept them from enjoying the rapport that Thatcher and Reagan had developed.

For Thatcher, the relationship was one based on mutual interest and history, businesslike without the broad-based trust she and Reagan shared. Thatcher saw Bush as more like the establishment politicians in her own party that she had beaten than the lonely voice for truth that she saw herself and Reagan as being. Upon Bush's election she wrote:

He was one of the most decent, honest, and patriotic Americans I have met. He had great personal courage, as his past record and his resilience in campaigning showed. But he never had to think through his beliefs and fight for them when they were hopelessly unfashionable as Ronald Reagan and I had had to do. This means that much of his time now was taken up with reaching for answers to problems which to me came quite spontaneously, because they sprang from my basic convictions.[10]

As that observation suggests, Thatcher's initial assessment of President Bush was ambivalent. Apparently, she worried about whether Bush would be tough enough to make the hard decisions that the President of the United States – leader of NATO and 'Leader of the Free World' – would be called upon to make. When the invasion of Kuwait occurred, she worried that Bush would 'go wobbly' and not show the determination to resist Hussein's aggression with force if necessary. She counselled him in the blunt language quoted above, and continued to press Bush as he considered his options. Again, her comments in her memoirs reveal much about her thinking at the time: :

The President that day [in August 1990] was an altogether more confident George Bush than the man with whom I had had earlier dealings. He was firm, cool, showing the decisive qualities which the Commander-in-Chief of the greatest world power must possess. Any hesitation fell away. I had always liked George Bush. Now my respect for him soared.[11]

145

The unspoken preface to these comments is that Thatcher had previously held Bush in some measure of respect, but not too much. Therefore, we can suggest that Thatcher tended to worry about Bush suffering from an excess of caution in situations that demanded more assertiveness. When we turn to the issue of how the Bush-Thatcher relations affected the managing of the end of the Cold War, we shall see how she pressed the president to move forward more decisively.

Twice in *A World Transformed*, Bush compares his relationship with Thatcher to the one she enjoyed with Reagan. Bush first expresses regret at not having forged a close relationship with Thatcher as Reagan had.[12] The second comparison is prompted by Thatcher's defeat as Conservative Party leader: 'While we had not been as close as she had been with Ronald Reagan, our relationship was excellent and it had grown steadily warmer over my time in office. I greatly respected and admired Margaret, and still do.'[13] But 'Margaret had a genuine respect and affection for Reagan. While Reagan usually set the tone at international meetings, he often seemed to turn the discussion over to Thatcher, let her speak for the two of them. She enjoyed talking on their joint behalf, frequently saying "Ron and I feel."'[14] For a president who placed high value in personal relationships, these comments betray a sense of wistfulness on Bush's part.

Bush's evaluation of Thatcher presents her as a British parallel to Reagan, which her own comments reveal is the way she saw herself. Recalling discussions among NATO leaders in 1989 on issues of nuclear weapons, Bush remembers one exchange with her in this way: 'This conversation was vintage Thatcher, strong and principled.'[15] Elsewhere, he says of Thatcher, 'She is a courageous woman of conviction. She had been a champion for democracy in the revolutions we had nourished, and a wise friend for the United States and myself. I valued her open and direct way of dealing with people, based on solid principles.'[16]

For both parties, the Bush-Thatcher relationship was apparently a paler version of the closeness that had bonded Thatcher and Reagan. Bush seemed to regret that he could not enjoy a special relationship with the governmental head of the country with whom America had a 'special relationship'. As for Thatcher, she liked Bush but seemed to regret the political retirement of her friend Ronald Reagan. They worked together to deal with the momentous events of the years when they were both in power. But it was a formal working relationship in which Thatcher would prod Bush to do what she thought he ought to have seen on his own as the right course of action.

George Bush and Margaret Thatcher were concurrently chiefs of their respective governments for only two years (January 1989–November 1990), but that period was marked by the swift and unexpected end of the Cold War and the emergence of a new international order. The leaders of Britain and the United States were active players in the world-changing events of this period, and the relationship between them affected how they were involved in those changes.

How did their relationship affect their involvement? The answer is not simple. Thatcher tried often to convince Bush to adopt the course that she wanted. But her relative success in persuading Bush depended on his own inclinations. On several key issues – the question of how warmly to embrace Gorbachev's perestroika, arms control and NATO, the question of German reuinification, and the Iraqi invasion of Kuwait – Thatcher was generally most successful at prodding Bush when her counsel reinforced his own inclinations rather than attempting to move him to a different course of action.

When Bush assumed the presidency in 1989, the United States had already begun to improve its relationship with Gorbachev's Soviet Union. In this policy Washington was joined by Britain; in 1984, after all, Thatcher had declared that 'We can do business' with Gorbachev, and had supported efforts to reduce tensions between East and West.

Bush did not want merely to continue in the policy of his predecessor. Consequently, he sent Moscow a set of carefully mixed signals. Shortly after the presidential inauguration in 1989, Bush's national security adviser, Brent Scowcroft, appeared on television to express scepticism about whether perestroika would lead to any major improvements in US–Soviet relations. The next day, the president telephoned Gorbachev to tell him that Bush wanted 'no foot-dragging' on improving relations, but that he intended to conduct a broad review of American foreign policy before embarking on any new initiatives.[17]

To that end, the president issued a directive ordering the State Department to conduct a 'national security review' assessing the current and possible future state of relations between the two superpowers, with a due date in mid-March 1989.[18] The subsequent review created a sort of 'pause' in diplomacy between Washington and Moscow, as the new administration evaluated its options.

At this point, Thatcher entered the picture. In February, Secretary of State James Baker met Thatcher, and the Prime Minister used the occasion to tell Bush's best friend and closest political associate that Bush's pause was taking too long: 'Don't let things linger,' she told him. 'Don't let them lie fallow.'[19] Baker indicated that the American administration was in no hurry to make a mistake, but conveyed to the President the pressure that had been placed on him by Thatcher and her government.

By April 1989, the review was still under way and Gorbachev was growing impatient. Meeting with Thatcher in London, on 6 April he told her that the American-induced 'pause' was becoming 'intolerable'.[20] Thatcher defended Bush's cautious approach to the Soviet leader, but immediately following the meeting she sent Washington a message summarising the conversation and indicating that the policy review was taking too long.[21]

Bush and his advisers were committed to maintaining a cautious approach to Gorbachev, but Thatcher's message joined a chorus of voices pressing the administration to move more quickly to grasp the possibilities opened by perestroika. The president thus decided to alter what American officials were saying about the state of Soviet-American relations, although he insisted he was not yet ready for any dramatic changes in policy. As Bush told his assistant Scowcroft, the White House needed to 'get moving, at least in the way we talk about this thing. We've got to make clear that we know important stuff is happening and we're not just sitting here on our duffs'.[22] Complying with that instruction, Scowcroft told a television interviewer that the administration was now seeing evidence that 'the West has won' the Cold War, but that no major policy change was needed.[23]

Bush was now moving toward a warmer embrace of Gorbachev and improvement in superpower relations, but he was still cautious in policy shifts. By May, however, the president himself was ready to speak publicly about changes in American policy toward the Soviet Union. On 12 May, 1989, he announced the conclusions reached by his administration's policy review: 'Containment worked . . . Our review indicates that forty years of perseverance have brought us a precious opportunity. And now it is time to move beyond containment to a new policy for the 1990s – one that recognises the full scope of change taking place around the world and in the Soviet Union itself'.[24] Bush said that he wanted to see reform in the Soviet system continue and succeed, but also cautioned that America's security 'must be based on deeds, and we look for enduring, ingrained economic and political change'.[25]

Bush had now made the public embrace of perestroika that Thatcher had wanted, but he did it his own way. While her prodding probably contributed to the shift in rhetoric in April and May, Bush would continue to exhibit caution in his policies.

In addition to the question of the overall American approach to Gorbachev, the newly inaugurated President Bush faced the issue of NATO policy towards arms control and allied defence. Over the spring of 1989, the Bush administration faced a situation in which the West German government of Chancellor Helmut Kohl, under domestic political pressure, pushed for NATO initiatives to reduce or even eliminate short-range nuclear forces (SNF) in Europe. Kohl's insistence on aggressive arms-control initiatives conflicted with both the American position on SNF and that of the Thatcher government in London.

When George Bush took office in January 1989, NATO had in place a plan to modernise its short-range nuclear forces in the near future. These plans were upset, however, when in February Chancellor Kohl called for postponing NATO SNF modernisation until after 1990. Kohl, whose governing coalition was under pressure to reduce tensions with East Germany and the Soviet Union, wanted to push back force modernisation until after the 1990 elections in the Federal Republic. Soon after this call, Kohl increased the pressure on the President by insisting that NATO open negotiations with the Soviet Union to reduce short-range forces, although NATO's established position was that any SNF negotiations with Moscow should come after NATO and Moscow had resolved issues relating to conventional force levels in Europe. Hans Dietrich Genscher, leader of the party that was Kohl's coalition partner, questioned the utility of any NATO nuclear force modernisation.[26] The upshot of these statements from German officials was to threaten the united NATO negotiating position vis-a-vis Moscow.

These activities occurred within the context of preparations for a major summit of NATO leaders in May, which would mark the fiftieth anniversary of the Alliance and present an especially inopportune occasion for dissension among the allies. German pressure was one problem that Bush faced. Another was a call from NATO's Secretary-General, Manfred Wörner (a West German politician himself), for Bush to take the lead in resolving not only the SNF issue but also finding a new overall direction for NATO in an era of perestroika and improved East–West relations.[27] Still another problem was Thatcher's strong opposition to any SNF negotiations with the Soviet Union, a position presented to the United States in April by British Foreign Secretary Geoffrey Howe.[28]

Thatcher created an additional problem for Bush. While her position coincided with Bush's own ideas about SNF negotiations, the Prime Minister wanted the president to leave the issue to her to work out with Kohl.[29] For Bush, this suggestion constituted a challenge to his role as leader of the NATO Alliance; it also illustrates a clash between the Thatcher and Bush approaches to foreign policy and their mutual relationship in operation.

Thatcher's suggestion that Bush step aside was consistent with her style. As she made clear in her memoirs, she thought it 'vital that the United States and Britain should stand firm'[30] against German pressure for hasty negotiations. For her, the issue was a matter of principle. Meeting with Chancellor Kohl, 'I was quite direct. I said that in putting the case for SNF to his people he should simply ask the fundamental question whether they valued their freedom.' To protect this principle, a unified NATO was essential: 'NATO had to modernise its weapons, otherwise the United States would sooner or later start to withdraw its troops from Germany. Britain and Germany together should give a lead.'[31]

Bush was not interested in stepping aside, because as President of the United States he was leader of the Alliance. While he generally agreed with Thatcher, he was more nuanced in his language and determined to demonstrate that he was capable of living up to the responsibilities of his role as Alliance leader: 'I think Margaret was unsure about how I planned to lead NATO and she took strong public positions on SNF, perhaps reasoning that this would make it more difficult for me to compromise with the Germans.'[32] Concerned about personal diplomacy, he also suspected 'that the Thatcher–Kohl relationship was not smooth'.[33] But he was particularly concerned about Thatcher's bluntness: 'She was even more unyielding than we, and far more emotional about the dangers of compromise.'[34]

This clash of styles between the 'Iron Lady' and the diplomatic professional-as-president meant that Bush and Thatcher had to rely on the mutual interests in NATO of their countries more than the personal relationship that the President valued. They saw themselves as needing each other's support in dealing with Germany, but because they had a mutual stake in the issue rather than because of personal connections.

As a result, the United States and Britain jointly pressed Kohl to maintain a united NATO front that supported SNF modernisation. Over the course of April and May 1989, they continued to work for a strong NATO position supporting modernisation, despite further German pressure for negotiations with the Soviet Union.

Bush and Thatcher remained in touch with one another, but there was a certain degree of parting of their ways. In May, the United States announced a new proposal for resolving the issue – a plan coupling successful conventional-force negotiations to progress on SNF – but released it without consulting Thatcher. The new plan was endorsed by Germany, but Thatcher was unhappy with it (although in public she supported it). Thatcher complains in her memoirs about not being consulted about the proposal,[35] but in his book Bush defends his circumvention of Thatcher by saying that he already knew what her reaction would be.[36] In the end, at the NATO summit in late May the allies agreed on a unified position, with Thatcher swallowing her objections in the interest of allied unity.

This conflicting approaches of the two leaders ultimately led President Bush to subvert one of his preferred techniques – personal relationships – in order to protect other values. Thatcher's approach kept her from being more influential with Bush, although it is probably the case that Bush regarded this issue as one of demonstrating his own leadership and reaffirming America's primacy in the NATO Alliance. Perhaps it was events like those of the spring of 1989 that kept Thatcher and Bush from developing the close relationship that had marked relations between Ronald Reagan and the British Prime Minister.

German reunification was one of the most emotional issues of the end of the Cold War. It was emotional for the Germans, who longed for national unity; for the French, who had historic fears of German power; and for other nations east and west of the Berlin Wall for whom the division of Germany was the central fact and symbol of the Cold War.

Bush saw the drive for German unity as part of a larger process of change sweeping Europe. Bush, the President who identified with professional diplomats, was a believer in processes – the methodical, step-by-step mechanics of working through difficult political issues – especially in the realm of diplomacy. It was an important issue, as was SNF in 1989, but the President viewed it as part of the larger process of managing the end of the Cold War.[37] His dealings with Thatcher on this issue were framed by this context.

Bush's approach to unification is best summarised by the statement he made in February 1990, when he and Chancellor Kohl spoke to reporters after a meeting in which the President endorsed the idea of German unity. After he spoke in favour of a unified democratic Germany and welcomed the wave of democratisation that swept Eastern Europe, Bush uttered a characteristic remark: 'The enemy is unpredictability, the enemy is instability.'[38] He wanted pro-democracy forces in Europe to triumph, but the conservative internationalist and the diplomatic professional in him feared instability that might provoke military action on the part of the still real Soviet armed forces.

In taking this position, Bush stood between the West German political establishment, who urgently desired unity, and Thatcher and some other NATO allies, who were much more sceptical about it. As Bush recounts one conversation with Thatcher early in 1990, 'It was clear Margaret still feared the worst from reunification and, like [French President Francois] Mitterrand, worried that the Germans might "go neutral" and refuse to permit stationing nuclear weapons on their soil.'[39] In other words, the French and British leaders feared that Kohl might be willing to accept a neutralisation of Germany (between NATO and the Warsaw Pact) as the price for Soviet acquiescence in reunification. They saw such a turn of events as a threat to their own security.

Bush was willing to take this middle line because of his own assessment of the political realities of Europe in 1989 and 1990, and because of his confidence in the value of personal relationships. As he put it in his memoirs following his comments on the fears of Thatcher and Mitterrand:

For my part, it seemed pretty clear reunification was on its way and we had to work with it. By the end of January, with the inability of the East German government to regain control of its affairs, I had accepted it as inevitable and welcomed it. Furthermore, I trusted Kohl not to lead the Germans down a special, separate path.[40]

Bush trusted Kohl and Gorbachev. He had made a commitment to Kohl in January 1990 to support unification so long as instability did not threaten; and by early 1990 he had come to trust that Gorbachev would not be an obstacle to the rapidly developing events in Europe.

While Bush's personal relations with key actors affected his actions, so did his diplomatic professional's trust in processes. Commenting on Thatcher's fears about the costs of German unity, the President remarked: 'While I did not agree with Margaret's concern about the implications of a united Germany, to so some degree I did share her worry about the adverse political effect reunification could have on Gorbachev. However, I thought we could manage these issues in a way that would obviate most of her concerns.[41]

Once again, Bush insisted on taking his own course in dealing with Germany. Thatcher was not able to prevail with him, because he had confidence in his own approach and in personal relationships. As with the SNF controversy, he found her position too rigid, and he was determined to be both leader of NATO and a facilitator of peaceful resolution of international disputes. When Helmut Kohl addressed the German people on the eve of reunification in October 1990, he went out of his way to 'thank the United States of America and above all President Bush' for their role in advancing German unity.[42]

The event in which Margaret Thatcher arguably had the greatest effect on the international behaviour of George Bush was in influencing his response to the invasion of Kuwait in August 1990. Ironically, her success was short-lived, for the President did not follow her counsel on how to proceed, nor was she in power long enough to participate in the most dramatic events of the Kuwait crisis in 1991.

Thatcher's influence with Bush appears to stem from the conjunction of two realities: that what she was urging Bush to do coincided with his own inclinations in the situation; and, the fact that by sheer coincidence she and Bush were meeting together when news of Iraq's invasion struck the world. In August 1990, the two leaders were together in Aspen, Colorado, where the Prime Minister and the President were to address a conference of the Aspen Institute. Thatcher was in Aspen when she learned of the invasion, and Bush was due to arrive the next day.

Shortly after the President arrived in Aspen, he and Thatcher met, and she was able to give him the full force of her argument. As Thatcher described their meeting later, 'George Bush just said to me, "Now Margaret, what do you think?', straight away"'.[43] Her response was direct and completely consistent with the core principles she had brought to office: 'Aggression must be stopped. That is the lesson of this century. And if an aggressor gets away with it, others will want to get away with it too, so he must be stopped, and turned back. You cannot gain from aggression.'[44]

Bush agreed with Thatcher on the principle involved in this situation. As he relates their meeting in his memoirs, 'Margaret and I saw the situation in remarkably similar ways, which I think was mutually reassuring.'[45] But Thatcher believed that her strong stand did more than reassure Bush, because he was receiving conflicting advice about how to respond to the invasion. As she explained to an interviewer, 'That's why it is so vital to get your own ideas sorted out and the reasons for them . . . It's not enough to say well, I can put things across. You must know the reasons, and we were on absolutely firm ground.'[46] She apparently saw her meeting with the President as a unique opportunity to ensure that he did what she and he believed was the right thing to do: respond forcefully to Iraq's aggression. As she would eventually tell Bush when he confronted the first situation – in late August 1990 – when force might have to be employed against an Iraqi vessel, 'Look, George, this is no time to go wobbly.'[47]

However strong their agreement on principle, Bush and Thatcher would come to disagree on the means for responding to Iraq's invasion. Bush pursued a United Nations-sponsored coalition to drive the invaders out of Kuwait, while Thatcher saw no need to rely on the UN, because 'it suggested that sovereign states lacked the moral authority to act on their own behalf'.[48] In this view she was opposed by Secretary of State James Baker – with whom Bush had a much longer and closer personal relationship – and other American officials. In the end, Bush's resolve that the invasion of Kuwait 'will not stand' was reinforced by Thatcher's strong arguments, but he arrived at his own means for translating their shared principle into action. Thatcher's government cooperated in the American-led coalition that ultimately drove Iraqi forces from Kuwait, but she lost her position as Conservative Party leader in November 1990 and Bush went on without her.

By the time Margaret Thatcher left power, George Bush was firmly in control of the diplomacy that led to the Gulf War in 1991. He regretted that they had not been closer friends, but his actions in office had repeatedly demonstrated his resolve to be the international leader that he believed the American President ought to be.

Bush's relationship with Thatcher was more than merely atmospheric. It probably made a difference in nudging the President to be more forthcoming towards Gorbachev and perestroika in 1989, and it certainly steeled Bush's resolve in responding to the invasion of Kuwait. But Thatcher was never able to say 'George and I think . . .' the way she had been able to tell the NATO allies how 'Ron and I feel . . .' There were too many differences in their own approaches to foreign policy for that to be possible. Thatcher, like Reagan, saw international affairs as an arena in which principles and decisiveness sway events. Bush, on the other hand, saw the arena as a place for cautious and nuanced professionalism.

Thatcher and Bush remained committed to the Anglo-American 'special relationship', but the differences between them prevented their own personal interactions from achieving the same level of closeness. They respected and liked each other, but were less partners than they were cautious allies.

Notes

1   See corresponding discussion in Ryan J. Barilleaux, 'George Bush, Germany, and the New World Order,' in *Shepherd of Democracy? America and Germany in the Twentieth Century*, pp. 161–72, edited by Carl C. Hodge and Cathal J. Nolan (Westport, Conn.: Greenwood Press, 1992), pp. 165–66.

2   George Bush and Brent Scowcroft, *A World Transformed* (New York: Knopf, 1998), p. 60.

3   Ibid., p. 69.

4   Quoted in Margaret Thatcher, *The Downing Street Years* (New York: HarperCollins, 1993), pp. 122.

5   Ibid, pp. 11–12.

6   'Interview with Margaret Thatcher, Prime Minister, United Kingdom,' oral history interview on the Persian Gulf War, Frontline page, website of WGBH-Boston [http://www.pbs.org/wgbh/pages/frontline/gulf/oral/thatcher/1.htm].

7   Quoted in Michael Beschloss and Strobe Talbott, *At the Highest Levels: The Inside Story of the End of the Cold War* (Boston: Little, Brown, 1993), p. 30. Emphasis in original.

8   Thatcher, p. 9.

9   'Interview with Margaret Thatcher,' loc. cit.

10 Thatcher, pp. 782–783.

11 Ibid., p. 820.

12 Bush and Scowcroft, p. 69.

13   Ibid., p. 410.

14   Ibid., p. 69.

15   Ibid., p. 69.

16   Ibid., p. 410.

17   Beschloss and Talbott, pp. 17–18.

18   Ibid., p. 24.

19   Ibid., p. 31.

20   Ibid., p. 49.

21   Ibid., p. 49.

22   Ibid., p. 51.

23   Ibid., p. 51.

24   Quoted in ibid., p. 70.

25   Ibid.

26   See Bush and Scowcroft, chapter 3.

27   Ibid.

28   Ibid., p. 67.

29   Ibid.

30   Thatcher, p. 785.

31   Ibid.

32   Bush and Scowcroft, p. 67.

33   Ibid.

34   Ibid.

35   Thatcher, p. 788.

36   Bush and Scowcroft, p. 72.

37   See Michael Mandelbaum, 'The Bush Foreign Policy,' *Foreign Affairs* 70, no. 1 (1990): pp. 5–22; see also Barilleaux, op. cit.

38   Quoted in Barilleaux, p. 165.

39   Bush and Scowcroft, p. 212.

40   Ibid., p. 213. Emphasis ours.

41   Ibid., p. 193. Emphasis ours.

42   Quoted in *New York Times* (October 3, 1990): A9.

43   'Interview with Margaret Thatcher,' loc. cit.

44   Loc. cit.

45   Bush and Scowcroft, p. 319.

46   'Interview with Margaret Thatcher' .

47   Ibid.

48   Thatcher, p. 821.

Margaret Thatcher:
Personality and Foreign Policy

Sir Bryan Cartledge

Mark Rozell's and Ryan Barilleaux's excellent essay stresses the importance which President George Bush attached to the health of his personal relationships with his fellow world statesmen and the care which he took to keep those relationships in good repair. The essay also makes it clear that in his defence and promotion of the interests of the United States and its allies, Bush was clear-eyed and dispassionate, basing his decisions more on objective appraisal than on pre-existing personal conviction.

Margaret Thatcher's diplomacy and conduct of policy was diametrically opposite in both respects. In the political arena, whether domestic or international, personal relationships were for her an irrelevance. This is not to say that personal chemistry played no part in her dealings with her fellow politicians and statesmen: it did, sometimes importantly, not least in her relations with President Reagan. The extent to which Margaret Thatcher and Mikhail Gorbachev struck sparks off each other was obvious to anyone who saw them together and could have been mistaken for flirtation; it gave rise to some unrepeatable Russian jokes. With Dr Garrett Fitzgerald, the Irish Taoiseach, the chemistry was also positive and helped to make Margaret Thatcher the improbable signatory of the Anglo-Irish Agreement of 1985. And it could work the other way. On her first overseas visit as Prime Minister, in May 1979, I remember watching the tightening of Margaret Thatcher's lips when President Giscard d'Estaing, having patronised her throughout the morning, exercised his presidential prerogative of being served first at the luncheon table in the Elysée

Palace; the chemistry thereafter was very negative indeed – as it was, for different reasons, with the Australian Prime Minister, Malcolm Fraser. But with Margaret Thatcher the chemistry either happened or it didn't: it would have been quite foreign to her nature to cultivate a personal relationship – or to flinch from extinguishing one if necessary. As Roy Jenkins famously remarked, 'as a proponent of the British case, she does have the advantage of being almost totally impervious to how much she offends other people.'

The other half of the contrast with President Bush is equally stark. Margaret Thatcher's decisions were taken with reference to a few deeply, even passionately, held personal convictions and beliefs against which proposals or individuals were measured: if found wanting, the proposal or individual was discarded without further ado. I recall one of her 'seminars' at Chequers, on Communism, at which she found the contribution of a participating academic insufficiently condemnatory of Soviet policies: 'I have had Mr "X", ' she rasped when the seminar was over and the unfortunate academic received no further invitations. Total, unremitting hostility to authoritarian systems of government was one of Thatcher's benchmark convictions; an unshakeable belief in the sanctity of national, and specifically of British, national sovereignty was another. From the very beginning she was impatient with and contemptuous of the forms and the ethos of the European Community and exasperated by its rhetoric. I remember accompanying her, as one of her Private Secretaries, to her first European Council meeting, in Strasbourg in 1979. The British Ambassador in Paris had sent his Rolls Royce for her use during her stay and I sat beside her as it drove her to the informal dinner with which these sessions traditionally begin, through streets lined with cheering Strasbourgeois who were waiting to catch their first glimpse of Britain's first woman Prime Minister. I was thoroughly enjoying myself until Margaret Thatcher suddenly turned to me and asked: 'Why do I have to go through with this? What is the point?' Seized by panic that the Prime Minister was about to order our driver to turn round and head for home, a Private Secretary's nightmare, I launched into an impassioned defence of the European Community and of Britain's role in it. My impertinent tutorial made not the slightest impression on the lady but at least it distracted her until the Rolls had drawn up at our destination, making retreat impossible.

This tension, between doing what had to be done and kicking against the traces every inch of the way, characterised Margaret Thatcher's relationship with Europe throughout her premiership; in addition, she enjoyed a good fight (so long as she won) and made sure that nearly every major Euro-meeting in which she took part turned into one. It has been argued that the battle over Britain's contribution to the European Community's budget, which dominated virtually every meeting of the European Council between Dublin in 1979 and Fontainebleau in 1984, could not have been won by any method other than the Thatcher tactic of relentless hand-bagging and furious rejection of opposing arguments in a style which often verged on contumely. I am not so sure. The substance of the British case was so strong that I believe that it would eventually have prevailed, even if advanced in a more orthodox manner – although it would probably have taken even longer. What is certain is that the positive achievements of Thatcher's European policy – essentially the budget settlement and the creation of the Single Market – were counterbalanced by a more negative legacy, unhelpful to British interests. In this there are two elements. The first, and shorter-lived, was the habit of resentment of Britain which Thatcher's bruising style and behaviour instilled in the bureaucracies and among the politicians of Europe; this survived her political demise and came to the fore most obviously during the crisis in Britain's relations with Europe over BSE, or 'mad cow disease', and the European boycott of British beef. Any sympathy for the British predicament which might normally have influenced the policies of her European partners was completely eclipsed by the pleasure of getting their own back – the behaviour of governments is not immune from human frailties. The same phenomenon was detectable in other, less public, contexts; but the advent of new faces round the European Council table, not least that of a British Prime Minister more positively disposed towards Europe, has probably now laid it to rest. The other, unintended, legacy of Thatcher's European policy is to be found in Britain itself. The pugnacity with which she defended British sovereignty against any perceived threat to it from Brussels, a defence which towards the end shaded into strident nationalism, articulated and had the unsought effect of breathing life into the latent xenophobia both within her own party and within the British population more generally, not least among its tabloid-reading majority. This has created a major obstacle in the way of the present British government's pursuit of the European policies which, at least in my view, British interests require. It is in good measure the 'Thatcher effect', as well as the absence of clear-cut leadership from Tony Blair, which has driven the British government back from advocacy of entry into Economic and Monetary Union with Europe to a desperate defence of the very principle of British membership of the European Union itself.

Thatcher, Bush, and Hussein: Developing a New Paradigm for Western Intervention in the Post-Cold War World

Frank J. Smist. Jr. and Zachary M. Stolz

On 2 August, 1990, 80,000 Iraqi troops invaded Kuwait and, in short order, proceeded to occupy Kuwait City and the rest of the tiny nation. In Washington, D.C., President Bush met with his key advisers and, during a photo session, told reporters, 'We're not discussing intervention.' When the media had left, the mood of President Bush and his advisers was one of shock and frustration. Iraq's invasion of Kuwait had clearly caught the administration by surprise.[1]

During the Cold War, the rivalry between the United States and the Soviet Union was the key determinant of American foreign policy. Containment of the USSR was the paradigm that guided America and the West from 1947 until the collapse of the Soviet empire began in 1989. Iraq's aggression against Kuwait in 1990 was the first international challenge in the post-Cold War world. In shaping the Western response to this challenge, the United States and Great Britain played leading roles and the actions of George Bush and Margaret Thatcher were of critical importance. Fortunately for George Bush, Margaret Thatcher was Prime Minister when this crisis began. Unfortunately, Mrs Thatcher no longer held her post when critical decisions had to be made during the final stages of the military action taken to expel Iraq from its occupation of Kuwait.

After 80,000 Iraqi troops occupied Kuwait, President George Bush was determined that this action would not stand. In public, Bush's initial comments were ambiguous. Writing in his memoirs, Bush notes that on 2 August, hours after the invasion, Helen Thomas of UPI asked him if the US would use force against Iraq. In response, Bush stated that he was not contemplating intervention. The reality though was quite different. Bush was contemplating intervention and he was determined that Iraqi forces would not remain in Kuwait.[2] As National Security adviser Brent Scowcroft observed:

The President's comment that he was not contemplating intervention has been taken by some to indicate he was passive or indecisive about the notion of doing anything about the Iraqi invasion until Margaret Thatcher 'put some stiffening in his spine' at their meeting later that day. Such speculation is wrong, although his choice of words was not felicitous.[3]

Despite Scowcroft's assertion, the public George Bush initially sent ambiguous signals as to what he would do about the invasion.

A careful examination of the record suggests that the President was determined from the very beginning to expel Iraq from Kuwait. However, President Bush could not consider Iraq in isolation. Aside from the actions in the Persian Gulf, the President had to consider the position of Soviet leader Mikhail Gorbachev. It was imperative to prevent Moscow from aiding its longtime ally Iraq. In addition, Bush had to assemble a coalition and build international support for sanctions and possible military action in the United Nations. Most importantly, the President had to retain the support of the American people and a Congress controlled by the opposition party.

In confronting Iraq, President Bush failed to decisively establish a new paradigm to replace the policy of containment founded in response to the Cold War. Instead of saying that Saddam Hussein was an aggressor who posed a key threat to vital American economic interests in the Persian Gulf, Bush equivocated. Human rights violations by the Iraqis were seized upon and Saddam Hussein himself was repeatedly compared to Adolf Hitler. To keep the thirty-nine nation coalition opposing Iraq together, military planning focused on ejecting Iraq from Kuwait and no planning was done to occupy Iraq and overthrow Saddam Hussein. After demonising the Iraqi leader and especially after equating him with Adolf Hitler, the failure to either arrest or kill Saddam Hussein at the end of hostilities would later pose significant long-term problems.

Unlike George Bush, Margaret Thatcher gave no mixed signals as to what should be done about the Iraqi aggression. For Thatcher, Iraq's action was totally unacceptable and immediate steps had to be taken to punish and evict the aggressor. As a young child, Thatcher had witnessed the appeasement of Hitler prior to World War II. The key event for her was the Munich Agreement of September 1938. Although Thatcher had hoped that Munich might lead to genuine peace, she was a realist. As she observed in her memoirs:

We knew by now [1938] a good deal about Hitler's regime and probable intentions . . . It was the Germans' subsequent dismemberment of what remained of Czechoslovakia in March 1939 that finally convinced almost everyone that appeasement had been a disaster and that war would soon be necessary to defeat Hitler's ambitions.[4]

Like Bush, Thatcher favoured expelling Iraq from Kuwait and punishing Saddam Hussein's regime. Unlike Bush, Thatcher did not have to worry about maintaining a relationship with Mikhail Gorbachev, keeping a diverse international coalition together, and playing political games. From the very beginning, she knew what needed to be done and attempted to do so in both her private and public actions.

Shortly after the invasion, Thatcher met with President Bush in Aspen, Colorado. Bush asked her what she thought. In reply Thatcher made two main points: First, aggressors must never be appeased. Second, because Saddam Hussein posed a serious threat to Saudi Arabia and other Persian Gulf neighbours, he had to be stopped quickly.[5] For Margaret Thatcher, there could be no equivocation in this matter. Unfortunately, the George Bush she dealt with in private was not as firm in his beliefs as she was. Later, after their meetings in Aspen, Thatcher flew to Washington and met with Bush at the White House. In her memoirs, she described the US leader she now encountered:

The President that day was an altogether more confident George Bush than the man with whom I had had earlier dealings. He was firm, cool, showing the decisive qualities which the Commander-in-Chief of the greatest world power must possess. Any hesitation fell away. I had always liked George Bush, now my respect for him soared.[6]

As Prime Minister, Margaret Thatcher never had any doubt as to what should be done about Saddam Hussein. She had lived through the 1930s and the appeasement of Hitler and that life experience shaped and affected her response to the Iraqi leader.

For George Bush, Margaret Thatcher was more than a close ally. Her determination and grit was crucial to reinforcing President Bush's own views that the Iraqi aggression must not be allowed to stand. As James Baker observed:

Desert Storm could have been a unilateral initiative. Legally the President was within his prerogatives to act under Article 51 of the United Nations Charter, which allows member states the right of self-defence to protect their national interests. Some of our allies thought that we should invoke Article 51, begin deploying American troops in the Gulf, and launch combat operations as soon as possible. Not surprisingly, the most prominent of these hawks was British Prime Minister Margaret Thatcher. On August 6, the President met in the Oval Office with the Prime Minister. Much has been written about the special relationship between the United States and Great Britain, and the bilateral ties forged between us over two centuries are every bit as durable as advertised. We have no better friends than the British. And the relationship is special. This gives the British a license others don't have – the licence of occasionally flexing our muscles. And sometimes they are quite adept at it. As her gutsy leadership during the 1982 Falklands war had amply demonstrated, Margaret Thatcher is a charter member of the do-what-you-must-now-and-worry-about-it-later school. She's never been reluctant to say what she thinks, and in this case she wasn't the least bit shy in expressing her serious misgivings about our preference for pursuing a multilateral course against Saddam. 'We simply can't let this stand,' she argued. 'We've got to take care of it now.'[7]

For George Bush, Margaret Thatcher was critical in helping him steel himself for the challenges that lay ahead. Supported steadfastly by Margaret Thatcher, George Bush assembled a thirty-nine nation coalition that sent almost 800,000 soldiers to the Persian Gulf to do battle with Saddam Hussein. The President worked with Mikhail Gorbachev, the United Nations, his coalition partners, and the American Congress to first impose economic sanctions on Iraq and then launch a forty-day air campaign and then a 100-hour land war against Iraqi forces in Kuwait. Unfortunately for Bush, Margaret Thatcher was forced from office before what was started could be brought to an end. In November 1990,

Thatcher was ousted from her position as Prime Minister. For George Bush, that day was one he would never forget:

That evening, Margaret suffered her Conservative Party leadership defeat. She had steadfastly worked through the entire meeting that day, although she looked nervous and it was clear that she had other things on her mind. She darted in and out to check on progress back in Britain. I left her at about five that afternoon, asking her if she had any word yet. She said it would be a couple of hours before she knew. I was saddened and surprised when I heard the news. Despite it, she courageously appeared for the dinner at Versailles, participating fully. Her downfall was amazing – so fast and almost unforeseen. While we had not been as close as she had been with Ronald Reagan, our relationship was excellent and it had grown steadily warmer over my time in office. I greatly respected and admired Margaret, and still do. She is a courageous woman of conviction. She had been a champion for democracy and the revolutions we had nourished, and a wise friend for the United States and myself. I valued her open and direct way of dealing with people, based on solid principles. It was a typical demonstration of Margaret's courage, and her determination that the coalition prevail, that in her 'farewell' letter to me a few days later, on November 22, she added a note confirming that Britain was sending additional troops and warships.[8]

For the United States, going to war against Iraq was the first war America had fought since Vietnam. More than 50,000 US servicemen had been killed in Vietnam and it left an indelible scar on America. Just before President Bush launched the air campaign against Iraq, Secretary of State James Baker met in Geneva with Tariq Aziz, the Iraqi Foreign Minister. At the end of the meeting, Tariq Aziz told Baker directly why Iraq did not fear American threats of military action: 'Your Arab allies will desert you. They will not kill other Arabs. Your alliance will crumble and you will be left lost in the desert. You don't know the desert because you have never ridden on a horse or a camel.'[9]

Unfortunately for Tariq Aziz and Iraq, the United States could fight and win in the desert. Any questions about America's forces due to its failure in the jungles of Vietnam could now be put to rest. The Arab members of the coalition remained intact as well. An air campaign of forty days was followed by a land invasion that ejected Iraq from Kuwait in less than one hundred hours. In their memoirs, President Bush and adviser Brent Scowcroft discussed at length how the war was conducted. It is clear that the key decisions were made exclusively by the President and his closest American advisers. In August 1990, Margaret Thatcher was a key player in shaping the strategy and tactics of the United States. At the end of the war, no one like her was there to shape the final outcome.

Did the absence of Margaret Thatcher affect the Gulf War's end? We believe that it did and that her absence adversely affected the quality of the decisions made by President Bush and his advisers. It is clear from reading the Bush-Scowcroft memoirs that critical decisions were made that had significant long-term implications and that Thatcher would have vigorously contested these decisions had she remained at Number 10 Downing Street. First, Saddam Hussein was allowed to remain in power and he was not even compelled to sign terms of surrender. Bush and Scowcroft explain why this was allowed to occur:

Trying to eliminate Saddam, extending the ground war into Iraq, would have violated our guideline about not changing objectives in midstream, engaging in 'mission creep', and would have incurred incalculable human and political costs. Apprehending him was probably impossible . . . We would have been forced to occupy Baghdad and, in effect, rule Iraq. The coalition would instantly have collapsed, the Arabs deserting it in anger and other allies pulling out as well. Under those circumstances, there was no viable 'exit strategy . . .'[10]

By making such a decision, George Bush allowed Saddam Hussein to remain in power and avoid any personal blame for the defeat of the Iraqi forces. For Margaret Thatcher, such a decision would have been unthinkable. As she noted in her memoirs:

One of my very few abiding regrets is that I was not there to see the issue through. The failure to disarm Saddam Hussein and to follow through the victory so that he was publicly humiliated in the eyes of his subjects and Islamic neighbors was a mistake which stemmed from the excessive emphasis placed right from the start on international consensus. The opinion for the UN accounted for too much and the military objective of defeat for too little. And so Saddam Hussein was left with the standing and the means to terrorise his people and foment more trouble. In war, there is much to be said for magnanimity in victory. But not before victory.[11]

When President Bush ordered a ceasefire on 27 February 1991, it appeared that the coalition led by the United States had won a significant victory. At the height of the war, 541,425 American soldiers were in the Persian Gulf region. Casualties had been incredibly light. There were 111 US service members killed in action and 395 wounded in action. Iraqi forces appeared to have suffered an over-whelming defeat. However, in this case, appearances were deceiving.

Saddam Hussein remained in power and, because he was allowed to contin-ue flying his helicopter gunships, forces loyal to him were able to crush Kurdish dissidents in northern Iraq and Shiite dissidents in the southern part of the nation. The allied coalition had not disintegrated as Iraq had expected and sov-ereignty had been returned to Kuwait. But, with Saddam Hussein remaining in power, more than 20,000 members of the US armed forces were required to remain in the Gulf. These men and women were still there in 2000.

Saddam Hussein's regime continues to pose a threat by seeking to build nuclear, biological, and chemical weapons of mass destruction. George Bush, who appeared invincible in the aftermath of the conflict with public approval ratings in the US exceeding 90 per cent, was defeated in the presidential election of 1992 and garnered a mere 38 per cent of the popular vote.[12] An opportunity to use the Gulf War to develop a new post-Cold War paradigm had been lost.

Since the war in the Gulf, neither President Bush nor President Bill Clinton has been able to develop and articulate a new paradigm to clearly identify US national interests in the post-Cold War world. As a result, US actions in this new era have been based largely on emotion rather than on a cold calculation of the national interest. America has lurched from crisis to crisis from Somalia to Haiti to Kosovo. At a unique moment in United States and world history, President Bush missed the opportunity to develop a new paradigm.

The loss of Margaret Thatcher at such a critical time in international politics has not gone unfelt either in the United States or in Great Britain. Her defeat meant that President Bush lost one of his great supporters and source of courage. The missed opportunities most likely would not have been as egregious had Thatcher maintained her dominance over British politics. She was a woman of incredible foresight who would not have let Saddam Hussein get away with the mass genocide of the Kurds and Shiites in Iraq. Lamentably, after Thatcher left office, Bush and Major backed down from their golden chance to remove one of the free world's greatest threats. Had Margaret Thatcher remained in office, Saddam Hussein would not have maintained his stranglehold over Iraq fopr so long. Without Thatcher, no new post-Cold War paradigm was developed and still has not been developed to this day. Hopefully, there is still a chance for this new world view to take shape.

We believe that such a new paradigm should distinguish between three levels of threat to the United States and the West. First, there exist situations in which the country could face imminent physical destruction. Just such a situation existed during the Cold War when US and Soviet nuclear missiles were aimed at each other. In the post-Cold War world, besides nuclear weapons, new and lethal arsenals of biological and chemical weapons could pose additional threats of imminent destruction. A second level of danger is the type of situation that would cause grave harm to US interests but not necessarily to US survival. For example, Iraqi control of Persian Gulf oil resources could have wreaked havoc on Western economies. Rogue states like Libya and North Korea could pose similar threats in the future. Finally, a third level of threat does not directly challenge US survival, but raises serious questions with respect to human rights and the humanitarian values we cherish. Here, situations such as those in Somalia, Haiti, Rwanda, and Kosovo readily come to mind. Had such a new post-Cold War paradigm been developed, US foreign policy would not have lurched from crisis to crisis since the end of the Gulf War.

Margaret Thatcher was critical in helping President George Bush steel himself for the challenge posed by Saddam Hussein. But the theoretical challenge presented by Saddam Hussein still remains largely ignored. Since the departure of Margaret Thatcher from the post of Prime Minister, no other Western leader has had the vision and perspicacity required to address the challenges and dilemmas that are a reality in the post-Cold War world.

Notes

1   Thomas L. Friedman and Patrick E. Tyler, 'From the First, U.S. Resolve to Fight,' *New York Times*, March 3, 1991, pp. 1, 12.

2   George Bush and Brent Scowcroft, *A World Transformed* (New York: Alfred A. Knopf, 1998), p. 315.

3   Ibid.

4   Margaret Thatcher, *The Path to Power* (New York: HarperCollins Publishers, 1995), pp. 26–28.

5   Margaret Thatcher, *The Downing Street Years* (New York: HarperCollins Publishers, 1993), p. 817.

6   Ibid., p. 820.

7   James A. Baker, III, *The Politics of Diplomacy* (New York: G. P. Putnam's Sons, 1995), pp.278–279.

8   George Bush and Brent Scowcroft, *A World Transformed*, p. 410.

9   Thomas L. Friedman and Patrick E. Tyler, 'From the First, U.S. Resolve to Fight,' p. 12.

10   George Bush and Brent Scowcroft, *A World Transformed*, p. 489.

11   Margaret Thatcher, *The Downing Street Years*, p. 828.

12   Peter Applebome, 'The Glory of the Persian Gulf Victory Fades as the Wounds Outlive the War,' *New York Times*, 16 January, 1992, p. A11.

The Special Relationship and the Falklands War

Dov S. Zakheim

———

The 'special relationship' between Britain and the United States, one of the lasting legacies of the Second World War, has actually functioned on three different levels: the political, the official, and the operational. The political level has involved presidents, prime ministers, and their ministerial subordinates. The official level has involved what in the Untied States are termed sub-cabinet posts, whose British counterparts are the mandarins of the civil service. The operational level includes both the military and the intelligence communities of both countries.

The 'special relationship' has suffered from the most fluctuations at the political level. The personal styles and predilections of the leaders of both countries governed the general nature of relations between them. John Kennedy and Harold Macmillan had a good relationship, and the two countries generally worked in harmony as Britain accelerated its process of decolonisation. On the other hand, relations between Harold Wilson and Lyndon Johnson were at times rather prickly, particularly because of the Labour government's lukewarm support for America's prosecution of the Vietnam conflict. There was also a marked contrast between the personalities of the two men. Wilson was an Oxford-educated intellectual; Johnson prided himself on his coarseness.

Although senior civil servants on both sides took their leads from their political masters, sometimes it was they who encouraged their ministers down a particular path. A most notable case in point was the 1962 American decision to cancel the Skybolt missile, upon which Britain had based its plans for modernising its strategic nuclear deterrent. Pentagon analysts concluded that Skybolt was not cost-effective, and paid little attention to the impact of cancellation on Britain's military posture, or, for that matter, on London's application for entry to the European Economic Community. Secretary of Defence Robert McNamara readily accepted the PA&E analysis, and passed it on to Kennedy. The President then delivered the bad news to a very unhappy Harold Macmillan.

Such vicissitudes have rarely plagued the operational level of the relationship. The two military establishments have long conducted a vast array of exercises, some more public than others, that often have gone beyond anything similar on the part of either of them with any third country. Co-operation likewise has been more intimate between the two military research establishments than either has had with that of any other state.

Finally, while many of the details of the Anglo-American intelligence partnership remain cloaked in secrecy, it is safe to say that the relationship between James Bond and Felix Leiter in the Ian Fleming series provides an excellent metaphor for the real-world co-operation between the Central Intelligence Agency and MI5: two partners who share the most intimate secrets and come to each others' aid when the chips are down. Neither time nor political leadership has eroded that relationship. When Margaret Thatcher took office in 1979, the 'special relationship' definitely took a turn for the worse at the political level. Thatcher had emerged from the right wing of the Conservative Party. Her views were not at all congenial with those of the left-of-centre President Jimmy Carter. Nevertheless, on a personal level she found Carter 'impossible not to like'.[1]

More importantly, she valued the 'special relationship' too highly to allow herself to criticise America's leader publicly; instead she voiced her support for the President with regard to the month-old Iran hostage crisis.[2]

Nevertheless, the differences between the two leaders ran deep, and prevented the development of a truly intimate partnership between them. Even as Carter pursued the last vestiges of détente, Thatcher struck a more hard-line tone vis-a-vis the Soviets. Her desire to loosen Britain's socialist bonds did not sit well with the White House. She felt that Carter 'was over-influenced by the doctrines ... that the threat from Communism had been exaggerated, 'that he 'had no large vision of America's future,' and that he had 'an unsure handle on economics'.[3]

Of the various candidates for the Republican nomination in 1980, only Ronald Reagan was truly at home with Thatcher's views. Like the British Prime Minister, he felt that the state was too involved in the American economy; that taxes were too high; that the Soviet Union was a force for evil that could only be held at bay by means of military strength.

Thatcher had first met Reagan at her room in the House of Commons on 9 April 1975. He had recently completed his second term as Governor of California while she was just settling in as Leader of the Opposition. The meeting between them was supposed to be a courtesy call, scheduled to last forty-five minutes. It ran for twice as long, as the two future leaders of their respective countries discovered that they had much in common. Reagan later recalled that 'it was evident from our first words that we were soulmates', and that he thought she would make 'a magnificent Prime Minister'.[4] Reagan also appreciated something else about the new Conservative leader: unlike the government, none of whose senior ministers were willing to see him, Thatcher treated him with the respect due a potential president. It was something Reagan never forgot.[5]

Reagan again met Thatcher in London in 1978; she was now well ensconced in her role as Leader of the Opposition, he was an ageing former Governor who had lost the 1976 nomination to Gerald Ford. Both of them continued to be viewed as rather extreme right-wingers; that did not bode entirely well for her prospects for the Prime Ministership or his for the presidency. When Thatcher did become Prime Minister in 1979, he was the first leading politician to phone her with congratulations.[6] Thatcher returned the favour early on 5 November, 1980. She recognised that Reagan's election 'was of immediate and fundamental importance, because it demonstrated that the United States . . . was about to reassert a self-confident leadership in world affairs . . . [F]rom the first I regarded it as my duty to do everything I could to reinforce and further Ronald Reagan's bold strategy to win the Cold War which the West had been slowly but surely losing'.[7] Thatcher ultimately succeeded. Reagan would later recall, 'throughout the eight years of my presidency, no alliance was stronger than the one between the United States and the United Kingdom.'[8]

Reagan's new foreign policy team was a mixed bag as far as Thatcher and Britain were concerned, however. Thatcher had not interacted much with Alexander Haig, Reagan's new Secretary of State, when Haig had been Supreme

Allied Commander Europe.[9] Nevertheless, his familiarity with Europe reassured the British, many of whom worried about the west coast orientation of the new administration.[10]

Thatcher had met Richard Allen, the new National Security Adviser, when he accompanied Reagan to the April 1975 meeting in the Commons. Allen had long been Reagan's leading adviser on national security policy. He had actively forged links between the original 'Reaganauts' and conservative thinkers in Europe and Asia, including Thatcher's own closest advisers.

Reagan's new Ambassador to the United Nations, Jeanne Kirkpatrick, was a tough-minded woman who in many ways resembled Thatcher herself. But, as Thatcher would later discover, Kirkpatrick's affinity for America's right-wing Latin American allies exceeded her sympathy for Britain. Kirkpatrick would prove to be a strong advocate of neutrality when Argentina launched its attack on the Falklands in 1982.

Reagan's choice for Secretary of Defence, Caspar Weinberger, does not appear to have interacted much with Thatcher prior to his taking office. But Weinberger was an Anglophile of long standing. That fact, combined with his total devotion to Reagan, and the commonality of his views with those of Thatcher on national security, the Soviets, and economic issues, made him a key ally of the British even before the onset of the Falklands War.

Several of Weinberger's key aides also had close ties to Britain. In particular, Secretary of the Navy John Lehman had earned his doctorate at the University of Cambridge, while Assistant Secretary of Defence Richard Perle had studied at the London School of Economics. Perle's attitude to Britain was crucial, because his office of International Security Policy was responsible for the Pentagon's relations with America's NATO allies.

There was one other appointment that later proved to be of crucial importance to Britain. Bobby Inman, a four-star Navy Admiral, took over as Deputy Director for Central Intelligence. Inman was a product of the Navy's Intelligence community, which, like the American intelligence community generally, had exceedingly close ties to Britain. He was also especially concerned with the Argentines' long standing efforts to develop a long-range ballistic missile, a matter he most certainly must have followed closely while serving as Deputy Director of the Defence Intelligence Agency in the mid-1970s.

It did not take long for the Defence Department to respond to the new relationship between the two leaders. At approximately the same time as Ronald Reagan was elected President of the United States, the Thatcher government discovered that the Ministry of Defence was about to overspend its cash limit because, as Thatcher put it, 'with the depressed state of industry, suppliers had fulfilled government orders faster than expected.'[12] She also speculated that her government's acceptance of a commitment to spend 3 per cent of Gross Domestic Product on defence meant that 'the MoD had little incentive to get value for money in the hugely expensive equipment it purchased'.[13]

The United States was, somewhat inadvertently, part of Thatcher's problem. Only a year earlier, she had requested that the United States sell Britain its latest submarine-launched ballistic missile, the Trident I (or C-4 missile), which Britain intended to deploy aboard a new class of Trident ballistic missile submarines. When the United States agreed to the British request,[14] however, it exacerbated Britain's cash flow difficulties.

Thatcher was in a quandary. She stood for a tougher British defence posture. Yet, it now appeared that her government would have to cut back on its defence spending. On 5 January 1981, just two weeks before Reagan took his oath of office, Thatcher replaced Pym at the MoD with John Nott, giving him 'the remit of getting better value for money from the huge sums spent on defence'.[15] Nott, who questioned the need to maintain the Royal Navy's surface fleet levels, quickly launched a Defence Review which entertained plans both to cut back on naval procurement and to close the Chatham shipyard, which serviced the submarine fleet. Worst of all, from the American perspective, the MoD also planned to reduce the RN surface fleet to fifty warships by decommissioning ships that had been designated for the protection of transatlantic convoys in the event of a war in Europe.

The incoming Pentagon leadership viewed the British financial crisis and progress of the Defence Review with great concern. The Thatcher government appeared to be downplaying the importance of the convoy protection mission at the very time that the United States was making the case for a larger Navy to support NATO operations in Europe. Moreover, senior Pentagon officials felt that the British Defence Review threatened to create a credibility problem for Reagan's own plans for significant increases in the US defence budget.

Even as it finalised its plans for releasing the results of its Defence Review in a White Paper on 25 June 1981,[16] the MoD appealed to the new administration for help. The Pentagon responded with enthusiasm. At virtually the same time as the Government publicly revealed its revised defence programme, the Department of Defence and the Ministry of Defence agreed to establish a US/UK Defence Review Working Group to address the Defence Review in general and MoD's cash flow concerns in particular. The British side was led by a senior civil servant, Michael Power, the Assistant Under Secretary of State (Naval Staff). I led the American inter-agency team.

The Working Group's initial task was to decide on the scope of the exercise. On the assumption that the group would address all aspects of the Defence Review, the US team offered an agenda that addressed the broadest possible range of subjects. These included:

- Maximising Naval/Maritime Force Levels and Availability, notably
- The disposal of older nuclear submarines;
- The British aircraft carrier acquisition programme;
- The status of the Royal Fleet Auxiliary, which provided logistics support to Royal Navy warships;
- Co-operation on NATO operations, including North Atlantic operations and Gibraltar.
- Co-operation outside the NATO area ('Out-of-area') including:
- US logistics ships in support of Royal Navy forces;
- Royal Marine Commando operations;
- Co-ordinated Maritime Patrol (primarily anti-submarine warfare) operations in the Persian Gulf;
- Co-operation in the Caribbean.

The scope of the agenda was remarkable not only for its breadth, but for the willingness of the British to have the Americans look into so many aspects of their affairs.[17]

The British felt that a number of matters were already being dealt with in other channels, and did not require further review. These included the question of access for American forces en route to locales outside the NATO area, a sub-

175

ject already being dealt with through prime ministerial, i.e., Cabinet Office and Foreign Office channels; the status of Britain's standby reserve force squadron; and, most sensitive of all, the fate of the Trident programme. On the last issue, the British responded with the preference that it remain the purview of ongoing interaction between the US Navy's Strategic Systems Projects Office (SSPO), and its MoD counterpart. The two offices had worked together on US-UK strategic matters for years; each trusted the other's discretion.[18]

Ultimately, the MoD agreed, with minor reservations, that all of the foregoing issues could be placed on the agenda.[19] The Defence Review Working Group met several times until mid-November 1981. The agenda had both expanded and been narrowed at the same time. The possibility of homeporting American ships at Britain's Portsmouth base was added to the list. So too was the possible acquisition by the US Navy of major British warships, including the aircraft carrier Invincible. By late October the Americans had accepted in principle proposals to help the British transfer surplus Polaris material to the US and to eliminate American charges for the use of facilities.

Although the talks appeared to be going smoothly, they stalled by late November.[20] There was some dispute over the magnitude of the research and development recoupment charges that would be added to the cost of the Trident II missile, should it be sold to the British. More troubling for the British was a DoD attempt to have some portion of the waived Trident research and development charges redirected within the RN budget to enable the procurement of surface warships that otherwise would not be funded.

British concerns became even more intense when it was reported on 10 November that Secretary of the Navy John Lehman had indicated that the British government was reconsidering its plans to reduce the size of the surface fleet.[21] The report prompted several interventions by the Labour Opposition during Parliamentary Question Time that day, which put the government very much on the defensive.[22]

The confluence of concerns led the MoD to suspend the entire working group exercise. At virtually the same time, however, the British Cabinet Office quietly approached the White House with a request to negotiate the sale of the Trident II (D-5) missile. The two sides quickly put together very small negotiating teams, with Deputy National Security Adviser Robert MacFarlane leading the

American inter-agency team and Robert Wade-Gery of the Cabinet Office lead-ing its British counterpart.[23]

The negotiations moved rapidly, as Thatcher wanted to announce the Trident purchase as soon as possible. By early February the agreement was close to com-pletion. The DoD agreed to waive the facilities use charges that were assessed on the C-4 missile, to set the researcha nd development recoupment charges at 'a fixed sum in real terms,' thereby protecting MoD against currency fluctuations,[24] and to waive provisions of the Buy American Act, to allow British companies to bid on sub-contracts for the Trident II missile.[25]

The US side drew on the work of the Defence Review Working Group in another respect, urging the British to retain some of their surface forces that had been slated for decommissioning. In particular, the DoD hoped the British would retain the recently commissioned aircraft carrier *Invincible* in conjunc-tion with the savings on research and development recoupment costs that were to accompany the Trident sale. Britain neither explicitly accepted nor rejected this suggestion, however, since the Defence Review had, in effect, put *Invincible* up for sale.[26] The deal did involve other provisions relating to the RN, including arrangements regarding RN amphibious ships that had been slated for decom-missioning.[27]

On 11 March, Thatcher formally wrote to Reagan 'to ask whether in place of Trident I missiles the United States would be ready to supply Trident II missiles' [28] The details of the Trident sale, with all the concessions that the United States offered, reflected the intimate relationship between the two countries. The pre-sumption on the part of the DoD was that the British needed help, and, to the extent possible, every effort had been made to provide that assistance. The deal as finally formulated allowed the Ministry of Defence some breathing room as it prepared its future budgets. It also permitted the RN more easily to support its surface fleet, including *Invincible* and its amphibious fleet, both of which played a crucial role in the Falklands War that broke out less than a month after the Trident sale was announced.

After a series of lesser incidents in late March involving landings by Argentine 'scrap metal dealers' on South Georgia Island, 800 miles southeast of the Falkland Islands, Argentine forces mounted a full-scale assault on the Falkland Islands on Friday morning, 2 April 1982. The following day the Argentine military landed on South Georgia Island and easily seized control of the undefended territory.

Britain had exercised full sovereignty over the Falklands ever since Captain James Onslow struck the Argentinian flag and hoisted the Union Jack on January 2, 1833. The Argentinians immediately protested to Lord Palmerston, the British Foreign Secretary, and continued their protests for the next 149 years.[29] When the newly installed Argentine junta reviewed the Falklands situation early in 1982, it found itself making little headway with London in the face of the approaching and highly emotive 150th anniversary of the islands' seizure by the British.[30] The military leaders of the junta also noted that Britain's commitment to the islands seemed to be increasingly hollow. This view was underscored by the fact that among the surface naval force reductions previewed in the Government's June 1981 White Paper was the decision to withdraw HMS *Endurance* from its Falklands patrol by April 1982. The *Endurance* was an ice patrol ship, 'the sum total of the British naval presence in the area.'[31] Henceforth, only a small detachment of Royal Marines would be permanently stationed on the islands; from the perspective of the junta, it appeared that Britain had no will to resist an invasion.[32]

When the junta authorised the invasion of the now virtually undefended islands, it no longer adopted the coy posture that had led it formally to disown the 'scrap dealers' landings of the previous months. It now said that it would under no circumstances relinquish the islands, and it had no expectation that Britain would do much about it.

As is now well known, the Argentines seriously underestimated the determination of Prime Minister Thatcher. They also underestimated the degree to which the United States would be prepared to assist its ally. Initially, Buenos Aires had little reason to expect anything other than an even-handed (that is to say, stand-offish) policy on the part of Washington. The US government, especially Thomas Ender, the Assistant Secretary of State for Latin American affairs, had shown little interest in the dispute prior to or even shortly after the March 18 landing of the scrap dealers.[33] Enders in particular continued to be dubious about Argentine intentions right up to the actual invasion; he was inclined to believe the assurances of Argentine Foreign Minister Dr Nicanor Costa Mendes.[34]

Thatcher pressed Reagan to intervene, and the latter responded with a phone call to General Leonardo Galtieri urging the junta leader not to proceed with the invasion. Reagan 'couldn't budge him'.[35] Haig, on the other hand, pressed by Foreign Secretary Lord Peter Carrington and worried about the escalating crisis, reluctantly agreed on 31 March that the United States would try to mediate the dispute.[36]

The initial American plan was for Vice-President George Bush to attempt to mediate the dispute. That idea was stillborn once the invasion commenced. On 5 April Reagan agreed that Haig should serve as the mediator.[37] By then the British had announced plans for a naval task force led by the carriers *Hermes* and *Invincible* to deploy to the region in order to evict the Argentine forces.[38]

While the State Department focused on mediation, Caspar Weinberger and the Pentagon concentrated on the implications for the US of a British attempt to retake the Islands. Weinberger felt strongly that 'if the British were going to mount a counterattack . . . we should, without question, help them to the utmost of our ability'.[39] Even as the British organised their task force, and Haig continued his futile attempts at shuttle diplomacy, the Pentagon and the MoD began consultations on providing whatever equipment the British thought essential for the successful prosecution of the campaign. On Monday 5 April, Assistant Secretary Perle, with the approval of the Secretary of Defence,[40] designated me to lead a DoD task force that would co-ordinate the Pentagon's responses to Britain's requests, as well as maintain liaison with other branches of the government, notably the State Department, that were themselves seized of the Falklands crisis.

Not everyone in the administration, nor for that matter, even in the Pentagon, shared Caspar Weinberger's enthusiasm for the British cause. The Ambassador to the UN, Jeanne Kirkpatrick, was notable for her sympathy for the Argentines.[41] So too was Thomas Enders. Enders has spent most of his career working on European affairs. But, like the senior diplomat he was, he quickly became a leading advocate for the interests of that region of the world which was his current purview: 'where you sit is where you stand' is a concept well entrenched in the State Department, as it is in other bureaucracies.

Finally, there were other senior Pentagon officials, with close ties to Latin America, who likewise worried that too much support for Britain would jeop-

ardise their efforts to repair years of friction with many Latin American governments that had been engendered by Jimmy Carter's policies. These officials were
not about to challenge Caspar Weinberger's pro-British enthusiasm, and they
tended to communicate their concerns only among themselves.

Haig, like Enders, was an Europeanist. But he was now firmly committed to
mediate the dispute. Haig was therefore unhappy with anything other than an
even-handed American posture, since any intimations of bias would undermine
his mediation efforts. He did agree to stop arms sales to Buenos Aires, but that
was all.[42]

Given Haig's attitude, the DoD's discussions with MoD were held sufficiently
closely to prevent too much visibility at the State Department. The British made
it clear that they were faced with a massive logistical challenge, as well as with
shortfalls of all kinds of equipment. Their only en route support facility was the
base and Wideawake airfield at Ascension Island, some 3,400 miles from the theatre of combat operations and, critically, beyond the un-refuelled combat radius
of all British aircraft.

The Ascension Island facilities were actually American; the British merely
held title to the land. The American base commander at Wideawake had some
reservations about turning the island into a rear echelon support base. With
Weinberger's blessing, the message was soon conveyed to the Commander that
the British would have unhindered use of the base and airfield.[43]

Starting in April, RAF C-103s and VC-10s began regular airlift missions from
the UK to Wideawake. Once British ships reached the facility, RAF and RN helicopters used Wideawake to transfer cargo to hastily loaded ships enroute to the
theatre. Two to four Nimrod reconnaissance aircraft were based at Wideawake
and extensively used for ocean surveillance.

In early May the Nimrods were equipped for refuelling, and then were able to
reach the theatre through a piggy back operation. Victor tankers, also based at
Wideawake, refuelled the Nimrods near the edge of their combat radius, and
would then turn for home while the Nimrods proceeded southwards. They
would then meet up with returning Nimrods to refuel them for the remainder
of the trip to Wideawake.[44]

Also starting in early May, three Harriers (and later F-4s) flew combat air
patrols out of Wideawake to protect the island from air attack. Beginning at

about the same time critical items were flown from Wideawake to the theatre in 40 C-130 Hercules combat missions. And beginning in May as well, Wideawake was the starting point for five Vulcan bomber missions against the Argentine forces at Port Stanley.[45]

With respect to the transfer of equipment, it was agreed that every item would actually be sold to the British. There were a number of outstanding sales to the UK that the Defence Security Assistance Agency, which was a part of the Office of the Secretary of Defence, had been in the course of processing when the war broke out. All new sales were simply tacked on to these prior 'cases', as they were called, so as to maintain the façade that not only was there no military assistance (in the sense of un-reimbursed aid) to the UK, but that transfers to London were merely 'business as usual'.

Even as the Pentagon's materiel support system got into high gear, the intelligence community also secretly supported the British effort. That secrecy was due in part to the special nature of intelligence work and in part to the exceedingly close relationship between the American and British intelligence communities. The decision to release all relevant intelligence to the British was taken by the President himself.[46] Later reports stated that, among other information, Weinberger authorised the release to the British of both signals intelligence and some satellite photography.[47] It was also reported that the Navy passed along its assessments of Argentine operational effectiveness,[48] and that a satellite was relocated to provide coverage of the South Atlantic.[49] Weinberger, in his memoirs, avoided getting into the specifics of just what was passed on to GCHQ, as British intelligence headquarters is termed.[50]

Getting the other parts of the intelligence community to cooperate with the DoD was not a foregone conclusion. Various intelligence agencies have been known at other times to be quite capable of bureaucratic stonewalling when they oppose a particular policy. But CIA Director William Casey was a Europhile, and a committed anti-fascist.[51] Like Weinberger, he was fond of quoting Churchill in his speeches.[52] And he had Bobby Inman as his deputy, who openly sided with the British during administration deliberations as the crisis exploded into war.[53]

It did not take long for the Argentines to get word of the supply effort, and for the State Department to attempt to rein in the Pentagon. Haig, still attempting to be the even-handed mediator, went so far as to suggest to Thatcher on 14 April that he issue a statement that henceforth British operations at Wideawake would be restricted so as not to 'go beyond the scope of customary patterns of co-operation'.[54] Thatcher was furious with Haig's proposal, and lobbied hard, and successfully, to have the language about Ascension Island removed from the statement.

Although Haig personally intended to come out in favour of the British if necessary, he hoped that he could avoid making that choice.[55] He and others (who did share his sympathy for the British) therefore continued to object to the level and scope of American support for Britain while the mediation proceeded.

The issue was constantly debated in many meetings of the National Security Planning Group, a sub-group of the National Security Council. Weinberger, who could be exceedingly stubborn, insisted that while the cost of supporting the British was low, the moral and political price of abandoning London was very high.[56] The Joint Chiefs generally supported him. Kirkpatrick 'vehemently opposed an approach that condemned Argentina and supported Britain'.[57] Casey 'broadly supported Britain but did not want to damage relations with Kirkpatrick'.[58] National Security Adviser Judge William Clark was more sympathetic to Argentina, but he was close to Weinberger personally and would not clash with him. Reagan invariably acceded to Weinberger's requests, although he was not prepared to terminate the Haig mediation. Weinberger was convinced that the President's sympathies were in any event with the British.[59]

By the time the British retook South Georgia Island, on 25 April, the Pentagon's supply system was in place. Five days later, the Haig mission collapsed (Haig later believed his failure cost him his job as Secretary of State);[60] President Reagan branded Argentina a military aggressor and announced that, henceforth, the United States would respond positively to British requests for military materiel. On 2 May Weinberger reiterated to Francis Pym, the new Foreign Secretary, and to Ambassador Sir Nicholas Henderson, his commitment to supply Britain's needs as quickly as possible.[61] Accordingly, the DoD swung into high gear as an adjunct to the British Ministry of Defence.

The British were concerned that, in spite of Weinberger's assurances, some of their requests might ultimately be denied – if only for the quite legitimate reason that the American military's own stocks of a particular item might be very low. The British therefore furnished the Pentagon with preliminary informal requests in order to determine the likelihood of their being fulfilled. For its part, the Pentagon committed itself to providing the British an indication regarding every requested item of equipment within twenty-four hours, or a few days at most.

When the British knew a request would be granted, they would make a formal submission for the item. The request would then be processed within a few days, and delivered shortly thereafter. Given the brevity of turnaround time, many of the supplies had to come from the DoD's own stocks of equipment. All British requests were lumped under an open-ended 'case' whose administrative details – including pricing – would be dealt with at a later date.

Each morning, the British presented a list to the US Joint Staff of items they required. The same list, often with military comments, was transmitted to me in the late afternoon. At times, the military services were reluctant to part with sensitive equipment from their own stocks, often because such equipment was in short supply. I would then prepare a new memorandum for the Secretary, through Under Secretary of Defence for Policy Fred Ikle, that itemised British requests, any military objections to the transfers, and our own recommendations. Weinberger sometimes overruled the military on some of the items that they preferred not to transfer. At other times I was able to compromise with the Vice Chief of the service in question, so that the Secretary would not be forced to make a ruling. In any event, in most cases the British knew within twenty-four hours whether their requests would be granted, and were able to plan accordingly.

Needless to say, the supply effort was a sharp departure from usual Pentagon practice. Foreign military sales 'cases' usually took months to process, and an equal time to be executed. Requests for new foreign military sales cases were treated individually, and certainly not in open-ended fashion. And, of course, prices and payment schedules were normally determined at the time the case was formulated.

On 2 May, 1982, in one of the most spectacular naval engagements of the war, the British nuclear-powered submarine HMS *Conqueror* sank the 10,560 ton Argentine cruiser *General Belgrano*.[62] The following day Weinberger met with John Nott at the regular gathering of NATO defence ministers. Nott stressed the importance of maintaining the façade that Britain could manage the operation on its own. Weinberger was sympathetic to Nott's concerns, and the DoD continued to treat the supply process with considerable discretion. It was the British who initially revealed any details of the magnitude and nature of the American supply effort.[63]

The list of British purchases ultimately was estimated to total in the region of $100 million.[64] Supplies were shipped to Britain, to Ascension Island, and ultimately to the Falklands.[65] Among the earliest requests were those for missiles to be employed in the campaign at sea, including the latest version of the Sidewinder air-to-air infra-red missiles, the AIM-9L, which, as Henderson[66] put it, were 'vital for the Harriers', Harpoon anti-ship missiles, and Shrike anti-radiation missiles. The Stinger air-to-surface missile was, in Henderson's words, 'particularly effective'. In addition, the U.S. provided 4700 tons of airfield matting for the rapid reconstruction of Port Stanley airport; helicopter engines, and submarine detection devices[67] and JP-5 aviation fuel.[68] The list was actually much longer.

As the task force approached the Falklands, and the planned D-Day seemed imminent, the British sent in urgent requests for additional equipment. One request caught my eye, that for radio receivers to communicate with 'intelligence gathering sources'.[69] The British wanted the radios in their hands in less than twelve hours. To have satisfied British needs required a superhuman effort. The desired materiel had to be located, shipped and placed in British hands in the South Atlantic, thousands of miles away – all while the paperwork was being completed – in the space of a day. But the United States military and the Department of Defence are remarkable institutions. The mission was accomplished; the British had their radios in six hours. The invasion of the Falklands was launched shortly thereafter, on 21 May 1982.

Throughout the process, the Department of Defence discreetly informed Congressional leaders of its activities. It helped that the Republican chairman of the Senate Armed Services Committee was the Anglophile and former student at the London School of Economics, John Tower. Under Secretary of Defence Fred Ikle and I briefed him privately on the size and scope of the sales programme. In addition, leading Democrats such as Joseph Biden and Daniel Patrick Moynihan, the latter a former Oxford scholar, had weighed in behind the British with a pro-British Congressional resolution in late April.[70] There were few naysayers in Congress, a remarkable event in itself.

The supply effort continued as British forces advanced on Port Stanley, the Falklands' capital. Within a few weeks, and after pitched battles, notably at Goose Green, Britain retook the islands. On 15 June 1982 Margaret Thatcher formally notified Parliament of the Argentine surrender.

The British success on the Falklands meant that London's defence budget crisis was no longer relevant. Funding for systems required to keep the peace in the South Atlantic was quickly forthcoming, and all talk of reducing the surface fleet came to a halt. Invincible was not sold. Two amphibious ships, *Fearless* and *Intrepid*, that the Government had planned to decommission, avoided mothballs or the scrap heap.[71] The British requested, and received from the United States, a cut-rate sale of F-4 aircraft. These planes, re-designated F-4S and retrieved from the inactive 'bone yard' at Davis-Monthan Air Force Base, were bought for less than a million dollars each, and then upgraded to British specifications.[72] In addition, the United States negotiated a new arrangement with the UK regarding the use of Ascension Island so as to give Britain considerably more latitude in the event of another Falklands flare-up.

The Falklands War may well have been Margaret Thatcher's finest hour. She demonstrated that Britain still was a force in international affairs, and that it continued to be counted among those who strongly opposed aggression and totalitarianism. Britain might have won the war without American help; but it would have been a very close call. Indeed, most analysts believe that without the support that the Department of Defence and other agencies offered their British counterparts, the war would not have been won.

The 'special relationship' has taken different forms over time, depending on who were the Presidents and Prime Ministers of the day.[73] It flourished again with Bill Clinton in the White House and Tony Blair at Number 10 Downing Street. But there can be no denying that, since the end of World War II, it reached a high point during the Falklands War, only to be matched when Margaret Thatcher returned the favour by telling George Bush not to 'go wobbly' and British soldiers, sailors and airmen fought alongside their American counterparts in the Desert Storm victory over Iraq's Saddam Hussein.

Notes

1   Margaret Thatcher, *The Downing Street Years*, (London: HarperCollins, 1993), p. 68.
2   Geoffrey Smith, *Reagan and Thatcher* (New York: W.W. Norton, 1991), p. 17.
3   Ibid., p. 68.

4   Ronald Reagan, *An American Life*, (New York: Simon and Schuster, 1999), p. 204.

5   For a discussion of Reagan's early meetings with Thatcher, see Smith, *Reagan and Thatcher*, pp. 1–8, passim.

6   Ibid., p. 11.

7   Thatcher, *Downing Street Years*, p. 157.

8   Reagan, *An American Life*, p. 357.

9   Thatcher visited NATO headquarters in 1979 before she became Prime Minister. Alexander M. Haig, Jr. *Caveat: Realism, Reagan and Foreign Policy* (New York: Macmillian, 1984), p. 274.

10   Smith, *Reagan and Thatcher*, p. 39.

11   Ibid., p. 3.

12   Thatcher, *Downing Street Years*, p. 125.

13   Ibid.

14   Margaret Thatcher to Jimmy Carter, 10 July, 1980; Carter to Thatcher, 14 July 1980; Secretary of Defence Harold Brown to Secretary of State for Defence Francis Pym, July 14, 1980; Pym to Brown, 15 July, 1980, all letters attached to press release, Office of the White House Press Secretary (15 July, 1980).

15   Thatcher, *Downing Street Years*, p. 249.

16   Statement on the Defence Estimates 1981: Cmnd. 8288 (London: HMSO, 1981).

17   'Agenda for UK/US Defence Review Working Group.' The paper is dated, in pencil, July 1981. It was prepared after the 20–21 July meetings and prior to the Perle-Quinlan meetings of 30–31 July.

18   Ibid.

19   Memorandum from Dov S. Zakheim to MG Richard Boverie, USAF, Dr. Richard Kugler, Dr. Jeanne Mintz, Rear Admiral Arthur Moreau, USN, 'Agreed Agenda for UK/US Defence Review Working Group' (July 31, 1981).

20   Michael Power wrote to me, 'I think we helped nudge things along a little.' Power to Zakheim, 8 October 1981.

21   Nicholas Ashford, 'Navy Cuts May Be Modified,' *The Times* (London), 10 November 1981.

22   'Navy Cuts 'Not Bering Reconsidered," *The Daily Telegraph*, 11 November 1981.

23   I served as the principal DoD representative.

24   Parliamentary statement of the Rt. Hon. John Nott, 11 March 1981

25   Late in May I led a joint DoD/US industry team to London to brief representatives of British industry on sub-contracting opportunities with respect to the missile system.

26   Thatcher, *Downing Street Years*, p. 185.

27   Dov S. Zakheim, 'Memorandum for the Assistant Secretary of Defence (ISP),' 11 March, 1982 UNCLASSIFIED.

28   Thatcher to Reagan, 11 March 1982.

29   Paul Eddy, Magnus Linklater and Peter Gillman, *The Falklands War: The Full Story* (London: Sphere, 1982), p. 37–38.

30   Ibid., p. 4.

31   Ibid., p. 19; the proposal to retire the Endurance emanated from the RN, which wished to minimise the impact of the Defence Review on its cruiser/destroyer fleet.

32   See Caspar Weinberger, *Fighting for Peace: Seven Critical Years in the Pentagon* (New York: Warner, 1990), pp. 204–205.

33 Freedman and Gamba-Stonehouse, *Signals of War*, pp. 32–34.

34 Ibid., p. 96.

35 Reagan, *An American Life*, p. 359.

36 Haig, *Caveat*, pp. 261–264; Freedman and Gamba-Stonehouse, *Signals of War*, p. 32.

37 Ibid., pp. 97–98, and 159-161.

38 Thatcher, *Downing Street Years*, pp. 179–83.

39 Weinberger, *Fighting for Peace*, p. 209.

40 Thatcher later wrote that 'from the first…Weinberger…was in touch with our ambassador, empha-
    sising that America could not put a NATO ally and long-standing friend on the same level as
    Argentina and that he would do what he could to help' (*Downing Street Years*, p. 188).

41 Freedman and Gamba-Stonehouse, *Signals of War*, pp. 159–60.

42 Freedman and Gamba-Stonehouse, *Signals of War*, pp. 188, 193.

43 Ibid., p. 190.

44 The British were able to use the Victors, normally assigned to NATO duties, because the United
    States provided aircraft to replace them in the theater. See Max Hastings and Simon Jenkins, *The
    Battle for the Falklands* (New York: Norton, 1983), p. 142. Weinberger calls the Hastings volume 'an
    excellent account of the entire operation.' *Fighting for Peace*, p. 25 f.n. 2.

45 Details of British use of the Wideawake facilities were outlined in an unclassified DoD Background
    Paper, 'US Support Related to Ascension Island During the Falklands Conflict,' no date given.

46 Smith, Reagan and Thatcher, p. 84.

47 Freedman and Gamba-Stonehouse, *Signals of War*, pp. 189–90.

48 Ibid.

49 Smith, *Reagan and Thatcher*, p. 84.

50 Weinberger, *Fighting for Peace*, p. 216. See also Hastings and Jenkins, *The Battle for the Falklands*, p. 142.

51 Mark B. Leidl ed. *Scouting The Future: The Public Speeches of William J. Casey*, compiled by Herbert
    E. Meyer (Washington, D.C.: Regnery Gateway, 1989), p. 10–11.

52 Ibid., pp. 137–41.

53 Freedman and Gamba-Stonehouse, *Signals of War*, p. 162.

54 Weinberger, *Fighting for Peace*, p. 205 termed this phrase 'one of [Haig's] more convoluted sen-
    tences.'

55 Smith, *Reagan and Thatcher*, p. 81.

56 Weinberger, *Fighting for Peace*, p. 207.

57 Haig, *Caveat*, pp. 268–69.

58 Smith, *Reagan and Thatcher*, p. 88.

59 Ibid; Weinberger's assessment was certainly correct. Reagan 'was never convinced that there was
    really …a role [as mediator] for the United States to play' (Smith, *Reagan and Thatcher*, p. 80).

60 Haig, *Caveat*, p. 298

61 Weinberger, *Fighting for Peace*, p. 208.

62 For a description of the sinking, see Freedman and Gamba-Stonehouse, *Signals of War*, pp. 260–69,
    and Eddy et. al., *The Falklands War*, pp. 156–59.

63 Weinberger, *Fighting for Peace*, p. 210.

64 Freedman and Gamba-Stonehouse, *Signals of War*, p. 190, cites a total of $60 million excluding

Sidewinder missiles and ship and jet fuel. There were other items that have yet to be made public.

65 Weinberger, *Fighting for Peace*, p. 214.

66 Henderson to DoD General Counsel William H. Taft IV, 27 September 1983; see also Weinberger, *Fighting for Peace*, p. 215.

67 Henderson to Taft, 27 September 1983. See also Hastings and Jenkins, *The Battle for the Falklands*, p. 142.

68 Freedman and Gamba-Stonehouse, *Signals of War*, p. 190.

69 The term is Weinberger's, *Fighting for Peace*, p. 216.

70 Ibid., p. 237.

71 Desmond Wettern, 'Rethink on Amphibious Ships,' *Daily Telegraph* (10 October 1983), p. 5.

72 Fifteen aircraft were sold at a cost of $936,000 each 'United States Department of Defence Letter of Offer and Acceptance,' Reference UKDPO Ltr P-1049, Case UK-P-SAA, 28 February 1983.

73 For a discussion see Dov S Zakheim, 'Wither the Special Relationship?'

Mrs Thatcher's War:
The Rise and Fall of an Ideologue

David Monaghan

———————

Prior to the outbreak of the Falklands War, Margaret Thatcher had a vision but only a partial narrative through which to express it. This vision was, as Tom Nairn described it, 'Janus- faced':[1] Britain must go backwards in order to move forwards towards a better future. Thatcher had little trouble in envisaging the shape that this future might take. The dead hand of socialism would be shaken off, thus leaving space for a spirit of free enterprise to flourish. As a result, everyone from the great captains of industry down to the humblest council house tenant would enjoy a 'higher standard of prosperity and happiness'.[2] However, Thatcher was much less precise about the nature of the journey into the past and, in fact, manifested a confusing tendency to shift between tempo-ral and timeless metaphors. Sometimes it seemed that Britain must recreate some key aspects of a particular historical period, never defined any more clearly than as prior to the post-war era of socialism and consensus. At other times, it seemed that Thatcher was looking to recapture a supra-historical national essence.

A complete and convincing narrative of national greatness regained was, of course, essential if Thatcher was to capture the imagination of a British public desperate for something more inspiring than either Conservative or Labour governments had been able to offer in the 1970s. Talk of what might be achieved through exchange rate mechanisms, popular capitalism, money supply, public sector borrowing requirements, privatisation and so on probably went down well in the board rooms of the nation. However, it did not mean much to the great mass of voters, especially during the Thatcher government's first three years in office when the promised boom failed to materialise and Labour's economic crisis deepened into the Tories' recession. It is therefore not surprising that by 1982, the profoundly disappointing Margaret Thatcher had become the least popular of all post-war prime ministers.[3]

At this low point in her career, the totally unexpected Argentinian invasion of the Falkland Islands on 2 April must have seemed like the last thing Thatcher needed. Long before the British troops recaptured Port Stanley on June 14, however, Thatcher had proven herself a brilliantly opportunistic ideologue by transforming what was in reality a diplomatic and intelligence fiasco into a thrilling story of British greatness reborn. At last, she had found her narrative.[4]

In ideological terms, the greatest value of the Falklands War resided in the opportunity it provided Thatcher for synthesising metaphors whose incompatibility had bedevilled her previous attempts at expressing what was involved in retrieving the national past. On the one hand, she could present the war as part of a recurring cycle of timeless moments when, in the mythic version of British or, more accurately, 'English' history that she favoured, the long slumbering nation rouses itself to defend freedom against tyranny, the weak against the strong, and 'our' way of life against alien creeds. Viewed in this perspective, the defeat of the Argentinians – a conclusion already scripted well before the British task force even reached the Falklands – stands alongside earlier transcendent moments of national destiny such as the rout of the Spanish Armada, a string of victories over the French, in venues as diverse as Agincourt, the Plains of Abraham, Trafalgar and Waterloo, and, most notably, that other triumph over fascism, the Second World War. According to this mythic reading of the significance of the Falklands War, Thatcher herself becomes the latest reincarnation of the archetypal British warrior hero who has earlier appeared in the form of Boedicea, Elizabeth I, Woolf, Wellington – the Iron Duke to her Iron Lady – and, towering above all others, Winston Churchill.

On the other hand, the particular circumstances of the Falklands War made it possible for Thatcher, who usually collapsed all distinctions between the Falklands and Britain itself, to present the task force's voyage as an almost literal journey back into two specific and highly charged times in the national past. First, since the Falklands still enjoyed colonial status, Thatcher often spoke of the conflict with the Argentinians as an imperial war of the kind so often fought by the Victorians during a period in which Britain was the globally dominant power. Second, she found it relatively easy, especially at a distance of 8,000 miles, to postulate the Falklands, with their all-white population of mainly British origins, exclusively rural economy, patriarchal family structures and semi-feudal system of government and employment, as the reincarnation of a pre-industrial Britain that had a deeply atavistic appeal for the country's profoundly nostalgic population. By restoring the islands to British rule, Thatcher could therefore claim to have given concrete form to her promise that she would 'make the Britain you have known, the Britain your children will know'.[5]

In order to cement the connection she had always claimed between the two halves of her Janus-faced vision, Thatcher gave an entrepreneurial twist to her interpretation of the significance that should be attributed to the Falklands War in an important speech delivered to the Party faithful on Cheltenham racecourse in July 1982. On this occasion, and for the first time, Thatcher ascribed that 'stir[ring]' and 'rekind[ling]' of 'the spirit which has fired [Britain] for generations past,' which she termed the 'Falklands Factor',[6] to entrepreneurial values rather than to acts of military heroism performed in a noble cause. Thus, Thatcher is lavish in her praise of commercial shipyard and aerospace workers for adapting ships and Nimrod aircraft in record time, thereby demonstrating the kind of commitment and ingenuity required if Britain is to succeed as a modern industrial power. The task force becomes the focus of attention only to the extent that it can be made to serve as a model of the 'professionalism'[7] needed for the creation of an efficient business.

By framing the historical foundations of the nation's economic future within such visionary concepts as 'our heritage' and 'our great past',[8] Thatcher succeeded in transforming her political agenda into something close to myth. As a result, in a process that has been brilliantly defined by Roland Barthes, she 'depoliticised' and made natural what was in reality 'contingent'[9] with the ultimate goal of transforming an ideological stance into a commonsense fact.[10]

For concrete evidence of the success of Thatcher's strategy, we need look no further than the elections of 1983 and 1987 when the Conservatives won such decisive victories that the death of the Labour Party seemed to be imminent.

However, for all her success in conferring the status of truth on the identification she forged between 'being British' and 'the restoration of competition and profitability',[11] Thatcher could never, of course, step completely off the field of ideological contestation. A fictional hint of the vulnerability of Thatcherism to a counter-narrative is provided by the title of this essay. As readers of Jonathan Coe's satirical novel, *The Winshaw Legacy or What a Carve Up!* (1994), will recognise, *Mrs Thatcher's War* is the deliberately misleading title given to a documentary made by a film student during the Falklands War. The main subject of the film is not, as we would expect, the Prime Minister's personal, political and military triumph in the Falklands but the very different wartime experiences of an old-age pensioner who also happens to be named Thatcher. The aim of this shift in focus, which the film's maker achieves by juxtaposing images of 'warships steaming into battle and extracts from the Prime Minister's speeches' with 'scenes from the life of her less eminent namesake: making trips to the shops, preparing frugal meals . . . and so on',[12] is to challenge the official version of events by constructing the Falklands War as a symbol, not of national rebirth, but of the triumph of hubris over concern for the poor and needy. This 'efficient if unsubtle piece of polemic' thus ends with two captions on an otherwise black screen: 'Mrs Emily Thatcher supports herself on a weekly income of £43.37;' 'the cost of the Falklands War has already been estimated at £700,000,000'.[13]

The fictional subversion of Thatcherite ideology embodied within the documentary film *Mrs Thatcher's War* finds its real life equivalent in the reshaping of the relationship between the Labour and Conservative Parties achieved by Tony Blair since his election to the leadership of the Labour Party in 1994. Throughout the Thatcher years, as I have already suggested, Labour was viewed as irretrievably old-fashioned. Margaret Thatcher insisted on this as early as her maiden speech to the Party Conference in 1975. The election of the elderly 'Worzel Gummidge' figure of Michael Foot as Labour's leader following the electoral defeat of 1979, the crushing blow to the union movement dealt by the failure of the miners' strike, and even the collapse of the Soviet Union all added fuel to the idea that the People's Party had become a 'worn out relic'.[14] Faced with his Party's poor image and with the fact that most of the positive connotations of the British past had been co-opted for the Conservative Party by Thatcher, Blair staked his hopes of achieving long-term electoral success on the literal rebranding of the Labour Party as 'New'. He was helped in this by the increasingly shopworn appearance of the Conservatives under the grey man, John Major, and then the young/old William Hague as well as by his own youthful and dynamic appearance, modern marriage to a successful career woman, and role as father of three, soon to be four, young children. However, Blair has built on the foundation created by these fortuitous circumstances by always treating 1994, the year in which he succeeded John Smith as leader of his Party, as a kind of Year Zero. Whatever came before that date in the history of the Labour Party must, according to the Blair credo, be either ignored or rejected. Blair's most notable expunging of the past was, of course, the abolition of Clause 4 of the party constitution and, as recently as February 2000, he dismissed Labour's first hundred years as a 'century of failure'.[15]

Although Blair has tended to praise rather than to actively bury Margaret Thatcher, the broader effects of his repositioning of Labour as the party of 'cool Britannia', Noel and Liam Gallagher, and 'e-commerce', and as the enemy of all forms of upper and lower case C/conservatism, has been to make Thatcher, and not just the Party that she once came close to establishing as the nation's 'natural' governors, look terribly old-fashioned. The transformation that Blair has wrought in the British ideological landscape was never more evident than in the media treatment of Thatcher's appearance at the 1999 Conservative Party conference. For Andrew Rawnsley, writing in the *Observer*, the audience reaction to Thatcher's speech was such as to demonstrate that 'almost a decade since the fall, the Conservative Party now belongs to Margaret Thatcher more completely than ever it did when she was actually Prime Minister'.[16] However, this identification of party and individual no longer has the positive connotations that it did in the 1980s. Once viewed as the great reformer and moderniser, Thatcher has now become, in Rawnsley's view, the icon of a party so out of touch with the realities of the contemporary political landscape that it is 'aboard a flight to cloud-cuckoo land'.[17] Even the right-wing *Daily Telegraph* allowed that, for all the attempts being made by William Hague and his team of front-benchers to 'spell out a new vision for the party', Thatcher and other old stagers such as Norman Tebbit had succeeded in turning the conference into 'a gathering of staggeringly old faces saying much the same thing that they have for more than a decade'.[18]

A final crucial contribution to Tony Blair's attempts to claim the new Millennium for Labour while consigning the Tories to that same dustbin of history once reserved for his own Party was made, ironically enough, by the once ideologically sure-footed Margaret Thatcher. First, she chose a cinema showing *The Haunting* as the location for her speech in support of General Augusto Pinochet, thus generating 'titters from the audience'[19] and a plethora of jokes in the media about Thatcher as a ghost come back to haunt 'wee Willie' Hague. Second, as part of her defence of Pinochet, Thatcher identified the former fascist dictator as 'this country's staunch, true friend in our time of need when Argentina seized the Falkland Islands'.[20] By so doing she destroyed whatever credibility still clung to the Falklands myth that had played such a major part throughout the 1980s in cementing both Conservative hegemony and her own reputation as Winston Churchill's successor as the champion of democracy and freedom against the threat of right-wing totalitarianism.

The complete reversal thus wrought in Margaret Thatcher's position within dominant British ideology can be aptly summed up by comparing two cartoon images. The first, drawn by David Hopkins for the cover of the 15 May, 1982 edition of *The Economist*, depicts a grim-faced but powerful and rigidly controlled Thatcher maintaining a firm grip on the ferocious British lion as it struggles to leap onto the Falkland Islands.[21] Through his use of an 1854 Punch cartoon as the model for his own, Hopkins seeks to enhance his dignified portrayal of Thatcher by connecting her to what he suggests is a still vital spirit of Victorian imperialistic militarism.[22] The second, Steve Bell's *Guardian* cartoon of 7 October, 1999, entitled 'The Haunting, Part Eighteen: The General's Daughter',[23] shows a much reduced and manic-looking Thatcher/Dracula rising from her coffin to greet the towering projected image of General Pinochet. Pinochet's slippers, cardigan and pipe, as well as the flying ducks and dog with *Daily Telegraph* that are located behind him, further suggest that, as 'the General's Daughter', Thatcher belongs, not to a vigorous tradition, but to an old-fashioned and distinctly 'uncool' part of the British past.[24] Most important of all, though, Bell's cartoon adds a moral dimension to a Blairite perspective that, at root, reduces politics to a question of style. For Bell, by choosing to champion the cause of Augusto Pinochet, Thatcher has identified herself as the ideological daughter of a fascist butcher rather than, as she had always claimed in the past, the man who saved Britain and its democratic ideals from the threat of Nazism. By so doing, she has stripped herself of the last vestiges of the moral authority that she earned by her conduct of the Falklands War.

Notes

1 Tom Nairn, *The Break-Up of Britain: Crisis and Neo-Nationalism* (London: New Left Books, 1977), p. 348.

2 Margaret Thatcher, 'To the Conservative Party Conference, Blackpool, 10 October 1975,' in *The Revival of Britain: Speeches on Home and European Affairs* (London: Aurum Press, 1989), p. 20.

3 Andrew Gamble, *The Free Economy and the Strong State: The Politics of Thatcherism* (Durham: Duke University Press, 1988) p. 20.

4 For a fuller discussion of the ways in which Margaret Thatcher gave meaning to the Falklands War, see David Monaghan, *The Falklands War: Myth and Countermyth* (London: Macmillan, 1998), pp. 1–38.

5 Thatcher, p. 22.

6 Anthony Barnett, *Iron Britannia* (London: Busby, 1982), pp. 151, 153, 150.

7 Barnett, p. 150.

8 Thatcher, p. 22.

9 Roland Barthes, *Mythologies* (London: Paladin, 1973), p. 155.

10 In the course of the speech that she delivered during the Honorary Degree ceremony held in her honour at Hofstra University on 27 March, 2000, Margaret Thatcher spoke strongly against the suggestion that her political position is in any sense 'ideological', John Nott, Minister of Defence during Thatcher's first term of office, responded to the paper published here by objecting strongly to my identification of ideological elements within Thatcherite discourse. From a far right perspective it would seem that, as a Marxist concept, ideology is a realm reserved for left-wing politicians and thinkers. The right, by contrast, deals only in truth and common sense!

11 Stuart Hall, 'The Great Moving Right Show', in *The Politics of Thatcherism*, eds Stuart Hall and Martin Jacques (London: Lawrence and Wishart, 1983), pp. 27, 29.

12 Jonathan Coe, *The Winshaw Legacy or What a Carve Up!* (New York: Vintage, 1996), pp. 280–1.

13 Coe, pp. 280, 281.

14 Patrick Wright, *On Living in an Old Country: The National Past in Contemporary Britain* (London: Verso, 1985), p. 138.

15 Patrick Wintour, '100 Years of Failure, Blair to Tell Party,' *Observer*, 20 February. 2000: 8.

16 Andrew Rawnsley, 'The Monster Raving Tory Party,' The *Observer*, 10 October. 2000.

17 Ibid.

18 Robert Shrimpsley, 'Highjacked by Iron Lady's Agenda,' *Electronic Telegraph*, 7 October 1999.

19   Ibid

20   'Pinochet was this country's staunch true friend:' Full text of Thatcher's speech to the Blackpool fringe, *Guardian*, 6 October 1999.

21   Hopkins cartoon is entitled 'Let him go?' and occupies the entire front cover of *The Economist*. In the foreground is the prow of a ship featuring two figures. The first, a male lion rears up on its hind legs and roars. The second is Margaret Thatcher. Her hair is impeccable and she is dressed in a long-sleeved top with ruffled collar and cuffs, an ankle-length skirt and low-heeled slip-on shoes. She is depicted with her grimly determined face turned towards the reader as she grasps the lion by the mane and braces herself to prevent it leaping off the ship. The lion's target is a rocky headland on which is mounted a white flag.

22   James Aulich, 'Wildlife in the South Atlantic': Graphic Satire

23   Bell's cartoon can be found on the *Guardian* website at www.guardian.co.ukunder 'Special Reports,' 'Conservative Conference, 1999'.

24   Most of Bell's cartoon, which is entitled 'The Haunting: Part Eighteen, The General's Daughter,' is occupied by a huge image of General Pinochet projected onto a cinema screen. He sits in an arm chair, screen centre. He is wearing carpet slippers, cardigan and tie. He clutches a pipe in his left hand and waves with his right. Pinochet's face is unsmiling and is made sinister by his pinprick eyes, heavily shadowed by the brim of his general's hat. Curtains almost cover a window to Pinochet's right and, on his left, three flying ducks are mounted on the wall and a seated dog holds the *Daily Telegraph* in its mouth. The centre of the stage in front of the screen is occupied by a coffin from which a demented looking Margaret Thatcher is emerging. The tiny Estate,' in *Framing the Falklands: Nationhood, Culture and Identity*, ed. James Aulich (Milton Keynes: Open University Press, 1991), pp. 105-7.

IV

Thatcher and British Culture

Virgin Queen, Iron Lady, Queen of Hearts: The Embodiment of Feminine Power in a Male Social Imaginary

Diane Antonio

From the perspective of feminist cultural studies, with its deep interest in philosophy of the body, Margaret Thatcher's rise to power qua embodied woman, demands fresh interpretation. What was 'that (expletive deleted) woman's' public power style? To what extent did it mirror the successful gendered style of an earlier British female leader, Elizabeth I? In contrast to Mrs Thatcher, how and why did Princess Diana fail to parlay her enormous influence for the public good into access to this iconic tradition of female power in Britain? Why, of these three public servants, did Diana alone fail to persuade that she was a serious presence on the political stage? To say that she did not hold elected office and was a titular princess does not suffice, in light of Diana's extraordinary gifts and work of reform. As Machiavelli has told us, for princes, perception is all.

In order to analyse the historical evolution of Western female political power-styles from Elizabeth to Thatcher to Diana, it is necessary to interrogate the English male Social Imaginary. Too often, with tragic results, the 'body images' of 'embodied subjects' who are gendered 'wome,,' have been largely shaped by the historical forces of a hostile 'masculine imaginary' (or, more properly, imaginaries, correspondent to class, race, epoch, religion). A Social Imaginary is 'the dimension, the register of all images, conscious or unconscious, perceived or imagined',[2] in a particular culture. It includes folkloric and mythical, philosophical and historical elements, often situated below the threshold of consciousness. The Social Imaginary also contains culturally-specific models of political vision and rationality.[3] Most importantly, the Social Imaginary delineates a gendered Imaginary Anatomy or 'culturally shared phantasy about male and female biologies',[4] Feminist theorist Moira Gatens writes:

The imaginary body is socially and historically specific in that it is constructed by a shared language; the shared psychical significance and privileging of the various zones of the body (for example, the mouth, the anus, the genitals) and common institutional practices and discourse (for example, medical, juridical and educational) which act on and through the body.[5]

Unique to its culture, the 'Imaginary Anatomy' is then inscribed upon individual 'body image'[6] – a schema of being and identity that exists as both an inner and outer image, sensorally and imaginatively accessible to self and others. The 'body image' as map of Freud's bodily ego (on which he bases all motility and intentionality or interaction with the world) is dynamic. As inner and outer psychical and libidinal cathexes change, 'the body image can shrink or expand; it can give parts to the outside world and can take other parts into itself'.[7] So the politically active body subject can 'introject' aspects of the outer world on to her 'body image'[8] (e.g., sceptre, crown, icons of divinity, etc.) 'Body image' is, moreover, a dramatic way to offer meaning to others.

As such, the concept of embodiment put forth by the dominant male imaginary has important normative and political dimensions. For instance, the dominant male imaginary defines and delimits which kinds of bodies ought to attain political power, how bodies excluded from such power can expand their scope in the society and what aspects of the imaginative world should be introjected on to the body image of a politically powerful woman if she is to be successful in the world of men. With its power to define who is worthy to rule, the male Social Imaginary shapes the politics of gender, science and art.

In Western culture, the construction of the dominant 'Imaginary Anatomy' not only privileges masculinity, it disparages the female body/ego:

the hegemonic imago of masculinity conforms with his status as sovereign ego . . . and that of women with the correlative status of the one who is made to conform to this ego. The male body

is understood as phallic and impenetrable, as a war-body . . . The female body is its opposite,
permeable, able to absorb all this violence . . . The genital markers of sexual difference . . . seem
to render the kinds of power relations attendant upon them as natural and inevitable.[9]

Cast in relief to the masculine corporeal then, and with epochal, class, and economic variations, Western female bodies are typically seen by self and others as
privation, that is, bereft of corresponding maleness. Embodied females are often
imagined to be lacking morally in *integritas*, with its etymological entrainment
of goodness, soundness, wholeness and fitness to rule ('Do you want her finger
on the atomic button during her time of the month?'). A woman body subject
may thus unconsciously deem herself to be without the ability or right to make
important ethical and political judgements , and so not run for that lofty office
or speak up at that crucial public meeting. She may also regard herself as lacking an unimpeded, other-respected and self-respecting 'embodied willfulness' to
carry out her ethical and political judgements. In the case of a female political
leader, a positive and empowering 'embodied willfulness' (adapted from Sara
Ruddick's term)[10] indicates her ability to 'move', 'resist', 'choose', and 'act' with
decisive authority on the public stage.

So how is it that Elizabeth I, an embodied woman, was able to manipulate the
dominant male Social Imaginary to garner political power? To help answer this
question, I will discuss the award-winning[11] 1998 British film *Elizabeth*, which
depicts the Virgin Queen's consolidation of power in her early years on the
throne. The film yields paradigm examples of both Renaissance and contemporary (dominant) male Western Imaginary perspectives in regard to the embodiment of worldly power by a gendered woman.

Essentially, the problem of 'feminine' political power hinges on the ambiguity of the female body as conceived by the dominant male Western Social
Imaginary. In this Western Imaginary, the female body historically appears in
two modes: 'Personal' and 'Impersonal'. The 'Personal Body', which is always
sexed and gendered, is composed of a unique set of attributes: physical size and
shape, beauty, strength, purity, grace, health, sexual expression, emotional style,
desire, speech acts, intellect, temperament, moral character and values (how she
treats other sexed and gendered bodies), and situated perspectives (related to
age, ethnicity, etc.) These qualities are graphed on to the ever-changing person-

al body image (or self-representation, including shifting zones of psychic and physical intensity).[12]

The Western white male body subject, likewise, manifests these singular attributes, or what I term the 'Personal Body'. However, his bodily subjectivity, as opposed to the irrational female 'Other', is already culturally associated with political power. Unless there are problematic ethnic, sex-preferential, or class considerations, white male bodyselves in positions of authority do not necessarily come into conflict with popular perceptions of what a political leader should be (such as, a warrior, a sage, a representative of God the Father, and so on). The very embodiment of strength and reason, he 'looks' (and sounds) the part. Therefore, as opposed to women of power, men of power do not typically have to be fragmented into 'Personal' and 'Impersonal Bodies' in order to be legible culturally.

What, then, is the phenomenology of the 'Impersonal Body' that must be conjured by women of power in the West? The 'Impersonal Body', first of all, is a self-embodying of political or spiritual power. To generate the 'Impersonal Body', the individual female bodyself must consult the collective imagination on the subjects of will, majesty and command. She must (more or less) consciously draw on the iconic, political/philosophical, literary or folkloric repertoire of her culture such that she is able to manipulate public perceptions of her woman-gendered body. In 'shedding' the encumbrance of her female Personal Body, she gains access to 'impersonal' forces (ideations, cultural myths, theological symbols, etc.). These forces then charge and act through her as the puissant Impersonal Body.

The 'Public' or 'Impersonal Body' assumes the divestiture of individual bodily facticity in favour of an animate gender type (like the Blessed Virgin) with a prescribed ethos and set of behaviours. Of course, it is not possible to divest oneself of one's concrete individuality. But one may give the illusion of having accomplished this clean separation from the 'Personal Body' as actors do. Or, one may actually repress authentic individualised emotions, belief, desires and needs filling up the physical corpus. This is what Elizabeth I does when she repudiates the man she loves to 'wed England'. With this psychic and theatrical strategy, she brings the suspiciously female-linked 'Personal Body' into consonance with the more male-friendly 'Impersonal Body' wherein traditional 'feminine' power resides.[13]

In her lyrical first scene, Princess Elizabeth is depicted as a vulnerably fluid Personal Body.[14] In a radiant meadow, she and her five young Ladies-in-Waiting are practising the dramatic dance called the 'Volta'. When Lord Dudley joins her in the dance, it becomes clear that it is loveplay. And throughout the film, the 'Volta' will be used as a metaphor for their turbulent erotic relationship. At this moment, Elizabeth is her mother's daughter, a Persephone whose carnal destiny will lead her into danger.[15]

With her flowing red hair and sash, clad in the sorbet colours of a fairy tale, Elizabeth is also the Renaissance ideal of feminine Beauty. She has what Castiglione called 'the air of feminine sweetness in her every movemen.t'[16] A creature of light and air, her woman-gendered bodystyle stands in contrast to the 'serious' male world of her half-sister, Queen Mary. In that shadowy, ugly Court, all, including the Queen, are dressed in somber black, according to the strict gendered dress code of the time. Men renounced the 'nonutilitarian' and 'conspicuous': make-up, jewelery, long hair, brightly coloured clothing, and so on. In Europe, important men now dressed in sober, neutral garb: when they appeared in public it was in black, grey or white. The male's social presence was thus euphemised under the aesthetic mask of the 'serious'. Any transgression of this code entailed a loss of credibility and effectiveness.[17]

In this scene, the joyous Elizabeth also flouts the prescriptions of restrained corporeal style for public figures of power. Centuries before the dress code took effect differences had emerged in the way men and women carried their bodies. Men had long been taught to discipline their movements, to keep their distance from one another, to stand proudly erect, to hold their tongues and to restrain their gestures. Women could manifest their differences by talking idly, carrying themselves supply, fluttering about, laughing raucously, or letting slip a shoe, handkerchief or lock of hair.[18]

Ominously, Elizabeth's sensual dance echoes the gestural grammar of the opening frame of the film, as the camera swirls around and around three flame-engulfed Protestant 'heretics' who are being burned alive by the fanatically Catholic 'Bloody Mary'. Until Elizabeth begins to manipulate the icon of female power, sheds her Personal Body and becomes a social paradox, that is, 'a woman by appearance, a man by role',[19] the camera will circle her too with hot, predatory interest. According to the myth of the film, as long as Elizabeth inhabits her

Personal Body, i.e., beautified, sexualised, desiring, emotionally labile, in love, she can only attain tenuous personal power over her subjects, such as Lord Dudley, body-to-sexual body.

For example, as a Personal Body – even with all her acumen and her early, inspired solution for the religious conflict that was ravaging England – the young monarch was particularly susceptible to brazen personal verbal attack from both nobles and clergy.[20]

As a Personal Body, Elizabeth was also a female corpus in chronic physical crisis. Her bodyself was the intense focus of interest by domestic and foreign cabals because to possess her Personal Body in marriage was to possess England. In the dominant Renaissance male Imaginary, as now, the Personal Feminine Body is a hole to be filled, a wilderness to be claimed, permeable and incoherent.

Most of all, the embodied woman, no matter how well-born, is in need of the rational ordering of a male mind. She has no place in the political realm. As Jean Bodin wrote of 'the order of women' in *The Six Bookes of a Commonweal* (1606): 'I think it meet for them to be kept far off from all . . . places of command, judements, public assemblies and counsels: so to be attentive only unto their womanly and domestical business'.[21] And in 1632, an English jurist penned the following: 'Women have nothing to do in constituting Lawes, or consenting to them, in interpreting of Lawes or in hearing them interpreted'.[22] Consequently, when she proposes the 'Act of Uniformity' to Parliament ('a single Church of England, one common Prayer Book, one common purpose') to end bloody religious strife, Elizabeth is publicly scorned as 'only a woman' by the assemblage. And she is pushed to bear a male heir by Lord Burleigh, her first, venerable adviser. Until she affiances a powerful man, he tells Elizabeth, she and her kingdom will be in grave danger. It never occurs to him that she could sustain her sovereignty by her own brilliance. As a result, Elizabeth's Personal Body becomes the public victim of sexual harassment by her noble French suitor.

Worst of all, as a Personal Womanbody, she is uniquely vulnerable to attempted assassination by the Spanish Crown and Papacy, and to violent political overthrow from within her own Court (Lord Norfolk).[23] Significantly, these murder attempts take place in a gender theatre. Her youthful body resplendent in carnival regalia, she is relaxing on a Thames pleasure barge with her lover, Dudley, when an arrow comes 'hurtling out of nowhere' and kills an attendant. The netting over Elizabeth's pale face is spattered with his blood in a parody of the epoch's 'red/white' formula of feminine pulchritude.[24] A second arrow pins her pale face to the barge, as if to underscore the Tudor commonplace that while her body, like that of all sensually directed women, had a head on her shoulders, that pretty head had clearly not been used for thinking.[25]

But, as the film's story goes, Elizabeth ('I am my father's daughter'.) self-consciously alters this collective perception of her pregnable Personal Body in the dominant male Imaginary. It is Burleigh who first hints at the need for sacrifice: 'Her Majesty's Body and Person are no longer her own property. They belong to the State'. But for much of the film, the sensual Queen fights the insight.

It is only in the penultimate scene that Elizabeth makes her surrender. Gazing up at a statue of the Virgin, she cries out to Walsingham: 'Am I to be made of stone, must I be touched by nothing? And the shrewd Walsingham replies: 'All men need something greater than themselves to look up to and worship. They must be able to touch the Divine here on earth'. Elizabeth now undergoes a dramatic transformation of bodystyle that will shape her political substance. She finally accepts that she is a Public Body who must 'live her life in the open'. And she comprehends that she must engage the loyalty not only of great men but of all men, or be de-throned. She begins to craft the 'Impersonal Body'. She models herself on the Catholic representations of Mary the Virgin Mother, whose pure, holy and de-sexualised Impersonal Body commanded men for centuries. She also exploits the associated popular tradition of reformer 'holy women'.

Gradually, like these 'consecrated women', beatas, beguines, healers and mystics, the Queen had been stripping away her Personal Body. She had already renounced all suitors, romance and marriage, and 'forgotten' her woman's 'heart' ('I will have no masters here'). Now she ritually transforms herself into 'Gloriana', an archetype of the Golden Age. She orders that her face and hands be painted an inch-thick with white paste to approximate a rigid Byzantine statue of the Virgin. Eerily reminiscent of the burning martyr, she has her hair cut off. It is an heroic act of 'matronage',[26] so that the force of miracles can play through her Impersonal Body. 'I have become a Virgin', Elizabeth says in awe.

Why a 'Virgin?' Of all holy martyrs, the most pleasing to God, and thus, the most powerful intermediary, was the 'virgin martyr'.[27] Further, for Christians of the time, virginity 'represented freedom' from the Personal Body. As self-transcending entities, virgins, symbolically at least, overcame the 'co-efficient of adversity' inherent in their biological and cultural situations. They were free to become 'mediators between natural and supernatural, inside and outside, self-ness and otherness, manhood and womanhood . . . The virgin . . . represented humanity's deepest dream: that everyone, male and female alike, should be . . . united'.[28]

In the final scene, an awesome and emblematic Queen Elizabeth enters the throne room. 'Observe, Lord Burleigh', she tells him in a new voice, 'I am married to England'. A 'Living Saint', she is de-featured, geometrised in her stiff white ruff and encrusted gown which is now done in credible, male black. As Cate Blanchett, the actress who played Elizabeth in the film, once commented, the camera no longer circles the young Queen in predatory fashion, hungering for her personal flesh. It now bows before her, as do her subjects, worshipping.

Wielding the impersonal forces of the wise virgin, Elizabeth inscribes a new face onto history. Her Impersonal Body 'expresses the inexpressible', a direct relation to the Deity.[29] She is now a conduit for the divinity which hedges round a king. It is a spiritual power, theologically and imaginatively associated with males as reflections of God-the-Father. But, in this case, God's power is embodied par excellence by female flesh.[30] The 'Virgin Queen' can only manifest this power of the Impersonal Body because of her exquisite manipulation of religious into secular myth. The spiritual ignites the political. As 'Gloriana', Elizabeth heals her people and leads them through a Golden Age.

Like Elizabeth I in her time, Mrs Thatcher was also seeking civil and international peace, as well as an economic, moral and even spiritual renewal of the British people. If these two leaders were to survive politically (and in Elizabeth's case, physically) they were constrained to gain the co-operation and respect of the male hierarchy. An analysis of Mrs Thatcher's embodiment of power, as well as of the poetic language and ethical subtext of her collected speeches, provides insight into the effective way she resurrected the profoundly gendered power-style defined by Elizabeth I five hundred years before.

As with Elizabeth I, Margaret Thatcher, too, came to wield impersonal power through her transcendence of the vulnerable female Personal Body. She appears stoic in crisis, affectless on camera, during addresses, hence the 'Iron Lady' epithet. She does not 'seek to bring her personality into the nation's living rooms, as her hero Winston Churchill had done.'[31] Besuited like a businessman, she presents herself without the cultural baggage of female sexuality, although we know she was a wife and mother. She sacrifices her Personal Bodily characteristics to achieve masculine-type impersonal power.

To be more specific, the 'Iron Lady's' body is no longer identified with an individual and fluid corporeal situation, including breast-size, shapeliness, or personal, passional history with its flux of messy relationships and commitments. Her body is now self-and-other-identified with an overarching cultural situation. As was Elizabeth Regina, Margaret Thatcher is England, but radical Tory England, le moi commun, whereby all political and ethical negotiation is made possible. And like the Virgin Queen, she cedes her natural liberty to express feelings openly, to move gracefully, to walk through public life as the Personal Body.

If Merleau-Ponty is right, and language is a sophisticated form of bodily gesture, it is also Mrs Thatcher's bodily verbal style that gives her political substance within the male Imaginary. In a parallel to Elizabeth's gender strategy, Mrs Thatcher conjures the male-friendly 'Impersonal Body' of feminine tradition. She becomes the Consecrated Woman, wielding more subtly the culturally acceptable feminine archetype assumed by the first Elizabeth. Being of a more cynical epoch, Mrs Thatcher does so not with virgin-white lacquer and black lace, but through her extraordinary speech acts.[32]

For Lady Thatcher, speech writing was 'an important political activity' in which she wholeheartedly participated. In her speeches, she turns secular myth (the liberal philosophy of J.S. Mill, the 'people's capitalism' of Adam Smith) into religious myth. Thus, in her first Party Conference speech,[33] Mrs Thatcher writes: 'I told my speech-writers that I was not going to make just an economic speech. The economy had gone wrong spiritually and philosophically. The economic crisis was a crisis of the spirit of the nation'.[34] Startlingly, she employs a traditional feminine appeal to emotion, beauty, mood in order to consolidate her political power. Her style is lyrical. A great speech, she said, 'was more like a piece of poetry than prose'; it is the ideas, sentiments and mood below the surface which count' and 'inspire the faithful'.[35]

In her political addresses over the years, the Iron Lady offers 'a creed' whose 'truths are written in the human heart'.[36] She explicitly speaks this creed 'as a

Christian'[37] and in sacred terms. Thus, she talks of angels' weeping, of 'disbelief' and 'distrust', of 'divine wisdom', of 'the Sphinx', a figure of female power,[38] of 'soul' and 'grace' and 'sacrifice',[39] of St. Francis' peaceful prayer,[40] of 'joy' and 'light'.[41] She rallies the people to 'honour', to 'great and good causes', to a holy war against Communism, economic malaise and hopelessness. She prophesies a good outcome, a 'new Renaissance',[42] because 'the better moral philosophy of the free society underlies its economic performance'.[43] She initiates 'healing' acts of will[44] for the 'body politic'[45] whose exuberant 'animal life' must prevail. She has 'visions' of 'hope' for children.[46]

Most importantly, like the Renaissance holy women, Margaret Thatcher defined virtue for a nation. It is Mill's 'freedom' as a 'way of pursuing one's own good'[47] 'democracy', 'self-government',[48] 'respect for others' freedom',[49] 'dignity',[50] the 'moral faculty' of choice',[51] 'purity of heart', 'integrity'[52] and an implicitly self-referential women's 'wisdom'.[53] Morality is no mere male abstraction. Attaining virtue, she says, is a matter of 'life or death' for Britain.[54] Moreover, it is ultimately dependent on the typically feminine powers: 'understanding and intuition'.[55] Lastly, in the Thatcherite moral psychology, the fruit of virtue will be the feminine ethic of care, cultivated in the private sphere, put into the polis: 'Our fellow-feeling develops from self-regard. Because we want warmth, shelter, food, security, respect and other goods for ourselves, we can understand that others want them too'.[56]

But 'evil' is palpable too; it eats away even at history:

We are witnessing a deliberate attack on our values, a deliberate attack on those who wish to promote merit and excellence, a deliberate attack on our heritage and our great past, and there are those who gnaw away at our national self-respect, rewriting British history as centuries of unrelieved gloom, oppression and failure.[57]

In summary, as speaking head of the Conservative Party, Mrs Thatcher was, by her own definition, 'the living flesh of British life'.[58] Or, to put it in Elizabeth's terms, as the Impersonal Moral Body, the lady was 'married' to Britain. Gloriana, albeit more modestly, once again ruled.

Contrary to Mrs Thatcher, Princess Diana seemed neither willing nor able to shed her Personal Body nor turn from the Personal Bodies of others. Unlike

Elizabeth and Margaret Thatcher, Diana never made the requisite sacrifice of the feminine corporeal to the exigencies of male-defined political power. Within the dominant male Social Imaginary, she was bound (as Simone de Beauvoir would say) to her animal rhythms, to her facticite. Not only was she wed to the Prince in order to be a breeder of kings, but she was exposed by the penny-press as being obsessively flesh-conscious to the point of bulimia. Furthermore, she exclusively did the feminine work of Care, not male Justice. She touched death, decay, disease, like any medieval tertiary, but without the protective aura of virgin sanctity. She loved not wisely. All of this effectively excluded Diana of Wales from the *temenos* of political power. In the Imaginary eye, she would remain a mere woman, the Personal Body to the bitter end – and beyond.

Most telling of her tragic failure to alter violent gender perceptions, Diana's landmark anti-landmine work was trivialised by some in the Western press. How piquant: a princess in a minefield. What would she have thought of next? American TV pundits were baffled at the sensation caused by her death. What had Diana ever accomplished? She was a clotheshorse who squandered British tax dollars. No true sovereign like Elizabeth I, nor even a magisterial Thatcher, what was Diana to England or England to Diana? Mother Teresa was the real saint. In the Museum dedicated to Diana's memory, her brother, the Earl, ambiguously included his sister's landmine costume in her gallery of gowns.

However, as we know, upon Diana's untimely death, there was a storm of grief and bouquets that challenged America's image of British stiff-upper-lippery. Damn the political power, the populace seemed to be saying. Love of the beauty, the passion, the grace of the Personal Body, of the unspeakable feminine, is alive and well in England.

Notes

1   *Margaret Thatcher, The Collected Speeches*, ed. Robin Harris (New York: Harper-Collins, 1997), p. 435. Margaret Thatcher herself refers to the epithet assigned to her by her rival, the Labour leader, Neil Kinnock, in her Party Conference Speech, 12 October, 1990): 'I gather there may be an adjec-

tive between "that" and "woman", only no one will tell me what it is'.

2   Roland Barthes, quoted by Dorothea Olkowski, 'From Work to Text', in *Josue V. Harari*, ed. Textual Strategies (Ithaca: Cornell, 1979), p. 76.

3   Moira Gatens, *Imaginary Bodies: Ethics, Power and Corporeality* (New York: Routledge, 1996), p.148. Gatens' comments are based on Spinoza's Ethics, Part IV. Roland Barthes, quoted by Dorothea Olkowski, 'From Work to Text', in *Josue V. Harari,* ed. Textual Strategies (Ithaca: Cornell, 1979), p. 76.

4   Gatens, p. 13. Gatens draws upon the ground-breaking work of Lacan in this study.

5   Gatens, p. 12.

6   The body image is, in fact, the premier cite of psychical and physical inscriptions, and their inter-actions.

7   Paul Schilder, *The Image and Appearance of the Human Body: Studies in the Constructive Energy of the Pysche* (New York: International Universities Press, 1978), p. 202, in Elizabeth Grosz, *Volatile Bodies, Toward a Corporeal Feminism* (Bloomington: Indiana University Press, 1994), p. 80.

8   Grosz, p. 83.

9   Catherine Waldby, 'Destruction: Boundary Erotics and Refigurations of the Heterosexual Male Body', in ed., Elizabeth Grosz and Elspeth Probyn, *Sexy Bodies, The Strange Carnalities of Feminism* (New York: Routledge, 1995), pp. 248–9. Although Waldby prefers the Lacanian term 'imago' to what she considers to be the weaker denomination, 'body image', I favour 'body image'. In my view, 'body image' is appropriate here because it preserves the sense of a dynamic relationality between a concrete biological body (which is always the lived body with a psychical/intellectual dimension in Merleau-Pontian terms) and its cultural overlay.

10 Sara Ruddick, 'Injustice in Families: Assault and Domination', in ed. Virginia Held, Justice and Care: *Essential Readings in Feminist Ethics* (Boulder: Westview, 1995), p. 215. It should be noted here that Sara Ruddick herself primarily defines 'embodied willfulness' as the ability to resist and repudiate others' and one's own projects of sociopolitical oppression.

11 The imaginary force of Elizabeth over its artistic community and audience is evident in its seven Nominations for Academy Awards, and its winning of five BAFTAS (British Academy Awards), as well as a Golden Globe Award (Foreign Film Critics).

12 The individual bodyself may or may not be conscious or directive of any of the structurations of her body image.

13 The 'Personal' and 'Impersonal' Bodies are not mutually exclusive. The 'Personal Body' with its unique entrainment of speech acts and gestures must inform and limit the presentation of the 'Impersonal Body'. The apparently 'denatured' 'Impersonal Body' modifies the body image sub-tending the 'Personal Body'. But what is the relationship between the Personal Body and body image? The 'Personal Body' is a collective concept of embodiment located in the Social Imaginary. It describes certain empirical qualities adhering to the individual body subject and, thus, to body image. These qualities are generally observable, not only by the person who is embodying them, but by others in the world. On the other hand, individual 'body image' is a complex superstructure upon which a particular woman (or man) fleshes out the notion of her own 'Personal Body'. It should be noted that 'body image' is an intensely volatile, moment-to-moment, 'raw' representa-tion of the bodyself, to which the self-imaging individual has a privileged psychic and sensate

access (although to a lesser degree, others may contact my body image through their own corresponding body images). The Personal Body appears more like a polished and continuous identity to self and others.

14   Sara F. Matthews Grieco, 'The Body, Appearance and Sexuality', in ed. Natalie Zemon Davis & Arlette Farge, *A History of Women' Renaissance and Enlightenment Paradoxes* (Cambridge: Harvard University Press, 1997), p. 48. In the dominant Renaissance English Imaginary, fluidity or wetness was considered 'open and vulnerable'. And, of course, women were necessarily more wet (menses, childbirth fluid, etc.) then were men.

15   Later, when she is contemplating signing Elizabeth's death warrant, Queen Mary taunts Elizabeth about her mother, Ann Boleyn. (By the way, unlike Elizabeth, who is portrayed as life-giving Anima Mundi or fecund, feminine Natura, Mary is barren and can produce only disease and death out of her body.) The stunted Mary suggests that Elizabeth's mother was executed by their mutual father, Henry VIII, because she was a 'whore'. That is, Ann Boleyn dangerously lived out the desires, energies and perspectives of the Personal Body on the public stage. Like Princess Diana, she loved not wisely.

16   Castiglione, The Book of the Courtier, 1528, p. 57, in ed. Natalie Zemon Davis and Arlette Farge, *A History of Women*.

17   Veronique Nahoum-Grappe, 'The Beautiful Woman', eds. Zemon and Farge, p. 91.

18   Nahoum-Grappe, p. 91.

19   Francoise Borin, 'Judging by Images', ed. Zemon and Farge, pp. 242-3.

20   Thus, on the urging of the bishops, Elizabeth's military leaders snidely send a pathetic army of children against her formidable political enemy to the North, Marie de Guise. Interestingly, Marie de Guise, who is portrayed as a beautiful seductress, is done in by her sexuality. She is murdered in bed by her traitorous 'lover', Walsingham. The suave Walsingham is, in actuality, the gifted torturer, secret serviceman and personal bodyguard of Elizabeth. Recalling the priests who counselled the 'holy women' and tertiaries of medieval and Reniassance England, Walsingham plays a dark 'father confessor' to the 'Impersonal Body' of the Queen.

21   Natalie Zemon Davis, '*Women in Politics*', p. 167, ed. Davis and Farge.

22   The Lawes Resolution of Women's Rights, 1632, ed. Davis and Farge, p. 167.

23   Ironically, as Norfolk is crowning her Personal Body, he calls her Britain's 'Undoubted Queen'.

24   Grieco, p. 46.

25   Borin, p. 212.

26   Elisje Schulte van Kessel, 'Virgins and Mothers Between Heaven and Earth', ed. Davis and Farge, p. 145. For the 'consecrated woman' or 'living saint', 'loving service to God was conflated' with heroic public service. This service was a species of 'redemptive suffering', entailing the 'sacrificial gift of her own life'.

27   van Kessel, p. 142.

28   van Kessel, p. 136.

29   Borin, p. 238.

30   In *Beyond God the Father, Toward a Philosophy of Women's Liberation* (Boston: Beacon Press, 1993), the feminist theologian Mary Daly, has described the Blessed Virgin as a 'diluted' Mother Goddess figure (p. 90). It seems to me that in Christian Europe, deliberately excavating this connection to the

'pagan' Great Mother could only further degrade a woman's ability to rule men. This would be so not only in religious terms, but also in Kristeva's postmodern psychological terms ('Psychoanalysis and the Polis,' The Kristeva Reader, ed. Toril Moi (New York: Columbia University Press, 1986), especially pp. 307-10. On this view, the will/desire of the Great Mother or 'female principle' does not appear in the Symbolic cultural realm and is beyond discourse. As something 'unnameable' and 'unsignifiable', the Great Mother as an authority-in-herself would not be a coherent or useable icon of power within the male Imaginary.

31   ed. Robin Harris, 'Introduction', Margaret Thatcher, The Collected Speeches (New York: HarperCollins, 1997), p. xii.
32   Robin Harris, adviser, member of the Prime Minister's policy unit, and editor of Mrs Thatcher's speeches corroborates their significance. In the 'Introduction' to her Collected Speeches, he says they are 'of relatively greater importance for any understanding of her character and philosophy than would be the case for her predecessors or contemporaries (or successors)'. (xiv) Why? Because,, he suggests, Mrs Thatcher is not split into Personal and Impersonal Bodies, There is only a Public/Impersonal Body generating as well as presenting those speeches: 'temperamentally, there was never much possibility of her believing one set of propositions and publicly subscribing to another'. (xiv)
33   Thatcher, Party Conference, 1975, II, pp. 305–6.
34   Thatcher, p. xv.
35   Thatcher, p. xii. First Party Conference Speech, II, p. 305. At the Aspen Institute, 1990, p. 410, in quoting T.S. Eliot, Mrs Thatcher said 'What a pity more poets were not also politicians. That is marvellous language, and its meaning so wonderfully clear'.
36   Thatcher, Party Conference, 1990, p. 442.
37   Thatcher, Speech at the Church of St. Lawrence Jewry, City of London, 1981, p. 121.
38   Thatcher, Conservative Political Centre, 1968, p. xv.
39   Thatcher, St. Lawrence Jewry, 1978, p. 71.
40   Thatcher, Statement on the Doorstep of 10 Downing Street, 1970, p. 93.
41   Thatcher, Aspen Institute, 1990, p. 414.
42   Thatcher, Zurich Economic Society, 1977, p. 56.
43   Thatcher, Speech to the Conservative Central Council, March 1975, p. 21.
44   Thatcher, Party Conference, 1975, p. 38.
45   Thatcher, Zurich Economic Society, 1977, p. 55.
46   Thatcher, Speech to the Conservative Party Conference, October 1975, p. 50.
47   Thatcher, Conservative Political Centre, October 10, 1968, p. 13.
48   Thatcher, p. 15.
49   Thatcher, Speech to the Conservative Central Council, 1975, p. 20.
50   Thatcher, Party Conference, 1975, p. 36.
51   Thatcher, MacCleod Lecture, 1977, p. 63.
52   Thatcher, Keith Joseoph Memorial Lecture, 1996, p. 572.
53   Thatcher, Pankhurst Lecture, 1990, p. 401.
54   Thatcher, Kensington Town Hall, 1976, p. 47.
55   Thatcher, Zurich Economic Society, 1977, p. 49.

56   Thatcher, MacCleod Lecture, 1977, p. 63.
57   Thatcher, Party Conference, 1975, p. 33.
58   Thatcher, MacCleod Memorial Lecture, 1977, p. 61.

British Film in the Thatcher Era

Leonard Quart

The two decades of British cinema before Thatcher's ascent to power saw formally imaginative, socially illuminating, and psychologically penetrating films
by directors like Nicholas Roeg, Ken Loach and Tony Garnett, and Joseph Losey,
but the vast body of British cinema remained mired in uninspired mediocrity
and predictability. It wasn't until the Thatcher era,1979–90, that genuine signs
of an English film resurgence could be seen again.

The British arts establishment were consistently antagonistic towards
Thatcher. They attacked her as much for her persona – voice, clothes, personal
tastes – as for her cutting state support to arts institutions and her overall political agenda. Though Thatcher never exhibited any particular interest in the arts
beyond a poem by Kipling or a Freddy Forsyth thriller, she was no more of a
philistine than Labour Prime Ministers like Wilson and Callaghan. Still, institutions like the Royal Shakespeare Company or the Royal Opera House 'that
depended on the public purse started at a disadvantage in the Thatcherite scale
of priorities . . . (and) had to justify their existence against ever stiffer presump-
tions of guilt.'[1]

Consequently, Thatcher treated the arts, and the film business – notwithstanding her dislike of film – no differently than any other business. For example, the Thatcher government passed a new Films Bill in 1984–85, one which
applied market principles to the movie industry. The Bill abolished the 1947
Eady Levy, a law which had distributed a per centage of box office receipts to
British-made films, and provided no replacement for these lost revenues. It also
abolished a 25 per cent tax break for investment in film production and privatised the NFFC (National Film Finance Corporation), thus eliminating the 'only

direct form of government involvement in the field of commercial film production in Britain'.[2]

The Thatcher government's denial of aid for British film production merely
compounded the long-term problems of a historically sick industry whose audience continued to decline – the average Briton attended the cinema on an average of once a year during that period. In contrast with the generous subsidy
policies of Western European countries like Sweden, British governments even
committed to state intervention rarely gave much economic support to film
production. The British film industry, of course, never freed itself of Hollywood
domination. This colonisation held for both the pre-eminence of American
films in British movie theatres and on television, as well as Hollywood's success
at weaning away many of England's top directors (e.g., Alan Parker, Ridley Scott,
Stephen Frears, Mike Figgis) to work in a secure and well-financed industry and
make more lucrative careers. Film in Britain also confronted the generally
pro-theatre, anti-cinematic bias of the arts establishment, and faced competition for an audience with some very striking and original television programming (e.g., Dennis Potter's *The Singing Detective*) and home video – Britain having one of the highest ownership and rental rates in the world. In contrast with
the film industry, television remained a heavily subsidised business in which
most film people, including directors like Ken Loach, Michael Apted, and
Stephen Frears, among others, have done a great deal of creative work. Another
difficulty that the industry faced was that two major chains, Rank and EMI, and
two smaller ones, Cannon-Classic and the Star Group, dominated national film
distribution. All of these chains were committed to showing Hollywood films,
making it difficult for independent, intellectually difficult, and stylistically
experimental British films to receive nationwide exposure.

Despite, however, the industry's economic precariousness and limited
resources, the 1980s saw an exciting renaissance of British film. The revival,
brought on by renewed American interest in British film because of *Chariots of
Fire*'s (1981) success, was fuelled by America's expanded cable television market.
More important for the development of a low-budget, intellectually (though
rarely formally) adventurous cinema was Channel Four. This adventurous
British television channel exhibited an interest in subsidising film production
and commissioned films from independent producers. During the 1980s, a

number of out-of-the-mainstream, commercially risky films like *The Draughtsman's Contract* (1982), *The Ploughman's Lunch* (1983), *Another Time, Another Place* (1983), and *My Beautiful Laundrette* (1985) received most of their funding from Channel Four, which allocated the greater part of its drama budget to producing feature films. These films were first released in movie theatres and subsequently shown on television. In addition, despite the Thatcher government's unwillingness to aid the film industry, it did establish a general climate that encouraged economic risk-taking (small production companies) and experimentation with new and more innovative business practices.

Thatcher's prime contribution to British film-making was not the business climate she produced, but the social atmosphere her policies and the culture she helped create provided British directors. Many of the films portrayed Britain as a volatile urban society – heterogeneous, socially divided, fractured, and permeated with large pockets of unemployment and poverty. With the unions playing a less central role in English life the films centred more on marginal groups and characters than on traditional working-class ones. These films, however, made no claim to providing answers to Thatcherism, but the ethos she created seemed to become the implicit or explicit subject of many of the period's best films. From Ken Loach's spare, documentary-style film about drifting, unemployed youth in Sheffield, *Looks and Smiles* (1981), to Peter Greenaway's stylised allegory of Thatcherite greed and vulgarity, *The Cook, The Thief, His Wife, and Her Lover* (1990), a large number of British films gained their impetus from Thatcherism.

The film that began this cinematic renaissance, and helped grant British directors the confidence to confront English subjects, was Hugh Hudson's Oscar winning *Chariots of Fire*. A favourite of President Reagan's, *Chariots* offered a conventional, inflated paean to a triumphant,1924 Olympic-winning England, one skillfully evoked by the use of a booming soundtrack, a great many slow motion shots of handsome young men running on the beach, rich period detail, and romantic superimpositions. Shrewdly, this film uses the victory of anti-establishment characters, at odds with the insidious bigotry and genteel snobbery and hypocrisy of the English Establishment, to exult in nationalistic feeling and implicitly endorse the Thatcherite ethos. The film's driven central figure, Harold Abrahams (Ben Cross), a Jewish immigrant financier's son who rejects his Cambridge University masters' idea of gentlemanly values, hires a professional coach to train him for the Olympics. Abrahams and his Italian-Arab coach, Sam Massabini (Ian Holm), are seen by the Cambridge masters as both ethnic outsiders and aggressive arrivistes – both their class and nationality are held against them. However, Abrahams wins the Olympic 100 yard dash and becomes a fully assimilated Englishman – a member of the Establishment he always hungered to enter.

Chariots of Fire remains overtly critical of an England built on calcified class demarcations and aristocratic hauteur, but in its stead it implicitly endorses the Thatcherite ethos of a nation based on a meritocracy of the ambitious, the diligent, and the gifted. In the film's vision, the Establishment's values begin to shift, becoming more tolerant of individual difference and comprehending that the future no longer rests solely within their control. But the film's idea of a more dynamic, diverse nation, one where a man like Abrahams has the chance to succeed, is depicted with as much uncritical sentimentality as the Cambridge masters treat their own hierarchal and racist vision of Britain. It's a fitting message for a Thatcher-ruled England where the traditional class lines give way to an emphasis on individual drive and achievement usually defined by wealth and status.

The 1980s films that were harder to export, tended to be less decorative and pictorial than heritage films like *Chariots of Fire* or Ivory/Merchant's *Room with a View,* and dealt with contemporary England rather than turning their gaze away from the turbulent present to some luminous historical moment or to a serene, pastoral Britain. The Britain depicted in the heritage films offered a portrait of a relatively balanced, hieratic world that, despite its imperfections and inequalities soothed rather than disturbed educated, middle-class audiences. These were films whose literacy and fidelity to period detail allowed audiences to distance themselves from their lives without there ever perceiving they were viewing escapist fantasies not that different in quality from much less high-toned Hollywood genre films.

In contrast to the heritage works, a small, quiet film like Richard Eyre's *The Ploughman's Lunch* (1983) deals directly with Thatcherism. Subsidised by Channel Four, this sardonic, literate, and stylistically conventional movie perceptively satirises London media life, as well as the political and social climate of

Thatcher's England. The film centers around an ambitious, opportunistic BBC radio news editor of working-class origins, James Penfield (a subtle, muted performance by Jonathan Pryce), who avidly pursues class, status, and an unattainable upper-class bitch, Susi (Charlie Dore). Penfield, an unpleasant character, is a fitting anti-heroic figure for an ethos which eschews social concern and commitment for the celebration of individual success. He's a man who can pretend his working class parents don't exist when it suits his purposes, and remains passively remote from his dying mother, the emotional desperation of a colleague, and the moral fervour of the anti-nuclear Greenham Common women. Penfield also displays a gift for adapting his political convictions to the person he's talking to – turning into a proponent of imperial England and the invasion of Suez when talking to his Conservative publisher, and anti-Suez and sympathetic to socialism when talking to a Left-leaning female historian.

The Ploughman's Lunch does more than focus on one driven careerist's saga. Eyre totally entwines James's fortunes with a pointed critique of the moral emptiness of British public life. The BBC news staff meetings function as gatherings of wary, cynical professionals who lack any moral or intellectual response to the news. They aim to find the right balance, to provide a great deal of soft news and avoid controversial stories like the Greenham Common women's protest which could upset the vision of a bland social order they wish to convey. In other spheres, book publishing turns into merely the packaging of commercial products, while advertising creates fabricated pasts like the supposed eighteenth century 'ploughman's lunch' – invented in the sixties in some London marketing office.

The apotheosis of the substitution of hype for reality, can be seen in Eyre's seamlessly fusing footage of the 1982 Tory Party conference in Brighton with his fictional story. At that conference, Margaret Thatcher makes political capital by inflating the significance of the successful Falklands invasion – treating it as a sign of the British national spirit's renewal. Like most of the 1980s films critical of Thatcher, *The Ploughman's Lunch* offers no left alternative to her ethos. The only socialist in the film, Ann Barrington (Rosemary Harris), a middle-aged historian, lives a life of affluence and total comfort in a grand Norfolk house, while still indulging in empty, reflexively Left critiques of the Labour Party. The prototype of the academic socialist, her insulated, privileged everyday life totally at odds with her leftist political convictions.

A more emotionally complex film than *The Ploughman's Lunch*, one that provides a direct and corrosive critique of Thatcherism, is Mike Leigh's *High Hopes* (1988). Leigh, a much more original, idiosyncratic film director than Eyre, and a man rooted in experimental theatre, is the master of behavioural nuance – capturing in his films the pathetic and the comic, the solemn and the absurd in human interaction. Leigh's films begin without a script, and evolve through lengthy periods of improvisation. As a result, his construction of character and narrative eschews the formulaic for the nuanced and unpredictable. His films usually use little camera movement, and shooting often in close-up and reaction shot avoids telegraphing emotion or glamorizing his characters – scrupulously and incisively observing in long take every revelatory facial tic and body movement. Leigh's characters often convey a complex sense of their own modest individuality, thereby granting intricate life to the sort of ordinary people that rarely appear in mainstream films.

In *High Hopes* Leigh evokes the social mood and class tensions of Thatcher's London by centring the film around three couples. The central, most sympathetic and nuanced characters – Cyril (Philip Davis) and Shirley (Ruth Sheen) – are shaggy-haired, woolly-sweatered, left-wing, and working-class. Cyril is a red-bearded, bohemian who plays chess, owns a cactus named Thatcher, and at thirty-five works at a dead end job as a motorcycle messenger. (The Thatcher era saw a decline in unionised, mass production jobs, and the growth of service industries.) They live in a small, shabby flat, filled with anti-war and anti-Thatcher posters, in a working-class neighbourhood near King's Cross railway station. Cyril is an outsider in Thatcher's Britain – a radical without desire for money, social status, and material goods in a society dominated by those values. He is angrily filled with class resentment (sensing class condescension in every gesture and word from those who have money and clout), and it takes little to set him off. Leigh neither reduces Cyril to the sum of his social and political positions, nor does he give him a set of personal characteristics to easily tag him by. Cyril is a complex character, who is both emotionally constricted and remote, sullen, and unseeing, but also can be tender and filled with feeling. His warmth is most clearly expressed in his ten-year relationship with Shirley. They are lovers and friends who smoke pot, fight, have good-humoured sex, talk intimately, and joke lovingly with each other.

Shirley is the most caring character in the film. She is buck-toothed and ungainly, but her radiance and warmth make her seem beautiful at times, and she is connected to the world in a more concrete, knowing, and less ideological way than Cyril. She is given to warm laughter, loves flowers and plants, and yearns for children. Still, Leigh doesn't sentimentalise and turn her into some ethereal, benign presence. Shirley is sufficiently tough, knowing, and quick-witted to sharply handle her brother-in-law Martin's crude attempt to come on to her.

Leigh himself is an active supporter of the Labour Party, and shares Cyril's rage at the existence of unemployment and poverty in Thatcher's Britain, but displays little use for leftist slogans or sentimentality. He incisively and sympathetically captures in Suzi, a friend of Cyril and Shirley's, the kind of leftist whose commitments have much less to do with political thought and action than with intense psychological need. Suzi is a frenetic woman who anxiously spouts left rhetoric about the social pain caused by Thatcher's policies and augments it with foolish talk about the coming English working-class revolution. Cyril puts her talk down as nonsense, harshly dismisses her weekly political meetings as useless and her fantasy about going to help the peasants in Nicaragua (which she mispronounces) as absurd. But he also ruefully and honestly admits, when Suzi asks him what he does politically, that he does nothing but sit on his 'arse'.

The film's animus, however, is not directed at the Left, but at the other two couples who adapt, in different ways, to the Thatcherite ethos. The snobbish Tory couple, the Booth-Braines, who live next door to Cyril's depressed, disconnected mother, Mrs Bender (Edna Dore), are venomous comic caricatures whom Leigh utilises to send up 1980s' Thatcherism. Leigh uses them to depict the upper-middle-class gentrification of working-class terraces, and his own revulsion with the whole Thatcherite ethos and creed. The fashionably dressed wife, Laetitia, is a sherry-drinking, brittle, cold package of inhumanity and class contempt, who, voice and all, sounds like a pint-sized Thatcher. She hesitates allowing Mrs Bender to use her 'lavatory' ('toilet' is Mrs Bender's term) and phone, as if she'd contaminate the meticulous, well-appointed house. In a voice drawling with disdain, Laetitia briskly advises 'you people', meaning Mrs Bender, that her house is a gold mine and wants to know if it has all its 'original features'. Her husband, stuffy, arrogant Rupert, augments her detestable behaviour by unselfconsciously blurting out his reactionary credo to Cyril that 'what made this country great was a place for everyone and everyone in his place'.

For a couple like this given to charity work, nights at the opera, expensive restaurants, weekends in the country, and expressions like 'jolly good', and 'post haste', Mrs Bender is a non-person, an embarrassment, someone to be condescended to, who only lowers the social tone and financial value of their house. Leigh's parody tends to be a bit broad here, for their unrelieved detestable behaviour seems excessive even for smug upholders of Thatcherite culture.

The third couple is also caricatured, but with greater pathos and genuine pain at the centre of the characterisation. The focus is on Cyril's sister, Valerie, a self-involved, manic, overdressed vulgarian – leopard skin coats, leather skirts – who puts her makeup on with a trowel. She lives in a detached, overstuffed suburban house, highlighted by a pink, neon-lit house number, and an unused expensive chess set with the pieces placed in the wrong order. Shirley's remark 'that everything in the house comes off the back of a lorry' aptly sums up its garish decor.

Valerie alternates between a shrill, abhorrent laugh and sullen irritation and complaint, and spends most of her time consuming, exercising, and cooking gourmet meals. She has found a fitting match in Martin (who Cyril and Shirley dub 'the weasel in the diesel') – a cigar-smoking oaf who knows how to make money, and cynically sees everybody as having a price. He treats other people, especially women, as if they're inanimate, disposable objects.

Valerie and Martin have a ruin of an abusive and alienated marriage. Their only compensation is that they own a great many things and have credit cards and money. They are exemplars for Leigh of Thatcher's new class and of one her governing ideas that class is not historically fixed, but a social situation that can be altered by personal ambition, application, and a hunger for money. Thatcher garnering her greatest political support from members of this self-made middle class, which she viewed as a new, vital force in capitalism; Martin and Valerie embodying the worst aspects of that class.

Valerie's apotheosis as a comic-pathetic figure is the gaudy birthday party that she imposes on her reluctant mum – a woman she blatantly neglects, resents, even hates. That fact is strikingly illustrated when Valerie toasts her mum, Mrs Bender, on her birthday, by blurting out from the recesses of her unconscious 'that it could be her last'. She catches herself, laughs hysterically then cries, drinks champagne, and what follows a few scenes later is general chaos and cacophony. Leigh intensifies the sense of bedlam that dominates the scene by shooting Mrs Bender, her head bent, in tight close-up and in a long take, and, at the same time, we can hear off-screen the carefully orchestrated babel of Cyril, Martin, Shirley, and Valerie's conflicting, raised voices. The ill-conceived, farcical party ends with the desperate Valerie's drunken, melancholy retreat to her bathtub, left only with the dog, that she pathetically lavishes all her love on, to attend to her.

In contrast to his satiric treatment of the smug, odious Tory couple, and the unhappy, selfish Valerie and her boor of a husband, Leigh depicts Cyril and Shirley in a richly detailed, naturalistic fashion. They are the only one of the three couples that Leigh treats utterly seriously, which only adds to the positive feelings audiences have towards them. It's obviously easier for audiences to emotionally connect with realistically depicted characters than ones that are given somewhat over the top, cartoon-like treatments.

Leigh holds out a touch of hope for Cyril and Shirley in a society riven with avarice and lack of compassion. Cyril himself has not given up his socialist high hopes for a new, more fashionable set of political and social values. He's an orthodox enough socialist to do obeisance to Marx and his ideas by reverentially standing and contemplating Marx's giant bust and grave in Highgate Cemetery, though his socialism derives as much or more from a moral revulsion with capitalist greed and consumer-driven lifestyles as from an adherence to a set of firm political-ideological positions. He is, however, aware that the world as presently constituted is unlikely to fulfil those dreams (pursuing Marx's vision of a classless society is now merely, in his words, like 'pissing in the wind') He can't run away from the reality that Thatcher's vision garnered support from a sizeable segment of the working class – a fact that does not bode well for the imminent arrival of the socialist revolution. Still, Cyril never permits his disillusion to harden into defeat. His sense of doubt never turns to cynicism or nihilism. Despite the overwhelming triumph of Thatcherism, he continues to adhere to a vision of a more equitable and just society.

Leigh has made a comic and sardonic film, whose overt rage towards Thatcher's ethos and the oppressive constraints of the English class system successfully avoids becoming a political polemic or allegory. Society may be unjust, avaricious, and closed to genuine change, family life difficult, even traumatic, but Leigh offers no political solutions. There are just people like Cyril and Shirley who are capable of surviving with their moral centre and capacity for human feeling intact amidst all the greed and callousness. The film does not conclude with the ringing good cheer and brilliantly contrived warmth of a film like Capra's *It's a Wonderful Life*, but for Leigh it's his version of a happy ending, people muddling through, making some contact (Cyril and Shirley will visit Cyril's mother, Mrs Bender, more often), achieving a bit of harmony, even look-ing towards the future. The family will now provide some solace and kindness along with the strong doses of alienation that have characterised their lives up to now. In the modestly optimistic vision of life projected by *High Hopes*, Cyril and Shirley are two people who offer this sort of hope.

In addition to *High Hopes*, other British films deal directly with Thatcherism, like Chris Bernard's small fable, *A Letter to Brezhnev* (1985), and David Drury's *Defence of the Realm* (1985). The former centres around two working-class women who feel permanently imprisoned in a depressed Liverpool suburb, until ironically a Russian sailor arrives to offer one of them hope. The latter film, a well-made, paranoid thriller, poses direct political questions about the func-tioning of Thatcher's police-state like security services, and the Conservative press' willing collaboration with their murderous activities.

More imaginative and intellectually suggestive than most of the British films of the 1980s were Stephen Frears and Hanif Kureishi's literate and ironic *My Beautiful Laundrette* (1985) and *Sammy and Rosie Get Laid* (1987). Both films depict Thatcher's England as dominated by racism, greed, and social injustice, but they eschew an orthodox Left perspective for a more ambiguous, unpredictable, skeptical point of view. Frears and Kureishi avoid sentimentalizing victims of prejudice or economic deprivation, and though men with Left sympathies, equally subvert both schematic left thinking and respectable authority. Sammy and Rosie satirises Left positions – under-standing just how chic leftists are trapped by their own contradictions. Both Sammy and Rosie can mouth radical sentiments, but have never examined how their lives relate to politics. For example, Rosie can inanely spout that rioting is 'an affirmation of the human spirit' while, at the same time, walking to a sexual assignation, through the heart of the riot, oblivious to what is happening all about her.

Kureishi and Frears' commitment is to an anarchic, impulsive, and sexual life. Consequently, they are sympathetic to characters with size and panache – even if they turn out to be capitalist rogues and authoritarian executioners. Their films project a radical perspective where all our social categories – oppressor-victim, black-white, male-female are – ironically subverted. No social group or individual in the films has a monopoly of virtue or wisdom. In fact, the only unqualified villain in the two films is an absurdly posh-accented, arrogant Margaret Thatcher.

That's the one political certitude that many of the directors, and films shared. It was as if directors of American politically oriented works of the same period, like *Country* and *Do the Right Thing*, had begun to punctuate their films with barbed and contemptuous remarks aimed explicitly at Ronald Reagan, and had turned him into the prime source of all that had gone socially and politically wrong during the 1980s. If most of the British directors of the Thatcher years (excepting Ken Loach whose explicitly socialist commitment to an increasingly beleaguered working class remained unchanged) did not have an antidote to Thatcherism, they shared, at least, a belief that Margaret Thatcher was at the heart of what they felt had gone wrong in Britain. Stating that England in the 1980s is too complex a phenomenon for any ideology to explain, director Michael Radford (*1984*) claimed that we inhabit a world where 'all the things we were taught to believe have crumbled away'.[3] For Radford, the only belief system functioning in England in the 1980s was Thatcherism, an ideology that utterly repelled him.

Directors and screenwriters like Leigh and Frears-Kureishi may not exactly echo Radford's sentiments, but they too convey that both the Thatcher ethos and the traditional Left political alternatives to her rule were no longer viable in the England of the 1980s. Cultural and social structures that once reverberated morally and politically – like left-wing politics, the unions, the church, and even the class system – no longer played the same social role. In her desire to transform Britain into a more assertive, efficient, profit-oriented society, Margaret Thatcher created a world of rapidly changing, often socially and morally alienated values that severed itself from many of the institutions and norms that once dominated British society. For eleven years she controlled and shaped the British political and social landscape, looming as a larger-than-life figure in the consciousness and vision of some of its best film directors. Most of their films expressed a revulsion with Thatcherism; still, their anger rarely turned to sectarian or simplistic polemics, but evolved instead into the complex formal texture and imagination of art. Thatcher never provided direct help to the film industry, but her powerful, self-righteous, dogmatic presence moved British film-makers to burnish their art for at least one decade.

Portions of this chapter appeared in a different form in Leonard Quart, 'The Religion of the Market', The Fires Were Started, edited by Lester Friedman, (Minneapolis, University of Minnesota Press, 1993), pp. 15–34.

Notes

1   Hugo Young, *The Iron Lady*, (New York, Farrar Strauss Giroux, 1989), p.413.
2   Nick Roddick, 'If the United States Spoke Spanish We Would Have a Film Industry...'. *British Cinema Now*, edited by Martyn Auty and Nick Roddick, (London, BFI, 1985), p.14.
3   James Park, *Learning to Dream: The New British Cinema*, (London, Faber & Faber, 1984), p.100.

Ken Loach and the Cinema of Social Conscience

Simon Doubleday

Ken Loach is the most intensely political director in British cinema today, and the most passionate in representing the plight of the poor and the marginalised. No film-maker has been more active in denouncing the human cost of Margaret Thatcher's policies or, for that matter, more scornful of the gradual Clintonisation of the Labour Party. Since the late 1960s, Loach has portrayed the working class and underclass in compelling fashion, generating emotional intensity from social realism and kick-starting the careers of some of Britain's most exciting young actors. Films like *Riff-Raff* (1991), which will be the focal point of this essay, are a useful barometer of social and political division, and reveal much about the culture of opposition. Loach has often been perceived as a didactic director. A perpetual gadfly, unfashionably ideological in an age of centrism, he is nonetheless riding a wave of renewed popularity. While his Trotskyist sympathies appear almost charmingly archaic, his social conscience clearly touches a nerve. His film, *My Name is Joe* (1998), was a critical and box-office success on both sides of the Atlantic, and was chosen as one of the British Film Institute's 100 best British films of the century. Although it addresses such themes as alcoholism, poverty and violence in contemporary Glasgow, the film's raw emotions are occasionally lightened by touches of fullmontyesque humour. Loach has learned to reach a wide cinema audience, eschewing some of his earlier, more explicit polemic. Yet the voice of social conscience is always contentious. Loach is often compared to another, albeit a less strictly, leftist director, Mike Leigh. But in contrast to Leigh's charming *Topsy-Turvy*, Loach's films are unlikely ever to win any Hollywood accolades; his forthcoming *Bread and Roses* (his first American-based feature) is a paean to US labour activism which should guarantee his continued alienation from the American cinema industry.

During the sixties, a propitious time for artistic confrontation, Loach had enjoyed great success with hard-hitting television dramas like *Cathy Come Home* (1966), often cited as the direct cause of the creation of the homeless charity Shelter.[1] His first feature films, *Poor Cow* (1967) and *Kes* (1969), were strikingly innovative in their depth of social observation. Over the next decade, his perspective became far more explicitly political, but he maintained momentum with high-quality television drama like *Days of Hope* (1975) and with political documentaries such as *Rank and File* (1971). In the late 1970s, the Labour Government even offered him an OBE, which he rejected on the grounds that he wanted to have nothing to do with the British Empire.[2] Yet Loach's voice became strangely muted in the Thatcher years; one leading critic has referred to this as 'the most blighted period of his career'.[3] Some emphasis should be placed here on Mrs Thatcher's financial neglect of the film industry, part and parcel of her so-called 'sado-monetarism'.[4] Loach has spoken forcefully of the impoverished state of the industry in the aftermath of the Thatcher years, and in particular the lack of government support for the distribution and screening of British-made films. Giving evidence to the National Heritage Committee of the House of Commons in 1995 (alongside Mike Leigh and Alan Parker), he decried the creative drought which resulted: 'If you think of the cinema or films as prose then the cinema should be as broad as a library, [but] what we have in the British cinemas really is a range of products which is equivalent to airport novels'.[5] As Leonard Quart has written, Thatcher's main contribution was simply to create the kind of contentious climate in which films like *High Hopes* (dir. Mike Leigh), *My Beautiful Laundrette* (dir. Stephen Frears), and *The Cook, The Thief His Wife and Her Lover* (dir. Peter Greenaway) could be made: all of them rejected, in their different ways, the Thatcherite appeal to avarice.[6] Still, she was hardly unique among British prime ministers in her attitude towards arts subsidies, and not even Loach would blame her alone for his troubles in the 1980s. Responsibility for the unofficial censorship of his four-part television documentary *Questions of Leadership* (1983), which attempted to show a betrayal of the union rank and file during recent industrial action, appears to lie with the relatively conservative Independent Broadcasting

Authority and the liberal board members of Channel 4, rather than with Thatcher or her government.

There was also a more internal, artistic crisis of direction. 'Frankly', Loach has admitted, 'I don't think I was very competent at film-making in that period. I see, in retrospect, that I'd lost any clarity in the work I was doing'.[7] His only feature film of the whole decade, *Fatherland* (1986), is an unusually elusive, and occasionally surreal, attempt to recast our vision of East and West. Its protagonist, Drittemann, is an East German songwriter whose independence of mind leads him to be as critical of Western capitalism as of the Communist world; but the critique is nebulous, and never fully explored. This is, perhaps, the least satisfying of all Loach's films. In *Hidden Agenda* (1990), he returns to the more concrete world of Northern Irish politics; he dramatises an alleged perversion of justice by British security forces (the so-called shoot-to-kill policy of the early 1980s) and suggests a conspiracy within the Conservative Party – during the 1970s – to replace Edward Heath with Margaret Thatcher as party leader. For some critics, this film marks the beginning of his artistic rejuvenation. But complexity of plot comes at the expense of the kind of deeper human drama at which Loach excels; his characters here remain two-dimensional, and our emotions are not fully engaged. It is interesting to read a diagnosis of Loach's cinematic skills late in 1990, shortly after *Hidden Agenda* was awarded a Special Jury Prize at the Cannes Film Festival: 'The years of struggling have sapped some of his vitality, and one senses that in his frustration, the direct political content, latent in all his work, has risen to the surface. Subsequently, his films have become more polemic, and in the process, more detached from the very people they were claiming to represent: authentic working class characters'.[8]

All this was to change emphatically with Loach's next feature film, *Riff-Raff*: the first in a series of deeply moving, brilliantly observed films concerned with the lives and hardships of ordinary working-class people. In returning to his natural milieu, Loach found renewed inspiration and coupled this inspiration with an urgent determination to show the scars which had been inflicted on the working class in the name of liberty. 'As Britain emerged from the spell that Thatcher had put on it', he has said, 'I and perhaps some other film-makers felt very dissatisfied with ourselves. We felt we hadn't really put on the screen the appalling cost in human misery that aggressive Thatcherite politics had brought on everybody'.[9] Many of his ensuing films would address the experiences of the under- and unemployed, during and soon after the Thatcher years. These experiences are heartrendingly portrayed in *Raining Stones* (1993), in which the unemployed Bob desperately attempts to raise the money he needs to buy his daughter her first communion dress. The film, set in Manchester, revolves in large part around inescapable debt, and the violence which surrounds it. Loach is perennially concerned with the forms of social brutality which are standard fare for this segment of society: the aggression of loan sharks, violence and arson, and the self-fulfilling cycle of domestic abuse, which is a central theme in the traumatic *Ladybird, Ladybird* (1994). By this stage, Loach had fully re-immersed himself in the lives of the powerless and marginalised; in this case, a single mother whose children are taken into care after a house fire. There is nothing romantic about the character of Maggie, nothing even very appealing – except for her ferocious, angry desire to survive in a society which victimises her.

Ladybird, Ladybird is also the first film to introduce a Hispanic character, Jorge: a refugee from an unnamed Latin American country, exiled and lonely in cold urban Britain. In this sense, it is an interesting foreshadowing of a concern which would take Loach first to Spain, then to Central America, and finally – a logical next step – to the poor Hispanic communities of the United States. As the 1990s progressed, Loach became increasingly absorbed by the foreign manifestations of ideological conflict. *Land and Freedom* (1995) is concerned with an archetypal ideological cauldron, the Spanish Civil War, and follows a young Liverpudlian to the Catalan war front, where he joins the anarchist militia known as POUM. If the Spanish conflict was the last romantic war, a war of belief and political principle in which men fought for utopia, it was also in Spain that romanticism died; leftist dreams of liberty are crushed by the heavy guns of Stalinism, which betray the people's revolution. Flashbacks and other narrative devices make the relevance to contemporary Britain emphatically clear. Loach's next project took him to the scene of another cause celebre of the British Left: the revolution of the Sandinistas, crushed this time by illegal US intervention. The spellbindingly beautiful *Carla's Song* (1996), which deals with the tragedy of Nicaragua through the eyes of a refugee and the Glaswegian bus driver who persuades her to return, is surely Loach's most underrated film.

But it was *Riff-Raff* (1991) which had really marked Loach's return to form, and which would set the tone for all his subsequent work. It had only limited distribution in Britain, being shown only in BFI cinemas, but won great acclaim on the Continent.[10] The film follows the fortunes and misfortunes of a young man from Glasgow, Patrick Logan, whose search for work brings him to a building site in London; here, like many of the other workers, he adopts an alias, 'Stevie'. Bill Jesse, the Scottish screenwriter, had in fact been working on a site at the time (tragically, he was to die before the completion of *Riff-Raff*). In the film, a hospital is being turned into a luxury apartment building; or in other words, compassion is being replaced by indulgence. It is 1990, the final year of the Thatcher regime; 250,000 construction workers alone, we are told, are unemployed. The building site is chaotic and unregulated. The scaffolding is extremely unsafe, the men have no goggles to protect them from shattering cement, and they work with the constant threat of electrocution; needless to say, they are also uninsured. Loach comments: 'The defeat of the unions in the eighties had opened the door for the return of the old days of the Lump, where building workers had no protection from danger, exploitation or instant dismissal. I remember talking to a group of building workers shortly after we did *Riff-Raff*, and they were saying that there had been eleven deaths of building workers in the previous two months in London. But nobody knew what their real names were. That's just Dickensian, isn't it?'[11]

In both *Riff-Raff* and *Carla's Song*, a good deal of the success rests on magnetic performances by Robert Carlyle. Carlyle had been a painter and decorator for five years before he became an actor: one of the factors, perhaps, that gives this film its compelling authenticity.[12] But his character's thick Glasgow accent is not the only one that had to be subtitled (and indeed translated) for American audiences; there is also a Cockney, two Liverpudlians, some West Indians, and a Geordie. The *New York Times* recently ran a remarkably offensive article decrying the unaccustomed sound of regional accents in recent British film, and concluding: 'the grittier the fiction, the muddier the diction. The British cinema isn't dead, it just isn't speaking so clearly'. The two journalists, in a virtuoso display of linguistic and cultural prejudice, referred to *My Name is Joe* as 'a film about a recovering alcoholic whose name we could never quite make out'.[13] But of course, the accents serve a purpose. In *Riff-Raff*, they remind us that the labourers who have come from Glasgow, Liverpool, Bristol and Tyneside, have come because there is no work in their native cities.[14] They also break the old monopoly of Merchant-Ivory, Home County, and BBC pronunciation, literally giving voice to those who are too easily overlooked. The improvised talking, the loose, overlapping dialogue, and the colour of local language, bring vigor to Loach's work. The preternaturally flexible Carlyle is the embodiment of these new voices. A native Glaswegian who is said to have cried for half an hour when Gary McAllister missed a penalty kick for Scotland in Euro 96, he would use his native accent again in *Carla's Song* and as Begbie in *Trainspotting*, but he is a equally convincing South Yorkshireman in *The Full Monty*, and as a working-class Londoner in Antonia Bird's gangland film *Face*.[15]

Soon after his arrival on the building site, Stevie finds a squat with the help of the other workers: an empty flat in a bleak, graffiti-ridden housing estate. Larry, from Liverpool, takes the lead, connecting the gas and electricity for him. Larry is played by the actor Ricky Tomlinson, who in a previous incarnation had been a plasterer and union activist; he had been arrested and jailed for leading flying pickets during the 1972 building strikes.[16] In prison, Tomlinson refused to wear prison uniform, confining himself to solitary, and for twenty-two days had gone on hunger strike. Blacklisted as a builder, he had turned to acting, and found a regular niche on a soap opera set on a Liverpool housing estate: Labour leader Neil Kinnock is reported to have said to him, 'When I watched you in an episode of *Brookside*, it was like watching a party political broadcast on behalf of the Labour Party.'[17] In *Riff-Raff*, his character Larry is sometimes a figure of fun; but he is also the voice of righteous anger, and by far the most politicised of the workers. Fixing up Stevie's squat, for example, he expresses his indignation about Mrs Thatcher's privatisation of industry: 'Can anyone explain to me why someone's got to make a profit every time you boil a kettle? Or every time a kid has a drink of water? Or every time a pensioner has a warm by the gas fire?'

But Larry's wisdom is not always welcome. 'Every time you open your mouth, it's like a bleeding parliamentary debate', says his mate, Shem. Loach is clearly poking fun not only at Larry's own speech-making, but at his own political passion. He is often accused of political didacticism, a complaint which he considers justified to a certain extent. He thinks of *Riff-Raff* as a deliberate attempt to lighten the tone, to inject humour and humanity into his political concerns after the grave documentaries of the 1980s. 'I think I'd got far too po-faced and heavy-handed', he says; in *Riff-Raff*, 'what we started getting was the zest and the whiff and taste of real experience'.[18] At the same time, accusations are didacticism are generally misplaced; it is as if the mere presence of political ideas is an offence to critical sensibilities. The attacks are particularly curious in the context of films like *Land and Freedom* and *Carla's Song*, in which Loach deals with two of the most naturally politicised subjects that one could possibly imagine. There are few scenes in British film more compelling than the prolonged and impassioned discussion of the merits of collectivisation which takes place among the villagers of *Land and Freedom*. To have muted political convictions would have been to overlook the most fundamental ingredient of the Spanish Civil War, and (for Loach) to run the risk of playing into the hands of woolly liberal democracy. Equally, to have silenced the ideological crossfire of *Carla's Song* would have been to sacrifice authenticity for entertainment. Paul Julian Smith, a distinguished scholar of Spanish cultural studies, suggests in a hostile review that 'the denunciation of the horrors of US policy in Central America is so insistent and hectoring that it leaves no opportunity for the audience to exercise its imagination', but this is to ignore the fact that the ideology of the so-called Cold War (all too hot in Central America) was insistent, pervasive and unrelenting. Smith's remark also overlooks the emotional magnetism of Oyanka Cabezas and the other Nicaraguan actors, as well as a nuanced and empathetic performance by Robert Carlyle. The call of ideology is balanced, and indeed explained, by the human face of suffering.[19] In reality, the charge of didacticism clearly reflects a narrowly artistic conception of the possibilities of film, and an almost universal revulsion towards Old Leftist political views per se. Furthermore, as Loach rightly recognises, Hollywood films are just as political as his own work, albeit only implicitly so. Paul Laverty, the Glaswegian lawyer and human rights activist who wrote the screenplay for *Carla's Song*, makes the point well: 'American movies are very reactionary because of their subtext. They seem to say that problems can be solved with a gun. And look at how the camera worships wealth and consumerism'.[20]

Regardless, in *Riff-Raff, Land and Freedom* and *Carla's Song* alike, Loach tries to leaven the heavy political message with a love affair. Early in *Riff-Raff*, Stevie finds a handbag on the building site; when he goes to return it to its rightful owner, it turns out to belong to an unemployed Irish girl, Susan (played by Emer

McCourt), who soon moves in with him – partly because she can't pay the rent on her own place. 'In the end there were two people who needed each other for a time – two ships that passed in the night', Loach explains. 'I enjoyed doing these scenes because Emer McCourt was good to work with, and I think if it had been all hairy-arsed builders we might have got a bit fed up with them'.[21] Unfortunately, Susan soon becomes emotionally dependent on Stevie, who is much the stronger character; his strength in turn is sorely tested when he has to travel back to Glasgow for his mother's funeral, where he meets his brother and his sister-in-law, both recovering heroin addicts who are planning to start a new life in Canada; we are not convinced of their chances. Tragically, when Stevie returns to London, he comes upon Susan shooting up. Here, Loach touches briefly on a theme that would play a conspicuous role in *My Name is Joe*: the role of drugs in decimating inner-city communities.

Much more central to *Riff-Raff* is the fragmentation and political incoherence of the British working class. Again and again, we see frustrations turned inwards, rather than against the management. When the foreman refers to the worker from Bristol as a 'sheepshagger', the man from the West Country bites his tongue, and instead takes out his aggression on the rats which scurry through the workers' kitchen. A furious argument breaks out when one of the West Indians asks for a commission for going to cash the men's pay checks. Again, Larry provides the only voice of political awareness, insisting that the workers on the building site have to unionise: 'We're just fighting among ourselves', he protests. But no one really wants to hear his lectures. And when he agrees to act as spokesman for the workers, and goes to talk about the physical dangers of the building site with the management, he is almost immediately fired. Stevie, meanwhile, has none of Larry's political clarity; indeed, he seems to have half bought into the Thatcherite gospel of free enterprise. 'I'm into merchandising', he tells Susan. 'That's where I'm heading. Boxer shorts. Coloured socks . . . I've got big plans'. But Susan laughs. This is indeed a laughable, picaresque dream, never expressed with any conviction, and divorced from the real world which Stevie inhabits. Several other characters harbour dreams that seem similarly likely to founder: Stevie's relatives dream of going to Canada, the black labourer 'Desmond' dreams of going to Africa, and Larry dreams (forever and alone) of class unity.[22]

For Ken Loach, the absence of working-class solidarity is a tragedy. His greatest anger has been reserved not for Conservatives, not even for Margaret Thatcher, whose political position is – for Loach – beneath contempt, but for those on the Left whom he believes to have betrayed the workers. This includes Tony Blair's Labour Party, and the allegedly irresolute union leaders of the 1970s and 1980s. It is a position that dates back to the mid-1960s, when Harold Wilson's Labour government came and disappointed. 'What we realised', Loach says, 'was that social democrats and Labour politicians were simply acting on behalf of the ruling class, protecting the interests of capital'.[23] His attitude was therefore well formed by the time he worked with the novelist and scriptwriter Jim Allen in producing *Days of Hope*, a historical drama about the General Strike of 1926, but it can only have been accentuated by the experience. In the original novel, Allen writes (through the mouthpiece of his Communist character Goldman): 'Socialism will not, and cannot be inaugurated by decrees; it cannot be established by any government . . . Everything that we have ever learnt about the Left Social Democrats tells us that these people will always support every revolution but the next one!'[24]

For Loach, conflict must continue until there is structural change. Meanwhile, his characters must be content with the little victories, the small triumphs of the human will: finding a job, a relationship, or a home.[25] Towards the end of *Riff-Raff*, the Liverpudlian Shem scores an important symbolic victory. He has borrowed the manager's cell phone while the boss is ordering the workers about; he calls his mother (who assumes he must be calling from prison, before he corrects her). But the boss angrily comes back, confronts Shem, and fires him. Shem hurls the cell phone from the roof. He is fired on the spot, and arrested. One of the workers, Mo, is on the point of throwing a brick at the police car as it drives away, but Stevie calms him down: 'There's more than one way of skinning a cat', he says. 'We'll do the bastards. You and me'. In the last scenes of the film, Stevie and Mo set fire to the building site in a massive arson attack: 'It's a classic case of alienation', Loach says: 'They had taken enough and just said, "to hell with it"'.[26] The final image of the film is ambiguous: we see panic-stricken rats, scurrying through the rubble as the building is set ablaze. Are they to be viewed as a symbol of the working class, the riff-raff of the animal kingdom, destined for pain and suffering? One critic, disliking the ending, has complained that the men 'may be thought of as rodents by their bosses, but certainly not by themselves'.[27] Or are the rats – as Loach has reluctantly implied – a representation of the bosses themselves, predatory and mean-spirited, a metaphor of Thatcherite culture?: 'The whole country has a rat-infested quality now', he has said.[28] Either way, the optimism of revenge is tainted by grim realism.

For some audiences, Loach is unacceptably pessimistic. His spirit seems to clash with the upbeat energy of recent Brit movies like *The Full Monty*, *Lock, Stock and Two Smoking Barrels*, and the less-heralded *B-Monkey*.[29] But there is also laughter in his films; any honest portrayal of the working class must recognise the psychological need for humour. 'Depressions are for the middle classes', says Stevie to Susan; 'the rest of us have an early start in the morning'. There are slapstick jokes in the builder's kitchen in *Riff-Raff*; a quixotic double-decker bus ride into the highlands of Scotland in *Carla's Song*; and the ramshackle football team of *My Name is Joe*, transformed into invincible Brazil with the unexpected acquisition of the requisite team strip. Humour can derail or defuse a political message, as *The Full Monty* perhaps illustrates; it can be (as it must sometimes be) an escape and an opiate. But in Ken Loach's hands, it is an effective mechanism. Humour gives his characters their humanity, and it is their humanity which affects us when tragedy strikes.

Humorous or tragic, Loach's voice is one that needs to be heard; in amongst the flood of commercial thrillers and romantic comedies, a place must be found for the cinema of social conscience. As one critic has written, 'Forget *Four Weddings and a Funeral*. I would much rather see One Building Site, One Failed Relationship, One Death and a Funeral.'[30] In 2000, for the first time, Loach will be bringing his compassion to bear on the United States, with his new film *Bread and Roses*, which addresses the ongoing 'Justice for Janitors' campaign in Los Angeles. After all, despite the rhetoric of universal prosperity, America continues to provide fertile ground for a Marxist critique; as Loach suggested to the *Los Angeles Times*, 'The inequalities are stark, the struggles heroic. The whole romantic notion of the working poor fighting for dignity is overlaid with issues of illegal immigration and, in some cases, revolution at home. And it all happens in the glamour capital of the world'. In a characteristic search for authenticity, Loach has used many of the real working janitors and union organisers who led the movement, while professional actors were required to work as janitors during the night-shift. Loach's producer says that she hopes the film will appeal to the huge Latino audience, and not just to the usual art house film goers. The janitors' campaign is embarking on a new offensive this year. [31]

And, there is always hope, as well as painful realism, in the films of Ken Loach. A few of his aspirations may have even been met in the age of New Labour. He predictably continues to reject what he describes as 'the Blairite project of trying to give a radical gloss to hard-line capitalist politics', and he has expressed public support for Arthur Scargill's extreme left-wing Socialist Labour Party.[32] Loach's politics are now even further from the mainstream of politics than they were in the intensely polarised Thatcher years, but he continues to believe that the ground is still fertile for socialism, precisely because of the impact of the Thatcher years: 'In Britain, the recurring themes don't go away', he has said. 'The human cost of the experiment in free market economics that Thatcher inflicted on us is still working itself out, because the policy hasn't changed and it won't change drastically under Tony Blair'.[33] Yet to many observers, the working-class poverty depicted in films like *Raining Stones* appears to have been alleviated in the late 1990s; Loach's concern with the North and with Scotland is positively fashionable in devolved, post-Thatcherite Britain. There is an air of optimism in the country which was not present to the same degree in 1990, and 'Cool Britannia' is as much an expression of this spirit as it is a political slogan. Ironically, if idiosyncratically, Ken Loach's own artistic revitalisation seems to exemplify the more general rejuvenation of Britain.

Notes

1   See Martin Banham, ch. 8 ('Jeremy Sandford') in *British Television Drama*, ed. George W. Brandt (Cambridge: Cambridge University Press, 1981). Sandford was the author of the original novel, *Cathy Come Home*.

2   Simon Hattenstone, 'Kitchen Sink Drama', *Guardian*, 31 October 1998.

3   Graham Fuller, *Loach on Loach* (London: Faber and Faber,1998), p. 63.

4   Patrick McFadden, 'Saturn's Feast, Loach's Spain: Land and Freedom as Filmed History', in George McKnight, ed., *Agent of Challenge and Defiance: The Films of Ken Loach* (Westport, CT: Greenwood Press, 1997), p. 152.

5   The British Film Industry, vol II: Minutes of Evidence (London: MSO, 1995), p. 60.

6   Leonard Quart, 'The Religion of the Market: Thatcherite Politics and the British Film of the 1980s', in Lester Friedman, ed., *Fires Were Started: British Cinema and Thatcherism* (Minneapolis: University of Minnesota Press, 1993), pp. 15–34.

7   Fuller, *Loach on Loach*, p. 60.

8.   Jonathan Hacker and David Price, *Take Ten: Contemporary British Film Directors* (Oxford: Clarendon Press, 1991), pp. 290–91.

9.   Fuller, *Loach on Loach*, p. 111.

10. 'Film for a Spanish Republic', Ian Christie, Sight and Sound, October 1995.

11   Fuller, *Loach on Loach*, p. 86.

12. Fuller, *Loach on Loach*, p. 85; 'Bobby Beats a Path to Glory', Jeremy Hodges, *The Times*, 12 November 1995.

13. 'Speech That Trips on the Tongue', Franz Lidz and Steve Rushin, *New York Times*, 14 February 1999.

14. Luciano De Giusti, *Ken Loach* (Milan: Editrice Il Castoro, 1996).

15. 'Hard Man, Soft Man', Katherine Viner, *Guardian*, 31 January 1997.

16. 'The Poor Man's Rasputin', Bill Burrows, *Guardian*, 24 September 1999.

17. 'TV's class warrior', Jasper Rees, *The Times*, 10 July 1999.

18. Fuller, *Loach on Loach*, p. 86.

19. Paul Julian Smith, 'Carla's Song', *Sight and Sound*, February 1997.

20. 'Champion of the Working-Class Joe', Richard Natale, *Los Angeles Times*, 5 February 1999.

21   John Hill, 'Interview with Ken Loach', in McKnight, ed., *Agent of Challenge and Defiance*, p. 166.

22   De Giusti, *Ken Loach*, pp. 82–88. Audiences from non-cricket-playing countries will not immediately grasp the reference to Desmond Haynes, the stalwart West Indian opening batsman.

23. Fuller, *Loach on Loach*, p. 11.

24   Jim Allen, *Days of Hope* (London: Futura, 1975), pp.172, 195.

25. McKnight, *Agent of Challenge and Defiance*, pp. 3–5.

26. Ibid., p. 166.

27. 'Out of the Past – Riff-Raff, directed by Ken Loach', *The New Republic*, 15 February 1993.

28. 'Sympathetic Images: Ken Loach interviewed by Gavin Smith', *Film Comment* 30.2 (March-April 1994), p. 62.

29. 'Air of Change, Not Despair, in New Films from Britain', Stephen Holden, *New York Times*, 16 April 1999.

30. 'Rough Humor', Candy Guard, *Sight and Sound* (January 1995) p. 69.

31. 'A Fight for Dignity', Nancy Cleeland, *Los Angeles Times*, 17 October 1999.

32   Extract from a brief autobiographical entry submitted, in vain, for a CD-Rom to be produced by the Foreign Office: quoted by Simon Hattenstone, 'Why FO Is Beyond Our Ken', *Guardian*, 21 November 1997.

33   Fuller, *Loach on Loach*, p.113.

The Thatcher Government and the Politics of the Family

Martin Durham

———

The rise of a New Right in Britain in the late 1970s coincided with the rise of the New Right in the USA. In America the newly formed Christian Right was highly visible in the 1978 and 1980 elections, and the early years of the Reagan government were marked by considerable dispute over abortion, school prayer and other issues that concerned religious conservatives. In Britain, the anti-abortion movement was far weaker than its American equivalent, evangelicals were far less involved in pro-family campaigning and neither considered themselves close to the Conservative Party. Nonetheless, Margaret Thatcher's celebrated defence of Victorian values and her pronouncements in support of the family and morality led a number of commentators to argue that the government that came to power in 1979 was following the same path as that advocated across the Atlantic by such groups as the Moral Majority. Abortion would be massively restricted, homosexuality denounced, sex education abandoned. If the new government got its way, critics claimed, not only the state or the unions but sexual pluralism would be rolled back. Such expectations, it should be noted, could be found not only among Margaret Thatcher's opponents but, in a number of cases, among supporters too. It is the contention of this essay, however, that such an expectation was misplaced and represents a fundamental misreading of how we should understand Thatcherism, the British Right and the politics of the family.

Four issues deserve particular attention. The first is abortion. In 1967, under a Labour government, abortion had been liberalised so that women could terminate a pregnancy if two doctors agreed that it was either medically or socially necessary. There was no explicit time-limit as to the age of the fetus while the grounds on which an abortion could be granted included not only rape or substantial risk of disability but the overall situation of the prospective mother. For opponents of abortion, repealing the Act in the long run and restricting it in the short was crucial and the arrival in office of the Thatcher government might have been expected to have been a boon to their cause. But it was not. Neither the introduction in 1981 of a new form in which doctors had to specify particular medical grounds for termination nor a government agreement with private clinics in 1985 that they would cease to perform abortions after twenty-four weeks was to have any significant effect on the abortion rate.[1] The rejection in 1981 by the Department of Health of the claim that the IUD caused miscarriage after conception and as such should be illegal caused ill-feeling between the government and LIFE, one of the two key anti-abortion groupings.[2] In early 1987 the other leading group, the Society for the Protection of Unborn Children (SPUC), described government support for a bill in the House of Lords to reduce the time-limit for all abortions to twenty-four weeks as a 'sop to win the Christian vote', and it was this issue that was to most dramatically mark the unhappy relationship between government and movement at the end of the 1980s.[3]

In late 1987 the Liberal MP David Alton announced his intention to introduce a bill to reduce the time-limit for abortions to eighteen weeks. 'The only way to tackle the abortion issue', he declared, 'is through numerous small measures, nibbling away at one area after another'.[4] As the bill's second reading approached, however, the Prime Minister announced to the House of Commons: 'as the bill is drafted at present, I could not support it'. Such a stance was 'disgraceful', LIFE proclaimed, and while the bill did succeed in passing its second reading it was to run out of time. The Prime Minister, Alton subsequently complained, had 'become an immovable object that almost single-handedly prevented Parliament from considering the abortion issue further', and while this was to prove somewhat premature with the government's announcement of a fresh vote on the issue, her own standing with the pro-life camp was somewhat less than strengthened by her declaration that she favoured a twenty four-week time-limit and it was regrettable that the Alton bill had not.[5] In April 1990 the majority of MPs supported a twenty-four weeks limit and removed any limit in the case of foetal abnormality or grave permanent injury to the mother. In 1989 SPUC had described the Thatcher government as having an 'appalling record' on the abortion issue. The results of the 1990 vote only served to inflame anti-abortion sentiment yet further, with LIFE describing the leader of the house, Sir Geoffrey Howe, and the secretary of state and minister for Health, Kenneth Clarke and Virginia Bottomley, as leading 'The campaign against the unborn in the Commons'.[6]

If the Thatcher government had proved mortally disappointing for the anti-abortion movement, those who were most concerned with obscenity or sex education found the new administration somewhat more amenable. The best known campaigner on the media's portrayal of both sex and violence, Mary Whitehouse, had already declared before the 1979 election that where Labour took an unacceptable stance on pornography, 'There is no doubt that Mrs Thatcher is genuinely in support of our fight to protect the child and the family'. During the 1987 election campaign, she continued to contrast Labour opposition and Conservative support, and after the fall of the Conservative leader from power, she continued to take such a view, commenting in 1992 that 'Mrs Thatcher left me in no doubt of her support for our campaign'.[7]

But the relationship between her organisation, the National Viewers and Listeners Association, and the government had not always been so comfortable. In its early years, the Thatcher government had rejected the liberalising proposals of the Williams committee on obscenity, placed restrictions on sex shops and supported a private members' bill to classify videos, a move that would ban some and reduce access to others. Towards the end of the 1980s, it had set up a Broadcasting Standards Council, brought television under the 1959 Obscene Publications Act and sought to move against foreign stations transmitting indecent material into Britain. But the restriction of sex shops had been attacked as still permitting them, pornographic videos had been restricted as to where they could be sold, not banned, attempts to move against so-called top-shelf magazines had failed and the government had failed to respond to repeated entreaties to introduce new legislation that would supersede what moral campaigners had regarded as an ineffective obscenity law. In the early 1980s Whitehouse had complained that Britain was 'becoming another Denmark . . . and this under a Conservative Government', while the leading figure in another campaigning group, the Festival of Light, had accused the government of subordinating moral issues to economic ones.[8] The good relations between the anti-obscenity movement and the Thatcher administration had not been unquestionably so, and the same could be said too of another issue of the period, sex education.

Here another group, the Responsible Society (subsequently Family and Youth Concern), was particularly visible. At the beginning of the 1980s, the government had shown itself to be resistant to calls for the right of parents to withdraw their children from sex education classes. Schools should be more open about what exactly they taught within such lessons, the government held, and should make clear whether or not parents could view teaching materials. Furthermore, some of the material issued by such groups as the Family Planning Association and the Brook Advisery Centre, bodies in receipt of government funding, was viewed with disfavour by the government and would no longer be made available.[9] But attendance at sex education continued to be compulsory, campaigners continued to object to much of what was taught and it was not until the 1980s that Family and Youth Concern, now joined by a new organisation, the Conservative Family Campaign, was in a strong enough position to persuade the government to substantially respond to its concerns. Following the introduction of an amendment to the 1986 Education Bill calling for sex education to be taught 'in the context of enduring family life', the government announced its intention to introduce a new clause stating that local education authorities, school governors and head teachers should 'take such steps as are reasonably practicable' to ensure that sex education, where provided, would be 'given in such a manner as to encourage . . . pupils to have due regard to moral considerations and the value of family life'. Valerie Riches, the leading figure in Family and Youth Concern, declared, 'We have been working at this for years and at last we have had success'.[10] The Department of Education announced that it was preparing a circular which would indicate that schools would allow parents access to teaching materials used in sex education but pressure groups were far from satisfied. Family and Youth Concern continued to call for the right of children to withdraw their children from sex education. 'Some teachers', they observed, had 'strange lifestyles and this could be reflected in their teaching'. The Conservative Family Campaign was likewise concerned that 'teachers living in irregular relationships' would use sex education classes 'as a means of proselytising to children', and amendments were put forward in Parliament both to allow parents to opt out and to emphasise that the family life that would be commended to children would be 'stable'.[11]

The government continued to oppose the notion of parental withdrawal of their children from classes but in a speech to the 1986 Conservative Party Conference the newly appointed Secretary for Education, Kenneth Baker, offered a compromise proposal whereby school governors would decide whether or not a school would offer sex education and whether particular parents would be able to opt out of certain classes if they were provided. The Conservative Family Campaign was subsequently to claim credit for the government's change of mind but at the time campaigning groups remained sceptical. For the former Festival of Light, now Christian Action, Research and Education (CARE), the Department of Education draft circular was at fault both in failing to refer to marriage or to define what was meant by a 'moral framework', while for Family and Youth Concern, local education authorities could define gay relationships as families for the purposes of sex education without the new legislation being able to stop them.[12]

Sex education had often been criticised in terms of how it discussed heterosexuality. But it was entangled too with homosexuality, and by early 1986 it was that aspect that was coming to the fore. Proposals by the local Labour Party in the London boroughs of Haringey and Ealing that children should be taught about homosexuality in a positive manner resulted in a ferocious backlash. In Haringey, the local Conservative Party chairman declared, 'No person who believes in God can vote Labour now. It is an attack on ordinary family life as a prelude to revolution', and a local Parents Rights Group threatened to withdraw their children from local schools altogether. Where the Department of Education demanded that both councils provide it with full details of their plans, the Conservative Family Campaign argued that it was the Department's own circular that had led to such developments.[13] National organisations took up the issue, both from the moral lobby and from the New Right (one organisation, the Freedom Association, produced a pamphlet on the question and gave the Parents Rights Group tactical advice; another, the Committee for a Free Britain, published press advertisements on the issue and provided the parents' group with funding.)[14] But having just amended the Education Act, the government remained unpersuaded that any new measures was called for and when a private members' bill on the issue was debated in the House of Lords at the end of the year, its proposal that local authorities would be forbidden from 'promoting homosexuality as an acceptable family relationship' was not supported by the government.[15]

By the time the bill reached its committee stage in the Commons, however, the government's response had somewhat changed. While still suggesting that the measure was unnecessary in light of the Education Act, the government spokesman announced that the government would not oppose it and that he himself supported it. The bill did not proceed, but the Prime Minister declared that it had been 'a great pity' that it had not succeeded and that she hoped it would do so in the next Parliament.[16] And, indeed, it was in the aftermath of the 1987 election that an amendment was introduced to the government's Local Government Bill which declared once more that councils should not promote homosexuality. The Local Government Minister, Michael Howard, announced that the government had always supported such a stance and it was to become law. The credit for passing Clause 28, as it was known, was claimed both by the Conservative Family Campaign and by another moral lobby organisation, the National Council for Christian Standards in Society. But they were not the only claimants to this honour. Margaret Thatcher, one newspaper reported, had been particularly keen to pass Clause 28 when others in her government had not.[17]

Having discussed pro-life disappointments over abortion, we have gone on to explore an area where campaigners had been largely happy with government's responsiveness and another where gains had been made but had been considerably more hesitant. My last example is once again one where the Thatcher government proved to be the opponent, not the friend, of moral campaigners – the provision of contraception to girls under sixteen.

As the 1979 election had approached, protests had begun to appear in a number of localities against the existence of local clinics providing birth control to young people without their parents' consent. This, campaigners discovered to their horror, was in line with a 1974 Department of Health and Social Security memorandum which suggested that while it would be 'prudent' to consult parents, this could not be done without the child's permission. The newly elected government announced that it would review the guidelines and in February 1980 the Prime Minister wrote to a group that had delivered a five-thousand signature petition on the issue that she believed that wherever possible the family should be 'the first source of support and advice' and that the points the group had raised would receive 'particular attention' in the government's consideration of the matter.[18] The group's central figure, Victoria Gillick, had already begun to emerge as the leading campaigner on the issue and when the government's new guidelines appeared, she was to be bitterly disappointed that while they noted that doctors 'should always seek to persuade the child to involve the parent or guardian', they also held that medical confidentiality forbade doctors from informing the parents regardless. The government, the Responsible Society's Valerie Riches declared, had surrendered 'to the tide of permissiveness. We are not just surprised that the present government could act in this way – we feel betrayed'. Gillick, having unsuccessfully sought to obtain a promise from her area health authority that it would not give contraception to any of her daughters under the age of sixteen without her consent, resorted to the courts.[19]

In July 1983, the court ruled that parents did not have an absolute right to be consulted before the provision of contraception. Her appeal against this decision, however, initially met with success when it was ruled in December 1984 that the Department's guidelines were unlawful and that she was entitled to a guarantee that only in an emergency or by leave of the court would one of her under-sixteen daughters receive contraception. The Health Minister, Kenneth Clark, however, appealed the case to the House of Lords which in October 1985 decided by three to two that a girl under sixteen could receive medical treatment without parental consent. Gillick, who was to remain highly visible on the issue, was to author two books on the case. In one, she was to describe the government's 1980 guidelines as an 'abominable duplicitious trick'. Traditional values and stable families, she claimed, had merely been 'electioneering humbug' on the part of the Conservatives, while as for the decision to appeal against the government's defeat to the House of Lords, 'How Mrs Thatcher dared to do such a thing . . . is a measure of how hard-nosed politicians can be in defence of departmental policies'.[20]

Rather than pursue a moral majority strategy, the Thatcher government took a far more complex approach to such issues as abortion or sex education. On the former, although individual Conservative MPs played a prominent part in the anti-abortion movement, election manifestos avoided any identification with the issue and both Thatcher and leading ministers were unwilling to agree to pro-life demands for serious restrictions on abortion. Sex education was importantly different. Under pressure from both backbench MPs and an array of pressure groups, the government shifted its stance on the issue towards a standpoint which presented the family as particularly endangered by the encouragement of homosexuality. Those who campaigned in the name of parents' rights found the government willing to take up at least some of their demands on sex education, but exactly the same notion from opponents of the provision of contraception to under-sixteen girls met with far less success. For Gillick, the Thatcher government was a false friend – and a real enemy – of family values. (Like previous governments, she claimed, it was in thrall to a 'pagan state'.[21]) Yet for the anti-obscenity campaigner Mary Whitehouse, Margaret Thatcher was a genuine supporter of the issues she had espoused since the 1960s. Why the differences?

Two questions deserve particular attention. One concerns the groups to be found on the opposite side from the moral lobby. The Thatcher government was unlikely to be impressed by groups that it saw as tied to its political opponents or espousing an incompatible political agenda. But it was likely to listen to medical opinion, even if such opinion might not be what ministers wanted to hear. In the case of contraception and the young, the Responsible Society cited a report in the medical publication, *Pulse*, to argue that, along with key civil servants, it was the British Medical Association who had caused ministers to come 'full circle' on the issue. In the case of abortion too, LIFE's denunciation of 'Mrs Thatcher's disgraceful decision' not to support the Alton bill had been accompanied by an attack not only on the media but on the BMA.[22]

If we were to examine the development of government policy on AIDS, we would find once again an area where medical and scientific opinion was on one side, and moralists within and without the Conservative Party on the other.[23]

If one factor concerns the credentials of those who opposed the moral lobby, the other question that needs careful consideration is electoral. Evangelicals did not have the numerical strength or political involvement in Britain to mean that a party of the Right would believe that a pro-family stance needed to be pushed to the fore. Catholics were of importance in a number of localities but opposition to abortion never became a mobilising issue capable of drawing those of them who were pro-life away from support for the Labour Party. If neither

Catholics nor born again Christians seemed reachable through a moral majority argument, could Labour voters be won over (or ex-Labour voters be stopped from going back) by a Conservative appeal as the party – and the government – that defended parents? In 1986 the chance of associating London Labour, and by extension the party nationally, with the promotion of homosexuality, seemed to suggest just such a possibility. Addressing the Conservative Central Council in October 1986, the Party Chairman, Norman Tebbit, accused the Labour-run Inner London Educational Authority of distributing 'explicit books which no decent parents would want their children to see' and the following year the enthusiastically pro-government *Daily Mail* gave front page coverage to plans to use a special election poster 'to go for Labour's throat in a ruthless attack on the hard Left and its corruption of Britain's schoolchildren'. The poster showed three booklets, one criticising the police, one concerned with sex education and one for gay youth, the poster's caption asking 'Is This Labour's Idea Of A Comprehensive Education?'[24]

If Conservative pro-family arguments were particularly aimed at Labour, it was not their only target. In 1982 the Prime Minister, addressing the Conservative Central Council, declared that 'permissive claptrap' had meant that for over two decades standards had been under attack and 'The time for counter-attack' was 'long overdue'. In a report in the Conservative-supporting *Daily Express* immediately afterwards, it was suggested that this was the beginning of a concerted campaign against Roy Jenkins, once the Labour Home Secretary associated with many of the legislative changes to which morality campaigners most objected and now the leading figure in the newly emerged Social Democratic Party, initially seen as a major threat to Conservative hegemony. 'Top Tories', the *Express* reported, believed that 'the campaign for traditional values is 'a potential vote-winner', and in the opening speech of the election campaign the following year, Margaret Thatcher attacked the ex-Labour leading figures of the SDP for their past involvement in closing down selective schools, extending nationalisation and undermining 'respect for the family in the name of permissiveness'.[25]

For the Thatcher government, evocation of pro-family themes could prove highly useful in trying to block the rise of the SDP or seeking to win votes from the Labour Party. But if it was unable to satisfy much of the moral lobby, it could not please the most moralist sections of the New Right either. The Conservative Family Campaign, which at its peak claimed the support of thirty MPs, had been specifically set up in 1986 to work for the Conservative Party to prioritise the defence of the family, and while in the 1987 election campaign it had called for prayer for the re-election of the Prime Minister and 'the destruction of the Labour Party', one of its founders, Robert Whelan, had already accused the government of undermining the family while one of the speakers at its fringe meeting at the 1986 Conservative Conference had referred to the government's 'neutralist stance on questions of morality'. Following the 1987 victory, the CFC was to claim that the party's manifesto had failed to refer to the family because 'the government's own record in office' opened it to 'charges of duplicity'.[26] It was not the only such comment.

In the late 1980s, the Freedom Association published a pamphlet by the editor of its journal in which he argued that the government had failed to concern itself with the defence of the family. In the mid-1980s, one writer in the traditionalist conservative magazine, the *Salisbury Review*, praised the Prime Minister's opposition to permissiveness but complained that in practice the government's commitment to market economics was not matched by a rigorous stance on moral issues. Perhaps most striking of all, in a pamphlet produced in the early 1990s by the Centre for Policy Studies, the very body set up in the mid-1970s by Margaret Thatcher and Keith Joseph to renew Conservatism, a particularly prolific writer on the subject of the family in moralist and New Right publications, Patricia Morgan, declared that the 1980s had been a period in which divorce and illegitimacy had risen, taxation had discriminated against marriage and 'sexual deviants' had been increasingly tolerated. 'In the very decade the traditional family needed support, government – Conservative Government – failed it'.[27]

But if some of the New Right were at odds with the Thatcher government's treatment of pro-family issues, we should not conclude that the New Right, any more than the Thatcher government, prioritised such issues as abortion or homosexuality. Like the government itself, and unlike its American namesake, the British New Right prioritised the market economy and trade union reform and gave little attention to sexual politics. Yet if, as we have tried to argue, it is impossible to read British events through an American lens, there is, as the quote from

Patricia Morgan should alert us, one way in which pro-family politics did become important to the Conservative Party. It is not abortion, or sex education, or homosexuality, we should be looking at here. Instead, it is single-parent families. In the USA, both the work of Charles Murray and the Republican leadership's introduction of legislation after the 1994 Congressional victory has drawn considerable attention to the argument that the welfare system has been guilty of encouraging certain forms of family arrangement and that fundamental reform was needed to either end that support or go further and give positive support to marriage. In Britain too, where Murray's work has also drawn attention, the Institute of Economic Affairs had already begun to take up the issue at the beginning of the 1990s, and this argument came to the fore during the ill-fated attempt by certain ministers in the Major government to link John Major's call for a return to basics to a denunciation of what was seen as the spiraling cost and toxic social effects of single parent families. As the first volume of Margaret Thatcher's memoirs were to reveal, she had become 'increasingly convinced during the last two or three years . . . in office that . . . we could only get to the roots of crime and much else by concentrating on strengthening the traditional family'. Although there were limits to what politicians could do, she noted, 'by the time I left office my advisers and I were assembling a package of measures'.[28]

This was a development which could not have been foreseen at the beginning of the 1980s. Instead, for many social scientists, the Thatcher government and the British New Right were to be identified with a moral majority agenda. For Tim Newburn, 'the Thatcherite New Right' had been engaged in an 'ideological battle over the nuclear family and legitimate sexual expression' while for Stuart Hall, the Thatcher government had been 'all too willing' to take a moralist stance on abortion, homosexuality and sex education. For Tessa ten Tusscher, family issues were central to Thatcherism while for Ivor Crewe, how illiberal voters were towards abortion and pornography was a key indicator of how strong Thatcherism was within society.[29] Such interpretations are very different from those that circulate among much of the moral lobby and sections of the New Right, views perhaps most brutally espoused in an article which appeared in the *American Spectator* shortly after Margaret Thatcher's fall from power in which the author, an assistant editor of the pro-Conservative *Sunday Telegraph*, cited the critical views of leading figures of the Society for the Protection of Unborn

Children and Family and Youth Concern during an argument in which he accused the former Prime Minister of appearing not to give 'a fig about the fetus' and of having pursued a 'consistently liberal' social policy.[30] But as we have seen, government policy towards the family cannot be understood as either consistently embracing or rebuffing the concerns of the moral lobby. It was shaped by very different factors from those that gave birth to pro-family politics in America, and those who wish to understand the Thatcher government's record on the family will need to address the different pressures, the accident and the political calculation that underlaid its complex character.

Notes

1 *Church Times,* 29 January 1982; *Human Concern,* Spring 1982; *Catholic Herald,* 29 January 1982, 2 August 1985; *Guardian* 20, 30 July 1985.

2 *Catholic Herald,* 25 September 1981; *LIFE News,* Summer-Autumn 1981.

3 *Buzz* March 1987.

4 *Catholic Herald* 2 October 1987; *Universe* 15 January 1988.

5 House of Commons Debates 21 January 1988; *Daily Mail* 23 January 1988; *Universe* 1 June 1988; *Times* 3 February 1989.

6 *Human Concern* Spring 1989; *LIFE News* Summer 1990.

7 *Wolverhampton Express and Star* 28 April 1979; (Hornsey) Journal 22 May 1987; *Viewer and Listener* Spring 1992.

8 *Sunday Telegraph* 25 October 1981; Crusade January 1982.

9 *Daily Telegraph* 1 April 1980; House of Commons Debates 1 April, 4 August 1980; *Times Educational Supplement* 31 July 1981.

10 *House of Lords Debates* 15 April 1986; *Daily Telegraph* 4 June 1986; *Daily Express* 4 June 1986.

11 *Times Educational Supplement* 15 August 1986; *Times* 8 September 1986; Conservative Family Campaign, *Sex Education and Your Child* (Epsom: CFC, n.d., 1986).

12 *Guardian* 13 September 1986; *Times Educational Supplement* 10 October 1986; *Baptist Times* 25 January 1990; *Evangelism Today* December 1986; Family and Youth Concern 1986 Annual General Meeting.

13 *(Hornsey) Journal* 9 May 1986; *Times Educational Supplement* 26 September 1986; *Guardian* 21 August, 10 September 1986.

14 Rachel Tingle, *Gay Lessons* (London; Pickwick Books, 1986); City Limits 9-16 July 1987; *Times* 10 June 1987; Channel 4, *A Week in Politics,* broadcast on 9 December 1987.

15 House of Lords Debates 18 December 1986.

16 House of Commons Debates 8, 14 May 1987.

17 House of Commons Standing Committee A on Local Government Bill, 8 December 1987; Monthly

News Bulletin October 1988; Conservative Family Campaign, *The Family Needs Friends* (Epsom: CFC, n.d., c1989); *Guardian* 8 April 1988.

18   All England Law Reports 1984: 367-8; *Pulse* 9 June 1979; Victoria Gillick, Dear Mrs Gillick (Basingstoke: Marshalls, 1985), p. 74; *Daily Mail* 22 February 1980.

19   All England Law Reports 1984, pp. 368-9; *Daily Telegraph* 13 January 1981.

20   All England Law Reports 1984, pp. 365-75, 8 March 1985, pp. 533-59, 8 November, pp. 402-37; Victoria Gillick, *A Mother's Tale* (London; Hodder and Stoughton, 1989), pp. 210, 250-1.

21   Gillick 1989, p. 307.

22   Family Bulletin Summer 1980; *Daily Mail* 23 January 1988.

23   For the Conservative Family Campaign's declaration that the government's advertising campaign was 'offensive and an encouragement to experiment with immoral sex and drugs', see *Family Matters* February 1987; for Family and Youth Concern's view, see *Family Bulletin* Summer 1987.

24   *Times* 8 October 1986; *Daily Mail* 15 May 1987.

25   *Sunday Times* 28 March 1982; *Daily Express* 29 March 1982; *Financial Times* 14 May 1983.

26   *Independent* 28 May 1987; Prag Easter 1986; *City Limits* 16-23 October 1986; *Family Matters* August 1987.

27   Philip Vander Elst, *The Future of Freedom: Agenda for the 1990s* (London: Freedom Association, n.d., c1987), pp. 2, 4-7; *Salisbury Review* April 1985; Patricia Morgan, 'The Family: No Possibility of Ethical Neutrality' in Digby Anderson and Gerald Frost (eds.), *Hubris. The Tempting of Modern Conservatives* (London: Centre for Policy Studies, 1992), pp. 35-6.

28   Margaret Thatcher, *The Downing Street Years* (London: HarperCollins, 1993), pp. 628-30; for the Institute of Economic Affairs and the family see, for instance, Charles Murray, *The Emerging British Underclass* (London; IEA Health and Welfare Unit, 1990); Norman Dennis and George Erdos, *Families Without Fatherhood* (London; IEA Health and Welfare Unit, 1992); Patricia Morgan, *Farewell to the Family? Public Policy and Family Breakdown in Britain and the USA* (London; IEA Health and Welfare Unit, 1995).

29   Stuart Hall, T*he Hard Road to Renewal: Thatcherism and the Crisis of the Left* (London: Verso, 1988), p. 90; Tim Newburn, *Permission and Regulation: Law and Morals in Post-War Britain* (London; Routledge, 1992), pp. 187-9; Tessa ten Tusscher, 'Patriarchy, capitalism and the New Right' in Judith Evans et al. (eds.), *Feminism and Political Theory* (London: SAGE, 1986), pp. 73, 78-81; Ivor Crewe, 'Has the Electorate become Thatcherite?' in R. Skidelsky (ed.), *Thatcherism* (Chatto & Windus, 1988), pp. 33-4.

30   *American Spectator* February 1992.

Bibliography

Conservative Family Campaign (n.d., 1986), *Sex Education and Your Child*, Epsom, CFC.

Conservative Family Campaign (n.d., c1989), *The Family Needs Friends*, Epsom, CFC.

Crewe, I. (1988), 'Has the Electorate become Thatcherite?' in R. Skidelsky (ed.), *Thatcherism*, London, Chatto & Windus.

Dennis, N. and Erdos, G. (1992), *Families Without Fatherhood*, London, IEA Health and Welfare Unit.

Gillick, V. (1985), *Dear Mrs Gillick*, Basingstoke, Marshalls.

Gillick, V. (1989), *A Mother's Tale*, London, Hodder and Stoughton.

Hall, S. (1988), *The Hard Road to Renewal: Thatcherism and the Crisis of the Left*, London, Verso.

Morgan, P. (1992), 'The Family: No Possibility of Ethical Neutrality' in D. Anderson and G. Frost (eds), *Hubris. The Tempting of Modern Conservatives*, London, Centre for Policy Studies.

Morgan, P. (1995), *Farewell to the Family? Public Policy and Family Breakdown in Britain and the USA*, London, IEA Health and Welfare Unit.

Murray, C. (1990), *The Emerging British Underclass*, London, IEA Health and Welfare Unit.

Newburn, T. (1992), *Permission and Regulation: Law and Morals in Post-war Britain*, London, Routledge.

ten Tusscher, T. (1986), 'Patriarchy, capitalism and the New Right' in J. Evans et al. (eds), *Feminism and Political Theory*, London, SAGE.

Thatcher, M. (1993) *The Downing Street Years*, London, HarperCollins.

Tingle, R. (1986), *Gay Lessons*, London, Pickwick Books.

Vander Elst, P. (n.d., c1987), *The Future of Freedom: Agenda for the 1990s*, London, Freedom Association.

More Estonians than Etonians: Mrs Thatcher and the Jews

Charles Dellheim

'More old Estonians than old Etonians' – that was Harold Macmillan's verdict on Margaret Thatcher's second cabinet. There is something vaguely unpleasant, or, at least, unsettling, in the old fox's quip, for it suggests that the opposite ratio would have been preferable as if the dominance of Etonians, and a quota for Jews, was closer to the natural order of things. Intentions apart, however, Macmillan's statement highlights the Prime Minister's often-professed and often-cited philo-Semitism as well as the changing nature of the Tory front ranks. Like many 'Jewish questions', the question of whether Mrs Thatcher had a 'special relationship' with Jews makes many uneasy. Surely this topic worried, provoked, or embarrassed a number of the British politicians, managers, and clergy that I interviewed in the course of writing my book, *The Disenchanted Isle: Mrs Thatcher's Capitalist Revolution.*

And not without reason: even those who wisely reject the 'lachrymose' view of Jewish history, as Salo Baron called it, know well enough that singling out Jews for anything but Nobel Prizes is rarely, if ever, good news for anyone but anti-Semites. Such anxieties might seem out of place in modern Britain, a relatively tolerant, and humane society in which hatred of Jews, vile as it sometimes, remained largely social rather than political: a matter of exclusion from schools, clubs, and boardrooms. Nevertheless, it is also worth bearing in mind that English Jews (who number only about 400,000) often refer in conversation to the 'English' as if they themselves were still aliens, uncertain guests visiting an ancient manor house where they are not really welcome. Even so apparently

English a gentleman as the late Sir Isaiah Berlin, a Russian-Jewish immigrant from Riga who became one of the most heralded intellectuals of his generation, distinguished between 'Englishmen' and 'Jews'. I am not suggesting that we should take such distinctions literally, much less uncritically. But it is worth mentioning that English newspapers are hardly above mentioning the Jewish origins of insalubrious folk including many of the figures implicated in the Guinness Scandal. The fact that one of the principal culprits, Ernest Saunders, was an Anglican convert and a stalwart of his local church, made no difference.

Modest as the size of the Jewish community may have been in England from the early modern era to the present, Jews have occupied an important place in the English imagination. This was true, as James Shapiro has argued in *Shakespeare and the Jews*, because the English traditionally used the Jews as a foil against which to define their religious, political, social, and economic identities. This essay examines how and why Jews and Judaism came to occupy a significant place in Margaret Thatcher's political career and economic ethics. The answer to this question lies in her religious beliefs, family background, social marginality, and political experience. An outsider to the Tory squirearchy and a long-time MP for a constituency with a substantial Jewish population, Mrs Thatcher turned to free marketeers, many of whom were Jews, as she sought an alternative to the post-war social democratic consensus. Jewish politicians and businessmen became key figures in the capitalist revolution because they shared her evangelical commitment to entrepreneurship, work, family, and self-help. During the Thatcher years, representations of Jews and 'Jewish values' became a flash point for broader debates about the virtues and vices of the 'enterprise culture'. Such controversies may have had little to do with Judaism per se, but they still offer a window on the capitalist revolution.

Let me begin with how and why Jews came to play a significant role in Mrs Thatcher's world-view. In her memoirs, the Prime Minister made much of her respect for Jews. 'I have enormous admiration for the Jewish people, inside and outside Israel', she wrote. Her philo-Semitism was not unheard of among British statesmen and politicians. Oliver Cromwell, Arthur Balfour, Winston Churchill, and Harold Wilson were all known for their Jewish sympathies. And this is, of course, to say nothing of Benjamin Disraeli whose dip in the baptismal font did not efface his fascination with Jews and Judaism.

Nevertheless, anti-Semitism was commonplace (while Jews were not) in old Tory squirearchy and indeed in the world of small provincial towns in which Margaret grew up. Grantham, Lincolnshire, was a world without Jews. This market town and railway centre in middle England linked London and the North but exhibited few traces of cosmopolitan sophistication or entrepreneurial grit. As a grocer's daughter from a classic lower-middle class background, one would have predicted that Margaret Roberts would have been more likely to have been an anti-Semite than a philo-Semite, and it is to her credit that for all the provincial prejudices she was prey to, she did not regard Jews as capitalist usurpers undermining 'the little man'. The sole Jewish connection that we know of in Mrs Thatcher's early life was a young woman named Edith who was a pen pal of her sister Muriel. This Austrian refugee came to Grantham after the *Anschluss* before departing for South America. Her visit had been arranged by the local Rotary club, in which Alfred Roberts was active. The fact that the Nazi had crushed Germany's Rotary Clubs was one sign of their perfidy. Edith lived with the Roberts family for a time and her testimony alerted Margaret to the plight of the Jews.

What accounts for Margaret Thatcher's interest in, and sympathy for, Jews? As an ambitious, aggrieved outsider striving for social acceptance, economic security, and political influence, it was natural for her to see Jews as kindred spirits. After all, many Jews had triumphed over adversity much as she had – through intelligence, determination, and work. Furthermore, Mrs Thatcher's Protestant ethic accorded well with certain Jewish values: reverence for education, dedication to hard work, belief in self-reliance, and admiration for achievement. Born into a humble background without much money, the romance of poverty was as foreign to her as it was to most Jews. Although Jewish tradition was not universally hospitable to the pursuit of wealth, generally it took a far more positive view of business than the genteel, anti-industrial ethic that shaped English intellectual culture since the later nineteenth century if not before.

Margaret Thatcher's identification with Jews stemmed partly from her deep Methodist concern with the meaning of the Old as well as the New Testament. The historical and spiritual links between certain varieties of inner light Protestantism and Judaism were a source of sympathy and conflict. English Bible-readers may have been suffused with the spirit and ethics of the ancient

Hebrews, but they often frowned on their modern Jewish heirs. After all, the continuing presence of those who refused to acknowledge that the Messiah had come did nothing to strengthen the English claim to be the true successors of the Chosen People. Even so, there is a certain Hebraic tinge to the Methodist milieu in which Margaret Thatcher was reared and which helped shape her world-view and ethic.

In *Culture and Anarchy*, Matthew Arnold's highly influential, if not always accurate, anatomy of the failings of mid-Victorian English Liberalism, and especially provincial nonconformity, he described and derided the 'Hebraism' that supposedly flourished in the great industrial centres of the North such as Manchester and Leeds. Oversimplified and unsympathetic as Arnold's portrait is, the faults he ascribed to nineteenth-century liberal politicians and manufacturers apply equally well to Margaret Thatcher: excessive individualism, materialistic philistinism, insensitivity to the plight of the poor, and a distrust of the state. The 'Hebraic' character of the Methodist ethic helps explain Mrs Thatcher's elective affinity with Jews and Judaism. By contrast, the intellectual culture of the English writers, artists, and academics who opposed Mrs Thatcher so bitterly bore the impress of what Arnold called Hellenism, the Greek idealisation of beauty and contemplation.

Such cultural preferences aside, Margaret Thatcher's political career strengthened her links with the Jewish community.

During her many years as an MP, she represented one and only one parliamentary district – Finchley. About a half hour north of central London on the Northern line (when the Northern line is running properly, that is), Finchley is an ordinary North London suburb that is neither particularly charming nor unpleasant. Finchley is solidly middle class, but it is surely a poor relation of Hampstead, a pocket of the London intelligentsia and altogether richer in capital, architecture, and style. For our purposes, though, the point is that Finchley has a substantial Jewish population, about 15 per cent according to one estimate. Finchley's Jews tended to be upwardly mobile, many were small businessmen or accountants one generation out of the East End. In terms of class, then, they usually fell into the top two social classes used by English demographers. It is easy to see why Margaret Thatcher would feel a kinship with middle-class Jews dedicated to family, education, hard work, and self-help and why, in turn such folk would find her so attractive. Her Jewish constituents tended to be conservative in politics and traditionalist in religion. At any rate, they were further to the Right and closer to the straight and narrow than their more intellectual or assimilated brethren. Such mutual values made it easier for Mrs Thatcher to move from her husband's gin-and-tonic set to her constituency's bagel-and-lox set.

And yet it was no more inevitable that English Jews would vote Conservative than for American Jews to vote Republican. While it is easy to exaggerate the Jewish love affair with the Left, there is no doubt that the East European Jewish immigrants and their children were likely both to side with the working class politically and to try to escape from it economically. Though a certain proportion of English Jews, notably certain well-heeled grandees, were inclined to vote for the Tories since the later nineteenth century, most looked askance at what John Stuart Mill once called 'the stupid party'. For even though dumb Jews are more abundant than either anti-Semitic mythology or Jewish pride would allow, the bluff, unthinking rural English squire living off his tenants' sweat was a most unlikely hero for any sane or self-interested Jew. Though Jews became increasingly likely to vote Conservative as their social status and economic position improved, traditional sympathies for the Liberal or Labour Party proved reasonably durable. In short, there was a rough English equivalent to the American dictum: Jews earn like Episcopalians but vote like Puerto Ricans.

Even the rabid opposition of certain segments of the Labour Party to the creation of the State of Israel did not do the Conservatives as much as good as it might have, because of their own dubious record on the same and related issues. Moreover, the Conservative Party National Office consciously decided against aggressively pursuing the Jewish vote, even though they left local party associations free to do just that. Some did and the 'Jewish vote' was a significant factor in a number of key constituencies in which an electoral swing of a few per cent could spell victory or defeat. However, the prospect of a united 'Jewish vote' was steadfastly denied and discouraged by the Board of Deputies who feared that the appearance of a Jewish lobby would only exacerbate anti-Semitism. Finchley was not immune from social discrimination against Jews. In the late 1950s, the Finchley Golf Club (like many of its ilk) was 'officered by prominent Conservatives' who excluded Jews from membership.

This backdrop made Margaret Thatcher's philo-Semitism all the more welcome to Jewish voters. Always a hard-working constituency MP, as Finchley's long-time representative she had the opportunity and motivation to get to know Jews individually. On occasion, she attended services in a local synagogue or spoke to a local Jewish organisation. Mrs Thatcher particularly admired the fact that Jews took care of each other in her district and elsewhere. 'In the thirty-three years I represented it, I never had a Jew come in poverty and desperation to one of my constituency surgeries. They had always been looked after by their own community', she noted.[1]

But Mrs Thatcher's political ties to Jews went beyond Finchley's confines much as her respect for Jews went beyond her commitment to self-help. In short, Jews played a major role in conceiving and executing the ideology, strategy, and goals of the capitalist revolution. Let me emphasise that my point is not that Jews had an essential gift for, or inclination to, business. Nevertheless, social discrimination kept most Jews out of large-scale enterprises in economic sectors such as automobiles, telecommunications, oil, and chemicals. Ironically, this was the case even in certain companies founded partly by Jews – among them Shell and Imperial Chemical Industries. Eager to keep ownership and management in the same hands – their own – Jews tended to gravitate to rapidly growing industries where the barriers to entry were few and the prospects for profit many. The marginal social position of Jews combined with a commercial tradition founded on necessity stoked their entrepreneurial drives. And Jews focused such drives in small businesses, often family firms. Given Mrs Thatcher's undying idealisation of her father the grocer, the nature of Jewish entrepreneurial activity was bound to appeal to her – and so it did.

It was, therefore, no accident that Jewish politicians, businessmen, and intellectuals were so significant a force in shaping Mrs Thatcher's capitalist vision, her alternative to Disraelian One Nation Toryism. This had little, if anything, to do with Judaism which often stressed the social responsibilities of the wealthy and the moral dangers of wealth. But it had a lot to do with how Jews responded to their historical situation and social position in Christian Europe. Not all of the free-market theorists were Jews – Friedrich von Hayek, for one, was not. And, as Ian Buruma has suggested, the free-market capitalist philosophy put forth by Karl Popper, Milton Friedman, and von Hayek could easily be read as an Anglophile homage to Victorian liberals such as Richard Cobden and John Bright.

The fact remains, though, that Jews figured prominently among the captains of the capitalist revolution. None was more important or influential than Mrs Thatcher's mentor, Sir Keith Joseph. The son of a Lord Mayor of London who was the founder of Bovis, a successful building concern, Sir Keith belonged to the Jewish elite and attended Harrow and Magdalen College, Oxford. But this once moderate Tory with a social conscience, in tune with 'the middle way' between capitalism and socialism, had a political conversion experience. In its wake, he became a born again free-market Conservative dedicated to revitalising entrepreneurship by disciplining the trade unions and dismantling the welfare state.

In search of ideas and power, Sir Keith and Mrs Thatcher tried to form a conservative counter-establishment opposed to the social democratic consensus that had informed post-war British politics. And so they turned to an assortment of outsiders including Alfred Sherman, an East End Jew and former Communist, who became Director of the Centre for Policy Studies, a leading think tank for market capitalism. A number of businessmen joined the fold. They included David Wolfson of Great Universal Stores and Norman Strauss of Unilever, both of whom were Jews, and John Hoskyns, who was not. They brought to the new Conservative counter-establishment business perspectives that were foreign to more conventional Tories.

Not all Jews, however, looked favourably upon Thatcher or Thatcherism. Many continued to support the Labour Party or the Liberal Party. During the general election of 1979, seventy-four Jews stood for Parliament and thirty-three were elected: of these only eleven were Conservatives, and twenty-one were Labour.[2]

Once in power, Mrs Thatcher's political ties with Jews became even more apparent. In her memoirs, she explained, 'There have always been Jewish members of my staff and indeed my cabinet. In fact, I just wanted a cabinet of clever, energetic people – and frequently that turned out to be the same thing'.[3] Whatever the cause, there was a remarkably large number of Jews in the various Thatcher governments. At one time or another, they included Sir Keith Joseph, Nigel Lawson, David Young, Leon Brittan, Malcolm Rifkind, and Michael

Howard. Though this company included more old Estonians than old Etonians, as Macmillan put it, Mrs Thatcher's Jews were a largely secular, assimilated lot. The principal reason that Mrs Thatcher opted for so many Jewish cabinet Ministers was that they provided a welcome counter-weight to the paternalistic Tories of the old school.[4] And, for their part, Jewish Tories, inside and outside of the Cabinet, had good reason to welcome a new regime that challenged the club-by old boy network that was unlikely to welcome them into the seats of power. Hugo Gryn, an Auschwitz survivor, charismatic Reform rabbi and well-known broadcaster, offered a more personal explanation of Mrs Thatcher's kinship with the Jews: her ideal man was the good Jewish husband and father, a reliable, hard-working type like Alfred Roberts.[5]

At all events, the Thatcher government generally pursued strongly pro-Israel policies especially after 1983. But it was not entirely free from the anti-Zionist, if not anti-Semitic attitudes that pervaded the Foreign Office, some of whose officials evidently thought that they were Lawrence of Arabia reincarnated. In 1980, Lord Carrington, the aristocratic Foreign Secretary, had the temerity to state that the PLO was not 'a terrorist organisation' and must, therefore, be brought into a peace settlement. The Foreign Secretary's position was grossly hypocritical given the British government's attitude to the IRA which, by his logic, was as pacific and harmless a group as the PLO. In any event, Carrington's words led to a series of synagogue meetings in north-west London in which the Jewish vote was, as Geoffrey Alderman suggested, 'openly flaunted as a weapon against the government, and specifically against the Prime Minister'. The Reverend Leslie Hardman, for instance, urged his audience, 'especially those in Mrs Thatcher's constituency', to inform their MPs that they cannot vote for a Conservative Party adopting the present stand on the Middle East.[6] Such idiocy provoked an uproar in the Jewish community. Eager to calm the waters, Mrs Thatcher admitted that the PLO had terrorist links – which makes as much sense as saying that the Nazis had SS associations.

Jews and Jewish values also played a part in the debate over the impact of the capitalist revolution. Its terms and tenors recalled the condition-of-England question raised by the social impact of industrialism.

Fundamental to Margaret Thatcher's project was the attempt to reverse Britain's long relative decline by destroying socialism and renewing capitalism.

In the course of her long premiership, this vision was associated increasingly with the struggle to make Britain an enterprise culture, a fine and private place where only the employed dare embrace and which embraced only the employed. For all the considerable economic achievements of the Thatcher governments, there is no denying the human costs of policies that helped certain regions and classes at the expense of others. Even if a shake-out was inevitable in view of Britain's institutional rigidities, we need not subscribe to the view that Mrs Thatcher and Co. could not have, or should not have, done more to soften the blows.

The suffering of the unemployed, the poor, and the homeless aroused the ire of Mrs Thatcher's critics who were less impressed by the glories of enterprise than they were depressed by its discontents. In this connection, no single document was as telling as the Archbishop of Canterbury's report, *Faith in the City*, which railed against the capitalist revolution's excessive individualism and unbounded materialism. Researched and written at a time when unemployment was at its height, *Faith in the City* refused to accept the official government line that 'nothing could be done' to help the jobless. And its authors were no more willing to accept the fact that the pain of rationalising industry fell on those least able to absorb it. The communitarian message of the report was unmistakable: it held that the 'creation of wealth must go hand in hand with just distribution . . . There is a long Christian tradition, reaching back to the Old Testament prophets . . . which firmly rejects the amassing of wealth unless it is justly obtained and fairly distribution. If these provisos are not insisted upon, the creation of wealth cannot go unchallenged as a first priority for national policy'.[7] This passage takes for granted the ability of the individual or the nation to create wealth or jobs. It blurred the fact that Jewish and Christian economic ethics were not the same and indeed that there was considerable variation within each faith. And the passage does not explain precisely what 'just distribution' actually means. (Is it just that those who do work must support those who refuse to do so?) Yet the report did not take an entirely negative stance towards Thatcher policies. It did, for instance, make some mention of the value of local enterprise and of small business. But this was hardly a dominant theme in a document which the Archbishop himself characterised as a Christian critique with political implications.

By far the most controversial response to *Faith in the City* came from the man often referred to as the Prime Minister's favourite clergyman, Sir (later Lord) Immanuel Jakobovits, the Chief Rabbi of the British Empire. Not one to turn away from controversy, the German Jewish émigré from Nazism who had served as Chief Rabbi of Ireland before a stint at a Fifth Avenue synagogue in New York was one of the few notable orthodox Jews to criticise Israeli policy on the West Bank and to call for better treatment for Palestinian refugees. Liberal on foreign policy Sir Immanuel sometimes was, but no such description applied to his domestic social attitudes. Opposed to any force which, in his view, detracted from the family, he was highly critical of both feminism and homosexuality.

Sir Immanuel was also a good soldier of the capitalist revolution. Having criticised the Welfare State as early as 1977 for encouraging a 'get something for nothing attitude' at odds with Jewish tradition, the Chief Rabbi took on the Established Church in *From Doom to Hope* (1985), a spirited defence of self-help, individual responsibility, and the work ethic. (In a similar vein, his successor, Dr Jonathan Sacks, legitimised aspects of Mrs Thatcher's social philosophy by recourse to the Hebrew Bible in a 1985 pamphlet entitled 'Wealth and Poverty'.) Certain that 'cheap labour is better than a free dole', Sir Immanuel argued that government policy should promote work rather than welfare even though he recognised the importance of the safety net for the unfortunate. Work provided a means to build self-respect and nurture pride, both of which were cornerstones of economic success.

Rather than look to government for aid as the authors of *Faith in the City* recommended, Sir Immanuel offered a very different approach to the people of the inner city. He exhorted ethnic minorities, particularly West Indian blacks, to emulate the example of Jewish immigrants whose prosperity came from their own efforts; who took care of their own people; and who respected the law. What the Chief Rabbi failed to address, however, was the degree to which the unique culture and experience of European Jews really could provide a model for those who did not have the benefit of a highly literate tradition and strong families that valued educational achievement and supported economic ambitions. The fact that Sir Immanuel's message was similar, in certain respects, to that preached by Black Muslims, who also called for self-help, did not make it any less inflammatory. More to the point, Sir Immanuel's individualistic creed

failed to give sufficient attention to the Jewish emphasis on communal obligation and charitable work. By 1990, though, he articulated a more moderate position, emphasising his dissatisfaction with the harmful impact of Thatcher policies on the decline of public services, particularly the threats to the National
Health Service.[8]

Within the 'Jewish community' and indeed within the far larger category
known as 'non-Jews', the Chief Rabbi's response to the bishops caused a major
flap. His position was no shock to conservative Jews in areas of north-west
London such as the Prime Minister's own Finchley constituency which was full
of middle-class business and professional families who had worked their way up
from modest circumstances and out of the East End. But even those who agreed
with the Chief Rabbi, voted for Margaret Thatcher, and endorsed the enterprise
culture, feared an anti-Semitic backlash from too close an identification with
her policies. Other Jews were embarrassed by Sir Immanuel's refusal to buckle
under to the bishops or, at least, to keep duly quiet. Liberal or left-wing Jews,
courageous or craven, were particularly eager to dissociate themselves, for obvious reason, from any link between Jewishness and Thatcherism.

Though the Chief Rabbi spoke for a certain strand of conservative Jewish
opinion, he did not speak for those like Reform rabbi and Social Democratic
activist Julia Neuberger. Actively involved in a wide range of social work and
charitable causes, she was certainly aware of the importance of the issues raised
by *Faith in the City*. But she considered its social, economic, and political analysis deeply flawed. The strengths of the report were its success in calling attention to the plight of the poor and its often moving account of the problems
they faced. While Neuberger considered the Chief Rabbi's response 'profoundly unhelpful', and indeed irrelevant to the British situation, she totally rejected
the Bishops' 'bias to the poor'. It wrongly assumed that the poor were morally
superior to the rich. What made this position particularly objectionable was
that it often came from parish clergy who decried the fruits of capitalism while
often living comfortable lives in lovely towns and villages in the South of
England.

The bias to the poor had little resonance in Jewish tradition which had no
equivalent to the Franciscan ideal of poverty. Indeed, it found considerable
attractions (as well as dangers) in being rich, not the least of which was the abil-

ity to use money to do good for the community and to help the needy. A strong, but not uncritical advocate of entrepreneurship, Neuberger was impatient with the genteel hypocrisy of those who found inherited wealth more or less acceptable but liked to look down on those who made fortunes by building business. Eschewing the extremes of the Left and the Right, she sought a balance between competition and compassion. Her centrist approach combined her Reform Jewish roots with her commitment to the Social Democratic/Liberal Alliance. Encourage a free market but temper its excesses and mitigate its inequities by welfare and cooperation – this was her position.[9]

Nevertheless, certain left-wing and right-wing journalists emphasised the affinities between Mrs Thatcher and 'Jewish values'. In a *Guardian* column written around the time of the Prime Minister's first official trip to Israel, Hugo Young wrote that she 'is in some senses an honorary Jew herself'. Furthermore, he implied that Mrs Thatcher was overly influenced by Jewish values and indeed by the state of Israel. He stopped short of urging a return to Christian virtues, but some believed that this was his subtext. Peregrine Worsthorne, the deputy editor of the conservative *Daily Telegraph*, also announced that Judaism is the new creed of Thatcherite Britain – a claim that was not entirely welcomed by all Gentiles or Jews.[10] But such identifications of Thatcherism and Judaism were highly partial and misleading. They failed to consider not only the strong links between Jews and socialism or the 'Jewish values' that had little place in Thatcherism – notably the emphasis on charity and the social responsibilities of wealth.

In her address to the General Assembly of the Church of Scotland in Edinburgh in 1988, Margaret Thatcher finally responded in depth to her ecclesiastical critics. The irony of the uproar over her social and economic policies was that she was the most religious of twentieth-century Prime Ministers. Furthermore, her Government arguably took a more serious interest in matters religious than any of its predecessors since Gladstone.[11] Giving almost equal weight to the testimony of the Old and New Testaments, Mrs Thatcher emphasised the Christian roots of her emphasis on personal responsibility. The subtext was as interesting as the message: the address reaffirmed her Christian credentials. Thus, Mrs Thatcher implicitly countered the notion that she had been 'Judaised' – a commonplace allegation lodged for centuries against those who were sympathetic to Jews. In other words, there may have been more 'old

Estonians' than 'old Etonians' in her cabinet, but the fact remained that for all her respect for Jews and Judaism, she was a good Christian, even if she was not to the manor born.

In Tony Blair's Britain, 'Jewish questions' have attracted little notice. Certain Jews occupy influential positions in 'New Labour' as in 'Old Labour', but their religious origins are largely irrelevant. 'Old Estonians' and 'Old Etonians' remain on the scene. But the question of whether entrepreneurial value are 'Jewish' or 'Christian' is moot. Now we are all capitalists, happily or not.

Notes

1   Margaret Thatcher, *The Downing Street Years* (New York: Harper Collins, 1993), p. 509.
2.   Geoffrey Alderman, *The Jewish Community in British Politics* (Oxford: Clarendon Press, 1983), p. 175.
3   Ibid., p. 509.
4.   Geoffrey Alderman, *Modern British Jewry* (Oxford: Clarendon Press, 1992), Alderman, 357.
5   Interview with Hugo Gryn.
6.   Alderman, *The Jewish Community*, pp. 170–171.
7   *Faith in the City: A Call for Action by Church and Nation* (London: Church House Publishing, 1985), p. 52.
8   Interview with Lord Jakobovits.
9   Interview with Julia Neuberger.
10   *Daily Telegraph*, 10 January, 1988.
11   David Martin, 'The Churches: Pink Bishops and the Iron Lady', in Dennis Kavanagh and Anthony Seldon, *The Thatcher Effect* (Oxford: Clarendon Press, 1989), p. 335.

V

Leadership and the Monarchy

From Thatcher to Blair:
Different Conceptions of Political Leadership

Wayne Hunt

Tony Blair has declared his express admiration for Margaret Thatcher. The relationship between the two leaders has been the subject of much journalistic discussion, but it has only recently received more sustained attention. On one level it can be pointed out that each leader reflects the expectations of a specific era and that each, in turn, embodies a conception of political leadership which reflects those expectations. There is much to be learned from a classificatory scheme which looks at these expectations from a historical perspective. But classifications alone fail to give the full story of the Thatcher's impact – and the legacy of what came to be called Thatcherism. There is another level to this, and at this level it has to be understood that, at the peak of her powers, she restored faith both in the efficacy of government and in the ability of government to solve problems. But she represents more than this. She upset the status quo. She was a true radical. This essay presents the thesis that the Iron Lady's radicalism made it possible for Tony Blair to be radical. His initiatives were shaped and defined by what she bequeathed to him, and to the Labour Party. The nation-state is at the centre of a Thatcherite philosophy. Tony Blair also has views on the place of a nation-state in a global order but his views are more amorphous. Where Thatcher had a red-blooded commitment to the nation-state, Tony Blair took – and continues to take – a more detached view, seeing the nation-state as a malleable construct which can be reconfigured as circumstances demand.

In order to appreciate the difference between the two leaders, it is first necessary to underline the fact that Thatcher was at the centre of a social and economic revolution. She established the political framework which gave force and direction to these changes while engaging in a style of leadership that was rooted in a sense of moral certainty.[1] There is a larger context to this. Two broad approaches to the study of leadership provide a useful starting point for the analysis which follows. The first approach comes from the United States. Stephen Skowronek's innovative study of leadership patterns in the American polity, entitled *The Politics Presidents Make*, argues that those who occupy the Oval Office are persistent agents of change, continually disrupting and thereby transforming the entire political landscape. The same axiomatic set of assumptions can be applied to Great Britain, allowing the American author's methodology to extend beyond the borders of the United States to a different institutional context. But there are limitations to the Skowronek model. Omitted from this view of events is a satisfactory account of the role of communications technology. Successful political leaders are obliged to adapt to the dominant form of their era's communications. In examining the manner by which political leaders construct a narrative and then persuade a number of politically relevant publics that this narrative has utility, a second methodology is needed. This second methodology must be more broadly interdisciplinary in its approach. One entry to a second approach was supplied by a theorist who made Britain his home, Isaiah Berlin. Famously, Berlin adapted the metaphor of foxes and hedgehogs to his own purpose. The aim was to show how a fundamental divide in the approach to life can yield strange, and unexpected, insights into the way in which ideas are translated to a wider community.

Skowronek's purpose was more limited. His aim was to take down the walls that had been erected by those who studied presidential politics in his own country. A distinction, which he found to be arbitrary and misleading, had been erected between modern politics and a pre-modern period. He argued that the experiences of the pre-modern period had much to tell us about how the office is working today. He examined recurrent patterns of presidential politics, juxtaposing earlier periods with parallel periods 'in political time', to use the phrase which he adapted and made his own. At the heart of his enterprise was a paradox. The Oval Office, as depicted in this rendering, is a blunt and disruptive force. Presidents must thereby face the task of reconciling two opposites. Or as he put it, 'the order-shattering implications of the exercise of presidential power' had to come to terms 'with the order-affirming purposes of the institution itself'.[2] In other words, the Chief Executive is part of a fluid dialectical process which initiates political change. 'Reconstructive' Presidents vanquish an old order, change the terms of the political debate, and create lasting political alignments. Included in this category were Andrew Jackson, Abraham Lincoln, Franklin Roosevelt and Ronald Reagan. 'Affiliated' Presidents, as the name suggests, take their legitimacy from a prior legacy. They consolidate the changes which were associated with their predecessors. George Herbert Walker Bush and Herbert Hoover had presidential careers which could be assessed on those terms. Finally there were 'Pre-emptive' Presidents who mix antithetic doctrines. Leaders who fit this description take the cause of their opponents and re-make them in their own image. The paradigmatic example of this tendency came with the career of Bill Clinton. In this he joined company with Dwight Eisenhower, John Tyler and Andrew Johnson as well as Woodrow Wilson and Richard Nixon. Each tried to find a new middle ground on a field largely defined by his opponents. Clinton's use of the 'third way' was the latest example of that tendency. Skowronek's point is that they do not abide by existing orthodoxies. As he put it : 'Theirs is a mongrel politics which offers ... an aggressive critique of the prevailing political categories'.[3] They draw policy positions from either side of polarised debates and recombine them in a synthesis. But it is a synthesis which ultimately bears the imprint of their own personalities as much as their own personal policy preferences.

Viewed from this perspective, Tony Blair would be counted a 'pre-emptive' leader; Margaret Thatcher, 'reconstructive'. Thatcher reconfigured national politics and changed the terms of national debate in the same way that Disraeli did in the nineteenth century. Analogies with Lloyd George in the early part of the twentieth century have also been invoked. But more typical are the comparisons with contemporary leaders. The distance between Thatcher and Blair is greater than Skowronek's categories alone suggest. At this point Isaiah Berlin's celebrated distinction between two polarities of artistic and intellectual expression can offer certain insights.[4] Berlin separated those writers and thinkers who relate everything to a single, all-embracing, all-absorbing system and those who pursued many, often contradictory, ends at the same time. The latter were foxes, pluralist in outlook and cunning in the way that they seized advantage where they found it. Improvisers all, they had an instinctive grasp of the diversity of life.

Aristotle, Erasmus, Shakespeare, Goethe and Balzac were foxes; Plato, Dante, Hegel, Dostoevsky and Nietzsche, hedgehogs. So too it was with political leaders in their moments of highest glory. Lloyd George, Franklin Delano Roosevelt and François Mitterrand could be counted as foxes; Winston Churchill, a hedgehog. In this, the last named historical figure was joined with Konrad Adenauer and Charles de Gaulle. Ronald Reagan and Margaret Thatcher are often included in the second category as are Helmut Kohl and Jacques Delors. But it has to be remembered that the Oxford don's original essay was crafted around the life of Leo Tolstoy. Berlin's point, often neglected, was that the venerated Russian novelist was at one side of the chasm and wished to be at the other. Berlin hypothesised that 'Tolstoy was by nature a fox, but believed in being a hedgehog'.[5]

The argument can be transferred into the arena of partisan politics. In one sense it can be said that all those who strive for public office are foxes who wish to be hedgehogs; this is the nature of the trade. The term 'hedgehog' is identified with statespersonship while to be a fox is to be a mere politician – by common reference a man, or a woman, on the make. This is no mere accident of history. Statespersons have made the grand geopolitical decisions which committed the nation and by extension, the citizens of that nation to a particular course of affairs, of which the decision to go to war was the most consequential. By tradition, statespeople are identified with foreign policy and matters of 'high' politics while politicians, in this use of the term, are identified with the 'low' politics of domestic policy and internal party manoeuvres. By inference, hedgehogs are identified with the moments of high drama in the life of a nation-state. Classifications of this sort, as Berlin allows, are over-simplifications. When pressed they are artificial but 'like all distinctions which embody any degree of truth' they offer a starting-point for genuine investigation.[6] It is in this sense that the categories of hedgehog and fox have a particular resonance for Margaret Thatcher and Tony Blair. There was no sense of 'critical distance' between the private and the public person in Margaret Thatcher. Thatcher was very critical of leaders who cultivated a distance between the two. Francois Mitterrand fell into this category.[7] It could be said of her, as it was said of Ronald Reagan, that she 'talked it like (sic) she walked it'. Not so for Tony Blair, and even less for Bill Clinton. Politicians in Western democracies have been said to cultivate a sense of ironic detachment. The political trade has been called 'applied cynicism'.[8]

Parenthetically it should be noted that irony is used in a specific sense here: as the 'scene' of relations of power which, in turn, are based upon a system of communications.[9] Reasons for this have to do with the great issues of state. The cold war has ended and western democracies have not fought a major ground war in a decade. (As the experience in Kosovo demonstrated, different strategic calculations over the issue of ground troops separated Britain and the United States).[10] But the larger point remains: the issues which dominate the public agenda are managerial in nature.[11]

Hedgehogs are able to adapt to the prevailing communications technology of their era. For Churchill this was radio, for Reagan, as for Thatcher, it was television. To master these technologies it was necessary to talk in 'high concept' terms. Put another way, it was necessary to manufacture a discourse which could be readily understood and assimilated. The neo-conservatism of Reagan and Thatcher functioned in that manner. It was a public philosophy which acted as a morality tale. Individuals have to be held responsible for their own actions. To blame it on societal conditions is wrong. Hence Margaret Thatcher's oft-quoted statement that there is no such thing as society. Rights have to be balanced by responsibilities. Blair took these priorities and made them his own as well as those of his party. The result was the modernising effort to create a New Labour Party. Those sympathetic to the project could say that the objective of economic strength in a new world had always been the goal of the pioneers in the history of the Labour Party.[12] Doctrinal purists were less easily convinced. But as a leader Blair needed a story-line that was understandable to a wide audience. He experimented with notions like a 'stakeholder' society or a 'decent' society. These did not have popular electoral currency but the 'Third Way' did. Clinton had already used the concept in the United States and it worked with electorates there.

Like his famous predecessor but one, Tony Blair was accused of using authoritarian tactics within his own party; and again like his famous predecessor, but one he is not enamoured with, the bulky formality of full cabinet sessions.[13] But the points of comparison end upon a matter of style: the current resident of No.10 Downing Street does not cultivate the imperial presence. His is very much the approach of the 'therapeutic' politician, although unlike his friend across the Atlantic, he has never claimed to 'feel your pain'. Politics must operate within a certain frame which is provided by the so-called 'celebrity culture'. As one historian acknowledges, this 'serves as a form of collective emotional memory, which supports the creation of our social identities, not because we owe allegiance to the state and its institutional occasions, but because we connect the stages of our lives to public people and their doings'. [14]

This did not come as the work of a day. It was the product of a number of structural changes. The first of these was geopolitical. As previously noted, the ending of the Cold War removed the nuclear threat from the public imagination in Western democracies, without, unfortunately, removing the nuclear threat in its entirety. The second structural change is driven by technological innovations and the need for e-strategies. The last generation of hedgehog leaders was identified with broadcasting. Broadcasting has given way to narrow-casting. Advertisers are able to target a number of demographically defined target audiences in a more sophisticated manner and political marketeers are able to ply their trade in a parallel manner. Critics allege, and not without cause, that there is not a sense of greater purpose here. No national vision emerges from the coalition-building. Allied to that is the third structural change. It has to do with the role of nation-states in a global order. Hedgehogs are able to articulate the goals and aspirations of a populace in a modern nation-state; foxes must come to terms with the post-modern state. In this second state of affairs, nations are no longer concerned with balance of power security interests and are willing to pool resources.[15] At the same time a parallel process takes place as the boundaries between public and private lives are rendered less visible. People are made aware of the intrusive part played by the media and more generally by the role of mediating institutions. But there is a paradox in this. A 'post-modern cynicism' explicitly debunks both the image and the process around the image-maker even as it implicitly accepts both of them at the same time.[16] On a larger scale, the nation-state must also compete with transnational corporations and non-governmental organisations for the allegiance of its citizenry.

It is in response to these last named forces that New Labour was obliged to make its most decisive break with the legacy of Margaret Thatcher. Thatcherism forced social democrats in Britain to be more free thinking than their counterparts on the Continent. Thus they felt compelled to emphasise what was 'new' about New Labour.[17] The 'modernisers' around Tony Blair believed, as the Prime Minister himself believed, that statist intervention in the economy would cost the party key votes in that volatile constellation of middle-class electorate, which was their target audience. But the 'modernisers' insisted that a greater purpose was to be served: the aim was to construct a progressive coalition.[18] With these constraints in mind, it made it nearly impossible to seriously tamper with the market-oriented essentials of the Thatcher Revolution. In a classic example of 'pre-emptive' leadership more independence was given to the Bank of England to set interest rates without direct governmental (read: political) intervention.

This was a government that was determined to get its own story out on its own terms. By necessity, this required a high degree of hype and hyperbole. Blair was determined to show that he could be as radical as Thatcher had been in her time in office. In a political tract on the 'Third Way', Blair claimed that modernisation meant moving beyond an 'old Left preoccupied by state control, high taxation and producer interests' even as it moved beyond a 'laissez-faire Right championing narrow individualism and a belief that free markets are an answer to every problem'.[19] Commentary about the various 'Ways' tended to be negative. The Labour Party, as David Marquand pointed out, had a long history of uneasy and ambiguous relations with the intelligentsia.[20]

The Economist was not about to break with this tradition. They argued that Blair was 'convinced that you could do Tory things on the basis of Labour beliefs and be thanked for it'.[21] In order to accomplish this Labour strategists made a self-conscious decision to separate the cultural realm from the economic realm.[22] A distinction was made between a market society and a market economy.[23] (Thatcher's policies had, presumably, erased such distinctions.) But it was with the political institutions themselves that Blair's government was prepared to make radical changes, involving the House of Lords as well as with elected assemblies in Scotland and Wales. Added to this were (possible) experiments with proportional representation and a directly elected Mayor of London. These were features the Iron Lady would never countenance. As one analyst describes it, the neo-conservatism of the Thatcher era was premised on the political hierarchy 'in which the autonomy of the central state from both local and supranational sources of authority was paramount'.[24] Simply put, the socialist threat came as much from 'Red Ken' Livingstone as from Jacques Delors. (The same discovery came later to Tony Blair – after 'Red Ken' was elected Mayor of London, despite Blair's ham-fisted efforts to prevent this eventuality.) Or as the

Iron Lady announced in the second context, Britain had not successfully rolled back the frontiers of the state at home only to see them re-imposed from Brussels as a European superstate (as she [in]famously declared in her Bruges speech of September 1988).

New Labour's public philosophy is predicated on the belief that the Thatcher position on globalisation was defensive. The same was thereupon said to apply to her position on Europe. In contrast, Labour's 'modernisers' wanted to show themselves open to change. But the strength of the Eurosceptics meant that they had to be far from open in their support of a single European currency. Blair indicates his position by way of subtext and coded messages. His is an ironic position. There is another issue which he has failed to define on his own terms as well: genetically modified organisms (GMOs). This is a problem which does not fit the conventional categories. The controversy was made emotional because of vivid memories of the mishandling of the controversy over BSE (Bovine Spongiform Encephalopathy) by public officials in 1996. Ranged on one side of the issue was Tony Blair (or to be more precise, the early Tony Blair – the Prime Minister tended to move with public sentiment on this issue); on the other, Prince Charles. Celebrities such as Paul McCartney and other cultural icons sided with the Prince. There is a clash of cultures here. On one side stands the belief that technology can result in progress; on the other, the precautionary principle – and a cluster of views which are arranged around this principle. On the one side there is a consumerist and metropolitan lifestyle, on the other a rural lifestyle that was given worldwide exposure by events such as the countryside march on London which took place early in the present Prime Minister's tenure. On the one side are those who embrace and take a proactive stance toward globalisation, on the other are those who adopt a more sceptical approach. Falling into this last mentioned category is the present Mayor of London, Ken Livingstone. Included as well are an older variety of anti-globalists, a loosely defined assemblage which George Orwell, in an earlier context, called radicals for countryside and cricket, railways and real ale. This second tradition owes its inspiration to the 'Little Englanders'. It springs from a belief in self-reliance at home which is tempered by a cautious attitude towards what have been called 'entangling alliances' beyond their country's borders.[25] Thatcher gave a clarity of focus to such forces. Prince Charles, in a less ideological man-

ner, brings some of the elements of these enthusiasms into his public pronouncements. The Heir to the Throne has always been known as an enthusiast
for organic farming. On this issue however, he is taking on the role of unofficial
Leader of the Opposition. His stance shows Charles to be a hedgehog. This leads
to the paradoxical thought that the potential future head of a pre-modern institution, the monarchy, might see that institution put to a post-modern purpose,
the separation of the environment from corporate control. Public opinion in
Britain and France and in many other societies has moved towards the Prince
on this matter. He is the one who is acting without irony or artful contrivance.

The same cannot be said of Tony Blair. People knew where they stood with
Margaret Thatcher. She had a clear sense of where she wanted to take her nation.
As she frankly acknowledged, at first she failed to develop her instincts 'into a
coherent framework of ideas or into a practical set of policies for government'.[26]
This changed, and changed dramatically, when her command of government
became more assured. At this point, her former Press Secretary, Sir Bernard
Ingham, could forthrightly say that she knew her own mind, and he knew it as
well. But as one commentator has noted, with Tony Blair, presentation was at the
heart of all that he and his government did. And with Alastair Campbell, the
present incumbent, the job of Press Secretary 'entered another dimension'. But
there was a price to be paid. The clarity disappeared. One Labour activist put it
in these terms: 'When you heard Bernard Ingham speaking, you heard Margaret
Thatcher and when you heard Margaret Thatcher speaking you heard Margaret
Thatcher. When you hear Tony Blair, very often you hear Alastair Campbell'.[27]

The contrast was best explained by Henry Kissinger in *Diplomacy*. Kissinger
sketched out, to the point of caricature, two revolutionaries who stood at the
beginning of the contemporary European state system. The dilemmas they
faced, Kissinger intoned, set the pattern for succeeding generations. On the one
side, the former Secretary of State to Richard Nixon drew a portrait of Napoleon
the Third. The French leader's foreign policy collapsed 'not because he lacked
ideas but because he was unable to establish any order among his multitude of
aspirations or any relationship between them and the reality emerging all
around him. Questing for publicity, Napoleon never had a single line of policy
to guide him'. In Kissinger's estimation, Napoleon had to be judged a failure in
the longer view of history. He represented the 'trend of gearing policy to public

relations' and as such he never moved beyond the merely tactical, never 'bridged the gap between the formulation of an idea and its implementation'. On the other side of this was the Prussian leader, Otto von Bismarck. His legacy was the opposite. He 'did not lack the confidence to act on his own judgements'. He 'brilliantly analysed' the underlying reality of a situation and the available avenues of opportunity. But there were problems with Bismarck's legacy: 'Where he failed was in having doomed his society to a style of policy which could only have been carried on had a great man emerged in every generation'.[28] Substitute the name Thatcher for that of Bismarck, and the same observation applies; substitute the name Blair for that of Napoleon the Third and the observations are given even greater force.

The legacy of both Tony Blair and Margaret Thatcher will be decided over Europe. In the distance between the two periods faith in government has been eroded. Technological and geopolitical changes have undermined the independence of nation-states. But Britain has not been excluded from these changes. As Manuel Castells has noted, 'a renewed Atlantic connection seems to have established itself as the axis of the global economy' but as he sees it, networks 'rather than countries or economic areas, are the true architecture' of this new economy.[29] Those within Tony Blair's circle of intellectual advisers have pushed for an 'internationalist' new 'Way' which would have a human rights orientation. It would focus on issues of international criminal justice, poverty, and the regulation of financial markets.[30] Tony Blair himself exhibits an enthusiasm for markets which borders on neo-liberalism. He has made it his mission to take an Anglo-Saxon form of capitalism into Europe. Should he succeed in making European labour markets more flexible, and in removing the heavy hand of the state from European business practice, his natural career trajectory would be to move towards the Presidency of the European Commission.

Thatcher's most direct legacy lies with the combined emphasis on free markets and on the continuing autonomy of individual nation-states. Those who follow in the Thatcher tradition prefer to be part of a strategic alliance of independently minded nation-states rather than part of an organisation that would allow sovereignty to devolve downwards or evolve upwards on a piecemeal basis. They are returning to their Atlanticist roots by championing the idea of an 'Anglosphere' which would link North America and the United Kingdom.

Samuel Huntington has called this phenomenon 'kin-country rallying'.[31] The Old Commonwealth of New Zealand, Australia and South Africa would fit into an 'Anglosphere' while Japan, as long as it is overly-regulated and protectionist, would not.[32] Conrad Black, a Canadian media baron, has taken up a Thatcherite cause, as have many of the editorialists in his papers. He maintains that the United Kingdom should join the North American Free Trade Agreement (NAFTA). Black argues that further political integration in Europe would be a calamity. His route of preference would be to join Norway and others in the European Economic Area. This would give the United Kingdom the benefits of the free trade while, in the words of *The Economist*, it would be a way 'to bash the sovereignty-destroying, regulation-loving statists who really run Europe'. Thus it is seen as 'the next big thing' for the Right. Republican Senators have expressed an interest in the concept because they see it as a way to move the European Union away from its 'closed' trading practices.[33] Conservatives, as Huntington has duly noted, resent intrusions on national sovereignty from international organisations, courts and supranational regimes.[34]

Blair's radicalism was defined by the Thatcher Revolution. But in one crucial measure he has fallen short. He has failed to reorder British society. Wide-ranging constitutional changes have taken place under his watch but commentators look in vain to try and find a deeper impulse at work which will explain the transformation in terms of Blair's own core belief system. Many of these changes involved ideas that Blair inherited from his predecessor in the Labour Party, John Smith. They do not have a carefully thought out sense of purpose, or more importantly, a visceral commitment, behind them. What is clear is that Blair wishes to reconfigure the foundations of the nation-state while Thatcher sought to reinforce them. Each impulse sprang from a different world-view. The clash of these visions will continue to frame British public life for the foreseeable future, even as it is played out in other societies.

Notes

1   For an extended discussion see Dennis Kavanagh, *Thatcherism and British Politics, The End of Consensus?* (Oxford: Oxford University Press, 1987), pp. 9–22.

2   Stephen Skowronek, *The Politics Presidents Make, Leadership from John Adams to Bill Clinton* (Cambridge: Harvard University Press, 1997), p. xv.

3   Skowronek, p. 449.

4   For a more elabourate exploration see Wayne A. Hunt, 'Postmodern Foxes', *British Journal of Canadian Studies* 9:1 (1994), pp. 87–97.

5   Isaiah Berlin, *The Hedgehog and the Fox* (London: Weidenfeld and Nicolson, 1967 ed.), p. 4.

6   Berlin, p. 2.

7   See Margaret Thatcher, *The Downing Street Years* (New York: HarperCollins, 1993), pp. 797–798.

8   William Chaloupka, Chapters 10 and 11, *Everybody Knows, Cynicism in America* (Minneapolis: University of Minnesota Press, 1999), pp. 129–154.

9   A usage which is based upon Linda Hutcheon, Irony's Edge, *The Theory and Politics of Irony* (London: Routledge, 1994), p. 2.

10   For a more extended assessment see Gwynne Dyer, 'The End of History? The End of War?', *Queen's Quarterly* 106: 4 (1999), pp. 489–503.

11   The most celebrated assessment of the geopolitical and philosophical implications of this state of affairs came with Francis Fukuyama and his essay 'The End of History?'. The argument was elabourated upon in Francis Fukuyama, *The End of History and the Last Man* (New York: Free Press, 1992).

12   This is the approach adapted by Geoffrey Foote, *The Labour Party's Political Thought: A History, Third Edition* (New York: St. Martin's Press, 1997), p. 345.

13   There is a long history of cliques around power and authoritarian 'court government' in England. For an elaboration of this thesis see David Marquand, 'The Paradox of Tony Blair', *New Statesman* (20 March, 2000), pp. 25–27. An extended version appears in Marquand's article 'Democracy in Britain', *The Political Quarterly* 71: 3 (July–September 2000), pp. 268–276.

14   Leo Braudy, *The Frenzy of Renown, Fame And Its History* (New York: Vintage, 1997), p. 600

15   The classic article on this came from Robert Cooper, 'Is There a New World Order', in Geoff Mulgan, ed. *Life After Politics, New Thinking for the Twenty-First Century* (London: Fontana, 1997), pp. 312–324. Cooper drew a contrast between pre-modern and post-modern societies. The former had lost their purchase on the legitimate organisation of force while the latter had gathered state agencies into larger supranational units. Somalia, Sierra Leone, Liberia and Afghanistan qualify for the first category, the European Union, for the second. For an attempt to place these developments in a longer historical frame see Martin van Creveld, *The Rise and Decline of the State* (Cambridge: Cambridge University Press, 1999).

16   For a more extended argument refer to Daniel Hallin, 'Sound Bite News', in Shanto Iyengar and Richard Reeves, eds. *Do The Media Govern?* (London: Sage, 1997), pp. 57–65.

17   A point which was fully appreciated in Anthony Giddens, *The Third Way, The Renewal of Social Democracy* (Cambridge: Polity, 1998), p. ix.

18   See the account in Philip Gould, *The Unfinished Revolution, How the Modernisers Saved the Labour Party* (London: Little, Brown, 1998), pp. 396–399.

19   Tony Blair, *The Third Way, New Politics for the New Century*, Fabian Pamphlet 588 (London: Fabian Society, 1998), pp. 1–20.

20   David Marquand, *The Progressive Dilemma, From Lloyd George to Blair, Second Edition* (London: Phoenix, 1999), p. ix.

21   'The Third Way, Goldilocks Politics', The *Economist* (12 December, 1998), p. 75.

22   Perri 6, 'Governing by Cultures', in Geoff Mulgan, ed, *Life After Politics*, pp. 260–285.

23   In June of 1999 the German Chancellor, Gerhard Schroeder and the British Prime Minister, Tony Blair published a tract entitled 'Europe: The Third Way – Die neue Mitte. Lionel Jospin, a social democrat who at present is the French Prime Minister, refused to sign. Jospin argued that socialists in France had been in power for two decades and did not have to show that they were 'new'. For a critique of the artificial nature of the distinction between a market economy and a market society as well as a more general critique see Ralf Dahrendorf, 'The Third Way and Liberty', *Foreign Affairs* 78: 5 (1999), pp.13–17.

24   Perri 6, *On the Right Lines, The Next Centre-Right in the British Isles* (London: Demos, 1998), p. 25.

25   For a fuller account of the future implications of this force see Richard Gott, 'Little Englanders: The Confused Legacy of a Splendid Anti-Imperial Tradition', in Attila Pok, ed, *The Fabric of Modern Europe, Studies in Social and Diplomatic History* (Nottingham: Astra, 1999), pp. 65–75.

26   Thatcher, *The Downing Street Years*, p. 14.

27   Peter Oborne, *Alastair Campbell, New Labour and the Rise of the Media Class* (London: Aurum Press, 1999), pp. 150,153.

28   Henry Kissinger, *Diplomacy* (New York: Simon and Schuster, 1994), pp. 119,135,136.

29   Manuel Castells, 'Information Technology and Global Capitalism', in Will Hutton and Anthony Giddens, eds., *On The Edge, Living With Global Capitalism* (London: Jonathan Cape, 2000), p.61.

30   Anthony Giddens and Will Hutton, 'Fighting Back', in Hutton and Giddens, *On The Edge*, p. 217.

31   Samuel Huntington, *The Clash of Civilisations and the Remaking of World Order* (New York: Simon and Schuster, 1996), pp. 272–291.

32   See John Lloyd, 'The Anglosphere Project', *New Statesman* (13 March, 2000), pp. 20–23.

33   See 'Britain and NAFTA, Dream on?', *The Economist* (15 April, 2000), p. 56.

34   Samuel Huntington, 'Robust Nationalism', *National Interest* 58 (1999/2000), p. 38.

Margaret Thatcher:
A Test Case of Political Leadership

Dennis Kavanagh

───────

The literature on Margaret Thatcher and Thatcherism is already immense: there is an industry on the subject. Only Winston Churchill compares in the extent to which a British political leader has seized the public and intellectual imagination. Her political record and ideas and their alleged consequences are still a matter of controversy, not least in the Conservative Party. Some commentators and scholars have concentrated on her personality to a greater degree than has been the case for other leaders, while others have emphasised the circumstances which enabled her to flourish for much of her time as Prime Minister.

Mrs Thatcher was a remarkable political figure, not least because she defied so many conventions about the exercise of leadership in British politics. In this essay I shall try to explain the context in which political leadership is exercised in Britain and then examine Margaret Thatcher's significance as a political leader.

The British political system has offered little scope for the heroic leader. Strong political institutions – notably the cabinet and Parliament – and long established political parties have provided obvious constraints on personal leadership. Within government the fact that departments have the budgets, staff, expertise, policy networks and the Secretary of State has the statutory powers, have often checked Prime Ministers. Indeed, the ministers' resources often make the Prime Minister and Number 10 Downing Street look threadbare in comparison.

Any enumeration of the Prime Minister's powers should be accompanied by a warning of the practical limits in exercising them. Timing a dissolution of

Parliament is obviously a political advantage. But if the premier gets it wrong, in the sense of calling and losing the general election – like Harold Wilson in 1970, Ted Heath in February 1974 and James Callaghan in 1979 – he usually pays a heavy political and personal price. The power to hire and fire ministers is also subject to limits. A Prime Minister risks making enemies if he wields the axe too often or does not promote those who regard themselves as eminently qualified. The two politicians most instrumental in Mrs Thatcher's downfall were Michael Heseltine and Sir Geoffrey Howe, both of whom had felt force to resign from her cabinet in 1986 and 1990 respectively, on the grounds that she was acting in an overbearing manner and not abiding by collective cabinet government.

A Prime Minister actually has few direct levers. He or she can intervene in the odd department, as Tony Blair has in Northern Ireland, health and welfare, but at the cost of virtually ignoring other areas. For most of the time Number 10 is catching up or reacting to developments in the rest of Whitehall. This means that Prime Ministers usually shape policy and strategy via their ministers. Yet all recent Prime Ministers, including Margaret Thatcher, have felt frustrated by recalcitrant departments; in her case, she was persistently suspicious of the Foreign Office and Treasury.

That we often classify Prime Ministers as 'strong' or 'weak' reminds us that they vary in their performance. The British system has not been kind to strong Prime Ministers, even those who make their mark on history. Strong leaders usually fall spectacularly. When the Conservative Party withdrew from David Lloyd-George's coalition in 1922 he immediately resigned and was never a serious force again. Winston Churchill, the great war leader, received a humiliating election rebuff at the height of his powers in 1945. Mrs Thatcher fell when nearly 40 per cent of her MPs refused to support her in the leadership election in 1990, a stunning vote of no-confidence.

The point is underscored by the results of a December 1999 BBC poll, among historians and political scientists, on the most successful Prime Minister in the twentieth century. Winston Churchill was ranked first and Lloyd George second. Mrs Thatcher was placed fifth of the nineteen. The two men achieved greatness as successful war leaders, and were single issue politicians, dedicated to achieving national survival. They thrived in crisis conditions, when the normal political checks and balances were relaxed. Their particular strengths and skills suited *the times* when their demeanour and words expressed the national mood: Churchill once said that he was chosen to give the lion's roar. Both, however, were less successful as peacetime leaders and for most of their careers they were not good party men. They took an instrumental view of party and placed what they regarded as key policies above party. Lloyd George, as Prime Minister, was also no respector of cabinet. As exceptions, they proved the rule about the rarity of heroic or mobilising political leaders in Britain.

For much of the post-war period, Britain's relative economic and international decline has diminished the standing of governments and Prime Ministers. A weak economy has not been a suitable platform for exercising international leadership or achieving popularity at home. In the 1970s Britain attracted attention as a classic case of ungovernability. A senior civil servant spoke of governments' task as the 'orderly management of decline'. President Ford in a farewell interview in 1976 warned Americans: 'It would be tragic for this country if we went down the same path and ended up with the same problems that Great Britain has'. In these years, statist ideas dominated the thinking of political parties, commentators, academe, much of the media, and interest groups. Successful political leadership was thought to require the skills of brokerage and compromise with the main interests.

A problem with many analyses of leadership is the lack of clear criteria for success. Winston Churchill once wrote, admiringly, of politicians who 'made the weather'. He had in mind the strong-willed Joseph Chamberlain – but this was a back-handed compliment, for Chamberlain split two political parties in succession and kept each one out of office for several years.

Two reasonable criteria of successful leadership would seem to be:

1. Winning general elections, an indispensable requirement for exercising power. Mrs Thatcher scores highly on this test, winning three general election victories by large margins both in seats and votes. The electoral coalition she assembled was largely English, and southern at that, home-owning, and drawn from the skilled working class as well as the middle-class and self-employed;

2. Achieving a large part of a political programme, and perhaps an enduring shift in the political agenda.[1] Again, Thatcher was successful. If one compares the central policies of 1979 and 1990, one can point to big shifts in the following:

- **Taxation.** By the latter date Britain had substantially lower marginal rates of income tax, particularly at the top rates, and a shift from direct to indirect taxation. Taxes rose a share of GDP but the rate was slower than that achieved in most other states.
- **Privatisation.** The sale of state-owned assets was on the scale not seen since Henry VIII's dissolution of the monasteries in the sixteenth century.
- **Macro economic policy.** The objective of full employment had already been abandoned under the Labour Chancellor, Denis Healey. What was different was that Mrs Thatcher and her Chancellors, Sir Geoffrey Howe and Nigel Lawson, were open about the change and the priority that they now accorded to price stability.
- **Trade unions.** The bargaining power of the unions was substantially reduced and their political influence on government was effectively terminated. The abandonment of prices and incomes policies, meant that anti-inflation policy was effectively de-politicised.

All these policy changes had been widely considered to be politically impossible in 1979. Over time, however, they were gradually accepted by Labour and, as a result, removed many of the party's 'negatives', i.e. the reasons people gave for not voting Labour. Mrs Thatcher's high scores on the above two criteria may make her the most successful peacetime Prime Minister of the twentieth century.

Having over-hyped Mrs Thatcher as the cause of so many political changes, there is now the danger of an overreaction in the other direction. One part of the revisionist picture claims that she was extremely lucky and that favourable circumstances were much more important than her own skills and decisions. She was, for example, not a central player in the Heath government's U-turns over prices and incomes policy and intervention in industry, and not close to the leader. To Ted Heath's chagrin she not only disowned his government's record but was widely seen as offering a sharp break with it. She was lucky that more fancied and senior candidates refused to stand against Ted Heath on the crucial first ballot for the leadership in February 1975. When others joined in on the second ballot, she already had a head start. She was lucky again when Jim Callaghan, the Labour Prime Minister, rather than calling an expected general election in autumn 1978, soldiered on and suffered the humiliating Winter of Discontent at the hands of the trade unions which effectively destroyed Labour's claims to govern. She was lucky, finally, in blundering into the Falklands in April 1982 and managing to achieve a decisive military victory. This confirmed her reputation as a warrior leader, one who could be relied on to defend the state. Yet all successful leaders require luck. The acid test is if they have the skills to take advantage of circumstances.

Electorally, she was helped by the unrepresentative first past the post electoral system and the suicidal behaviour of sections of the Labour Party. For some 42 per cent of the popular vote she gained over 60 per cent of seats in the House of Commons. On policy, she was helped by the widespread perception that the post-war policy settlement was running into the sands. On inflation, employment, economic productivity, living standards, as well as quality of government and social cohesion, the politicians and the political system were not delivering. In the Decade of Dealignment, Professors Svarlvik and Crewe show how even many of Labour's supporters had abandoned the party's core policies on public ownership, welfare and trade unions by 1979.[2]

Thatcher also profited from the efforts of some notable precursors who made the case for a change of direction. Enoch Powell, Sir Keith Joseph, the Institute of Economic Affairs and sympathetic commentators helped to change the climate of opinion. In international affairs, she was helped by the coincidence of the United States, like Britain, having its most right-wing and populist leader in the post-war era.[3]

Another part of the revisionist case points to Mrs Thatcher's failure to change many of the collectivist and social democratic values of the British public.[4] During her tenure the majorities favouring tax increases and further public spending on public services over those favouring tax cuts steadily increased. It is, however, open to question about the extent to which these survey questions tap fundamental political values. They were certainly at odds with voting behaviour in the 1980s. It is the case that Mrs Thatcher was never a popular leader, in spite of landslide election victories. In her last year as Prime Minister her opinion poll ratings were regularly 3 to 4 per cent behind those of her party and she fell to the lowest ever satisfaction ratings for a Prime Minister. This was in spite of the strong tabloid press support for much of her premiership. The papers regularly portrayed her as 'Battling Maggie' and supported her against the 'loony Left' Labour local authorities and unpopular trade unions. She was a gift for the style of tabloid political journalism which was spreading in these years. It relied on simplified analysis, bold headlines, and stories which pitted the goodies against the baddies (particularly the Labour Left and foreigners). Her populist and authoritarian views on crime, capital punishment, the IRA, the trade unions, the EC, Michael Foot, Neil Kinnock and Arthur Scargill were strongly supported by the right-wing tabloids.

Finally, it is asserted that Mrs Thatcher, assisted by commentators, has falsely endowed a series of ad-hoc, reactive and sometimes incoherent interventions with consistency and coherence. Moreover, too much is claimed both for the radicalism of the measures (i.e. they had been attempted before), or there were other (non-Thatcher related) more important factors which produced the outcomes.[5]

Mrs Thatcher was of course helped by luck, circumstances and changes in ideas. But these alone do not determine outcomes. It was up to her to give history a push in the direction she desired and which circumstances allowed.

On the positive side, perhaps Mrs Thatcher's greatest achievement was to restore the authority of government. This had been severely compromised by the failed prices and incomes policies of preceding governments and by the manner, including the virtual collapse, of the election defeats of governments in 1974 and 1979. The corporatist approach in Britain proved to be less successful than in other countries, largely because of the absence of a broad consensus about social and economic policy, and the trade union and business leaders' lack of authority over their members. It is striking to recall that in the 1970s general elections were essentially about which political party could best deliver a prices and incomes policy, and this boiled down to who could get the consent of the trade unions. The question placed the Conservatives at a severe disadvantage.

The New Right, however, argued that the government's reach was exceeding its grasp. It should rein back its responsibilities and concentrate on essentials – maintaining law and order, defending the realm and protecting the value of the currency. It took time and persistence to win this debate among opinion-formers. In 1981 the bulk of the economics profession called for the abandonment of the Thatcher government's economic policies and return to Keynesianism.

Significant sections of the Conservative Party were also still wedded to incomes policies and intervention in industry.

In overturning so much of the post-war policy package, Mrs Thatcher also ended the dominance of the 'wets' in the Conservative Party. In the early years this outcome did not look assured. Her first cabinet was dominated by members of the Heath government and by ministers who had voted for him over her on the first ballot of the leadership election.

But overturn it she did – witness the changes in the Labour Party after 1987. One of the cleverest writers on Conservative politics at the time was the late Professor Jim Bulpitt.[6] He argued that by 1975 the Conservative Party was suffering a crisis of what he calls *statecraft*, essentially, how to win general elections and govern effectively. Mrs Thatcher's own agenda, aided by Labour ineptitude, helped to win elections and her reliance on monetarism rather than incomes policies and on privatisation of the nationalised industries, helped the government to achieve a degree of autonomy from pressure groups. Monetarism, for example, meant that ministers no longer required an incomes policy and deals with the trade unions. Bulpitt is one of those who does not detect any great consistency in ideas in the first Thatcher government, but emphasises the greater importance of its search for 'a governing competence' via a reassertion of 'traditional central autonomy.'

She also successfully challenged the wisdom about the significance of unemployment and voting behaviour. Only a few years earlier it would have seemed unthinkable for a government to win an election, having presided over a doubling of the numbers unemployed to more than three million. This loosening of the relationship between the state of the economy and voting behaviour involved educating voters into accepting that other issues were also important and that the government was no longer primarily responsible for economic outcomes. It also needed the Labour Party to behave in such a way that voters doubted that it could do any better.[7]

Thatcher's impact on the premiership as an institution was limited. Of all her post-war predecessors only Harold Wilson in 1964 entered office with less cabinet experience. Wilson, the creator of a Political Office in Number 10 in 1964 and a Policy Unit in 1974, left more of an institutional legacy. Over time she appointed more advisers but her staff numbers were still modest, certainly when compared to Tony Blair's. At its peak, her Political Office, Policy Unit and the handful of advisers amounted to no more than a dozen staff. Blair has over thirty. There was no Prime Minister's Department and, in spite of urgings from her more zealous supporters, no politicisation of the top tiers of the civil service.[8]

But she certainly left behind an example of what a Prime Minister with a strong personality, sense of direction, will power, and self-confidence backed by a large parliamentary majority and other favourable circumstances, could achieve. She expanded, even strained, the parameters of the premiership. Some critics, aware of the decline in the number of cabinet meetings and of papers distributed to it, as well as her reliance on ad-hoc committees and informal working parties, have argued that she weakened the cabinet. She also made fewer statements and speeches in the House of Commons than most of her predecessors.

In retrospect, we can now see that these features were part of a longer-term trend in the premiership. Tony Blair's approach to cabinet has been decidedly Thatcherite and, indeed, he has expressed admiration for her approach. Research by a team at the London School of Economics also shows that during the course of the twentieth century Parliament has been making fewer demands on the time of the Prime Minister.[9] Interestingly, Blair, like Thatcher has also expressed impatience at times with what he dismisses as 'the forces of Conservatism', particularly in the public sector.

Thatcher (like Blair again) also practised what some US commentators have called 'spatial leadership'.[10] Presidents Reagan and Clinton, to take two recent examples, frequently called on voters to support them against the claims of the federal government and of special interests. They cultivated, as it were, a sense of detachment from their own government. When she became leader in 1975 Thatcher was already something of an outsider, partly because she was a woman in a male-dominated profession and partly because she had challenged the incumbent for the leadership. As Prime Minister she frequently distanced herself from her colleagues, notably the wets. These were the target for her famous Conference speech in 1981 when she warned, 'U-turn if you want. The lady's not for turning'.[11]. At an early stage, one commentator observed: 'Mrs Thatcher seems more of an external pressure group on her cabinet than the traditional resolver of the conflicting forces. She hectors, bullies and bashes ministers mercilessly'.[12] The press often led with such headlines as that 'Maggie Steps In' as she intervened to sort out some mess caused by her colleagues. This was a Prime Minister who once described herself as 'the cabinet rebel', in contrast to Clement Attlee who saw his role as 'to collect the voices of the cabinet'.

There was little evidence of cronyism in her ministerial appointments. There was rarely a Thatcherite majority in her cabinets and by 1990 most of the cabinet had probably lost sympathy with her. In her memoirs she writes of various cabinet ministers, including Chris Patten, Malcolm Rifkind, Ken Clarke and William Waldegrave, as 'not of my persuasion'. But she appointed them because of their ability.

One has to be cautious about assuming that the party in Parliament or in the country was fully behind her. During the 1980s grass roots party membership steadily declined and surveys suggest that members were far from enamoured of her policies. Professor Philip Norton has calculated, on the basis of his analysis of Conservative MPs' voting records and signature of Early Day Motions, that less than a fifth were true Thatcherites.[13] Nearly 60 per cent were what he called party faithful, MPs who were primarily concerned to have a leader who could keep the party united and win a general election. By 1990 Mrs Thatcher was failing to do either. She was destabilising the Cabinet, particularly on Europe. A growing number of colleagues now regarded some of her qualities as weaknesses. Ironically, the new generation of Conservative MPs elected in 1992 and 1997 proved to be truer 'Thatcher's children'. Given the reservations which many ministers and MPs had about her, it is remarkable that Mrs Thatcher achieved so much.

Britain may have what Mrs Thatcher's Press Secretary, Bernard Ingham, has termed a pendulum pattern in political leadership. One type of leadership, pushed to an extreme, breeds a reaction against it. In 1916 the dynamic Lloyd George followed Asquith ('wait and see'), and he in turn was succeeded by the colourless Bonar Law. Mrs Thatcher followed the laid-back Wilson and Callaghan and she in turn was followed by John Major, a very different kind of Prime Minister. Indeed, when she stepped down as leader in 1990, all three candidates to succeed her pledged to restore cabinet government and listen to MPs – code for being more collegial. John Major in turn has bred a reaction in the shape of the more activist and commanding Tony Blair. There is something in this, although I believe that over time the trend has been for Prime Ministers to exercise more of a strategic oversight of government and also to strengthen themselves vis-a-vis their colleagues.[14]

Mrs Thatcher offered what might be termed a mobilising rather than a conciliatory style of leadership. The former is primarily concerned with the achievement of objectives, even if this involves offending significant interests. Lloyd George was a famous predecessor, in peace and in war, as was Joseph Chamberlain. To be effective, and to gather popular support, the approach requires widely identified enemies, as in a war or an economic crisis or an impatience with the status quo. Margaret Thatcher won her battles with the Labour left, trade unions, corporatism, and General Galtieri. By 1990, however, she had run out of credible enemies and the abrasive, handbagging style found fewer takers. That was a mark of success but it also proved to be her undoing in the end. The qualities that helped to make her successful eventually undermined her because the circumstances had changed.

Notes

1   Dennis Kavanagh, *Thatcherism and British Politics* (Oxford: Oxford University Press, 1990).

2   Bo Särluik and Ivor Crewe, *The Decade of Dealignment* (Cambridge: Cambridge University Press, 1983.

3   On the ideas, see John Ranelagh, *Thatcher's People* (London: Fontana, 1992), special issue of Contemporary British History, 1996 and Dennis Kavanagh, *The Reordering of British Politics* (Oxford: Oxford University Press, 1997), chapters 5 and 7.

4   Ivor Crewe, 'Values, The Crusade That Failed', in Dennis Kavanagh and Anthony Seldon.

5   David Marsh and R.A.W. Rhodes (eds.), *Implementing Thatcherite Politics: Audit of an Era*, Brighton: Open University Press, 1992.

6   Jim Bulpitt, 'The Thatcher Statescraft', in *Political Studies*, 1986.

7   Dennis Kavanagh and Anthony Seldon, *The Powers Behind the Prime Minister* (London: HarperCollins, 1999)

8   Ibid.

9   Patrick Dunleavy et al, 'Leaders, Politics and Institutional Change: The Decline of Prime Ministerial Accountability to the House of Commons, 1868–1990', in R.A.W. Rhodes and Patrick Dunleavy (eds.), *Prime Minister, Cabinet and Core Executive* (London: St. Martin's Press, 1995).

10   Michael Foley, *The Rise of the British Presidency* (Manchester: Manchester University Press, 1993).

11   Peter Norton, 'The Lady's Not For Turning; But What About the Rest?', in *Parliamentary Affairs*, 1990.

12   *Economist*, 4 October 1980.

13   Norton, p. 45.

14   Dennis Kavanagh and Anthony Seldon, *The Powers Behind the Prime Minister*.

Margaret Thatcher and Innovative Leadership

Jeremy Moon[1]

[Leadership is] an instrument of goal achievement . . . leadership transforms followers, creates visions of the goals that may be attained, and articulates for the followers the ways to attain these goals.[2]

Margaret Thatcher has been interpreted in various ways. Some authors argue that there was a Thatcher effect and that this was a good thing.[3] Others claim that she made a difference and that this was a bad thing.[4] A third group argues that her governments were associated with major change but the underlying cause was in the structure of the economy[5] or ideological.[6] A fourth group is sceptical about Thatcher having distinctive impacts due either to failure on her part or to the 'realities' of politics.[7] Thus the question as to whether Thatcher was instrumental in policy changes in Britain during the 1980s remains contested.

Different approaches to the question of Thatcher's political leadership generate different conclusions about her impacts. This chapter presents a 'mixed approach' to evaluating Thatcher's leadership in the policy areas of unemployment, trade unions and privatisation. It concludes that Thatcher should be regarded as an innovative leader in these areas because she was indispensable to policy changes therein. It offers an implicit critique of those who explain these policy areas in the 1980s without reference to a 'Thatcher effect'. But it cautions against extrapolating from these cases due to variability in Thatcher's capacity to lead and to the differential interplay of her leadership with institutions on the one hand and circumstances or 'fortuna' on the other.

Assessing political leadership in democracy is difficult for a number of reasons. Because it is a normatively loaded term, commentators are often reluctant to ascribe leadership to those whose politics they disapprove of. Leadership is often confused with the simple holding of office such that any actions of a Prime Minister are described as leadership. Thirdly, it is difficult to isolate leadership effects from other political phenomena because democracies are highly complex and inter-dependent systems. It is therefore difficult to be sure about what would have transpired without the actions of the leader – the counterfactual problem. Fourthly, although leadership is about rhetoric, style and substance, rhetoric and style can sometimes be confused with substance: after all most con-tenders for office claim to offer leadership. These conceptual and methodologi-cal difficulties are compounded when the candidate for the epithet leader has had as contentious a profile as Thatcher.

This essay offers an approach to Thatcher's leadership which is analytical rather than normative. It focuses on her impacts rather than on the powers of a British Prime Minister. Recognising the complexity of policy-making, it distills leadership effects through the use of a simple model. Comparison is used to establish the relative significance of her impacts and to address the counterfac-tual problem. The substance is distinguished from the style of Thatcher's lead-ership by testing the connection between her goals, the means deployed to pur-sue these and the political outcomes. It does not rely on Thatcher's self-assess-ments. In order to highlight the distinctive features of this approach, two other methods of evaluation of the Thatcher effect are first presented.

Scholars tend to use one of two sorts of yardstick to evaluate leadership effects. First, there are a priori models, whereby behaviour is assessed against some specified general criteria of leadership. Secondly, there are a posteriori approaches which judge behaviour in terms of its own significance, usually through comparison with similar cases. Both approaches been deployed in the case of Thatcher.

A Priori Approaches

The attraction of a priori approaches to evaluation is the promise of verification which is based on criteria devised 'outside' the experience of the politics in ques-tion. Marsh and Rhodes use Sabatier's test of top-down implementation.[8] They do so partly to challenge Savage and Robins'[9] conclusions that 'there was a clear

Thatcher effect [in] housing, industrial relations, privatisation and local government'.[10] According to Sabatier, perfect implementation consists of perfect continuity between outcomes and intentions. Applying this to Thatcher, Marsh and Rhodes argue that there is considerable evidence of outcomes not achieved and of change being caused by factors other than Thatcher's policies. Yet they also note that:

policy-making is not a simple, top-down process. It is subject to short falls at every stage. Given the conditions required for effective implementation, no government, not even one with illusions (sic) of grandeur, is either omnipotent or omnicompetent.[11]

Thus Marsh and Rhodes demonstrate that this is too strong a test of a Thatcher effect. If no government can pass the test, then it does not assist investigating whether one Prime Minister had a greater than usual impact on policy change.[12] But this is not to say that the a priori approach has no value in helping us to understand leadership and an alternative test is presented below.

A Posteriori Approaches

A posteriori approaches base conclusions about politics on the comparative significance of the data themselves. One obvious technique is to compare Thatcher's impact with those of other peacetime prime ministers who shared the broad institutional context of that office. Most such comparisons conclude that few of her predecessors matched Thatcher's activist style and impact. Clarke argues that only Gladstone matches Thatcher's ability to set political agendas and to mobilise support. Of both prime ministers he concludes that: 'their own outlook and gifts chimed in with the contemporary mood, anticipating rather than simply echoing it, so that they were able literally to speak to the concerns of the people'.[13]

King concludes that other twentieth-century peacetime prime ministers did not have a distinctive impact because they generally adopted a collegial approach to government; were relatively cautious so as to avoid party rebellion; and did not have agendas distinctive from those of their cabinet colleagues.[14] Thatcher, in contrast, had a broadly based agenda of her own which she was determined to pursue even at the risk of defeat (and some of her proposals were defeated). As a result, King concludes, she won often and government changed dramatically.

Jenkins singles out Thatcher for her domination of cabinet and her personal stamp on the full range of government business.[15] Likewise, Young comments on the hold 'she exerted over a quite unusually high proportion of the policies her government pursued. What she supported tended to happen. What she neglected or opposed tended not to happen'.[16] Finer concurs: 'She impressed herself upon government as nobody has done since the war years of Churchill'.[17]

But it could be objected that it is inappropriate to compare leaders in such different historical circumstances. Another a posteriori approach is therefore to compare Thatcher with heads of other governments of her day. Marsh and Rhodes reject the view that Thatcher had a distinctive impact on British industrial relations by noting that the contemporaneous Spanish industrial relations reform constituted a yet more dramatic attack on trade union power.[18] But the significance of this point is unclear given that trade unions had enjoyed a much longer period of workplace and political legitimacy in Britain than in Spain. Whilst other heads of government also grappled with the problems Thatcher faced, such as fiscal stress, inflation, unemployment and industrial adjustment, the significance of their impacts is obscured by their different political and socio-economic circumstances.

The Thatcher-Reagan comparison is frequently invoked due to some similar domestic agendas. But the utility of the comparison is questionable. In order to pass domestic legislation, US presidents face two houses of Congress in which, even in the rare event that their party is in the majority, the relative lack of party discipline means that government bills are not assured. Thereafter, legislation is vulnerable to judicial review.[19] Similarly, in most parliamentary systems, cabinets and legislative majorities consist of coalitions often reflecting proportional electoral systems. In some, upper houses are hostile and powerful. Others are federal or have constitutionally entrenched local government. Because Thatcher, like most British prime ministers, had fewer institutional constraints on her legislative initiative than most of her contemporary counterparts, it could be argued that comparison with most contemporary leaders in democracies is too weak a test of the Thatcher effect.

A Mixed Approach to Innovative Leadership

A mixed approach combines a priori elements with a posteriori tests of

Thatcher's impact. I offer an a priori model of innovative leadership in which goals, means and outcomes need to be identified and connected in such a way as to explain the behaviour of followers and the achievement of substantive changes. The significance of these impacts is tested by appropriate a posteriori comparisons.

The adjective innovative signals leadership that is associated with substantial change, whether this be in terms of its scope, scale or speed. It therefore contrasts with the leadership which brings stability in times of crisis. Following Bass's definition of leadership (above), for the model of innovative leadership to be met, the following conditions to be established:

1   that the leader intended innovative change – goals;
2   that they pursued these through the means of strong political will and strong policy capacity tempered by a sense of proportion, and;
3   that these means contributed to follower beliefs and behaviours and to substantive political outcomes that would not otherwise have been expected.

If we know a leader's goals, we have some yardstick for evaluation and can check that responsibility for outcomes is not only claimed with the benefit of hindsight. The terms in which political goals are stated vary. Sometimes they are programmatic, as in the case of the 1974 Labour government. Sometimes they are posed in terms of a broad vision to which policy details must conform, as in de Gaulle's project of 'grandeur' for Fifth Republic France. Within the context of such broad visions, particular goals may be set iteratively and revised in response to circumstances. In either case there is the possibility of dynamic agenda-setting in which goals and means are selected and amended in response to changing circumstances.[20]

Some of Thatcher's goals were policy specific and others combined conservative and neo-liberal ideology. Though some analysts give explanatory pre-eminence to the ideology itself,[21]

It is ideas in the form of economic theories and the policies developed from them, that enable national leaders to chart a course through turbulent economic times, and ideas about what is efficient, expedient, and just that motivate the movement from one line of policy to another.

Structural accounts can tell us a great deal about the constraints facing policy-makers, but policy making is based on creation as well as constraint.[22]

Secondly, the model requires evidence of means adopted to secure the goals. These means can be conceptualised in different ways. I distinguish political will and policy capacity. When these are strong, the means for leadership are maximised. This contrasts with the three other possible combinations of these variables:

1   weak political will and strong policy capacity which yield managerialism;
2   weak political will and weak policy capacity which yield inertia; and
3   strong political will and weak policy capacity which together yield zealotry.[23]

Strong political will refers to an unusual commitment to goals even in the face of opposition or obstacles. Thatcher possessed this, presenting herself and being perceived as a conviction politician. She understood politics in moral rather than pragmatic terms. Her 'political style . . . always depended to an unusual degree on this search for "rightness".[24] In contrast, her Conservative predecessors usually conformed to Lord Salisbury's preference for scepticism and pragmatism.[25] Thatcher's political will was applied to the full range of government activity compared with the more selective and delegatory approaches of her predecessors. One could never imagine Thatcher subscribing to Attlee's view that 'being Prime Minister left more spare time than any other job that he had done'.[26] Thatcher's strong political will is conveyed by Kavanagh's claim that: "her own perception of herself (courageous, persistent, and sticking to a course no matter how unpopular), is matched by public perception . . . for nearly ten years now voters have agreed about her strength of personality and outspokenness."[27]

Strong policy capacity is required to channel political will in pursuit of innovative goals. Two key components of policy capacity can be distinguished: cognitive and instrumental. These need to be tempered by a sense of proportion.

Cognitive capacity is the ability to understand issues and the implications of alternative responses: 'the ability to match policy goals with political possibilities' and 'a knowledge of the centre of political gravity'.[28] Thatcher's appetite for policy is legendary:

From the first hour she established her desire to see everything and do everything. At the end of the first week, one of her officials told me, 'She reads every paper she gets and never fails to write a comment on it' . . . She was at the beginning, incurably interventionist. This was partly by calculation . . . [B]ut it was also a matter of instinct . . . As she discovered things, however, there was soon a change of mood. In a very short time, a process of mutual education impressed itself on her and her staff . . . She was good at taking a brief, even though she invariably challenged the first draft, and she was particularly admired for attention to the footnotes.[29]

Instrumental capacity denotes organisational mastery, the command of forces to secure intended purposes. This is illustrated by its lack in John Major, Thatcher's successor, who was very dependent on the cabinet's 'big beasts' in time his unwillingness or inability to assert himself lead to charges of weakness, and letting circumstances and the push and pull of other people determine issues.[30]

Thatcher's instrumental capacity was founded on ensuring that cabinet members and her immediate advisers were the right kind of people. She used ad hoc groups and cabinet committees to prepare the ground before proposals reached cabinet: '[I]f there is a problem or a proposal she'll call a meeting involving those immediately concerned. She may also invite someone who will be important when it comes to selling it in cabinet'.[31]

However, for the 'passions' of political will to be tempered by cognitive and instrumental resources, leaders also require some distance from politics or, a sense of proportion. As Weber puts it: 'the decisive psychological quality of the politician: his ability to let realities work on him with inner concentration and calmness'.[32] Weber argued that leaders need to avoid vanity when political objectives become replaced by 'personal self-intoxification': 'the politician inwardly has to overcome a quite trivial and all-too-human enemy: a quite vulgar vanity, the deadly enemy of all matter of fact devotion to a cause [in order to maintain a] distance towards one's self'.[33] Again, this can be illustrated in its deficiency in John Major, who is said to have suffered from personal insecurity, a thin-skinned over sensitivity to criticism, and perhaps an emotional need to be liked by or to please others, which meant that when the political going got harder, he did not have the inner resources to provide steely leadership.[34]

Political will and policy capacity are dynamic. They may wax as through experience leaders learn about and seek to improve their means of securing their goals. They may also wane as leaders lose their sense of proportion. For the most part, Thatcher was able to subordinate her considerable pride so as to effectively channel her equally considerable convictions. Hence she deferred to cabinet colleagues on approaches to the welfare state and the National Health Service, for example. On other issues, though, her leadership was undermined by her lack of distance when she maintained strong political will in the absence of corresponding cognitive and instrumental capacities.

Finally, as with any model of leadership, we need to establish Thatcher's relations with followers. As Burns observes, 'One man leadership is a contradiction in terms'.[35] Whilst leaders 'influence more than they are influenced'[36], their relations with followers are not uni-directional. In setting directions, leaders must attend to the often unspoken inclinations and capacities of those they are claiming to lead. In this model, three concentric circles of followers can be distinguished: leadership networks; the faithful and the masses. Empirically, however, these categories overlap and the boundaries shift.

Leadership networks refer to those closely involved in the leadership project. They enhance a leader's capacity by providing suggestions and sounding boards. Thatcher's leadership networks included some cabinet members, a small No10 Downing Street team and close friends with whom she tested ideas.[37]

The faithful are those who support the leader's basic goals and in parliamentary systems; this usually means their party. Thatcher was at times the darling of the grass-roots Conservatives but she was more isolated within the Conservative Parliamentary Party than her predecessors.[38] She did not provoke a cultural revolution among MPs, only a minority of whom could be described as Thatcherite.[39] Her support rested on the energy she put into winning their loyalty and persuading them that she would deliver electoral victory:

Where Heath despised backbenchers, and often did not know their names, Mrs Thatcher set about cultivating them with manic energy and involving them, or so they imagined, in the making of policy. As many as seventy-five policy groups existed at one time, many of them peopled by backbenchers."[40]

The third circle of followers, the masses, is the electorate. Whilst in terms of seats, she had three huge election victories, 'Thatcher never won the support of vast numbers of voters, suggesting that there was no Thatcherite transformation of attitudes or behaviour among the British public. If anything, the British have edged further away from Thatcherite positions as the decade has progressed. The Thatcher governments have undoubtedly transformed the British political economy, overturned the political agenda, and permanently altered the social structure. But this had been without a cultural counter-revolution in the thinking of ordinary people.'[41]

The fact that Thatcher was not guaranteed followers suggests either that her policy agenda conformed with changing opinion or it risked offending party members and voters. The latter explanation could rest either on her assumption that sufficient numbers would be persuaded of the wisdom of her policies notwithstanding their scepticism about its ideological mainsprings, or on her ability to read attitudinal shifts before they were more widely apparent. Any of these explanations is consistent with leadership.

Thatcher possessed the general prerequisites for innovative leadership. She had distinctive goals, strong political will and policy capacity. She was usually able to maintain a sense of proportion in policy-making. She had a loyal leadership network and she worked hard to compensate for the lack of wider ideological support. But prerequisites for innovative leadership are just that, qualifying characteristics. We now investigate her leadership in the policy areas of unemployment, trade unions and privatisation. Thatcher's impacts will be evaluated against the requirements of my particular a priori model of innovative leadership and against comparative a posteriori evaluations.

Unemployment

It had been axiomatic for post-war British governments to act to reduce threatened increases in unemployment on pain of electoral punishment.[42] Although unemployment had been steadily rising since the early 1970s, it increased dramatically in the early 1980s. This prompted previous governments to reflate the economy and make selective interventions through industry and regional development policies. Despite the fact that Thatcher highlighted unemployment in the 1979 election campaign with the slogan 'Labour Isn't Working', it was clear from Thatcher's initial macro-economic policy that she intended to break the nexus between unemployment and government responsibility. Given the high salience of unemployment in the British political consciousness, this policy departure represented a major political risk.

Once in office, she signalled a distinctive approach by asserting that 'there is no alternative' and 'the Lady's not for turning', references to Edward Heath's 'U turns' in response to rising unemployment. Believing that unemployment results from malfunctions in the economy due to inappropriate government interventions, Thatcher's approach was to tolerate rises in unemployment whilst addressing such other issues as sound money and the enterprise culture which she saw as fundamental to 'real' employment growth. The numbers of people without work rose steeply in the early years of the government, passing two symbolic milestones in quick succession: two million in 1980 and three million in 1983.

Three means were used to legitimise Thatcher's approach which combined strong political will and policy capacity. First, Thatcher and her ministers sought to redefine unemployment by presenting it not as a government responsibility but a result of Britain's structural economic weakness combined with a global downturn.[43] Secondly, placebo policies (e.g. employment subsidies, work experience and training programmes) were introduced to offset the most politically sensitive aspects of unemployment (e.g. youth). Thirdly, the government revised the eligibility criteria for unemployment benefits with the overall effect of reducing the official magnitude of the problem. Whilst such strategies were not entirely new, Thatcher's approach was the most consistent and explicitly related to the goal of tolerating increasing unemployment. The test of its political efficacy would be public attitudes to the government's depiction of unemployment and to its relatively 'hands-off' approach.

Attitudinal change among the electorate to unemployment does suggest a leadership effect. This was an area in which Thatcher met with cabinet opposition but persevered and was vindicated by shifts in public opinion. Although unemployment continued to be designated 'the most important issue facing the country' for the first half of the 1980s, perceptions of government responsibility for and capacity to restore employment declined dramatically[44] such that 'there [was] widespread public acceptance of inflation and unemployment as relatively stable factors in Britain's economic condition'.[45] Whilst Norpoth's research suggests that popular prioritisation of unemployment as a pressing social issue was already declining in 1979, this does not detract from Thatcher's political risk.[46] Though there was probably some Falklands War effect in the 1983 election[47], if unemployment had retained its pivotal status in British political sensibilities, one can only conclude that the opposition would have had much more success in mobilising opinion against Thatcher. Even Secretary of State for Employment, Norman Tebbit, commented in 1983 that he did not expect the Conservatives to be re-elected if they could not reduce unemployment below three million.[48] Yet Thatcher's government was handsomely returned in the 1987 election with official unemployment figures at this level.

Thatcher had a clear aim to de-couple government responsibility from unemployment both as an end in itself and as part of a general re-orientation of government priorities. The success of this strategy rested on public acceptance of this shift. Thatcher and her ministers engaged in various legitimation techniques to justify their stance. Their success was evident in a wholesale revision of public opinion on the question of unemployment.

Trade Unions

Thatcher's goal of reducing trade union power was clear from the 1979 election campaign.[49] She saw excessive union power as part and parcel of socialism, the main problem facing Britain. Yet another cornerstone assumption in post-war British politics was that trade unions should enjoy considerable industrial power to protect the wages and conditions of workers. Thatcher's goal thereby risked offending large sections of public opinion as well as inviting union militancy which had mortally wounded the governments of Heath in 1973–74 and Callaghan in 1978–79. Moreover, Prime Minister Wilson had failed to implement his industrial relations reforms in the 1968 White Paper *In Place of Strife*, in the face of union opposition. In the light of these precedents, Thatcher might have been expected to moderate her ambitions here.

Yet Thatcher demonstrated her strong political will on the issue by persistently attacking trade unions power during her decade in office. The strength of her policy capacity was illustrated in the lessons drawn from the debacle of Heath's wholesale approach to industrial relations and she adopted an incremental approach to the problem backed up with a well-conceived symbolic victory. Instead of proclaiming a single comprehensive industrial relations act, her

301

government introduced four Employment Acts (1980, 1982, 1988 and 1989) and a Trade Union Act (1984). These were not presented as explicit attacks on union power. Instead they dealt with the workings of trade unions and were presented as making them more democratic (e.g. by requiring secret ballots for union elections and for decisions to take industrial action) and as improving workers' rights to work (e.g. by reducing trade unions' power to exclude non-members from employment). Secondly, they narrowed the legal scope of industrial action, specifically to ban political and secondary action. But unlike the Heath legislation, these were set in civil rather than criminal law such that penalties consisted of fines and sequestering of union funds rather than imprisoning union leaders. This reduced the possibility of trade union martyrs who could prompt further mobilisation as in the 1973–74 disputes.

This indirect approach to trade union power was calculated to minimise opportunities for union mobilisation and enabled the government to portray its legislation to the public in relatively positive terms. The government was also careful to avoid conflicts that it might lose. It therefore delayed repealing the Dock Labour Scheme until 1989. It backed down in the National Union of Mineworkers (NUM) 1981 pay claim. Instead, it bided its time and prepared for an expected showdown with the NUM. It replaced a consensus-style National Coal Board Chairman, Sir Derek Ezra, with the more combative Ian MacGregor. It diversified energy sources required in power stations and stockpiled coal at power stations and railway yards. When the expected industrial action occurred in 1984–85 the government had ensured that the public and industry were not inconvenienced with power shortages (as in industrial disputes in the 1970s). Moreover, it used its new legislation to limit the spread of industrial action and deployed well-equipped police to enforce the legislation. The upshot was a humiliating loss for the NUM, in which its leadership was discredited and a rival coalminers' union formed. The NUM was even disowned by other unionists and Labour MPs. This single action served as a powerful demonstration effect of Thatcher's distinctive approach to industrial relations and it was repeated in the 1986 Wapping Printers' dispute.

Thus Thatcher won two symbolic victories in which the new legislation was upheld and public opinion remained behind the government. Moreover, con-

302

ventional indicators reveal a decline in union industrial power in the 1980s.[50] Contrary to received wisdom, this did not provoke an electoral backlash against Thatcher possible because she was moving in step with shifting opinion on trade unions.[51] But this was not understood in 1979, 1983 and 1987 when Thatcher's views on trade unions were put to the electorate. Jenkins reports that whereas in 1979 73 per cent of the electorate saw trade unions as the most important issue facing the country, by 1988 only 1 per cent thought so.[52]

Two qualifications could be made to the interpretation of a Thatcher effect here. First, her instinct had been for wholesale industrial relations reform, but she was persuaded by the Minister of Employment, Jim Prior, to pursue a piecemeal approach. But her ability to recognise the intelligence of this approach and to persist with it suggests her sense of proportion subordinated her combative instincts. Secondly, it is possible that rising unemployment deterred unionists from taking industrial action against her policies. But conversely unemployment could have been used to widen and intensify working-class mobilisation against her. Even accepting the proposition that workers were intimidated by the prospect of unemployment, Thatcher demonstrated a leadership trait of turning her circumstances to her political ends.

Industrial relations changes of the 1980s could not have been imagined without Thatcher. Her strong political will, policy capacity and sense of proportion resulted in a purposeful but incremental approach which muted hostility to the changes and enabled government to enhance its capacity as each step was achieved echoing Lindblom.[53] More generally, her approach to trade unions was indicative of a wider theme in Thatcher's approach to politics: that government should govern. Her government also reduced the role of unions in policy-making by winding down inherited neo-corporatist policy-making arrangements (e.g. prices and incomes policy, the Manpower Services Commission). Similarly, it weakened the political influence of a much wider set of producer groups, including lawyers, doctors and teachers. This constitutes a singular departure from the generally consensual approach to group power adopted by previous post-war prime ministers.[54]

Thatcher had a clear goal to weaken the power of organised labour. Unlike her predecessors she selected incremental and indirect means to this end which led to a change in the legal and political context of industrial relations. The success of her approach was reflected in decreasing public support for trade union militancy and in substantive changes in workplace relations.

Privatisation

In 1979 there were key shared assumptions about the value of a substantial public sector in Britain, resting on its steady enlargement over the twentieth century by Labour and Conservative governments.[55] By 1990 a succession of privatisations[56] had reduced the public sector to a shadow of its former self. This raises the question of a Thatcher effect.

The Thatcher government did not come to power with a clear plan for privatisation. The 1979 manifesto only promised sales of organisations nationalised by the previous Labour government. The interest in privatisation resulted from problems the Thatcher government had had in its first term in dealing with nationalised industries and from the increasing salience of the views that economic freedom would increase with a larger private sector; that the private sector was more efficient than the public; that privatisation would loosen the power of trade unions; and that there would be budgetary gains from privatisation.[57] Thus, privatisation was not an explicit policy goal until the 1983 election campaign. But this lack of an initial blueprint and a single underlying justification for privatisation does not distinguish the Thatcher government from that of Attlee, which was the major agent of nationalisation. It too came to power without plans for nationalisation. That Thatcher's privatisation and the Attlee government's nationalisation agendas developed in office and for a number of different reasons does not detract from their innovative significance in respect of the size and scope of the British public sector.

Thatcher's political will and policy capacity increased with experience as privatisation was identified as a solution to diverse problems of governing in a 'learning curve of radicalism'.[58] Heald distinguishes the phases of 'Limited Horizons', 'Growing Ambition' and 'Finishing the Job'.[59] This step-wise approach was in one sense born of necessity: the stock market could not have absorbed a greater intensity of flotations. But from the perspective of policy capacity, the incremental approach enabled the government to focus on the merits of each candidate for privatisation and thereby minimise ideological contests over the public sector as a whole. Each case of public divestment provided an opportunity to improve policy capacity in what became a rolling agenda of privatisation. As a result government became better at: persuading public sector employees, and the managements in particular, of the advantages of privatisation; highlighting public benefits of privatisation, especially in terms of improved services, public expenditure savings and widened shareholding; and working with the new policy communities which emerged with each case.

The impacts of these changes on the structure of the public sector and labour market, on fiscal capacity, on share ownership and on the functioning and government of the economy have been formidable. In 1979 the UK public sector was one of the largest in Western Europe. By 1990 it was among the smallest. One million workers were transferred from the public to the private sector between 1979 and 1991. Fiscal policy was eased by the sales and by reduced recurrent expenditure on nationalised industries. The proportion of the population owning shares nearly tripled from 7 per cent to 20 per cent, across the decade. All this is consistent with Thatcher's view of her distinctive mission.

Crewe and Searing find that there was a parallel shift in public opinion towards privatisation through the 1980s.[60] But this does not detract from the political risk that Thatcher took in undertaking and renewing the privatisation agenda. As in the case of unemployment and trade unions, if she had adhered to the wisdom of the age, she would have held back, fearing the political costs of offending the British consensus of support for a large public sector.

Thatcher's agenda for privatisation grew with the experience of office. Although for practical purposes the government was obliged to adopt an incremental approach, Thatcher exploited this to present each privatisation on its own merits rather than in ideological terms. The success of her approach is illustrated in mass attitudes and in the substantive decline of the public sector.

Leadership, Institutions and Circumstances

We have established that Thatcher met the criteria for innovative leadership in unemployment, trade unions and privatisation. The connection of her distinctive goals, appropriate means and consistent outcomes and transformation of followers conforms with the a priori model. Comparisons have confirmed that her recent predecessors had either not entertained such policy developments or had tried and failed. In each case study, Thatcher's approach was at odds with expectations based on a reading of commentaries on British politics of the day. Describing Thatcher's role in these areas as innovative leadership is not to deny that others, particularly cabinet ministers and senior civil servants, were involved in the processes. Rather, our findings provide little basis for imagining these changes without her. The cases of council house sales; civil service and inter-governmental relations reform; and the radical restructuring of the taxation system could be analysed with similar conclusions.

Given the comparative institutional advantage that British prime ministers enjoy, it could be argued that Thatcher does not pass the cross-national a posteriori test. It is, perhaps, no coincidence that the other country which experienced very comparable political change in the 1980s was New Zealand[61] which, by Lijphart's criteria[62], then surpassed the UK in its 'majoritarian-ness'. However, this is insufficient reason to rule out the innovative leadership explanation of the policy changes we have considered. This is for the reasons of our intra-British comparative conclusions. Despite having similar institutional opportunities, none of Thatcher's predecessors made the similar impacts. As Jenkins noted, "whereas Eden talked of property owning democracy, Heath sold a few council houses, Churchill privatised steel and road haulage, Healy tinkered with monetarism, and Callaghan started the debate on education, Thatcher was a 'doer'."[63] Although the Attlee government was responsible for a similar scale of change, its policies hardly resulted from a Prime Minister effect as its agendas were broadly shared by the ministerial teams.

The analysis of Thatcher's leadership informs the following conclusions:

1 according to the a priori test, she was instrumental in the three policy areas considered, and ;
2 although she was greatly assisted by the comparative institutional advantage that occupancy of Number 10 Downing Street usually affords;
3 she exploited this advantage to a much greater extent than did previous incumbents to pass the a posteriori test and confirm a Thatcher effect.

This does not mean that Thatcher succeeded across the board. In many areas, her aims were not achieved and in some cases preferred outcomes were frustrated. The poll tax proved publicly unacceptable. Overall, public expenditure

and taxation increased in the Thatcher years. It is unclear that monetarist measures explained price stabilisation in the mid-1980s. There was no upward investment in British industry. Three related factors seem to explain this uneven
record: leadership variation, institutions and circumstances.

Leadership varies because of the human element. Even the best leaders make
mistakes in the selection of their goals, the application of political will and the
deployment of policy capacity. For much of Thatcher's premiership she was particularly adept at making these choices. King notes her ability to switch between
'deliberative' to 'declaratory' approaches to Cabinet leadership according to the
issue in question.[64] She often proved herself capable of pragmatic judgements
about what would work. In the case of the Poll Tax, however, she ignored the
considerable intelligence gathered about local taxation in favour of a fatal
declaratory policy seemingly informed by impatience and dogma. In short, she
had no sense of proportion here and strong political will was deployed without
correspondingly strong cognitive or instrumental policy capacity. This spelt
zealotry and proved fatal to Thatcher's relationship with all circles of followers.
This combination of factors also figured in the Westland and Spycatcher
episodes and in her policy reversal on the EU.

Whilst Thatcher made better use of the institutional latitude afforded to most
twentieth-century British prime ministers, institutions also imposed constraints, most obviously in the form of regular elections. Thus, in contrast to her
preparedness to challenge assumptions about British political opinion in the
case studies, in other areas, where adverse public reactions to proposals were
anticipated, goals of NHS and welfare reform were suppressed. Despite
Thatcher's large parliamentary majorities she suffered defeats in the Commons
(e.g. the abolition of SERPS, student grants). Thus, her ambition was modified
by the basic institutional feature of representative democracies, elections, and
the way these were anticipated by their main beneficiaries, MPs. That institutions contribute to explaining the limits of the Thatcher effect is nowhere better
illustrated than in her demise. The collapse of her support base resulted from
Conservative MPs' doubts about Thatcher's electoral standing.[65]

For Machiavelli, *fortuna* explains about half of the Prince's success. The weak
Labour Party was Thatcher's most auspicious circumstance, as it prevented sustained and coherent opposition. Moreover, after several senior Labour figures

formed the Social Democratic Party, Thatcher was able to win massive parliamentary majorities in the 1983 and 1987 general elections with only around 40 per cent of the votes. Thatcher was able to exploit the Falklands War victory to substantiate her self-projection as a national leader, though there is a sense in which she created her own circumstances by her manifestly risk-laden approach to the conflict.

Whilst Thatcher was able to exploit Britain's parlous economic circumstances to legitimise attacks on organised labour and some privileging of private capital, these circumstances also constrained her ambitions in such areas as inflation, exchange rates, growth and employment. Although in some policy areas Thatcher was able to uncouple her policies from the logic of 'inheritance'[66] in the area of public expenditure, the commitments of past governments made it difficult to radically shift welfare entitlements, for example.

But as we have noted with Hall, 'policy-making is based on creation as well as constraint'.[67] In the cases examined, Thatcher exploited institutions and circumstances to transform followers' attitudes and achieve substantive policy change. She thereby conforms to the picture of "the transforming leader [who] articulates principles of creation and renewal in a neo-institutional world by stimulating new preferences, by creating new coalitions of interest, and by identifying new missions."[68]

She did so by presenting radical goals in key areas of British politics and pursuing these with unusually strong political will and policy capacity tempered by a sense of proportion. These enabled her to maintain her pioneering journey, adapting to new challenges and opportunities that presented themselves along the way in what became a series of 'rolling agendas'. Thatcher's leadership provides the explanation to Gamble's 'puzzle of . . . . the capacity of Thatcherism to renew itself and regain its radical momentum',[69] when most British political commentary and political science literature would have expected this radicalism to have long petered out.

Notes

1   This chapter was written when I was a Visitor at the Institute for Advanced Study, Princeton. I am grateful to Ruth Abbey and Meena Bose for comments on a draft.

2   Bernard Bass, Bass and Stodgill's *Handbook of Leadership Research: Theory, Research and Managerial*

Applications (New York: Free Press 3rd ed, 1990), p. 15.

3   e.g. Shirley Letwin, *The Anatomy of Thatcherism* (London: Fontana, 1992); David Willetts Modern Conservatism (London: Penguin, 1992).

4   e.g. Andrew Gamble, *The Free Economy and the Strong State: The Politics of Thatcherism* (London: Macmillan, 1988); Sir Ian Gilmour, *Dancing with Dogma: Britain under Thatcherism* (London: Simon and Schuster, 1992).

5   e.g. Bob Jessop, et al Thatcherism: *A Tale of Two Nations* (New York: Polity, 1988); Peter Taylor, 'Changing Political Relations' in Paul Cloke ed *Policy and Change in Thatcher's Britain* (Oxford: Pergamon, 1992).

6   e.g. Joel Wolfe, 'State Power and Ideology in Britain: Mrs Thatcher's privatisation programme' *Political Studies* 39: 237–52, 1991.

7   e.g. Jim Bulpitt, 'The Discipline of the New Democracy' *Political Studies* 36: 19–35 1986; Dave Marsh and RAW Rhodes, 'Implementing Thatcherism: Policy Change in the 1980s' *Parliamentary Affairs* 45:33–51, 1992.

8   Paul Sabatier','Top-Down and Bottom-Up Approaches to Implementation Research' in Daniel Mazmanian and Paul A Sabatier, eds *Implementation and Public Policy* (Glenview, Illinois: Scott Foresman, 1983).

9   Stephen P. Savage and Lynton Robbins, eds *Public Policy under Thatcher* (Basingstoke: Macmillan,1990).

10   Marsh and Rhodes, p. 33.

11   Marsh and Rhodes, p. 34.

12   Jeremy Moon, 'Evaluating Thatcher: Sceptical and Synthetic Approaches' *Politics* 13: 43–49, 1994 criticises Marsh and Rhodes' approach. They respond in 'Evaluating Thatcherism: Over the Moon or Sick as a Parrot?' *Politics* 15: 1 49–54, 1995. I reply in 'Evaluating Thatcher: Did the Cows Jump Over? A Reply to Marsh and Rhodes' *Politics* 15: pp. 113–116, 1995.

13   Peter Clarke, 'Margaret Thatcher's Leadership in Historical Perspective' *Parliamentary Affairs* 45: 1–17 1992, p.2.

14   Anthony King, 'Margaret Thatcher as a Political Leader' in Robert Skidelsky ed *Thatcherism* (London: Chatto & Windus, 1988).

15   Roy Jenkins, 'Changing Patterns of Leadership: From Asquith via Baldwin and Attlee to Thatcher' *Contemporary Record* Summer pp. 20–24, 1988. He views Thatcher's parliamentary and media skills as relatively deficient.

16   Hugo Young, *One of Us: A Biography of Margaret Thatcher* (London: Pan, 1990), p. 464.

17   SF Finer, 'Thatcherism and British Political History' in Kenneth Minogue and Martin Biddiss, eds *Thatcherism: Personality and Politics* (London: Macmillan, 1988), p.140.

18   Marsh and Rhodes, 1995.

19   Presidential powers in defence and foreign relations yield a different comparative story.

20   Marsh's assumption that only her goals set prior to 1979 are admissible for identifying a Thatcher effect is too strong (in Dave Marsh, 'Explaining 'Thatcherite' Policies: Beyond Uni-dimensional Explanation' *Political Studies* XLIII: 595 – 613, 1995). It denies the vitality of democratic politics and the possibility of governments innovating by adapting to changing environments in pursuit of their broad goals.

21   e.g. Wolfe.

22   Peter Hall, ed (1989) *The Political Power of Economic Ideas* (Princeton: Princeton University Press, 1989), pp. 361–2.

23   Jeremy Moon, *Innovative Leadership in Democracy: Thatcher in Perspective* (Aldershot: Dartmouth, 1993), p. 40.

24   Young, p. 216.

25   But Heath adopted programmatic approaches to local government and industrial relations.

26   Roy Jenkins, p. 23.

27   Dennis Kavanagh, *Thatcherism and British Politics: The End of Consensus* (Oxford: Oxford University Press, 1987), p. 273.

28   David Bell, et al 'Skill in Context: A Comparison of Politicians' *Presidential Quarterly* 29: 3, 2000, pp. 529–30.

29   Young, pp. 158–9.

30   Bell, et al, p. 536.

31   in Peter Hennessy, 'The Prime Minister, Cabinet and the Thatcher Personality' in Minogue and Biddiss eds, pp. 62–3.

32   'Politics as a Vocation' in *From Max Weber: Essays in Sociology* (New York: Oxford University Press, 1919 [1946])), p.115.

33   Weber, p.116.

34   Bell, et al, p. 535.

35   James McGregor Burns, *Leadership* (New York: Harper and Row, 1978), p. 452.

36   HH Gerth and CW Mills, *Character and Social Structure* (New York: Harcourt, Brace and World, 1953), p. 405.

37   John Ranelagh, *Thatcher's People* (London: Harper Collins, 1991).

38   Anthony King, 'Margaret Thatcher: The Style of a Prime Minister' in A King ed *The British Prime Minister* (London: Macmillan 2nd ed, 1985).

39   Philip Norton, 'The Lady's not for turning but what about the rest? *Parliamentary Affairs* 43: 41–58, 1990; 'Mrs Thatcher and Conservative MPs' *Parliamentary Affairs* 43: 249–259, 1990.

40   Young, p.119.

41   Ivor Crewe, 'Values: The Crusade that Failed' in Denis Kavanagh and Anthony Seldon eds *The Thatcher Effect* (Oxford: Clarendon Press, 1989), p. 241.

42   see Samuel H. Beer, *Modern British Politics* (London: Faber & Faber, 1965); Peter Jay 'Englanditis' in R Emmett Tyrrell, ed *The Future that Doesn't Work* (New York: Doubleday, 1977).

43   On occasions unemployment was also linked to individual responsibility as illustrated in Norman Tebbit's injunction that the unemployed should 'get on a bike' to find work.

44   See Jeremy Moon and JJ Richardson, *Unemployment in the UK: Politics and Policies* (Aldershot: Gower, 1985).

45   Anthony Harrison, 'Economic Policy and Expectations' in Roger Jowell and Colin Airey eds *British Social Attitudes: The 1984 Report* (Aldershot: Gower, 1984), p. 50.

46   Helmut Norpoth, *Confidence Regained: Economics, Mrs Thatcher and the British Voter* (Ann Arbor: University of Michigan Press, 1992).

47   Psephologists debate this: see William Miller, 'There was no Alternative! The British General Election of 1983' *Parliamentary Affairs* 37:3, 1984; Peter Saunders, et al 'Government Popularity and

the Falklands War: A Reassessment' *British Journal of Political Science* 17: 3, 1987.

48   Butler and Kavanagh, *The British General Election of 1987* (London: Macmillan, 1988), p.178.

49   Ibid.

50   E.g. union membership, number of strikes, numbers of workers involved in strikes and the number of working days lost to strikes.

51   Ivor Crewe and Donald Searing, 'Ideological Change in the British Conservative Party' *American Political Science Review* 82: 362–384, 1988.

52   Peter Jenkins, 1988.

53   C Lindblom, 'The Science of Muddling Through' *Public Administration Review* 19: 79–88, 1959.

54   see JJ Richardson and AG Jordan, *Governing Under Pressure: The Policy Process in a Post-Parliamentary Democracy* (Oxford: Martin Robertson, 1979).

55   Prior to 1979 privatisations had been rare: the Iron and Steel Industries (1950s); and the Thomas Cook travel agency, the Carlisle pubs and some BP shares (1970s).

56   It refers here only to denationalisation, though elsewhere privatisation refers to deregulation, contracting, the use of markets and the introduction of private sector techniques.

57   The goals of widening share ownership and employee share ownership were added.

58   Jeremy Richardson, et al 'The Dynamics of Policy Change: Lobbying and Water Privatisation' *Public Administration* 70: 157–175, 1992.

59   David Heald, 'The United Kingdom: Privatisation and its Political Context' *West European Politics* 11: 31–48, 1988.

60   Crewe and Searing, 1988.

61   Jonathan Boston, 'Thatcherism and Rogernomics: Changing the Rules of the Game – Comparisons and Contrasts' *Political Science* 39: 129–152, 1987.

62   Arendt Lijphart, *Democracies: Patterns of Majoritarian and Consensus Government in Twenty-One Countries* (New Haven: Yale, 1984).

63   Peter Jenkins, p. 374.

64   King, 1988

65   RK Alderman and Neil Carter, 'A Very Tory Coup: The Ousting of Mrs Thatcher' *Parliamentary Affairs* 44: 2, 1991.

66   Richard Rose, 'Inheritance Before Choice in Public Policy' *Journal of Theoretical Politics* 2: 263 – 291, 1990.

67   Hall, p.362.

68   Erwin Hargrove, 'Two Conceptions of Institutional Leadership' in Bryan Jones ed *Leadership and Politics* (Lawrence Kansas: Kansas University Press, 1989), p.58.

69   Gamble, p.222.

Two Queens:
Thatcherism and the Monarchy

Ben Pimlott

———————

What happens in a constitutional monarchy when the chief executive and head of state disagree?

Fundamental to the British Constitution as it evolved in the twentieth century has been the principle of the political neutrality of the sovereign. Constitutional monarchy as such does not require it, and in the nineteenth century there were several occasions on which the monarch displayed partisanship, or sought to do so. In the last hundred years, however, political necessity evolved into a firm convention, and it became a basic understanding that the head of state's authority depended on and required strict even-handedness. Residual powers remain – to appoint a Prime Minister in the event of political deadlock, for instance – but it has long been accepted that these cannot be exercised in a one-sided way. Indeed, on the last important occasion on which the monarch intervened independently in government forming (in 1931), the head of state sought to establish a National Government based on consensus.

Not only may the monarch not act in a partisan way: he or she must not express publicly – or privately, if there is a danger of the opinion leaking – a party-political opinion or preference. In this respect, the King or Queen is unique among the 'hereditary' parts of the Constitution. The Consort or the Heir to the Throne are discouraged from expressing controversial opinions. If they do so, however, the resulting row is unlikely to cause a constitutional crisis unless they commit the offence too often. By contrast, the rule for sovereigns is absolute, and courtiers are extremely careful to ensure that it is obeyed. By the same token, it is fully understood that the monarch, when acting or speaking 'on advice' – that is, on the explicit advice of the Prime Minister – has no liberty, and therefore is not to be blamed for what is said.

This system has worked well, and there have been remarkably few occasions on which it has caused any difficulty. There is, however, one area of potential dilemma. Since the nineteenth century, and especially since the expansion and development of the Commonwealth from the 1950s, the position of the British monarch as head of state simultaneously of a number of other countries which are in other respects self-governing, and the separate position of the British sovereign as 'Head of the Commonwealth' – a title invented for the present Queen in 1952 – has meant that conflicting 'advice' on the same issue can come from different parts of the globe.

So far, this potential problem has been headed off. From time to time, however, it has put the monarch in a difficult position, underlining the anomaly of the 'multiple-constitutional-personality' head of state – a strange, mutated descendant of the Queen-Empress or King-Emperor. At least one of these occasions occurred during the premiership of Margaret Thatcher. Although the conflict was smoothed over, the fleeting row showed how tensions could arise if a conjunction of strains were present at the same time – in this case, a difference of approach to an international problem between a British Prime Minister and British sovereign; a simultaneous difference between the British premier and the Commonwealth collectively; and a broader sense that the British premier was expressing 'extreme' opinions which jeopardised domestic harmony. When such factors were combined with personal coolness between British Prime Minister and head of state, the danger of mutual embarrassment naturally increased.

In general, the present Queen – as British head of state and head of state of many other countries – has enjoyed good relationships with her UK Prime Ministers, partly on the basis of her weekly meetings with them à deux while Parliament is sitting. Inevitably, such audiences have varied and changed in character over the years. Winston Churchill, the Queen's first Prime Minister, treated the monarch fondly as if she were a favourite great-niece, while Tony Blair, her tenth, apparently treats her respectfully as if she were his granny. Some have been gallant, like Macmillan, others formal, like Heath. Almost all, however, have valued their relationship and spoken of it with pride.

If there have been differences, a highly intrusive press has so far failed to win-kle them out: except in one case, that of the first British woman Prime Minister. It is, indeed, ironic that the traditionalist occupant of a highly conservative insti-tution should have got on least well with the most right-wing premier of the post-war period, who also happened to be female. Yet such was the case. Indeed, it is interesting that, in researching my own study of the Queen and the monar-chy, I found some of the greatest scorn for the role of Buckingham Palace, and even a tacit or passive republicanism, among keen and close supporters of the Queen's longest serving premier.

The Queen had a friendly relationship with Harold Wilson and James Callaghan, a largely formal but mainly unproblematic one with Edward Heath. In the case of Margaret Thatcher, by contrast, the monarch-Prime Minister interface seems to have bristled with difficulties.

Contrary to rumours, the problem was not – or not mainly – personal. Neither was it a matter of scorn for the hereditary principle. Indeed, Margaret Thatcher not only dismissed any suggestions that the hereditary House of Lords should be reformed, she actually recommended parliamentarians for new hereditary peerages – a practice discontinued by Wilson in 1964, and notably not revived by his Conservative successor, Edward Heath, after 1970. 'Mrs Thatcher's views were very supportive of the Queen's institution', one senior Tory minister suggested to me, when I was writing my book. 'She had an instinc-tive respect for its dignity'.[1]

There was never anything as dramatic as a public clash. There was a famous rumour that, when the Prime Minister appeared to treat the Queen's role as head of state of the Caribbean island of Grenada casually, the monarch expressed her fury by failing to invite Mrs Thatcher to sit down at their next audience. Since, however, such audiences were held without witnesses, and what took place at them was confidential, the source of the tale would have had to be one or other participant which, given the discretion of both, seems implausible. There could scarcely be a more tight-lipped British sovereign than the present one, while Margaret Thatcher – renowned for the exceptional depth of her curt-seys – was punctilious in her public and private demonstrations of loyalty.

Nevertheless, if there was no identifiable or provable personal animosity, there was certainly a lack of rapport. Tales of a stiffness between them began early. The evidence is fragmentary, but cumulatively powerful. Thus Wilson's press secretary, Joe Haines, recalls Wilson gleefully reporting that the Queen did not like the new Conservative leader; while a leading churchman – who must remain nameless – tells a story about Mrs Thatcher, perhaps because of a bout of flu, fainting not once but twice at royal events. 'She's keeled over again', remarked the Queen heartlessly, following Mrs Thatcher's second mishap.[2]

After Mrs Thatcher became premier, the stories became more frequent, though they remained elusive: nothing that would stand up in a court of law, but such a ubiquitous impression that it is hard to discount. The problem was often present-ed as one of status: who was really the monarch? 'The weekly meetings between the Queen and Mrs Thatcher – both of the same age – are dreaded by at least one of them', wrote the respected commentator Anthony Sampson, who had close Palace contacts, in 1982. 'The relationship is the more difficult because their roles seem confused; the Queen's style is more matter of fact and domestic, while it is Mrs Thatcher . . . who bears herself like a Queen'.[3] As Mrs Thatcher became grander and more imperial, so this particular difficulty was perceived to increase. Following the Falklands War, irritation was expressed – supposedly shared in the Palace – at Mrs Thatcher's usurpation of the Queen in the place of honour at the victory parade. There was a wider gender difficulty: while the Queen was used to male gallantry from her Prime Ministers, Mrs Thatcher was used to eclipsing any powerful woman who came within range. Some saw Mrs Thatcher as uncharac-teristically nervous. 'Why does she always sit on the edge of her seat?' the Queen once asked a Tory peer.[4] The premier regarded the Balmoral trips as purgatory – and got away as quickly as she decently could.

At the same time, there was also a mutual condescension. If the Palace regard-ed Thatcherite fervour as vulgar, Mrs Thatcher's retainers considered the Palace irrelevant, effete and – most damaging word in the Thatcherite lexicon – wet, identifying the Court with old-style noblesse oblige and social deference. It became a Number 10 convention to treat the monarchy as a bore. 'The Palace was on a mental checklist', according to one former Thatcher adviser. 'it was a matter of kicking yourself about its involvement' – about, for example, a foreign trip that technically required the monarch's permission.[5] 'The Prime Minister might curtsey deep', points out another official adviser, but 'I am not sure how important she thought the Queen was'.[6]

How important was she? Such an attitude on the part of a premier may be regarded as politically trivial: and, given the nature of the British Constitution, an accurate assessment of the state of affairs. However, on at least one significant occasion, the sense that the monarch and her Prime Minister did not take the other as seriously as each might have wished surfaced in a way that raised issues that extended beyond purely British concerns. The problem became much more than merely personal when speculation began – hardening into an assumption – that the Queen and her courtiers had a greater concern for the Commonwealth and hence a greater interest in the opinions of Commonwealth leaders than was true of the Queen's own UK government.

The dimensions involved certainly transcended the personal, however much lack of personal sympathy may have acted as an incubus. Here was a clash, involving distinct elements of the monarch's constitutionally divided self, that was waiting to happen. 'My whole life', the Queen as Princess Elizabeth had declared in a famous Cape Town speech in 1947, would be devoted to 'the service of our great Imperial family to which we all belong'.[7] The Empire became Commonwealth, but there were always echoes, in the Queen's behaviour and interests, of that vow. As Queen, she had visited every Commonwealth capital, and she had known some of the older Commonwealth politicians for decades. Though first and foremost Queen of the United Kingdom, she did not accept the right of the British government to impose a view of the Commonwealth upon her, and indeed her headship-of-state of other countries would have become untenable if she had yielded this small remaining area of authority. Moreover, the position was not just technical: more than any single individual the Queen had not only symbolised, but represented and provided a passionate if necessarily muted leadership to, the evolving international institution of which she was titular head.

On one occasion, the Queen's relationship with Commonwealth governments may have been helpful to Mrs Thatcher. At the Commonwealth heads of government meeting at Lusaka in 1979, the Queen – according to some witnesses – intervened personally with heads of the so-called front-line states to such emollient effect that a settlement over Rhodesia – later sealed as the Lusaka Accord – became possible. The incident demonstrated the bridge the Queen was able to provide between her own government, at one extreme on African affairs, and some of the African leaders, on the other. The same position – in the middle, pulled both ways – could also be the cause of friction.

There was the Grenada incident. There was also, more significantly, the response to the Queen's Christmas 1983 royal broadcast, shortly after the Brandt Report, which had drawn attention to global inequalities. Each year on Christmas Day, the BBC broadcast worldwide a message from the monarch that was not 'on advice' – in other words, a statement written for the Queen by her own personal advisers and not by the government. Normally, the Palace sought to avoid controversy, but on this occasion, it aroused it. 'The greatest problem in the world today', the monarch declared, perhaps unguardedly, 'remains the gap between rich and poor countries, and we shall not begin to close that gap until we hear less about nationalism and more about interdependence'. Even more challenging, she went on to declare that one of the main aims of the Commonwealth was 'to make an effective contribution towards redressing the economic imbalance between nations'.[8] Worse was to come: in the course of the programme, the Queen was shown talking to Mrs Ghandi about technological co-operation and development. Mrs Thatcher said nothing: but some members of the Thatcherite New Model Army of neo-liberals were outraged at this alleged slap in the face by a British monarch at the policies of the UK government, and her readiness – as they saw it – to be used as a pawn by Commonwealth Marxists.

Rumbles on the Conservative benches, however, reflected more than the Queen's alleged sympathy for greater redistribution in the direction of the Third World. Thatcherites were becoming anxious about evidence that the Palace was less than enthusiastic about Mrs Thatcher's domestic policies as well, in a harsh economic climate, and in the absence, because of the Labour Party's marginalisation, of an effective political opposition.

The rumbles coincided with the first tremors of what, in the early 1990s, was to become a major earthquake in the relations between the British public and the family of the head of state. In the Thatcherite 1980s, social deference of the traditional type was dying: and with it royalty's hitherto taken-for-granted immunity from press criticism. Leading the change was the Rupert Murdoch press, owner not just of the tabloid and semi-scatological Sun and News of the World, but also of The Times newspapers, which had been placed in the hands of editors who, to a greater or lesser degree, gave voice to their proprietor's impatience with monarchy. Thus, when the monarch began to give indications of an opinion that differed – even mildly – from that of her Prime Minister, the media's tradition of reticence came under exceptional strain. The Commonwealth was the catalyst – but other matters added to the fission.

The core issue was apartheid in South Africa, and Britain's attitude to the pol-icy of sanctions against the regime in South Africa. These had long been demanded by a majority of Commonwealth states – but resisted by Mrs Thatcher on the grounds that they were both ineffective, and bad for Britain's economic interests. Worse – from the monarch's point of view – the British Prime Minister made increasingly clear her contempt for an organisation dom-inated by representatives of the Third World. In the summer of 1986, this heat-ed question threatened to tear the Commonwealth apart.

From the Palace's point of view, it was the nightmare scenario: given the Queen's predilection for keeping her head down, what could she do? To side with the Commonwealth against the British government was obviously impossible. Yet to appear to give unequivocal support to her British Prime Minister, and to ignore the feelings of Commonwealth ones – whether or not she was, in any par-ticular case, head of state of the country concerned – would be damaging to her relations with them, as well as being personally disagreeable. She seems, there-fore, to have decided on a policy of maximum tact: saying nothing that could be interpreted as criticism of the UK line, while privately giving the Commonwealth heads a non-committal hearing. Unfortunately, even the subtlest of nuances, in an institution that took care over every comma, looked like taking a position.

When some countries threatened to boycott the Commonwealth Games in Edinburgh in protest, the London *Sunday Times* – edited by the rumbustious and not-at-all-monarchist Andrew Neil – decided to make the most of the Queen's constitutionally split persona. On 15 June it claimed that the monarch was 'increasingly concerned' about the sanctions issue, and the risk of the Commonwealth disintegrating as a result, and claimed that she had expressed her concerns in an audience. Never slow on a topic with a royalty angle, other papers took up the theme. How free was the Queen on Commonwealth matters? 'Certainly', wrote the respected historian, John Grigg, 'in what she chooses to say about the Commonwealth as such, she is not bound by the advice of her UK ministers'.[9] In July, *The Times* gave a similar opinion, reminding readers that Elizabeth II was 'seventeen queens in one person and more besides', which inevitably forced her, on occasion, to face in different directions. [10] Meanwhile, Peregrine Worsthorne accused the Queen in the *Sunday Telegraph* of a left-wing, going-native-on-the-Commonwealth stance.[11]

There was the question of what the monarch might actually do. 'Will she, will she have to, can she blow the whistle if divisions within the Commonwealth get out of hand?' asked Malcolm Rutherford in the *Financial Times*.[12] Media interest increased still further, as it became clear that the cabinet itself was split on the sanctions issue, with Sir Geoffrey Howe, the Foreign Secretary, signalling his disagreement with the Prime Minister's point of view on sanctions. Thus with tension all round – Mrs Thatcher against the Commonwealth, the Foreign Secretary against Mrs Thatcher, and the two sides of the Queen's constitutionally divided personality against each other – the fuse was lit.

The bomb went off on 20 July 1986, in the *Sunday Times*. In the pages of Britain's most widely read Sunday broadsheet, the paper's political editor, Michael Jones, and another journalist, Simon Freeman, announced what they boldly described as the most fundamental disagreement between a British monarch and British Prime Minister for fifty years. Quoting 'sources close to the Queen' – which could only mean a senior official at Buckingham Palace – they claimed irrefutable proof that the Queen regarded the whole approach of Mrs Thatcher as 'uncaring, confrontational and socially divisive'.[13] There had been several briefings from the Palace, and the information was supposedly specific. It also related to much more than South Africa: the government's harsh response to the 1984 miners' strike was cited, and so was the Prime Minister's eagerness to offer UK bases to the Americans for the US punishment raid on Libya in April 1986; finally there was, allegedly, a general royal dissatisfaction or alarm at Mrs Thatcher's abandonment of the nation-sustaining post-war consensus in British politics. Recasting the Queen as 'an astute political in-fighter who is quite prepared to take on Downing Street when provoked', the paper concluded that on many issues the monarch was left of centre, and took a keen interest in race relations and inner urban decay.

Such a critique went far beyond the constitutionally ambiguous territory of the Commonwealth, and the question immediately arose of whether the newspaper's information was soundly based. The Palace quickly issued haughty denials, but the *Sunday Times* insisted that its sources were 'unimpeachable'. Immediately the hunt was on for a name. On 27 July, the rival *Observer* pinpointed the Queen's press secretary, Michael Shea. This rapid discovery, in the wake of official protests, pushed the Palace on to the defensive. There followed a long, and still unresolved, controversy about the nature, tone and mutual understanding of the conversations that took place, and who said what to whom. Shea maintained (and maintains) that he merely answered questions of the 'Is the Queen very keen on the Commonwealth?' variety – affirmatively. Nevertheless, there was little doubt – and he did not deny – that he co-operated with Simon Freeman, his interrogator.[14]

Despite the Palace's disclaimer, most other papers assumed that the conversations not only took place but that – with a little embellishment – the *Sunday Times* account of the Queen's attitudes was essentially correct. The Left rejoiced publicly, wets in the cabinet rejoiced privately, while in Downing Street there were pained faces, lip-biting, and stoical resistance of the temptation to hit back. 'There was a lot of dismay around', according to Sir Bernard Ingham.[15] Another aide put it to me less mildly. 'The idea that the Queen was pissed off with Mrs Thatcher was the last thing we needed', he maintained.[16] According to Ingham, Mrs Thatcher was herself greatly concerned, and the feeling was part and parcel of a strained relationship between Number 10 and the Royal Household. 'She went out of her way not to appear to be irritated', according to a senior ministerial colleague. 'There was a feeling around Buckingham Palace that people there were amused by Mrs Thatcher', according to Ingham, 'people who derived amusement from Mrs Thatcher's passion, unspecified people who looked down their noses at her, as a kind of Johnnie-come-lately;'[17] in other words, classic British social snobbery. Meanwhile, the Commonwealth Secretariat, which worshipped the Queen and loathed Mrs Thatcher, glowed with satisfaction.

In a sense it was a scoop that wasn't. There was certainly no intention to embarrass Mrs Thatcher, and thereby doubly to embarrass the Queen – which was what happened – and Michael Shea caused himself a lot of trouble as a result of what occurred. At the same time, the 'revelations' contained little that was not rumoured already. Once it was clear that the monarch herself was not directly involved, talk of a constitutional crisis faded. What the story did do was to crystallise a growing – and historically unusual – distance between Palace and Prime Minister, of a kind that had not existed for a long time, and has not so far recurred. When a story breaks apparently giving substance to what is widely believed, the question is whether it reflects a general truth: in this case, the general truth was that the Queen and her advisers were less comfortable with the Thatcher Government than with any of its predecessors, and this was a truth that Buckingham Palace – and Downing Street – found impossible to evade.

How much did it matter? In the Commonwealth, it seems to have acted as a tonic, enabling politicians to draw a clear line between a government with which they sharply disagreed, and the head of an institution of which they were members, and which they continued to find useful. When Howe visited Zambia a short time later and faced the cameras alongside Kenneth Kaunda, the Zambian President was vigorous in denouncing Mrs Thatcher who 'has kissed apartheid'. At the same time, he expressed his appreciation of the Queen. He made clear to the Zambian press that he was welcoming the Foreign Secretary because of his 'love and respect' for the British monarch, rather than as a representative of her Government. At home, the incident was a mild reminder that the monarchy could not be regarded entirely as a political cipher, but formed part of the system of checks and balances, when the political system tipped too far one way.

What does it tell us about Thatcherism? There were a number of paradoxes contained within the affair: a right-wing Prime Minister impatient with a conservative institution of which, in principle, she heartily approved – and for which, it should be said, Mrs Thatcher was later to make the most generous and satisfactory financial settlement of the reign; two strong women getting on worse with each other than each generally got on with powerful men; an hereditary ruler showing more immediate concern for the nation's and the world's oppressed than did a premier from a humble background; the influential advisers of a dominant government made to feel socially uncomfortable by the courtiers of a constitutionally marginal figurehead. The affair also highlighted how little a neo-liberal yet nationalistic government, prepared to fight a perilous colonial war to retain almost the last of British colonial possessions in the South Atlantic, cared about the Empire's cultural echo, the Commonwealth.

The incident pointed to the contradictions that still existed within the British political and social system. The Thatcher-monarch clash over South Africa, and the highlighting of difference between Downing Street and Palace, provides an historical reminder that Margaret Thatcher, scourge of socialism, elective dictator, ruler of almost all she surveyed, was not – and not quite ever – a full member of that indefinably miasmic layer of the British elite, known as the Establishment, however much she might aspire to be so. At the same time, it indicated how far the same Establishment, once regarded as seamless, had fragmented by the end of the twentieth century. Indeed it displayed the British Establishment with its pants down. The press, Commonwealth leaders, the civil service, the monarchy, the Royal Court and a Conservative Prime Minister – who in the middle of the century would naturally have fallen in behind each other at any moment of embarrassment – graphically revealing the tensions that now pulled them apart.

Notes

1 Confidential interview.
2 Confidential interview.
3 Anthony Sampson *The Essential Anatomy of Britain* (London: Hodder & Stoughton, 1982)
4 Confidential interview.
5 Confidential interview
6 Confidential interview.
7 *Manchester Guardian*, 21 April 1947.
8 *Guardian*, 21 January 1984.
9 *Daily Telegraph*, 17 July 1986.
10 *The Times*, 16 April 1986.
11 *Sunday Telegraph*, 20 July 1986.
12 *Financial Times*, 19 July 1986.
13 *Sunday Times*, 20 July 1986.
14 Michael Shea: interview.
15 Sir Bernard Ingham: interview.
16 Confidential interview.
17 Sir Bernard Ingham: interview. See also Ben Pimlott, *The Queen: A Biography of Elizabeth II* (London: HarperCollins, 1996 and New York: John Wiley & Co, 1997).

Thatcher and the monarchy

Stuart Prall

———

This topic has two sides: the monarchy as an institution and the role of the Queen as a person. My remarks will touch upon both. Perhaps no one other than Lady Thatcher and the Queen herself are as well informed about this relationship as Ben Pimlott. His biography of the Queen was based upon a great number of unattributed interviews which I have not been able to duplicate. My remarks are limited to what has been recorded in the press and in the published works of Lady Thatcher, Ben Pimlott himself, Vernon Bogdanor, and Lady Thatcher's chosen successor, John Major. Of course, *The Times* of London, the *Sunday Times* and the occasional radio and TV programme also have been followed.

Lady Thatcher claims, and I think all agree with her, that she has always had the greatest respect for the institution of the monarchy. That she curtsied more deeply before the Queen than any other woman could be taken as proof of her great regard for the institution. However, it has been suggested by a few that the curtsy was her way of mocking the institution. I do not accept that nasty interpretation. On a personal level only the Queen and Lady Thatcher know the truth about their relationship. The weekly audience, generally on a Tuesday evening, was religiously adhered to. These audiences are totally private; no one else is in the room. No notes are taken; no summary is composed later by either participant. By tradition the Palace is always silent about such things; also by tradition no Prime Minister, or any other minister, reveals private talks with the monarch until after the death of that monarch. Five of the Queen's former prime ministers are already dead. By outliving her ministers much of this personal history will never be recorded. John Major's biographer, Bruce Anderson, has written:

For eleven and a half years, I asked almost everyone who worked closely with Margaret Thatcher what the true state of affairs was between monarch and Premier. Naturally, one took the elementary precaution of waiting to pose the question until the gossip was flowing and the glasses had been filled. But I always got the same answer: that Mrs Thatcher never discussed her dealings with the monarch. It seems improbable that Her Majesty was any less discreet. All the supposed reports turn out to be nothing more than recycled rumour.[1]

Anderson also reminded his readers that a few days after her retirement the Queen bestowed the Order of Merit upon her. The OM is one of the highest honours that she can bestow on her own initiative.

What the Queen really thought about her Prime Minister, and doubts about the Queen's own discretion, became a major media event following a *Sunday Times* article on 20 July, 1986, referring to 'sources close to the Queen'. The source was said to be Michael Shea, the Queen's press secretary, who in an 'off the cuff' interview seemed to suggest that the Queen thought Mrs Thatcher did not care sufficiently for the poor and needy; that her policies were socially divisive; that she had gone too far in opposing the miners' strike in 1984; and that she should not have helped the US bomb Libya. Ben Pimlott has covered this fracas in great detail in his biography of the Queen. I think it is fair to conclude that both Lady Thatcher and the Queen were anxious to put the story behind them, and that the views may well have been true, but that the Queen was not responsible for the leak. Lady Thatcher still treated Shea with respect, but within a few months he took retirement.

The story of the Queen's real views about her Prime Minister did, however, come at a time when real differences between Queen and Prime Minister of a constitutional nature did clearly exist. Soon after becoming Prime Minister, Mrs Thatcher was expected to attend the bi-annual meeting of the Commonwealth chiefs of government conference, held that year in Lusaka, Zambia. Edward Heath before her clearly found these meetings annoying. Mrs Thatcher's reluctance to go at all was clear. But go she did, once it was clear that nothing would stop the Queen from playing her role as head of the Commonwealth. The Queen takes her role, and the Commonwealth itself, very seriously. She is still head of state for seventeen of its members. Without the monarch's personal headships the whole structure could well collapse. (Suggestions that the headship should rotate among its membership are absurd.) By attending such conferences with the Queen, but then being treated as just one of fifty or so equals; having no right to attend the Queen's private audiences with each of the other leaders; and being the butt of anti-apartheid rhetoric at the plenary sessions clearly annoyed Mrs Thatcher, as her own *bête noire* Edward Heath had been annoyed.

As interest in the Commonwealth declines within the UK itself, the Queen's personal commitment to it does have potential dangers for the monarch. No British Prime Minister can in the long run allow the Queen to forget that she is first and foremost the British monarch. All the rest is icing, not the cake.

There is another, and similar problem, regarding the church. I know from personal interviews – kept unattributed – that the Queen takes her role as Supreme Governor of the Church of England seriously. Not only does she take an interest in the C of E, however, but in the wider Anglican Communion, the clerical leader of which is the Archbishop of Canterbury. Archbishops and monarchs should potentially have views and interests that transcend the UK, and the C of E The Prime Minister does not, and probably will not, always share these wider vistas.

On the whole complex matter of the royal finances, Mrs Thatcher seems to have played both a traditional and a supportive role. The tradition since the accession of George III in 1760 is that the sovereign turns the revenues from the crown lands over to the Treasury, receiving back the annual subsidy called the Civil List. The post-world war II inflation led George VI and Elizabeth II to seeking periodic revisions to keep up with inflation. In addition many expenses were directly carried by other branches of the government. In 1971 the Heath government had adopted a ten year rule for Civil List revisions. In the subsequent Wilson and Callaghan administrations, accompanied by even higher inflation, annual debates in Parliament, if not annual revisions, became the ugly norm. In July 1990 Mrs Thatcher announced a return to the ten-year rule. She also continued to protect the monarch's private income from public scrutiny and debate. It was not until the Major administration that the Queen's private tax exemption became a hot issue, resulting in her offer to pay income tax on the private income.

The Falkland Islands war provided an opportunity for those who saw the Thatcher relationship with the Queen strained. Where, on the one hand, she informed the Queen on 25 April, 1982 that 'one of your islands' (South Georgia) had been recovered, she also 'usurped' the Queen's place at the 'victory' service at St Paul's Cathedral once the war was over. The forces involved in the actual fighting, however, continued to show traditional loyalty to the sovereign. Mrs Thatcher was not a substitute for the Queen among the serving ranks themselves.

I now want to turn to a topic that no one else has ever described the way I shall. I may be right; I may be wrong; but here it is. Prior to Prince Andrew's marriage it was assumed that he would be created Duke of York at some appropriate date, such as at his marriage. Since Harold Wilson became Prime Minister in 1964 no heredity peerages or baronetcies had been bestowed. For the Queen to so recognise her son Prince Andrew would create a chasm between royalty and the rest of society. Mrs Thatcher helped prepare the way by advising the Queen to bestow three hereditary peerages in 1984 – two viscounties – George Thomas and Willie Whitelaw. The former was a bachelor; the latter was married but childless. Neither would actually have an heir to inherit. On the other hand, former Tory Prime Minister Harold Macmillan, with a living son and grandson, was given an earldom. This would be and was truly hereditary. Why Macmillan, who stood for all that she despised in the grandee, landed paternalistic, 'middle-way' post war Tory party? But that was the point: Macmillan could not be faulted by traditionally main stream Tories and was the kind of Tory that the Labourites and the Liberals could accept as being preferable to Thatcher herself. At the time I was convinced that these titles were designed to make it easier for the Queen to ennoble Andrew. Some assumed that the Macmillan title was just her own bid to be made a countess upon her own retirement. Of course, that has not happened; she received a life peerage in the tradition of Wilson and Callaghan. Upon her retirement it was her husband Denis who received a hereditary baronetcy. I thought at the time, and I still think, that Mrs Thatcher was doing her bit to help the Queen, her sovereign.

A final thought: when one compares Tony Blair's relationship with royalty, one can see that Mrs Thatcher was very traditional. That Blair walked down Whitehall in June 1997, attracting press attention away from the Queen's own carriage procession, was not Thatcherite, and has never been done again. The rather low-key wedding for Prince Edward compared with the spectacular weddings for Charles and Andrew may or may not have had prime ministerial input, but I suspect the spectacles of the 1980s are not Blair's style, whether or not it is the Queen's.

Whatever the personal chemistry between the two women, except for the victory service at St Paul's, Margaret Thatcher was indeed a loyal subject and servant of her Queen.

Notes

1   Bruce Anderson. *John Major: The Making of the Prime Minister* (London: Fourth Estate, 1991), p. 139.

Margaret Thatcher:
A Study in Strong Leadership

The Rt. Hon Brian Mulroney

———————

This volume is really all about remembering the Thatcher years, its principal players and the manner in which they helped changed the world. Presidents and prime ministers everywhere of all political stripes have at least one thing in common: they soon wonder and worry how history will deal with them. Not all have the self-confidence of Churchill who, when asked how he expected to be treated by history, responded. 'History will treat me very well – because I plan to write it myself!'

After a while, many of us evince some of the nostalgia and insecurity of Thomas d'Arcy McGee, an Irish immigrant to Canada who became one of our Fathers of Confederation. In one of his poems, McGee asked:

Am I remembered in Erin
I charge you, speak me true
Has my name a sound, a meaning
In the scenes my boyhood knew.

Margaret Thatcher will not have to worry about this because she is remembered pretty well everywhere – from Erin to Estonia, from Maryland to Madagascar from Montréal to Monterey. Margaret Thatcher does not enter history tentatively – she does so with panache. At home and on the world stage, hers were not the pallid etchings of a timorous politician. They were the bold strokes of a confident and accomplished leader.

Many of you have known Margaret Thatcher longer and better than me. Some of you worked with her daily for years and bring that unique insight to these deliberations. I knew her as a fellow G-7 leader with whom I shared moments of high drama on the world stage during one of the most explosive decades in modern history. We became friends and I saw her often when questions of world peace or war were being determined. In that most scalding of political cauldrons, I observed Margaret Thatcher closely. That is the perspective I will try to share with you in this essay.

In his seminal work on leadership, James MacGregor Burns segregates 'transactional' from 'transforming' leadership. He writes that it is the transforming leader who 'raises the level of human conduct of both leader and led . . . who responds to fundamental hopes and expectations and who may transcend and even seek to reconstruct the political system rather than simply operate within it'.

Many suggest that great, inexorable currents of history themselves – and not individual leaders – seal our fate. In my judgement, however, Carlyle was on target when he observed that the right person in the right place at the right time can completely change the course of history. I believe that to be true because some of us were there to see it happen.

In a brilliant address delivered some years ago in Canada, Theodore Sorenson – himself a skilled observer of powerful leaders – said:

Once in office those who wish to stand up and stand out and leave something enduring behind must build new institutions, not new images. They must look to the next generation not merely the next election. They must talk in terms of fundamental values, not merely costs. They must appeal to our hopes as well as our needs, to what we long to be and what we know is right. That's leadership.

Does this remind you of anybody?

If today you asked the British people if they think Margaret Thatcher was a 'transforming' Prime Minister or simply a 'transactional' one, what do you think they would reply? Look around you, they would say, the Thatcher Revolution and its powerful effects on freedom, economic prosperity, the private sector and the public good are clearly visible both to contemporary Britain and to history.

Margaret Thatcher reignited and personified the optimism and confidence of the British people to themselves and to the world. She bolstered the spirit of Britain, restored national strength and the ability to succeed. The word 'malaise' was never part of her vocabulary.

Even those who did not agree with her – and they were legion – respected Margaret Thatcher because she was unwavering in what she believed was right for Britain. No ambiguity, no deception, no cynicism. What you saw or heard was precisely what Margaret Thatcher meant.

The impact of significant public policy decisions is often unclear in the early years. It sometimes takes a considerable period – frequently decades – before the full consequences of an important initiative become apparent.

As Reinhold Niebuhr reminded us: 'Nothing worth doing is completed in our lifetime; therefore we must be saved by hope. Nothing fine or beautiful or good makes complete sense in any immediate context of history; therefore we must be saved by faith'. It is in this perspective that great and controversial questions of public policy must be considered.

Time is the ally of leaders who placed the defence of principle ahead of the pursuit of popularity. And history has little time for the marginal roles played by the carpers and complainers and less for their opinions. History tends to focus on the builders, the deciders, the leaders, because they are the men and women whose contributions have shaped the destiny of their nations.

Theodore Roosevelt had courageous leaders like Margaret Thatcher in mind I suspect when he spoke at La Sorbonne and said:

It is not the critic who counts; not the man who points out how the strong man stumbles, or where the doer of deeds could have done better. The credit belongs to the man who is actually in the arena, whose face is marred by dust and sweat and blood . . . who spends himself in a worthy cause, who, at the best, knows in the end the triumphs of high achievement and who, at the worst, if he fails, at least fails while daring greatly, so that his place shall never be with those cold and timid souls who know neither victory nor defeat.

I thought of these lines when I watched Margaret Thatcher in her final appearance in the House of Commons and her departure from Number 10 – her heart broken but her dignity fully intact and her historic legacy fully ensured.

On this tenth anniversary of Margaret Thatcher leaving office however, some early judgements are appropriate.

The world was a very different place when Margaret Thatcher took office in 1979 from when she left it in 1990, and worlds apart from what it has become since. Leonid Brezhnev then ruled the fifteen Republics of the Soviet Empire, a vast federation in some decline, but still powerful, aggressive and hostile. Cold War tensions prevailed and regional conflicts abounded. The Soviets refused to discuss arms control at Geneva, even as they became embroiled in regional wars from Afghanistan to Africa. Communist leaders firmly agreed with Mr Krushchev's threat to the West that 'we shall bury you' – and conducted themselves with a swagger that meant clearly it was only a matter of time.

Some in the West during the early 1980s, believing both systems – Communism and democracy – were equally valid and viable, advocated a policy of 'live and let live'. Others, while deploring the tragic human injustices and economic flaws inherent in the Soviet system, saw it as a country much more powerful and successful than it really was, and viewed it as worthy at least of Western tolerance, if not muted praise. In contrast, Margaret Thatcher saw Communism as an insidious menace to be contained, challenged and confronted in the genuine belief that its underpinnings of brute force, destruction of individual liberties and widespread moral decay would fall swiftly to the gathering winds of freedom and the shining achievements of democracy. Provided, as she said, that NATO and the Western industrialised democracies stood firm and united.

And provided as well, as she said, that Western leaders transform their nations into strong, productive free market economies based on individual freedom and economic opportunity. They did and we know now who was right.

Some years ago over the Christmas holidays I read the autobiography of Prime Minister Callaghan, Mrs Thatcher's predecessor, for whom I have a high personal regard. When I put the book down, however, it occurred to me how profoundly Mrs Thatcher had in a decade transformed Britain.

Mr Callaghan spoke of the difficult time he had had negotiating with the Trade Unions' Congress at Number 10 Downing Street before legislation could even be brought to the House of Commons. He wrote of meetings with the International Monetary Fund which threatened to withhold borrowing authority from Her Majesty's Government unless certain fiscal measures were accepted by Westminster. He spoke of miners' strikes that crippled the government's will, lowered peoples' hopes and diminished the nation's horizons.

All of this changed with Margaret Thatcher. There were no sudden miracles in the UK and the British disease was not cured overnight.

Slowly but surely, however, this resolute and principled leader articulated a compelling new future for Britain – competitive, prosperous, influential and proud.

And then Prime Minister Thatcher set out to give life to this vision persuading the nation to accept massive and often painful change, together with challenges like to the Falklands that lifted the spirit and enriched the soul of the country to a point that, by the late 1980s, had attracted for Britain a degree of attention and admiration the world had felt for her so long ago when all of us were young.

In 1999 one of America's leading historians said: 'That's what leadership is all about – staking your ground ahead of where opinion is and convincing people, not simply following the popular opinion of the moment'. Well, that is what Margaret Thatcher did and that is why I believe historians will view much of what she accomplished as visionary. They will say decades from now that she had the courage to take decisions not for easy headlines in ten days but for a better Britain in ten years.

In specific terms, Prime Minister Thatcher's achievement was to smash the post-World War II political consensus among all parties in Britain, which supinely accepted high taxation, nationalised industries, state provision – a culture of dependency, over-powerful trade unions which could not be challenged, constant strikes, and declining British influence in the world as simply inevitable and unchangeable .

She replaced it with:

- lower taxes, down from a high of 98 per cent so that people had an incentive to work harder and could decide how to spend their money rather than have government do it for them;
- popular capitalism under which far more people enjoyed ownership of homes and stores. Government and local authority housing was sold to the occupiers;

- trade unions subject to the law, with secondary picketing outlawed and consequently a dramatic fall in strikes. The breaking of the coal miners strike in 1984–5 was a cathartic event;
- privatisation of the nationalised industries to get government out of business and give a better service to the public;
- smaller government with a greatly reduced civil service;
- making Europe a genuine single market and getting a square deal for Britain's financial contribution to Europe;
- a much more self-confident Britain in the world, based on victory in the Falklands proving that Britain once again mattered in the world;
- a major role, with Ronald Reagan and other G-7 leaders, in bringing down communism and winning the Cold War.

In other words, she brought about a cultural revolution in Britain and a renewed respect for Britain in the outside world, largely by force of personality and by focusing on the very big issues. Thatcherism was not so much an ideology as a cold shower. Its success depended in some measure on there being like-minded allies doing the same thing in the US and Canada and elsewhere. But, above all, its success was due to the extraordinary vision, discipline and single-mindedness of an entirely unique leader, Margaret Thatcher.

May our common future and that of our great nations be guided by wise men and women who will remember always the golden achievements of the Thatcher era and the success that can be theirs if the values of freedom and democracy are preserved, unsullied and undiminished, until the unfolding decades remember little else.

I conclude with a line from the great Irish writer William Butler Yeats: 'Think where man's glory most begins and ends, and say my glory was I had such friends'. Mila and I have been blessed with such friends as Margaret and Denis Thatcher. I am grateful that our paths have crossed and that our lives have touched. We shall always remember them with deep admiration and affection and we shall always feel honoured by the journey we travelled together in the course of better and more peaceful tomorrows for all God's children, everywhere.

VI

The Thatcher Legacy

The Thatcher Years:
Repudiating the Conventional Wisdom

Caspar W. Weinberger

———————

One of the ways of testing and establishing Lady Thatcher's greatness is to imagine a world in which she had not been here. Just think of all of the differences we would have had today had she not served in office for such a very long and a very fortunate time for all of us as Prime Minister of Great Britain, but also as one of the world's statesmen who made a very real and a very major difference at all times in her remarkable career. What she did that was so very great was to repudiate the conventional wisdom, and that's not an easy thing to do. The conventional wisdom is basically established by people who are generally considered experts in their field, people who have had distinguished records of their own – usually not in office but in their fields – and to conclude that perhaps that conventional wisdom was not all that wise and needs to be questioned, and occasionally needs to be reversed, requires great personal courage and great personal insight, and, more important almost than that, great conviction. And the difference between conviction and consensus office holders, I think, is the difference between Lady Thatcher and a great many of her predecessors and successors. And that is, I think, one of the things that enabled us all to understand the remarkable record that she achieved.

The conventional wisdom basically before Lady Thatcher was that you would have, depending on which party was in, a little more or a little less government interference and government authority; that you'd have basically steady or increasing taxation, no slight suggestion of any reduction in taxes; certainly no suggestion that there should be any reduction in the power and strength of gov-

ernment; and that you accepted as a kind of a given the complete and permanent domination of labour unions. This was a fact of life that couldn't really be
challenged, and when people were asked in the previous government to hers
who really ran Great Britain, whether it was the government or the labour
unions, there were not many people who hesitated very long by saying, well,
basically, of course, the labour unions. And we accept that, and what we have to
do is to work with them. We have to work together. The idea of confrontation
was not only basically wrong but couldn't possibly work because in any confrontation with labour unions, there couldn't be any conceivable outcome
except that the basic union demands would succeed. Otherwise, there would be
strikes, the country would be crippled, and so on. Well, in a sense, that's how she
came to office. There had been strikes, and the country was crippled. And the
economic situation of Great Britain of 1978–79 is very hard to remember now
but it was something that clearly needed fixing in ways other than simply a little more of this or a little less of that, or a little of anything. It required a major
surgical overhaul, and that is in fact what actually happened.

There was no suggestion before that time of privatisation. Privatisation is one
of the things that has caught on now and is followed in an astonishing number
of countries around the world, in all of the continents. And it works because
what's happened is, of course, that when nationalised industries are privatised,
they work much better. They work more efficiently, they cost less, and the government gets a fair amount of money for having sold the assets, and it can use
that for either other purposes or perhaps – as scarcely heard of before – tax
reduction. And so this was a very major thing. And the important thing, really,
wasn't the amount of money that was saved, or the number of industries that
were denationalised or privatised. The important thing is that the power and
size and strength of government was being reduced, and that was vital because
as the power of government increases, the power and ability of the individual,
or the area of personal freedom, diminishes. You can't have the two together.
When the power of government expands, that diminishes the ability of the individual to be free. The greatest challenge to liberty is the expansion of governmental power. And Mrs Thatcher was able to see that, did understand that, and
proceeded with privatisation in a way that brought bitter criticism for a very
long time, just as did her attempts – which stretched from virtually 1982 to 1988

– to corral the unbounded power that the unions exercised over the economy and the daily life of everybody – union member and non-union member – in Great Britain.

The great achievement was that somebody was willing to challenge the conventional wisdom. Somebody was willing to substitute for it a consistent, coherent theme, and to do more than talk about it, but to put that into effect. And as a result, the English economy grew and strengthened, and the whole idea carried through many different areas of English life. Because of the privatisation, stockholding became very much more popular, very much more a thing in which more and more people participated. And as more and more people participated, they had a real stake in the strength of the economy, just as did the idea of selling privately the publicly owned, publicly constructed housing, which had been virtually unheard of – nobody even had thought of suggesting it before. And yet this gave the people who could buy their own house now the public housing that they'd been living in, maybe for years and years, sometimes generations, they could own that, they could have a stake in it, they could have a basic real interest in improving it and becoming, in effect, a landowner, which was enormously important then and now.

So that all of this was done, and was done in a way that, as we say, violated the conventional wisdom, but left a legacy for Great Britain of a vastly improved economy, of inflation that was reduced, of budget deficits that were reduced and sometimes substituted for surpluses as the privatisation went on. And the size of government and the most important thing, the power of government, was reduced. The actual number of civil servants was reduced during her years by over 22 per cent. And cost-cutting in local government was more difficult because here the local councils had virtually unlimited ability to incur costs that would have the effect, of course, of raising local taxes. She took care of the problem rather neatly in London, I thought. She abolished the London County Council, and also, at the same time, put a lid or ceiling on the amount of expenditures that could be made on the amount of public spending that could be done by local government. And while that didn't necessarily reduce all local government costs, it made a major stab in that direction, and it also did what had been felt to be impossible before, and that is start to reduce and get a hold on and put a lid on this other very largely rising amount of government expenditures, aside from the national government.

So all of this was a total and complete change, a total and complete violation of the conventional wisdom, and it was a matter of surprise to the British people. It was part of her campaign, it was part of her platform, as we would say here. And just before or just after she took office, there was a remarkable manifesto that was signed by 364 certified conventionally wise standard economists all over the country. These were people who were great experts in their field, they were people whose views and opinions had been very much respected. They were certified to be properly politically correct. And their manifesto was to the effect that the new policies Lady Thatcher had advocated and was about to put into effect with her newly chosen government could not possibly work and should be avoided. The 364, at last report, were still writing manifestos. Lady Thatcher changed the world.

So this is a series of accomplishments that I think we would be very wrong to ignore, we would be very wrong not to pay tribute to, because again, the difficulties of achieving them can scarcely be realised now, so many years after. The reason they can scarcely be realised is that her ideas have – and perhaps this is her greatest tribute – become the conventional wisdom. Privatisation is copied all over the world in countries that had been socialist for years, and the idea of more and more people getting a stake in the economy by buying their own property and owning some of it, all of that now is something that is accepted, as is the attempt to limit and reduce the costs of government, because along with that you're reducing the power of government and increasing individual freedom and individual liberty. So this is now something that is so completely accepted and completely understood, not only is the whole dialogue – political dialogue and economic dialogue – been changed, but it has been changed in a way that has literally turned it around to the point where this is now what is accepted. And that is, I think, as good a measure of greatness as you can imagine, because without her, I have very, very strong doubts as to whether any of this would happen – certainly not happen all at once, certainly not happen as completely, or not happen this quickly. And that, I think, can certainly fairly be said to be one of the measures of greatness. But try to imagine now – and it's hard to do – what the world would have been like had she not had the courage, the conviction, the decision to take this kind of course no matter how much criticism it brought. And it's very hard now to re-create and remember the barrage of criticism for the actions that finally made labour unions a responsible member of the economy, with wage demands that did not add to inflation and that enabled them and their individual members to have a far better quality of life.

Well, that's quite enough, but it wasn't all, because Lady Thatcher was one of those very few prime ministers, one of those very few people, who were able to make a major difference in foreign policy as well as domestic. And in foreign policy, again, the conventional wisdom is now so far behind us that it's very hard to realise. But what that conventional wisdom was was basically that there was going to be always a very large amount of at least socialism throughout the world; that it could never really be challenged; that you could elect different governments and different parties, but your changes were going to be minuscule. And there might be some that would have a little less attempts to deal strongly with things like the Cold War, which are virtually forgotten now. The way you did that, of course, was very much the same way you dealt with domestic affairs. First of all, you cut defence spending, because defence spending is clearly not popular. I suppose I'm one of the leading American authorities on how unpopular defence spending is in democracy, but that was part of the conventional wisdom. And another part of the conventional wisdom was that there couldn't ever be any confrontation or anything like real opposition.

During the Cold War, there were three or four words that guided our philosophy for a long time, until Mrs Thatcher and President Reagan were in office, and those words were, first of all, containment. Containment was the idea that you couldn't possibly oppose the Soviet Union's growth or their goal of world domination. What you could do would be to try to contain it, and then, after several decades, it would implode upon itself and so you didn't really have to do anything at all. Just try to contain it. This overlooked the fact that the Soviet Union, with a basic agenda of world domination – they used to deny they had that, but all of the writings and all of the teachings showed that they did – they didn't want to be contained, and they didn't join in this idea that containment was going to, in effect, keep many of the gains they had made at the end of World War II and at the same time make some more, all in the nature of having basically only a desire for safe quarters. The Soviets, in common with their

Russian predecessors – and, I might say, their Russian successors – are very concerned always about whether or not their quarters are safe. Well, this is understandable enough, but in order to secure that, they want these buffer zones. And the buffer zones extended pretty well across most of Europe on the one side, and well into the Pacific on the other side. And as these buffer zones got bigger and bigger, it became quite apparent that there was not going to be anything in the way of containment that was really going to work.

Well, we tried other things. We tried détente, in which we were supposed to try to get along with the Soviet Union. Then there was a thing called 'moral equivalence'. I know a little bit about moral equivalence because, as Lady Thatcher remembers, I had to debate at Oxford University on the subject that resolved that there is no moral difference between the foreign policy of the United States and the USSR. Our embassy was quite naturally extremely alarmed that I had accepted an opportunity to debate that subject, and I told them that as far as I was concerned, it was too late to back out, even if I had concluded I should. And so we went ahead and conducted the debate. It was against primarily a self-admitted Marxist professor named E. P. Thompson. And at the end, we were able to prevail that there was indeed a difference, a moral difference, between the two foreign policies. But that moral equivalence was an argument that was quite strong for a long time, and it was, again, more or less of an excuse, a kind of a reason for not pursuing any policy of confrontation.

And then the other one that we ran into in that time was always convergence: that the two policies were going to basically come together and yes, you would have a communist system over here and you'd have a capitalist or semi-capitalist system over here, and the two could converge, and pretty soon there would be no real differences or no real need for anything in the way of confrontation because the two could simply exist together. Well, again, it took quite a lot of strength to oppose that kind of rather comforting sort of theory as to why we should never have confrontation and never really do anything to stop the growth and the expansion and the strength of the then Soviet Union. In fact, it became very unfashionable to do so. And people who have spoken in an anti-Communist tone were considered to be either basically partisans of Senator McCarthy or otherwise rather unreliable and not very safe people to have around conferences or other gatherings. And it took a lot to repudiate that.

That was repudiated. There was a recognition finally that coexistence was not possible, and I always admired Winston Churchill's statement about this. He said that he always had a great deal of difficulty maintaining neutrality as between the fire brigade and the arsonist. And it seemed to me that that was a pretty good way to phrase the idea of trying to stay neutral in this enormous struggle.

Mrs Thatcher and President Reagan were those who recognised that you couldn't really have this convergence, or this moral equivalence, or the two could work together, and it was indeed an evil empire that we were opposing in the Soviet Union. And some of you may remember the anguished cries of the conventional wisdom people when Mr Reagan used this term, because it sort of upset all of the careful theories that were supposed to lead to a living together and a working together. And his idea was very simple. He said that you basically could not live and work together with a system that did not honour freedom, or human rights, or the rule of law, or elementary justice. And again, these were extraordinarily strong and basically unpopular statements to be making about that time, and yet it was the making of those statements and the adherence to the principles that were involved that did allow us to win the Cold War. Mrs Thatcher was one of those few people who could see that, and could see how strength in opposition was necessary.

I remember when we had to bomb some of the sites in Libya that had been connected with the export of terrorism. We had many planes based in England at that time, and Mrs Thatcher gave permission immediately, without the slightest hesitation, that those planes could be used in attack on terrorist targets in Libya. Another country, whom I won't name except to say that it was France, declined to do that, and as a result, we had to fly some 1,800 miles in addition, with radio silence and four extra refuellings – and a refuelling with radio silence is an interesting experience that none of you who are not skilled pilots would want to undertake. But in any event, that again was an example of how the observation and the judgement and the conclusion was there that, no matter how unpopular it might have been at home – and it was unpopular for her at home – that it was the right thing to do, and it would be done.

I don't think it's necessary to mention very much about the Falklands, but there again was a difference between accepting with a sort of a shrug the inva-

sion and the seizure of the Falkland Islands under British sovereignty by a corrupt military dictatorship in Argentina. And a lot of people were willing to make
that shrug and in effect to say, well, it's not really very important, and anyway,
there's nothing we can do about it. Eight thousand miles, as Mrs Thatcher mentioned in her very eloquent convocation speech earlier this afternoon, with only
a single stop in between for refuelling, and by a military force that had been
reduced, this was considered basically not possible. And her military chiefs so
advised her, and our military chiefs advised me that it basically was not going to
be possible. Mrs Thatcher took all of this in stride and she uttered to me what
was always a very memorable comment. She said, 'The possibility of defeat simply does not exist'. And it did not exist because of that kind of attitude and that
kind of strength and that kind of spirit, and the magnificent fighting qualities of
the British military forces. So that again you had an example of a dictatorship,
an aggressor – a very brutal aggressor – a tyrant, and appeasement, as Mr
Churchill always said, encourages tyranny. That was stood up to and successfully opposed, and it told the world that this kind of aggression was not going to
succeed.

It was very much the same kind of thing that Britain and the United States,
and twenty-nine other nations, demonstrated in the Gulf War: that we were not
going to allow an aggressor to seize the small neighbouring country of Kuwait
and impose his will on it, and not do anything about it. Tyranny could not be
encouraged in that way.

So all of this, I think, was basically the kind of spirit that applied domestical-
ly and made such an enormous difference in the domestic policy of Great
Britain, and indeed the world, and led the way. And then it was again done many
times over in foreign policy. Negotiations with a corrupt dictator, with an
aggressive tyrant, cannot succeed, and there is no peace process, there is no arms
control talk, that is going to succeed because you know in advance that the
promises that are being made are not going to be kept. And we've had ample
authority for that, ample examples of that, in the way in which Saddam Hussein
has declined to allow any UN inspections, despite all of his promises made at the
end of the Gulf War that that would happen. So I think it is important that we
have in mind these as lessons of the Cold War: that you can negotiate all you
want, but every time you give away something, and give away in return for a

promise, the promise is not going to be kept. Had that policy been followed with the Argentines in the Falklands, they would still have the Falklands, and we would have had various negotiations that could have enabled some to say, well, we have brought peace. We would have brought peace at far too high a price had that been the case. Fortunately, we didn't have to put that to a test.

To sum this up: the contributions that have been made by Lady Thatcher to the world, and they are very great – to her own country, and to us, and to all people who love freedom – is to mention a statement made by an Italian parliamentarian. An Italian parliamentary victory had finally been won by a basically reasonably conservative coalition. And Mrs Thatcher was writing to them to urge them to carry out many of the policies that she had carried out, and that they would have, she felt, the same result on the economy of Italy, which was in serious trouble at that time. The Italian parliamentarian wrote back to her and said, yes, he would like to do that. But of course they couldn't do that for a wide number of reasons. He said, 'We have all these things against us. We have a system of proportional representation, we have to have coalitions, we don't have strong parties. Our party is only in by agreeing with a number of other parties to get a simple majority. Our people would never tolerate any kind of reduction in social services. And all of these things we have against us, and these are all reasons why we can't do it'. But he said, 'On the other hand, we have one thing that you don't'. And Mrs Thatcher said, 'What is that?' And he said, 'We have your example'.

Myth and Reality:
The Impact and Legacy of Margaret Thatcher

Philip Allmendinger

Like many things in life, first impressions matter. And my first impressions of Margaret Thatcher were to colour my interest in her and politics. As a small boy my class-mates and I received a daily bottle of free milk – a policy introduced many years before in an attempt to improve the health of children. As Secretary of State for Education in the Heath government of 1970–74 Margaret Thatcher abolished this state handout. The chant 'Thatcher the milk-snatcher' was a popular one at the time.

The second impression came when I started work for a local council in the late 1980s. I had been studying articles and books by many eminent academics and commentators on how the Thatcher governments were slashing red tape here and budgets there. But on starting work in one of these hated bureaucracies the reality seemed very different. Little appeared to have been cut in budgets or services, the rhetoric of 'jobs in filing cabinets' did not appear to have been translated into change on the ground and, where change had occurred, those imaginative enough had been simply replacing reduced red tape with regulation of another kind to achieve the same ends. I was not alone in feeling that there seemed to be an hiatus between what we were led to believe would happen and what actually did happen.

These two characteristics – myth and reality – are central to any understanding of the impact and legacy of Thatcherism. Helmut Kohl once said that dealing with Margaret Thatcher was like taking alternate hot and cold baths. For me, this neatly sums up the frustrations, complexities and attractiveness involved in studying Thatcherism – just when you think you have a grip on a theme or thread, its slips away.

One cannot detract from some of the achievements of Margaret Thatcher: she was the first female Prime Minister in British history, she won three elections, held office for eleven years – a period longer than any other Prime Minister of the twentieth century, led Britain into a successful war against military advice and gave her name to a phenomenon that we are reflecting on here. Once, when asked what she had changed, she replied, 'Everything'. How can one reconcile the obvious achievements with evidence that points to different conclusions? The answer partly lies in what we mean by Thatcherism.

This volume presupposes that there is such a thing as Thatcherism though that is by no means agreed. In the UK at least, any perspective on Thatcherism depends as much on intangible criteria as objective assessment of policy impact and implementation. Like Churchill, her style and attitude were more suited to some situations than others; 'Thatcherite' is as often used as a pejorative adjective as a complimentary one. Indeed, the term 'Thatcherism' was coined by left-wing critiques of the style and substance of her approach[1] though such criticisms often masked admiration and envy of the conviction with which she pursued her beliefs. Marxists saw Thatcherism as the crude championing of capitalism. More perceptive left-wing critiques also perceived the strong authoritarian element that accompanied the pursuit of the free market: 'free economy, strong state' as it was termed.[2] The Left has been particularly important in helping define and explore Thatcherism. In helping to characterise the phenomenon they filled the vacuum left by some right-wing commentators many of whom rejected the idea of any coherence or identifiable ideology to Thatcherism. Instead, they preferred to see it as a collection of personal beliefs about the relationship between human beings and society.[3] Partly, this ambivalence derives from distrust within the Conservative Party of theory above 'common sense', a distrust that Margaret Thatcher played on with her kitchen sink homilies concerning fiscal prudence. Consequently, the idea of a coherence which we associate with Thatcherism largely derived from political opponents.

There are also further issues of coherence and consistency.

First, evolution. One tries hard to reconcile the Thatcher of the early 1970s with that of the late 1980s. The early Thatcher seemed to be a follower, particularly of the ideas associated with Keith Joseph and Enoch Powell. It was Joseph in particular who was developing and expounding ideas concerning reductions in state activity, taxation and more supply side incentives for economic growth. At this time, Margaret Thatcher had free market instincts but, according to some, she was not elected as a Thatcherite.[4]

Second, pragmatism. No government starts with a clean slate and the first Thatcher administration was no different. It inherited an economy where inflation was rising and continued to rise throughout 1980s to a high point of 22 per cent. This led to a rise in taxes in the first budget though mostly through indirect taxation. The 'Iron Lady' who was 'not for turning' frequently did. This happened most notably on economic policy and the loosening of fiscal targets which, while politically popular, eventually fed inflation in the late 1980s. During the 1983 general election campaign she boasted about government spending on welfare and that the existing level of expenditure was 'about right'.[5]

Third, like all leaders there were concessions to be made with the party. The election of Margaret Thatcher as leader in 1975 did not signal a wholesale shift to monetarist thinking. A number of leading Tory thinkers were extremely hostile to the shift away from Keynesian economic orthodoxy.[6] This battle within the party was by no means won by 1979 or even well into the 1980s. The manifesto of 1979 looked remarkably like the Heath one of 1970 and contained no mention of policies such as privatisation that were later to be seen as the leitmotif of Thatcherism.

Finally, events and luck played a significant role in the Thatcher years. Most notably, the Falklands War provided the basis for Thatcher to demonstrate her convictions while a continually divided Labour Party provided little, if any, effective opposition

Overall, I do not subscribe to the view of some that Thatcherism is an ideology or a coherent body of thought. This is not to say that there is no such thing as Thatcherism. It may be harder to pin down than, say, Marxism but it also has a similar visceral confidence. Rather than an ideology I think it is more accurate to see it as a set of ideas, prejudices and instincts that often compliment each other but also, at times, contradict each other. I do, however, subscribe to the majority view of Thatcherism that it is comprised of two broad tenets: a free-market liberalism and a strong-state authoritarianism. The translation of liberalism and authoritarianism into approaches to government varied and depended upon the issue and, crucially, upon time and space. In my own area of study, local government and environmental regulation, liberalism and authoritarianism were translated into three broad approaches.

First, there is an emphasis upon market mechanisms. Supply-side constraints were attacked in a move to encourage risk-taking and entrepreneurship. 'Rolling back' the state, however, did not go as far as many, particularly liberals, of the New Right would have wished.

Second, there was a related emphasis on a rule of law. Where state intervention was necessary, discretion and the uncertainty and ambiguity that accompanied it were to be replaced by explicit regulations and frameworks that could be taken into account by those making investment decisions.

Finally, there was a strong centralising component to Thatcherism. This had a number of origins, including a distrust of democracy and particularly social democracy, a dislike of the public sector and a desire to resist popular change.

I do not want to present these three broad approaches as the only aspects of Thatcherism, nor do I see them as necessarily coherent. A lot of academic debate has focused upon the intellectual roots of Thatcherism or the New Right and this has added to a growing mythology of coherence and omnipotence that we are, perhaps, also feeding here. There is some coherence to the various elements of Thatcherism. Liberals want a strong system of law to protect the market and do not object to authoritarian measures to enforce it. Authoritarians are muted in their support for the market but find its harsh discipline a useful means of imposing authority. But the abstract coherence of liberalism and authoritarianism masks problems with policy detail that led to compromise and in some cases outcomes being contrary to that desired. Let me give an example.[7]

As part of the supply-side emphasis on reducing red tape, local discretion and creating a more explicit and rule-of-law-based approach to regulation, the Conservative government quickly turned their attention to the UK's intricate approach to land use planning and environmental regulation. The highly centralised nature of UK government still left a good deal of discretion in the hands of professionals such as planners, architects and others at the local level. There was much suspicion of such characters and their middle-class socialist leanings within the Conservative Party. Throughout the 1980s proposals emerged to curb these 'excesses' and release entrepreneurial spirit and economic growth.

Policy papers were drawn up and legislation introduced with highly ambitious objectives that talked of 'lifting the burden' and seeking to create areas without any form of control or fiscal link to government. Good, combative, typical Thatcherite rhetoric. A plethora of changes were introduced to land use regulation and local government throughout the Thatcher years. Roughly fifty Acts of Parliament concerning local government and around twenty-three concerning planning and environmental control were passed during the Thatcher decade. This is not to mention the changes in secondary legislation and government advice. With large majorities in Parliament and a centralised governmental system (Thatcher abolished six metropolitan councils and the Greater London Council in 1986 for no reason other than malice) the will of the government should have been implemented.

Here, today, it is clear that little actually changed in this and many other areas of state control.[8] One study found that

The government experienced major implementation problems. Some of these problems are common to all governments: conflicting objectives, insufficient information or limited resources. However, some problems were clearly exacerbated by the Thatcher government's approach to policy-making.[9]

Why did little change? There are many reasons. One could point to the conflict between the neo-liberals and authoritarians within the party. Liberals wanted to see wholesale deregulation while authoritarians felt the need to protect Britain's heritage from the ravages of unplanned development. A related reason was the support from the mainly rural based constituency of the Conservative Party who saw the threat of wholesale deregulation as a threat to house values.

The outcome was confusion. But it was not just that such changes were ineffective. Those charged with implementing changes that were supposed to create 'certainty and flexibility' (how one reconciles those two was never explained) could and actually did use the proposed changes to increase regulatory control.

Another set of reasons was hinted at above and has been developed from a policy analysis perspective.[10] This highlights that the Thatcher governments lacked:

- clear and consistent objectives;
- adequate causal theory or sufficient information about the problem and its causes;
- appropriate policy tools and sufficient resources to implement the policy;
- control over implementing officials;
- the support of, or compliance from, the interest groups/agencies affected by the policy;
- stable socio-economic contexts that do not undermine political support.

In short, the very reasons why the Thatcher government was lauded, e.g., strong, uncompromising leadership, etc. were also the source of its problems. The rejection of consultation and negotiation, for example, alienated those groups who were charged with implementing policy who then failed to co-operate or comply with that policy.

I do not want to suggest that all the changes introduced during the Thatcher years were failures. The government did manage to abolish the seven democratically elected councils as mentioned earlier and there were obviously some high-profile achievements. But these achievements have been mythologised into a governing competency that did not exist. Partly, this is because attention has tended to focus on the 'big picture' in assessments of Thatcherism and consequently, some of the less high profile impacts have been overlooked.

More than a decade after she stepped down it is often forgotten (particularly by Conservatives) that John Major ruled for nearly as long as Margaret Thatcher. The 1990s were still the Conservative decade. However, by the time Major took office in 1990 the Thatcher governments had succeeded in alienating much of the party's popular support.[11] Despite this the Conservatives won the 1992 general election more because of the distrust of Labour than an endorsement of Major or Conservatism. Did Thatcherism come to an end in 1990?

There is no doubt that important elements of Thatcherism continued under John Major in the years 1990–97. This has led some to dub the Major years 'late

Thatcherism'.[12] The rhetoric did change in some respects. From the harsh and strident tones of Thatcher's 'There Is No Alternative' (TINA) to Major's talk of a 'classless society'. Behind this, however, was a Thatcherite, if not more radical Thatcherite set of policies.[13] Privatisation, for example, was extended to areas such as rail, coal, mail and the prison service that caused a revolt in the party. This is not to say that the Major governments were any more successful in implementing policy.

This brief assessment of the Major years does raise another important aspect in any assessment of Thatcherism: the extent to which we should view Thatcherism per se as homogenous. Although some studies approach Thatcherism (including the Major years) from a perspective that highlights the evolving approaches and policies,[14] most assume a consistency that simply did not exist. It would not be uncontroversial to claim that the first Thatcher government of 1979–83 hung on by its fingertips, was still working out detailed policy prescriptions and was extremely unpopular. Similarly, it is widely recognised that the 1987–90 government was the most radical of Mrs Thatcher's administrations. What also changed were policies. Following the success of the Green Party in the 1989 European Elections, for example, the Conservatives noticeably shifted towards a more pro-environmental stance.

To this temporal evolution I want to add a further dimension of space. Just as Thatcherite policies and success varied throughout the 1980s and 1990s so they also varied across the country. From high-profile differences such as the poll tax to more local interpretations of policy such as found in local government one cannot talk of a spatially neutral Thatcherism.

Notwithstanding the continuation of Thatcherism under Major it has been the latter who has been blamed for 'deviating' from the path. The myth of Thatcher did not stop in 1990. There has been a growth in the mythology after 1990 that saw her as a strong leader, willing to take on difficult groups such as the European Union or difficult issues such as the growth in union power. Major was widely portrayed as weak and vacillating. But Major has let it be known through his memoirs[15] that Margaret Thatcher played far more than a passive role in this mythologising and re-writing of history.

However, John Major is not the only subsequent leader to have been accused of diluting Thatcherism. It is now almost a cliché to claim that one of Thatcher's biggest achievements was to force the Labour Party to become electable again. However, the Conservative Party under its next leader, William Hague, accepted the Labour government's introduction of a minimum wage – hardly a Thatcherite policy. Notwithstanding this, the party is now shifting much further to the right than under Margaret Thatcher particularly over Europe. The former Chancellor Geoffrey Howe recently argued that even in her most strident phase there was still some tolerance of the left within the party.[16] Although a Thatcherite minister himself, Hague has ruthlessly purged his shadow cabinet of Thatcherites associated with the 1980s.

It is now more than a decade since Margaret Thatcher stepped down as leader of the Conservative Party and Prime Minister of the UK. Since that time the very word Thatcherism has become shorthand for either aggressively anti-state, laissez-faire and authoritarian dogma or pro-market, strong leadership and nationalistic pride depending on your view. Such a polarisation of opinion makes it difficult to make objective assessments. This is complicated by the myths that surround the Thatcher years. The low taxation, anti-state, market-orientated image can be refuted with evidence to the contrary – the Thatcher governments had, at best, a mixed bag of results.

What is for certain is that Thatcherism will remain a label. A recent letter in the *Independent* talked of Thatcherism being alive and kicking. Myth and reality are still at work.

Notes

1   Stuart Hall and Martin Jacques (eds) *The Politics of Thatcherism* (Lawrence and Wishart, London 1983).

2   Andrew Gamble, *The Free Economy and the Strong State. The Politics of Thatcherism* (London: Macmillan, 1988).

3   Shirley Robin Letwin, *The Anatomy of Thatcherism* (London: Fontana, 1992).

4   Anthony King, 'Margaret Thatcher: The Style of a Prime Minister', in Anthony King (ed) *The British Prime Minister* (London: Macmillan, 1985).

5   E. J. Evans, *Thatcher and Thatcherism* (London: Routledge, 1997).

6   See, for example, Sir Ian Gilmour, *Inside Right* (London: Hutchinson, 1977).

7   For a fuller account see Phillip Allmendinger, and Huw Thomas, *Urban Planning and the British New Right* (London: Routledge, 1998).

8   For assessments of the period see Paul Cloke, (ed) *Policy and Change in Thatcher's Britain* (Oxford: Pergamon Press, 1992); Dennis Kavanagh, and Anthony Seldon, (eds) *The Thatcher Effect. A Decade of Change* (Oxford: Oxford University Press, 1989).

9   David Marsh, and R. A. W. Rhodes, (eds.) *Implementing Thatcherite Policies. Audit of an Era* (Buckingham: Open University Press, 1992).

10   David Marsh, and R.A.W. Rhodes, ibid.

11   S. McAnulla, 'Explaining Thatcherism: Towards a Multidimensional Approach', in D. Marsh, J. Buller, C. Hay, J. Johnston, P. Kerr, S. McAnulla, M. Watson, *Post-war British Politics in Perspective* (Cambridge: Polity Press, 1999); pp. 189-207.

12   Kerr, P., McAnnulla, S. and Marsh, D. 'Charting Late-Thatcherism: British Politics Under Major', in S. Lancaster (ed) *Developments in Politics* (Ormskirk: Causeway, 1997), pp. 101–126.

13   A. Barker, 'Major's Government in a Major Key: Conservative Ideological Aggressiveness Since Thatcher', *New Political Science*, 1995, 33, 125-50. in Stuart Hall, and Martin Jaques, (eds) (1983) *The Politics of Thatcherism* (London: Lawrence and Wishart, 1983).

14   See for example, Jessop, B., Bonnet, K., Bromley, S. and Ling, T. (1988), *Thatcherism: A Tale of Two Nations*, (Cambridge: Polity Press, 1988) or Kerr, P. and Marsh, D. 'Explaining Thatcherism: Towards a Multidimensional Approach', in D. Marsh, J. Buller, C.Hay, J. Johnston, P. Kerr, S. McAnulla, M. Watson, *Post-war British Politics in Perspective* (Cambridge: Polity Press, 1999), pp. 168–187.

15   *John Major, The Autobiography* (London: HarperCollins, 1999).

16   Geoffrey Howe, 'Where should William Hague Go Next? To the Centre Ground, of Course', *Independent*, 4 January 2000, p. 18.

New Labour as a Thatcher Legacy

Dennis Kavanagh

―――――

The concept of New Labour – a Labour Party transformed in its policies, institutions and ethos – is indelibly associated with Tony Blair and his fellow-modernisers. But the idea of modernising Labour, to take account of changes in social structure, public opinion and the economy predates Blair. Neil Kinnock after 1987, the Labour right-wingers who exited to form the SDP in 1981, and Hugh Gaitskell and his fellow-revisionists in the 1950s all blazed this trail. All operated within the political centre left. From outside, however, Margaret Thatcher may also be considered as a midwife of New Labour.

I shall argue in this essay that New Labour is both a product and vindication of Thatcherism. The sweeping changes which the party has made to its structure, policies and ethos since the late 1980s mark the success of the Thatcher project. On the eve of the 1997 general election she said: 'Britain will be safe in the hands of Mr Blair'. Effectively, she was expressing confidence in the safety of her legacy. John Major has reflected in retirement that his 1992 general election success, against the odds, had the effect of killing off socialism in Britain.

Political agendas rarely change. This is because the necessary combination of political actors, circumstances, and new ideas or 'doable' policy alternatives are rarely found together.[1] The 1945 Labour government achieved a breakthrough in terms of establishing a policy framework that lasted largely intact for the next thirty years. The Conservative Party, often in government in the succeeding years, accepted the package of state-financed welfare provision, full employment, public ownership of major industries and utilities, and the importance of the trade unions.

Just as the stability of a new constitution requires its acceptance by a successor government, so the durability of a new political agenda depends on its acceptance by later governments. In the case of Thatcherism, this depended on the behaviour of both her Conservative successor in 1990 and the new Labour government in 1997. Ten years after her departure from office, one can offer an interim verdict on her impact on the agenda.

It is worth highlighting some of the big changes in the public policy framework which came about during the 1980s. Curbing inflation rather than achieving full employment became the central task of economic policy. Trade unions now operate in a more restrictive legal framework. The ending of quasi-corporatist decisions about prices and incomes meant that wage-bargaining was depoliticised. The market – not the state – is acknowledged as the prime engine of economic growth. The major utilities were sold off to private investors rather than being owned by the state. Marginal rates of income tax have been substantially lowered to provide incentives for hard work and enterprise, and to promote freedom. An increased degree of conditionality, including the encouragement of greater self-reliance and means-testing, has been attached to welfare benefits. The role of the state and local government has been defined in terms of being a regulator and enabler rather than provider.

Political parties have identities born of their history, supporting social groups, shared values and interests. These are forces for continuity. But a party also has to cope with changed circumstances, not least the success of the opposition party in building winning electoral coalitions and reshaping the agenda. The British Conservative Party, as the normal party of government, has been a remarkably successful catch-all party, appealing across social classes and wearing ideology lightly. Adaptation has not been easy, given the growth in size and assertiveness of the working class and trade unions after 1945 and the emergence of a more collectivist and egalitarian thrust to public policy in the 1970s. Yet the Conservative Party after 1945 provides one of the most successful cases of party adaptation to a changed political agenda. A key architect of the recovery was R. A. Butler who remarked, after the 1945 humiliation, that if the British people wanted to have full employment policies and a welfare state then 'they can have it but under our auspices'.[2]

The Labour Party, on the other hand, has historically found it more difficult to adapt to social and cultural change. It possessed an ideology (expressed in the party's 1918 constitution), was deeply rooted in the industrial working class, was largely created and financed by the trade unions and its party structure gave power to the activists. The result was that the party was usually more geared to respond to the interests of party activists and producer groups than Labour voters.

Yet Labour Party leaders, at least from the time of Hugh Gaitskell (1955–63) onwards, have often been revisionists, struggling to come to terms with social change. They were modernisers before the term had been invented. In large part they were driven by new work patterns, changing values, particularly increasing individual choice, and a run of Conservative electoral successes. After a third consecutive Conservative election victory in 1987, Neil Kinnock embarked on the process of party reform and changing party policies. The party leaders could refer to the ample survey evidence as well as candidates' personal contact with ordinary voters which confirmed the Labour Party's unpopularity.[3] The party had to adapt to meet the aspirations of a more affluent society and the changes wrought by a decade of Conservative government.

It is worth recalling that Labour was well on the way to becoming a new party before Tony Blair was elected leader in 1994. There had already been big shifts in policy following the 1983 election defeat. On defence, membership of the European Community, many of the industrial relations reforms, privatisation of the utilities and sales of council (public) houses, Labour had moved in the direction of the Conservative Party. The leadership espoused a new vocabulary of the enabling state, working with the market, promoting opportunity and fairness rather than equality and asserting the right of consumers over those of producers. The party also took steps to distance itself from the trade unions. A new Policy Forum was set up to clip the wings of the activist-dominated party Conference, and activists were to be further weakened by holding membership ballots for the selection and reselection of parliamentary candidates. A powerful leader's office was established and the NEC weakened. All the changes were designed to make the party more voter-responsive and enable it to move to the new 'middle ground'.[4]

Yet one has to admit that modernisation was incomplete by 1992, when Neil Kinnock resigned as leader or even by 1994, when Blair became leader. Labour was still not fully trusted when it came to handling the trade unions, taxes and crime – the reasons which people gave for not supporting the party. Clause IV of the party constitution, and its commitment to widespread public ownership, was a symbol of old Labour. Getting rid of it would be a dramatic break with the past and a symbol of New Labour. Tony Blair's revised Clause IV praised the Thatcherite themes of enterprise, markets, and competition, but with the proviso that they should operate 'in a just society'.

By the time he became leader, Blair had already concluded that the centre left parties in the West were in trouble. People were resistant to paying more taxes, demanded public services which were more responsive and provided greater choice, and did not identify with state-owned enterprises. In a *Spectator* lecture in 1995 he signalled a new approach to welfare, when he spoke not of entitlements, but of 'rights' matched with 'responsibilities' and 'duties'. He thought that politics at the end of the twentieth century had to move beyond the battle between socialism and capitalism and between Left and Right. Labour had to respond to the aspirations of ordinary people, occupy the middle ground and govern from the political centre. Research by John Curtice suggests that by 1997 Labour had even moved to the right of the median voter on a number of key issues.

A number of forces contributed to the emergence of New Labour and its convergence with the Conservative policy. They include:

- Changing public opinion. Labour's survey research showed how during the 1980s the Conservative Party had captured the themes of choice, ownership, prosperity and educational standards. Labour modernisers were challenged by further research after the 1992 election defeat which showed how former Labour voters and 'soft' Conservatives in the south-east felt that Labour might be good for 'losers' and 'have nots', but that it also held back the ambitious and those wanting to get on, i.e. people like themselves. Mrs Thatcher, according to Philip Gould (Blair's polling adviser), had changed Britain and Labour had to follow. The research shaped a largely conservative set of social and economic policies. Labour was in the business of being a preference-accommodating rather than a preference-leading party.[5]
- Circumstances The passage of time meant that it was impractical for Labour to maintain its 1983 pledges of reversing many Conservative measures. The trade union reforms, income tax cuts, and council house sales were all pop-

ular with the voters. Britain was now too entwined in the European Community to contemplate withdrawal. Returning privatised utilities to public or part public ownership would be expensive, and compensating shareholders would be a major drain on public finances and preclude spending on other more popular programmes.

- Globalisation and the interdependence of states. The experience of the Mitterrand government in France in the early 1980s showed that socialism – or even Keynesianism – in one country was no longer possible. Regimes converged around business-friendly policies of low taxes, low borrowing and flexible Labour markets. There was nothing new in Labour being tamed by international markets. Labour governments had had trouble in 1931, were forced to devalue in 1949 and 1967, and subject to IMF intervention in 1976. But now the liberalised financial markets and mobility of capital imposed further constraints.
- Shifts in the Left. The collapse of Communism in Eastern Europe and break-up of the former Soviet Union in the late 1980s, and the decline of faith in the state as a solution to problems affected centre left political parties everywhere. Awareness of these limits meant that parties of the left in Australasia and much of Western Europe turned away from state ownership and intervention in the economy, and squeezed entitlements to welfare benefits. Collectivist institutions like the trade unions, local government and nationalised industries had all been weakened by the end of the 1980s, as a result of Conservative policies. In common with much of the left in Western Europe, Labour became interested in a non-economic agenda, embracing policies for the environment, women's rights, welfare reform and the incorporation of the European Union's social chapter.
- Constitutional Reform. Labour's acceptance in the mid 1990s of what had traditionally been a Liberal party agenda was in large part a reaction to the long period of Conservative rule. Such measures as devolution for Scotland and Wales and proportional representative for all non Westminster elections and reducing the number of hereditary peers in the House of Lords were designed to help centre left forces. The two party system had failed to be competitive after 1979; hence the interest in constitutional reform as a means of providing the balance between government and opposition the that party system that had failed to promote.

359

- New campaign techniques. These include a greater use of public relations and focus groups, an emphasis on the party leader, the development of simple message and centralised control of party communications. Of course, the promotion of the leader and disciplined adherence to a centrally devised message encouraged the centralisation of authority in the party. The party learned much from Clinton's successful campaign for the US Presidency in 1992. But before then Labour had been impressed by the campaigning superiority of the Conservative Party.[6]

It is true to say that a number of other forces were at work in making New Labour. They include Blair's own Christian Socialist beliefs, his willingness to come to terms with a hostile press, his determination to recruit votes from traditionally non-Labour voters in so-called 'middle England', and the ideas about policy and the campaign techniques of Bill Clinton in 1992. But the Thatcher governments played an important role in assisting virtually every one of the factors discussed above. It did this, negatively, by removing or weakening many of the unpopular policies and institutions associated with Labour and more positively in terms of policies which Labour came to accept.

Finally, it is important to look beyond Britain in the 1980s. In western Europe and Australiasia centre left political parties accepted, often grudgingly and fitfully, the ideas of economic liberalism – privatisation, deregulation, downgrading full-employment policies and curbing the growth of public spending. In a brilliant essay, David Marquand noted:

Just as conservative and Christian democratic parties accommodated themselves to the collectivism and dirigisme of the 1940s, so social-democratic and even Communist parties have struggled, with varying degrees of success to accommodate themselves to the reborn economic liberalism of the last twenty years. [7]

Mrs Thatcher had been much impressed with Sir Keith Joseph's use of the ratchet metaphor in 1975 to describe how her Conservative predecessors regularly sold out to the Labour Party. Joseph claimed that in the interests of policy continuity and pursuit of the middle ground, Conservative leaders had too readily accepted the measures and policies of Labour governments. But, so he claimed,

Labour governments then moved to more new left-wing ground – in the form of more public spending, extending public ownership and regulations on business, and imposing higher taxes – and the mid point moved to the left. This was the so-called ratchet effect.

Since 1983 there has been a reversal of Joseph's ratchet. The convergence between the Conservative and Labour parties on many policies has been in one direction, from Labour to Conservative. In a recent book, Richard Heffernan points to the close correspondence between Labour's economic priorities in 1997 and the 1979 Conservative election manifesto. The latter promised to: control inflation as a first priority; curb public spending; reduce public borrowing; oppose punitive taxation; restore incentives for business and enterprise; and regulate trade unions. Labour in 1997 shared all these economic priorities.[8] In other words, New Labour has provided more policy continuity than discontinuity and Blair, like Mrs Thatcher might add, 'There is no other way'.

New Labour's occupation of much of the ground occupied by the Conservatives is a back-handed compliment to Mrs Thatcher. Her governments did much to force or facilitate the factors that led to New Labour. It did this by promoting certain social and economic changes, shifting popular expectations about government and offering a style of personal leadership. Ironically, this success in turn has created problems for the Conservative Party today. Traditionally, the Conservatives have thrived by stealing their opponents' clothes. But as many Conservative themes of the 1980s have been accepted by Labour and many of the well-defined 'enemies' of 1979 (high income tax, nationalised industries, and powerful trade unions) have been vanquished, so the party finds itself seeking new clothes.

Notes

1   On how agendas change, see Dennis Kavanagh, *The Reordering of British Politics* (Oxford: Oxford University Press, 1997). For discussion about whether there was an agenda change under Mrs Thatcher, see David Marsh, et. al., *Post-War British Politics in Perspective* (Cambridge: Polity Press, 1999) and Howard Glennerster, *British Social Policy since 1945* (Oxford: Blackwell, 1995).

2   For an historical perspective see Samuel H. Beer, *Modern British Politics* (London: Faber, 1965). It is

interesting to compare his book with his early impressions of Thatcher in *Britain Against Itself* (London: Faber, 1982).

3   On popular perceptions of Labour over a forty-year period, see Mark Abrams and Richard Rose, *Must Labour Lose?* (London: Penguin, 1960) and Phillip Gould, *The Unfinished Revolution* (London: Little Brown, 1998).

4   Eric Shaw, *The Labour Party since 1945* (Oxford: Blackwell, 1996).

5   For a stimulating discussion on this topic see, Colin Hay, 'That was Then, This is Now: The Revision of Policy in the 'Modernisation' of the British Labour Party – 1992–1997', *New Political Science*, vol.20, 1998 and his 'Labour's Thatcherite Revisionism: Playing the 'Politics of Catch-up'', *Politics Studies,* vol. 42, 1994.

6   See Dennis Kavanagh, *Election Campaigning. The New Marketing of Politics*

7   David Marquand, 'After Socialism', *Political Studies,* vol. 41, 1999, p. 45.

8   Richard Heffernan, *New Labour and Thatcherism* (London: Macmillan, 2000).

How Mrs Thatcher Saved the Labour Party (and Destroyed the Conservative Party)

Tony Wright

Soon after Margaret Thatcher became leader of the Conservative Party, the right-wing journalist Peregrine Worsthorne wrote an article in which he advised her to make an effort to understand British socialism and British socialists. He suggested a reading list, with the writings of R. H. Tawney at the top. It was good advice, which Mrs Thatcher almost certainly (and characteristically) did not take. As on other fronts (with Europe as the permanent example) she preferred to deal in caricatures rather than in real understanding. This became a serious disability, with eventually damaging political consequences – not least for her own fortunes (and that of her party). It also helped to save the Labour Party.

Had she taken Peregrine Worsthorne's advice and read some Tawney, she would have encountered the kind of ethical socialism that has always been central to the British Labour tradition. When the Labour Party had to remake itself, after the travails of the 1980s, these were the materials it used. Moreover, it was a tradition which extended beyond the organisational confines of the Labour Party and encompassed the broad swathe of progressive opinion. At the beginning of the twentieth century it had been described as 'liberal socialism' (by a Liberal) and it represented the intermingling of liberal and socialist ideas that has long constituted a strong and distinctive strand of British political thinking. Indeed, it may well constitute majority opinion, if survey evidence is to be believed.

Yet Mrs Thatcher knew little or nothing about it. This is directly relevant to arguments about liberty (with which her name is linked in the title of the conference). A reader of Tawney would have encountered the argument that 'freedom for the pike is death for the minnow', that it should be understood in terms of practical capacity, and that freedoms can be enlarged rather than diminished when public action constrains market power. Here was a social democratic view of freedom, which recognised that it could be threatened both by state power and market power, and which was far removed from the political caricatures of Thatcherism.

By not understanding this tradition, Mrs Thatcher led her party into an intellectual and political cul-de-sac from which it has not yet been able to escape. This also explains the oft-noticed puzzle that the electoral success of Thatcherism was not matched by its ability to change the underlying political and social values of the British people. Even when they voted for Mrs Thatcher, they were not Thatcherised. Instead they remained stubbornly social-democratic in their basic values. What they lacked, in the 1980s, was an effective social democratic party to vote for, such was the sorry and fractious state of the Labour Party at that time.

It was too easy, in the political climate of the day, for the Thatcherites to persuade themselves that they were the pioneers of a wholly new political culture in Britain. There was a deliberate cutting adrift from older traditions, including their own. 'It was only in April 1974 that I was converted to Conservatism', proclaimed Keith Joseph, Mrs Thatcher's leading intellectual lieutenant. 'I had thought I was a Conservative, but now I see that I was not really one at all'. This involved a rupture from domestic traditions of an explicit kind. The New Right takeover of the Conservative Party persuaded it to repudiate the whole philosophy of social justice and social equality. The zealous embrace of a creed of market authoritarianism (free economy, strong state) seemed to carry all before it. Yet it was a chimera. The journey to a promised land was really to be a journey into the wilderness. It was ungrounded, anchored only in the shallow and exceptional political circumstances of the time.

This is the real significance of Mrs Thatcher's notorious remark about there being 'no such thing as society'. The point is not whether the remark was misunderstood or wrenched out of context, but that it acquired a deep and symbolic resonance because it offended against a political culture that took community seriously. At a philosophical level, Mrs Thatcher did not understand that markets are grounded in cultures, institutions, and communities. At a political level, her flag-waving nationalism could not conceal her misunderstanding of the enduring political instincts of her people. It was a grievous error, for which she and her party were to pay dearly. It brought her down, at the hands of her own party. It also meant that she converted the most successful party of government into a warring sect of zealots.

So it is not simply that Mrs Thatcher saved the Labour Party by forcing it to undergo the shock therapy of prolonged opposition. The story is more complex than that. Labour's defeats were largely self-inflicted. What the arrival and ascendancy of Thatcherism did achieve was to shatter illusions on the Left about a range of its own previous assumptions and contribute to the tide of revisionism. In this sense Mrs Thatcher could be said to have helped save the Labour Party, rather as Tony Blair will (eventually) turn out to have helped save the Conservative Party. In the same vein, Mrs Thatcher has good claim to be regarded as the real progenitor of Britain's current constitutional revolution. By exposing and exploiting the unchecked power available to a government in Britain, she provoked a movement for constitutional and political reform in a way that she could not have anticipated and with consequences she would certainly loathe.

But the real point, which is far more interesting than the familiar law of unintended political consequences, is that Mrs Thatcher's misreading of British political culture meant that she was unable to secure the long-term hegemony of the Conservative Party that her electoral successes seemed to promise. She was saved for a long time by the Labour Party, but ended up as an electoral liability who finally had to be assassinated by her own followers. Crucially, she had failed to construct a political position which could establish itself as the new common sense in Britain. It looked for a time as though she might do so; but she failed. In failing, she not only revealed her own limitations but opened up a political space that a reconstructed Labour Party, and a new social democracy, could profitably fill.

It is in this decisive sense that Mrs Thatcher saved the Labour Party. Her extraordinary achievement was to unscramble the whole box of tricks that was the post-war settlement. That began to fall apart in the 1970s and was beyond repair by 1979. This paralysed the practitioners of post-war politics. If Labour had won the 1979 general election (which it might well have done had it been held in late 1978), it would not have known what to do with its victory. The old compasses did not work any more and those who tried to steer by them hit the rocks. The Thatcherites' delight in dancing on these broken compasses was matched only by their confident march into the new and uncharted territory.

On any test Mrs Thatcher shook things up. In key areas – such as trade union power, or the disciplines of the market – she cleared roadblocks and opened up new directions. There is no doubt that much of this was to prove helpful to the Labour Party as it struggled to escape from old positions. The beneficiary should have been the Conservative Party, and seemed to be so for a period; but it can at least be argued that the real beneficiary was the Labour Party. This is certainly the belief of Gerhard Schröder, who regularly explains that the SDP has found it more difficult than the Labour Party to renew and modernise itself because Britain had the experience of Margaret Thatcher. Britain had been shaken up, in the way that Germany under Kohl had not.

This is the sense in which Mrs Thatcher is the midwife of Blairism. She did not create Blairism, nor – emphatically – is Thatcherism the same as Blairism. Both are modernising creeds, but one is market modernisation, the other inclusive modernisation. One knows the distinction between a market economy and a market society, the other did not. But she certainly helped to make Blairism possible. This may even come to be seen as her lasting legacy. At this distance she already looks like a transitional figure, a product of the period between the collapse of the post-war settlement and the making of a new political consensus. This consensus, which likes to describe itself as a third way between Old Left and New Right, is a post-Thatcherite consensus. Unlike Thatcherism, it grounds itself in powerful strands of the British political culture, even when it mixes these strands in new ways. It mixes public and private, state and market, collective and individual, duties and rights in a potent synthesis. Its claim to combine dynamic markets with social justice is an objective that is widely shared.

It is also a claim that would once have been shared by much of the Conservative Party, until its Thatcherite takeover. Having unscrambled post-war British politics, Mrs Thatcher failed to put it back together again. She may have danced on the grave of the post-war settlement, but she failed to establish a new settlement of her own. This was a failure of historic proportions, not least for the future of her party. She ended as a beleaguered and isolated figure, not the architect of a new political and intellectual hegemony but the symbol of a kind of politics that had brought the Conservative Party to its knees. Her removal was a desperate bid for survival by her party.

In the short term this was successful, in that the 1992 general election was narrowly won. Yet this turned out only to be a stay of execution, for Mrs Thatcher's achievement was to have converted her party into an ungovernable sect. All those characteristics which had made the Conservative Party such a formidable and successful political force she had managed to extinguish. Yet it could (and, in some sense, should) have been so different. A different kind of leader could have consolidated her achievements into a new consensus, but she was not such a leader. The narrowness of her vision proved a fatal (and tragic) disability. Her replacement by John Major in 1990 should have been one of those moments in Conservative Party history when the party effortlessly adapted itself to a new environment, summoning up those elements in its own history, ideas and traditions which had enabled it to make such adaptations in the past. John Major was well cast for such a role and clearly wanted to perform it. His tragedy, and the tragedy for his party, was that Mrs Thatcher had bequeathed him a party that made this impossible.

This provided the Labour Party with its opportunity. A space had opened up in the middle ground of British politics that a Thatcherised Conservative Party had willfully vacated. Mrs Thatcher had provided a lifeline to a Labour Party whose obituaries had been confidently written. Once Labour had determined to grasp this lifeline, there occurred one of the most remarkable reversals of political fortunes in British political history. Labour came back from the dead, while the Conservatives interred themselves. Mrs Thatcher was decisive in both.

Margaret Thatcher:
Revised, Revisited, Re-examined,
and Reappraised

Michael A. Genovese

It is not a principle of the Conservative Party to stab its leaders in the back, but I must confess that it often appears to be a practice.

Arthur Balfour, 1922

The loyalties which centre upon number one are enormous. If he trips, he must be sustained. If he makes mistakes, they must be covered. If he sleeps, he must not be wantonly disturbed. If he is no good, he must be pole-axed.

Winston Churchill

Loath as I am to lend a note of reality to this 'love-in', it behooves me to introduce just a few prickly facts and counter-arguments to this very festive celebration of the achievements – and they are considerable – of Baroness Margaret Thatcher. You see, I come to praise Margaret Thatcher – not to bury her . . . But the vote was close! After all every leader has their strengths and weaknesses, good and bad points, successes and failures. In this, Lady Thatcher must be evaluated for the totality of her record; for the scope of the problems surfaced and the solutions she offered; for the short- and long-term consequences of her tenure; for what she did and failed to do; for her achievements and her shortcomings.

And yet, Margaret Thatcher is not your everyday, run-of-the-mill political leader. She mattered more than most, left huge footprints in the political land-scape, was a force for change. She was, in James Burns' phrase, 'a transforming leader'.

So how is one to make sense of Margaret Thatcher? Analogies might be use-ful, poetry perhaps more useful. But ultimately, they fail to capture the peculiar, even paradoxical nature of Margaret Thatcher's rise and accomplishments. Even the lofty language of the Bard might prove inadequate to the task of explaining Margaret Thatcher.

In many ways, Margaret Thatcher is a political phenomenon. Not only was she England's first woman Prime Minister, but she served in that capacity longer than anyone in this century, won three consecutive elections, reshaped much of the British political landscape, ranks as one of the most important prime min-isters in modern British history, finds herself compared with Clement Atlee and Winston Churchill, and is the only British Prime Minister with an 'ism named after her. There can be no doubt that Margaret Thatcher has stamped her imprint on British politics. How did she do it?

How did so seemingly unlikely a character rise to the top of a male world in the most suffocatingly traditional bastion of male supremacy, the British Conservative Party? And how did she so thoroughly dominate her party and political scene as to transform British politics from old Churchill/Attlee post-war consensus to a new, different political and economic orientation? For it is indeed no exaggeration to say that Margaret Thatcher has transformed British politics, and stamped her mark on government and society.

The Context

Events of the twentieth century had been very unkind to the British Empire. At the turn of the century, Britain ruled one-fifth of the globe, was widely recog-nised as hegemon of the West, exerted vast economic, political, and diplomatic leverage throughout the world, possessed a mighty military machine, and basked in the glory and rewards of empire. But in less than a generation Britain was stripped of empire, might, and glory. Starting with World War I, extending to the depression of the 1930s, and culminating in World War II, Great Britain's rapid decline in economic, military, and geopolitical power led from Pax Britannica to Pax Americana.

In the period immediately following World War II, Britain was forced to accept a world role dramatically reduced from the days of empire, as Britain became a peripheral power to the American core. 'British decline' became a phrase of common usage.

The post-World War II 'consensus' (or settlement), which came to so utterly dominate British politics, emerged out of Churchill's wartime consensus government and post-war recovery plans, but came to full fruition under the Prime Ministership of Clement Attlee. The consensus consisted of an agreement on the part of both Labour and the Conservatives over how post-war Britain should be governed. Its elements included agreement on both the foreign policy and domestic/economic components of British politics. The foreign policy elements included a bipartisan approach to problem-solving, support for NATO, decolonisation (in the thirty years after World War II, over thirty nations achieved independence from British rule), and Britain as a nuclear power. The domestic/economic elements of the consensus consisted of a bipartisan commitment to full employment, greater acceptance of trade unions in the political arena, more public ownership of industry, the pursuit of a mixed economy of public and market orientation, active economic management of the economy by the government, and the rise of the social welfare state. This required an active government, significant public expenditures, and high taxation.

This consensus was remarkably durable. It resulted in a striking continuity between governments and parties, and resulted in a marriage of sorts between modern capitalism and social democracy.[1] But the great successes of the consensus, and the economic and political recovery it engendered did not last forever. As economic and political problems rose in the 1970s, cracks in the consensus began to emerge.

The solidity of the post-war consensus was jeopardised by a combination of factors, none more menacing than the economic and trade union problems which beset England in the early 1970s. The centre could not hold. As Peter Jenkins noted, 'Economic failure had gradually taken its toll on the social cohesion and stability which had made Britain for so long one of the political wonders of the world'.[2] England's post-war recovery, sluggish by European standards, went into a tailspin, and with it, the consensus began to unravel. Britain began to be seen – and to see itself – in a state of decline and de-industrialisation.

It was not until the mid-1970s that the consensus came to be seen as the enemy of economic growth. Britain came to be seen as 'ungovernable' and an 'overloaded' state. The government seemed on the verge of economic bankruptcy and political insolvency. Britain was seen as 'the sick man of Europe', trade union strikes increased in number and severity and came to be seen as 'the British disease'.

By the mid and late 1970s, a window of political opportunity opened for those wishing to challenge the consensus. The economic downturn exposed a weakness in the consensus as the government's performance could not match public expectations. All that was missing was a viable challenger with a sellable alternative. At first, that person did not appear to be Margaret Thatcher, for up until her Prime Ministership, Thatcher was an unlikely rebel: a woman, a traditional Tory Conservative, a team player.

The Path to Power

After the Conservatives' defeat in two General Elections of 1974, the party was prepared to jettison Ted Heath and embrace a new leader. But Heath did not give up power easily. After a good deal of political manoeuvering, after several of Heath's most likely challengers withdrew from the contest, Thatcher entered the leadership battle. While Thatcher charted a course to the political right of Ted Heath, it was not yet clear just how far right or how much of a conviction, or ideological leader Thatcher was to become.

After losing three of four elections in a ten-year period, the Conservatives were ready for change of leadership. Margaret Thatcher emerged as head of the Conservative Party. The party had chosen an outsider, a dissident, and a woman as its new leader.

Thatcher was, as Chris Ogden notes, 'no one's first choice',[3] but she was the only true Conservative challenger to emerge, and in a time when the centrist/right consensus politics of Ted Heath was held to ridicule, even as unlikely a candidate as Margaret Thatcher became viable. Harris argues that Thatcher became head of the party 'as the result of a series of accidents', and was 'a mistake that should never have happened'.[4] Thatcher herself told a newspaper reporter six months earlier that 'It will be years before a woman either leads the party or becomes Prime Minister. I don't see it happening in my time'.[5]

While there were some early indications that Thatcher was a radical conservative, her years as leader in opposition belied this. Her shadow cabinet was dominated by unreconstructed Heathites, and her policy advocacy seemed moderate and cautious. Thatcher's caution reflected the precariously fragile perch upon which her leadership rested. But public appearances aside, Thatcher was determined to chart a new, more radical brand of conservatism for Britain.

In the late 1970s, the New Right, or the more radical right, gained ground within the Conservative Party. Rejecting the politics and policies of the old consensus-oriented wing of the party, the intellectual centre of the Conservatives began to slowly drift to the right. Thatcher, always skating on political thin ice as party leader, slowly and cautiously moved the party right. She knew her hold on the party was precarious and a major blunder could cause her demise. She repeatedly said, 'I shall have only one chance', for there were always political sharks waiting to depose her.

While in opposition, Thatcher witnessed the collapse of yet another government, as Labour was unable to solve the economic and trade union problems which plagued Britain. Thatcher began to develop economic policies in sharp contrast to the consensus model, and as economic conditions worsened, this new economic philosophy gained adherents – not so much because it was convincing, but because it was an alternative, the only alternative, to the status quo. Margaret Thatcher was again winning by default.

In the general election of 1979, the in-party was thrown out, and the out-party was put in. Owing her election more to the failure of the Callaghan Labour government than to the attractiveness of her policies or her personality, Thatcher was once again a leader on shaky ground. But she was the leader. She was the Prime Minister.

How did Thatcher win? First and foremost, Labour lost. The 1979 election was a 'throw 'em out' election. Secondly, the ideas which animated Thatcher's drastic social revolution were not yet fully formed and thus the election was about change, but it was always unclear just how much change was involved. Third, the 1970s were at a time of international economic malaise, and Britain suffered more from this than most. Worldwide, in-parties were thrown out, and Thatcher benefited from this trend. Fourth, while gender mattered, other factors dominated the election, and gender – while important – was overshadowed by the failure of Labour and the desperation of Britain's economic condition. All these factors, and many more coalesced to bring an unlikely person to power. As Young points out, she was 'a cluster of paradoxes'.[6]

And what was the Thatcher agenda? In many ways it was as surprisingly simple as it was challengingly radical: to transform Britain from a social welfare state to an entrepreneurial state.

Margaret Thatcher seemed an unlikely rebel. How could this small town girl grow up to be a radical, anti-consensus revolutionary? How did she change Britain? Margaret Thatcher's policies – if not her politics – are conservative, perhaps radically so. She attributes her policy formation not to any abstract philosophical principles, but to the everyday experiences she learned at the foot of her father.

Thatcher's goal was to break down the post-war consensus and revitalise Britain with a free-market, entrepreneurial public philosophy. The fact that the old consensus was seen as a failure created a window of opportunity through which Thatcher was determined to take Britain. In economic policy primarily, but also in defence, domestic, and social policy, Great Britain would be recast from top to bottom.

In economic terms, the revolution was to be accomplished by curbing public spending, lowering taxes, liberating the entrepreneurial spirit, tight money control, lowering inflation, reducing government regulations, moving towards privatisation of publicly owned industries, and busting unions. It was of course, an amazingly ambitious plan, but one which Thatcher was driven to put into place. Her goal, she said, was to use economics to change people, 'Economics are the method, the object is to change the soul'.[7] One may wish to forgive a bit of messianic language, after all, it's revolution about which we speak.

On inflation, after some early successes, Britain's inflation rate soared to double digits – one of the highest inflation rates in Europe.

On public spending the goal of controlling growth was only marginally successful. The rate of growth was reduced but not significantly. What is more interesting is not so much the rate of spending as the shift of priorities – more money went to defence and law and order; less went to housing, education and public transportation.

Thatcher also sought to rid the public sector of the nationalised industries. This effort at privatisation continued apace in the 1980s as the assets of several key industries were sold. Industries such as British Petroleum, British Aerospace, Rolls Royce, British Steel, British Telecom, Jaguar, British Airways, and British Gas were privatised under Thatcher.

There was, as promised, a cut in the top tax rate (from 83 to 60 per cent), as well as the standard rate of income tax (from 33 to 30 per cent). But the Value Added Tax (VAT) rose from 8 to 15 per cent and the employer's national insurance contributions also rose. In 1988 taxes were cut even further with the top rate dropping to 40 per cent, and the standard rate going down to 25 per cent. Overall, however, taxes have not gone down. There was a shift from direct to indirect taxes, but not a cut.

As the 1980s drew to a close, Thatcher proposed, and passed into law, a poll tax, aimed at shifting the burden of taxes away from the wealthy and on to the middle and lower classes. This tax, the level of which was determined in large part by local authorities, and in which almost everyone had to pay an equal tax total, was presented as a tax reform, but was really a way to try and dump the tax blame on to the local (or liberal) governments. The poll tax was highly unpopular and short-lived.

Due in part to increased revenues from North Sea oil which offset declines in manufacturing, Britain experienced economic growth during the 1980s. While the growth was not dramatic, approximately 2 per cent, it did mark an increase over the very sluggish (less than 2 per cent) growth of the 1970s, but was lower than the growth of the 1960s.

Union-busting efforts were designed to eliminate what Thatcher saw as the stranglehold trade unions had over the government. Thatcher was determined to bring the trade unions down, and proved to be unrelenting in this goal. She was very successful.

Strikes, which so often crippled Britain, were met with firm resolution, and eventually became politically insignificant. Thatcher succeeded in busting union power in Britain.

Linked to the decline in union power was the dramatic rise in unemployment. Upon taking office, Thatcher faced an unemployment rate of 5.4 per cent. This doubled under Thatcher. High unemployment, which may have been a policy goal linked to lowering wages, lowering inflation, and busting unions, did have the effect of weakening labour's bargaining power, and, as long as high unemployment did not create significant social repercussions, could be tolerated by the Thatcher government.

Thatcher's policies raise questions about winners and losers. Clearly labour and the underclass were losers. Under Thatcher, the tax system became less progressive, social services were cut, and unemployment rose. The number of homeless skyrocketed, government support for housing dropped. The disabled, the weak, the poor and the elderly all suffered under Thatcher's policies. Under Thatcher, inequality and poverty rose adding to what Neil Kinnock has called the 'archipelago of poverty' in Britain. There was no measurable 'trickle-down'. The big winners in this are the upper class. In short, under Thatcher, the rich got richer and the poor got poorer, and, according to Chris Ogden, 'a meaner and greedier society' was created.[8]

Thatcher's goal of freeing the economy came at a high cost in human terms. It also required a strong state to implement these goals. That a free economy would go along with a strong, centralised, more intrusive state, runs counter to the traditional Conservative goals. But that is precisely what has taken place in Britain. Thatcher, more of an authoritarian Conservative than a libertarian Conservative, gave lip service to the rhetoric of the minimalist state, but her activist government expanded the power of the central state, and pursued what one of her ministers called 'the smack of firm government'.[9] Thatcher attempted to enforce a 'moral' code of competitive capitalism. This required government rule-making as well as a good deal of persuasion. The government's education policy serves as an excellent example of the contradictions in a system of heightened governmental control in a less controlled economy. The state intrudes more often as guide and rule enforcer, as Thatcher divests the government of nationalised industries and attempts to create a new model of economic man for Britain.

Military and Defence Policy
When Margaret Thatcher took office in 1979, Britain's international standing was quite low. The heady days of empire had ended, and the 'sick man of Europe' had limited power and little prestige. On top of that, Thatcher herself had no prior experience in foreign affairs.

Thatcher's early foreign policy goals were clear: increase defence spending, maintain a nuclear arms deterrent, support the United States, oppose the Soviet Union and Communism, support NATO, but maintain cool relations regarding Britain's membership in the EEC. But Thatcher's policy goals were very quickly overshadowed by her style in foreign affairs: resolute, unyielding, nationalistic, rigid. It wasn't long before the sobriquet 'the Iron Lady', given to Thatcher by the Soviet news agency, TASS, became both a fitting appellation, but also a description of her style of governing.

After eleven years in office, Thatcher faced several seemingly intractable foreign policy problems. She was unable to make headway into the problems of Northern Ireland, faced severe criticism for her support of the white minority government in South Africa, and stubbornly fought the move to a more truly United European community, leaving Britain outside the inner circle as Europe moved towards unity in 1992.

On the more positive side of the foreign policy ledger, Thatcher was successful at strengthening the already strong ties between Britain and the United States. In fact, so close was Margaret Thatcher to Ronald Reagan that the mutual fawning society between the leaders, while it helped each leader in their respective countries, actually masked a deeper unease which Thatcher felt towards Reagan. While Thatcher and Reagan competed in public to see who could heap higher praise on the other, in private Thatcher had grave doubts about Reagan's ability. 'Poor dear', she once said, 'there's nothing between his ears'. After a meeting with Reagan, Thatcher remarked, 'Not much grey matter, is there?'

Thatcher's relationship with Mikhail Gorbachev and the Soviet Union represents one of the few cases where Margaret Thatcher actually changed her mind. Beginning her term as a rabid anti-communist, Thatcher was captivated by Gorbachev, concluding that, 'We can do business together'. Thatcher helped persuade Ronald Reagan that indeed he could do business with Gorbachev.

On 19 March 1982, a small group of Argentinians landed on the Falkland Islands. The islands just off the coast of Argentina (which the Argentines called the Malvinas) were claimed by Argentina but had been controlled by Britain since 1833. The Thatcher government responded swiftly and forcefully, sending British forces to the islands to recapture them.

376

The war itself was in part the result of gross errors of judgement and policy by the Thatcher government. Several steps were taken just prior to the Argentine invasion which served as indications that Britain was unwilling to fight for or defend the Falklands. This led Hugo Young to conclude that 'the war to reclaim the Falkland Islands from Argentinean occupation was the result of a great failure in the conduct of government: arguably the most disastrous lapse by any British government since 1945'.[10] But the errors in judgement ended up being the greatest thing which ever happened for Margaret Thatcher's leadership. For in the aftermath of Britain's Falkland victory, Thatcher emerged in a stronger position than ever. After victory was assured, Thatcher emerged from seclusion and announced, 'Today has put the Great back in Britain', and indeed, that is the way many in Britain saw it. The Falkland victory proved to be the seminal event in Thatcher's years in power. She was now seen as the leader of Britain, with virtually no challengers. And from that point on, Thatcher acted with a bolder, more self-confident style. Thatcher was virtually unstoppable.

Almost overnight her hold on power was solidified. Thatcher was now a world figure who halted Britain's retreat and brought victory. Her popularity skyrocketed. Her style, seen as abrasive and strident before the war, was now applauded as firm and resolute. The Falkland victory dramatically transformed Thatcher's leadership and power, and from that point on she dominated, even overwhelmed the political scene.

Domestic and Social Policy

While Margaret Thatcher was determined to transform Britain through a new economic policy, the domestic and social policy agenda was to contribute to and compliment the Thatcher Revolution. Thatcher opposed increases in welfare, hoping instead to shrink the welfare state, reduce its costs, and break the chain of dependency which she felt it created. The problem was not merely economic, but was also political, for the social welfare programmes were extremely popular. Thatcher therefore was able to make only marginal changes in funding and policy.

In education, while no drastic cuts took place, Thatcher so politicised the issue that morale plummeted, resulting in a crisis in the educational system. As part of her effort to discredit the leftist-leaning Greater London Council (which she eventually disbanded) which controlled local policy, Thatcher also disbanded the Inner London Education Authority, which controlled local schools. Thatcher was upset that too much social engineering was taking place in the London school system (e.g. each school was required to implement an anti-racism programme) and was determined to purge the schools of liberal content, regardless of the cost in educational quality. This led Thatcher – in spite of her public statements honouring local control – to further centralise education policy by establishing a national curriculum and national assessment programme. Public pronouncements to local control aside, this was centralisation on a massive scale. Thatcher thus displayed her willingness to violate her philosophy (conservative, local control) in an effort to gain her desired political ends (control of the schools).

Thatcher's policy towards British higher education was even more devastating. In both rhetoric and action, Thatcher made it clear that the university system was a political enemy, and her harsh rhetoric and frugal policies created a crisis in higher education. The result has been a brain drain (especially in the sciences, but in other academic areas as well) where the very best British scholars left England for greener and more welcome academic pastures abroad.

On the environment, Thatcher's record began with benign neglect, but by the end of the 1980s, Thatcher discovered environmental protection as an issue, and began to modestly increase government activity. But Britain, long considered the dumping ground for European refuse (toxic and otherwise), has serious environmental problems which were addressed in only the most peripheral manner.

The Thatcher Revolution made only a marginal impact on health policy. In the late 1980s, the Thatcher government began an attempt to place a Conservative hue on to the health services system, but the health system was highly popular, and nearly immune from deep budget cuts. On crime, the government's policy had little impact as crime and violent crime remained major problems.

A government in office for a dozen years is bound to face ethical problems from time to time. How did Margaret Thatcher handle such crises? Her first significant ethical challenge came in 1983 when a *Daily Mirror* headline blared about a 'love child'. Thatcher's valued cabinet minister and campaign manager Cecil Parkinson, had been having an affair with his secretary Sara Keays, who was pregnant. How did Thatcher, the strident advocate and protector of

Victorian values respond? She supported Parkinson. But as events unfolded, and as the political heat was turned up, it became clear that Parkinson had to go. The messy scandal, however, revealed that the Prime Minister was willing to over-look scandal when it suited her; however, when self-interest dictated, she would jettison even her most trusted aides.

In early 1986, the Thatcher government faced a much more serious political scandal: the Westland affair. This scandal was to reflect very poorly on Margaret Thatcher's credibility and her character. Due to carelessness, poor management, and the desire to cover up wrongdoing, Thatcher engaged in what Hugo Young called 'the darker political arts'.[11]

Westland was a small helicopter company, the only British company in fact which made helicopters. It was facing bankruptcy, and went to the government for assistance. Thatcher was a devout opponent of public money going to save businesses, but since Westland was defence related, it merited a second look. Michael Heseltine, a member of Thatcher's cabinet, but seen as a rival for power, was at the time Minister of Defence.

He opposed a buy-out deal by the American Sikorsky Company, and instead favoured purchase by a European consortium.

From this point on the affair took a variety of twists, turns, and backstabs. Thatcher, in part to issue a slap at rival Heseltine, sided with Trade and Industry Minister Leon Britain in favour of the Sikorsky sale. What followed were a series of behind-the-scenes promises and deals, press leaks and lies, accusations and deceits. Thatcher claimed ignorance of all wrongdoing, a claim unconvincing to even the staunchest Thatcherites. At the height of the scandal, Thatcher told one associate, 'I may not be Prime Minister by six o'clock tonight'. But amazingly, the opposition could not strike the fatal blow. Thatcher was blessed from the begin-ning with a weak, divided opposition and the Prime Minister weathered yet another political storm. While the Prime Minister's reputation suffered, she hung on to power and soon the Westland scandal was forgotten.

Margaret Thatcher always had as her stated goal in domestic and social pol-icy to provide less government and promote more individual responsibility. The individual and the entrepreneur were her heroes. The group, the society, the community were secondary. She told an interviewer in 1987, 'There is no such thing as society. There are individual men and women and there are families'.[12] Hardly the comment of a Burkean conservative! As was the case with education and local government control, the goal of less government was often superseded by a narrower, more partisan question of whose ox was being gored. Thatcher was not immune to violating principle when that meant hurting political opponents.

But Thatcher made only very limited headway in these policy areas. By over-politicising many of these issues she ended up having limited impact and few successes. Most social and domestic problems worsened under Thatcher, and after nearly twelve years in power, the intellectual cupboard on Conservative social policy seemed bare.

Thatcher's Leadership Style

How did Margaret Thatcher exercise power? What was her style of political leadership? In many ways – not solely because she is a woman – Thatcher was a different type of political leader.

Margaret Thatcher was a bold, innovative, ideological leader, a populist radical who relied on a strong sense of self, a warrior image, self-confidence, determination, and 'conviction'. In fact she called herself a conviction leader. 'I am not a consensus politician', she once said, 'I am a conviction politician'.[13] At another time she said 'The Old Testament prophets did not say "Brothers, I want a consensus". They said: "This is my faith. This is what I passionately believe. If you believe it too, then come with me".' Thatcher came to power determined to end the era of consensus politics which had characterised British politics for over thirty years. Consensus was, to her, the problem.[14] Thatcher was an outsider bent on breaking the consensus. There was thus a crusading zeal about her, a strong sense of belief or conviction which harboured few doubts and allowed little dissent. On taking office she said she wanted a conviction government and would not waste time with any internal arguments.

The sense of moral rigidity and mission led Thatcher to continually ask of subordinates, 'Is he one of us?' meaning, is he ideologically pure and temperamentally strong enough? This question was the test, which after the first two or three years, all would-be ministers had to answer before being allowed into the corridors of power. This let Thatcher to develop a highly (perhaps overly) personalised and somewhat imperious style of leadership. Inside the executive office, one had to either submit to the cult of her leadership or be dismissed. Few felt free to tell the emperor she had no clothes.

Thatcher's leadership traits emote a paradoxical quality , and could be seen as a series of dichotomies: her single-mindedness was often dogmatic; conviction was often rigidity; strength was often an aggressive drive for control; her determination was often contentiousness; forcefulness was combative; her moralism was often quarrelsome.

Thatcher was a true believer determined to lead a moral crusade. Her Messianic spirit was capture in her pre-prime ministerial comment, 'You can only get other people in tune with you by being a little evangelical about it'.[15] Her messianism fit comfortably with her warrior style in which she set policy by full frontal assaults on her cabinet, party, and political system. She saw governing as an adversarial, not a collegial process. Getting her way was everything, and she used fear, threat, intimidation, and all other means of persuasion to win. There may be a type of method to this madness in that since Thatcher had not won the hearts of the British people (public opinion polls reflect only lukewarm support for Thatcher and her policies) she tried to get her way by bullying the cabinet and party.

Thatcher's jarring personality and sheer force of will coupled with her Churchillian rhetoric were formidable political tools. Where others sought to build a consensus, Thatcher attempted to dominate allies and adversaries into submission. 'I am not ruthless', she once said, 'but some things have to be done, and I know when they are done one will be accused of all sorts of things'.[16] Thatcher's style of leadership was quite unique when compared with styles of her predecessors. Thatcher was generally more ambitious, more of a centraliser, more autocratic, less collegial, more confrontational, and more ideological than her predecessors. As Anthony King wrote, Thatcher 'leads from the front. She stamps her foot, raises her voice. For a British Prime Minister, she is extraordinarily assertive'.[17] This assertive style was essential to Thatcher's success. Not only did she take her cabinet and party by storm, she also took them by surprise. Thatcher was different, and the difference often worked.

Leading in Cabinet

Thatcher's aggressive style was very evident in her dealings with the cabinet. The tradition of collegial decision-making gave way to prime ministerial rule.

Thatcher's vision of collegiality saw her cabinet falling into line behind her. Just prior to becoming Prime Minister Thatcher described this vision, saying, 'As Prime Minister I couldn't waste time having any internal arguments'.[18] And after she solidified her power, Thatcher chose her cabinet more on the basis of loyalty and obedience than on ability and experience. It was to be a conviction cabinet.

Her first cabinet was a mixture of old Tory conservatives with a few true believers. But over time Thatcher replaced the traditionalists with a cabinet more loyal to her. 'Is he one of us?' was the question so often asked by Thatcher, or is he 'wet' or 'dry'.[19] It was her cabinet, her party, her government. Decisions were not generally agreed to after debate and discussion. Often, Thatcher would tell her cabinet what she wanted, then try to bully them into submission. She was often successful.

Cabinet meetings were often tense and full of conflict. Former cabinet minister David Howell remembered that 'some arguments just left such acrimony and ill feeling . . . I think the general atmosphere in the government of which I was a member was that everything would start as an argument, continue as an argument and end as an argument'.[20] Thatcher controlled her cabinet through fear and intimidation, by controlling the agenda, by sheer force of personality and conviction, and by creatively using cabinet committees for her purposes. But even with her formidable skills, when matters reached the cabinet level for decisions, Thatcher was on the losing end of the cabinet vote 'on more numerous occasions than any other post-war Prime Minister'.[21] Thus, Thatcher's bullying style proved a two-edged sword. She was sometimes able to force her will upon her cabinet, but when given the opportunity, the cabinet often struck back.

There is the story, circulated in London towards the end of Lady Thatcher's tenure, of the evening Mrs Thatcher and her entire cabinet went to the Savoy for dinner. The waiter approached Mrs Thatcher and asked what she would like for starters (the English word for appetisers). Mrs Thatcher responded: shrimp cocktail. The waiter then asked, 'And for the main course?' 'Beef Wellington', was her reply. 'And for the potatoes?' 'Mashed'. 'And for the vegetables?' 'Oh', Mrs Thatcher replied, 'they'll have the same thing'.

Thatcher often seemed an outsider in her own cabinet. She once refereed to herself as 'the cabinet rebel'. This allowed or compelled her to overly personalise everything, and look upon cabinet meetings as contests to be won. And how was one to win in cabinet? Usually by bullying. Thatcher saw the cabinet as a group organised to endorse her policies, not as a collegial body designed to discuss issues and arrive at decisions.

While Thatcher did not significantly altered the machinery of cabinet government, she did succeed in bending it to her will. She increasingly surrounded herself with weak men, to the point where Dennis Healy called the cabinet 'neutered zombies'. And Shirley Williams remarked after one of Thatcher's periodic cabinet reshuffles, 'She has replaced the cabinet with an echo chamber'.[22]

Thatcher and Parliament

In general, when the cabinet collectively decides, the Parliament usually follows. As leader of her cabinet and party, Thatcher commanded a good deal of power. This was heightened by the inability of the Labour opposition to mount any sustained challenges to Thatcher's leadership. Being able to bully her cabinet, dominate her party, usually ignore or scoff at her opposition, made Thatcher the preeminent force in government. While she did not structurally alter the government, she dominated it.

All of this add up to a style of leadership more presidential than prime ministerial in nature, and while one is cautioned against stretching the analogy too far (British power is 'fused' or 'unified', American power is separate and often divided), Thatcher clearly preferred the presidential operating style.

In both the style and ideological substance of what she has done, an 'ism has been created: Thatcherism. It is about force of will, depth of conviction, and personal drive. It is also about bullying, rigidity and closed-mindedness. Thatcherism is about dogged determination, clarity of theme, Victorian values, a crusading approach; it is also about a combative style and a rejection of consensus, about radical economic Conservatism, and jingoistic patriotism, about promoting inequality and rough justice. She has earned a variety of caustic nicknames from 'The Iron Lady' to 'Leaderene', from 'Her Malignancy' to 'Attila the Hen', from 'Boadicea' to 'Virago Intacta'. But regardless of how one views her, no one can doubt that she has made an enormous difference.

The Fall

The fall of Thatcher came, as falls so often do, not as the result of a single dramatic event, but from the culmination of a series of smaller acts which, one by one, opened the political window of opportunity for Thatcher's critics, and eventually pulled her down.

Thatcher had been vulnerable before, but she always managed to fight off potential challenges and retain power. This is partly a function of being blessed with a weak and divided opposition party, but was also a function of Thatcher's political skill and savvy. But by 1989, time and good fortune seemed to be running out for Thatcher. She had been in office nearly a dozen years, and many were tiring of her bullying style of leadership. The economy, which during the 1980s was one of her claims to fame, worsened as unemployment and inflation were rising, and economic growth was declining. In this atmosphere, a series of blows to Thatcher's power occurred which led to her downfall.

One can trace the beginning of the end to the resignation in protest of Chancellor of the Exchequer Nigel Lawson in October of 1989. From that point on, criticism of Thatcher became harsher and more biting, especially relating to the widely unpopular poll tax and Thatcher's intransigence over European unity. When on 1 November 1989, former Thatcher loyalist and Deputy Prime Minister Sir Geoffrey Howe resigned from the cabinet, and on 13 November, made a devastating House of Commons speech in which he attacked Thatcher, saying that her style of leadership was leading to 'a very real tragedy' for herself, and 'running increasingly serious risks for the future of our nation', and accusing her of a failed policy towards European unity, the floodgates of Thatcher-busting broke loose. In resigning, Howe invited 'others to consider their response' to his 'conflict of loyalty'. This invitation to insurrection was not lost on Michael Heseltine, who saw this as his opening to challenge Thatcher for leadership of the Conservative Party.

The flamboyant Heseltine (referred to as Tarzan), a former Defence Minister under Thatcher, sensed the rumblings of discontent within the Conservative Party, and after five years of quietly but unceasingly campaigning for Thatcher's job, made his move, and openly challenged Thatcher for control of the party. Thatcher accepted the challenge. Heseltine's challenge proved viable not merely on policy differences (which were rather insignificant) but on political grounds. Increasingly, Conservatives came to believe, and their opinion polls verified this, that the Conservative Party was likely to lose the next general election with Thatcher at the helm.

After a very brief leadership campaign the party voted. Of the 372 votes, Heseltine garnered 152 to Thatcher's 204. Under the party's leadership selection formula, Thatcher did not receive enough votes for a win (falling two votes short), and was forced into a run-off. Vowing to 'fight on. I fight to win', Thatcher retreated and prepared for the next battle. But the momentum was shifting, and Thatcher soon found her top ministers deserting her sinking ship.

In spite of her pronouncement to 'fight on', it soon became clear that the party was deserting Thatcher. Minister after minister met with Thatcher and finally persuaded her that the only way to stop Heseltine, whom she detested, was to pull out of the race and allow a cabinet ally to enter. She reluctantly did so, announcing that, 'Having consulted widely among colleagues, I have concluded that the unity of the party and the prospect of victory in a general election would be better served if I stood down to enable cabinet colleagues to enter the ballot for leadership'. Two did: Douglas Hurd and John Major. Thatcher let it be known that she supported Major, who eventually won.

Major, Thatcher's forty-seven-year-old Chancellor of the Exchequer, became the youngest British Prime Minister since 1894. He was, in many ways, a Thatcher clone. He was not born to privilege, but worked his way up. This self-made man appeared to be a true believer in the Thatcherite creed. But it was not long before Major began to undo some of the more extremist of Thatcher's policies, including an abandonment of the poll tax in March of 1991.

Thatcher's Performance

It is especially difficult to evaluate Thatcher's performance in office because (1) she is so controversial; (2) her style was so abrasive; and (3) the long-term consequences of her actions are unknown to us. Few people are neutral about Mrs Thatcher. She evokes strong emotions. One thing, however, is quite clear. Thatcher was, as Anthony King has noted, a person of 'extraordinary personal force'.[23] She has got her way. She has imposed her will. She has won.

But how deep is Thatcher's success? Was she good or merely important? By almost all accounts, Thatcher's victories are personal victories, not party or ideological victories, and some are quite ephemeral. She has changed Britain's policies, but has not won the hearts and minds of the people. As Ivor Crewe notes, 'She (Thatcher) is both intensely admired and deeply loathed'.[24]

People respect Thatcher, but do not like her. In short, the electorate has not become Thatcherite. She has won few converts with her missionary style. Her effort to transform the British people from a dependency culture to an enterprise culture has not succeeded in a deep sense. There was no revolution in social values.

One can examine Thatcher's success in political, policy, and personal terms. Politically, Thatcher had been in office nearly twelve years, won three general elections, and had utterly humiliated the opposition. In policy terms, the record is mixed, but she did elevate Britain's international reputation, moderated the pace of British decline, and established the Conservative agenda in the political sphere. In personal terms the record is also mixed. It is true she has won, but she has not sold Thatcherism to the British people. She was powerful, but there is a shallowness in many of her victories. She was respected, but unloved, powerful, but a temporary force.

Thatcher was one of the most powerful prime ministers in this century, and she succeeded in implementing almost all of her agenda. She has changed Great Britain, remaking it in her image. As Harris writes, 'Only Gladstone, perhaps, has had such a profound personal effect on government and politics, on shaping society according to a vision'.[25]

The Gender Factor

To what extent did gender matter in Thatcher's rise to power and in the way she exercised power? How did this non (many would say, anti) feminist woman rise in a male society, male party, male political system, to govern a nation? Thatcher is, in Wendy Webster's words, 'a conspicuous figure in the world of sexual politics'.[26] Feminists are torn when it comes to Thatcher. After all, Thatcher benefited from the repercussions of the Women's Movement, without which she could never have achieved the prime ministership. But at the same time, Thatcher rejected, even vilified the Women's Movement. Webster writes of Thatcher:

For women Mrs Thatcher has often been an ambivalent figure. Some feminists have found little difficulty in reaching a verdict: she is an ardent servant of patriarchy, colluding with male power and male violence. She is not, and never has been, one of us. Others have felt the problems of attacking her, the dangers of sliding into misogyny, the need to disassociate themselves

from sexist slogans like 'Ditch the Bitch'. Those who have written about her from a feminist per-
spective have often felt a need to recognise that she has proved that a woman can be a Prime
Minister, that she is capable, well organised, articulate and courageous, that she has coped
extremely effectively with the demands of the job, and in that sense has not 'blown it for
women'. [27]

Thatcher used her femaleness when it suited her interest, but women were not a part of the Thatcher Revolution. Thatcher's political agenda was decidedly lacking in proposals designed to advance the cause of women's rights in Britain. In effect, Thatcher often enjoined women to stay at home, to raise families, to assume traditional roles. Do as I say, not as I do. There is, in the Thatcher Revolution, room for no more women. Gender was important to Thatcher, and she used it repeatedly and in a variety of ways. As Barbara Castle notes:

She's . . . shown almost a contempt for her own sex in the way she has used her power as Prime
Minister. Of course she has sex consciousness . . . she wouldn't bother so much about her
appearance, her grooming . . . if she weren't sexually conscious. But that's different from what I
mean. Her treatment of the services that matter so much to women, that liberate them from the
domestic servitude, all the social services . . . these don't arouse her interest at all. [28]

She surrounded herself with men, but rarely strong independent men. Thatcher's cabinet, and even her closest advisers, were usually fairly weak men willing to not only take orders, but suffer blistering public humiliation at the feet of Thatcher. Throughout her public life there seems to be only one woman whom Thatcher admired: India's Indira Ghandi.[29] Throughout her career, Thatcher was very adept at sexual style-flexing, using a variety of different approaches to her femaleness as circumstances dictated. Early in her career she assumed the public role of devoted housewife and mother, though in fact she spent little time at either task. [30]

Later she assumed the role of mother to the nation, firm nanny, wartime dominatrix, and still later, as androgynous leader. This style-flexing allowed Thatcher to pick and choose sexual roles to fit perceived needs. She didn't, she told the *Daily Mirror*, on 1 March 1980, regard herself as a woman, but as Prime Minister.

How did Thatcher's gender impact on her sense of self? Some argue that, 'she . . . discarded most of the significant gender traits and become for all practical purposes, an honorary man'.[31] Governing in a 'man's world' of politics, it is argued, forced her to jettison all aspects of femininity, and 'act like a man'. In fact, her style of leadership, dominating and bullying, is often characterised as a male style. As Prime Minister she led almost a womanless existence. Practically none of her staff or cabinet were women, and she spent her time in the company of men. She was almost always the lone female, surrounded by men.

Thatcher was a 'gender bender', floating back and forth between what are dimensionally seen as male and female roles, producing a synthesis, or a type of political cross-dressing. But if Thatcher's career was a tribute to the 'manly qualities' of toughness, aggressiveness, and power, how did she escape the scorn of society for being 'un-feminine?' The fact of the matter is that by her style-flexing, Thatcher was seen as different things at different times.

Often, Thatcher used gender differences as a political tool. In a way, being a woman proved to be one of her greatest advantages. Women have a great deal of experience dealing with men who hold positions of power, but men have virtually no experience dealing with women who are in positions of political power. Men were not accustomed to being in a subordinate position politically and Thatcher exploited this situation. Melanie Phillips noted, 'If she'd been a man, she would never have got away with half of it; she understood this and played it for all she was worth'. Phillips continued:

Mrs Thatcher simply didn't behave as men thought a woman should behave. She was rude, she shouted, she interrupted, she was tough, she was ruthless – male qualities that she used more effectively than the men who thought all this just wasn't cricket. If a male Prime Minister had behaved like this, it would have been thought entirely normal and his colleagues and opponents would have had no difficulty in using the same tactics against him.[32]

Just as being a woman helped Thatcher gain some early political appointments (the Conservative Party had few women in Parliament and thus Thatcher was tabbed for ministerial appointments prior to proving her ability), it also helped her in dealing with the men in her government. Many of the men in

her cabinet simply did not know how to deal with an assertive woman, especially one in a position of political superiority. Thatcher's bullying style got
the best of a number of her cabinet appointees. One, Jim Prior, wrote an
almost apologetic biography, in which he confesses his inability to stand up to
an aggressive woman.[33] Even opposition leader Neil Kinnock noted that 'Mrs
Thatcher is more difficult for me to oppose . . . I've got however much I try to
shrug it off an innate courtesy towards women that I simply don't have
towards men'.[34] Thatcher often showed men up, and by all indications, derived
a great deal of pleasure in such encounters. Webster notes that Thatcher
enjoyed demonstrating to an audience what they (men) really were – the
weaker sex. Conventional sex roles were reversed as men were lumped together as feeble and fumbling, a gang of 'wets' and craven yes-men, while Mrs
Thatcher alone carried the banner of masculine virtues – strong, decisive,
determined, courageous'.[35] In dominating her cabinet and colleagues, Thatcher
would, and could, engage in a variety of different styles and roles, filling her
approach to the situation. In all this she kept her cabinet off, and often at her
mercy. She was indeed different, and the men around her did not know how
to deal with her. Even the few skilled and strong men who would sometimes
fly into the Thatcher orbit (e.g. Michael Heseltine) had trouble dealing with
the Prime Minister. As Webster notes of the men in Thatcher's cabinet: 'They
simply did not know how to handle her'.[36]Overall, the gender factor helped
Margaret Thatcher. From her early political rise when the Conservatives needed 'a woman', to her tenure as prime minister, Thatcher has used gender issues
with skill and cunning. She used gender, sometimes relying on feminine wiles,
sometimes as nanny, sometimes as bully, sometimes to coax, cajole and flatter,
but always calculatingly. As Young notes, 'Without discarding womanhood,
she has transcended it'.[37] But Thatcher's success, and her style of governing are
not merely result of gender. Clearly she was driven by unbending ideological
conviction. She was a crusader whose forcefulness mixed with the gender issue
to produce a truly unusual politician. As she noted, 'If a woman is strong, she
is strident. If a man is strong, gosh, he's a good guy'.[38]

This represents a paradox of women in power. If they are strong they are criticised for not being a 'woman', if they are weak, they 'prove' that a woman simply can't govern. It's a no-win proposition.

Unusually, Thatcher was the beneficiary of the gender issue. She used her opportunities wisely and well, and seized power. As Wendy Webster notes, there was 'not a man to match her'.[39]

Conclusion

Margaret Thatcher came to power with the cards stacked against her. She had limited experience, did not have the support of a majority of her parties leaders, promoted a new and radical agenda, and she was a woman.

But while her level of political opportunity was not high upon assuming office, a dozen years later one is struck by just how many of her key agenda items have been implemented. Historians, looking back on the Thatcher years, will note that more than most prime ministers, she left her mark. She was powerful and purposeful, a force for change, a woman who dominated the political landscape of Britain. There is no question that Thatcher made a difference. She mattered. But were Thatcher's victories, Britain's also? She won, but did Britain?

Long-term evaluations must be left to historians, but Thatcher's record seems decidedly mixed. She left Britain more prosperous, but it is a prosperity not evenly shared. Thatcher's Britain in 1990 was in social disrepair, divided and unequal. The social cohesion and harmony which resulted from the welfare state has deteriorated. The wealthy, who were poised to profit from Thatcher's vision of an opportunity society, benefited greatly. As Peter A. Hall has written:

Nagging doubts remain. There is something ignoble about a regime that preaches the virtues of personal initiative and equality of opportunity while cutting back on social and educational programmes that generally extend such opportunities to those at the bottom of the ladder. If all revolutions have their shadows, this is the shadow that still hangs over Mrs Thatcher's moral revolution. [40]

Thatcher's philosophy of rugged individualism has opened entrepreneurial doors for the British, but is has also closed other doors. Britain is less a community, is more divided, has less which binds it together. Thatcher saw the choice as either self-interest or society; she chose the former. But clearly self-interest is not enough. The search for community must also be a part of the national quest. However, for Thatcher the invisible hand guides, the trickle down theory determines.

Thatcher was the first woman to head the government of a major Western nation, serve longer continuously than any modern Prime Minister, tamed the trade unions, revived Britain's pride and economy, led her country to victory in war, and overwhelmed her opposition. But her flaws were as big as her virtues. She turned a blind eye to the poor and dispossessed, was overbearing and domineering, and she left Britain a harsher, nastier place than she found it. She was a woman of firm conviction and great strength, but she had been running against the 'socialist past' for so long, many in Britain wonder if towards the end, she had a proactive vision.

Clearly, Thatcher changed Great Britain. She accomplished so much on the force of her will and the power of her ideas. Where most British governments ground to a halt due to failed policies, scandals, lack of leadership, or electoral shifts, Thatcher managed to not only stay in power for a dozen years, but to thoroughly dominate her party, and demoralise her opposition.

What is the future of Thatcherism? It is unlikely to survive. While Thatcher implemented a variety of changes, so much of her power was built on her persona. It has become apparent that Thatcherism as a style of governing cannot survive her. It was too dependent on Thatcher's unique style and drive. But what of Thatcherism as a policy approach? Robert Skidelsky has doubts, writing:

Thatcherism may have been necessary to break out of the corporatist and bureaucratic impasse of the late 1970s; but the analysis was oversimplified, the means crude and mean. More fundamentally, Thatcherism as an economic and social philosophy – as a basis for the long-term government of Britain – is seriously one-sided. [40]

One senses that Thatcher herself knows that Thatcherism is coming to an end. Her importance to the revolution is now lost. Thatcher once remarked, 'I think I have become a bit of an institution', and 'the place wouldn't be quite the same without this old institution'. [42]

Her hand-picked successor, John Major, while a true believer, was up against formidable odds at attempting to re-inject Britain with another dose of Thatcherism; one was Thatcher's apparent reluctance to truly step down from power. After all, shortly after announcing her resignation Mrs Thatcher publicly announced that she would make a 'good back-seat driver', leading a Labour critic to charge, when noting that Major's first cabinet contained no women (the only cabinet in all of Western Europe not to have a woman minister), 'Is the only woman in the cabinet the back-seat driver?' and other opposition politicians took to calling Major 'Mrs Thatcher's poodle'. This promoted Major to fire back, 'I am my own man'.

Less than two years after assuming office, John Major was required to call a national election. Amidst the worst recession in Britain since the Second World War, but facing weak opposition in Neil Kinnock and the Labour Party, Major and the Conservatives, while losing approximately forty seats, managed to maintain a slim majority in Parliament. It was the fourth consecutive national election victory for the Conservatives, and in some ways it served as vindication for Margaret Thatcher.

Margaret Thatcher was a revolutionary leader, not simply because she was a woman, not simply because she was a powerful woman, but because she was these things and more. She governed for a dozen years, one almost all of her major political goals, and vanquished her opposition. While her contemporaries are mixed (generally along partisan lines) regarding Thatcher's long-term impact, it is clear that a revolution has changed Britain. The nation is more prosperous but is a prosperity not evenly spread. The rich are richer, the poor poorer; the south of England is strong, the north weak. The union's have been weakened, and a sense of 'acquisitive individualism' has spread. Market liberalism has been increased, so too has poverty and unemployment. Inflation is down, inequality is up. Local governments have become less powerful, the central state more powerful. Whatever the long-term results, one knows whom to praise or blame: it has indeed been a Thatcher Revolution.

Notes

1   See Samuel Beer, *Modern British Politics,* London: Faber, 1965; and Dennis Kavanagh, *Thatcherism and British Politics*, Oxford: Oxford University Press, 1990, pp. 26–62.
2   Peter Jenkins, *Mrs Thatcher's Revolution* (Cambridge, Ma.: Harvard University Press, 1988), p. 30.

3   Charles Ogden, *Maggie* (New York: Simon and Schuster, 1988), p119.
4   Kenneth Harris, *Thatcher* (London, Fontana, 1989), p. 48.
5   Ogden, p. 119.
6   Hugo Young, *One of Us*
7   Ogden, p. 173.
8   Ogden, p. 335.
9   Kavanagh, p. 284 and 294.
10   Young, p. 258.
11   Young, p. 427.
12   Wendy Webster, *Not a Man to Match Her* (London Women's Press, 1990), p.57.
13   Jenkins, p.3.
14   Harris, chapter 3.
15   Harris, p. 126.
16   Young, pp 104–105.
17   Anthony King, ed. *The British Prime Minister* (London: Macmillan, 1986), p. 118.
18   Harris, p. 109.
19   Young, Preface.
20   H. Young and A. Solomon, *The Thatcher Phenomenon* (London: BBC, 1986), p.14.
21   Jenkins, p.184.
22   Ogden, pp. 176 and 197.
23   King, Introduction.
24   Ivor Crewe, 'Has the Electorate Become Thatcherite?' in P. Hennessy and A. Sheldon, eds., *Reeling Performance* (Oxford: Basil Blackwell, 1987), p. 45.
25   Harris, pp. 288–289.
26   Webster, p. 1.
27   Webster, pp. 1–2.
28   Gene Little, *Strong Leadership* (Melbourne: Oxford University Press, 1988), pp 110-111.
29   Young, p. 120.
30   Young, pp. 306–312.
31   Young, p. 304.
32   Harris, p. 66.
33   Jim Prior, *A Balance of Power* (London: Hamish Hamilton 1988)
34   Little, p. 109.
35   Webster, p. 117.
36   Webster, p. 118.
37   Young, p. 312.
38   Young, p. 543.
39   Wendy Webster, *Not a Man to Match Her* (London, Women's Press, 1990), p.57.
40   P.A. Hall, 'The Smack of Firm Government', *New York Times* Book Review. 2 October, 1989, p. 8.
41   R. Skidelsky, ed., *Thatcherism* (Oxford: Basil Blackwell, 1989), p. 23.
42   Young, p. 543.

Contributors

Leo Abse, lawyer, parliamentarian, social reformer and psycho-biographer, a Member of Parliament for thirty years, was responsible as a legislator for the liberalisation of Britain's divorce and homosexual laws. His published works include: *Private Member*, a psycho-analytical review of British politics; *Margaret, Daughter of Beatrice*, a psycho-biography of Margaret Thatcher; *Wotan, My Enemy*, a scrutiny of the German psyche; *Fellatio, Masochism, Politics and Love*, a study of current alienation. His latest work, published in April 2001, *Tony Blair, the Man behind the Smile*, is a psycho-biography of Britain's Prime Minister which has provoked widespread controversy in Britain.

Philip Allmendinger completed his PhD on the impact of Thatcherism in 1995 and since then has written widely on her legacy most notably *Urban Planning and the British New Right* (with Huw Thomas) (Routledge, 1998). He is currently researching the impact and influence of the Thatcher years upon the current Labour government with colleagues at the University of Aberdeen, Scotland. He is now Reader and Head of Department of Land Economy at the University of Aberdeen.

Alan Allport is a candidate for the Master of Arts degree in History at the University of Pennsylvania. His research interest is modern Britain, and in particular British political culture in the twentieth century.

Diane Antonio is an adjunct professor of Philosophy at Hofstra University and SUNY, Purchase. With a background in English literature and theatre, she has published in the fields of cultural history, philosophy of the body, and feminist theory. She has published fiction as well. Her doctoral dissertation, 'Moral

Bodies', theorises an ethics of embodiment through three Shakespearean 'comedies of ethics'.

Ryan J. Barilleaux is professor and chairman of the Department of Political Science, Miami University (Ohio). He is the author or editor of six books, including *The Post-Modern Presidency* and *Presidential Frontiers: Underexplored Issues in White House Politics*. His work has appeared in professional journals such as *Congress and the Presidency, World Affairs,* and *Catholic Social Science Review*. His current research (with Mark Rozell) focuses on interpreting presidential leadership in the first Bush administration.

Larry Bumgardner is associate professor of business law at Pepperdine University's Graziadio School of Business and Management. At the time of the Thatcher Conference, he was associate professor of political science and director of the Washington, D.C. programme for Pepperdine's undergraduate Seaver College. He previously served as executive director of the Ronald Reagan Presidential Foundation and Centre for Public Affairs in Simi Valley, California. A former journalist, he has written and commented in the media on a variety of legal and political issues.

Sir Bryan Cartledge, KCMG. After graduating from Cambridge University, he researched Russian history at Oxford, Stanford and Harvard Universities before entering the British Diplomatic Service in 1960. He served in Stockholm, Moscow (twice) and Tehran and as Head of the East European and Soviet Department in the Foreign Office in London. From 1977 to 1979 he was Private Secretary (Overseas Affairs) to the British Prime Minister, serving both James Callaghan and Margaret Thatcher in that capacity. His subsequent appointments included those of Ambassador to Hungary, Deputy Secretary of the Cabinet and Ambassador to the Soviet Union. On retiring from the Diplomatic Service, he was elected Principal of Linacre College, Oxford (1988–96). He is currently writing a history of Hungary.

Charles Dellheim earned his doctorate in modern European cultural history at Yale University. Formerly the Ella Darivoff Fellow at the University of

Pennsylvania's Centre for Advanced Judaic Studies, he is presently professor and chair of the History Department at Boston University. His publications include *The Disenchanted Isle: Mrs Thatcher's Capitalist Revolution* (W.W. Norton), *The Face of the Past: The Preservation of the Medieval Inheritance in Victorian England* (Cambridge University Press). Dellheim has held fellowships from the National Endowment for the Humanities, Harvard Business School, and the Littauer Foundation. He is a past president of the Economic and Business Historical Society and is on the executive board of the Western Humanities Alliance. His current research project is Becoming European: Jews, Art, and Citizenship.

Peter Dorey is Senior Lecturer in Politics at Cardiff University. He is author of *The Conservative Party and the Trade Unions, British Politcs since 1945*, and *Wage Politics in Britain: The Rise and Fall of Incomes Policies since 1945.*, as well as editor of *The Major Premiership: Politics and Policies under John Major, 1990–1997*. He has also written numerous articles and chapters on aspects of post-1945 British Conservatism.

Simon Doubleday is Associate Professor of History at Hofstra University, where he specialises in the history of Spain and Western Europe. He received his BA from Cambridge in 1988 and his doctorate from Harvard in 1996. He is currently completing a book on the ghosts of Spanish history.

Martin Durham is Senior Lecturer in Politics at the University of Wolverhampton. He has written extensively on conservatism and the politics of morality in Britain and the United States and has recently published *The Christian Right, the Far Right and the Boundaries of American Conservatism* (Manchester University Press, 2000).

Bruce Geelhoed is Director of the Centre for Middletown Studies and Professor of History at Ball State University in Muncie, Indiana. He is the author of *Charles E. Wilson and Controversy at the Pentagon* (1979); with Millicent Anne Gates, *The Dragon and the Snake: An American Account of the Turmoil in China*, (1986); and *Margaret Thatcher: In Triumph and Downfall*, (1992). He has also published articles in *Military Affairs, Michigan History, Presidential Studies Quarterly*, and *The History Teacher*.

Michael A. Genovese holds the Loyola Chair of Leadership Studies, and is Professor of Political Science at Loyola Marymount University in Los Angeles. He is the author of eleven books, most recently, *The Power of the American Presidency, 1789–2000*, published by Oxford University Press. He is currently editing *The Encyclopedia of the American Presidency* for Facts On File.

Candace Hetzner is Director of the M.S. in Management Program at Lesley University in Cambridge, Massachusetts. Dr Hetzner – a recipient of Woodrow Wilson and Ford Foundation Fellowships – has had a lifelong commitment to bringing interdisciplinary perspectives to bear on issues of management and public policy. She has written extensively about business–government relations, public personnel issues, and business ethics and corporate social responsibility in both the United States and Europe. She is the author of *The Unfinished Business of Thatcherism* which deals with value change in Britain since the late 1970s.

Arianna Huffington is a nationally syndicated columnist and author of eight books. She graduated from Cambridge University with a MA in Economics. At twenty-one she became President of the famed debating society, the Cambridge Union. Her latest book, *How To Overthrow The Government*, on the corruption of our political system and the need for reform, was a *New York Times* bestseller. During the 2000 presidential campaign, Arianna Huffington was the driving force behind Shadow Conventions 2000, a pair of alternative gatherings that ran parallel to the Republican and Democratic party conventions. Huffington's previous books include *The Female Woman* (1974), *After Reason* (1978), *Maria Callas: The Woman Behind the Legend* (1981), *The Gods of Greece* (1983), *Picasso: Creator and Destroyer* (1988), *The Fourth Instinct* (1994) and *Greetings From the Lincoln Bedroom* (1998).

Wayne A. Hunt is a Professor of Political Science at Mount Allison University in Sackville, New Brunswick, Canada. He has been a Visiting Scholar at Harvard's Kennedy School of Government and a Visiting Fellow at the Centre for

International Studies in the International Relations Department of the London School of Economics. He has written extensively on European politics. His latest work is on the political reaction to genetically manipulated organisms. This will be part of a broader study of the challenges posed by the biotech revolution.

Dennis Kavanagh, Professor of Politics at the University of Liverpool, is one of the leading authorities on British politics and political behaviour. He has written or edited over twenty books and is author of a wide range of scholarly articles. Along with David Butler he has produced the definitive study of every UK general election since 1974. He has written extensively on both the Thatcher and Major premierships. Together with Anthony Selden, he edited *The Thatcher Effect* (1989). Professor Kavanagh is also the author of *Thatcherism and British Politics: the End of Consensus?* (1987; 1990). His recent work includes *Election Campaigning: the New Politics of Marketing* (1995) and *The British General Election of 1997* (with David Butler). He is a regular feature writer for *The Times, Guardian* and *Independent* and is a commentator/consultant to a wide range of radio and television programmes.

Joseph S. Meisel is currently a programme officer at The Andrew W. Mellon Foundation in New York. He received a PhD in history from Columbia University, where he has also taught, and is the author of *Public Speech and the Culture of Public Life in the Age of Gladstone* (2001).

David Monaghan is a Professor of English at Mount Saint Vincent University, Halifax, Nova Scotia. He has published several books on Jane Austen and John le Carré. The most important product of his work on Margaret Thatcher is *The Falklands War: Myth and Countermyth* (Macmillan, 1998). Professor Monaghan has recently been working on British working class film in the 1980s and Jane Austen and Film. His most recent publication, 'Margaret Thatcher, Alan Bleasdale and the Struggle for Working-Class Identity' was published in the Spring 2001 edition of *Journal of Popular Film and Television*.

Jeremy Moon is Head of the School of Law, Governance and Information Management, The University of North London. His publications include *Innovative*

Leadership in Democracy: Thatcher in Perspective (Dartmouth UK, 1993). His current research includes a more general study of Leadership in Democracy.

The Rt Hon. Brian Mulroney, P.C., C.C., LL.D. led the Progressive Conservative Party to the largest victory in Canadian history in September 1984, becoming Canada's eighteenth Prime Minister. He was re-elected with a majority government four years later thereby becoming the first Canadian Prime Minister in 35 years to win successive majority governments and the first Conservative Prime Minister to do so in 100 years. He resigned in June 1993, having served almost nine years as Prime Minister. Mr Mulroney was born in Baie Comeau, Quebec, in 1939 and received his undergraduate degree from St Francis Xavier University and a law degree from Université Laval in Quebec City. He practised law in Montreal and served as President of the Iron Ore Company of Canada before entering politics by becoming Party Leader in 1983 and Leader of the Official Opposition in the House of Commons, to which he was first elected in 1983 and re-elected in 1984 and 1988. Upon resigning, Mr Mulroney rejoined the Montreal law firm of Ogilvy Renault as Senior Partner. Mr Mulroney has been awarded Canada's highest honour, Companion of the Order of Canada, and has received honorary degrees and awards from universities and governments around the world.

Ben Pimlott has been Warden of Goldsmiths College, University of London, since 1998. He was Professor of Politics and Contemporary History at Birkbeck College from 1987 to 1998. His books include *Labour and the Left in the 1930s* (1977), *Hugh Dalton* (Whitbread Prize, 1985), *Harold Wilson* (1992), *Frustrate Their Knavish Tricks* (1994), and *The Queen* (1996). He has bee a Fellow of the British Academy since 1996.

Stuart E. Prall is Professor Emeritus of History at Queens College of New York and the City University of New York Graduate School. He has been a visiting professor at Johns Hopkins University, the University of Tel Aviv where he was the Margaret Thatcher Lecturer in 1994, and the Hebrew University of Jerusalem. He served as the Chair of the History Department at Queens College (1985--88) as well as the Executive Office of the PhD Program at the CUNY Graduate School (1988–94). He was a Fulbright Scholar at the University of

Manchester and has been a Fellow of the Royal Historical Society since 1978. Among his many publications are *The Agitation for Law Reform During the Puritan Revolution, 1640–1660* (1966); *The Puritan Revolution: A Documentary History* (1968); *The Bloodless Revolution: England, 1688* (1985); *A History of England*, 4th ed., (1991); *Church and State in Tudor and Stuart England* (1993). His latest work, *The Puritan Revolution, 1640–1660* is in press.

Stanislao G. Pugliese is associate professor of modern European history and Italian Studies at Hofstra University. He is the author of *Carlo Rosselli: Socialist Heretic and Antifascist Exile* and the editor of a number of works, including *The Most Ancient of Minorities: The Jews of Italy, The Legacy of Primo Levi*, and *Frank Sinatra: History, Identity* and *Italian-American Culture*. His most recent book is *Desperate Inscriptions: Graffiti From the Nazi Prison in Rome, 1943-1944* and his anthology, *Fascism, Anti-Fascism and the Resistance in Italy* is forthcoming. He is presently writing a biography of the Italian anti-fascist writer Ignazio Silone to be published by Farrar, Strauss & Giroux.

Leonard Quart, Professor of Cinema Studies at the College of Staten Island and at the CUNY Graduate Centre. He has written essays and reviews for *Dissent, Film Quarterly, The Forward, London Magazine,* and *New York Newsday*. He is a Contributing Editor of *Cineaste*. His major publications include *How the War was Remembered: Hollywood and Vietnam* (Praeger, 1988) co-authored with Albert Auster, and the revised and expanded edition of *American Film and Society Since 1945* (Praeger, 1991). He has most recently co-authored *The Films of Mike Leigh* for Cambridge University Press, and a third edition of *American Film and Society* (2001).

Peter Riddell is political columnist and commentator of *The Times* (London). He has written two books on the policies of the Thatcher era: *The Thatcher Government* (1983) and *The Thatcher Decade* (1989, revised and expanded as *The Thatcher Era and its Legacy* [1991]). His most recent book is *Parliament under Blair* (2000). He has contributed chapters to a wide variety of other books on Thatcher and contemporary British politics. He has written for *The Times Literary Supplement* and the *New Statesman;* and for the *Journal of Legislative*

Studies, British Journalism Review, Contemporary British History and *Political Quarterly.* He is a regular lecturer at schools and universities. He is a member of the council of the Hansard Society for Parliamentary Government and vice-chairman of its Commission on the Scrutiny of Parliament and is on the board of the Institute of Contemporary British History. He is a fellow of the Royal Historical Society. He has been appointed Visiting Professor of Political History in the Department of History at Queen Mary and Westfield College, University of London, for three years from November 2000.

Mark J. Rozell is professor of politics at The Catholic University of America in Washington, D.C. He is the author of numerous books, articles and book chapters on presidential politics, media and politics, and social movements and interest groups.

Frank J. Smist, Jr. is Chair of the Department of Political Science, Director of Global Studies, and Pre-Law Adviser at Rockhurst University. He is the author of *Congress Oversees the United States Intelligence Community: 1947–1994* (second edition) and presently is working on a biography of David L. Boren.

Zachary M. Stolz is a Trustees' Scholar at Rockhurst University.

The Rt Hon. The Baroness Thatcher LG OM FRS, former Conservative Member of Parliament for Finchley, was Britain's first woman Prime Minister. She was appointed Prime Minister on 4 May 1979, following the success of the Conservative Party in the general election. When the Conservative Party subsequently won the general election of 9 June 1983 and 11 June 1987, Margaret Thatcher became the first British Prime Minister this century to successfully contest three consecutive general elections. She resigned as Prime Minister on 28 November 1990. In December 1990, she was awarded the Order of Merit by Her Majesty the Queen. On 30 June 1992, she was elevated to the House of Lords to become Baroness Thatcher of Kesteven. In April 1995, she was made a member of the Most Noble Order of the Garter.

Margaret Hilda Roberts was born on 13 October 1925. She was educated at Kesteven and Grantham Girls' High School, and won a bursary to Somerville

College, Oxford, where she obtained a degree in Natural Science (Chemistry). While an undergraduate, she was President of the Oxford University Conservative Association. She is also a Master of Arts (MA) of Oxford University. In June 1983, she was elected a Fellow of the Royal Society (FRS). In 1954 she was called to the Bar and practised as a barrister, specializing in taxation law. In 1959 she was elected to the House of Commons.

Lady Thatcher's first ministerial appointment came in 1961, when she became a Parliamentary Secretary to the then Ministry of Pensions and National Insurance. From 1964 to 1970, she was a front-bench spokesman for her party and from 1967 a member of the Shadow Cabinet. When the Conservatives returned to office in June 1970, she was appointed Secretary of State for Education and Science and was made a Privy Counselor. She was elected Leader of the Conservative Party and thus Leader of the Opposition in February 1975. Lady Thatcher was Chancellor of the College of William and Mary, Virginia and Chancellor of the University of Buckingham from 1992 to 1998. She is Chairman of the Board of the Institute of US Studies at London University. She has received a large number of awards and honorary degrees. Lady Thatcher is a patron of a number of charities and has established her own Foundation.

Lady Thatcher married her husband Denis in 1951 and they have a twin son and daughter, Mark and Carol, who were born on 15 August 1953.

Lady Thatcher's two volumes, *The Downing Street Years* and *The Path to Power*, were published in 1993 and 1995 respectively. A volume of her collected speeches was published in 1997.

Caspar W. Weinberger graduated from Harvard College in 1938 and received his law degree from Harvard Law School in 1941. He served in the army during the Second World War and later served in the California State Legislature. In 1970 President Nixon appointed him as Chairman of the Federal Trade Commission and later was Director of the Office of Budget and Management. In 1980 he was nominated by President Reagan to be Secretary of Defence and served in that post until 1987. In 1989, he was named publisher of *Forbes* as is presently serving as Chairman of the magazine. He is the author of several books including *Fighting for Peace: Seven Critical Years in the Pentagon.*

Duane Windsor received his PhD from Harvard University and is Lynette S. Autrey Professor of Management in Rice University's Jesse H. Jones Graduate School of Management, where he has been on the faculty since 1977. He teaches and publishes in the area of public and nonprofit financial management.

Dr. Tony Wright is the Labour Member of Parliament, first elected to the House of Commons in 1992 and re-elected in 1997. In 1997–98 he was Parliamentary Private Secretary to the Lord Chancellor, and is now Chairman of the Public Administration Select Committee. He has been Chairman of the Fabian Society, and is joint editor of the *Political Quarterly*. Before entering Parliament, Dr Wright was Reader in Politics at the University of Birmingham, where he is now an Honorary Professor. He is the author of many books, articles and pamphlets. His book *Socialisms Old and New* (1996) was described in a preface by Tony Blair as 'an important route-map' for the new politics. Other recent books include *Citizens and Subjects* (1994), *Why Vote Labour?* (1997), *The New Social Democracy* (joint editor, 1999) and *The British Political Process* (2000). Dr Wright was educated at the London School of Economics and Balliol College, Oxford, and was a Kennedy Scholar at Harvard University.

Dov S. Zakheim is Under Secretary of Defense for Finance with the present Bush Administration. He was a Corporate Vice-President of System Planning Corporation (SPC), a high-technology, research, analysis, and manufacturing firm based in Arlington, Virginia, and CEO of SPC International Corporation, specialising in political, military, and economic consulting, and international sales and analysis. In addition, he is an Adjunct Senior Fellow for Asian Studies of the Council on Foreign Relations, Adjunct Scholar of the Heritage Foundation, and a Senior Adviser at the Centre for International and Strategic Studies. From 1985 until March 1987, Dr Zakheim was Deputy Under Secretary of DefenSe for Planning and Resources. Dr Zakheim served the Reagan administration in a variety of other senior Department of Defense posts from1981 through 1985. He had served previously as Principal Analyst with the National Security and International Affairs Division of the Congressional Budget Office.

Index